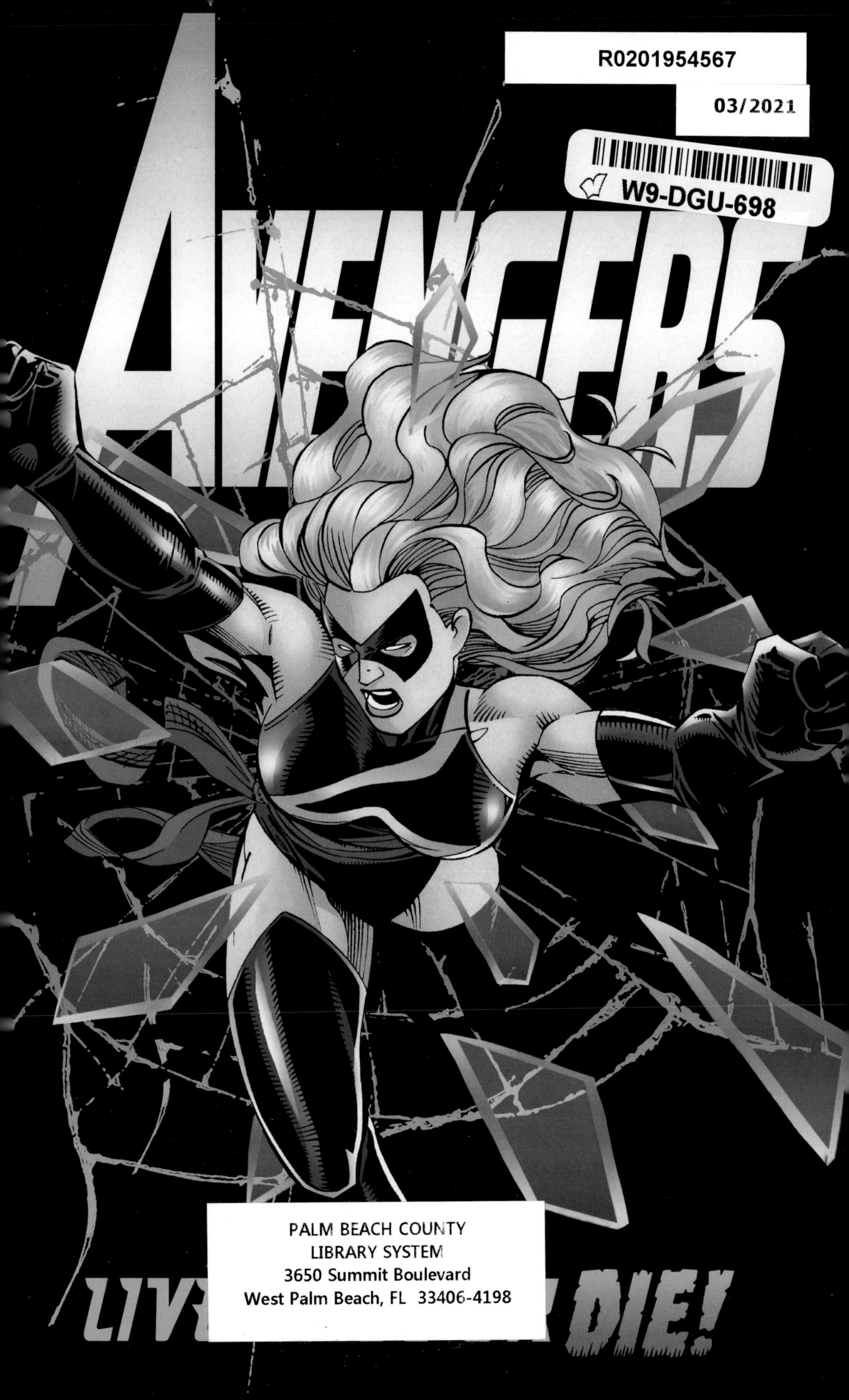
AVENGERS
DIE!

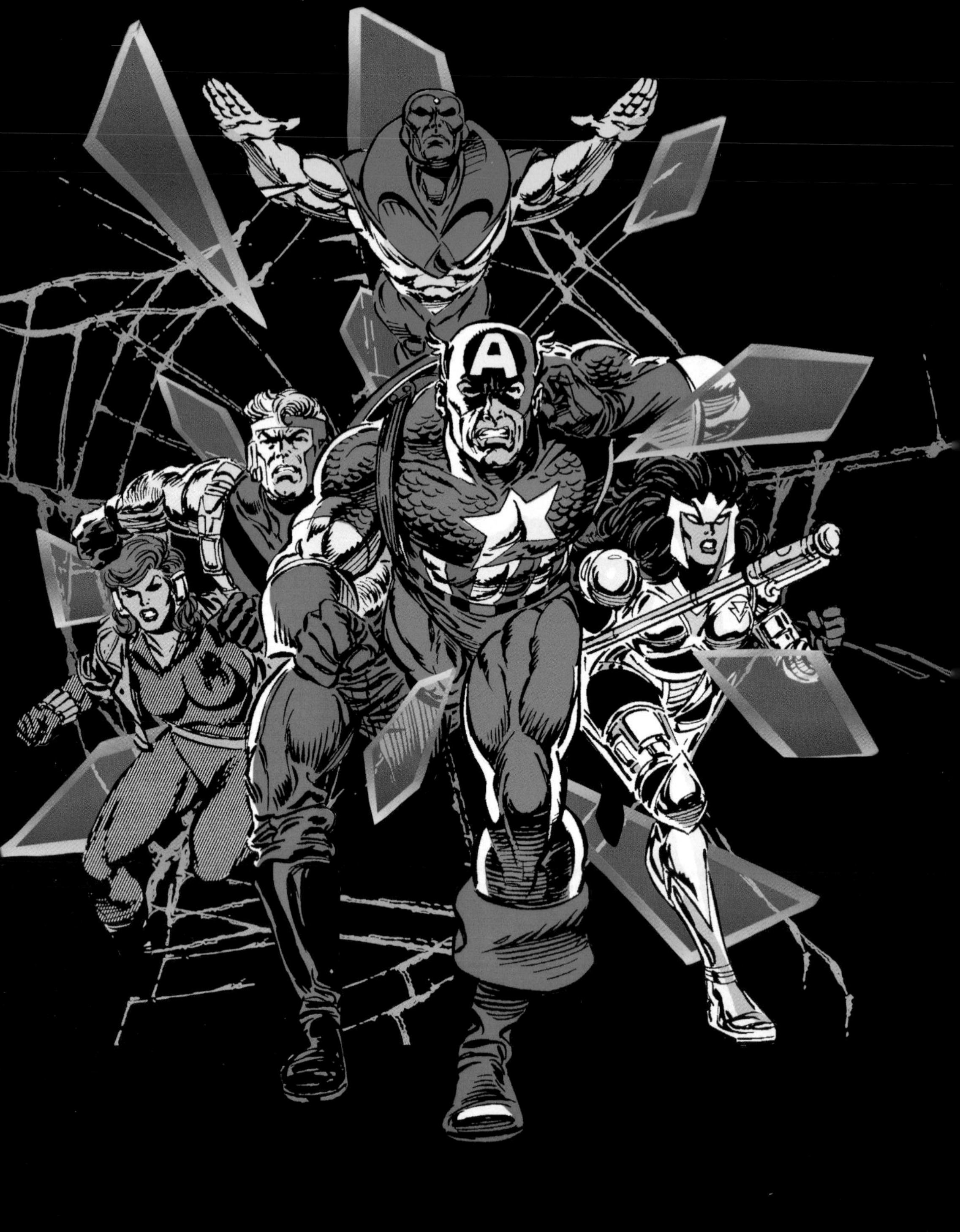

COLLECTION EDITOR: **MARK D. BEAZLEY** • ASSISTANT MANAGING EDITOR: **MAIA LOY** • ASSISTANT MANAGING EDITOR: **LISA MONTALBAN**
ASSOCIATE MANAGER, DIGITAL ASSETS: **JOE HOCHSTEIN** • SENIOR EDITOR, SPECIAL PROJECTS: **JENNIFER GRÜNWALD**
VP PRODUCTION & SPECIAL PROJECTS: **JEFF YOUNGQUIST** • RESEARCH AND LAYOUT: **JEPH YORK** • BOOK DESIGNER: **STACIE ZUCKER**
SVP PRINT, SALES & MARKETING: **DAVID GABRIEL** • EDITOR IN CHIEF: **C.B. CEBULSKI**

SPECIAL THANKS TO **TOM PALMER**

AVENGERS: LIVE KREE OR DIE. Contains material originally published in magazine form as AVENGERS (1963) #364-366 and #378-379, IRON MAN (1998) #7, CAPTAIN AMERICA (1998) #8, QUICKSILVER (1 #10, and AVENGERS (1998) #7. First printing 2020. ISBN 978-1-302-92318-1. Published by MARVEL WORLDWIDE, INC., a subsidiary of MARVEL ENTERTAINMENT, LLC. OFFICE OF PUBLICATION: 1290 Av of the Americas, New York, NY 10104. **Printed in the U.S.A.** KEVIN FEIGE, Chief Creative Officer; DAN BUCKLEY, President, Marvel Entertainment; JOHN NEE, Publisher; QUESADA, EVP & Creative Director; TOM BREVOORT, SVP of Publishing; DAVID BOGART, Associate Publisher & SVP of Talent Affairs; Publishing & Partnership; DAVID GABRIEL, VP of Print & Digital Publis JEFF YOUNGQUIST, VP of Production & Special Projects; DAN CARR, Executive Director of Publishing Technology; ALEX MORALES, Director of Publishing Operations; DAN EDINGTON, Managing Editor; S CRESPI, Production Manager; STAN LEE, Chairman Emeritus. For information regarding advertising in Marvel Comics or on Marvel.com, please contact Vit DeBellis, Custom Solutions & Integrated Advert Manager, at vdebellis@marvel.com. For Marvel subscription inquiries, please call 888-511-5480. **Manufactured between 6/5/2020 and 7/7/2020 by LSC COMMUNICATIONS INC., KENDALLVILLE, IN,**

10 9 8 7 6 5 4 3 2 1

AVENGERS
LIVE KREE OR DIE!

BOB HARRAS, KURT BUSIEK & MARK WAID WITH
RICHARD HOWELL, JOHN OSTRANDER & JOE EDKIN
WRITERS

STEVE EPTING, STAZ JOHNSON, SEAN CHEN, ANDY KUBERT, DEREC AUCOIN & GEORGE PÉREZ WITH **TOM GRINDBERG**
PENCILERS

TOM PALMER, JESSE DELPERDANG, RICH FABER & AL VEY WITH **RICH RANKIN, ERIC CANNON & SEAN PARSONS**
INKERS

TOM PALMER, JOHN KALISZ,
STEVE OLIFF, JASON WRIGHT,
JOE ROSAS, TOM SMITH & DIGITAL
CHAMELEON WITH KARL BOLLERS,
SCOTT MARSHALL & MIKE MARTS
COLORISTS

BILL OAKLEY, RICK PARKER,
JANICE CHIANG, TODD KLEIN AND
RICHARD STARKINGS & COMICRAFT'S
ALBERT DESCHESNE & CO.
LETTERERS

PAT GARRAHY, MATT IDELSON, POLLY WATSON,
PAUL TUTRONE, LYSA KRAIGER & GREGG SCHIGIEL
ASSISTANT EDITORS

RALPH MACCHIO, BOBBIE CHASE, MATT IDELSON,
MARK BERNARDO & TOM BREVOORT
EDITORS

STEVE EPTING, TOM PALMER & VERONICA GANDINI
FRONT COVER ARTISTS

GEORGE PÉREZ & TOM SMITH
BACK COVER ARTISTS

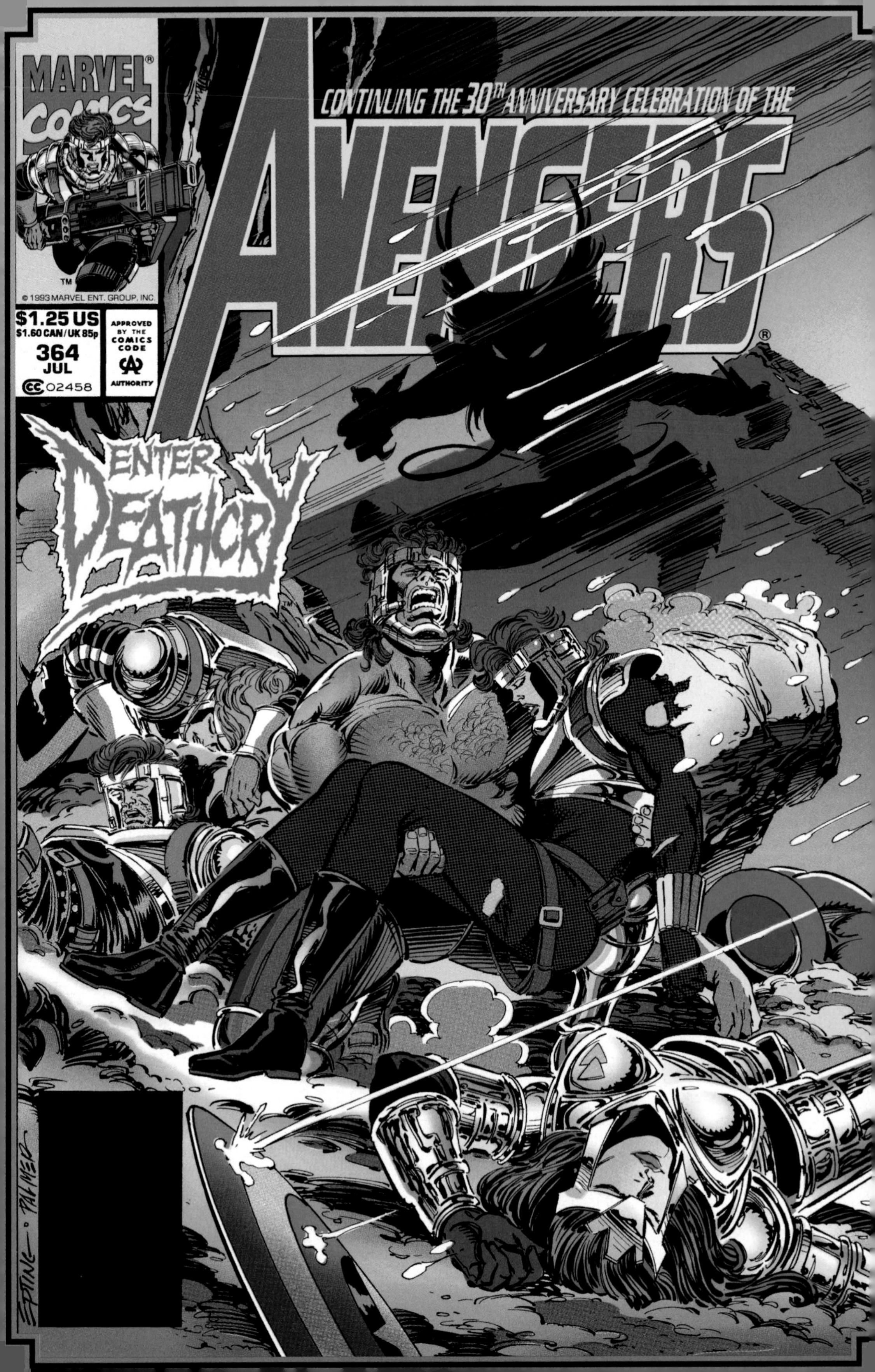
MARVEL COMICS
CONTINUING THE 30TH ANNIVERSARY CELEBRATION OF THE
AVENGERS
© 1993 MARVEL ENT. GROUP, INC.
$1.25 US
$1.60 CAN/UK 85p
364
JUL
02458
APPROVED BY THE COMICS CODE AUTHORITY
ENTER DEATHCRY

TO COMBAT THOSE THREATS WHICH NO SINGLE HERO CAN STAND AGAINST, EARTH'S MIGHTIEST HEROES HAVE FORGED A COVENANT TO UNITE IN BATTLE FOR THE PROTECTION OF ALL MANKIND!
STAN LEE PRESENTS . . . **THE MIGHTY AVENGERS!**

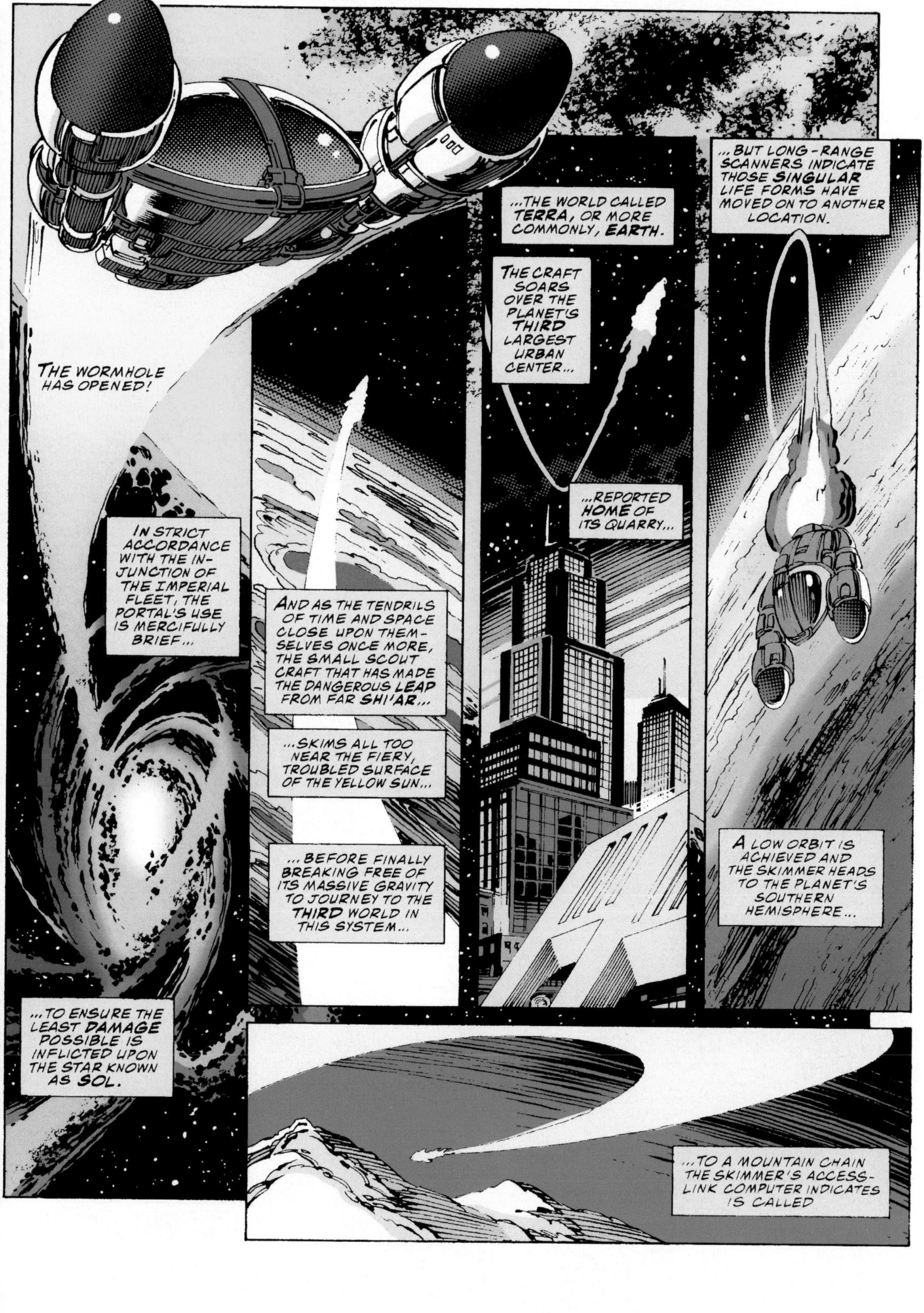

THE WORMHOLE HAS OPENED!
IN STRICT ACCORDANCE WITH THE INJUNCTION OF THE IMPERIAL FLEET, THE PORTAL'S USE IS MERCIFULLY BRIEF...
...TO ENSURE THE LEAST DAMAGE POSSIBLE IS INFLICTED UPON THE STAR KNOWN AS SOL.
AND AS THE TENDRILS OF TIME AND SPACE CLOSE UPON THEMSELVES ONCE MORE, THE SMALL SCOUT CRAFT THAT HAS MADE THE DANGEROUS LEAP FROM FAR SHI'AR...
...SKIMS ALL TOO NEAR THE FIERY, TROUBLED SURFACE OF THE YELLOW SUN...
...BEFORE FINALLY BREAKING FREE OF ITS MASSIVE GRAVITY TO JOURNEY TO THE THIRD WORLD IN THIS SYSTEM...
...THE WORLD CALLED TERRA, OR MORE COMMONLY, EARTH.
THE CRAFT SOARS OVER THE PLANET'S THIRD LARGEST URBAN CENTER...
...REPORTED HOME OF ITS QUARRY...
...BUT LONG-RANGE SCANNERS INDICATE THOSE SINGULAR LIFE FORMS HAVE MOVED ON TO ANOTHER LOCATION.
A LOW ORBIT IS ACHIEVED AND THE SKIMMER HEADS TO THE PLANET'S SOUTHERN HEMISPHERE...
...TO A MOUNTAIN CHAIN THE SKIMMER'S ACCESS-LINK COMPUTER INDICATES IS CALLED

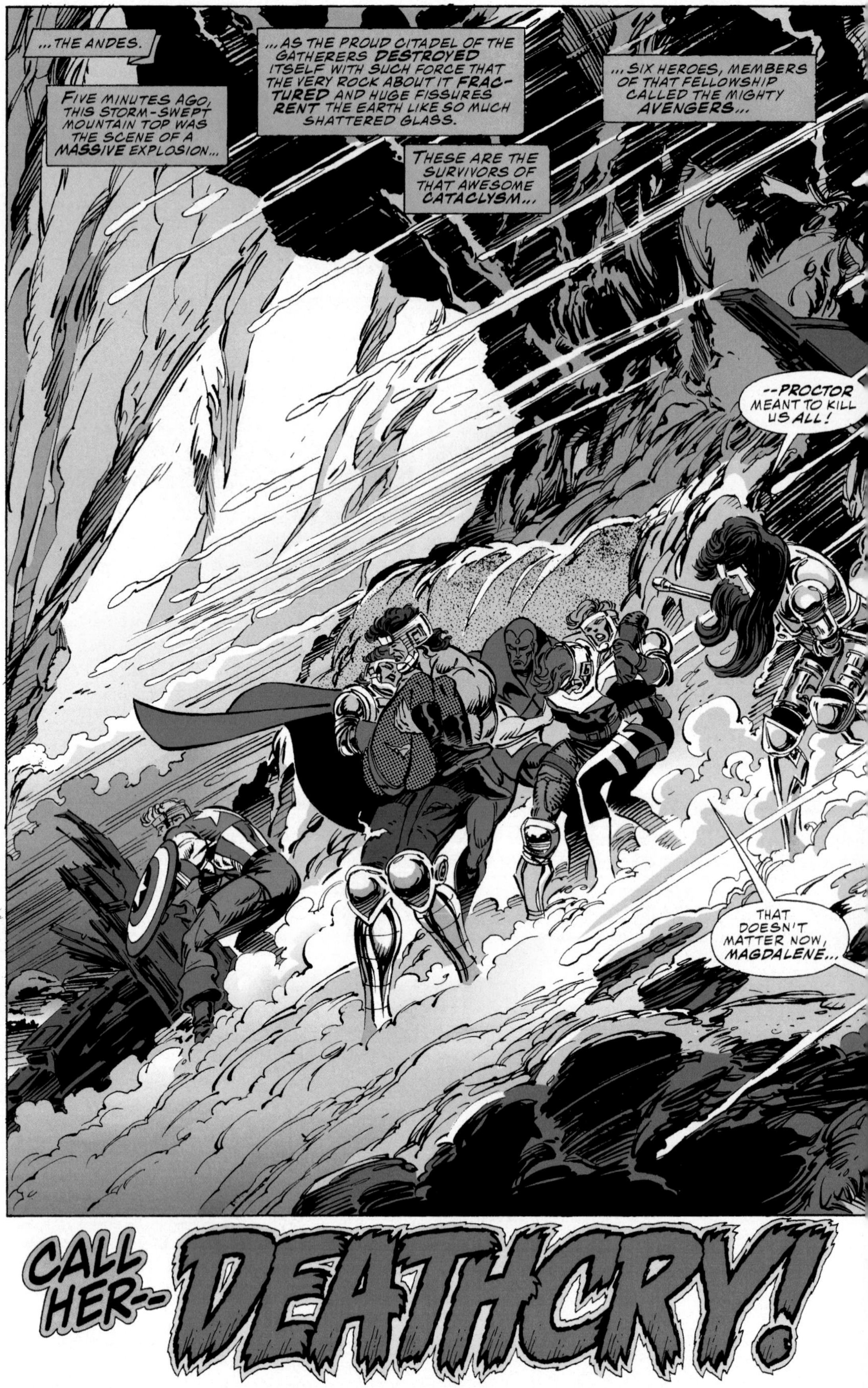
...THE ANDES.
FIVE MINUTES AGO, THIS STORM-SWEPT MOUNTAIN TOP WAS THE SCENE OF A MASSIVE EXPLOSION...
...AS THE PROUD CITADEL OF THE GATHERERS DESTROYED ITSELF WITH SUCH FORCE THAT THE VERY ROCK ABOUT IT FRACTURED AND HUGE FISSURES RENT THE EARTH LIKE SO MUCH SHATTERED GLASS.
THESE ARE THE SURVIVORS OF THAT AWESOME CATACLYSM...
...SIX HEROES, MEMBERS OF THAT FELLOWSHIP CALLED THE MIGHTY AVENGERS...
--PROCTOR MEANT TO KILL US ALL!
THAT DOESN'T MATTER NOW, MAGDALENE...

CALL HER-- DEATHCRY!

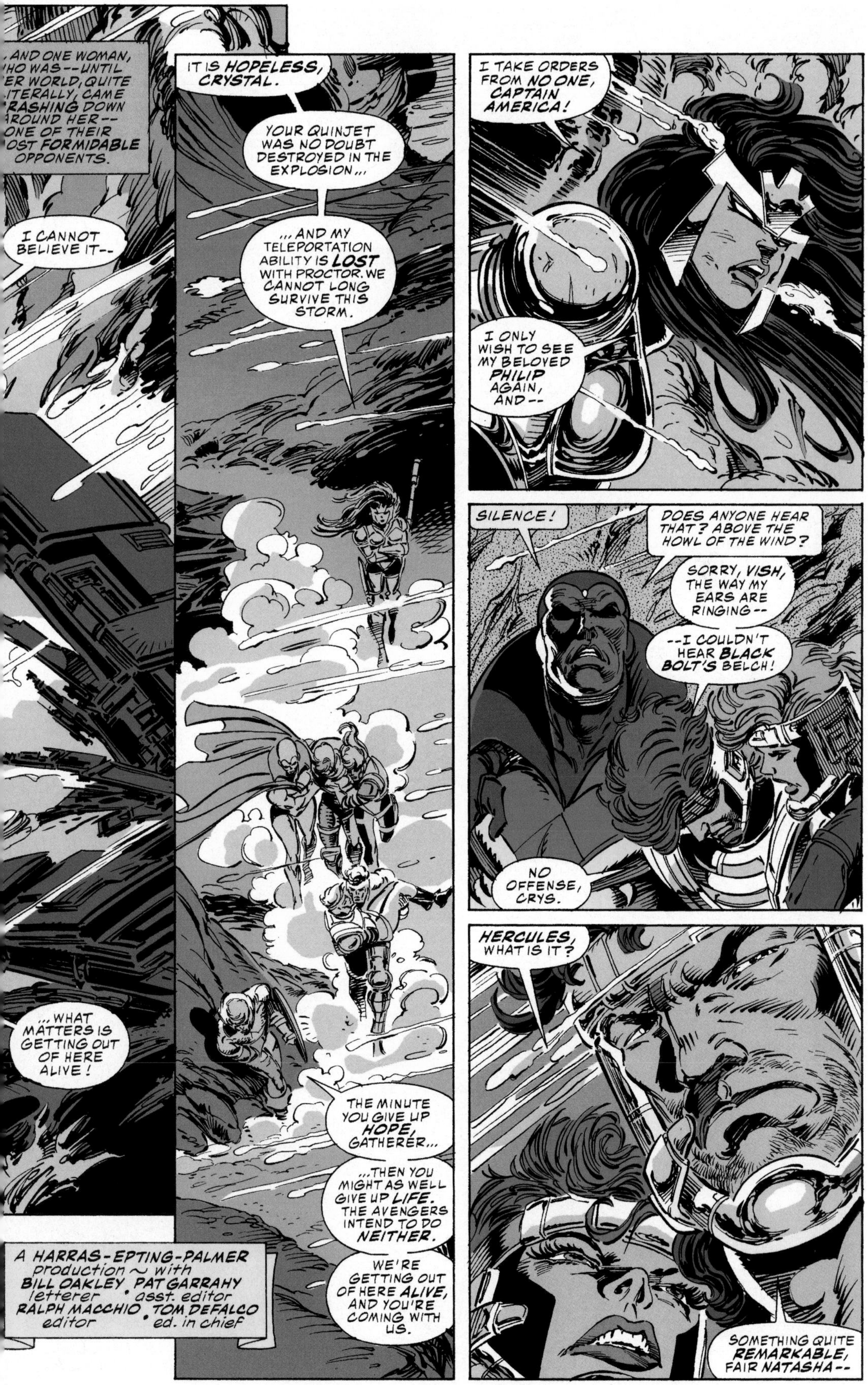
...AND ONE WOMAN, WHO WAS--UNTIL HER WORLD, QUITE LITERALLY, CAME CRASHING DOWN AROUND HER--ONE OF THEIR MOST FORMIDABLE OPPONENTS.
I CANNOT BELIEVE IT--
...WHAT MATTERS IS GETTING OUT OF HERE ALIVE!
IT IS HOPELESS, CRYSTAL.
YOUR QUINJET WAS NO DOUBT DESTROYED IN THE EXPLOSION...
...AND MY TELEPORTATION ABILITY IS LOST WITH PROCTOR. WE CANNOT LONG SURVIVE THIS STORM.
THE MINUTE YOU GIVE UP HOPE, GATHERER...
...THEN YOU MIGHT AS WELL GIVE UP LIFE. THE AVENGERS INTEND TO DO NEITHER.
WE'RE GETTING OUT OF HERE ALIVE, AND YOU'RE COMING WITH US.
A HARRAS-EPTING-PALMER production ~ with BILL OAKLEY letterer • PAT GARRAHY asst. editor RALPH MACCHIO editor • TOM DEFALCO ed. in chief
I TAKE ORDERS FROM NO ONE, CAPTAIN AMERICA!
I ONLY WISH TO SEE MY BELOVED PHILIP AGAIN, AND--
SILENCE!
DOES ANYONE HEAR THAT? ABOVE THE HOWL OF THE WIND?
SORRY, VISH, THE WAY MY EARS ARE RINGING--
--I COULDN'T HEAR BLACK BOLT'S BELCH!
NO OFFENSE, CRYS.
HERCULES, WHAT IS IT?
SOMETHING QUITE REMARKABLE, FAIR NATASHA--

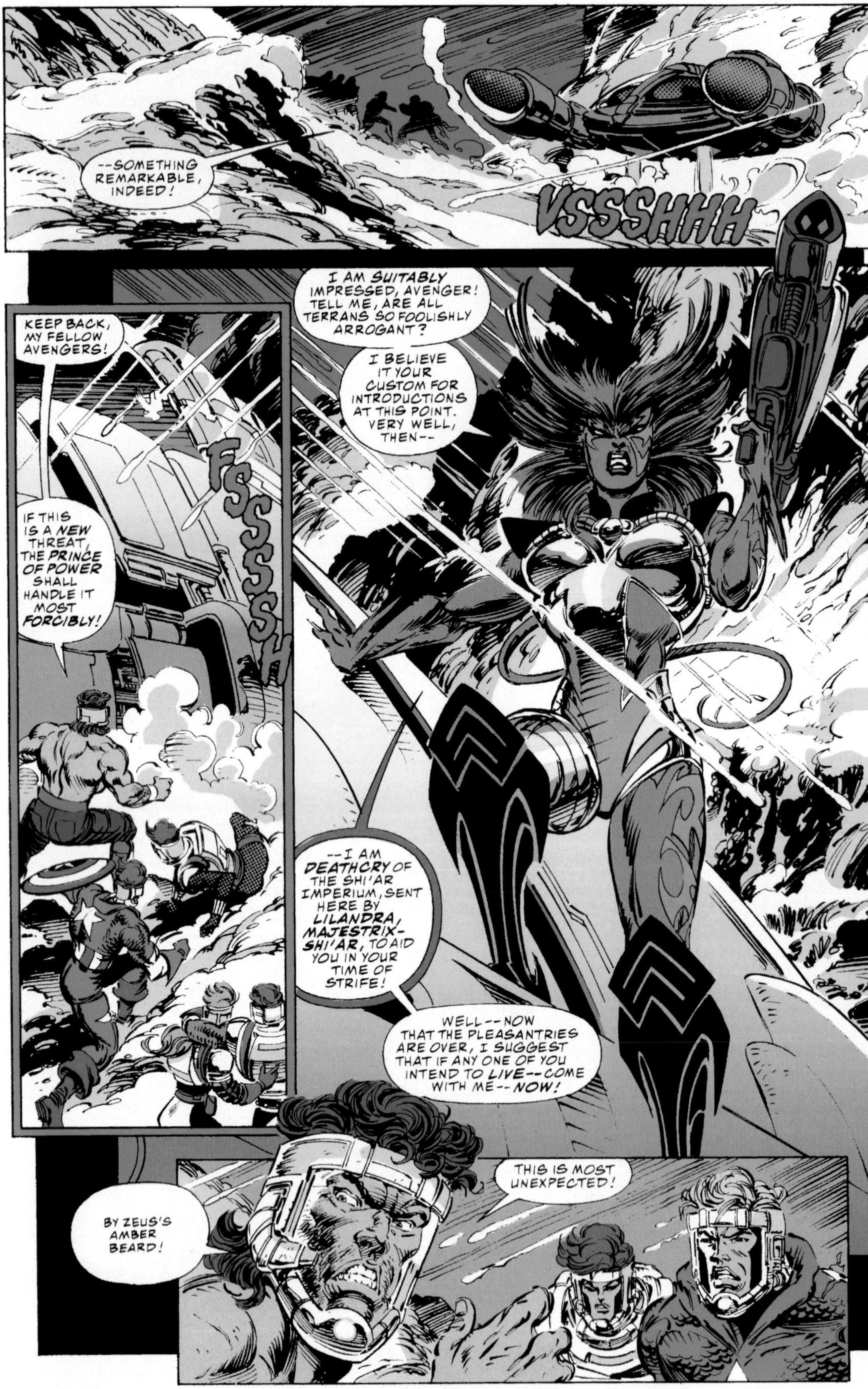

--SOMETHING REMARKABLE, INDEED!
VSSSHHH
I AM SUITABLY IMPRESSED, AVENGER! TELL ME, ARE ALL TERRANS SO FOOLISHLY ARROGANT?
I BELIEVE IT YOUR CUSTOM FOR INTRODUCTIONS AT THIS POINT. VERY WELL, THEN--
KEEP BACK, MY FELLOW AVENGERS!
IF THIS IS A NEW THREAT, THE PRINCE OF POWER SHALL HANDLE IT MOST FORCIBLY!
FSSSSSH
--I AM DEATHCRY OF THE SHI'AR IMPERIUM, SENT HERE BY LILANDRA, MAJESTRIX-SHI'AR, TO AID YOU IN YOUR TIME OF STRIFE!
WELL--NOW THAT THE PLEASANTRIES ARE OVER, I SUGGEST THAT IF ANY ONE OF YOU INTEND TO LIVE--COME WITH ME--NOW!
BY ZEUS'S AMBER BEARD!
THIS IS MOST UNEXPECTED!

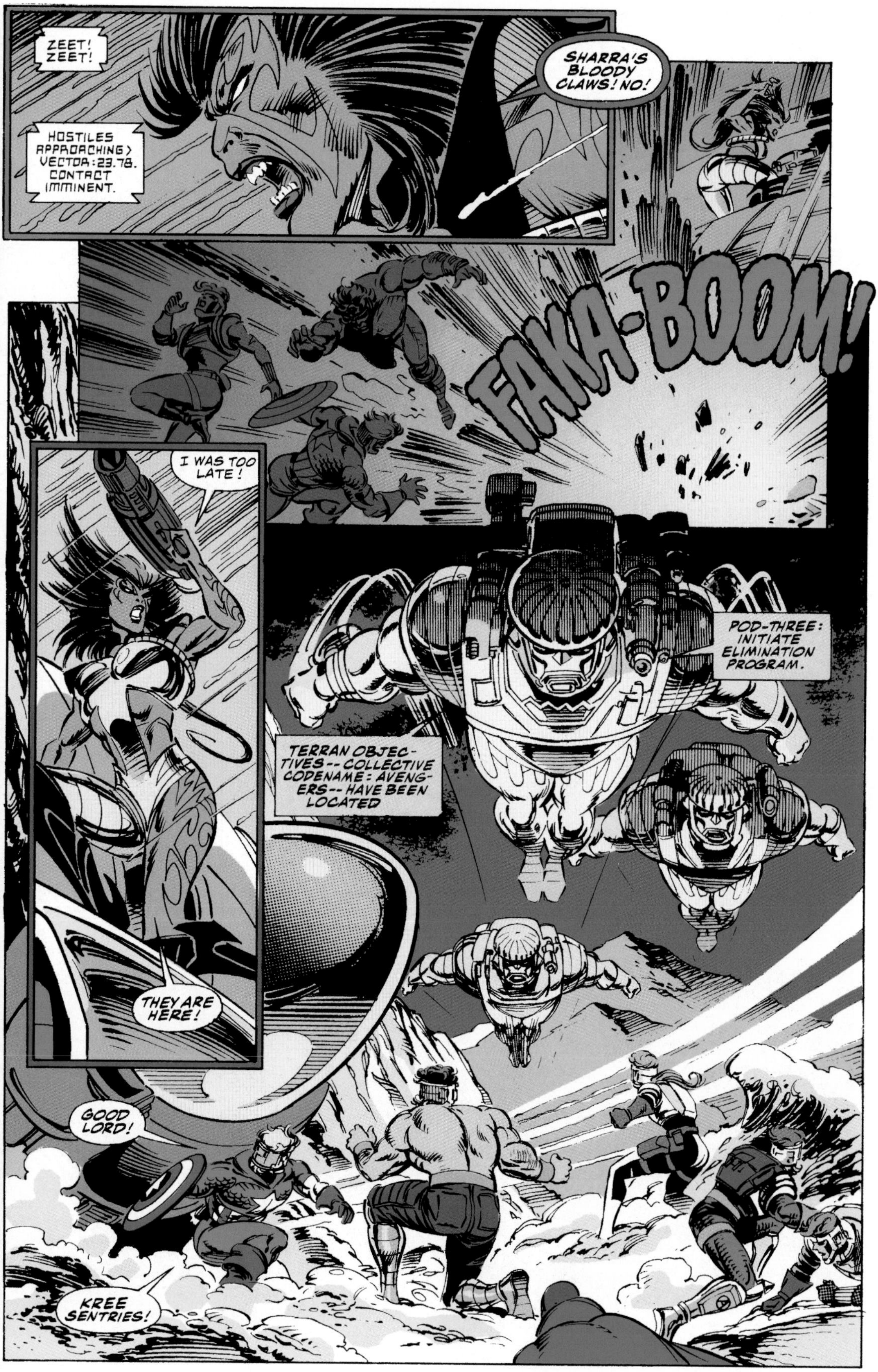
ZEET! ZEET!
HOSTILES APPROACHING > VECTOR: 23.78. CONTACT IMMINENT.
SHARRA'S BLOODY CLAWS! NO!
FAKA-BOOM!
I WAS TOO LATE!
THEY ARE HERE!
POD-THREE: INITIATE ELIMINATION PROGRAM.
TERRAN OBJECTIVES-- COLLECTIVE CODENAME: AVENGERS-- HAVE BEEN LOCATED
GOOD LORD!
KREE SENTRIES!

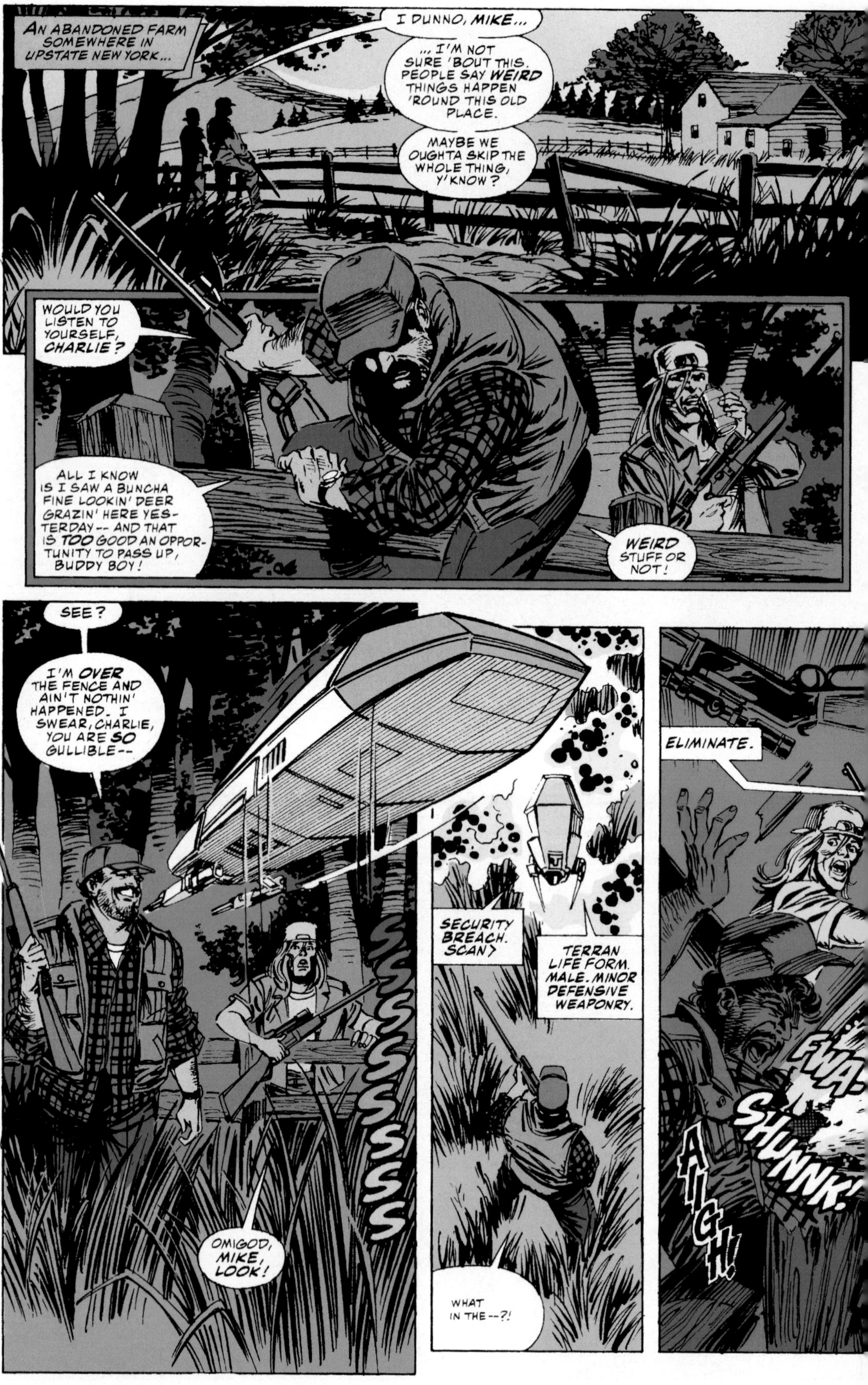
AN ABANDONED FARM SOMEWHERE IN UPSTATE NEW YORK...
I DUNNO, MIKE...
...I'M NOT SURE 'BOUT THIS. PEOPLE SAY WEIRD THINGS HAPPEN 'ROUND THIS OLD PLACE.
MAYBE WE OUGHTA SKIP THE WHOLE THING, Y'KNOW?
WOULD YOU LISTEN TO YOURSELF, CHARLIE?
ALL I KNOW IS I SAW A BUNCHA FINE LOOKIN' DEER GRAZIN' HERE YESTERDAY-- AND THAT IS TOO GOOD AN OPPORTUNITY TO PASS UP, BUDDY BOY!
WEIRD STUFF OR NOT!
SEE?
I'M OVER THE FENCE AND AIN'T NOTHIN' HAPPENED. I SWEAR, CHARLIE, YOU ARE SO GULLIBLE--
SSSSSSSSSS
OMIGOD, MIKE, LOOK!
SECURITY BREACH. SCAN>
TERRAN LIFE FORM. MALE. MINOR DEFENSIVE WEAPONRY.
WHAT IN THE--?!
ELIMINATE.
FWA-SHUNNK!
AIIGH!

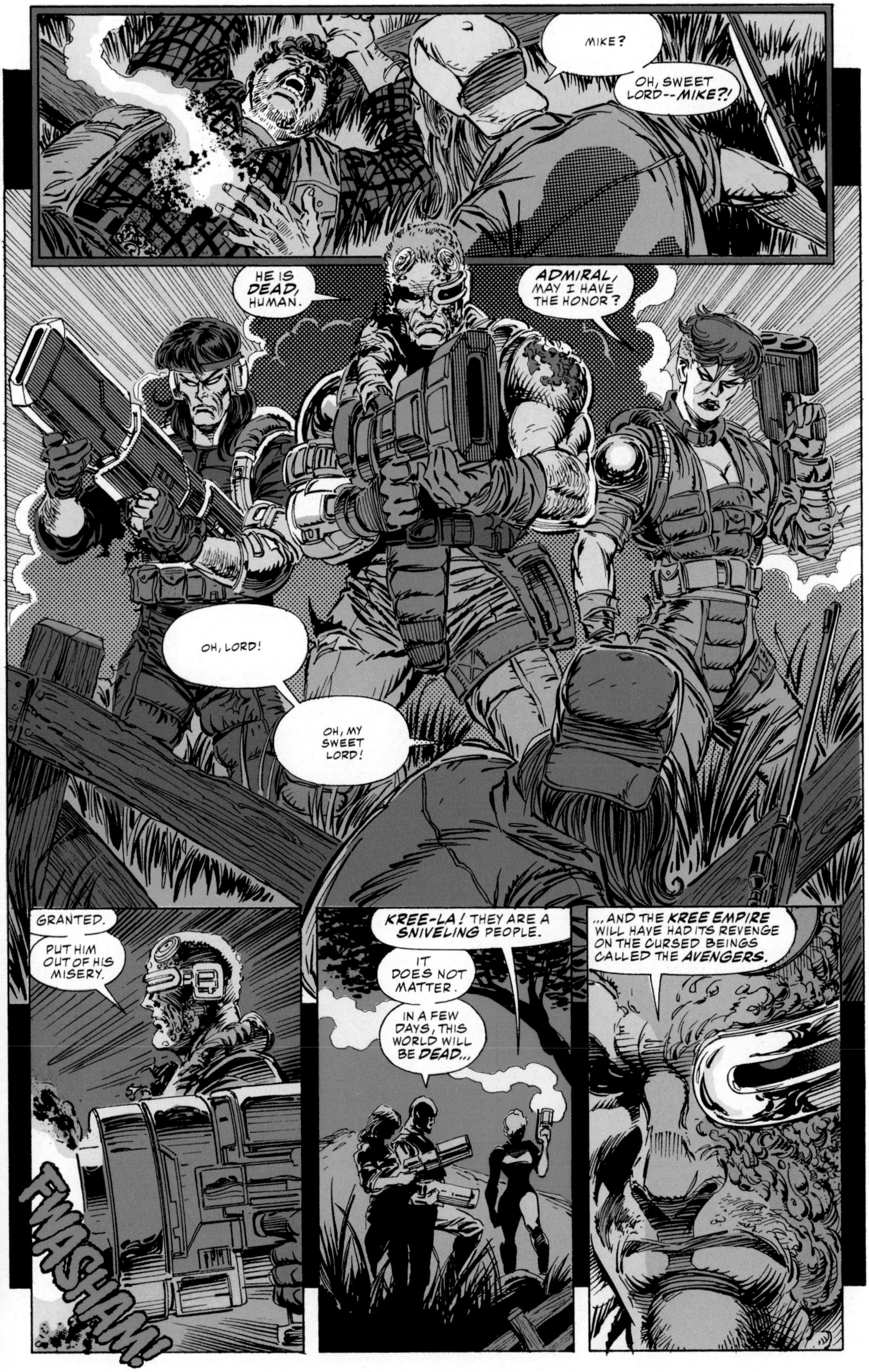
MIKE?
OH, SWEET LORD--MIKE?!
HE IS DEAD, HUMAN.
ADMIRAL, MAY I HAVE THE HONOR?
OH, LORD!
OH, MY SWEET LORD!
GRANTED.
PUT HIM OUT OF HIS MISERY.
FWASHAM!
KREE-LA! THEY ARE A SNIVELING PEOPLE.
IT DOES NOT MATTER.
IN A FEW DAYS, THIS WORLD WILL BE DEAD...
...AND THE KREE EMPIRE WILL HAVE HAD ITS REVENGE ON THE CURSED BEINGS CALLED THE AVENGERS.

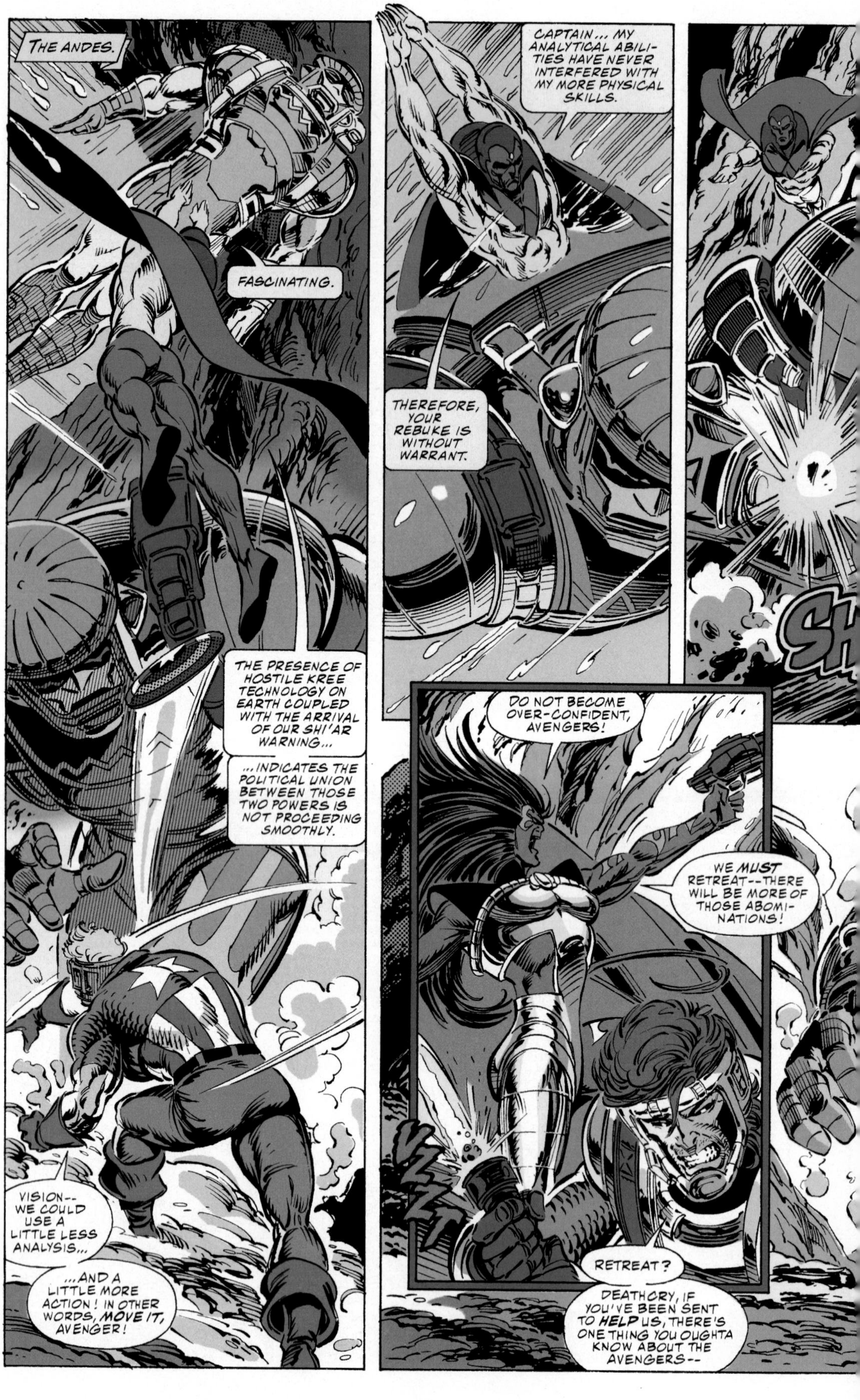
THE ANDES.
FASCINATING.
THE PRESENCE OF HOSTILE KREE TECHNOLOGY ON EARTH COUPLED WITH THE ARRIVAL OF OUR SHI'AR WARNING...
...INDICATES THE POLITICAL UNION BETWEEN THOSE TWO POWERS IS NOT PROCEEDING SMOOTHLY.
VISION-- WE COULD USE A LITTLE LESS ANALYSIS...
...AND A LITTLE MORE ACTION! IN OTHER WORDS, MOVE IT, AVENGER!
CAPTAIN... MY ANALYTICAL ABILITIES HAVE NEVER INTERFERED WITH MY MORE PHYSICAL SKILLS.
THEREFORE, YOUR REBUKE IS WITHOUT WARRANT.
DO NOT BECOME OVER-CONFIDENT, AVENGERS!
WE MUST RETREAT--THERE WILL BE MORE OF THOSE ABOMINATIONS!
RETREAT?
DEATHCRY, IF YOU'VE BEEN SENT TO HELP US, THERE'S ONE THING YOU OUGHTA KNOW ABOUT THE AVENGERS--

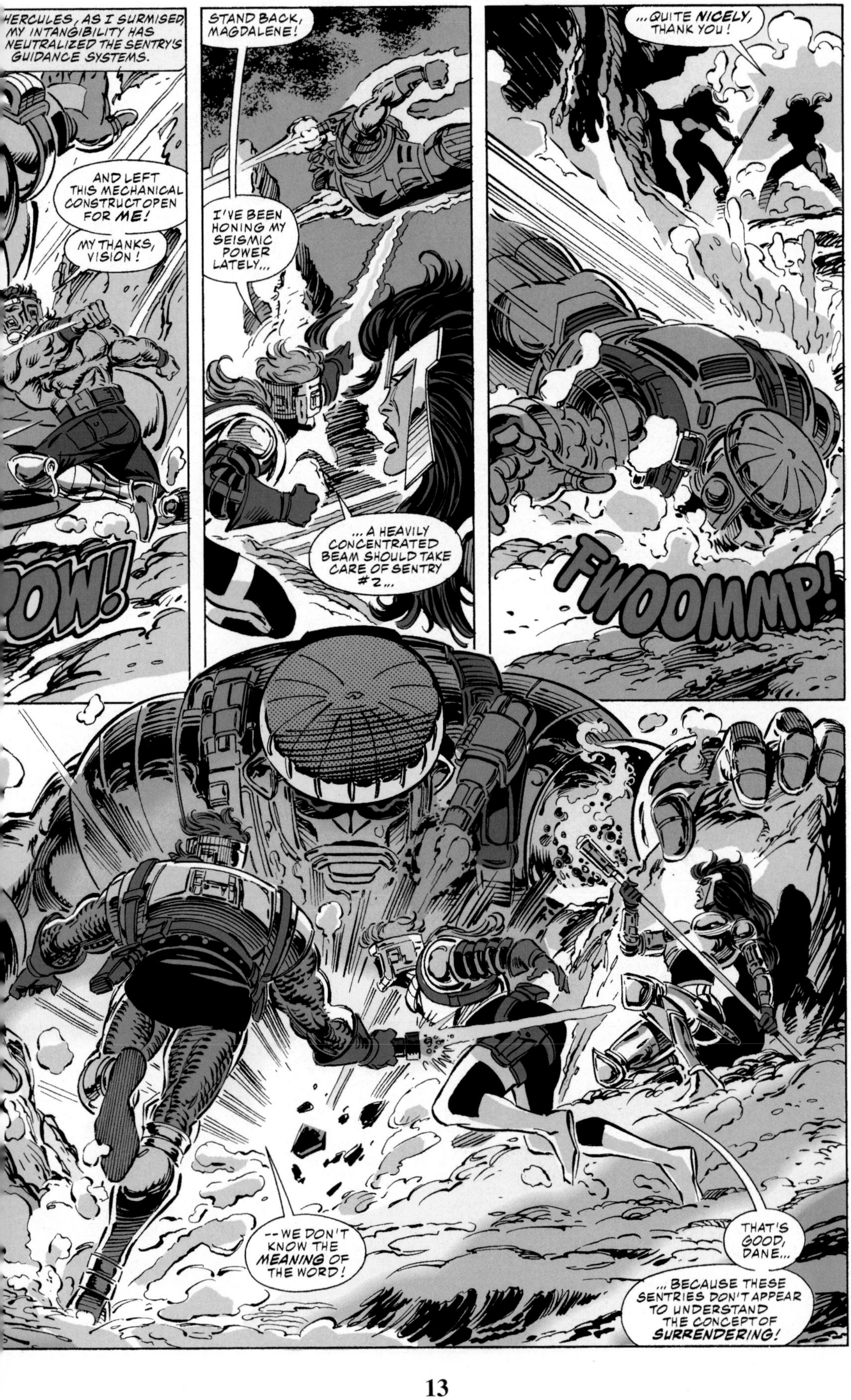
HERCULES, AS I SURMISED, MY INTANGIBILITY HAS NEUTRALIZED THE SENTRY'S GUIDANCE SYSTEMS.
AND LEFT THIS MECHANICAL CONSTRUCT OPEN FOR ME!
MY THANKS, VISION!
STAND BACK, MAGDALENE!
I'VE BEEN HONING MY SEISMIC POWER LATELY...
...A HEAVILY CONCENTRATED BEAM SHOULD TAKE CARE OF SENTRY #2...
...QUITE NICELY, THANK YOU!
FWOOMMP!
--WE DON'T KNOW THE MEANING OF THE WORD!
THAT'S GOOD, DANE...
...BECAUSE THESE SENTRIES DON'T APPEAR TO UNDERSTAND THE CONCEPT OF SURRENDERING!

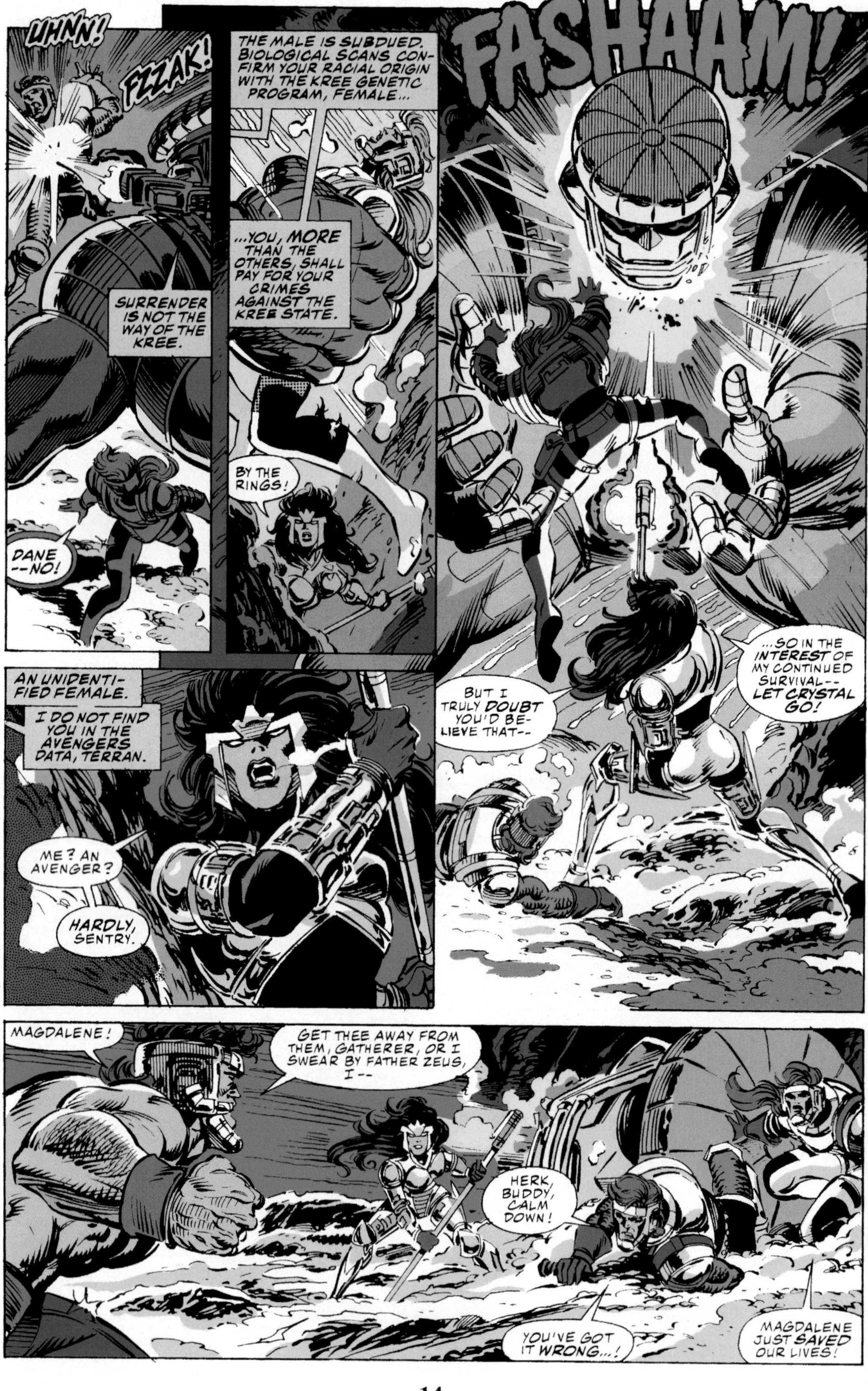
UHNN!
FZZAK!
SURRENDER IS NOT THE WAY OF THE KREE.
DANE --NO!
THE MALE IS SUBDUED. BIOLOGICAL SCANS CONFIRM YOUR RACIAL ORIGIN WITH THE KREE GENETIC PROGRAM, FEMALE...
...YOU, MORE THAN THE OTHERS, SHALL PAY FOR YOUR CRIMES AGAINST THE KREE STATE.
BY THE RINGS!
FASHAAM!
AN UNIDENTIFIED FEMALE.
I DO NOT FIND YOU IN THE AVENGERS DATA, TERRAN.
ME? AN AVENGER?
HARDLY, SENTRY.
BUT I TRULY DOUBT YOU'D BELIEVE THAT--
...SO IN THE INTEREST OF MY CONTINUED SURVIVAL-- LET CRYSTAL GO!
MAGDALENE!
GET THEE AWAY FROM THEM, GATHERER, OR I SWEAR BY FATHER ZEUS, I--
HERK, BUDDY, CALM DOWN!
YOU'VE GOT IT WRONG...!
MAGDALENE JUST SAVED OUR LIVES!

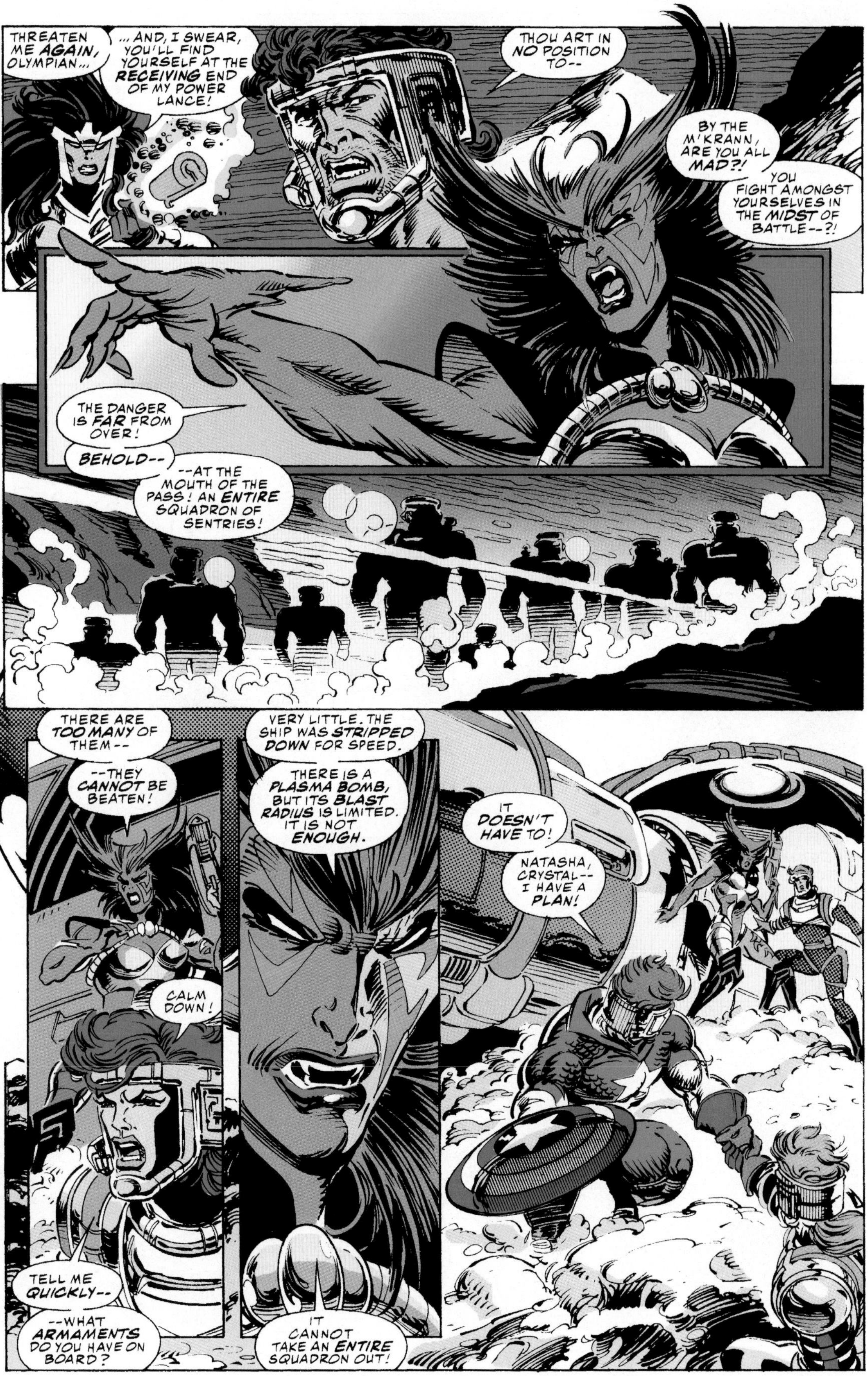
THREATEN ME AGAIN, OLYMPIAN...
...AND, I SWEAR, YOU'LL FIND YOURSELF AT THE RECEIVING END OF MY POWER LANCE!
THOU ART IN NO POSITION TO--
BY THE M'KRANN, ARE YOU ALL MAD?!
YOU FIGHT AMONGST YOURSELVES IN THE MIDST OF BATTLE--?!
THE DANGER IS FAR FROM OVER!
BEHOLD--
--AT THE MOUTH OF THE PASS! AN ENTIRE SQUADRON OF SENTRIES!
THERE ARE TOO MANY OF THEM--
--THEY CANNOT BE BEATEN!
CALM DOWN!
TELL ME QUICKLY--
--WHAT ARMAMENTS DO YOU HAVE ON BOARD?
VERY LITTLE. THE SHIP WAS STRIPPED DOWN FOR SPEED.
THERE IS A PLASMA BOMB, BUT ITS BLAST RADIUS IS LIMITED. IT IS NOT ENOUGH.
IT CANNOT TAKE AN ENTIRE SQUADRON OUT!
IT DOESN'T HAVE TO!
NATASHA, CRYSTAL-- I HAVE A PLAN!

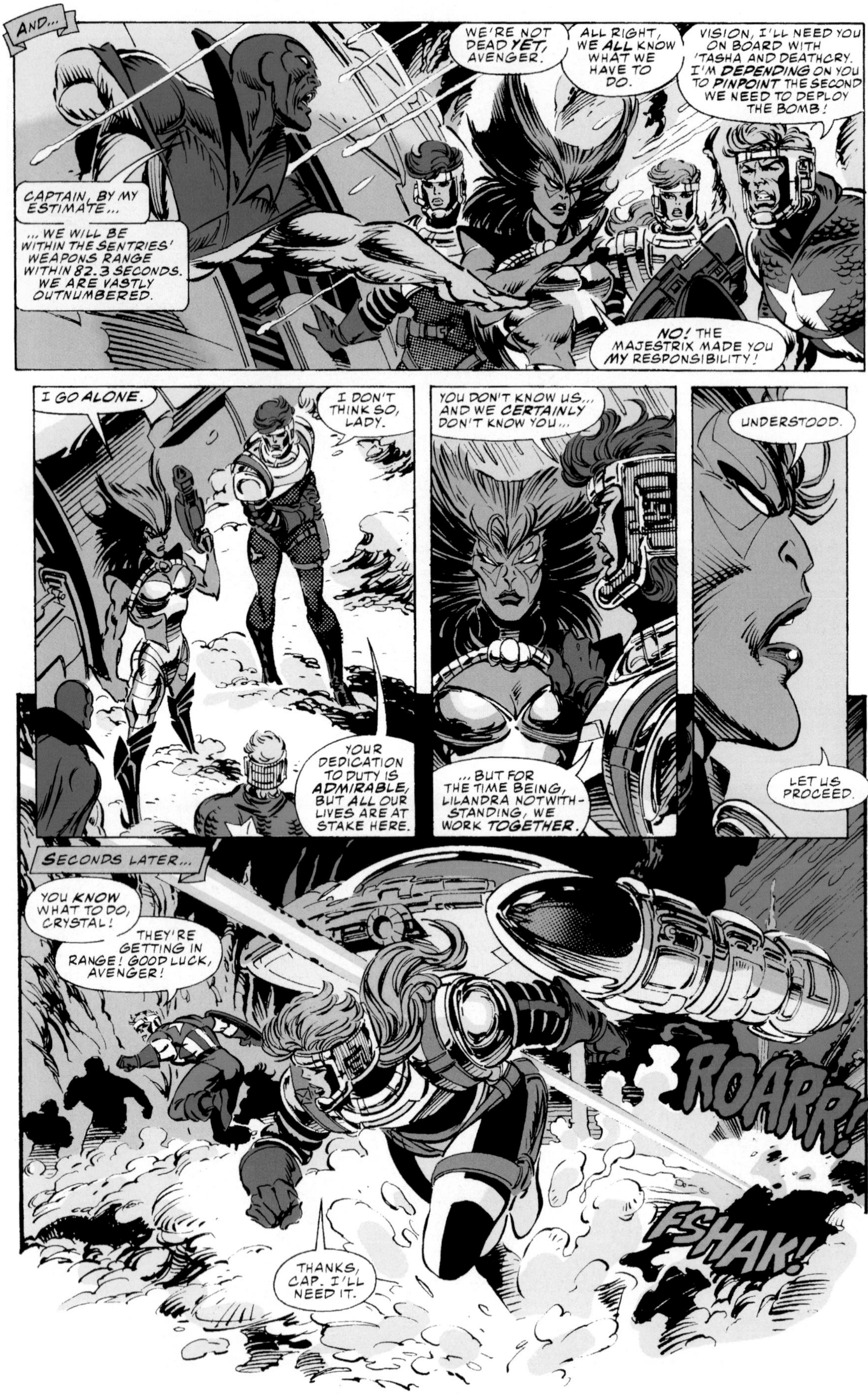
AND...
WE'RE NOT DEAD YET, AVENGER.
ALL RIGHT, WE ALL KNOW WHAT WE HAVE TO DO.
VISION, I'LL NEED YOU ON BOARD WITH 'TASHA AND DEATHCRY. I'M DEPENDING ON YOU TO PINPOINT THE SECOND WE NEED TO DEPLOY THE BOMB!
CAPTAIN, BY MY ESTIMATE...
...WE WILL BE WITHIN THE SENTRIES' WEAPONS RANGE WITHIN 82.3 SECONDS. WE ARE VASTLY OUTNUMBERED.
NO! THE MAJESTRIX MADE YOU MY RESPONSIBILITY!
I GO ALONE.
I DON'T THINK SO, LADY.
YOUR DEDICATION TO DUTY IS ADMIRABLE, BUT ALL OUR LIVES ARE AT STAKE HERE.
YOU DON'T KNOW US... AND WE CERTAINLY DON'T KNOW YOU...
...BUT FOR THE TIME BEING, LILANDRA NOTWITH-STANDING, WE WORK TOGETHER.
UNDERSTOOD.
LET US PROCEED.
SECONDS LATER...
YOU KNOW WHAT TO DO, CRYSTAL!
THEY'RE GETTING IN RANGE! GOOD LUCK, AVENGER!
ROARR!
FSHAK!
THANKS, CAP. I'LL NEED IT.

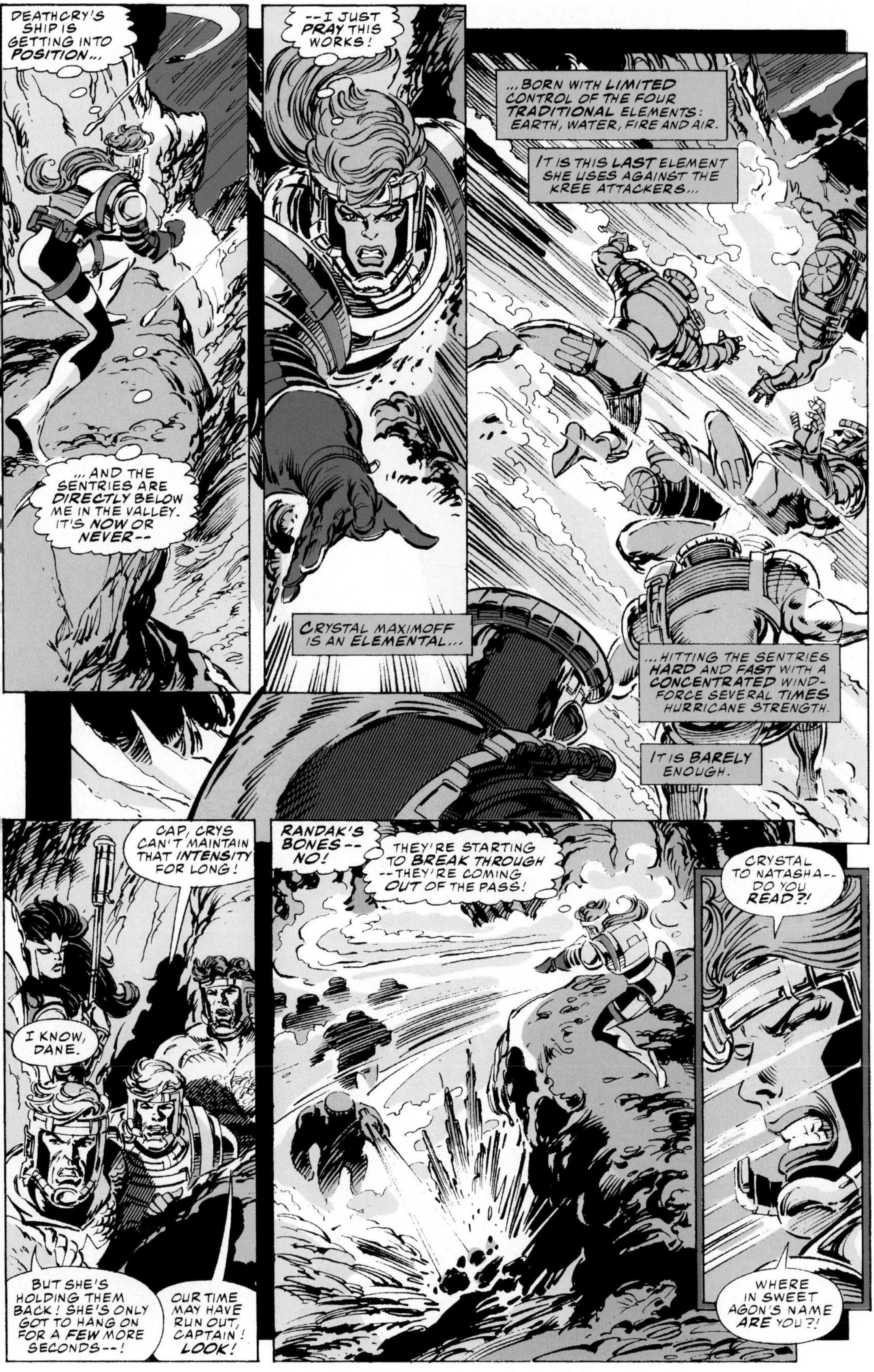

DEATHCRY'S SHIP IS GETTING INTO POSITION...
...AND THE SENTRIES ARE DIRECTLY BELOW ME IN THE VALLEY. IT'S NOW OR NEVER--
--I JUST PRAY THIS WORKS!
CRYSTAL MAXIMOFF IS AN ELEMENTAL...
...BORN WITH LIMITED CONTROL OF THE FOUR TRADITIONAL ELEMENTS: EARTH, WATER, FIRE AND AIR.
IT IS THIS LAST ELEMENT SHE USES AGAINST THE KREE ATTACKERS...
...HITTING THE SENTRIES HARD AND FAST WITH A CONCENTRATED WIND-FORCE SEVERAL TIMES HURRICANE STRENGTH.
IT IS BARELY ENOUGH.
CAP, CRYS CAN'T MAINTAIN THAT INTENSITY FOR LONG!
I KNOW, DANE.
BUT SHE'S HOLDING THEM BACK! SHE'S ONLY GOT TO HANG ON FOR A FEW MORE SECONDS--!
OUR TIME MAY HAVE RUN OUT, CAPTAIN! LOOK!
RANDAK'S BONES--NO!
THEY'RE STARTING TO BREAK THROUGH--THEY'RE COMING OUT OF THE PASS!
CRYSTAL TO NATASHA--DO YOU READ?!
WHERE IN SWEET AGON'S NAME ARE YOU?!

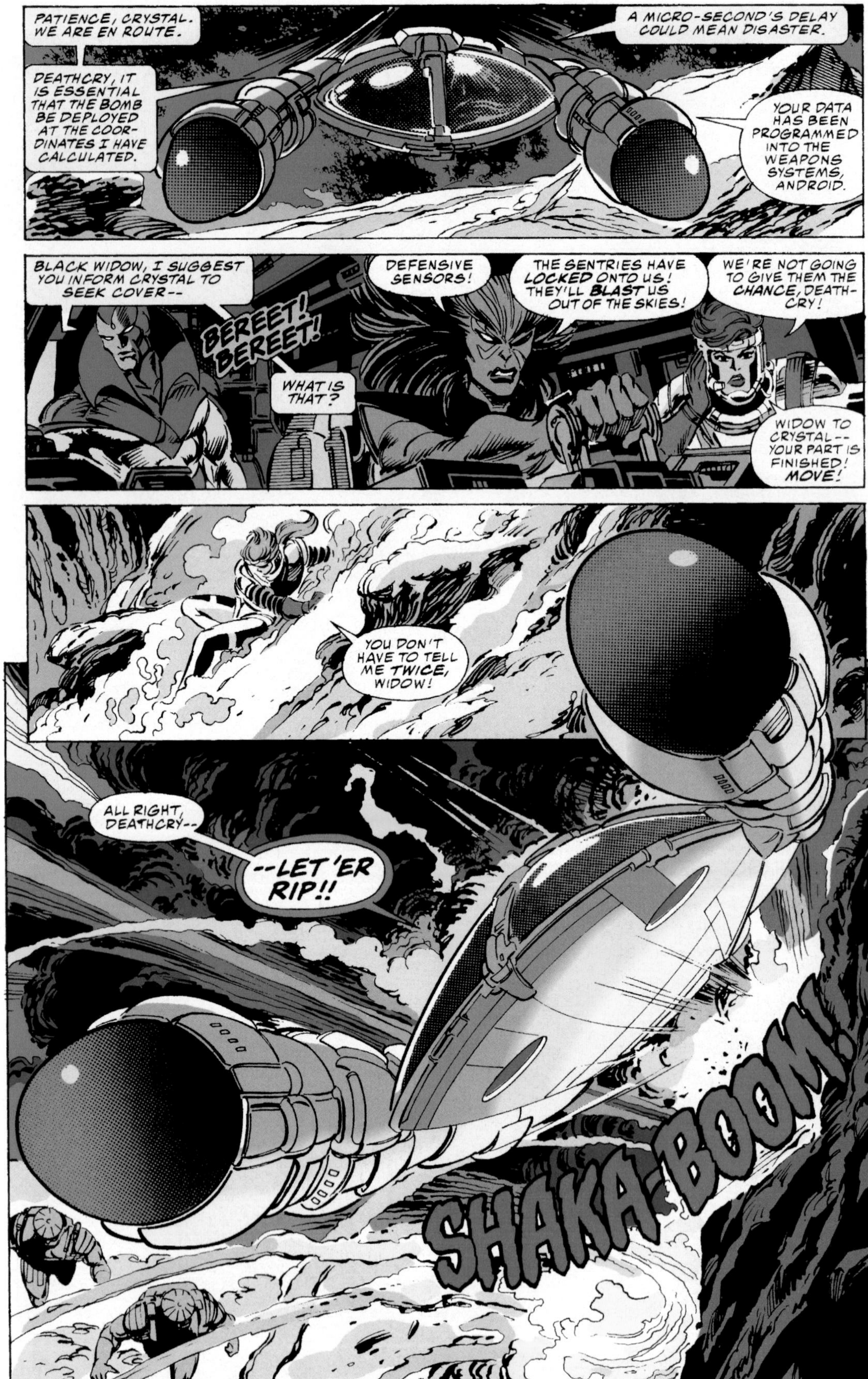
PATIENCE, CRYSTAL. WE ARE EN ROUTE.
DEATHCRY, IT IS ESSENTIAL THAT THE BOMB BE DEPLOYED AT THE COORDINATES I HAVE CALCULATED.
A MICRO-SECOND'S DELAY COULD MEAN DISASTER.
YOUR DATA HAS BEEN PROGRAMMED INTO THE WEAPONS SYSTEMS, ANDROID.
BLACK WIDOW, I SUGGEST YOU INFORM CRYSTAL TO SEEK COVER--
BEREET! BEREET!
WHAT IS THAT?
DEFENSIVE SENSORS!
THE SENTRIES HAVE LOCKED ONTO US! THEY'LL BLAST US OUT OF THE SKIES!
WE'RE NOT GOING TO GIVE THEM THE CHANCE, DEATHCRY!
WIDOW TO CRYSTAL-- YOUR PART IS FINISHED! MOVE!
YOU DON'T HAVE TO TELL ME TWICE, WIDOW!
ALL RIGHT, DEATHCRY--
--LET 'ER RIP!!
SHAKA-BOOM!!

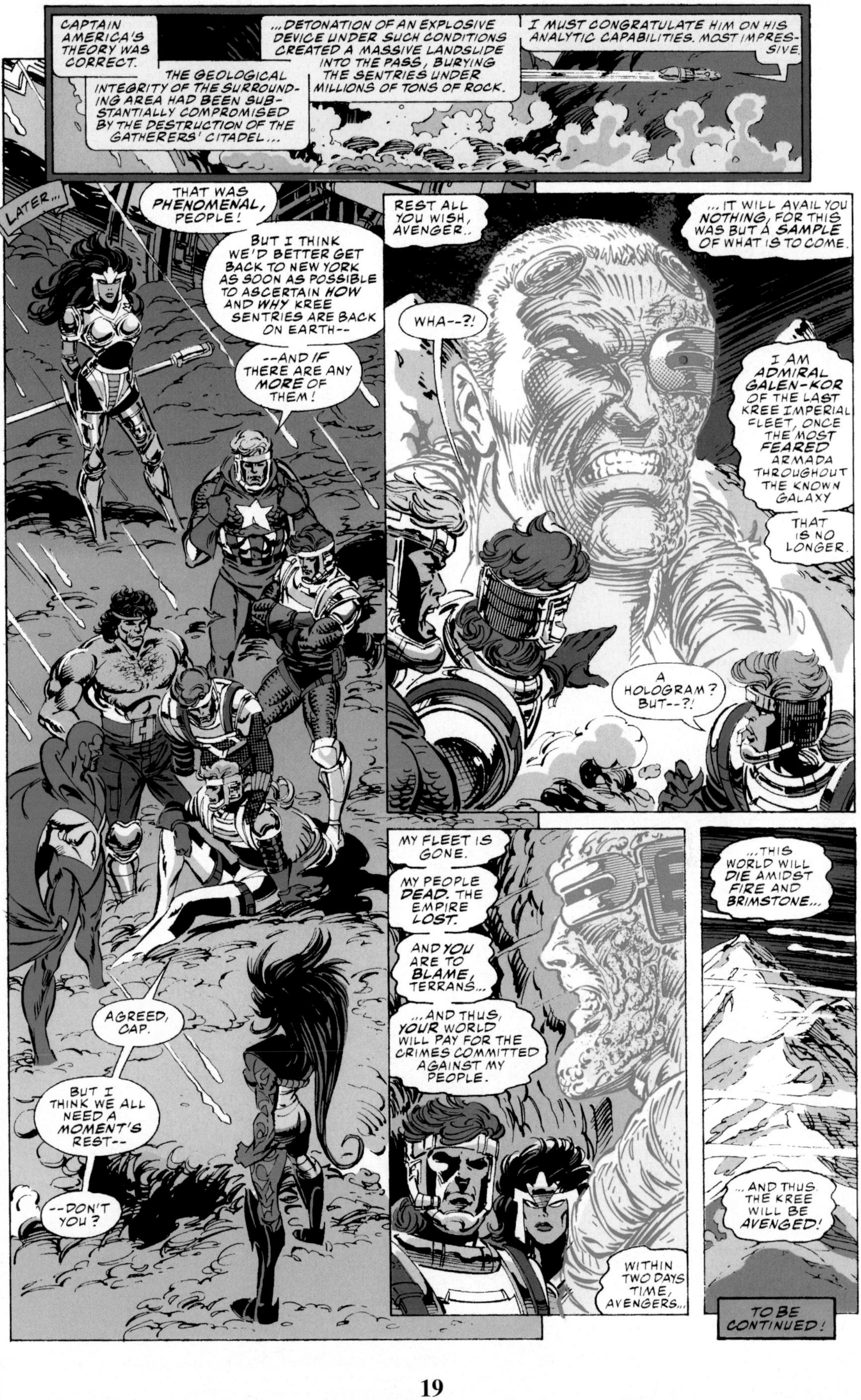
CAPTAIN AMERICA'S THEORY WAS CORRECT.
THE GEOLOGICAL INTEGRITY OF THE SURROUNDING AREA HAD BEEN SUBSTANTIALLY COMPROMISED BY THE DESTRUCTION OF THE GATHERERS' CITADEL...
...DETONATION OF AN EXPLOSIVE DEVICE UNDER SUCH CONDITIONS CREATED A MASSIVE LANDSLIDE INTO THE PASS, BURYING THE SENTRIES UNDER MILLIONS OF TONS OF ROCK.
I MUST CONGRATULATE HIM ON HIS ANALYTIC CAPABILITIES. MOST IMPRESSIVE.
LATER...
THAT WAS PHENOMENAL, PEOPLE!
BUT I THINK WE'D BETTER GET BACK TO NEW YORK AS SOON AS POSSIBLE TO ASCERTAIN HOW AND WHY KREE SENTRIES ARE BACK ON EARTH--
--AND IF THERE ARE ANY MORE OF THEM!
AGREED, CAP.
BUT I THINK WE ALL NEED A MOMENT'S REST--
--DON'T YOU?
REST ALL YOU WISH, AVENGER..
...IT WILL AVAIL YOU NOTHING, FOR THIS WAS BUT A SAMPLE OF WHAT IS TO COME.
WHA--?!
I AM ADMIRAL GALEN-KOR OF THE LAST KREE IMPERIAL FLEET, ONCE THE MOST FEARED ARMADA THROUGHOUT THE KNOWN GALAXY
THAT IS NO LONGER.
A HOLOGRAM? BUT--?!
MY FLEET IS GONE.
MY PEOPLE DEAD. THE EMPIRE LOST.
AND YOU ARE TO BLAME, TERRANS...
...AND THUS, YOUR WORLD WILL PAY FOR THE CRIMES COMMITTED AGAINST MY PEOPLE.
WITHIN TWO DAYS TIME, AVENGERS...
...THIS WORLD WILL DIE AMIDST FIRE AND BRIMSTONE...
...AND THUS THE KREE WILL BE AVENGED!
TO BE CONTINUED!

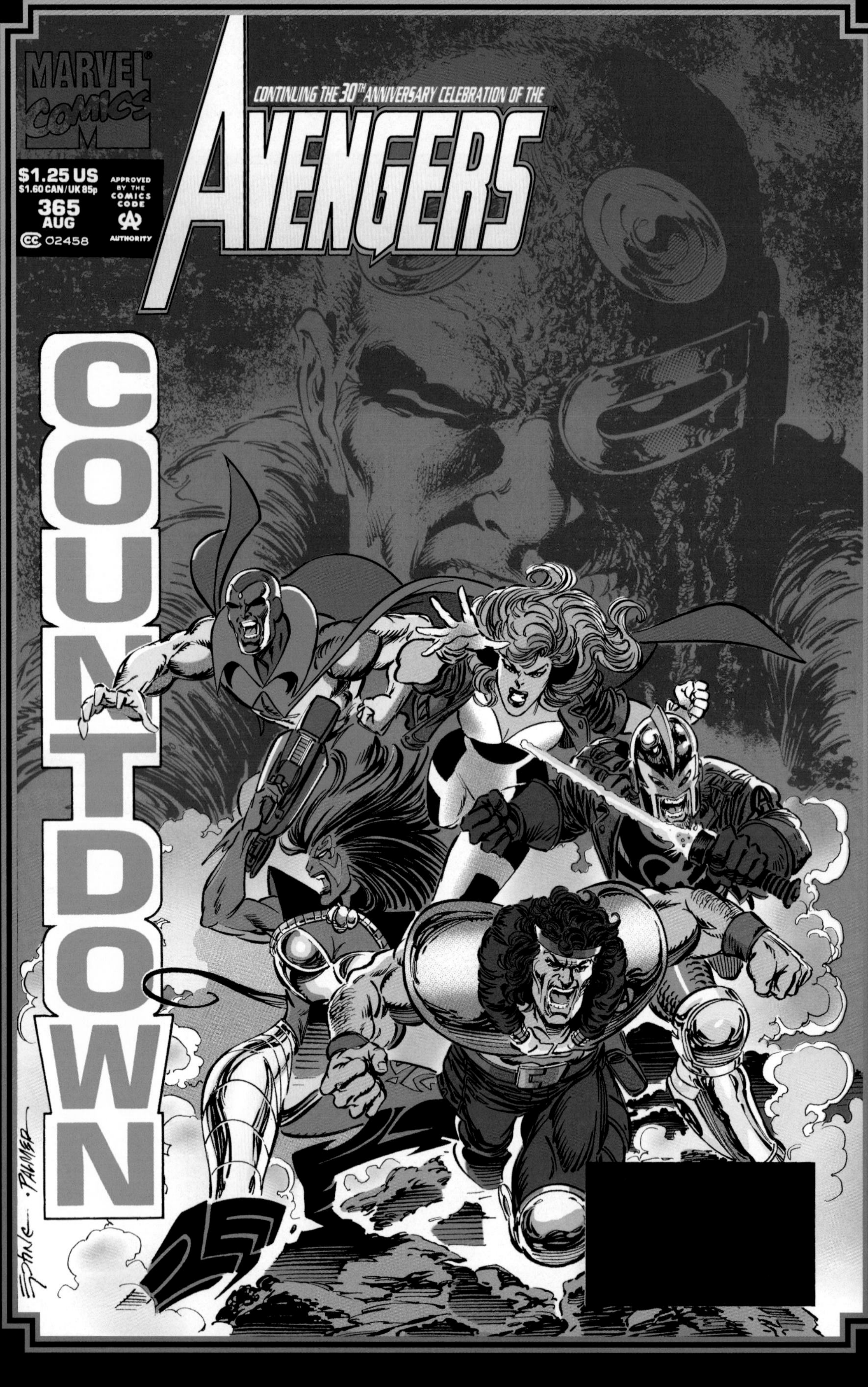
MARVEL COMICS
CONTINUING THE 30TH ANNIVERSARY CELEBRATION OF THE
AVENGERS
$1.25 US
$1.60 CAN/UK 85p
365
AUG
CC 02458
APPROVED BY THE COMICS CODE AUTHORITY
COUNTDOWN
PALMER

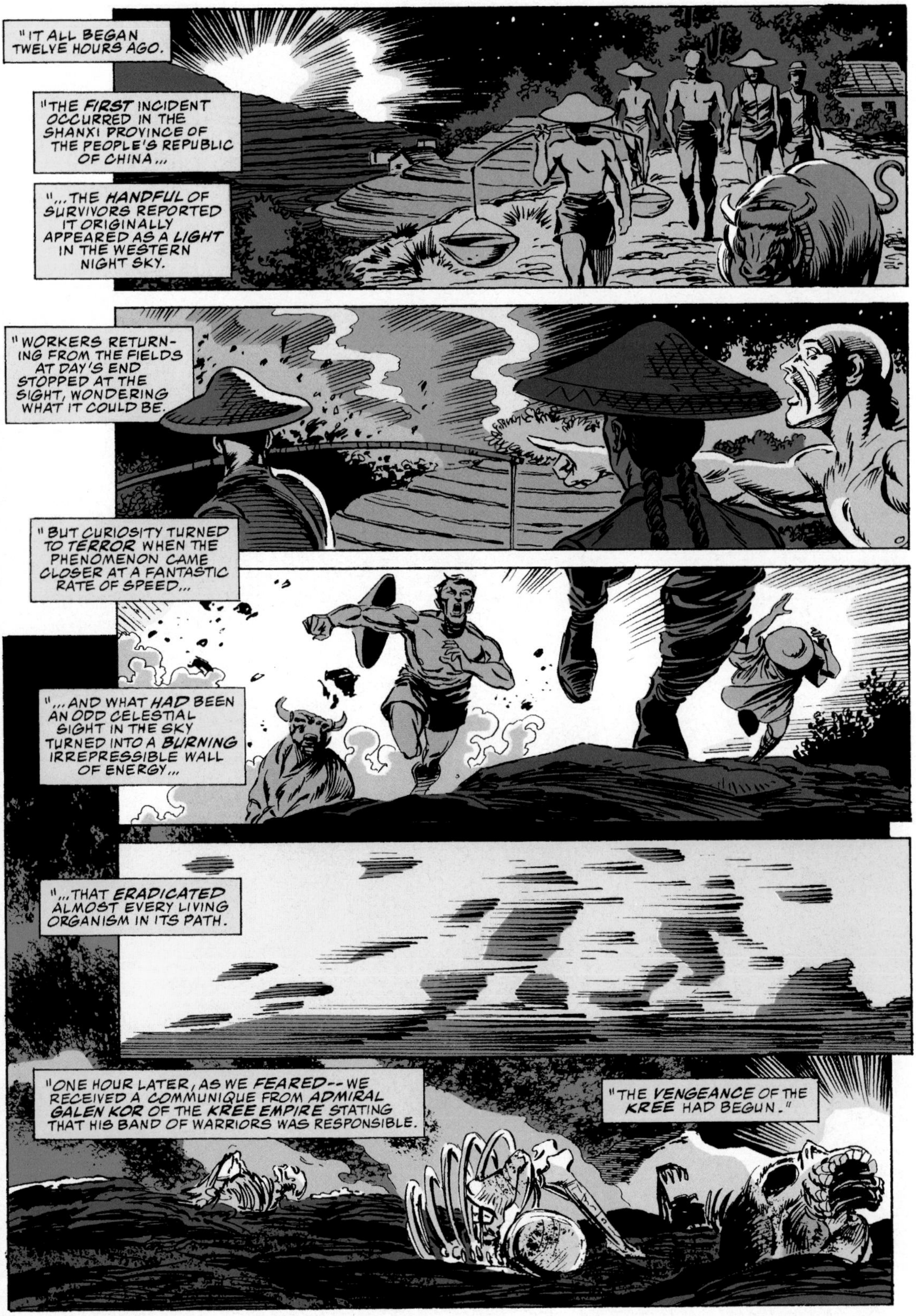
"IT ALL BEGAN TWELVE HOURS AGO.
"THE FIRST INCIDENT OCCURRED IN THE SHANXI PROVINCE OF THE PEOPLE'S REPUBLIC OF CHINA...
"...THE HANDFUL OF SURVIVORS REPORTED IT ORIGINALLY APPEARED AS A LIGHT IN THE WESTERN NIGHT SKY.
"WORKERS RETURNING FROM THE FIELDS AT DAY'S END STOPPED AT THE SIGHT, WONDERING WHAT IT COULD BE.
"BUT CURIOSITY TURNED TO TERROR WHEN THE PHENOMENON CAME CLOSER AT A FANTASTIC RATE OF SPEED...
"...AND WHAT HAD BEEN AN ODD CELESTIAL SIGHT IN THE SKY TURNED INTO A BURNING IRREPRESSIBLE WALL OF ENERGY...
"...THAT ERADICATED ALMOST EVERY LIVING ORGANISM IN ITS PATH.
"ONE HOUR LATER, AS WE FEARED--WE RECEIVED A COMMUNIQUE FROM ADMIRAL GALEN KOR OF THE KREE EMPIRE STATING THAT HIS BAND OF WARRIORS WAS RESPONSIBLE.
"THE VENGEANCE OF THE KREE HAD BEGUN."

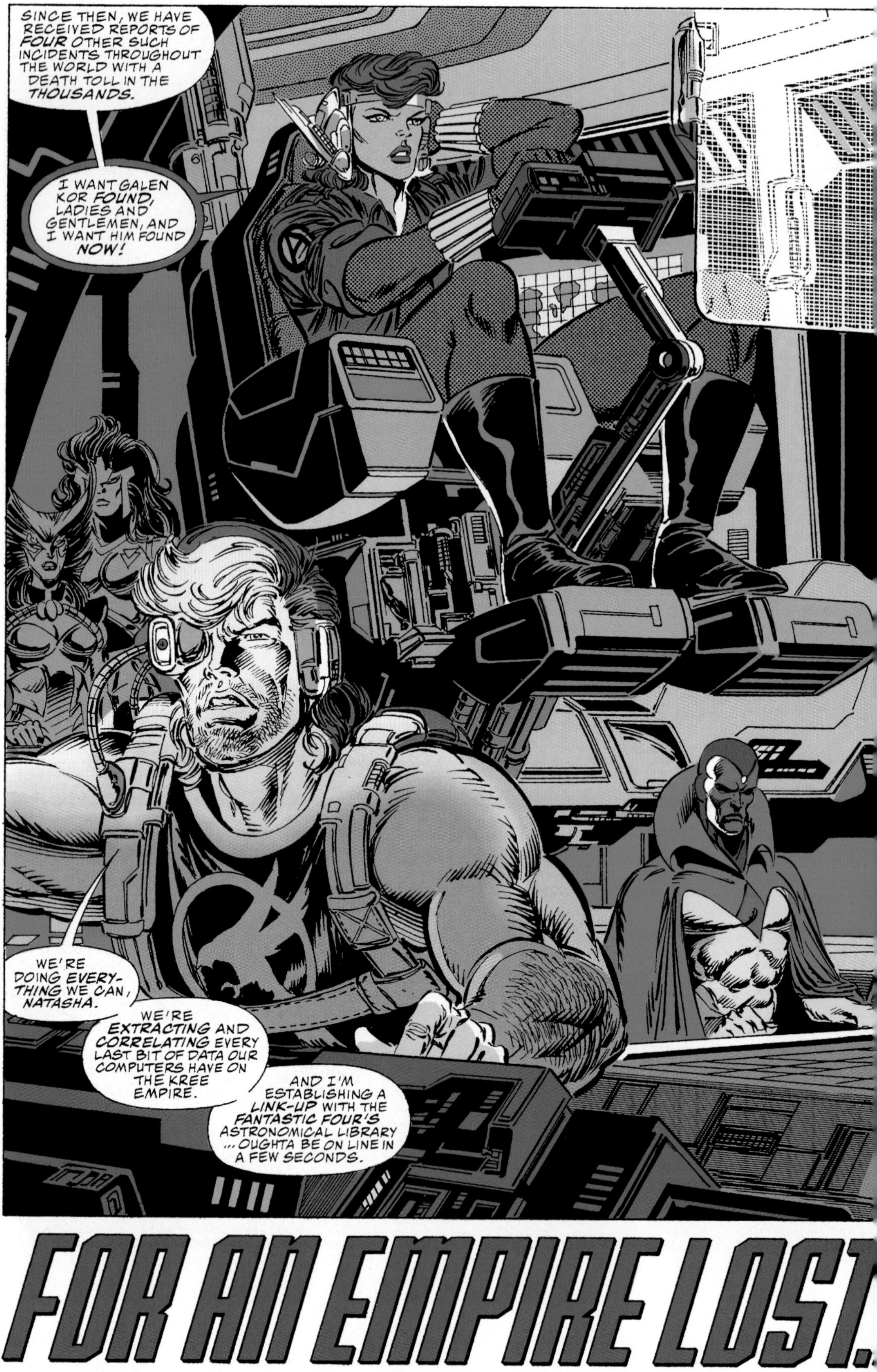
SINCE THEN, WE HAVE RECEIVED REPORTS OF FOUR OTHER SUCH INCIDENTS THROUGHOUT THE WORLD WITH A DEATH TOLL IN THE THOUSANDS.
I WANT GALEN KOR FOUND, LADIES AND GENTLEMEN, AND I WANT HIM FOUND NOW!
WE'RE DOING EVERY-THING WE CAN, NATASHA.
WE'RE EXTRACTING AND CORRELATING EVERY LAST BIT OF DATA OUR COMPUTERS HAVE ON THE KREE EMPIRE.
AND I'M ESTABLISHING A LINK-UP WITH THE FANTASTIC FOUR'S ASTRONOMICAL LIBRARY ...OUGHTA BE ON LINE IN A FEW SECONDS.
FOR AN EMPIRE LOST...

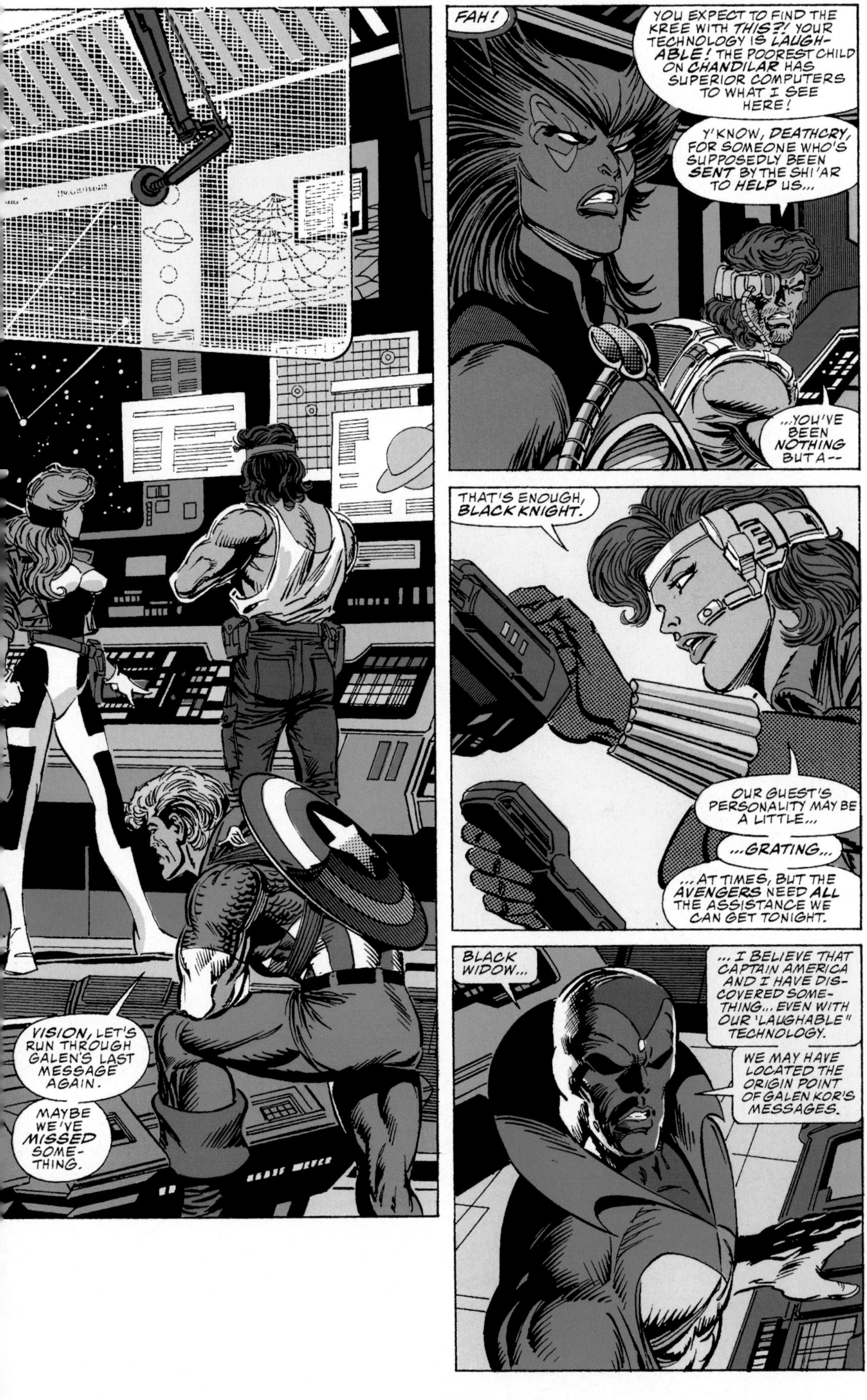
VISION, LET'S RUN THROUGH GALEN'S LAST MESSAGE AGAIN.
MAYBE WE'VE MISSED SOME-THING.
FAH!
YOU EXPECT TO FIND THE KREE WITH THIS?! YOUR TECHNOLOGY IS LAUGH-ABLE! THE POOREST CHILD ON CHANDILAR HAS SUPERIOR COMPUTERS TO WHAT I SEE HERE!
Y'KNOW, DEATHCRY, FOR SOMEONE WHO'S SUPPOSEDLY BEEN SENT BY THE SHI'AR TO HELP US...
...YOU'VE BEEN NOTHING BUT A--
THAT'S ENOUGH, BLACK KNIGHT.
OUR GUEST'S PERSONALITY MAY BE A LITTLE...
...GRATING...
...AT TIMES, BUT THE AVENGERS NEED ALL THE ASSISTANCE WE CAN GET TONIGHT.
BLACK WIDOW...
...I BELIEVE THAT CAPTAIN AMERICA AND I HAVE DIS-COVERED SOME-THING... EVEN WITH OUR 'LAUGHABLE" TECHNOLOGY.
WE MAY HAVE LOCATED THE ORIGIN POINT OF GALEN KOR'S MESSAGES.

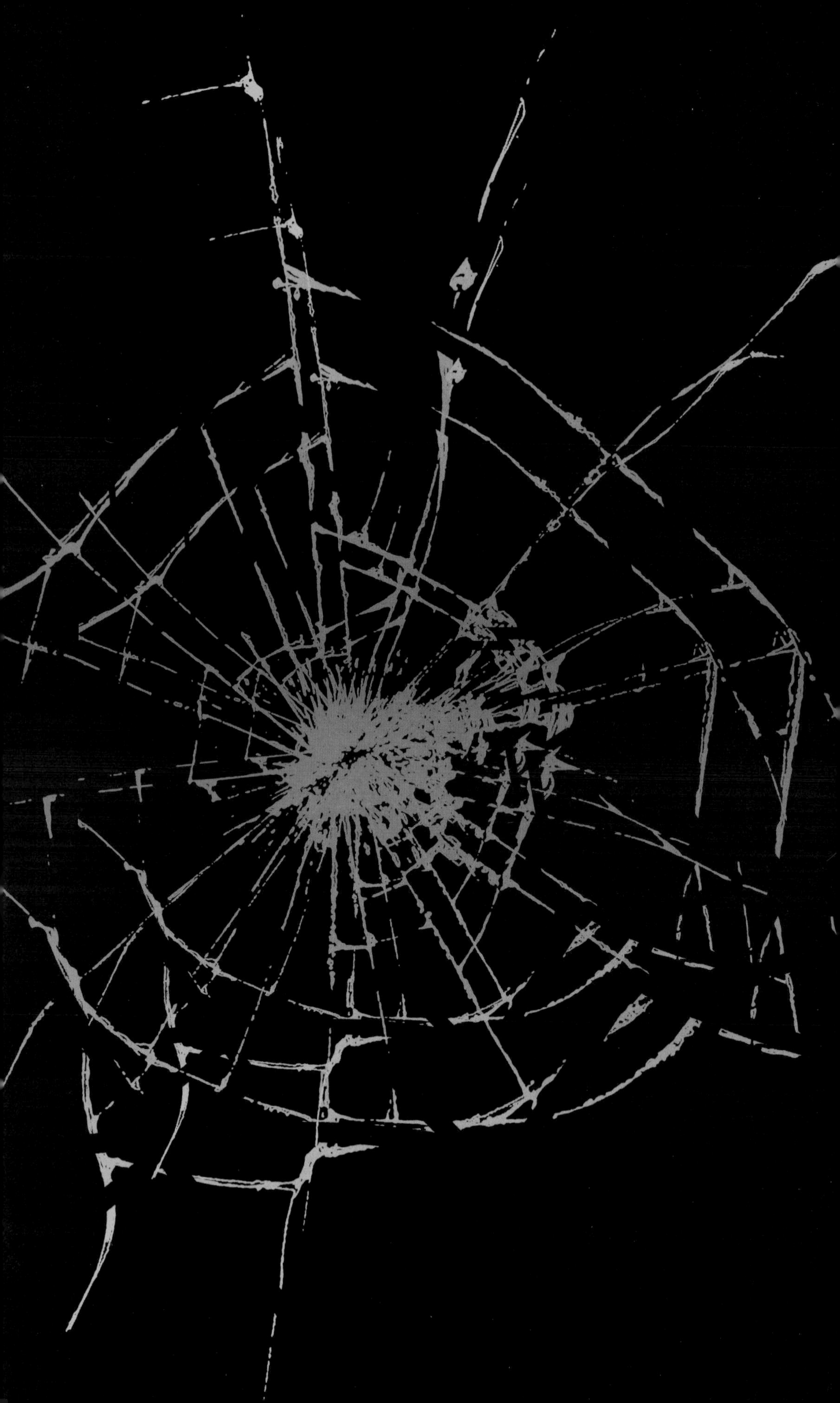

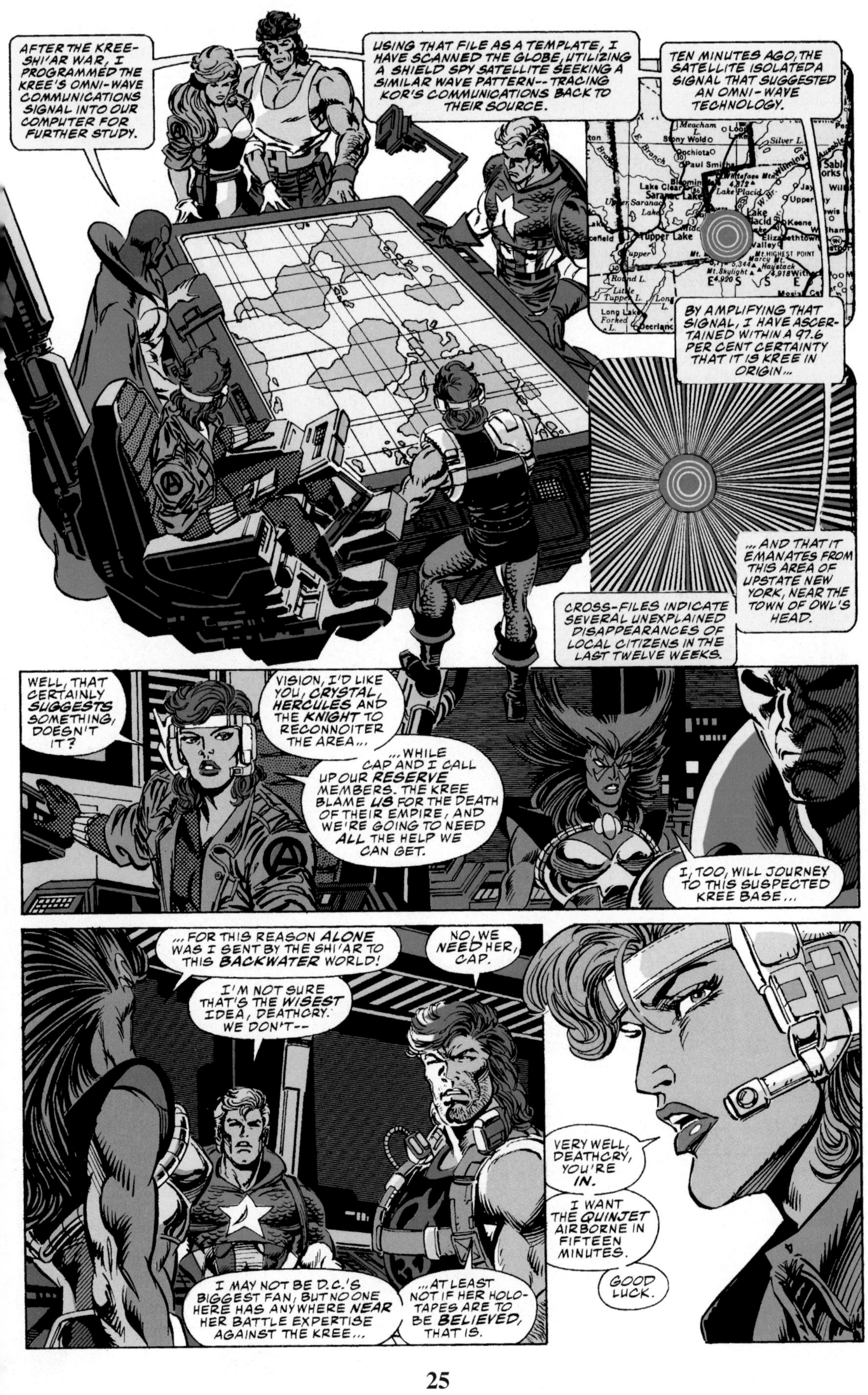

AFTER THE KREE-SHI'AR WAR, I PROGRAMMED THE KREE'S OMNI-WAVE COMMUNICATIONS SIGNAL INTO OUR COMPUTER FOR FURTHER STUDY.
USING THAT FILE AS A TEMPLATE, I HAVE SCANNED THE GLOBE, UTILIZING A SHIELD SPY SATELLITE SEEKING A SIMILAR WAVE PATTERN-- TRACING KOR'S COMMUNICATIONS BACK TO THEIR SOURCE.
TEN MINUTES AGO, THE SATELLITE ISOLATED A SIGNAL THAT SUGGESTED AN OMNI-WAVE TECHNOLOGY.
BY AMPLIFYING THAT SIGNAL, I HAVE ASCERTAINED WITHIN A 97.6 PER CENT CERTAINTY THAT IT IS KREE IN ORIGIN...
...AND THAT IT EMANATES FROM THIS AREA OF UPSTATE NEW YORK, NEAR THE TOWN OF OWL'S HEAD.
CROSS-FILES INDICATE SEVERAL UNEXPLAINED DISAPPEARANCES OF LOCAL CITIZENS IN THE LAST TWELVE WEEKS.
WELL, THAT CERTAINLY SUGGESTS SOMETHING, DOESN'T IT?
VISION, I'D LIKE YOU, CRYSTAL, HERCULES AND THE KNIGHT TO RECONNOITER THE AREA...
...WHILE CAP AND I CALL UP OUR RESERVE MEMBERS. THE KREE BLAME US FOR THE DEATH OF THEIR EMPIRE, AND WE'RE GOING TO NEED ALL THE HELP WE CAN GET.
I, TOO, WILL JOURNEY TO THIS SUSPECTED KREE BASE...
...FOR THIS REASON ALONE WAS I SENT BY THE SHI'AR TO THIS BACKWATER WORLD!
I'M NOT SURE THAT'S THE WISEST IDEA, DEATHCRY. WE DON'T--
NO, WE NEED HER, CAP.
I MAY NOT BE D.C.'S BIGGEST FAN, BUT NO ONE HERE HAS ANYWHERE NEAR HER BATTLE EXPERTISE AGAINST THE KREE...
...AT LEAST NOT IF HER HOLO-TAPES ARE TO BE BELIEVED, THAT IS.
VERY WELL, DEATHCRY, YOU'RE IN.
I WANT THE QUINJET AIRBORNE IN FIFTEEN MINUTES.
GOOD LUCK.

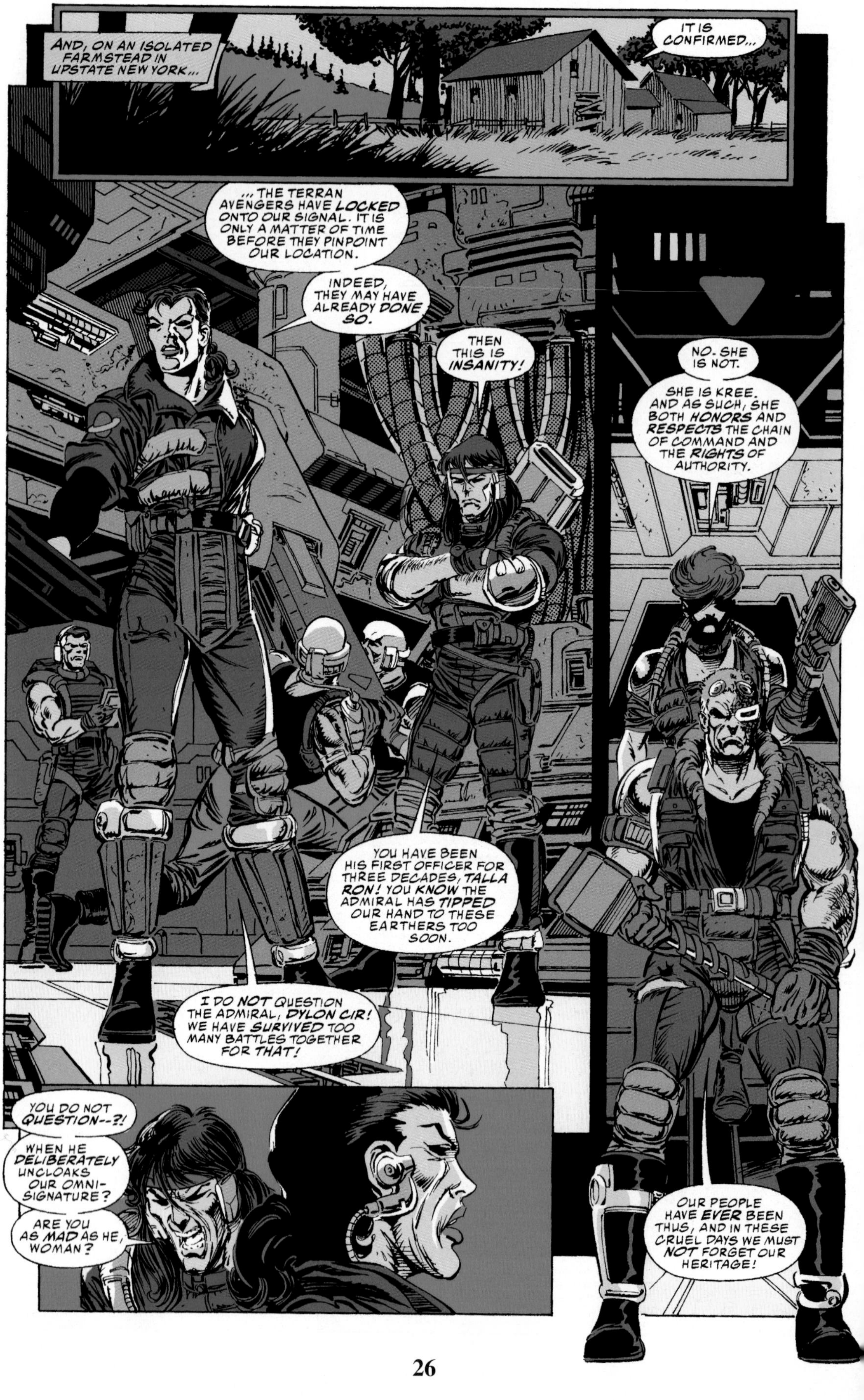
AND, ON AN ISOLATED FARMSTEAD IN UPSTATE NEW YORK...
IT IS CONFIRMED...
...THE TERRAN AVENGERS HAVE LOCKED ONTO OUR SIGNAL. IT IS ONLY A MATTER OF TIME BEFORE THEY PINPOINT OUR LOCATION.
INDEED, THEY MAY HAVE ALREADY DONE SO.
THEN THIS IS INSANITY!
NO. SHE IS NOT.
SHE IS KREE. AND AS SUCH, SHE BOTH HONORS AND RESPECTS THE CHAIN OF COMMAND AND THE RIGHTS OF AUTHORITY.
YOU HAVE BEEN HIS FIRST OFFICER FOR THREE DECADES, TALLA RON! YOU KNOW THE ADMIRAL HAS TIPPED OUR HAND TO THESE EARTHERS TOO SOON.
I DO NOT QUESTION THE ADMIRAL, DYLON CIR! WE HAVE SURVIVED TOO MANY BATTLES TOGETHER FOR THAT!
YOU DO NOT QUESTION--?!
WHEN HE DELIBERATELY UNCLOAKS OUR OMNI-SIGNATURE?
ARE YOU AS MAD AS HE, WOMAN?
OUR PEOPLE HAVE EVER BEEN THUS, AND IN THESE CRUEL DAYS WE MUST NOT FORGET OUR HERITAGE!

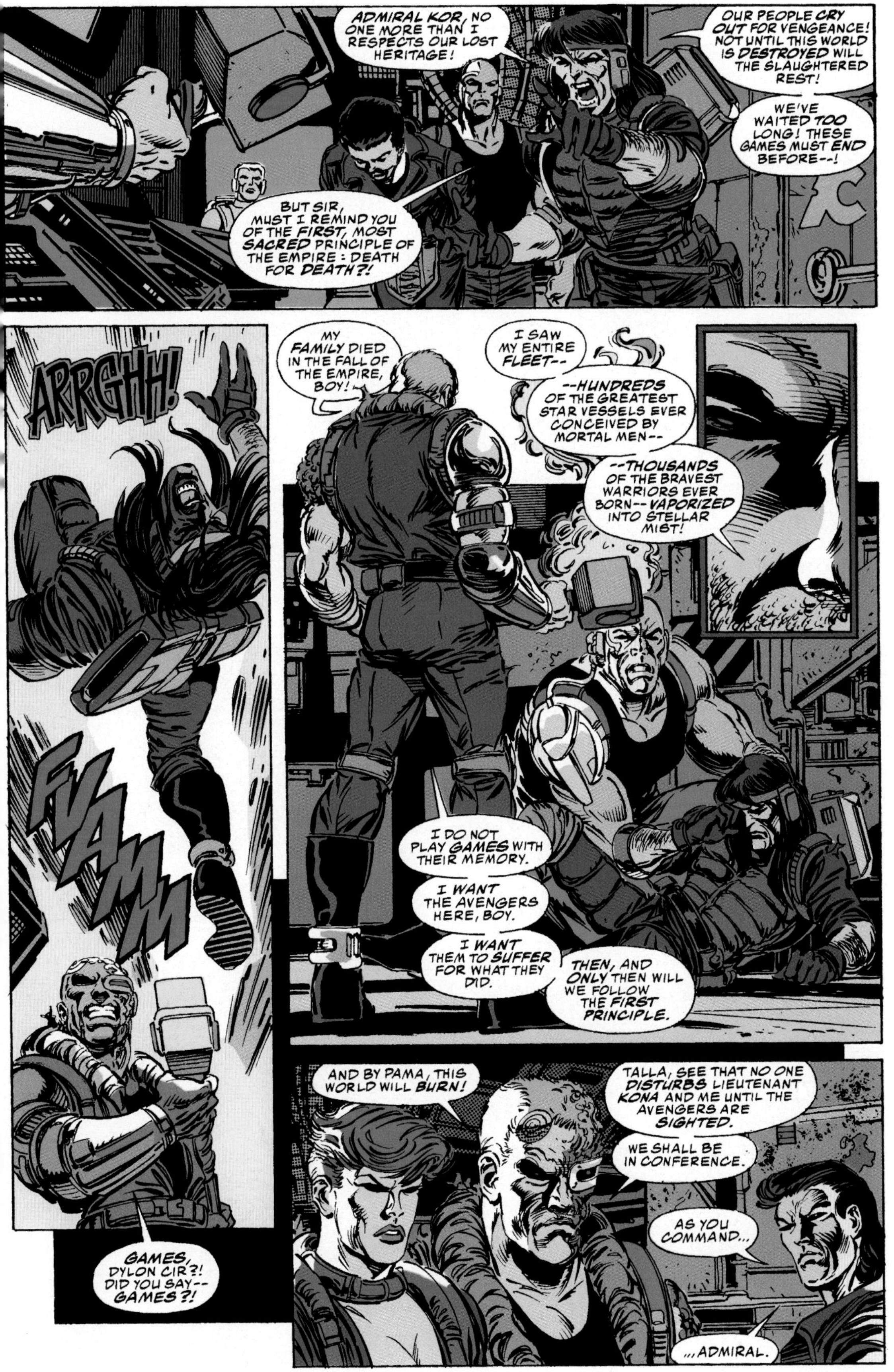
ADMIRAL KOR, NO ONE MORE THAN I RESPECTS OUR LOST HERITAGE!
OUR PEOPLE CRY OUT FOR VENGEANCE! NOT UNTIL THIS WORLD IS DESTROYED WILL THE SLAUGHTERED REST!
WE'VE WAITED TOO LONG! THESE GAMES MUST END BEFORE--!
BUT SIR, MUST I REMIND YOU OF THE FIRST, MOST SACRED PRINCIPLE OF THE EMPIRE: DEATH FOR DEATH?!
ARRGHH!
FVAMMM
GAMES, DYLON CIR?! DID YOU SAY--GAMES?!
MY FAMILY DIED IN THE FALL OF THE EMPIRE, BOY!
I SAW MY ENTIRE FLEET--
--HUNDREDS OF THE GREATEST STAR VESSELS EVER CONCEIVED BY MORTAL MEN--
--THOUSANDS OF THE BRAVEST WARRIORS EVER BORN--VAPORIZED INTO STELLAR MIST!
I DO NOT PLAY GAMES WITH THEIR MEMORY.
I WANT THE AVENGERS HERE, BOY.
I WANT THEM TO SUFFER FOR WHAT THEY DID.
THEN, AND ONLY THEN WILL WE FOLLOW THE FIRST PRINCIPLE.
AND BY PAMA, THIS WORLD WILL BURN!
TALLA, SEE THAT NO ONE DISTURBS LIEUTENANT KONA AND ME UNTIL THE AVENGERS ARE SIGHTED.
WE SHALL BE IN CONFERENCE.
AS YOU COMMAND...
...ADMIRAL.

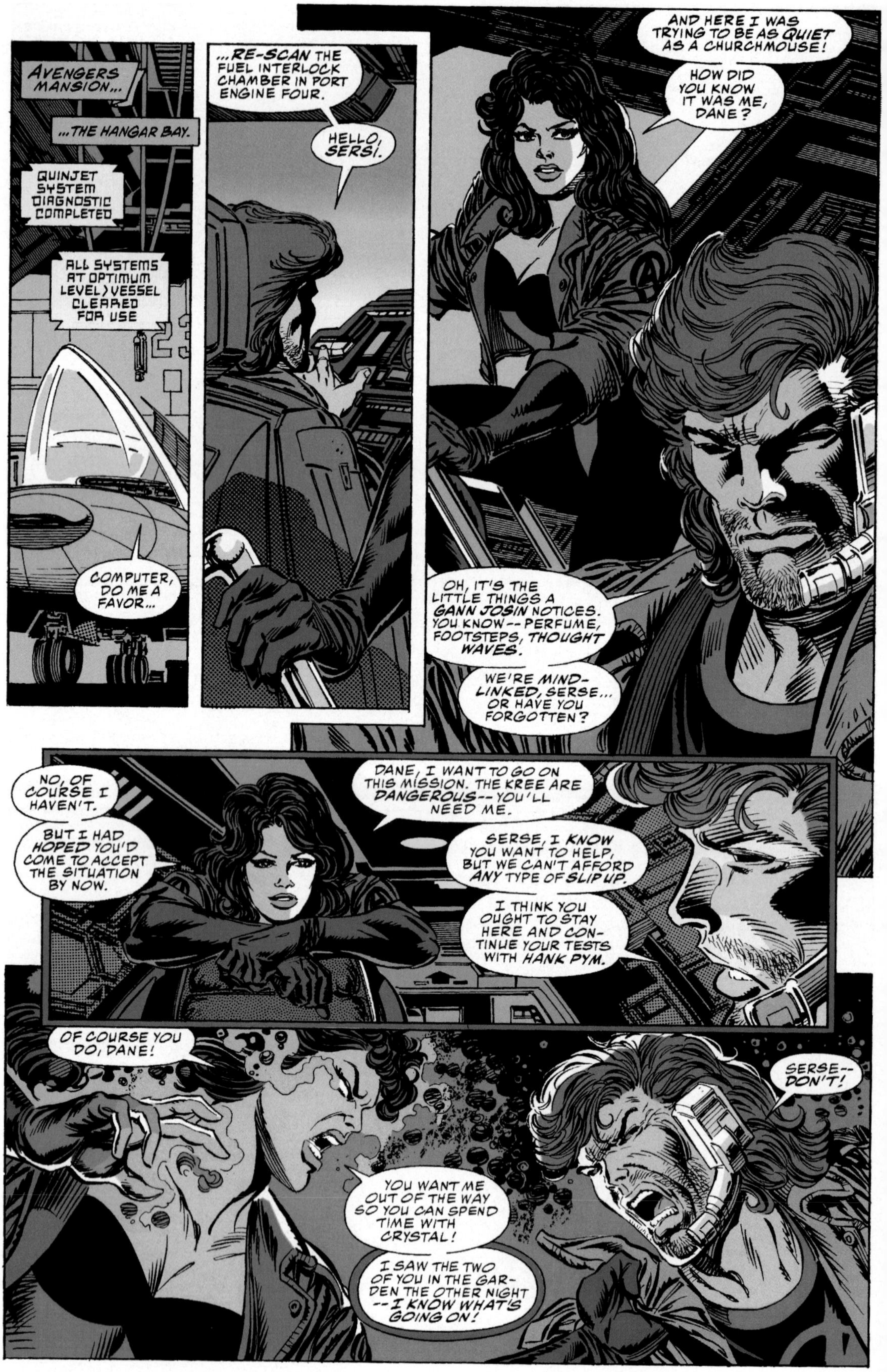

AVENGERS MANSION...
...THE HANGAR BAY.
QUINJET SYSTEM DIAGNOSTIC COMPLETED
ALL SYSTEMS AT OPTIMUM LEVEL) VESSEL CLEARED FOR USE
COMPUTER, DO ME A FAVOR...
...RE-SCAN THE FUEL INTERLOCK CHAMBER IN PORT ENGINE FOUR.
HELLO, SERSI.
AND HERE I WAS TRYING TO BE AS QUIET AS A CHURCHMOUSE!
HOW DID YOU KNOW IT WAS ME, DANE?
OH, IT'S THE LITTLE THINGS A GANN JOSIN NOTICES. YOU KNOW--PERFUME, FOOTSTEPS, THOUGHT WAVES.
WE'RE MIND-LINKED, SERSE... OR HAVE YOU FORGOTTEN?
NO, OF COURSE I HAVEN'T.
BUT I HAD HOPED YOU'D COME TO ACCEPT THE SITUATION BY NOW.
DANE, I WANT TO GO ON THIS MISSION. THE KREE ARE DANGEROUS--YOU'LL NEED ME.
SERSE, I KNOW YOU WANT TO HELP, BUT WE CAN'T AFFORD ANY TYPE OF SLIP UP.
I THINK YOU OUGHT TO STAY HERE AND CON-TINUE YOUR TESTS WITH HANK PYM.
OF COURSE YOU DO, DANE!
SERSE-- DON'T!
YOU WANT ME OUT OF THE WAY SO YOU CAN SPEND TIME WITH CRYSTAL!
I SAW THE TWO OF YOU IN THE GAR-DEN THE OTHER NIGHT --I KNOW WHAT'S GOING ON!

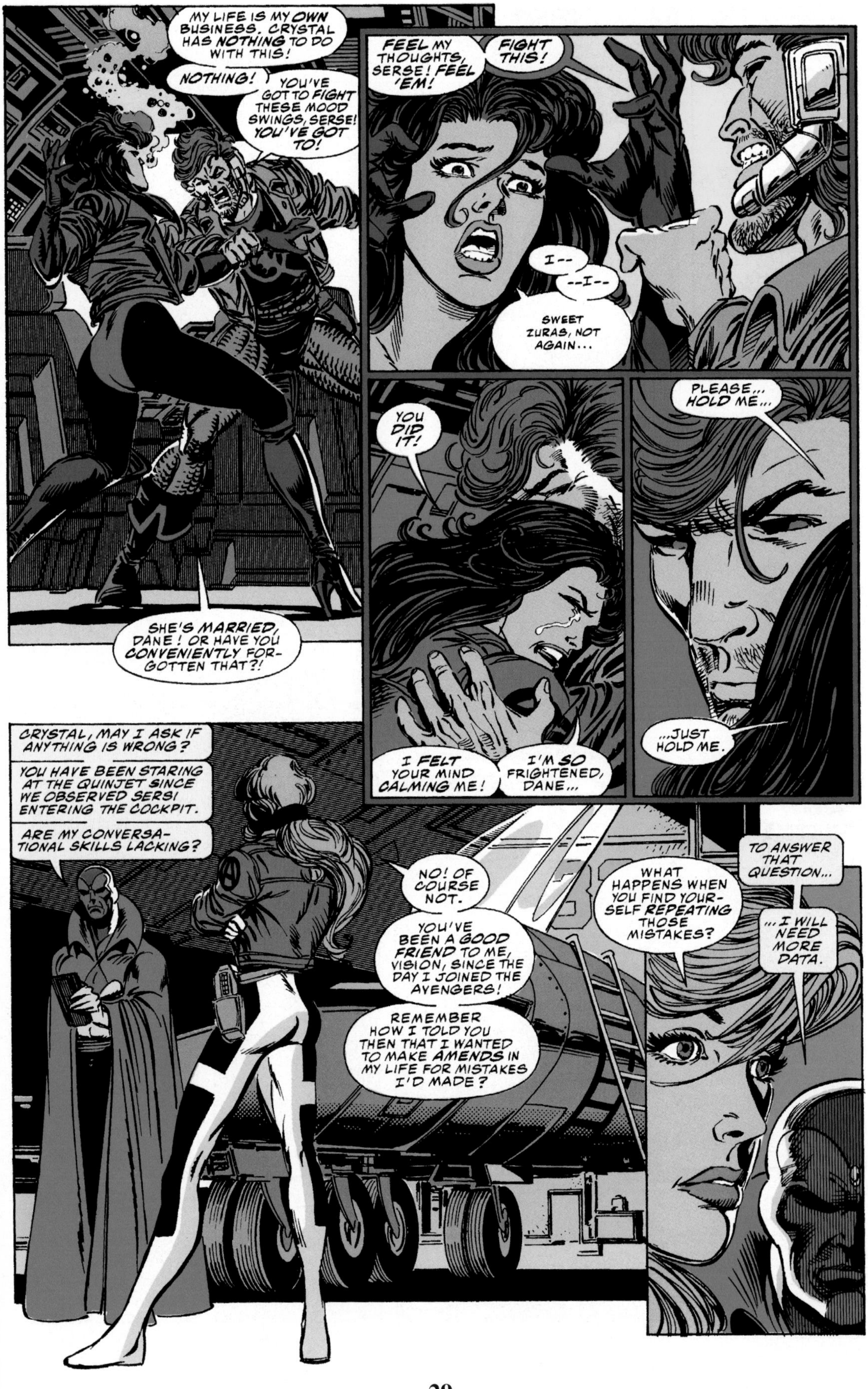

MY LIFE IS MY OWN BUSINESS. CRYSTAL HAS NOTHING TO DO WITH THIS!
NOTHING!
YOU'VE GOT TO FIGHT THESE MOOD SWINGS, SERSE! YOU'VE GOT TO!
SHE'S MARRIED, DANE! OR HAVE YOU CONVENIENTLY FORGOTTEN THAT?!
FEEL MY THOUGHTS, SERSE! FEEL 'EM!
FIGHT THIS!
I--
--I--
SWEET ZURAS, NOT AGAIN...
YOU DID IT!
I FELT YOUR MIND CALMING ME!
I'M SO FRIGHTENED, DANE...
PLEASE... HOLD ME...
...JUST HOLD ME.
CRYSTAL, MAY I ASK IF ANYTHING IS WRONG?
YOU HAVE BEEN STARING AT THE QUINJET SINCE WE OBSERVED SERSI ENTERING THE COCKPIT.
ARE MY CONVERSATIONAL SKILLS LACKING?
NO! OF COURSE NOT.
YOU'VE BEEN A GOOD FRIEND TO ME, VISION, SINCE THE DAY I JOINED THE AVENGERS!
REMEMBER HOW I TOLD YOU THEN THAT I WANTED TO MAKE AMENDS IN MY LIFE FOR MISTAKES I'D MADE?
WHAT HAPPENS WHEN YOU FIND YOURSELF REPEATING THOSE MISTAKES?
TO ANSWER THAT QUESTION...
...I WILL NEED MORE DATA.

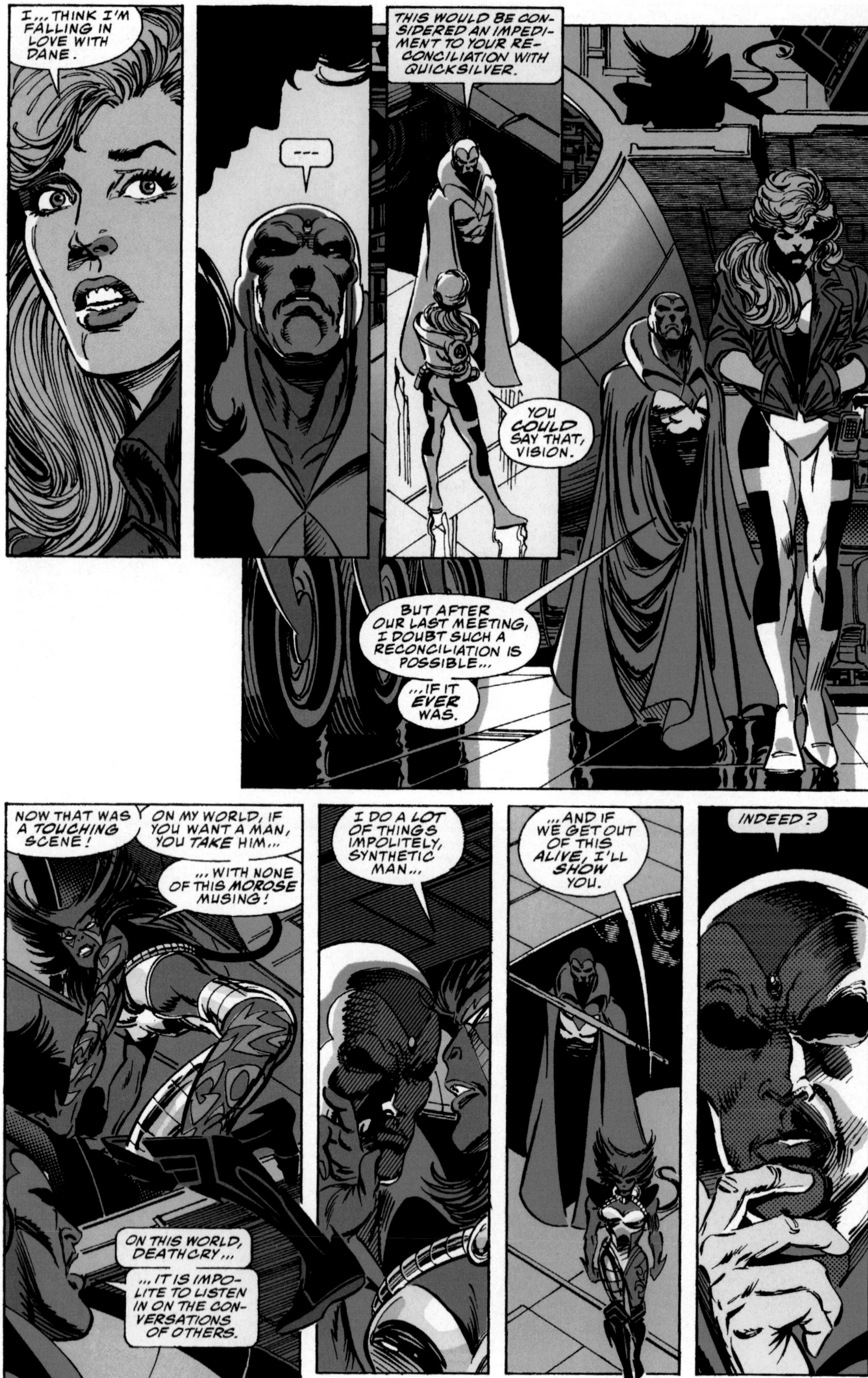

I... THINK I'M FALLING IN LOVE WITH DANE.

THIS WOULD BE CONSIDERED AN IMPEDIMENT TO YOUR RECONCILIATION WITH QUICKSILVER.
YOU COULD SAY THAT, VISION.
BUT AFTER OUR LAST MEETING, I DOUBT SUCH A RECONCILIATION IS POSSIBLE...
...IF IT EVER WAS.
NOW THAT WAS A TOUCHING SCENE!
ON MY WORLD, IF YOU WANT A MAN, YOU TAKE HIM...
...WITH NONE OF THIS MOROSE MUSING!
ON THIS WORLD, DEATHCRY...
...IT IS IMPOLITE TO LISTEN IN ON THE CONVERSATIONS OF OTHERS.
I DO A LOT OF THINGS IMPOLITELY, SYNTHETIC MAN...
...AND IF WE GET OUT OF THIS ALIVE, I'LL SHOW YOU.
INDEED?

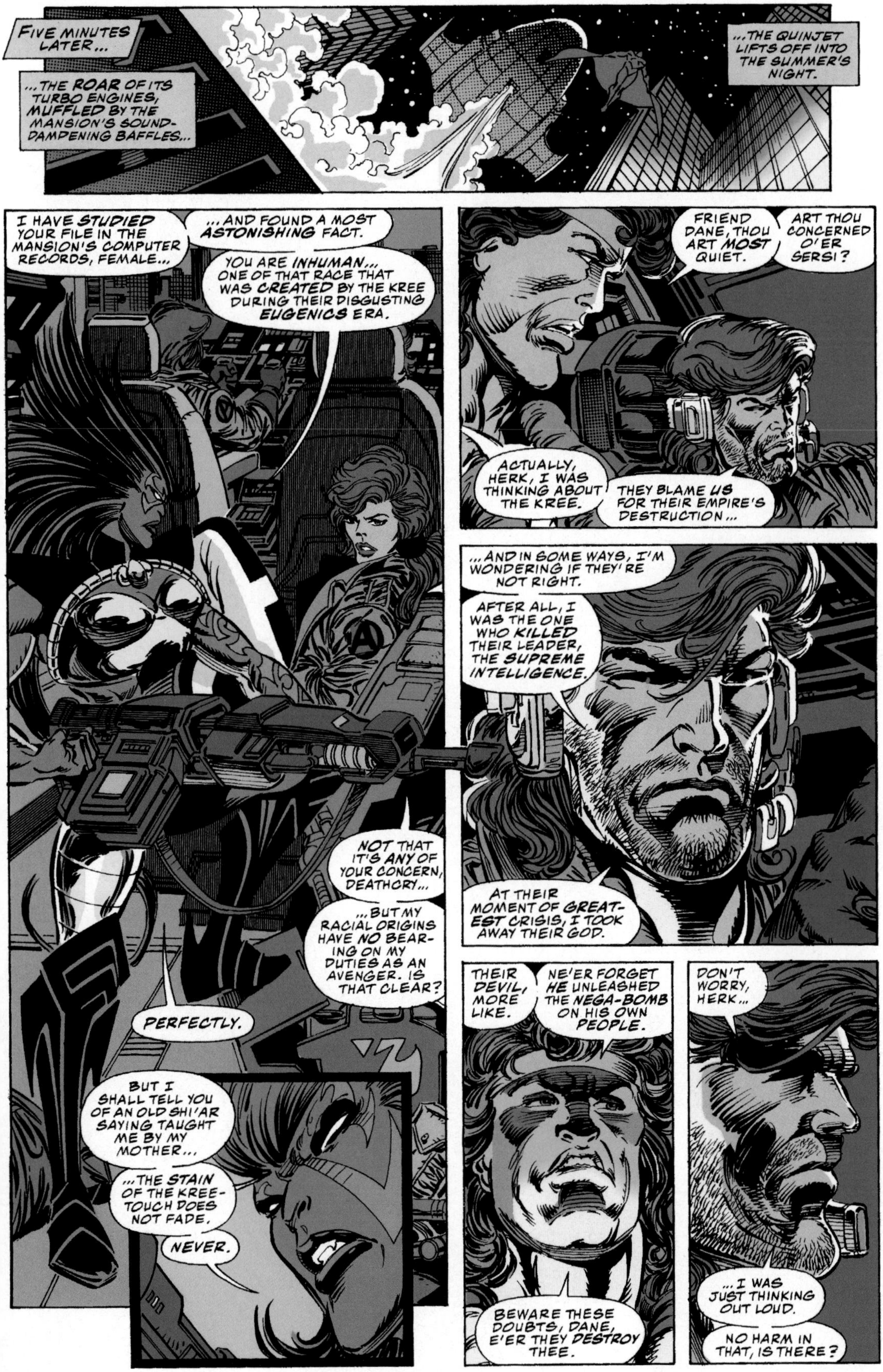
FIVE MINUTES LATER...
...THE ROAR OF ITS TURBO ENGINES, MUFFLED BY THE MANSION'S SOUND-DAMPENING BAFFLES...
...THE QUINJET LIFTS OFF INTO THE SUMMER'S NIGHT.
I HAVE STUDIED YOUR FILE IN THE MANSION'S COMPUTER RECORDS, FEMALE...
...AND FOUND A MOST ASTONISHING FACT.
YOU ARE INHUMAN... ONE OF THAT RACE THAT WAS CREATED BY THE KREE DURING THEIR DISGUSTING EUGENICS ERA.
NOT THAT IT'S ANY OF YOUR CONCERN, DEATHCRY...
...BUT MY RACIAL ORIGINS HAVE NO BEARING ON MY DUTIES AS AN AVENGER. IS THAT CLEAR?
PERFECTLY.
BUT I SHALL TELL YOU OF AN OLD SHI'AR SAYING TAUGHT ME BY MY MOTHER...
...THE STAIN OF THE KREE-TOUCH DOES NOT FADE.
NEVER.
FRIEND DANE, THOU ART MOST QUIET.
ART THOU CONCERNED O'ER SERSI?
ACTUALLY, HERK, I WAS THINKING ABOUT THE KREE.
THEY BLAME US FOR THEIR EMPIRE'S DESTRUCTION...
...AND IN SOME WAYS, I'M WONDERING IF THEY'RE NOT RIGHT.
AFTER ALL, I WAS THE ONE WHO KILLED THEIR LEADER, THE SUPREME INTELLIGENCE.
AT THEIR MOMENT OF GREATEST CRISIS, I TOOK AWAY THEIR GOD.
THEIR DEVIL, MORE LIKE.
NE'ER FORGET HE UNLEASHED THE NEGA-BOMB ON HIS OWN PEOPLE.
BEWARE THESE DOUBTS, DANE, E'ER THEY DESTROY THEE.
DON'T WORRY, HERK...
...I WAS JUST THINKING OUT LOUD.
NO HARM IN THAT, IS THERE?

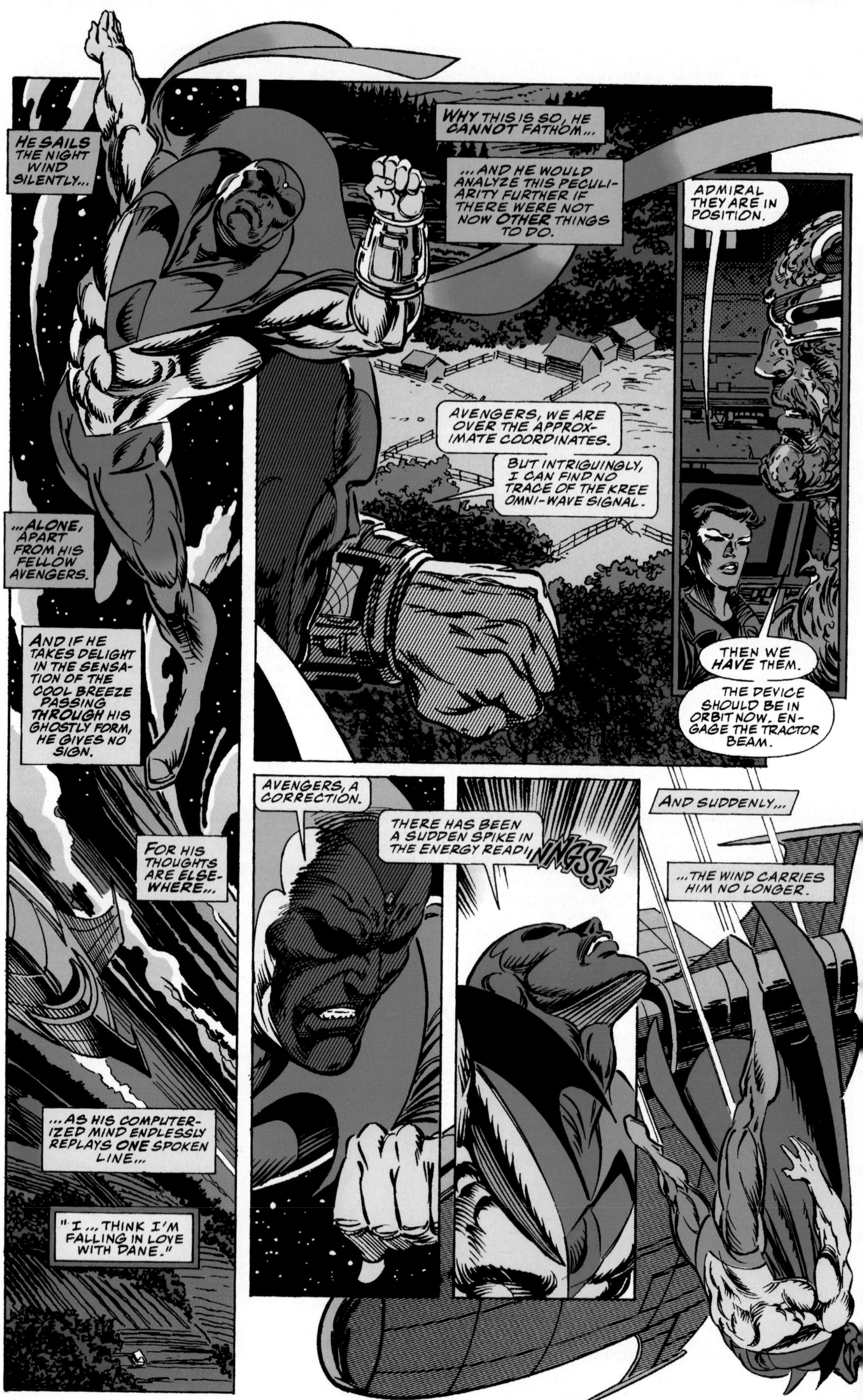
HE SAILS THE NIGHT WIND SILENTLY...
...ALONE, APART FROM HIS FELLOW AVENGERS.
AND IF HE TAKES DELIGHT IN THE SENSATION OF THE COOL BREEZE PASSING THROUGH HIS GHOSTLY FORM, HE GIVES NO SIGN.
FOR HIS THOUGHTS ARE ELSEWHERE...
...AS HIS COMPUTERIZED MIND ENDLESSLY REPLAYS ONE SPOKEN LINE...
"I... THINK I'M FALLING IN LOVE WITH DANE."
WHY THIS IS SO, HE CANNOT FATHOM...
...AND HE WOULD ANALYZE THIS PECULIARITY FURTHER IF THERE WERE NOT NOW OTHER THINGS TO DO.
AVENGERS, WE ARE OVER THE APPROXIMATE COORDINATES.
BUT INTRIGUINGLY, I CAN FIND NO TRACE OF THE KREE OMNI-WAVE SIGNAL.
ADMIRAL THEY ARE IN POSITION.
THEN WE HAVE THEM.
THE DEVICE SHOULD BE IN ORBIT NOW. ENGAGE THE TRACTOR BEAM.
AVENGERS, A CORRECTION.
THERE HAS BEEN A SUDDEN SPIKE IN THE ENERGY READI
NNGSS
AND SUDDENLY...
...THE WIND CARRIES HIM NO LONGER.

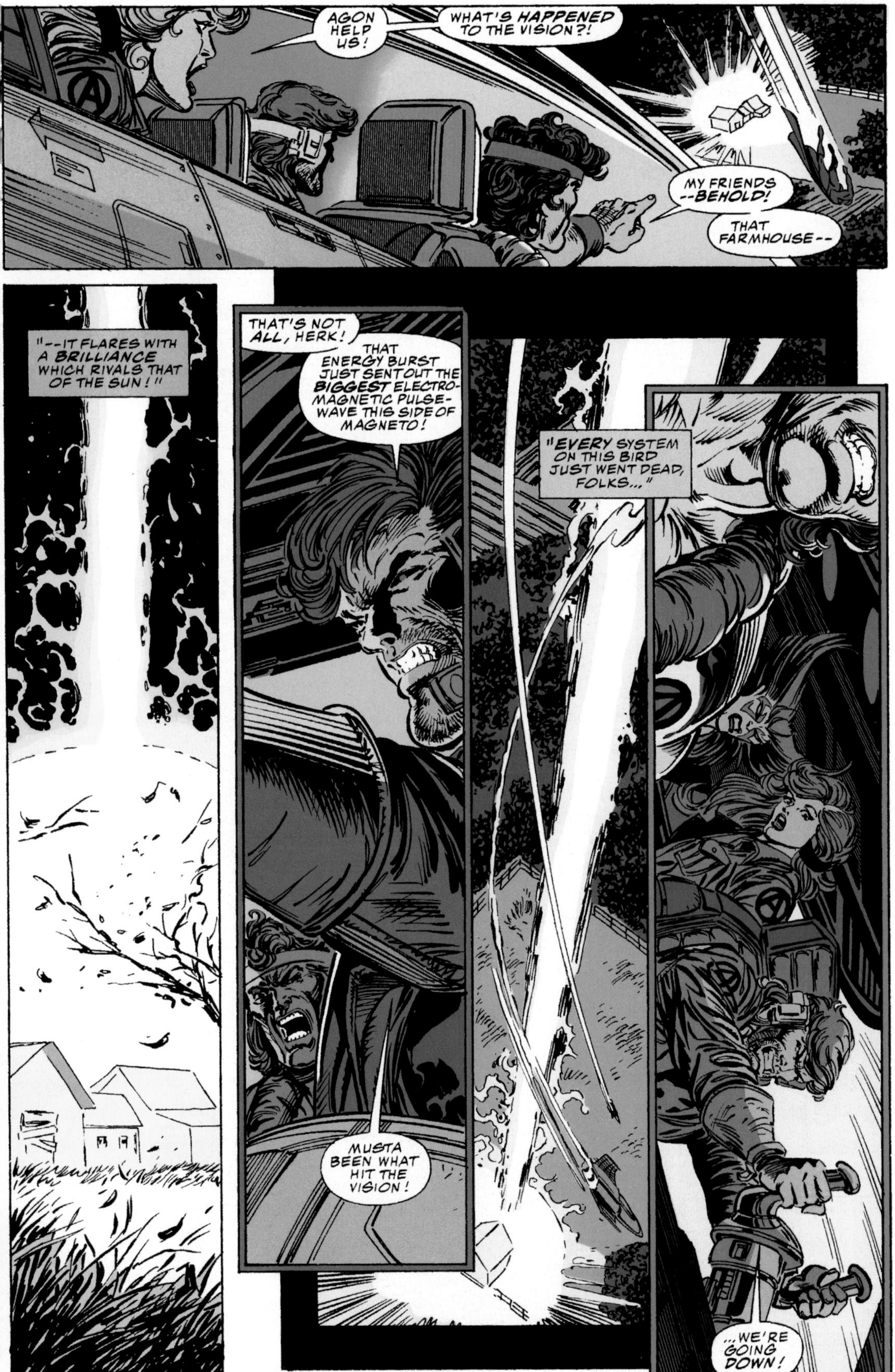
AGON HELP US!
WHAT'S HAPPENED TO THE VISION?!
MY FRIENDS --BEHOLD!
THAT FARMHOUSE--
"--IT FLARES WITH A BRILLIANCE WHICH RIVALS THAT OF THE SUN!"
THAT'S NOT ALL, HERK!
THAT ENERGY BURST JUST SENT OUT THE BIGGEST ELECTRO-MAGNETIC PULSE-WAVE THIS SIDE OF MAGNETO!
MUSTA BEEN WHAT HIT THE VISION!
"EVERY SYSTEM ON THIS BIRD JUST WENT DEAD, FOLKS..."
...WE'RE GOING DOWN!

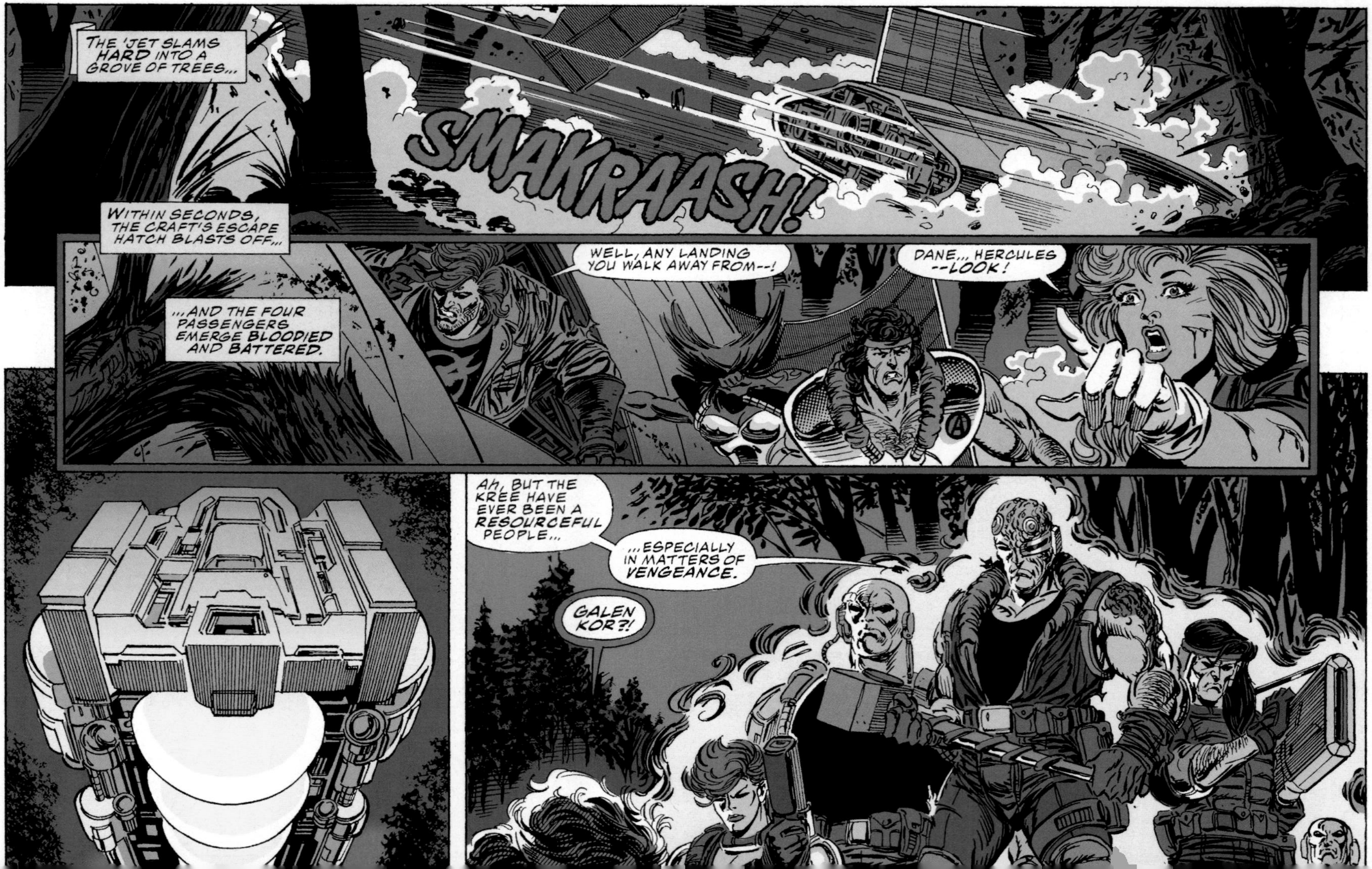
THE 'JET SLAMS HARD INTO A GROVE OF TREES...
SMAKRAASH!
WITHIN SECONDS, THE CRAFT'S ESCAPE HATCH BLASTS OFF...
...AND THE FOUR PASSENGERS EMERGE BLOODIED AND BATTERED.
WELL, ANY LANDING YOU WALK AWAY FROM--!
DANE... HERCULES --LOOK!
Ah, BUT THE KREE HAVE EVER BEEN A RESOURCEFUL PEOPLE...
...ESPECIALLY IN MATTERS OF VENGEANCE.
GALEN KOR?!

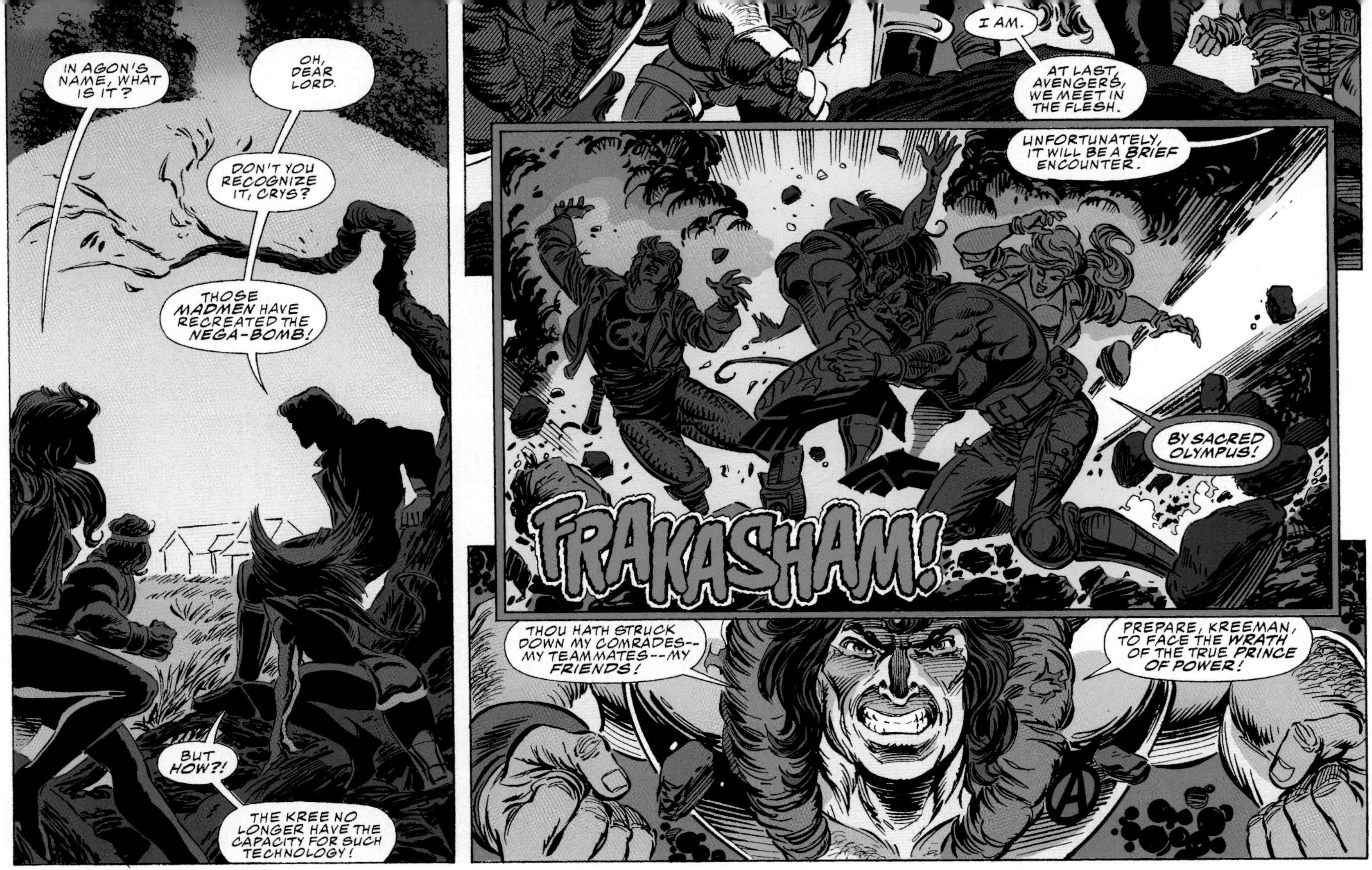
IN AGON'S NAME, WHAT IS IT?
OH, DEAR LORD.
DON'T YOU RECOGNIZE IT, CRYS?
THOSE MADMEN HAVE RECREATED THE NEGA-BOMB!
BUT HOW?!
THE KREE NO LONGER HAVE THE CAPACITY FOR SUCH TECHNOLOGY!
I AM.
AT LAST, AVENGERS, WE MEET IN THE FLESH.
UNFORTUNATELY, IT WILL BE A BRIEF ENCOUNTER.
BY SACRED OLYMPUS!
FRAKASHAM!
THOU HATH STRUCK DOWN MY COMRADES-- MY TEAMMATES--MY FRIENDS!
PREPARE, KREEMAN, TO FACE THE WRATH OF THE TRUE PRINCE OF POWER!

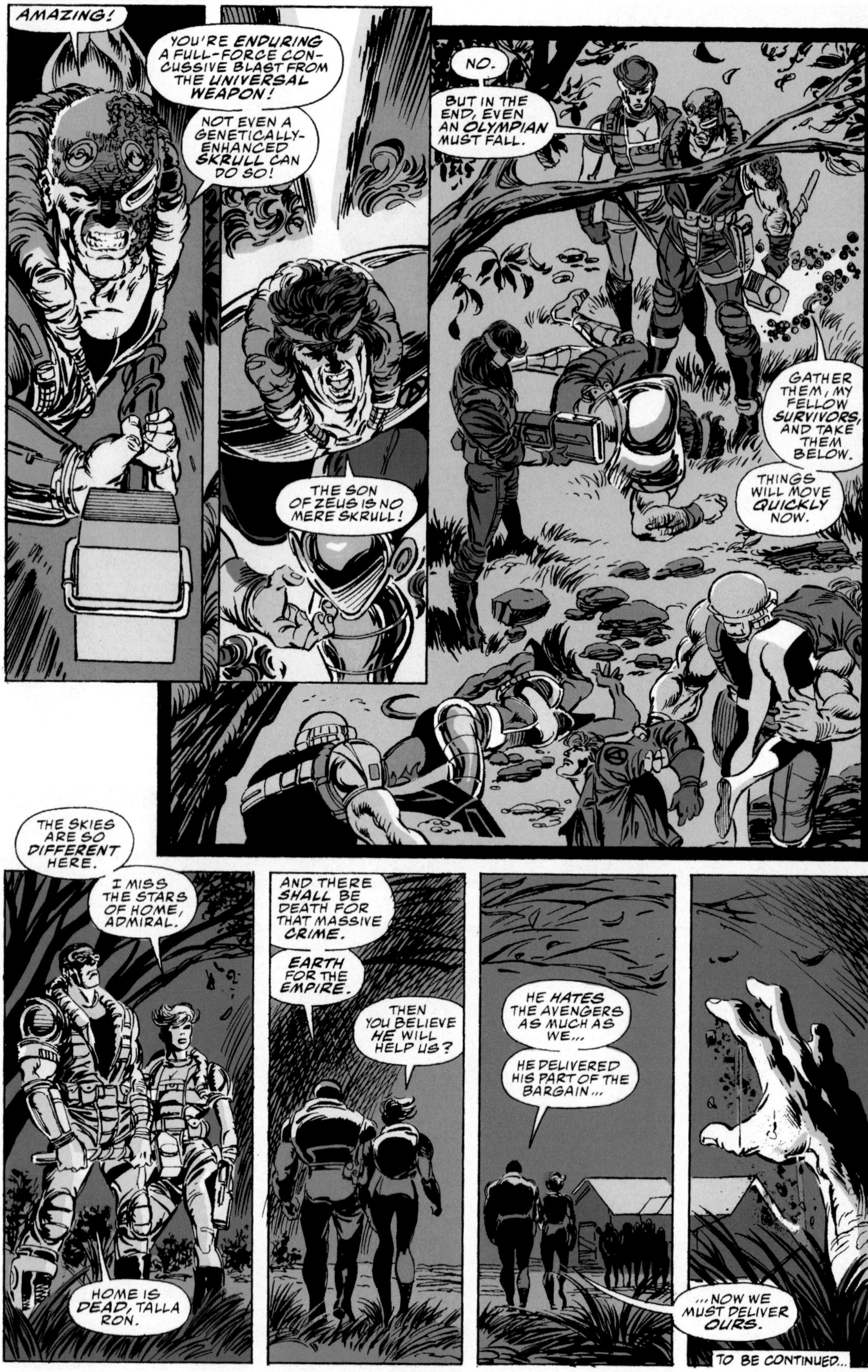
AMAZING!
YOU'RE ENDURING A FULL-FORCE CONCUSSIVE BLAST FROM THE UNIVERSAL WEAPON!
NOT EVEN A GENETICALLY-ENHANCED SKRULL CAN DO SO!
THE SON OF ZEUS IS NO MERE SKRULL!
NO.
BUT IN THE END, EVEN AN OLYMPIAN MUST FALL.
GATHER THEM, MY FELLOW SURVIVORS, AND TAKE THEM BELOW.
THINGS WILL MOVE QUICKLY NOW.
THE SKIES ARE SO DIFFERENT HERE.
I MISS THE STARS OF HOME, ADMIRAL.
HOME IS DEAD, TALLA RON.
AND THERE SHALL BE DEATH FOR THAT MASSIVE CRIME.
EARTH FOR THE EMPIRE.
THEN YOU BELIEVE HE WILL HELP US?
HE HATES THE AVENGERS AS MUCH AS WE...
HE DELIVERED HIS PART OF THE BARGAIN...
...NOW WE MUST DELIVER OURS.
TO BE CONTINUED...

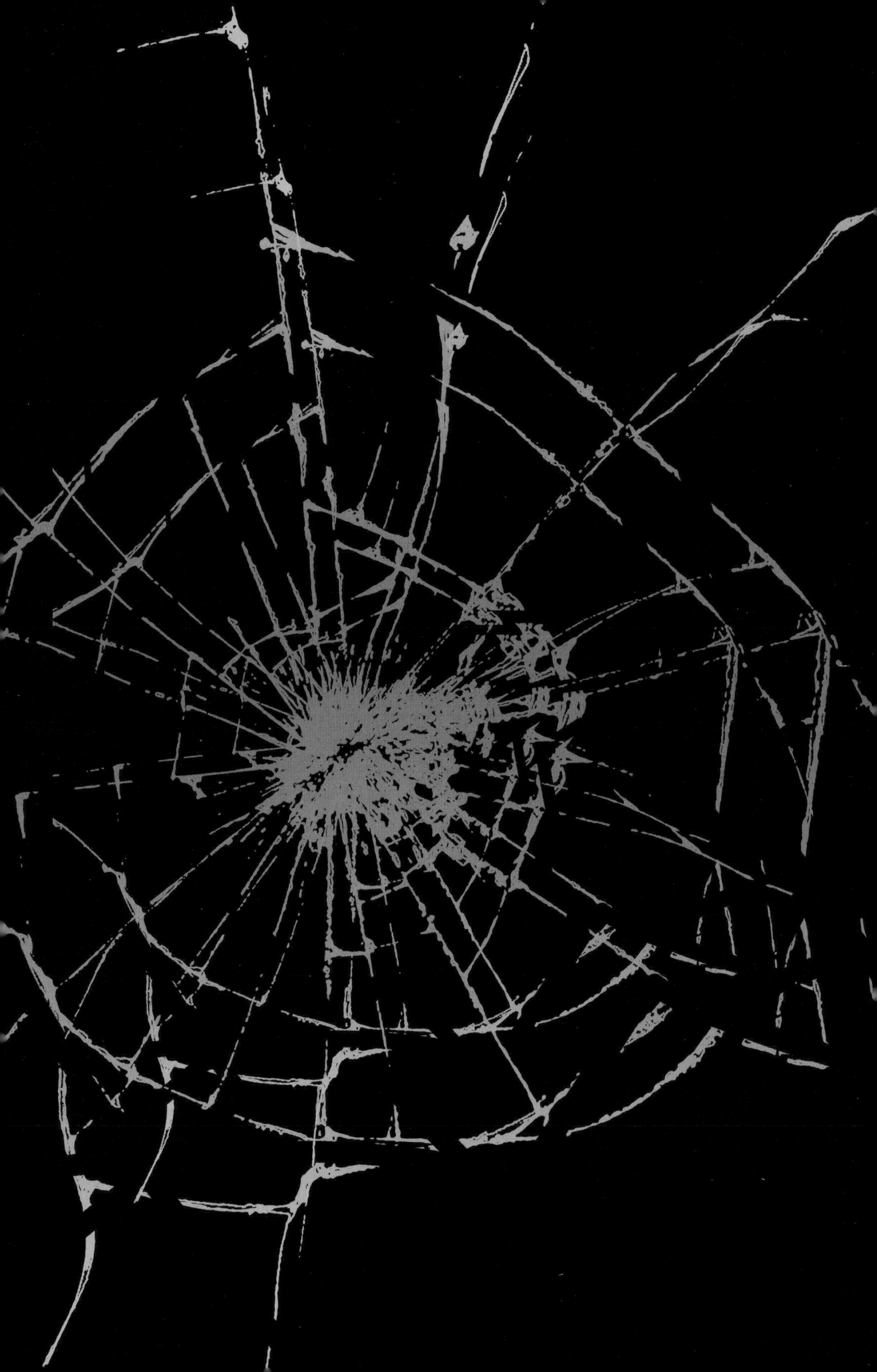

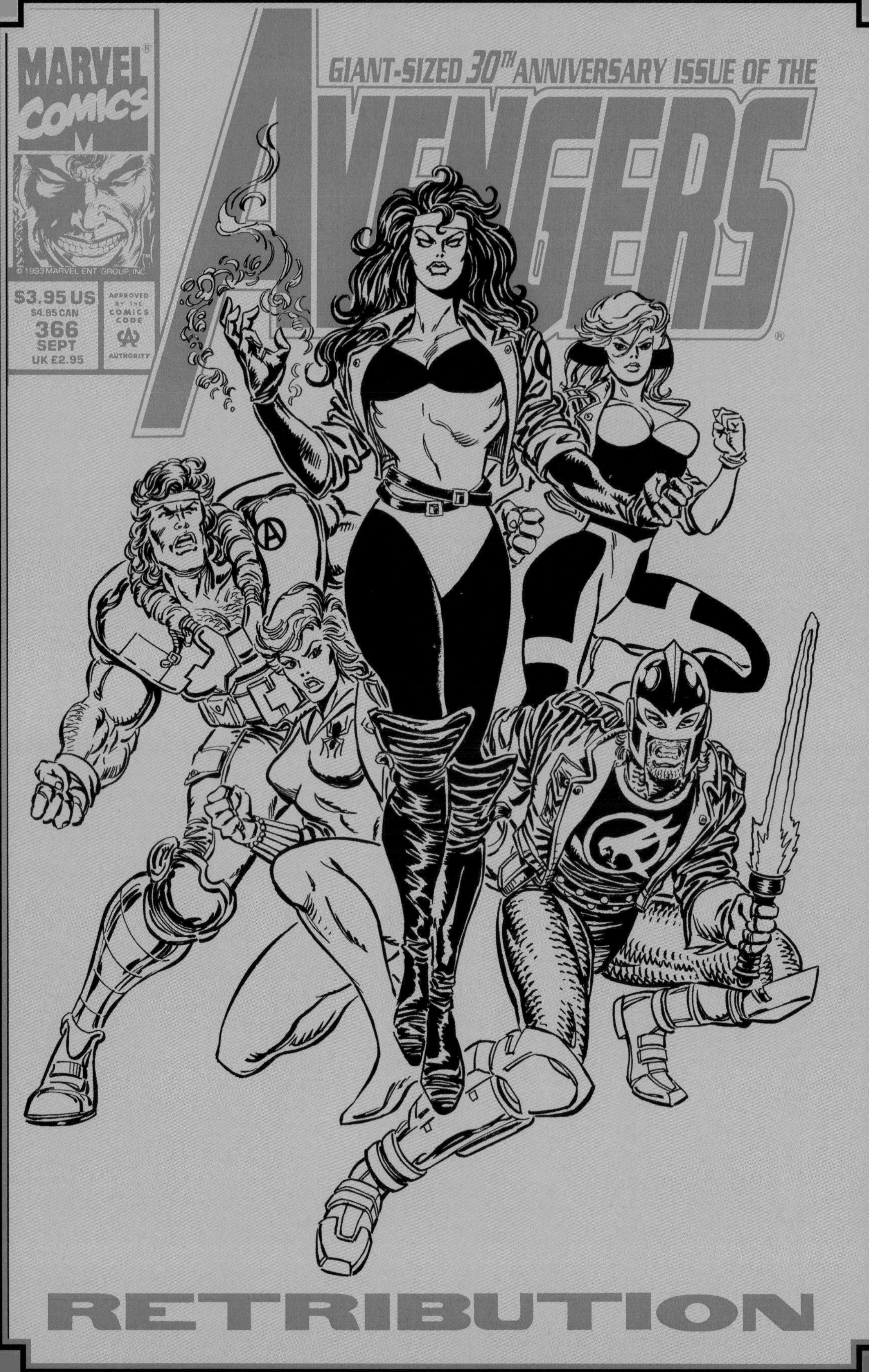
MARVEL COMICS
© 1993 MARVEL ENT. GROUP, INC.
$3.95 US
$4.95 CAN
366
SEPT
UK £2.95
APPROVED BY THE COMICS CODE AUTHORITY
GIANT-SIZED 30TH ANNIVERSARY ISSUE OF THE
AVENGERS
RETRIBUTION

TO COMBAT THOSE THREATS WHICH NO SINGLE HERO CAN STAND AGAINST, EARTH'S MIGHTIEST HEROES HAVE FORGED A COVENANT TO UNITE IN BATTLE FOR THE PROTECTION OF ALL MANKIND!
STAN LEE PRESENTS . . .
THE MIGHTY AVENGERS!

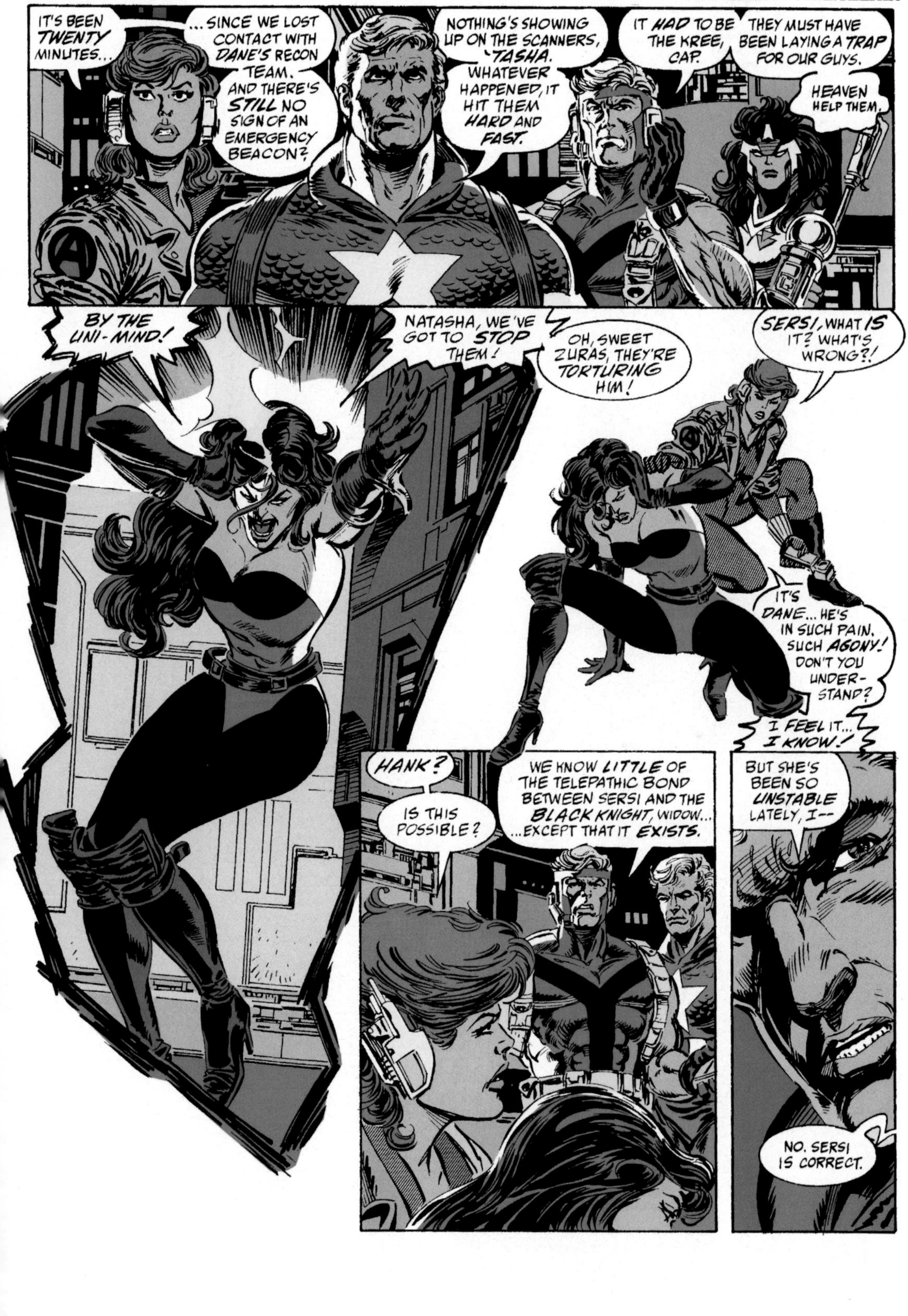

IT'S BEEN TWENTY MINUTES...
...SINCE WE LOST CONTACT WITH DANE'S RECON TEAM.
AND THERE'S STILL NO SIGN OF AN EMERGENCY BEACON?
NOTHING'S SHOWING UP ON THE SCANNERS, 'TASHA.
WHATEVER HAPPENED, IT HIT THEM HARD AND FAST.
IT HAD TO BE THE KREE, CAP.
THEY MUST HAVE BEEN LAYING A TRAP FOR OUR GUYS.
HEAVEN HELP THEM.
BY THE UNI-MIND!
NATASHA, WE'VE GOT TO STOP THEM!
OH, SWEET ZURAS, THEY'RE TORTURING HIM!
SERSI, WHAT IS IT? WHAT'S WRONG?!
IT'S DANE... HE'S IN SUCH PAIN, SUCH AGONY! DON'T YOU UNDER-STAND?
I FEEL IT... I KNOW!
HANK?
IS THIS POSSIBLE?
WE KNOW LITTLE OF THE TELEPATHIC BOND BETWEEN SERSI AND THE BLACK KNIGHT, WIDOW...
...EXCEPT THAT IT EXISTS.
BUT SHE'S BEEN SO UNSTABLE LATELY, I--
NO. SERSI IS CORRECT.

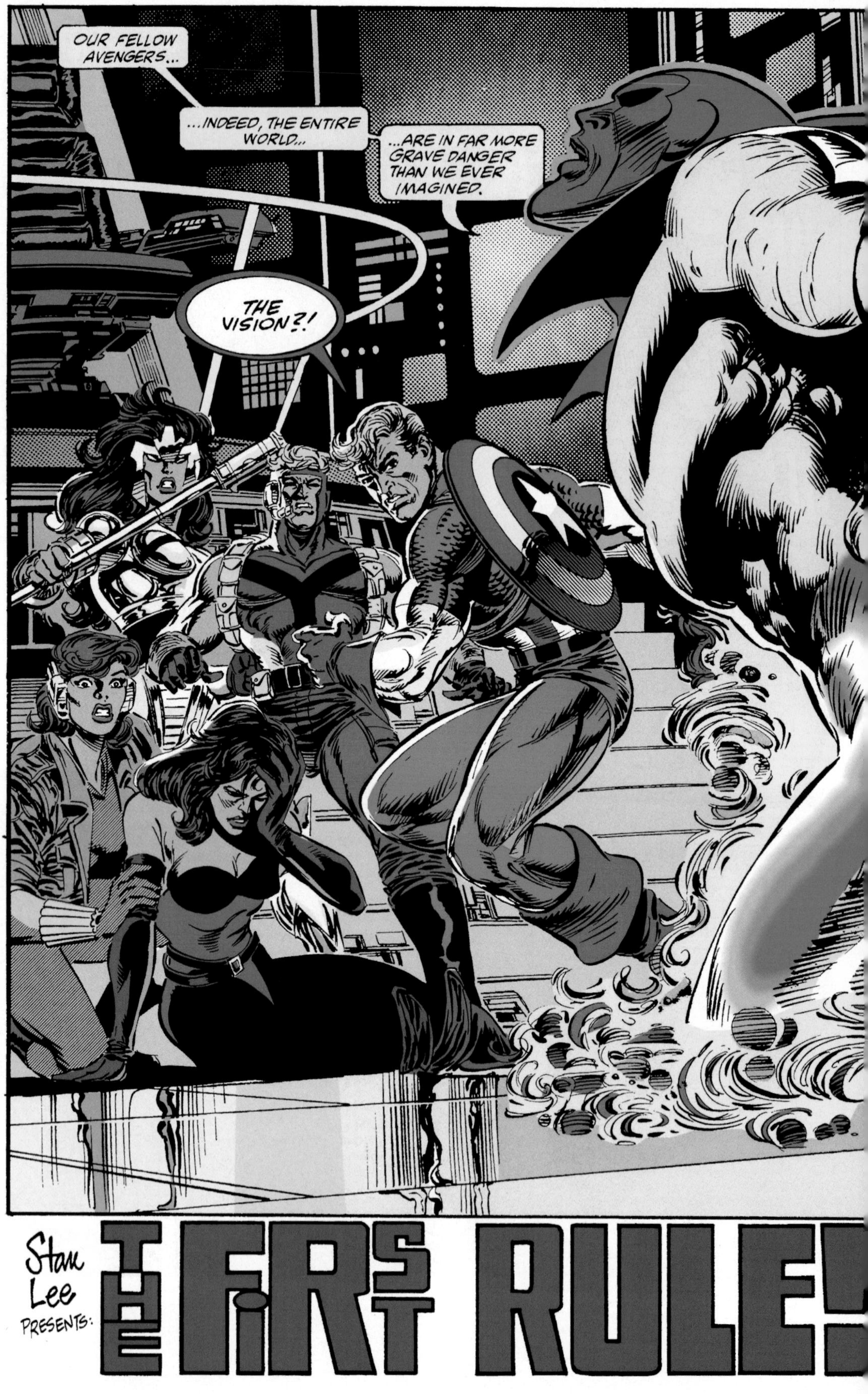
OUR FELLOW AVENGERS...
...INDEED, THE ENTIRE WORLD...
...ARE IN FAR MORE GRAVE DANGER THAN WE EVER IMAGINED.
THE VISION?!
Stan Lee PRESENTS:
THE FIRST RULE!

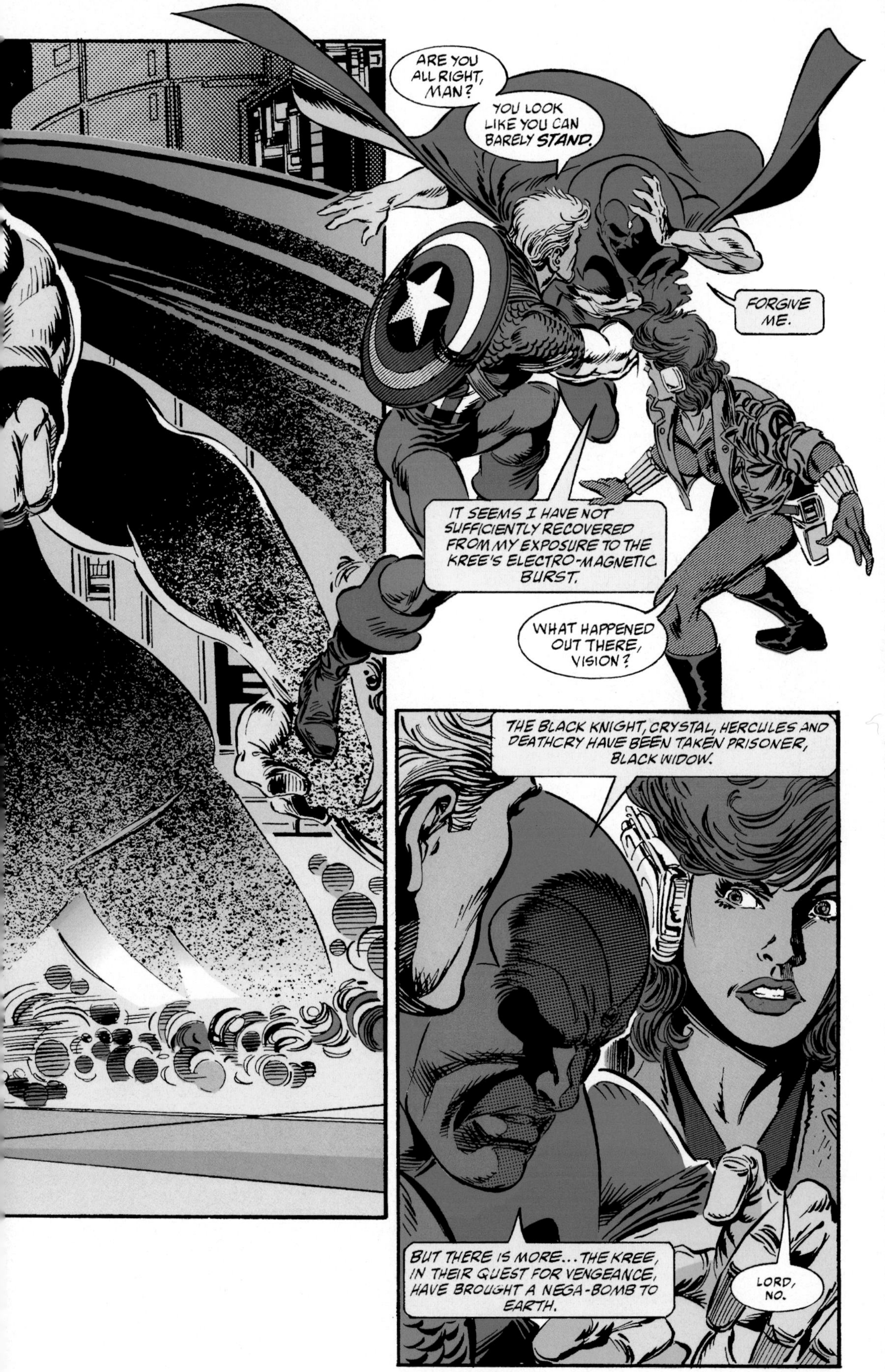

ARE YOU ALL RIGHT, MAN?
YOU LOOK LIKE YOU CAN BARELY STAND.
FORGIVE ME.
IT SEEMS I HAVE NOT SUFFICIENTLY RECOVERED FROM MY EXPOSURE TO THE KREE'S ELECTRO-MAGNETIC BURST.
WHAT HAPPENED OUT THERE, VISION?
THE BLACK KNIGHT, CRYSTAL, HERCULES AND DEATHCRY HAVE BEEN TAKEN PRISONER, BLACK WIDOW.
BUT THERE IS MORE... THE KREE, IN THEIR QUEST FOR VENGEANCE, HAVE BROUGHT A NEGA-BOMB TO EARTH.
LORD, NO.

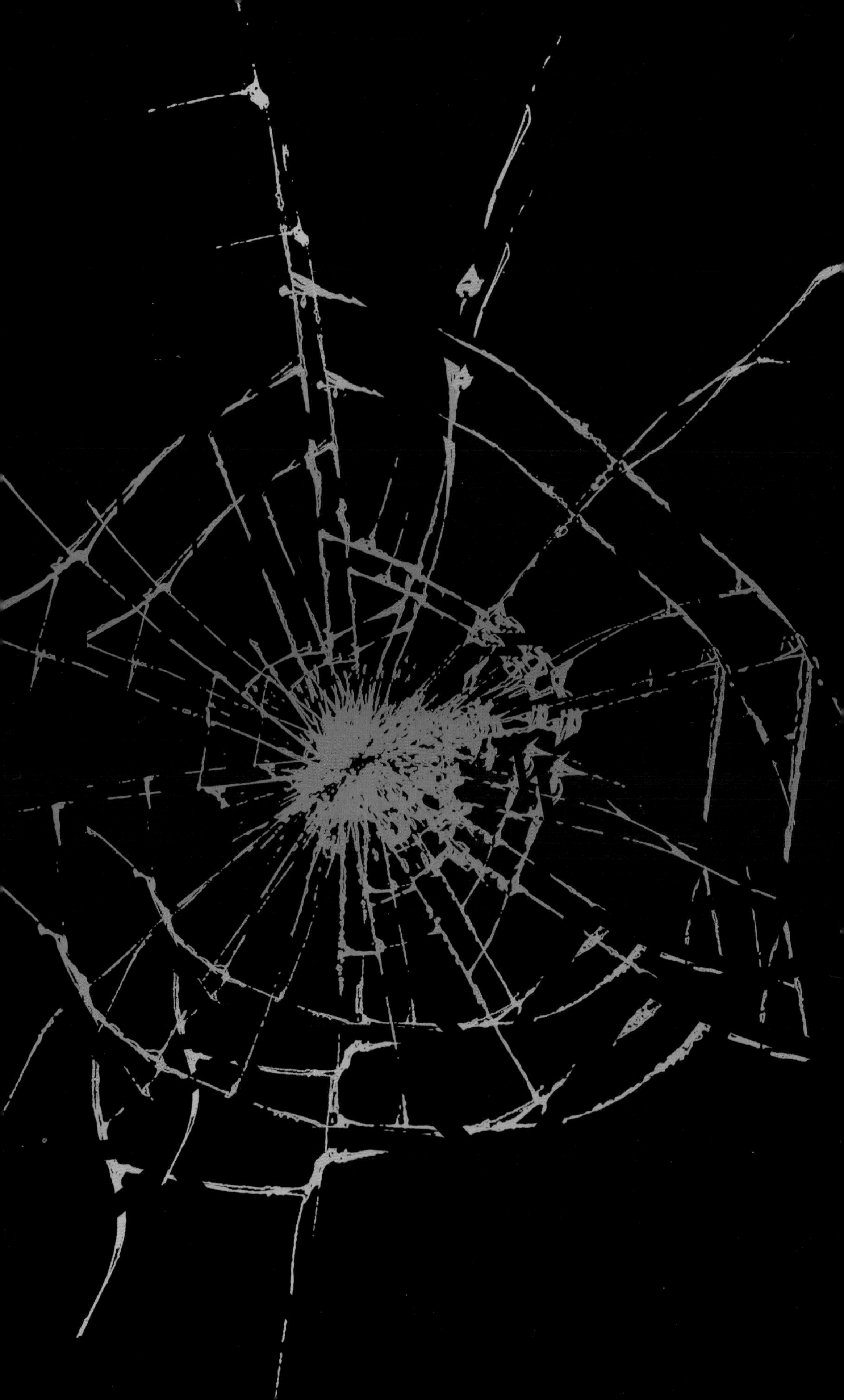

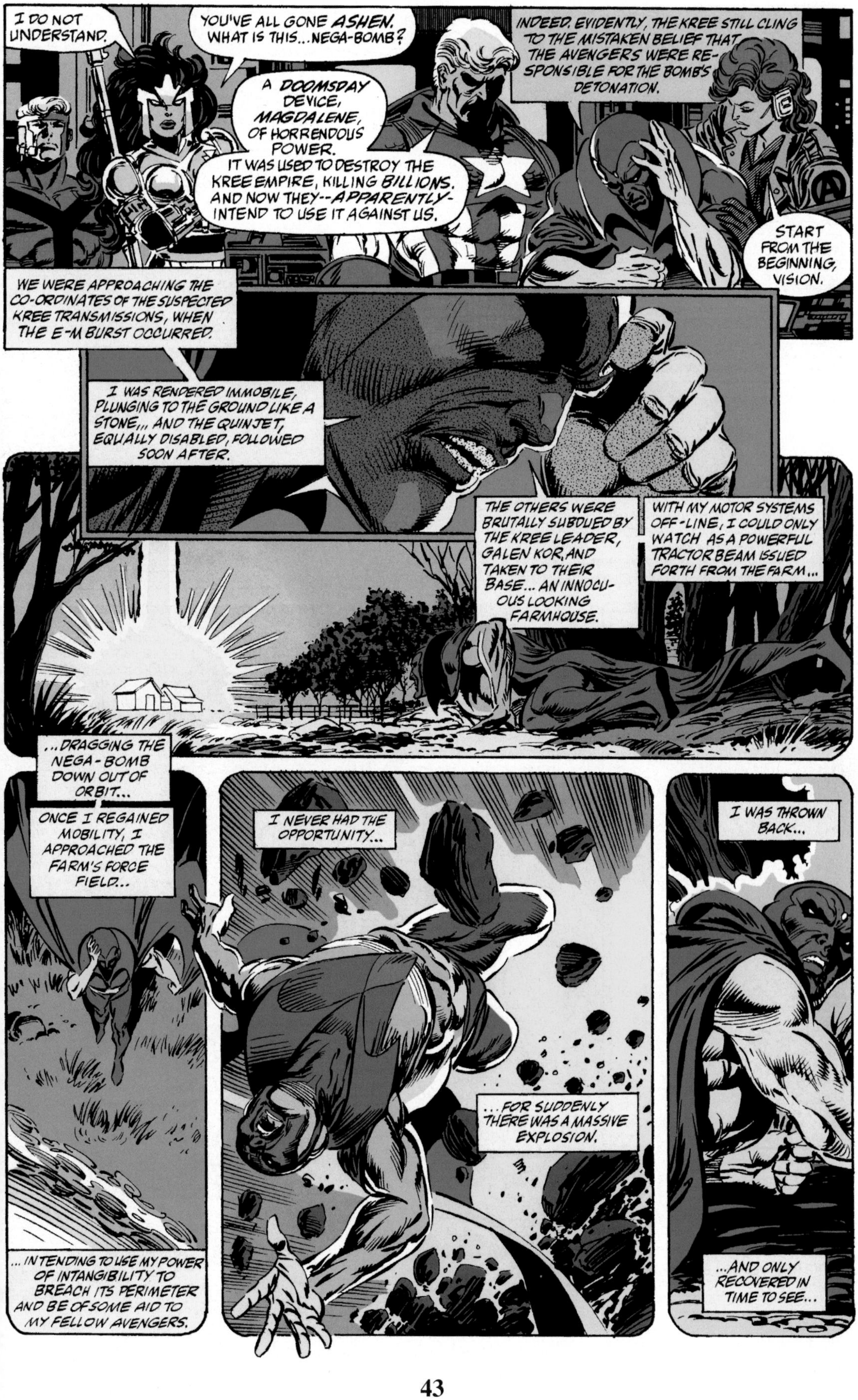
I DO NOT UNDERSTAND.
YOU'VE ALL GONE ASHEN. WHAT IS THIS...NEGA-BOMB?
A DOOMSDAY DEVICE, MAGDALENE, OF HORRENDOUS POWER.
IT WAS USED TO DESTROY THE KREE EMPIRE, KILLING BILLIONS. AND NOW THEY--APPARENTLY-INTEND TO USE IT AGAINST US.
INDEED. EVIDENTLY, THE KREE STILL CLING TO THE MISTAKEN BELIEF THAT THE AVENGERS WERE RESPONSIBLE FOR THE BOMB'S DETONATION.
START FROM THE BEGINNING, VISION.
WE WERE APPROACHING THE CO-ORDINATES OF THE SUSPECTED KREE TRANSMISSIONS, WHEN THE E-M BURST OCCURRED.
I WAS RENDERED IMMOBILE, PLUNGING TO THE GROUND LIKE A STONE... AND THE QUINJET, EQUALLY DISABLED, FOLLOWED SOON AFTER.
THE OTHERS WERE BRUTALLY SUBDUED BY THE KREE LEADER, GALEN KOR, AND TAKEN TO THEIR BASE... AN INNOCUOUS LOOKING FARMHOUSE.
WITH MY MOTOR SYSTEMS OFF-LINE, I COULD ONLY WATCH AS A POWERFUL TRACTOR BEAM ISSUED FORTH FROM THE FARM...
...DRAGGING THE NEGA-BOMB DOWN OUT OF ORBIT...
ONCE I REGAINED MOBILITY, I APPROACHED THE FARM'S FORCE FIELD...
...INTENDING TO USE MY POWER OF INTANGIBILITY TO BREACH ITS PERIMETER AND BE OF SOME AID TO MY FELLOW AVENGERS.
I NEVER HAD THE OPPORTUNITY...
...FOR SUDDENLY THERE WAS A MASSIVE EXPLOSION.
I WAS THROWN BACK...
...AND ONLY RECOVERED IN TIME TO SEE...

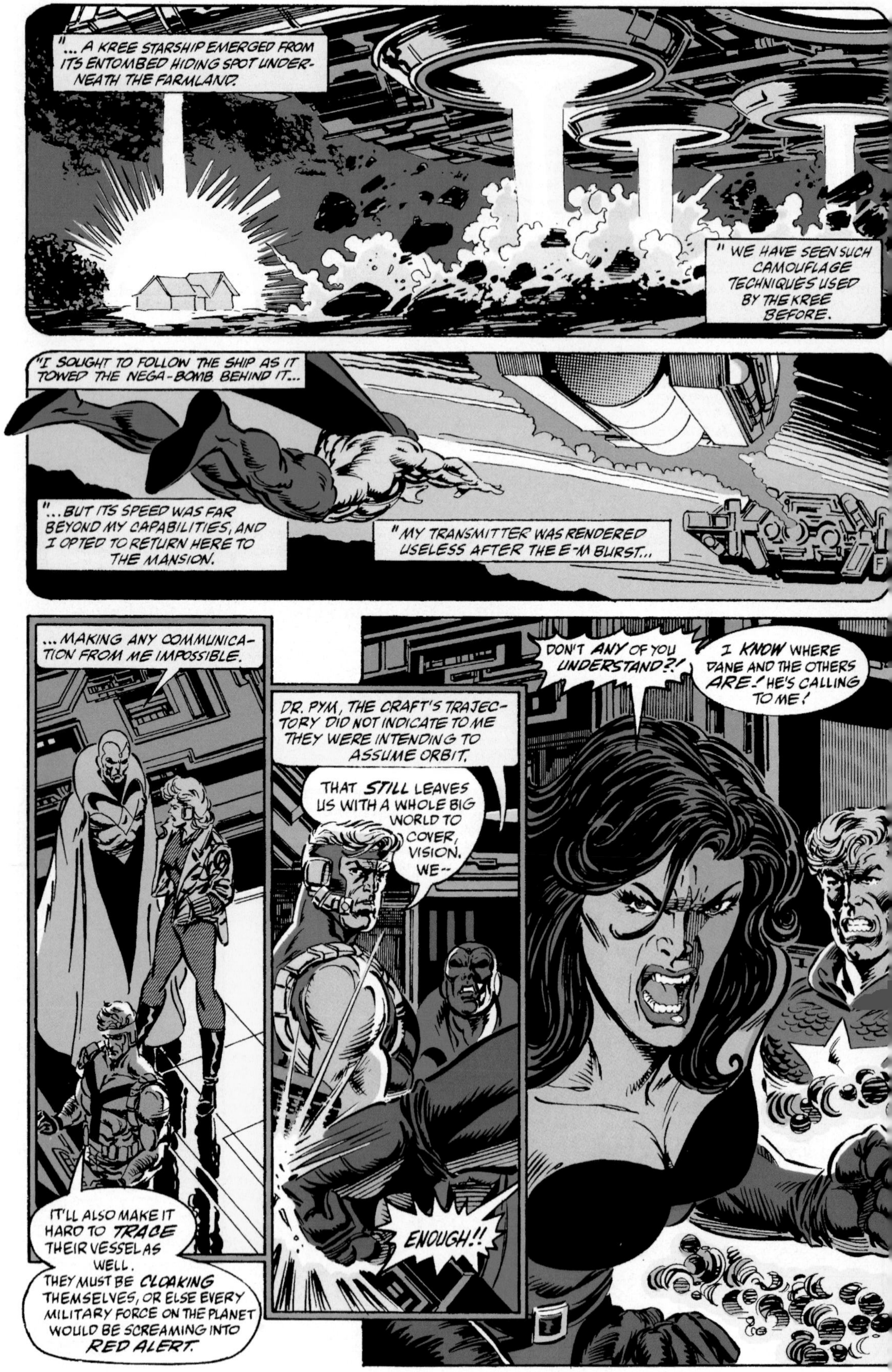
"...A KREE STARSHIP EMERGED FROM ITS ENTOMBED HIDING SPOT UNDERNEATH THE FARMLAND.
"WE HAVE SEEN SUCH CAMOUFLAGE TECHNIQUES USED BY THE KREE BEFORE.
"I SOUGHT TO FOLLOW THE SHIP AS IT TOWED THE NEGA-BOMB BEHIND IT...
"...BUT ITS SPEED WAS FAR BEYOND MY CAPABILITIES, AND I OPTED TO RETURN HERE TO THE MANSION.
"MY TRANSMITTER WAS RENDERED USELESS AFTER THE E-M BURST...
...MAKING ANY COMMUNICATION FROM ME IMPOSSIBLE.
IT'LL ALSO MAKE IT HARD TO TRACE THEIR VESSEL AS WELL.
THEY MUST BE CLOAKING THEMSELVES, OR ELSE EVERY MILITARY FORCE ON THE PLANET WOULD BE SCREAMING INTO RED ALERT.
DR. PYM, THE CRAFT'S TRAJECTORY DID NOT INDICATE TO ME THEY WERE INTENDING TO ASSUME ORBIT.
THAT STILL LEAVES US WITH A WHOLE BIG WORLD TO COVER, VISION. WE--
ENOUGH!!
DON'T ANY OF YOU UNDERSTAND?!
I KNOW WHERE DANE AND THE OTHERS ARE! HE'S CALLING TO ME!

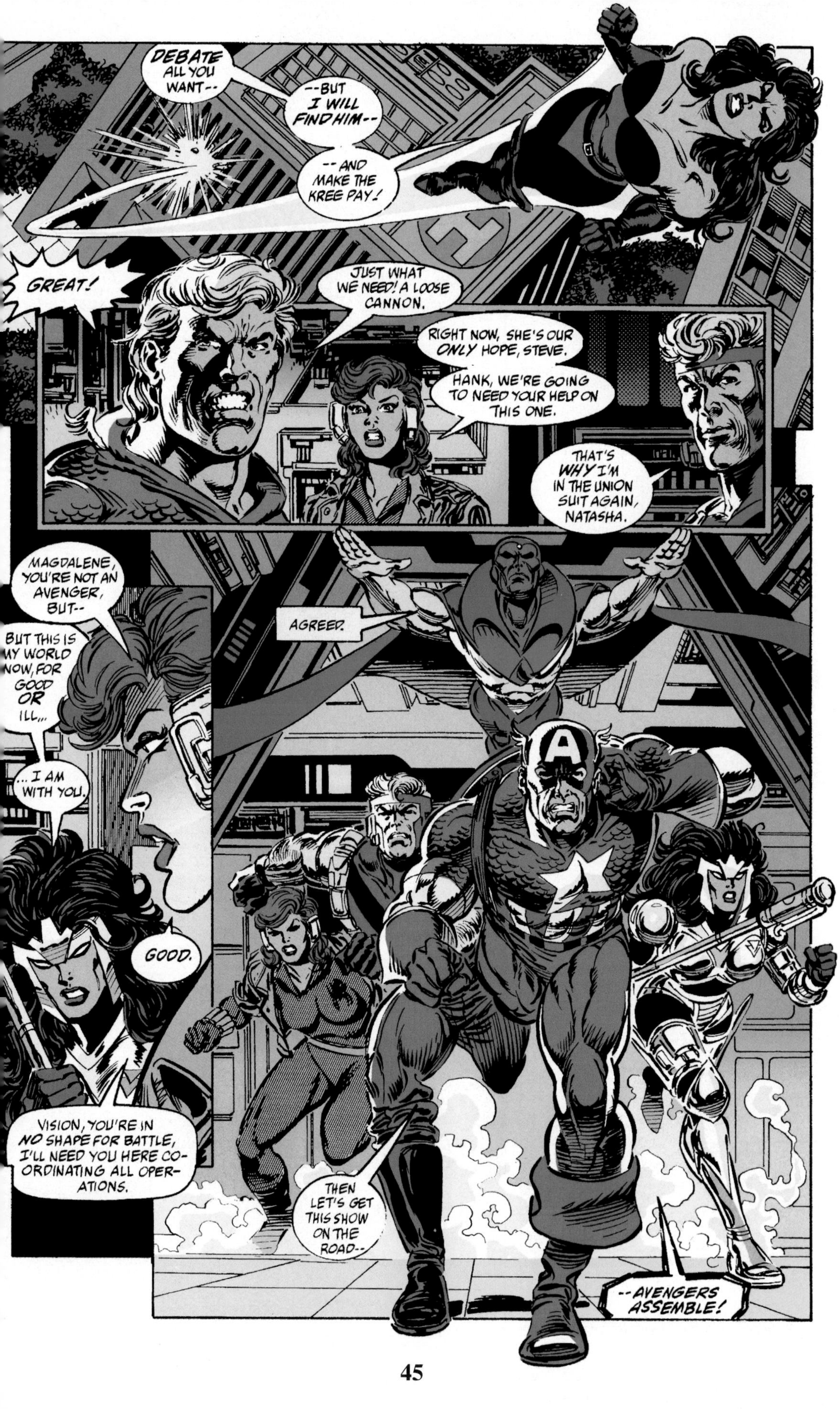
DEBATE ALL YOU WANT--
--BUT I WILL FIND HIM--
--AND MAKE THE KREE PAY!
GREAT!
JUST WHAT WE NEED! A LOOSE CANNON.
RIGHT NOW, SHE'S OUR ONLY HOPE, STEVE.
HANK, WE'RE GOING TO NEED YOUR HELP ON THIS ONE.
THAT'S WHY I'M IN THE UNION SUIT AGAIN, NATASHA.
MAGDALENE, YOU'RE NOT AN AVENGER, BUT--
AGREED.
BUT THIS IS MY WORLD NOW, FOR GOOD OR ILL...
...I AM WITH YOU.
GOOD.
VISION, YOU'RE IN NO SHAPE FOR BATTLE, I'LL NEED YOU HERE CO-ORDINATING ALL OPER-ATIONS.
THEN LET'S GET THIS SHOW ON THE ROAD--
--AVENGERS ASSEMBLE!

A TINY ISLAND...

...SOMEWHERE IN THE SOUTH PACIFIC...

AARRGHHHH

TORTURE IS A KREE SPECIALTY... AN ARTFORM, IF YOU WILL... AND YOU HAVE ENDURED *MUCH*, AVENGERS.

I AM IMPRESSED.

STILL, THE ASSA OF OUR LORD, THE *PREME INTELLIG* AND A KREESPAW *HUMAN* DESE NO LESS THAN VERY *BES*

BY PLUTO'S COLD EYES-- WHY WILL THOU *NOT* LISTEN?!

REMOVE THESE TWO.

THEY ARE NOT *WORTHY* OF FURTHER TREATMENT.

FRIEND DANE! GOOD CRYSTAL!

ANSWER ME IF THOU CAN, MY FRIENDS.

DO NOT *DESPAIR* FOR--

OLYMPIAN, YOU SHOULD KNOW WE EXPECT *SILENCE* FROM OUR PRISONERS.

HOLD YOUR TONGUE OR I SHALL HAVE IT *RIPPED* FROM THE BASE OF YOUR MOUTH.

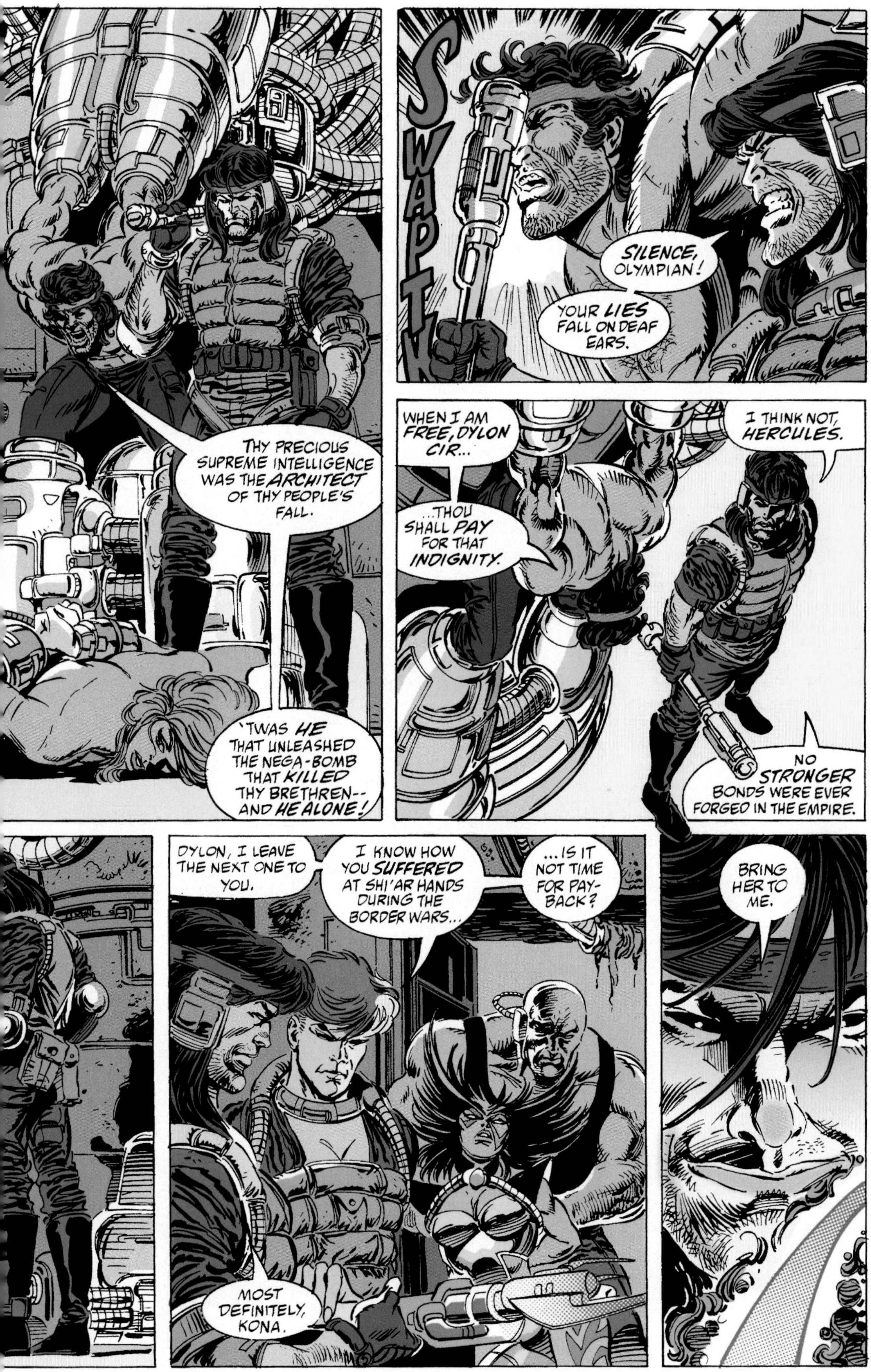
SWAPTK
SILENCE, OLYMPIAN!
YOUR LIES FALL ON DEAF EARS.
THY PRECIOUS SUPREME INTELLIGENCE WAS THE ARCHITECT OF THY PEOPLE'S FALL.
'TWAS HE THAT UNLEASHED THE NEGA-BOMB THAT KILLED THY BRETHREN-- AND HE ALONE!
WHEN I AM FREE, DYLON CIR...
...THOU SHALL PAY FOR THAT INDIGNITY.
I THINK NOT, HERCULES.
NO STRONGER BONDS WERE EVER FORGED IN THE EMPIRE.
DYLON, I LEAVE THE NEXT ONE TO YOU.
I KNOW HOW YOU SUFFERED AT SHI'AR HANDS DURING THE BORDER WARS...
...IS IT NOT TIME FOR PAY-BACK?
MOST DEFINITELY, KONA.
BRING HER TO ME.

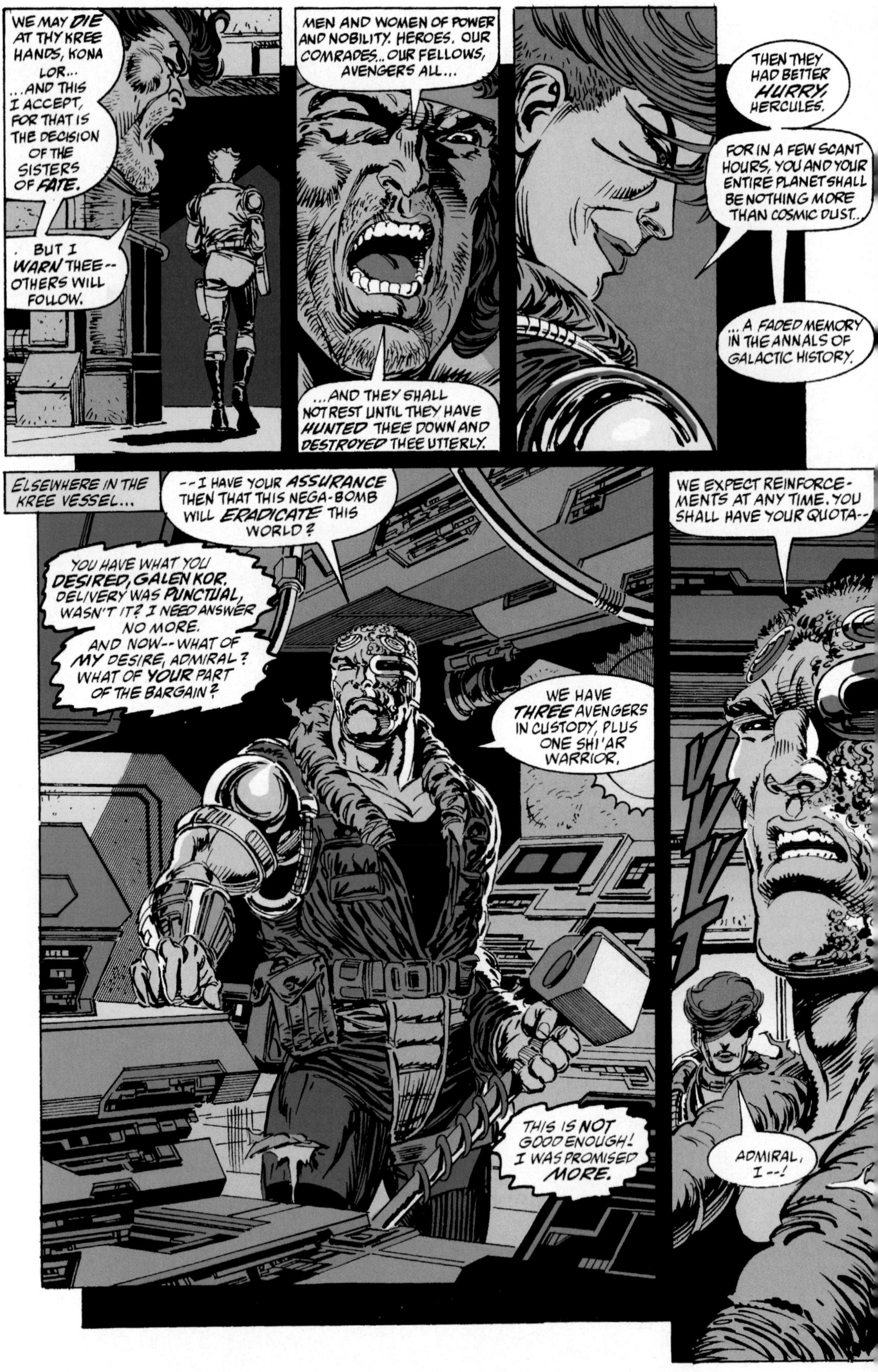

WE MAY DIE AT THY KREE HANDS, KONA LOR...
...AND THIS I ACCEPT, FOR THAT IS THE DECISION OF THE SISTERS OF FATE.
BUT I WARN THEE-- OTHERS WILL FOLLOW.
MEN AND WOMEN OF POWER AND NOBILITY. HEROES. OUR COMRADES... OUR FELLOWS, AVENGERS ALL...
...AND THEY SHALL NOT REST UNTIL THEY HAVE HUNTED THEE DOWN AND DESTROYED THEE UTTERLY.
THEN THEY HAD BETTER HURRY, HERCULES.
FOR IN A FEW SCANT HOURS, YOU AND YOUR ENTIRE PLANET SHALL BE NOTHING MORE THAN COSMIC DUST...
...A FADED MEMORY IN THE ANNALS OF GALACTIC HISTORY.
ELSEWHERE IN THE KREE VESSEL...
--I HAVE YOUR ASSURANCE THEN THAT THIS NEGA-BOMB WILL ERADICATE THIS WORLD?
YOU HAVE WHAT YOU DESIRED, GALEN KOR. DELIVERY WAS PUNCTUAL, WASN'T IT? I NEED ANSWER NO MORE.
AND NOW--WHAT OF MY DESIRE, ADMIRAL? WHAT OF YOUR PART OF THE BARGAIN?
WE HAVE THREE AVENGERS IN CUSTODY, PLUS ONE SHI'AR WARRIOR.
THIS IS NOT GOOD ENOUGH! I WAS PROMISED MORE.
WE EXPECT REINFORCE-MENTS AT ANY TIME. YOU SHALL HAVE YOUR QUOTA--
ADMIRAL, I--!

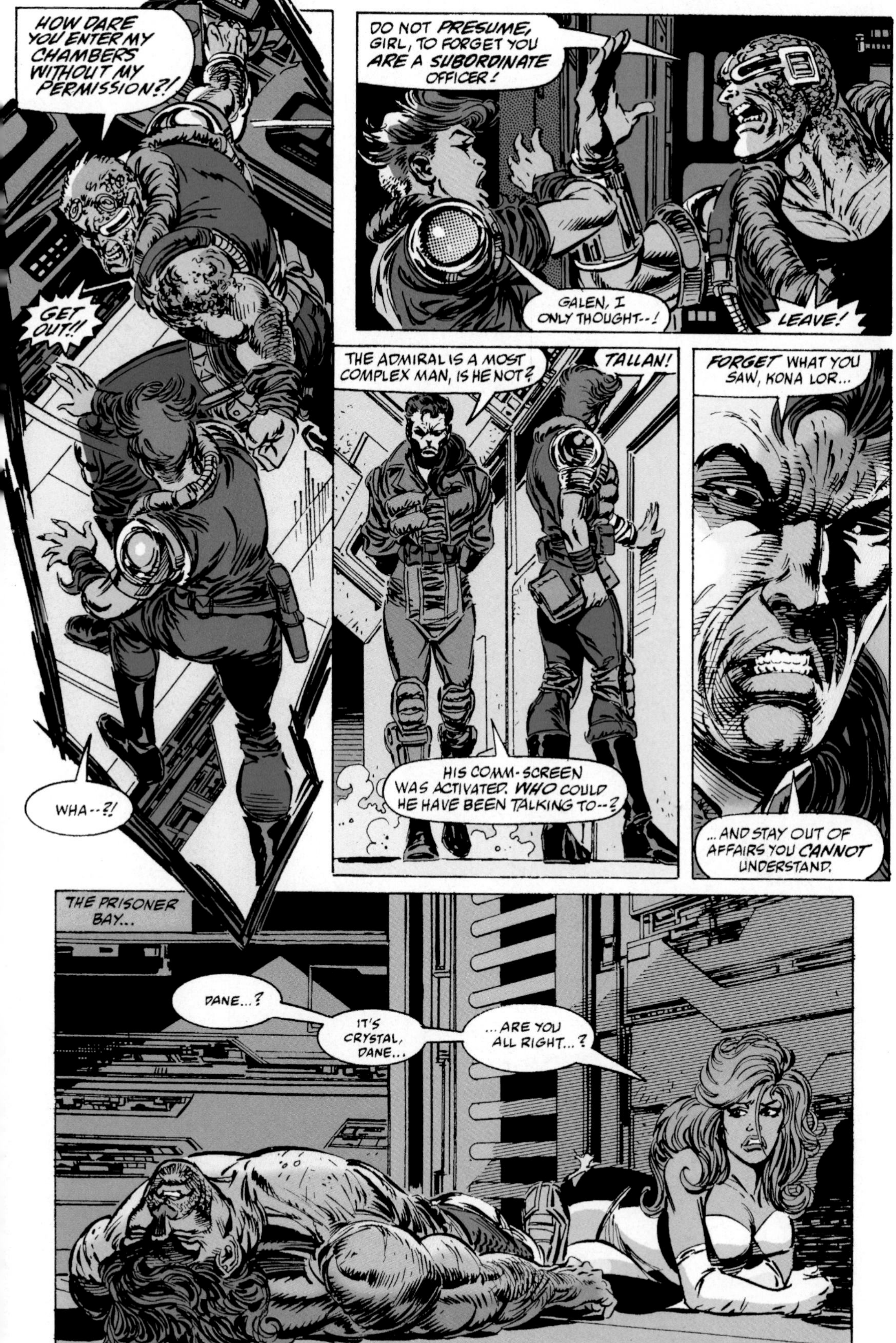
HOW DARE YOU ENTER MY CHAMBERS WITHOUT MY PERMISSION?!
GET OUT!!
WHA--?!
DO NOT PRESUME, GIRL, TO FORGET YOU ARE A SUBORDINATE OFFICER!
GALEN, I ONLY THOUGHT--!
LEAVE!
THE ADMIRAL IS A MOST COMPLEX MAN, IS HE NOT?
TALLAN!
HIS COMM-SCREEN WAS ACTIVATED. WHO COULD HE HAVE BEEN TALKING TO--?
FORGET WHAT YOU SAW, KONA LOR...
...AND STAY OUT OF AFFAIRS YOU CANNOT UNDERSTAND.
THE PRISONER BAY...
DANE...?
IT'S CRYSTAL, DANE...
...ARE YOU ALL RIGHT...?

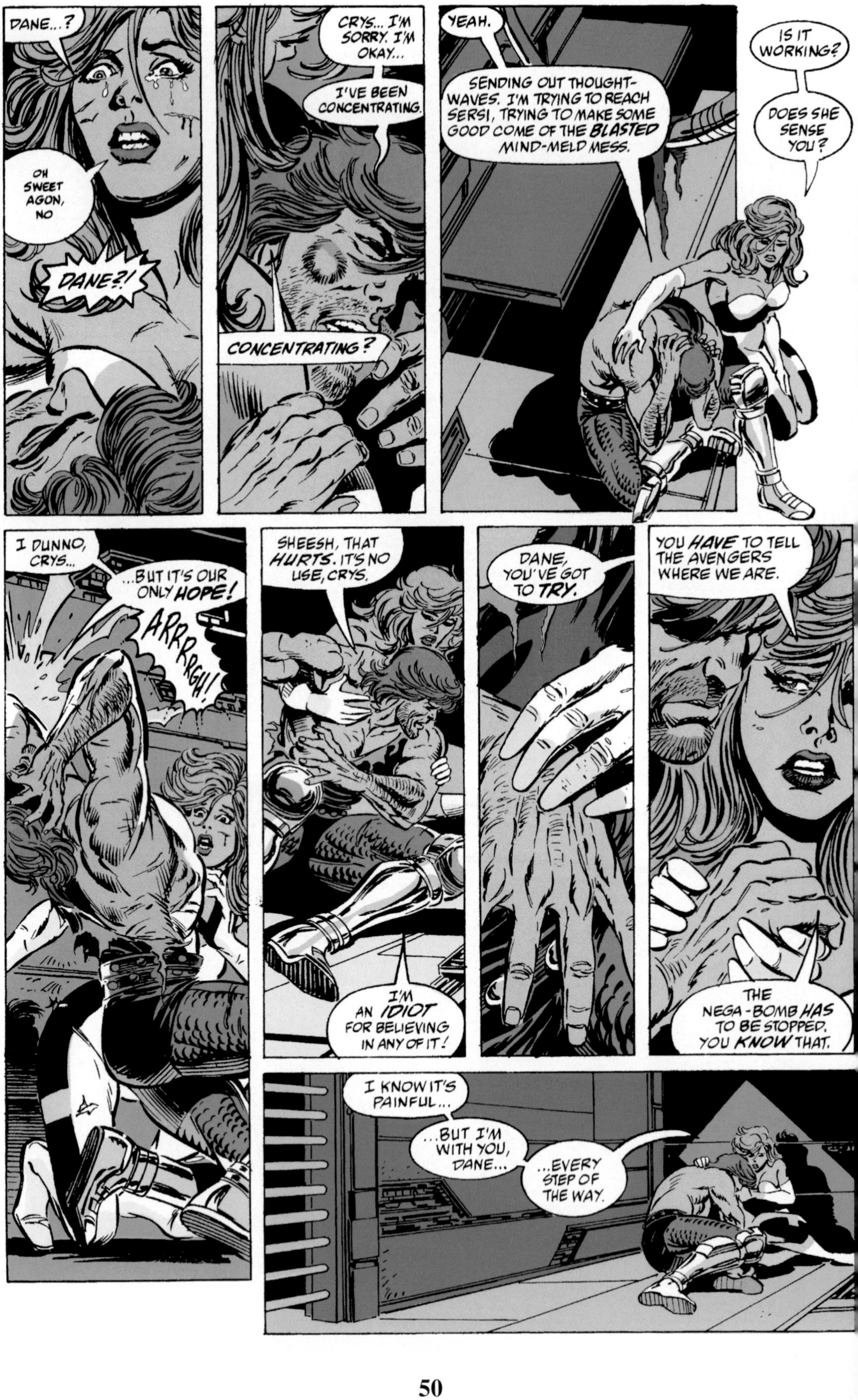
DANE...?
OH SWEET AGON, NO
DANE?!
CRYS... I'M SORRY. I'M OKAY...
I'VE BEEN CONCENTRATING.
CONCENTRATING?
YEAH.
SENDING OUT THOUGHT-WAVES. I'M TRYING TO REACH SERSI, TRYING TO MAKE SOME GOOD COME OF THE BLASTED MIND-MELD MESS.
IS IT WORKING?
DOES SHE SENSE YOU?
I DUNNO, CRYS...
...BUT IT'S OUR ONLY HOPE!
ARRRRGH!
SHEESH, THAT HURTS. IT'S NO USE, CRYS.
I'M AN IDIOT FOR BELIEVING IN ANY OF IT!
DANE, YOU'VE GOT TO TRY.
YOU HAVE TO TELL THE AVENGERS WHERE WE ARE.
THE NEGA-BOMB HAS TO BE STOPPED. YOU KNOW THAT.
I KNOW IT'S PAINFUL...
...BUT I'M WITH YOU, DANE...
...EVERY STEP OF THE WAY.

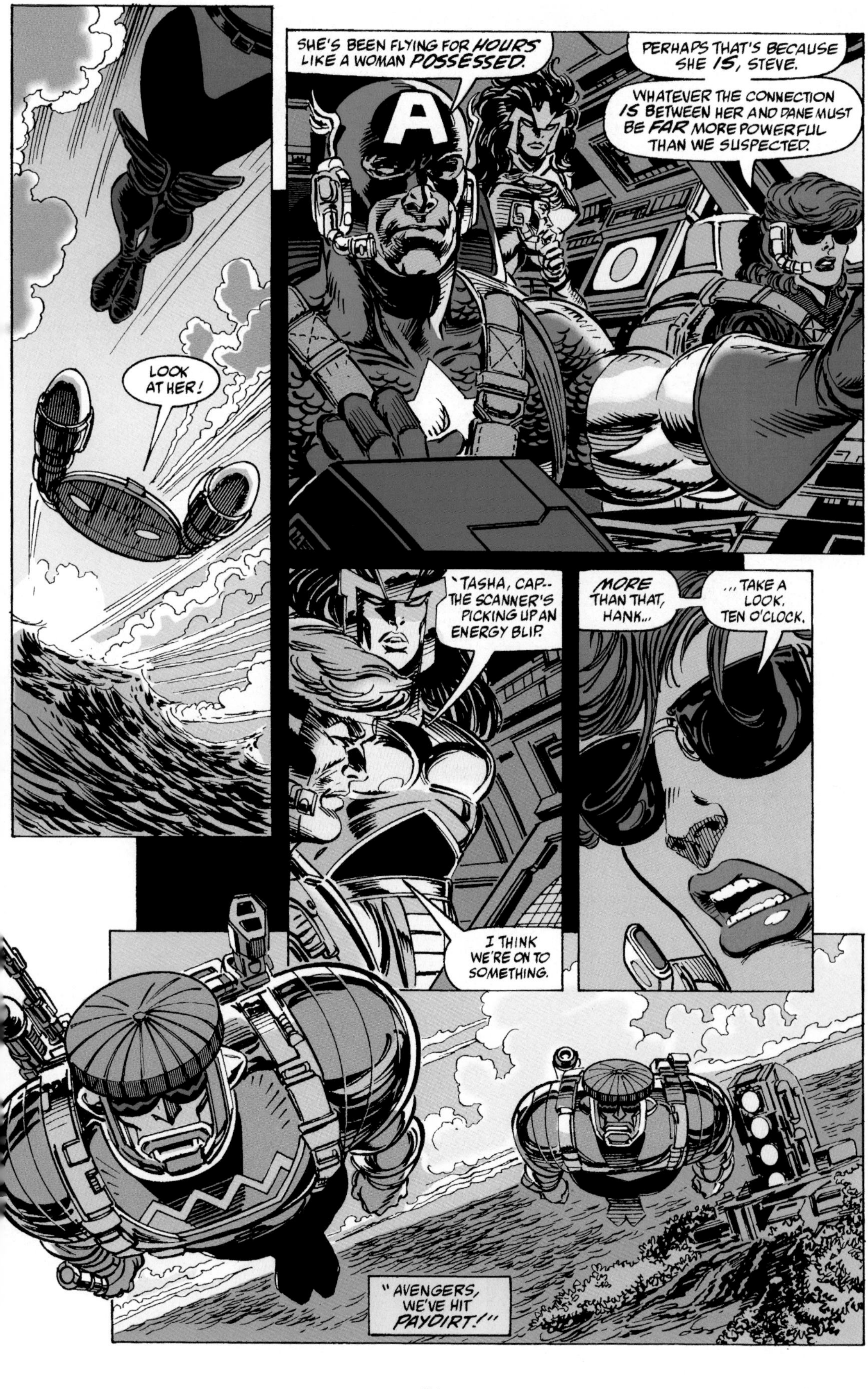

LOOK AT HER!
SHE'S BEEN FLYING FOR HOURS LIKE A WOMAN POSSESSED.
PERHAPS THAT'S BECAUSE SHE IS, STEVE.
WHATEVER THE CONNECTION IS BETWEEN HER AND DANE MUST BE FAR MORE POWERFUL THAN WE SUSPECTED.
`TASHA, CAP-- THE SCANNER'S PICKING UP AN ENERGY BLIP.
I THINK WE'RE ON TO SOMETHING.
MORE THAN THAT, HANK...
...TAKE A LOOK. TEN O'CLOCK.
"AVENGERS, WE'VE HIT PAYDIRT!"

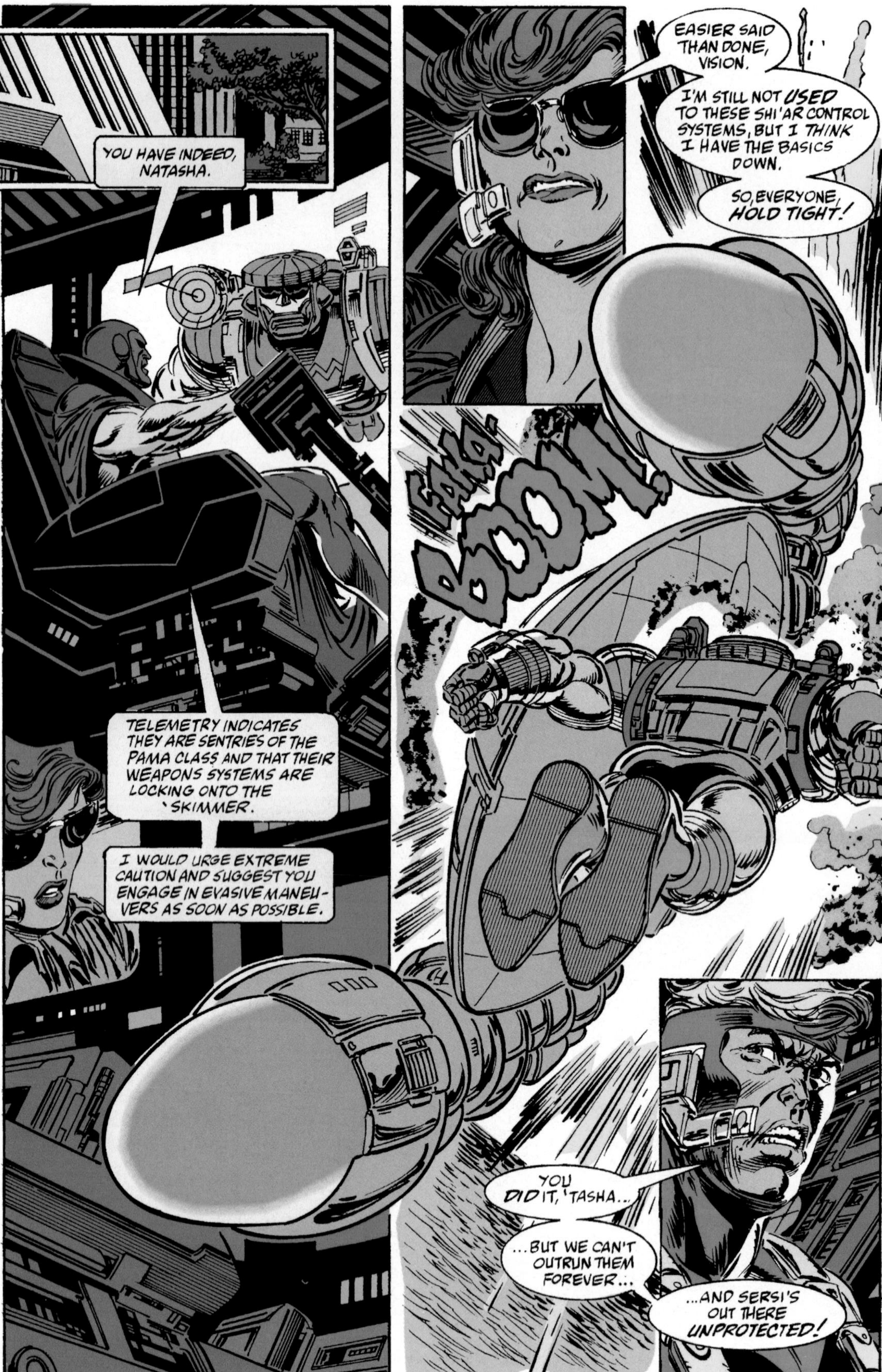
YOU HAVE INDEED, NATASHA.
TELEMETRY INDICATES THEY ARE SENTRIES OF THE PAMA CLASS AND THAT THEIR WEAPONS SYSTEMS ARE LOCKING ONTO THE 'SKIMMER.
I WOULD URGE EXTREME CAUTION AND SUGGEST YOU ENGAGE IN EVASIVE MANEU-VERS AS SOON AS POSSIBLE.
EASIER SAID THAN DONE, VISION.
I'M STILL NOT USED TO THESE SHI'AR CONTROL SYSTEMS, BUT I THINK I HAVE THE BASICS DOWN.
SO, EVERYONE, HOLD TIGHT!
FAKA-BOOM!
YOU DID IT, 'TASHA...
...BUT WE CAN'T OUTRUN THEM FOREVER...
...AND SERSI'S OUT THERE UNPROTECTED!

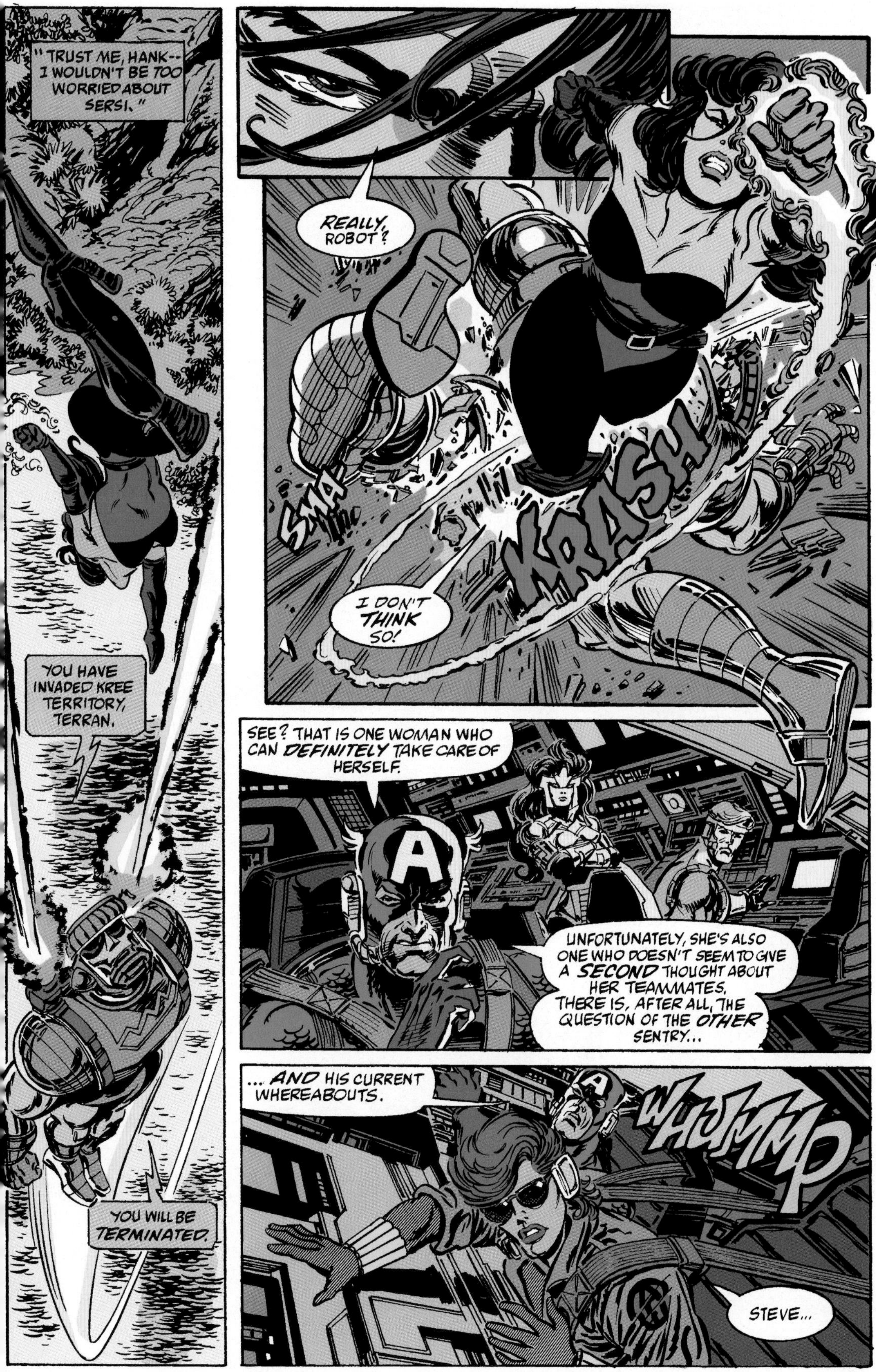
"TRUST ME, HANK-- I WOULDN'T BE TOO WORRIED ABOUT SERSI."
YOU HAVE INVADED KREE TERRITORY, TERRAN.
YOU WILL BE TERMINATED.
REALLY, ROBOT?
SMA
KRASH
I DON'T THINK SO!
SEE? THAT IS ONE WOMAN WHO CAN DEFINITELY TAKE CARE OF HERSELF.
UNFORTUNATELY, SHE'S ALSO ONE WHO DOESN'T SEEM TO GIVE A SECOND THOUGHT ABOUT HER TEAMMATES. THERE IS, AFTER ALL, THE QUESTION OF THE OTHER SENTRY...
...AND HIS CURRENT WHEREABOUTS.
WHUMMP
STEVE...

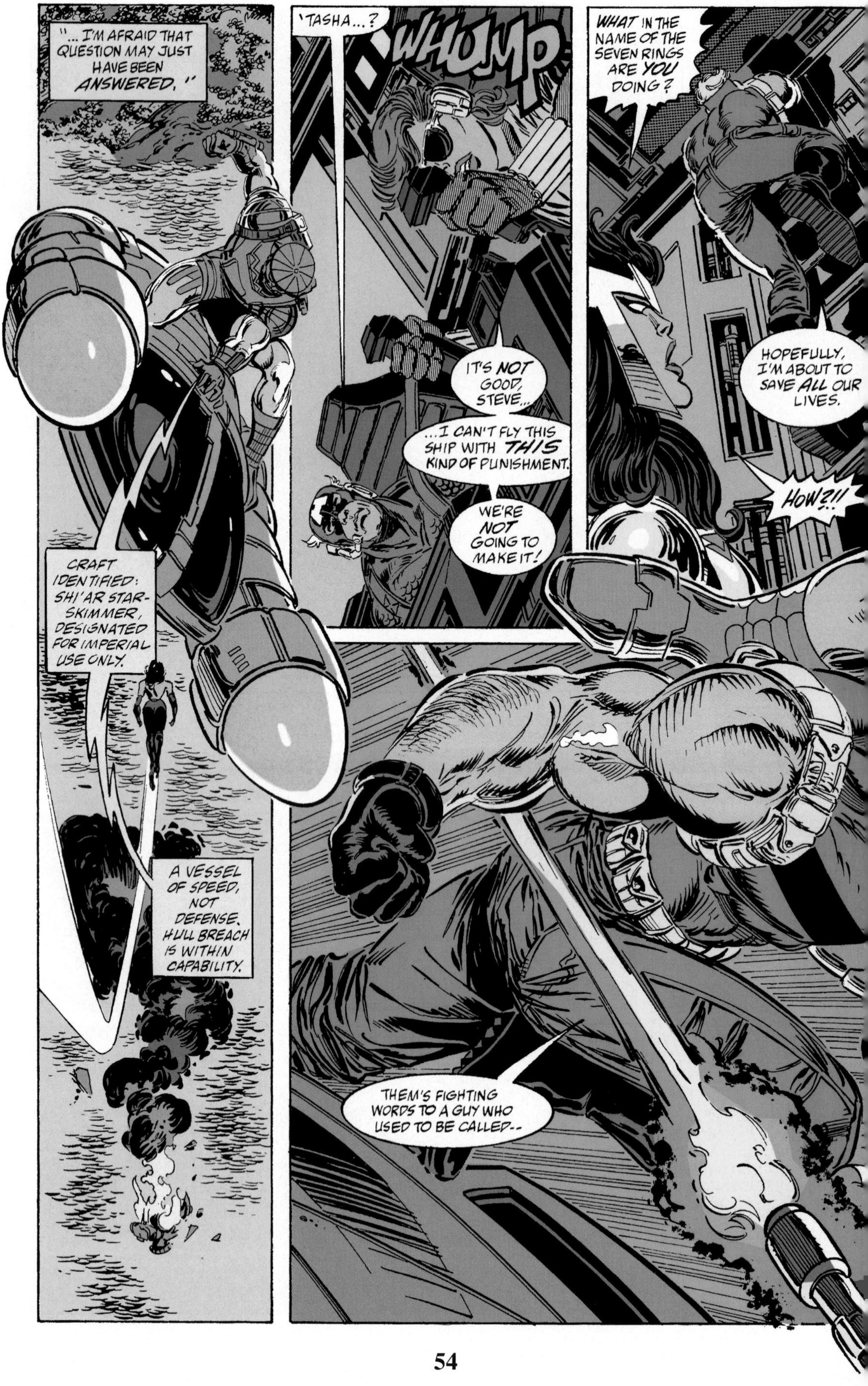
"... I'M AFRAID THAT QUESTION MAY JUST HAVE BEEN ANSWERED."
'TASHA...?
WHUMP
IT'S NOT GOOD, STEVE...
...I CAN'T FLY THIS SHIP WITH THIS KIND OF PUNISHMENT.
WE'RE NOT GOING TO MAKE IT!
WHAT IN THE NAME OF THE SEVEN RINGS ARE YOU DOING?
HOPEFULLY, I'M ABOUT TO SAVE ALL OUR LIVES.
HOW?!!
CRAFT IDENTIFIED: SHI'AR STAR-SKIMMER, DESIGNATED FOR IMPERIAL USE ONLY.
A VESSEL OF SPEED, NOT DEFENSE. HULL BREACH IS WITHIN CAPABILITY.
THEM'S FIGHTING WORDS TO A GUY WHO USED TO BE CALLED--

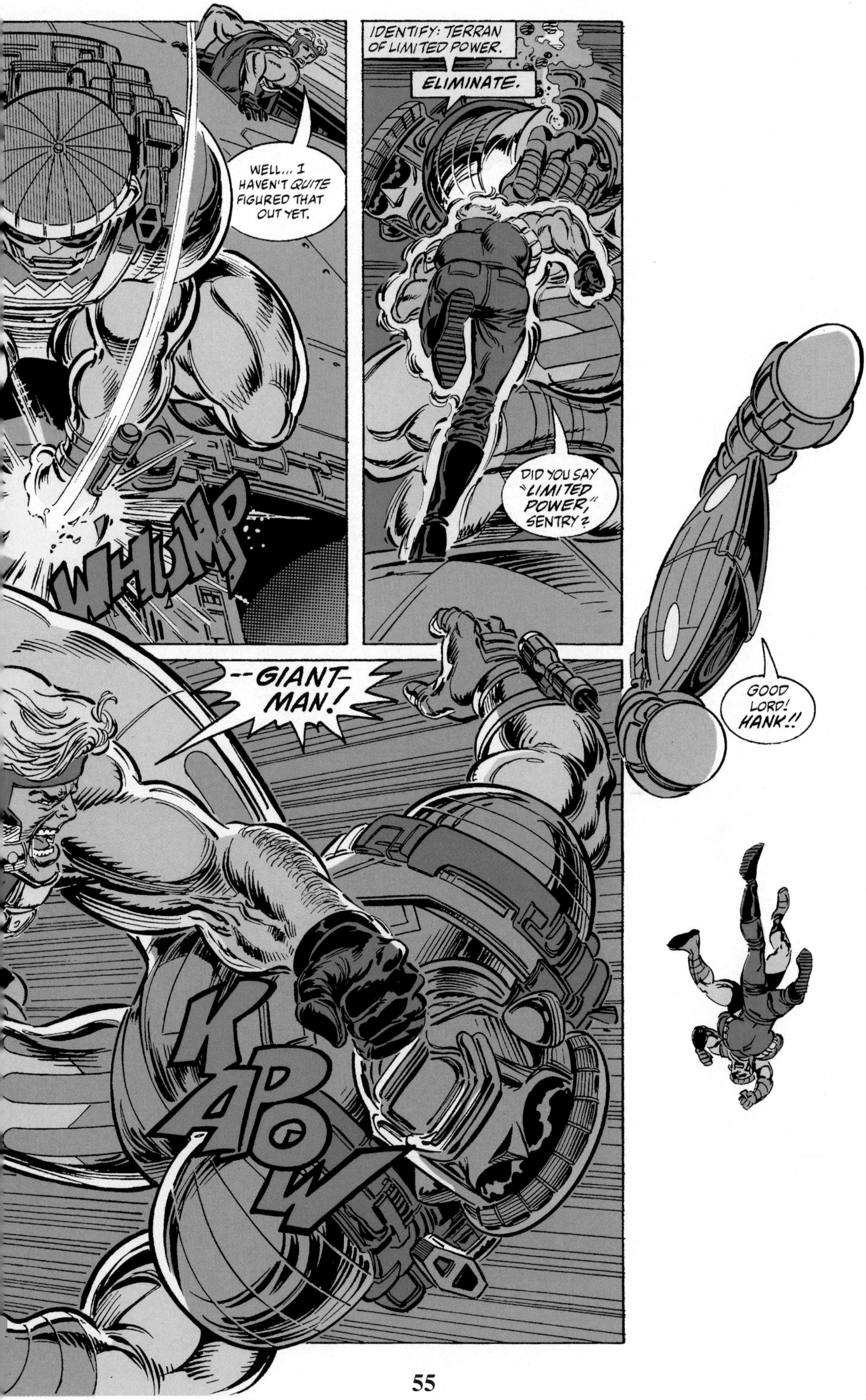
WELL... I HAVEN'T QUITE FIGURED THAT OUT YET.
WHUMP
IDENTIFY: TERRAN OF LIMITED POWER.
ELIMINATE.
DID YOU SAY "LIMITED POWER," SENTRY?
--GIANT-MAN!
GOOD LORD! HANK!!
KAPOW

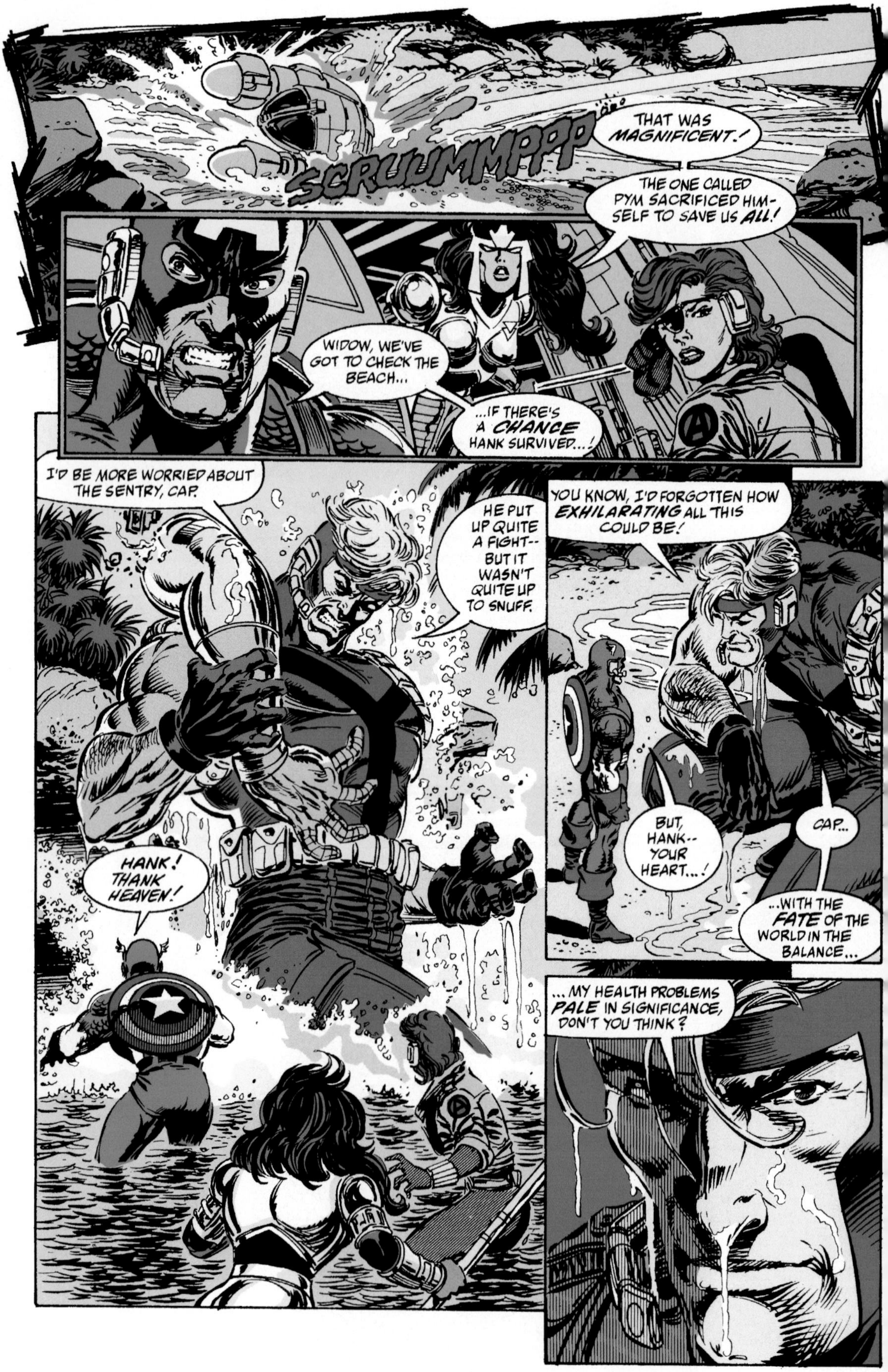
SCRUUMMPPP
THAT WAS MAGNIFICENT.!
THE ONE CALLED PYM SACRIFICED HIMSELF TO SAVE US ALL!
WIDOW, WE'VE GOT TO CHECK THE BEACH...
...IF THERE'S A CHANCE HANK SURVIVED...!
I'D BE MORE WORRIED ABOUT THE SENTRY, CAP.
HE PUT UP QUITE A FIGHT-- BUT IT WASN'T QUITE UP TO SNUFF.
HANK! THANK HEAVEN!
YOU KNOW, I'D FORGOTTEN HOW EXHILARATING ALL THIS COULD BE!
BUT, HANK-- YOUR HEART...!
CAP...
...WITH THE FATE OF THE WORLD IN THE BALANCE...
... MY HEALTH PROBLEMS PALE IN SIGNIFICANCE, DON'T YOU THINK?

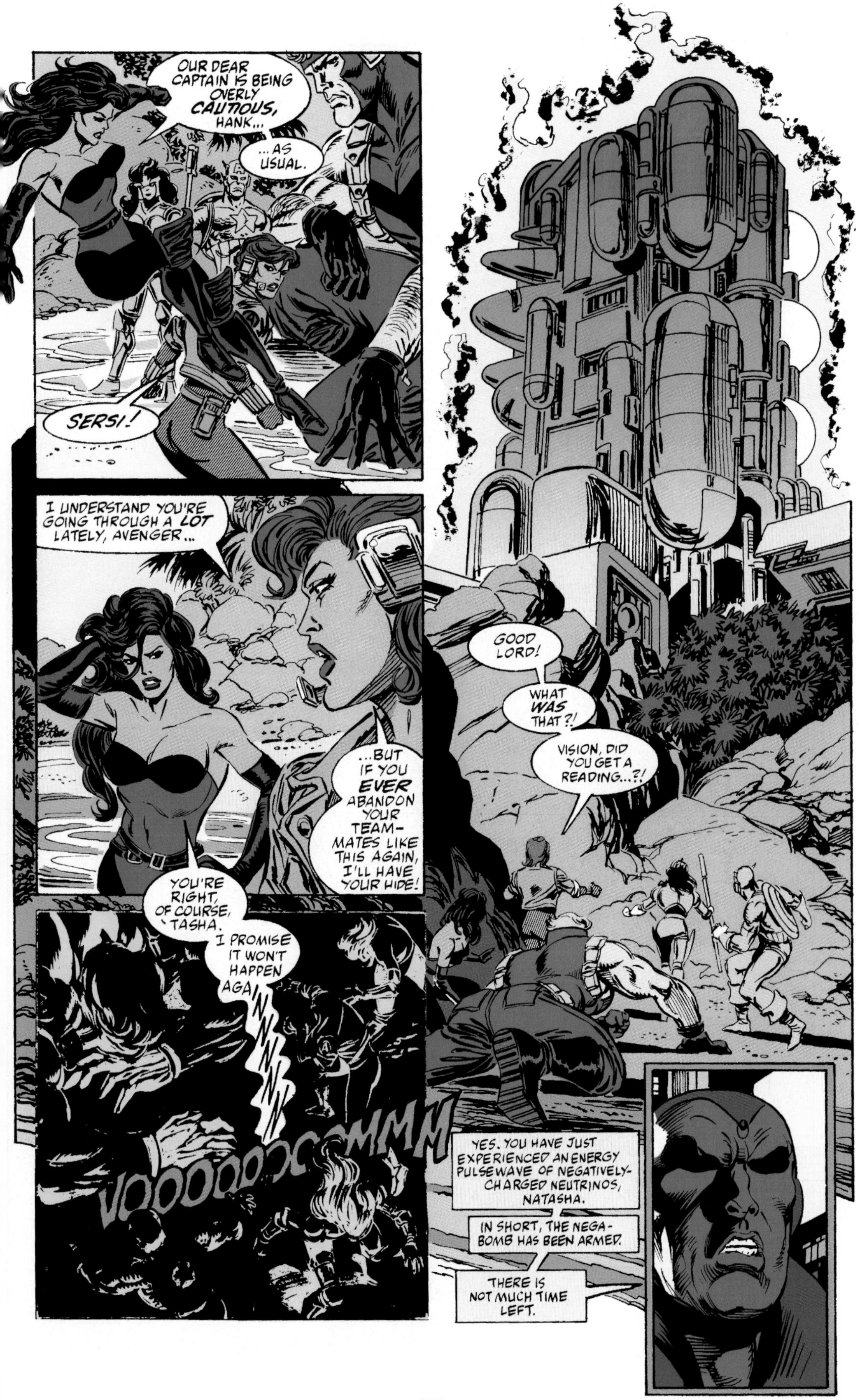

OUR DEAR CAPTAIN IS BEING OVERLY CAUTIOUS, HANK...
...AS USUAL.
SERSI!
I UNDERSTAND YOU'RE GOING THROUGH A LOT LATELY, AVENGER...
...BUT IF YOU EVER ABANDON YOUR TEAM-MATES LIKE THIS AGAIN, I'LL HAVE YOUR HIDE!
YOU'RE RIGHT, OF COURSE, 'TASHA.
I PROMISE IT WON'T HAPPEN AGAINNNNN
VOOOOOOOOMMMM
GOOD LORD!
WHAT WAS THAT?!
VISION, DID YOU GET A READING...?!
YES. YOU HAVE JUST EXPERIENCED AN ENERGY PULSEWAVE OF NEGATIVELY-CHARGED NEUTRINOS, NATASHA.
IN SHORT, THE NEGA-BOMB HAS BEEN ARMED.
THERE IS NOT MUCH TIME LEFT.

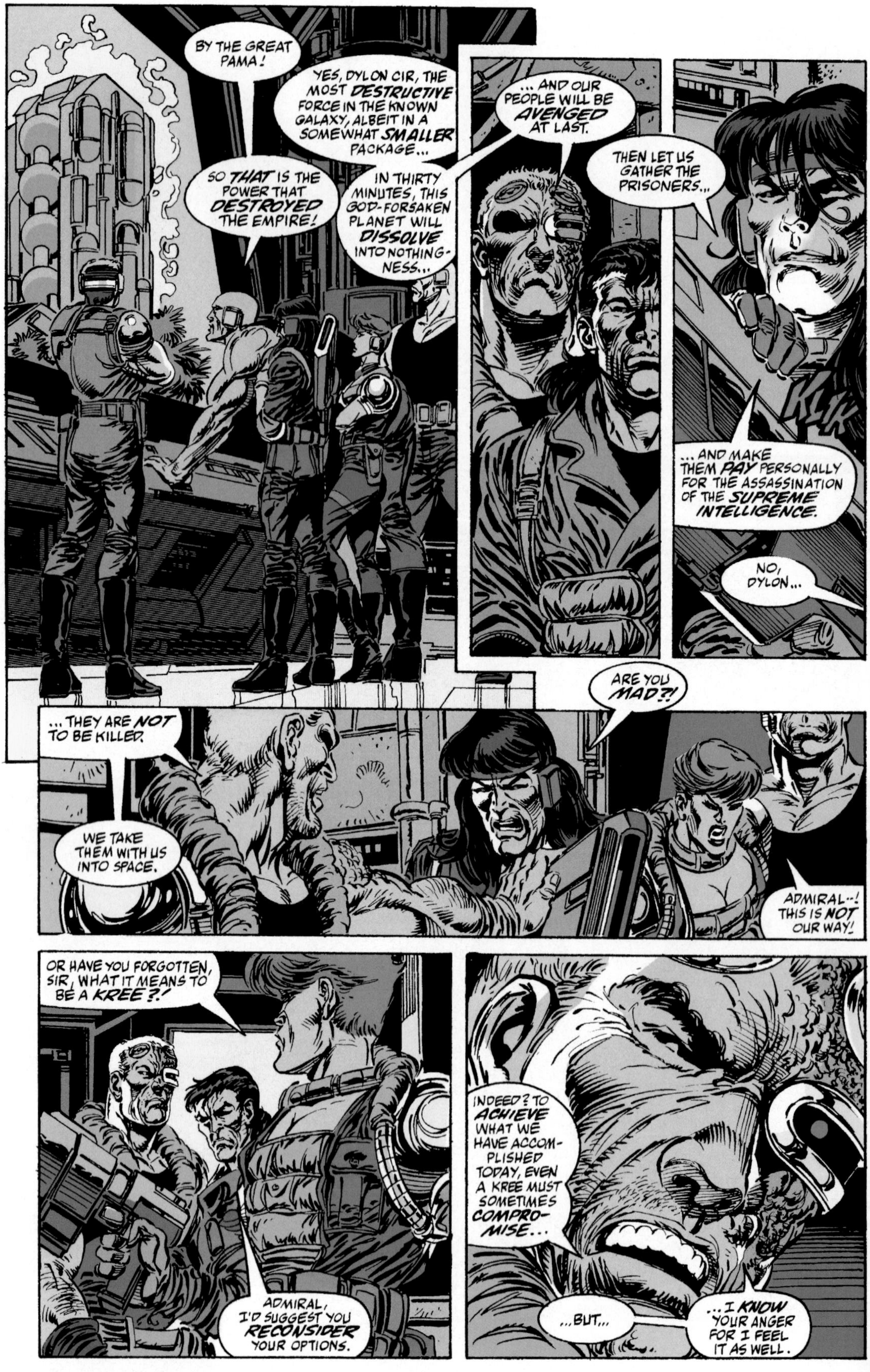

BY THE GREAT PAMA!
YES, DYLON CIR, THE MOST DESTRUCTIVE FORCE IN THE KNOWN GALAXY, ALBEIT IN A SOMEWHAT SMALLER PACKAGE...
SO THAT IS THE POWER THAT DESTROYED THE EMPIRE!
IN THIRTY MINUTES, THIS GOD-FORSAKEN PLANET WILL DISSOLVE INTO NOTHINGNESS...
... AND OUR PEOPLE WILL BE AVENGED AT LAST.
THEN LET US GATHER THE PRISONERS...
KLIK
... AND MAKE THEM PAY PERSONALLY FOR THE ASSASSINATION OF THE SUPREME INTELLIGENCE.
NO, DYLON...
... THEY ARE NOT TO BE KILLED.
WE TAKE THEM WITH US INTO SPACE.
ARE YOU MAD?!
ADMIRAL--! THIS IS NOT OUR WAY!
OR HAVE YOU FORGOTTEN, SIR, WHAT IT MEANS TO BE A KREE?!
ADMIRAL, I'D SUGGEST YOU RECONSIDER YOUR OPTIONS.
INDEED? TO ACHIEVE WHAT WE HAVE ACCOMPLISHED TODAY, EVEN A KREE MUST SOMETIMES COMPROMISE...
...BUT...
... I KNOW YOUR ANGER FOR I FEEL IT AS WELL.

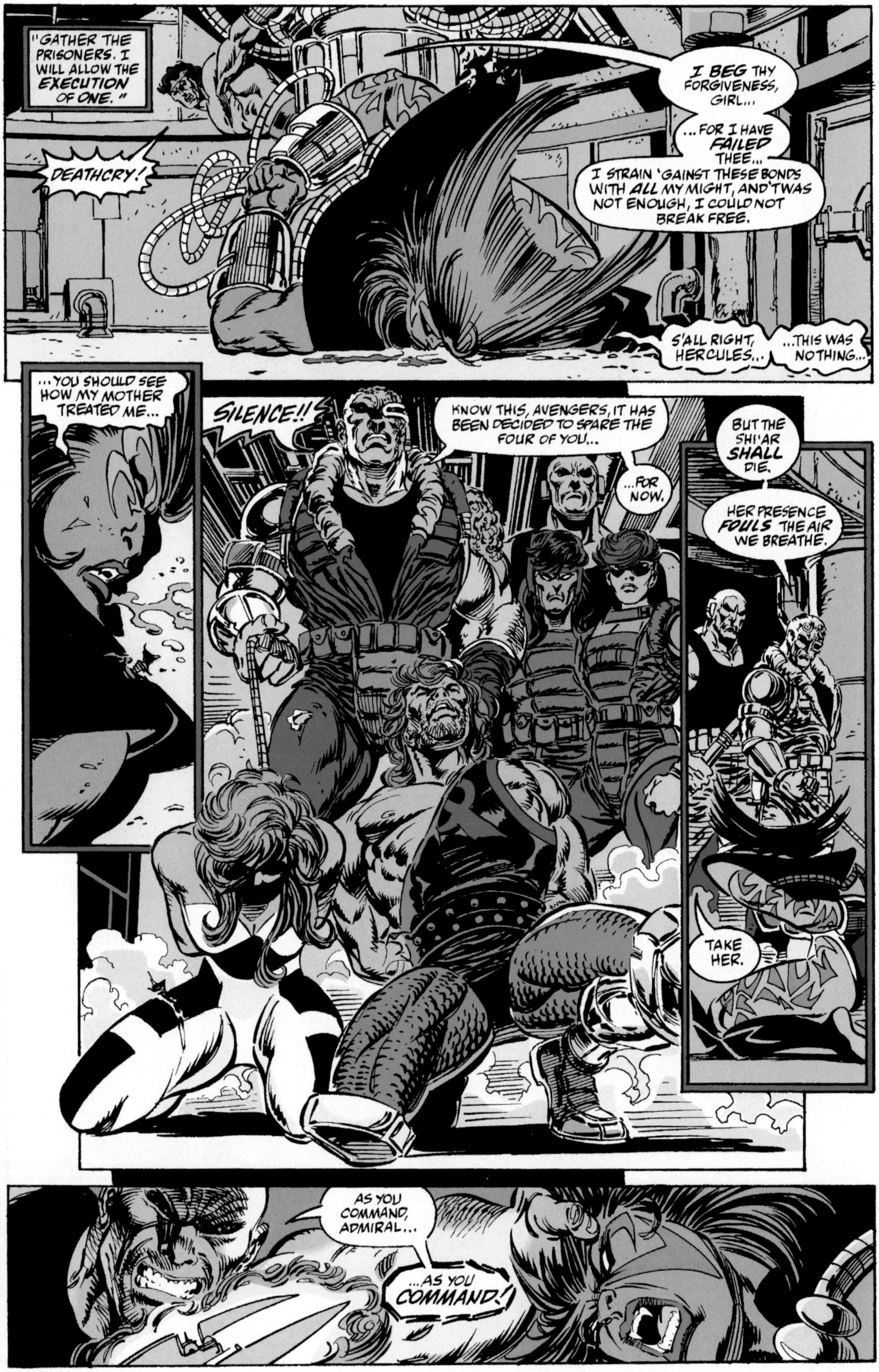
"GATHER THE PRISONERS. I WILL ALLOW THE EXECUTION OF ONE."
I BEG THY FORGIVENESS, GIRL...
...FOR I HAVE FAILED THEE...
I STRAIN 'GAINST THESE BONDS WITH ALL MY MIGHT, AND 'TWAS NOT ENOUGH, I COULD NOT BREAK FREE.
DEATHCRY!
S'ALL RIGHT, HERCULES...
...THIS WAS NOTHING...
...YOU SHOULD SEE HOW MY MOTHER TREATED ME...
SILENCE!!
KNOW THIS, AVENGERS, IT HAS BEEN DECIDED TO SPARE THE FOUR OF YOU...
...FOR NOW.
BUT THE SHI'AR SHALL DIE.
HER PRESENCE FOULS THE AIR WE BREATHE.
TAKE HER.
AS YOU COMMAND, ADMIRAL...
...AS YOU COMMAND!

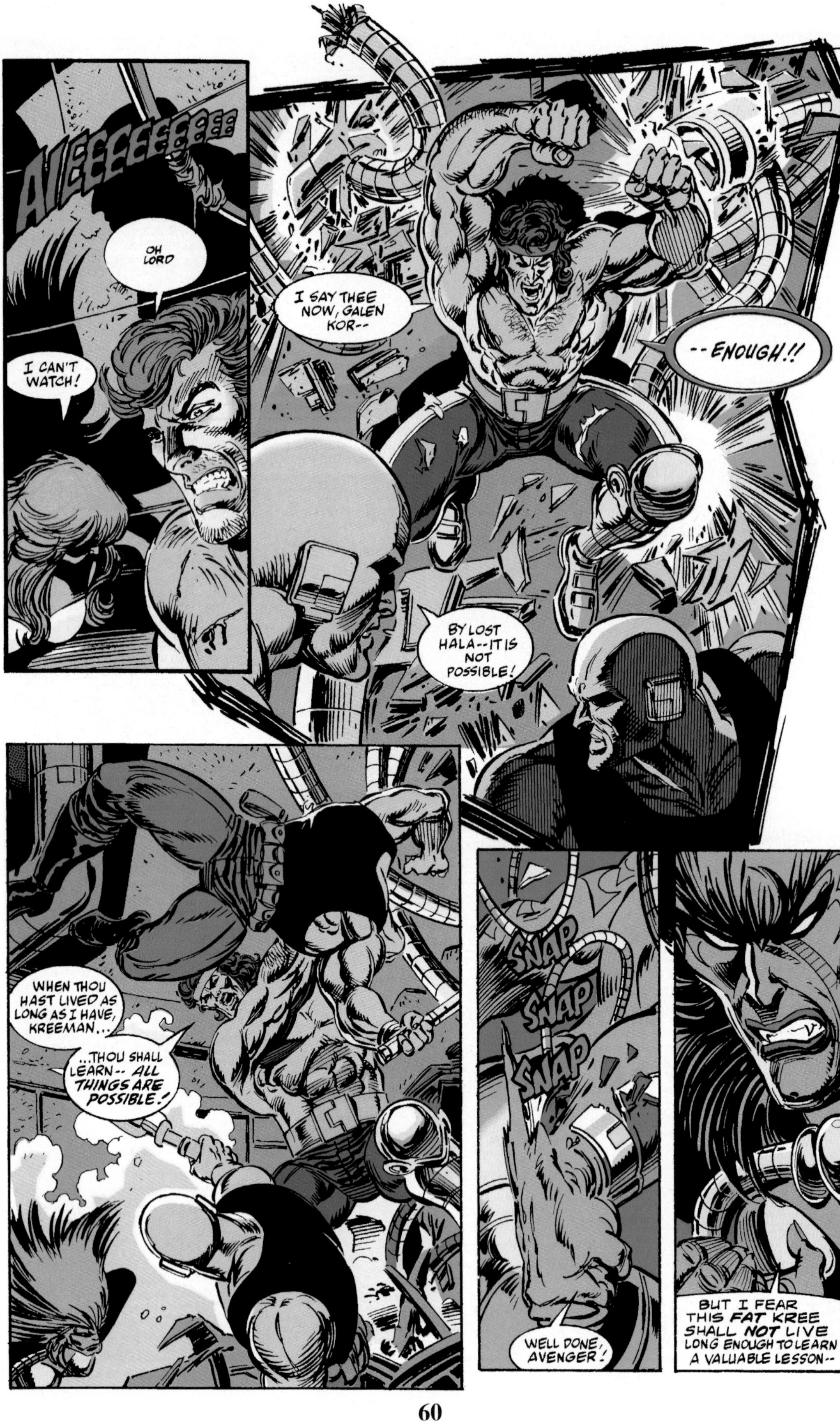
AIEEEEEEEEEE
OH LORD
I CAN'T WATCH!
I SAY THEE NOW, GALEN KOR--
--ENOUGH!!
BY LOST HALA--IT IS NOT POSSIBLE!
WHEN THOU HAST LIVED AS LONG AS I HAVE, KREEMAN...
...THOU SHALL LEARN-- ALL THINGS ARE POSSIBLE!
SNAP
SNAP
SNAP
WELL DONE, AVENGER!
BUT I FEAR THIS FAT KREE SHALL NOT LIVE LONG ENOUGH TO LEARN A VALUABLE LESSON--

-- FOR HE SHALL *PAY* FOR WHAT HE DID.

SLASHKTTT!

ARGGHHH

SO SWEARS *DEATHCRY!*

KILL THEM BOTH!

FASHA'SMMMM

THY FOOLISH WEAPONS WILL NOT *SAVE* THEE FROM THE *PRINCE OF POWER!*

I SHALL *TEAR* THIS SHIP DOWN AROUND THEE!

RO-RO-RIPP

WHAT'S GOING ON?! THE SHIP IS SHAKING?!

LOOK! AT THE HULL!

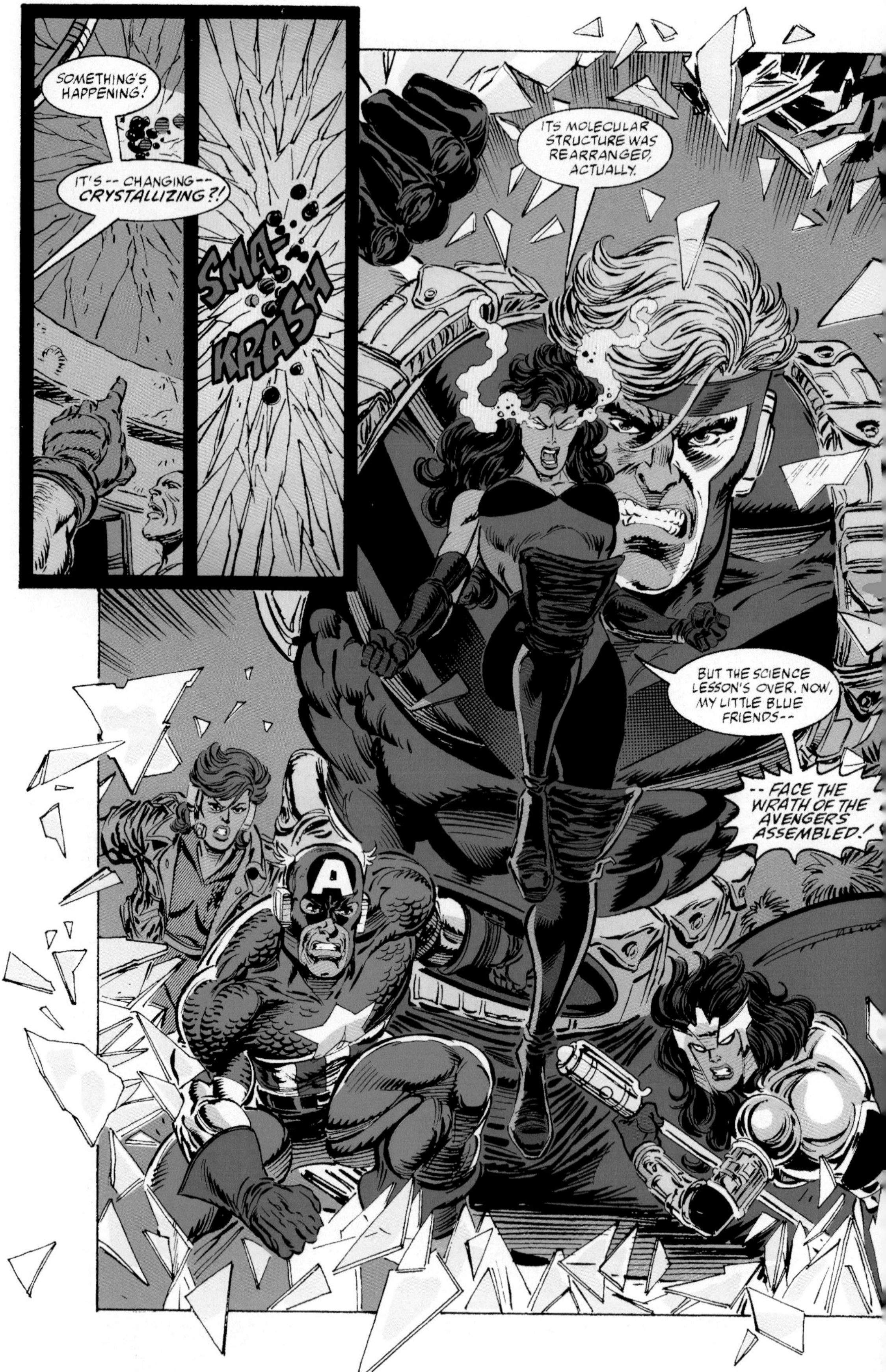
SOMETHING'S HAPPENING!
IT'S -- CHANGING -- CRYSTALLIZING?!
SMA-KRASH
ITS MOLECULAR STRUCTURE WAS REARRANGED, ACTUALLY.
BUT THE SCIENCE LESSON'S OVER, NOW, MY LITTLE BLUE FRIENDS --
-- FACE THE WRATH OF THE AVENGERS ASSEMBLED!

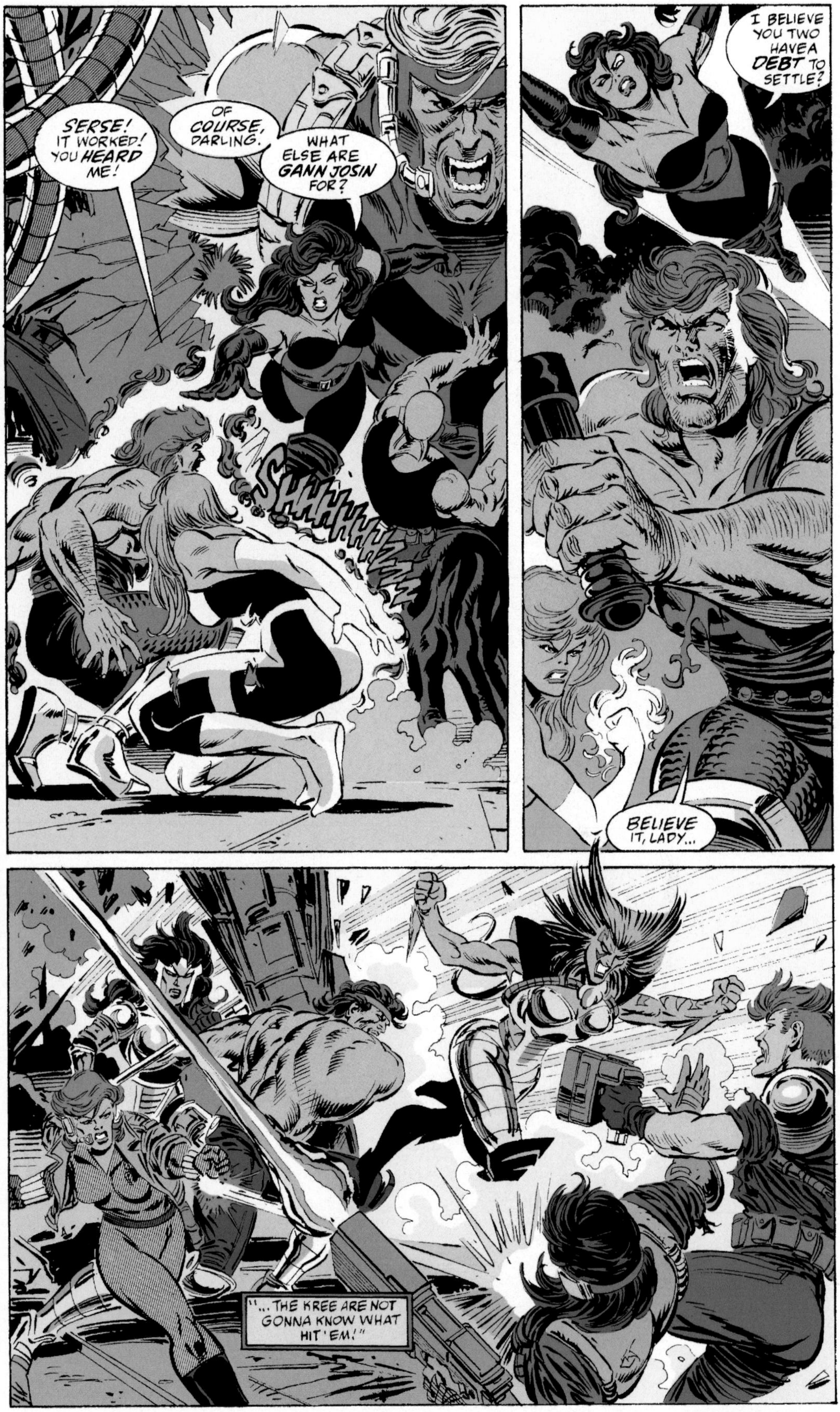
SERSE! IT WORKED! YOU HEARD ME!
OF COURSE, DARLING.
WHAT ELSE ARE GANN JOSIN FOR?
I BELIEVE YOU TWO HAVE A DEBT TO SETTLE?
BELIEVE IT, LADY...
"...THE KREE ARE NOT GONNA KNOW WHAT HIT 'EM!"

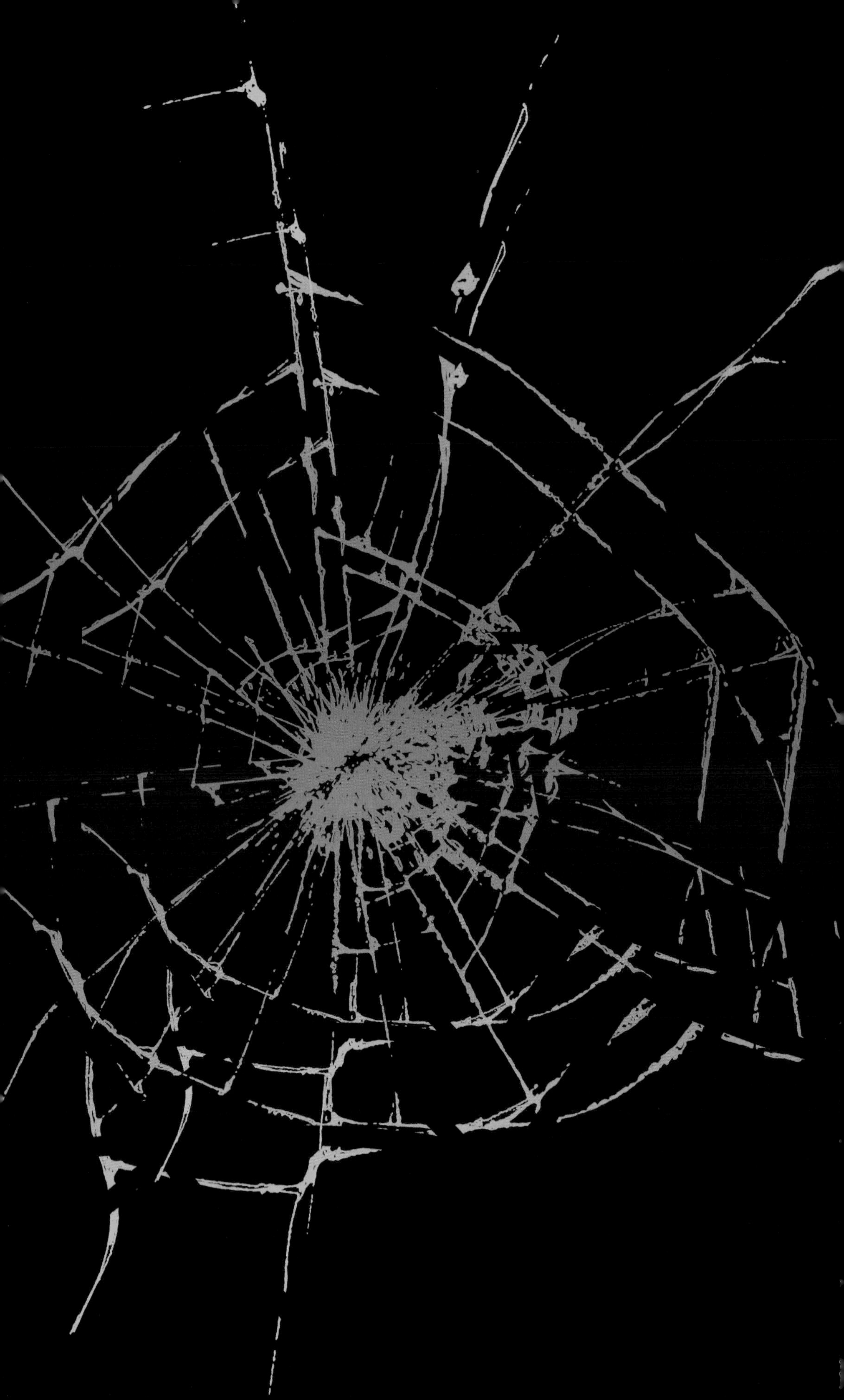

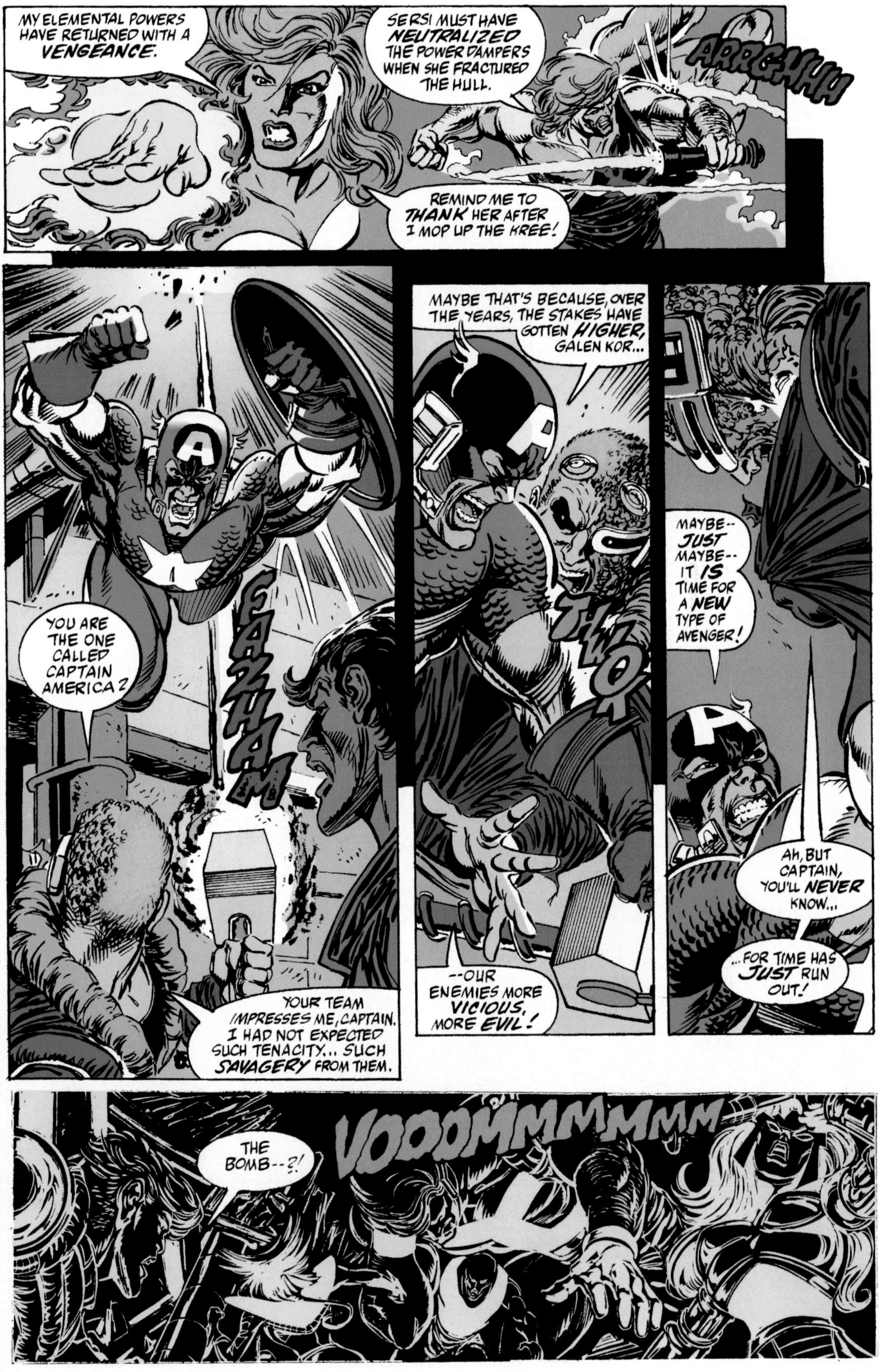
MY ELEMENTAL POWERS HAVE RETURNED WITH A VENGEANCE.
SERSI MUST HAVE NEUTRALIZED THE POWER DAMPERS WHEN SHE FRACTURED THE HULL.
ARRGHHH
REMIND ME TO THANK HER AFTER I MOP UP THE KREE!
YOU ARE THE ONE CALLED CAPTAIN AMERICA?
CHAKHAM
YOUR TEAM IMPRESSES ME, CAPTAIN. I HAD NOT EXPECTED SUCH TENACITY... SUCH SAVAGERY FROM THEM.
MAYBE THAT'S BECAUSE, OVER THE YEARS, THE STAKES HAVE GOTTEN HIGHER, GALEN KOR...
THWOK
--OUR ENEMIES MORE VICIOUS, MORE EVIL!
MAYBE-- JUST MAYBE-- IT IS TIME FOR A NEW TYPE OF AVENGER!
Ah, BUT CAPTAIN, YOU'LL NEVER KNOW...
...FOR TIME HAS JUST RUN OUT!
VOOOMMMMMMM
THE BOMB--?!

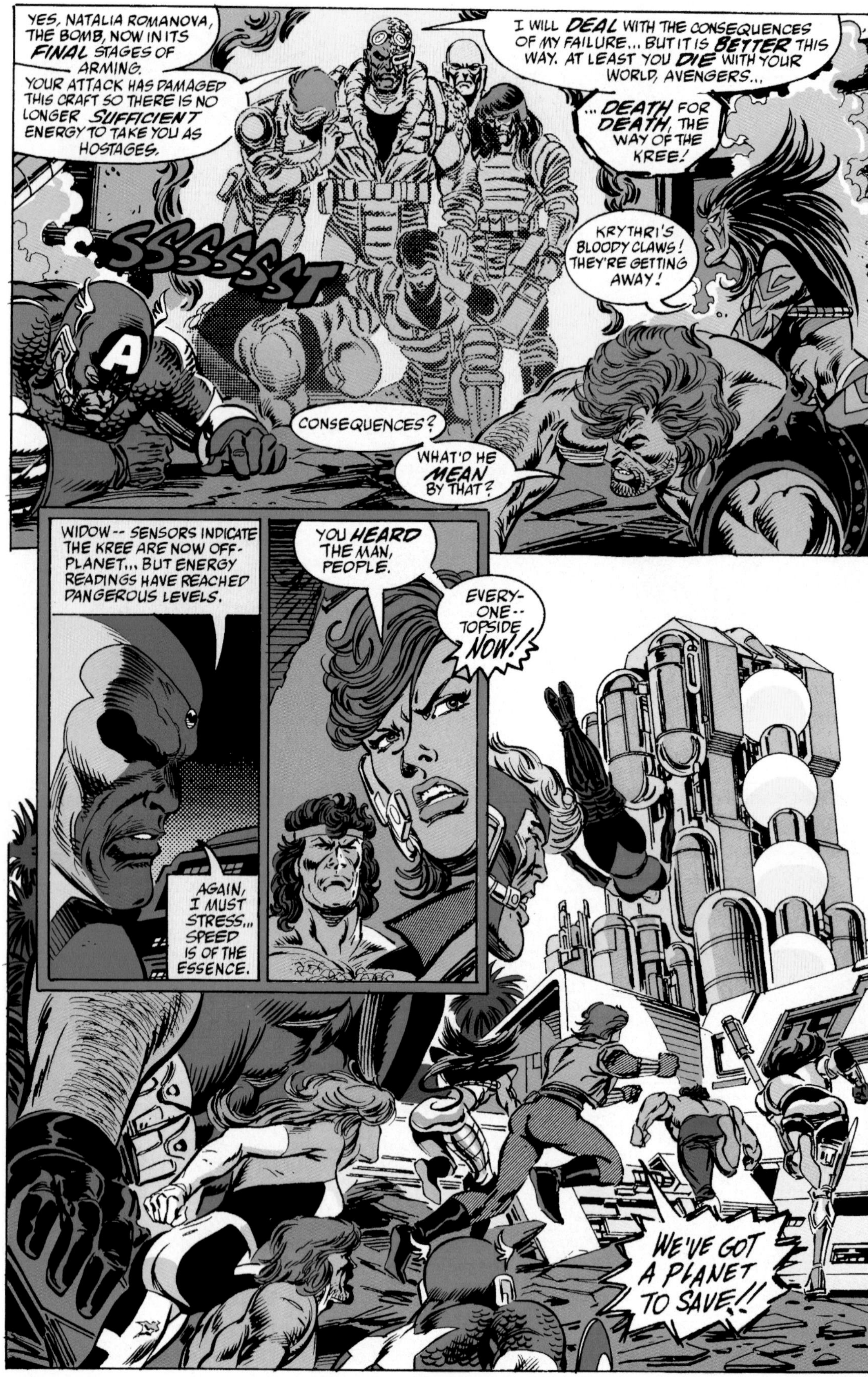
YES, NATALIA ROMANOVA, THE BOMB, NOW IN ITS FINAL STAGES OF ARMING.
YOUR ATTACK HAS DAMAGED THIS CRAFT SO THERE IS NO LONGER SUFFICIENT ENERGY TO TAKE YOU AS HOSTAGES.
I WILL DEAL WITH THE CONSEQUENCES OF MY FAILURE... BUT IT IS BETTER THIS WAY. AT LEAST YOU DIE WITH YOUR WORLD, AVENGERS...
...DEATH FOR DEATH, THE WAY OF THE KREE!
SSSSSST
KRYTHRI'S BLOODY CLAWS! THEY'RE GETTING AWAY!
CONSEQUENCES?
WHAT'D HE MEAN BY THAT?
WIDOW -- SENSORS INDICATE THE KREE ARE NOW OFF-PLANET... BUT ENERGY READINGS HAVE REACHED DANGEROUS LEVELS.
AGAIN, I MUST STRESS... SPEED IS OF THE ESSENCE.
YOU HEARD THE MAN, PEOPLE.
EVERY-ONE-- TOPSIDE NOW!
WE'VE GOT A PLANET TO SAVE!!

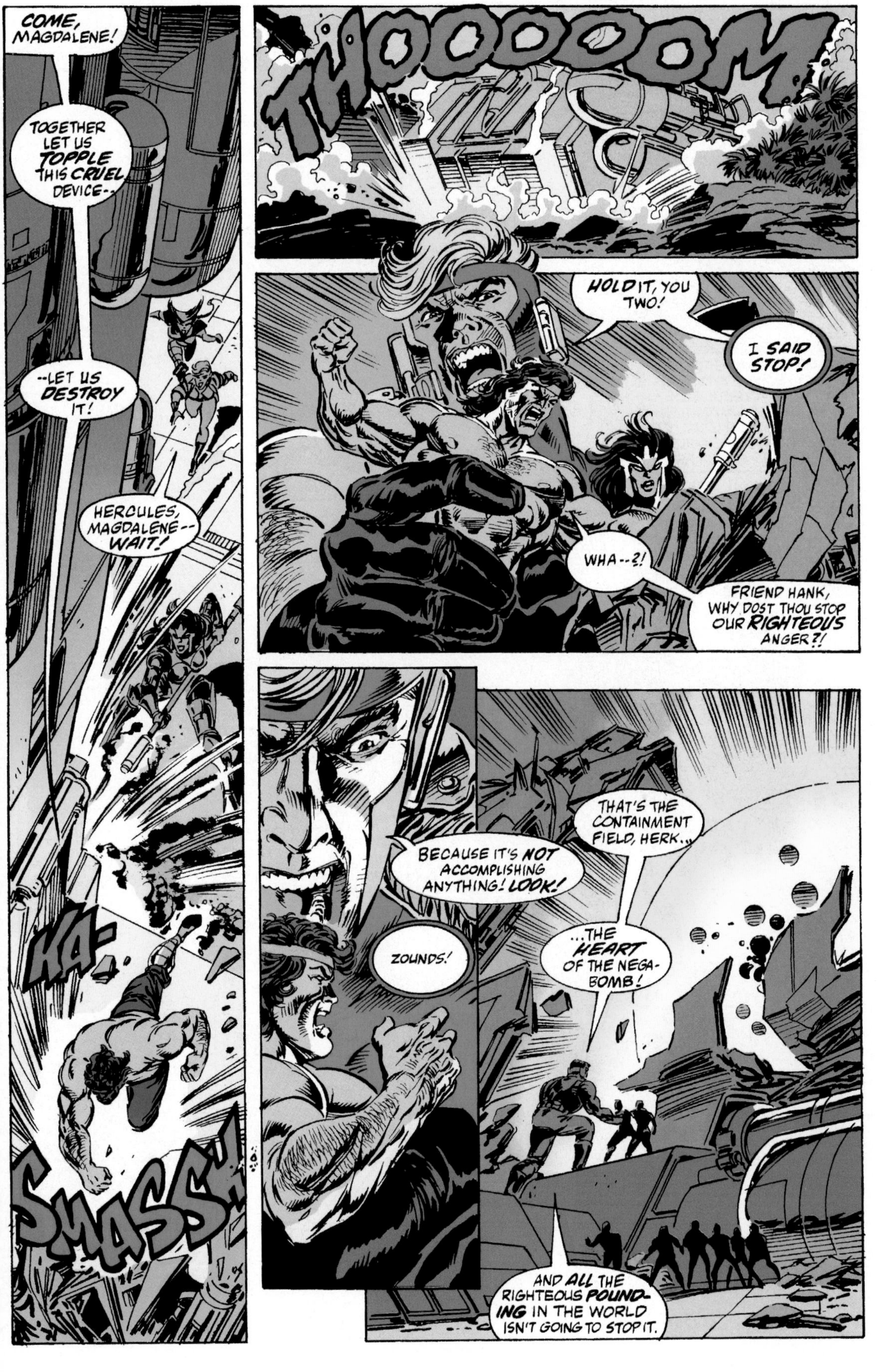
COME, MAGDALENE!
TOGETHER LET US TOPPLE THIS CRUEL DEVICE--
--LET US DESTROY IT!
HERCULES, MAGDALENE-- WAIT!
KA-
SHASS!
THOOOOOOM!
HOLD IT, YOU TWO!
I SAID STOP!
WHA--?!
FRIEND HANK, WHY DOST THOU STOP OUR RIGHTEOUS ANGER?!
BECAUSE IT'S NOT ACCOMPLISHING ANYTHING! LOOK!
ZOUNDS!
THAT'S THE CONTAINMENT FIELD, HERK...
...THE HEART OF THE NEGA-BOMB!
AND ALL THE RIGHTEOUS POUNDING IN THE WORLD ISN'T GOING TO STOP IT.

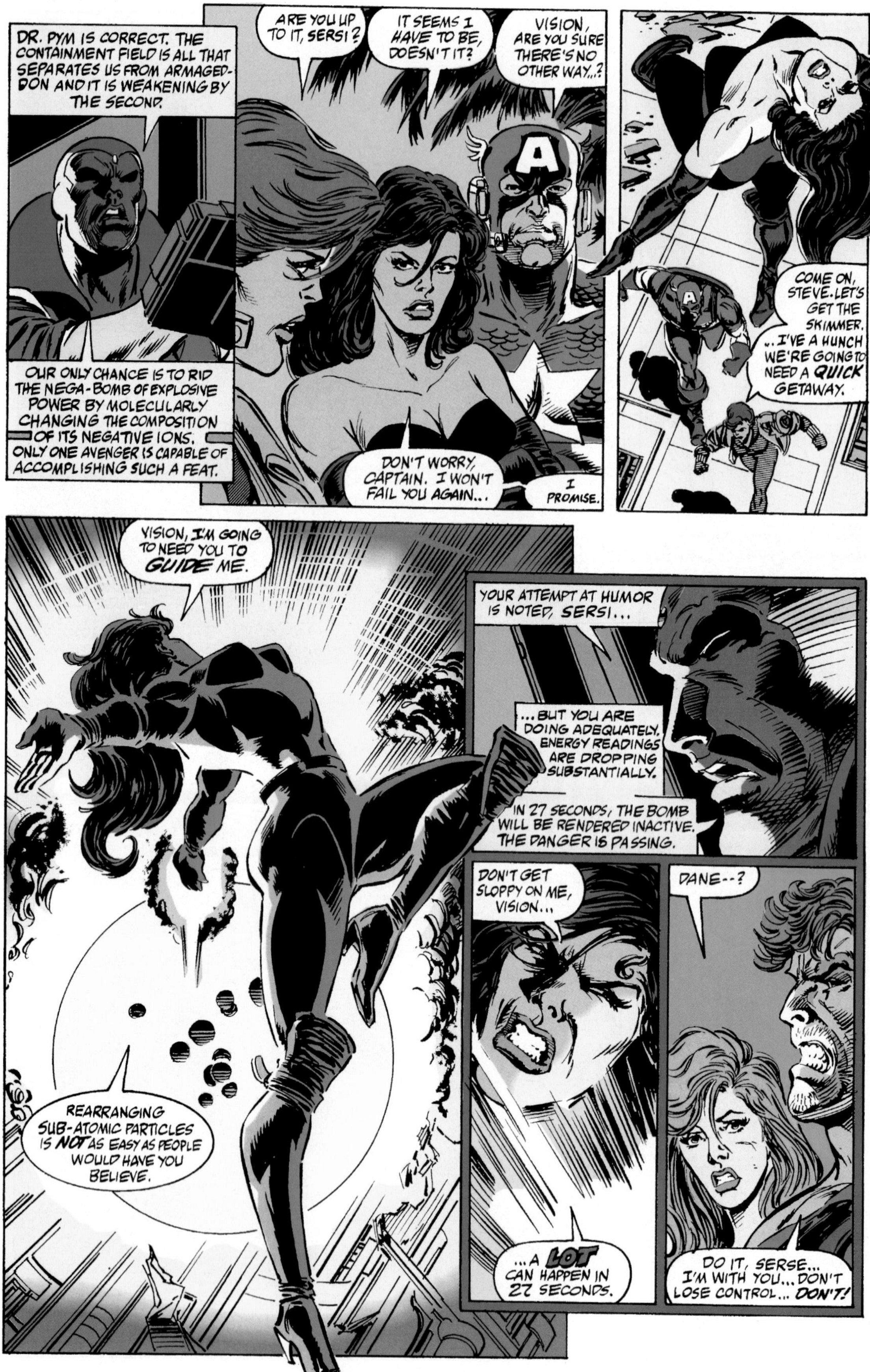

DR. PYM IS CORRECT. THE CONTAINMENT FIELD IS ALL THAT SEPARATES US FROM ARMAGEDDON AND IT IS WEAKENING BY THE SECOND.
OUR ONLY CHANCE IS TO RID THE NEGA-BOMB OF EXPLOSIVE POWER BY MOLECULARLY CHANGING THE COMPOSITION OF ITS NEGATIVE IONS.
ONLY ONE AVENGER IS CAPABLE OF ACCOMPLISHING SUCH A FEAT.
ARE YOU UP TO IT, SERSI?
IT SEEMS I HAVE TO BE, DOESN'T IT?
VISION, ARE YOU SURE THERE'S NO OTHER WAY..?
DON'T WORRY, CAPTAIN. I WON'T FAIL YOU AGAIN...
I PROMISE.
COME ON, STEVE. LET'S GET THE SKIMMER.
..I'VE A HUNCH WE'RE GOING TO NEED A QUICK GETAWAY.
VISION, I'M GOING TO NEED YOU TO GUIDE ME.
REARRANGING SUB-ATOMIC PARTICLES IS NOT AS EASY AS PEOPLE WOULD HAVE YOU BELIEVE.
YOUR ATTEMPT AT HUMOR IS NOTED, SERSI...
...BUT YOU ARE DOING ADEQUATELY. ENERGY READINGS ARE DROPPING SUBSTANTIALLY.
IN 27 SECONDS, THE BOMB WILL BE RENDERED INACTIVE. THE DANGER IS PASSING.
DON'T GET SLOPPY ON ME, VISION...
...A LOT CAN HAPPEN IN 27 SECONDS.
DANE--?
DO IT, SERSE... I'M WITH YOU... DON'T LOSE CONTROL... DON'T!

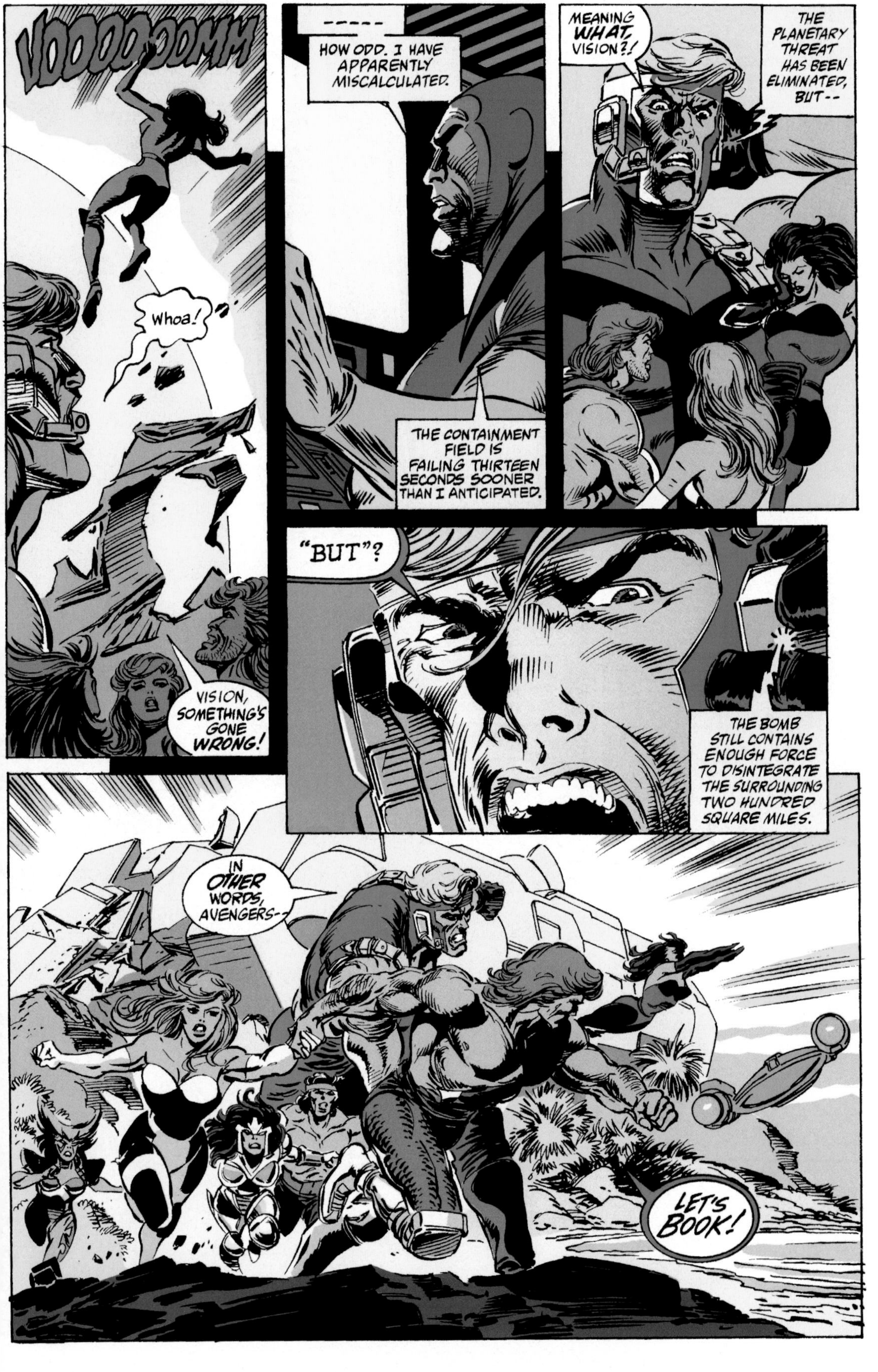
VOOOOOOMM
Whoa!
VISION, SOMETHING'S GONE WRONG!
HOW ODD. I HAVE APPARENTLY MISCALCULATED.
THE CONTAINMENT FIELD IS FAILING THIRTEEN SECONDS SOONER THAN I ANTICIPATED.
MEANING WHAT, VISION?!
THE PLANETARY THREAT HAS BEEN ELIMINATED, BUT--
"BUT"?
THE BOMB STILL CONTAINS ENOUGH FORCE TO DISINTEGRATE THE SURROUNDING TWO HUNDRED SQUARE MILES.
IN OTHER WORDS, AVENGERS--
LET'S BOOK!

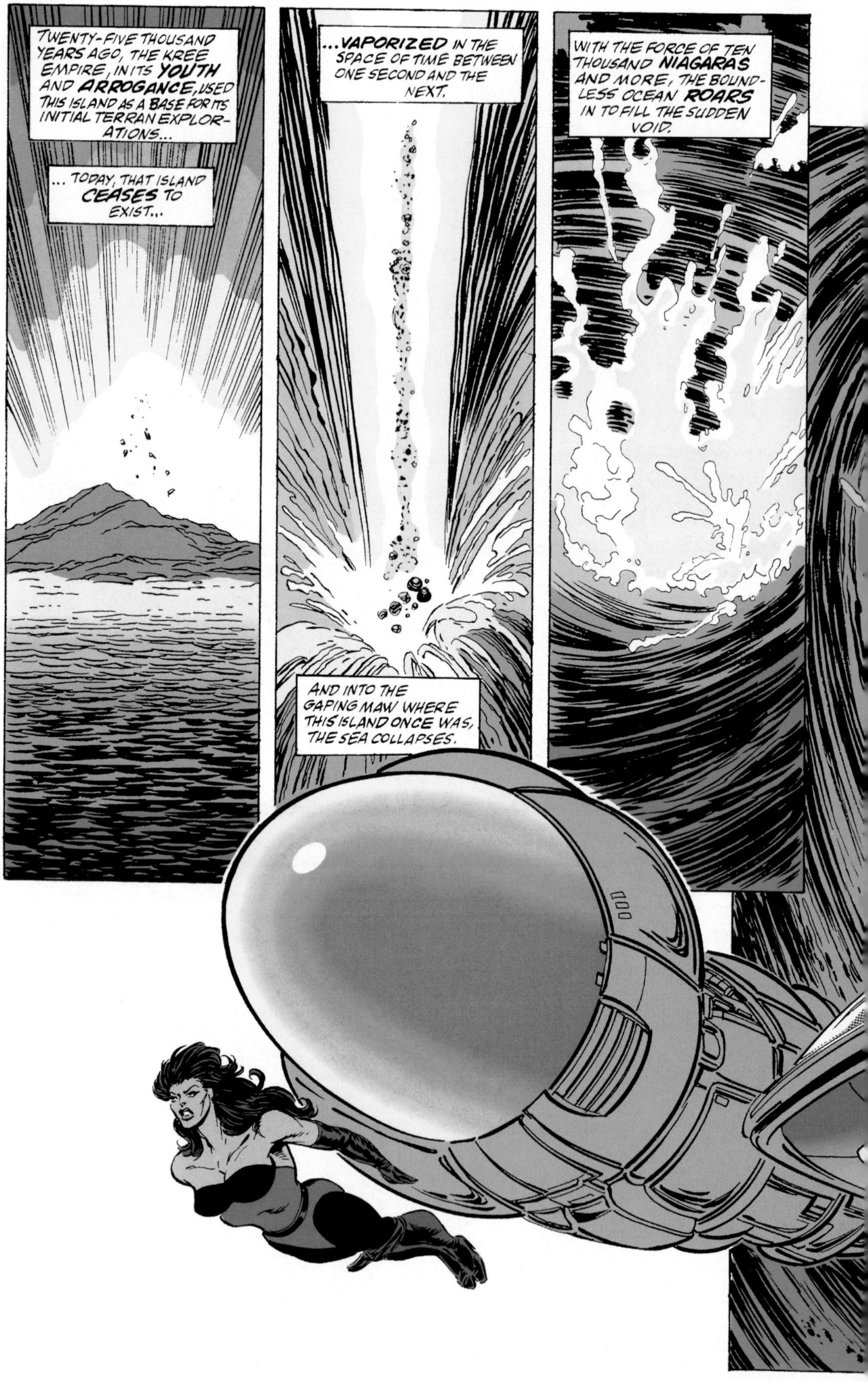
TWENTY-FIVE THOUSAND YEARS AGO, THE KREE EMPIRE, IN ITS YOUTH AND ARROGANCE, USED THIS ISLAND AS A BASE FOR ITS INITIAL TERRAN EXPLOR- ATIONS...
... TODAY, THAT ISLAND CEASES TO EXIST...
...VAPORIZED IN THE SPACE OF TIME BETWEEN ONE SECOND AND THE NEXT.
AND INTO THE GAPING MAW WHERE THIS ISLAND ONCE WAS, THE SEA COLLAPSES.
WITH THE FORCE OF TEN THOUSAND NIAGARAS AND MORE, THE BOUND- LESS OCEAN ROARS IN TO FILL THE SUDDEN VOID.

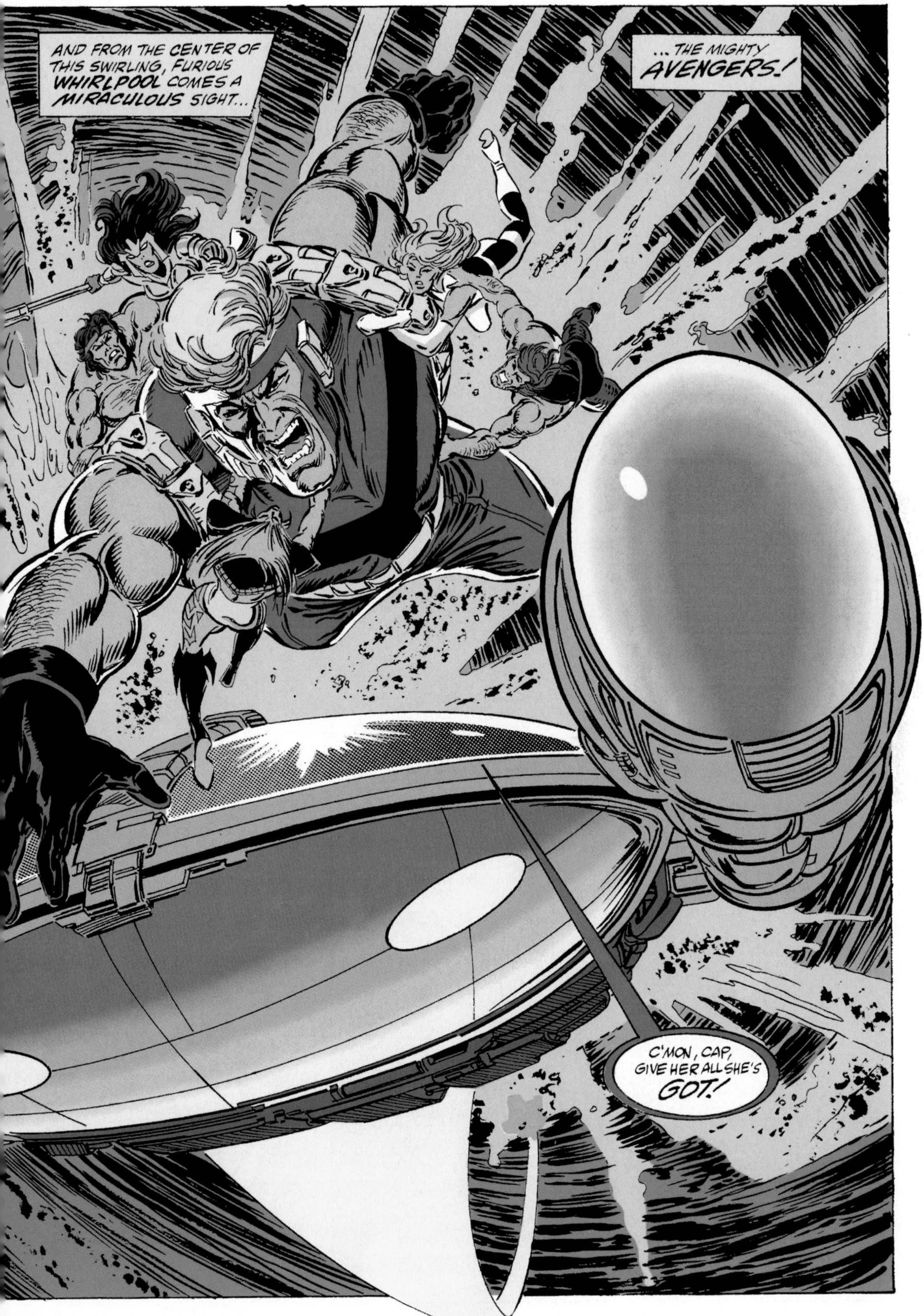

AND FROM THE CENTER OF THIS SWIRLING, FURIOUS WHIRLPOOL COMES A MIRACULOUS SIGHT...
... THE MIGHTY AVENGERS!
C'MON, CAP, GIVE HER ALL SHE'S GOT!

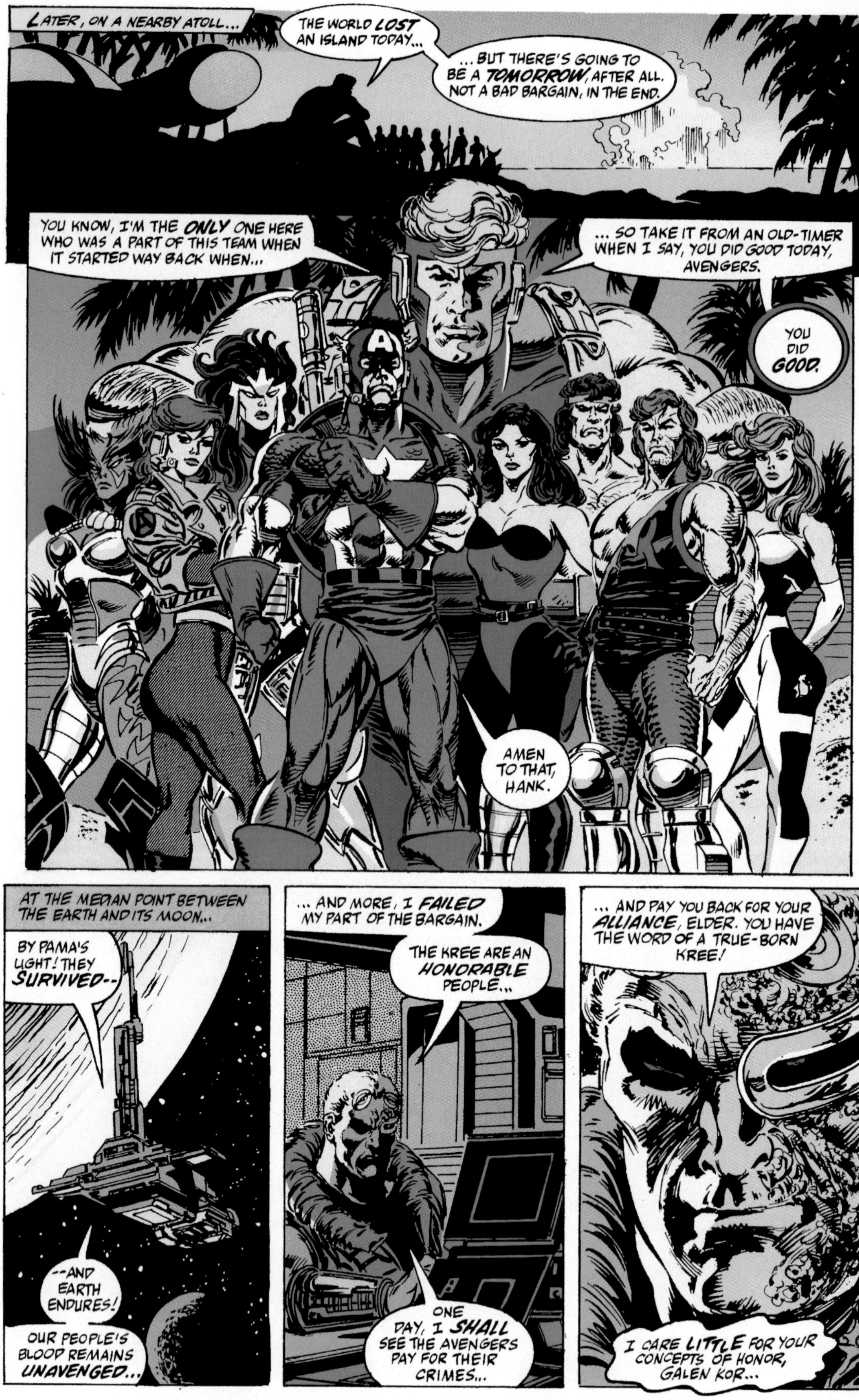
LATER, ON A NEARBY ATOLL...
THE WORLD LOST AN ISLAND TODAY...
...BUT THERE'S GOING TO BE A TOMORROW, AFTER ALL. NOT A BAD BARGAIN, IN THE END.
YOU KNOW, I'M THE ONLY ONE HERE WHO WAS A PART OF THIS TEAM WHEN IT STARTED WAY BACK WHEN...
...SO TAKE IT FROM AN OLD-TIMER WHEN I SAY, YOU DID GOOD TODAY, AVENGERS.
YOU DID GOOD.
AMEN TO THAT, HANK.
AT THE MEDIAN POINT BETWEEN THE EARTH AND ITS MOON...
BY PAMA'S LIGHT! THEY SURVIVED--
--AND EARTH ENDURES!
OUR PEOPLE'S BLOOD REMAINS UNAVENGED...
...AND MORE, I FAILED MY PART OF THE BARGAIN.
THE KREE ARE AN HONORABLE PEOPLE...
ONE DAY, I SHALL SEE THE AVENGERS PAY FOR THEIR CRIMES...
...AND PAY YOU BACK FOR YOUR ALLIANCE, ELDER. YOU HAVE THE WORD OF A TRUE-BORN KREE!
I CARE LITTLE FOR YOUR CONCEPTS OF HONOR, GALEN KOR...

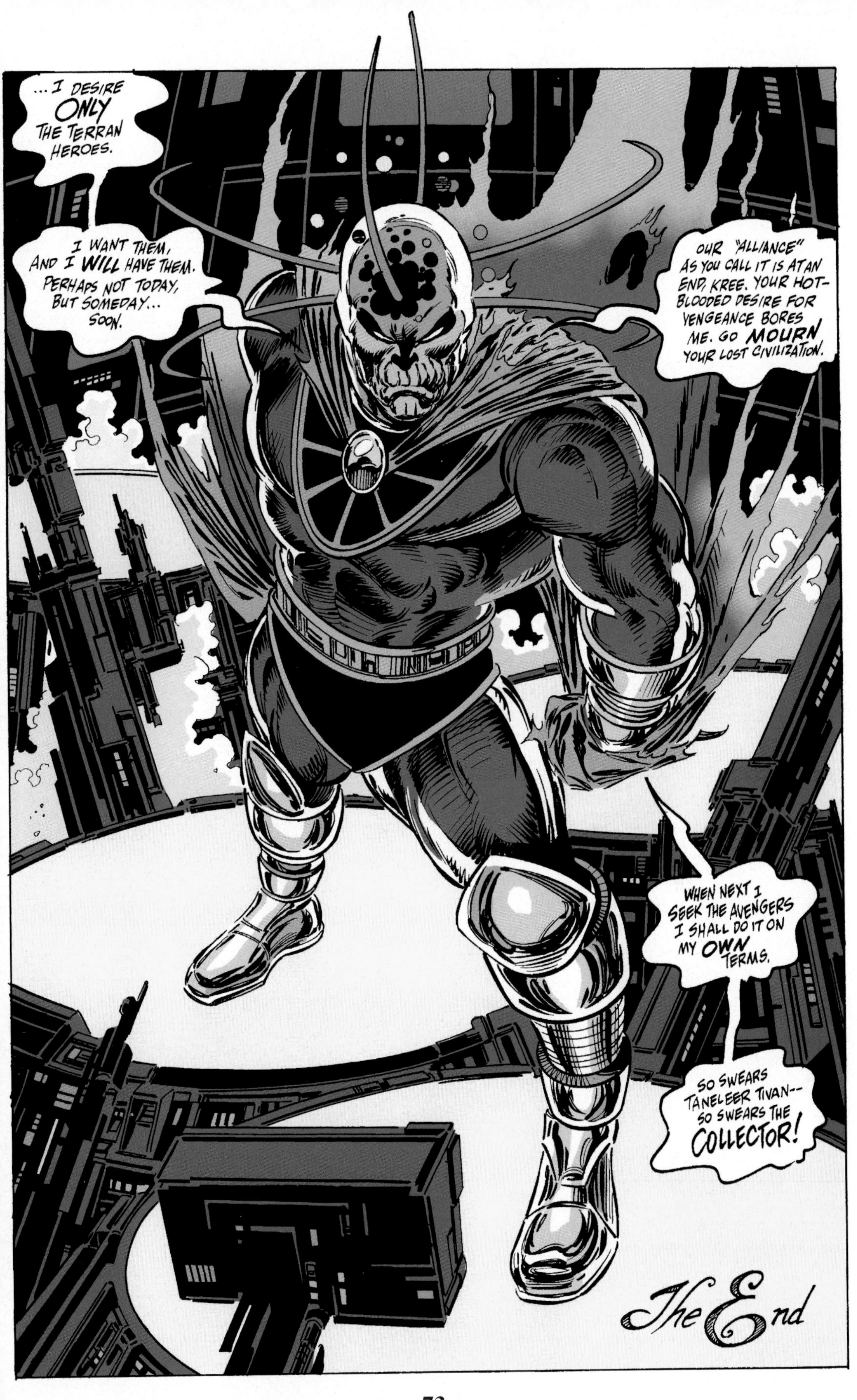
...I DESIRE ONLY THE TERRAN HEROES.
I WANT THEM, AND I WILL HAVE THEM. PERHAPS NOT TODAY, BUT SOMEDAY... SOON.
OUR "ALLIANCE" AS YOU CALL IT IS AT AN END, KREE. YOUR HOT-BLOODED DESIRE FOR VENGEANCE BORES ME. GO MOURN YOUR LOST CIVILIZATION.
WHEN NEXT I SEEK THE AVENGERS I SHALL DO IT ON MY OWN TERMS.
SO SWEARS TANELEER TIVAN-- SO SWEARS THE COLLECTOR!
The End

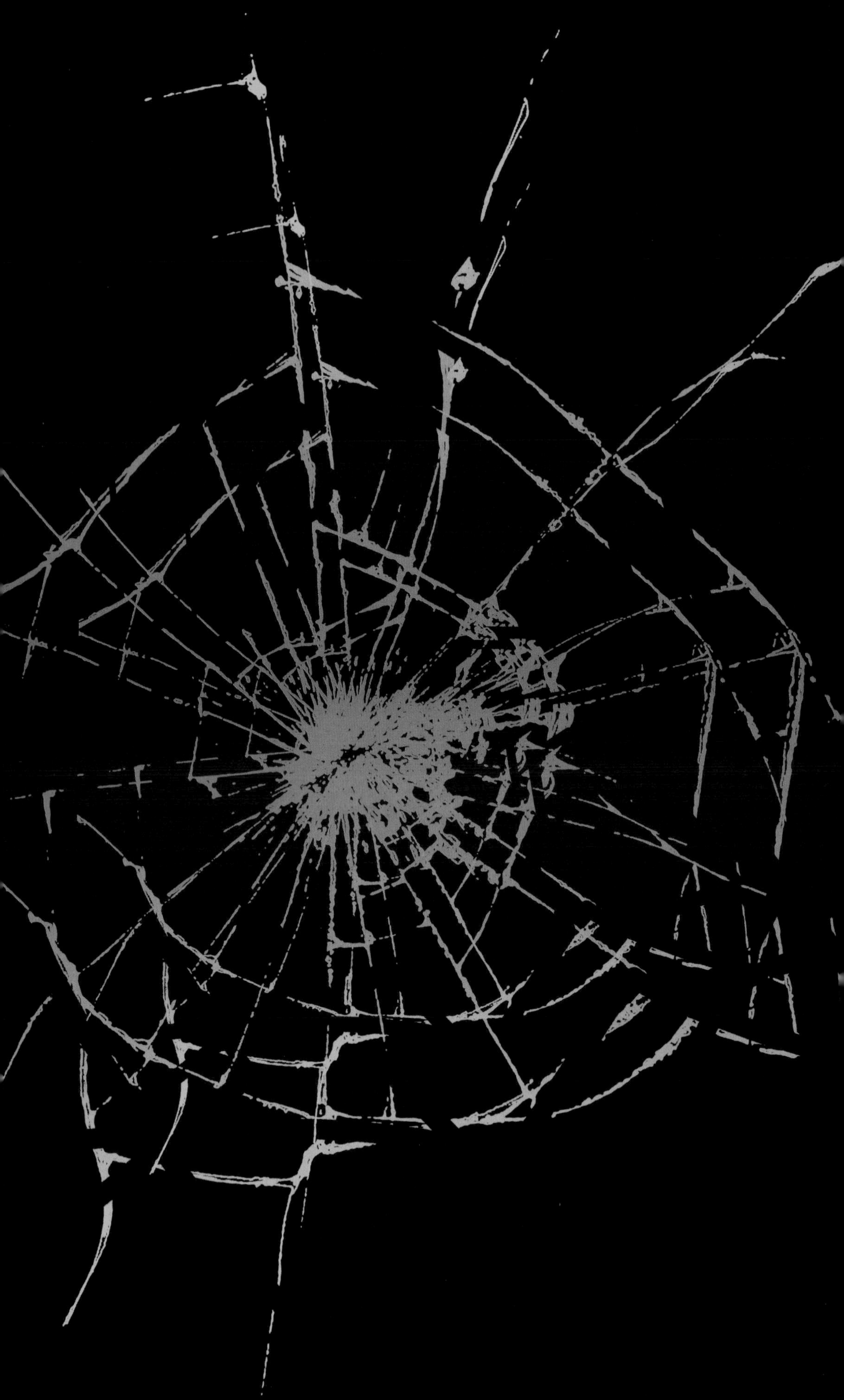

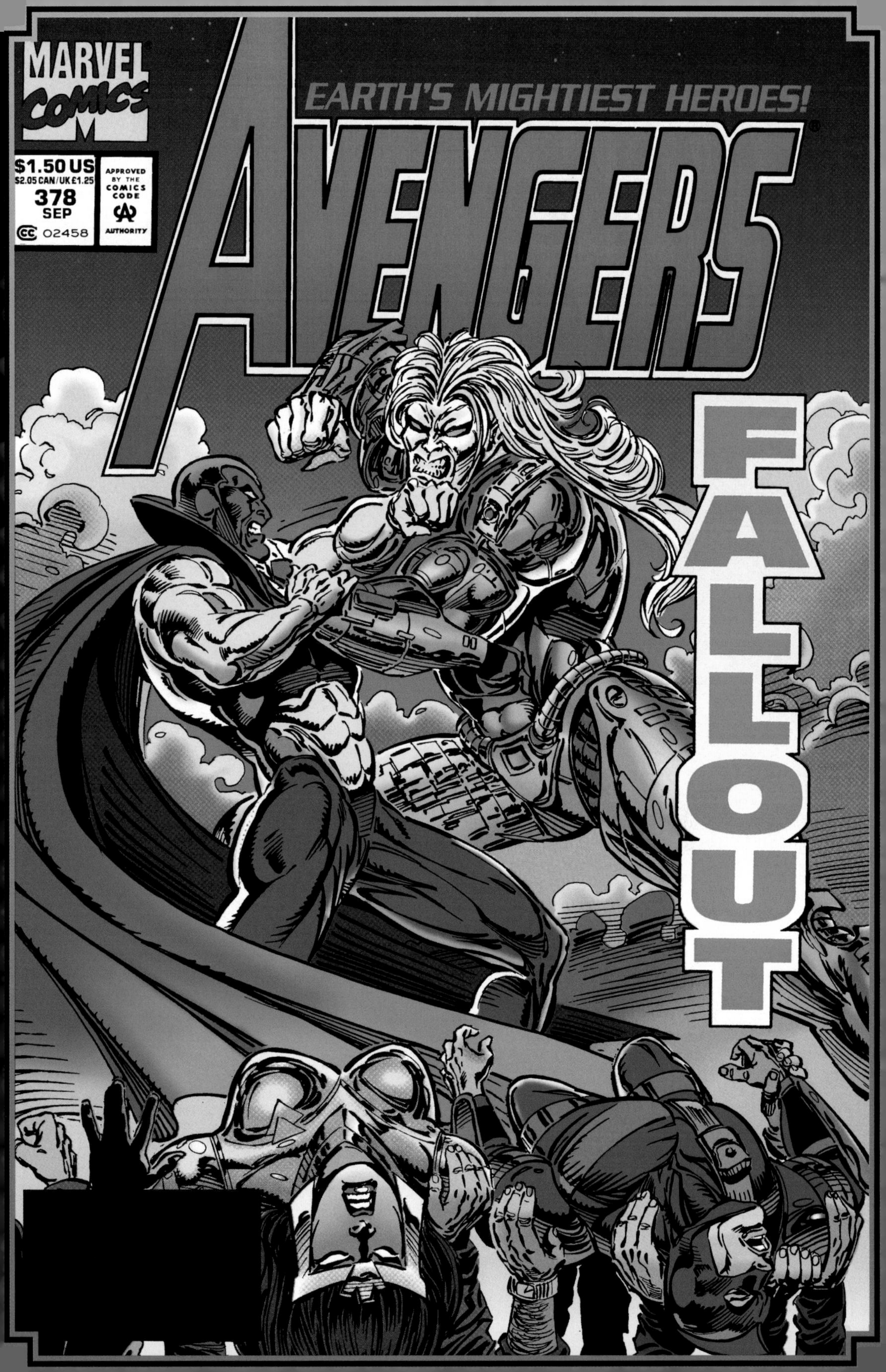

MARVEL COMICS
EARTH'S MIGHTIEST HEROES!
AVENGERS
$1.50 US
$2.05 CAN/UK £1.25
378
SEP
02458
APPROVED BY THE COMICS CODE AUTHORITY
FALLOUT

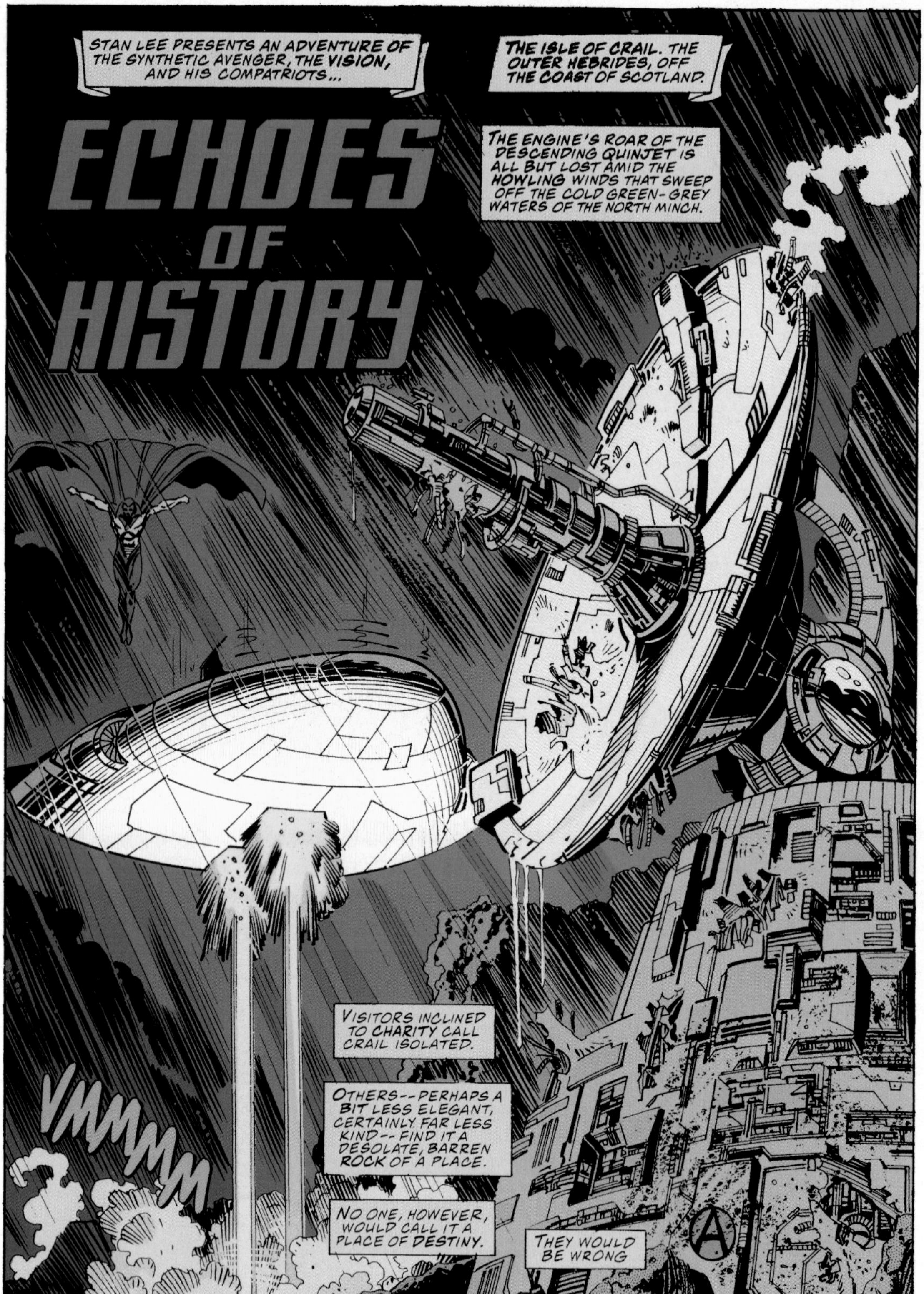
STAN LEE PRESENTS AN ADVENTURE OF THE SYNTHETIC AVENGER, THE VISION, AND HIS COMPATRIOTS...
THE ISLE OF CRAIL. THE OUTER HEBRIDES, OFF THE COAST OF SCOTLAND.
ECHOES OF HISTORY
THE ENGINE'S ROAR OF THE DESCENDING QUINJET IS ALL BUT LOST AMID THE HOWLING WINDS THAT SWEEP OFF THE COLD GREEN-GREY WATERS OF THE NORTH MINCH.
VMMMMM
VISITORS INCLINED TO CHARITY CALL CRAIL ISOLATED.
OTHERS--PERHAPS A BIT LESS ELEGANT, CERTAINLY FAR LESS KIND--FIND IT A DESOLATE, BARREN ROCK OF A PLACE.
NO ONE, HOWEVER, WOULD CALL IT A PLACE OF DESTINY.
THEY WOULD BE WRONG
BOB HARRAS WRITER
STEWART JOHNSON PENCILER
TOM PALMER INKER
BILL OAKLEY LETTERER
JOHN KALISZ COLORIST
RALPH MACCHIO EDITOR
TOM DEFALCO EDITOR IN CHIEF

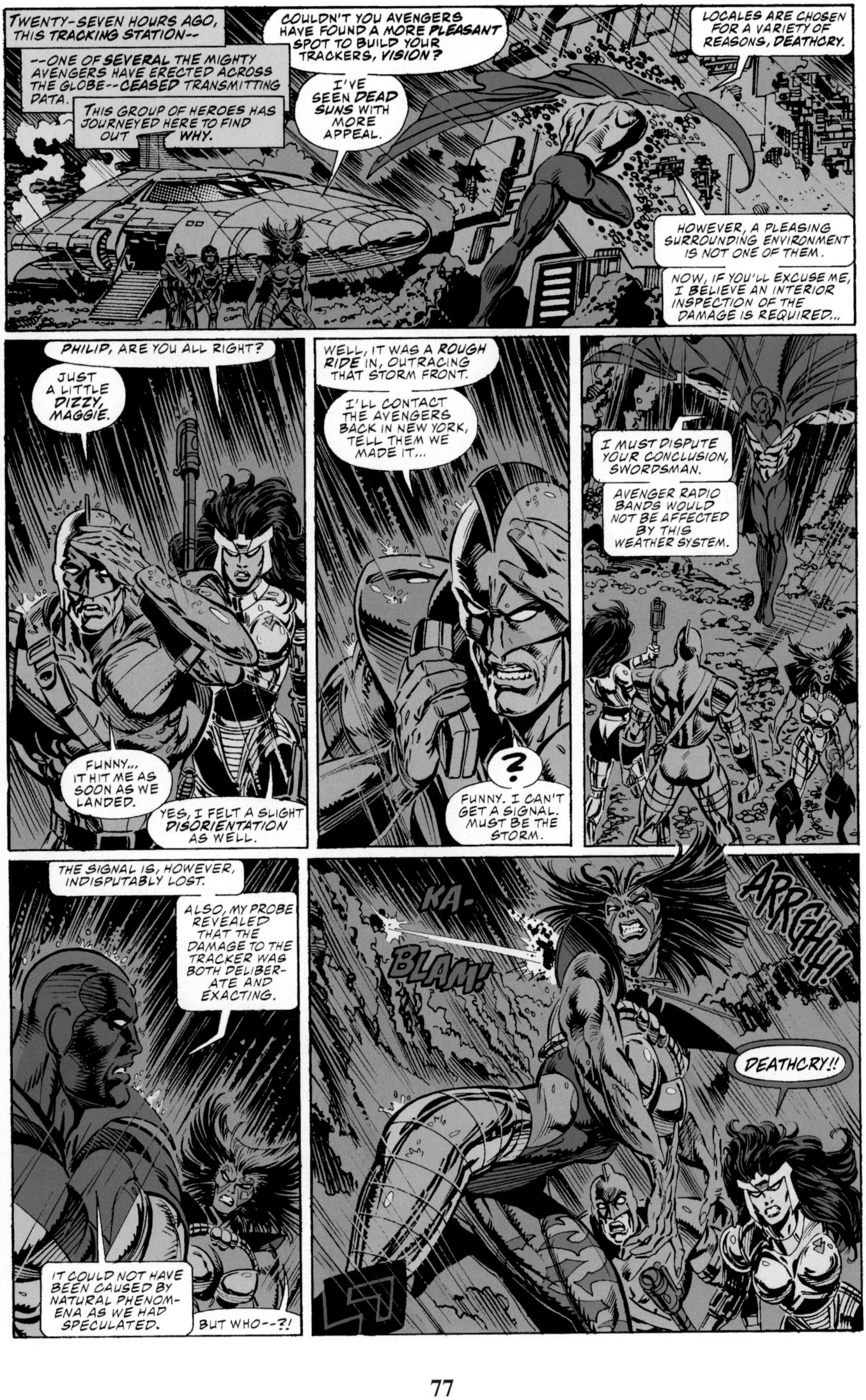
TWENTY-SEVEN HOURS AGO, THIS TRACKING STATION--
--ONE OF SEVERAL THE MIGHTY AVENGERS HAVE ERECTED ACROSS THE GLOBE--CEASED TRANSMITTING DATA.
THIS GROUP OF HEROES HAS JOURNEYED HERE TO FIND OUT WHY.
COULDN'T YOU AVENGERS HAVE FOUND A MORE PLEASANT SPOT TO BUILD YOUR TRACKERS, VISION?
I'VE SEEN DEAD SUNS WITH MORE APPEAL.
LOCALES ARE CHOSEN FOR A VARIETY OF REASONS, DEATHCRY.
HOWEVER, A PLEASING SURROUNDING ENVIRONMENT IS NOT ONE OF THEM.
NOW, IF YOU'LL EXCUSE ME, I BELIEVE AN INTERIOR INSPECTION OF THE DAMAGE IS REQUIRED...
PHILIP, ARE YOU ALL RIGHT?
JUST A LITTLE DIZZY, MAGGIE.
FUNNY... IT HIT ME AS SOON AS WE LANDED.
YES, I FELT A SLIGHT DISORIENTATION AS WELL.
WELL, IT WAS A ROUGH RIDE IN, OUTRACING THAT STORM FRONT.
I'LL CONTACT THE AVENGERS BACK IN NEW YORK, TELL THEM WE MADE IT...
?
FUNNY. I CAN'T GET A SIGNAL. MUST BE THE STORM.
I MUST DISPUTE YOUR CONCLUSION, SWORDSMAN.
AVENGER RADIO BANDS WOULD NOT BE AFFECTED BY THIS WEATHER SYSTEM.
THE SIGNAL IS, HOWEVER, INDISPUTABLY LOST.
ALSO, MY PROBE REVEALED THAT THE DAMAGE TO THE TRACKER WAS BOTH DELIBER-ATE AND EXACTING.
IT COULD NOT HAVE BEEN CAUSED BY NATURAL PHENOM-ENA AS WE HAD SPECULATED.
BUT WHO--?!
KA-
BLAM!
ARRGH!!
DEATHCRY!!

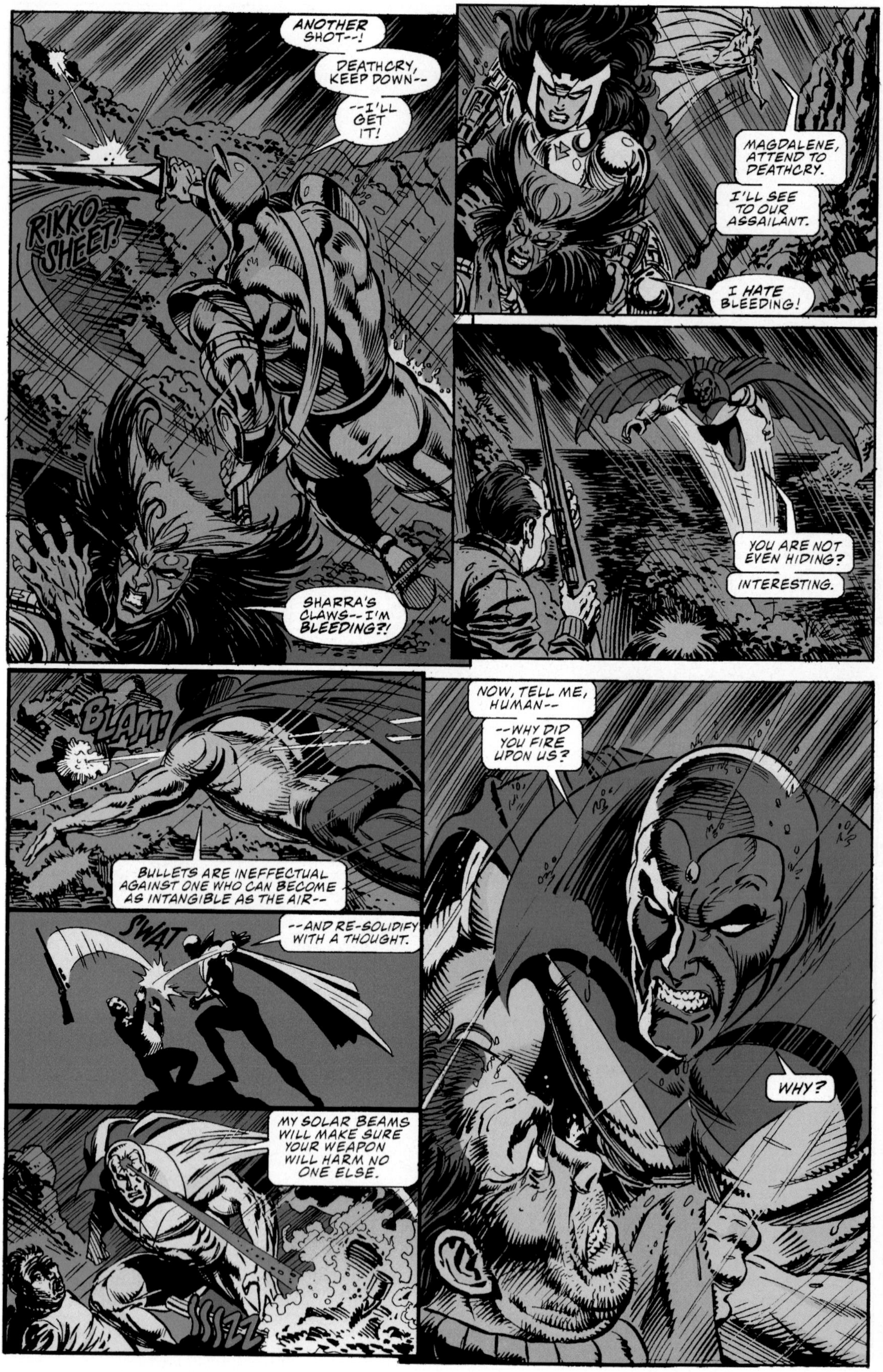
ANOTHER SHOT--!
DEATHCRY, KEEP DOWN--
--I'LL GET IT!
RIKKO-SHEET!
SHARRA'S CLAWS--I'M BLEEDING?!
MAGDALENE, ATTEND TO DEATHCRY.
I'LL SEE TO OUR ASSAILANT.
I HATE BLEEDING!
YOU ARE NOT EVEN HIDING?
INTERESTING.
BLAM!
BULLETS ARE INEFFECTUAL AGAINST ONE WHO CAN BECOME AS INTANGIBLE AS THE AIR--
SWAT
--AND RE-SOLIDIFY WITH A THOUGHT.
MY SOLAR BEAMS WILL MAKE SURE YOUR WEAPON WILL HARM NO ONE ELSE.
SSIZZ
NOW, TELL ME, HUMAN--
--WHY DID YOU FIRE UPON US?
WHY?

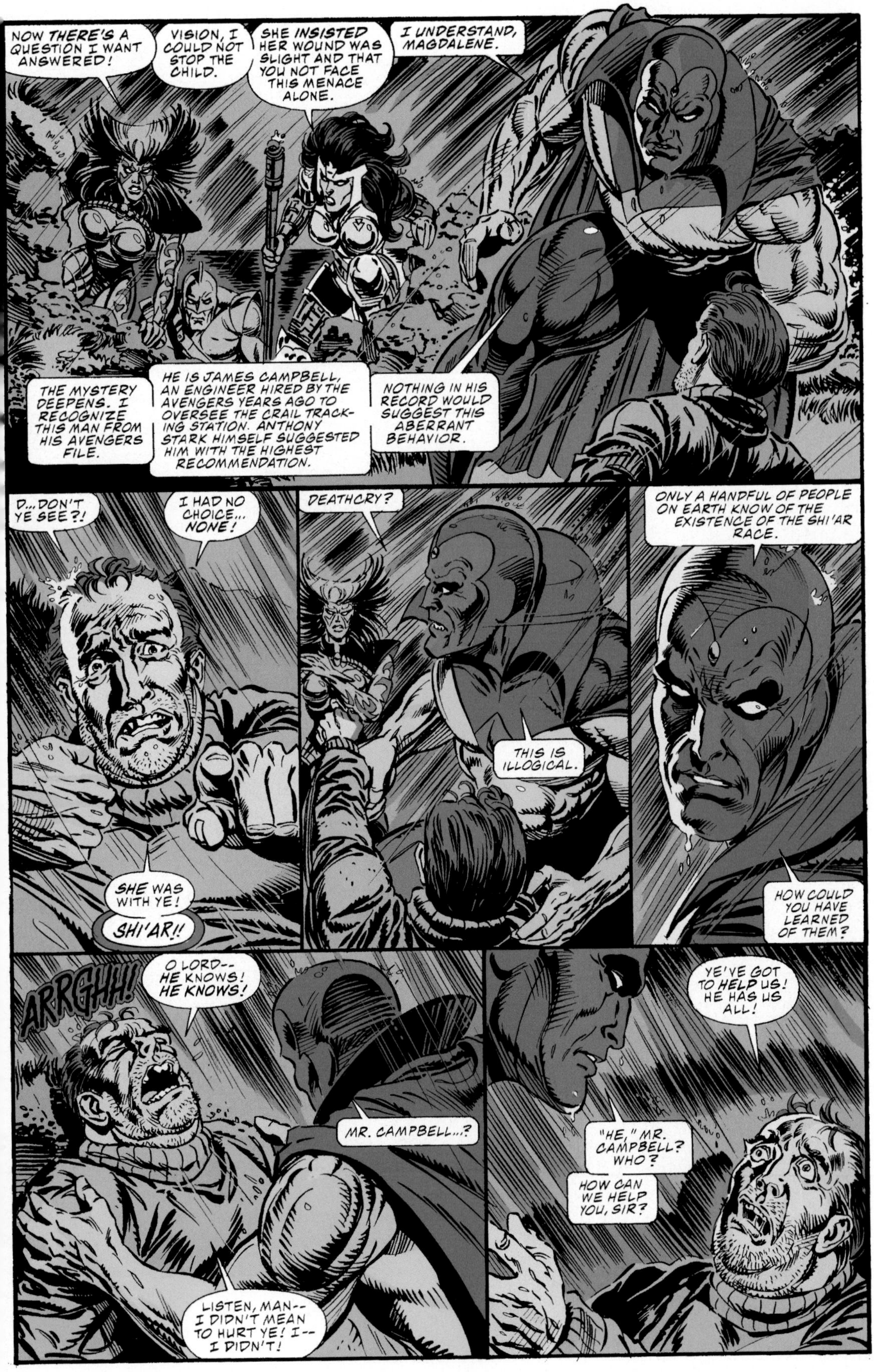

NOW THERE'S A QUESTION I WANT ANSWERED!
VISION, I COULD NOT STOP THE CHILD.
SHE INSISTED HER WOUND WAS SLIGHT AND THAT YOU NOT FACE THIS MENACE ALONE.
I UNDERSTAND, MAGDALENE.
THE MYSTERY DEEPENS. I RECOGNIZE THIS MAN FROM HIS AVENGERS FILE.
HE IS JAMES CAMPBELL, AN ENGINEER HIRED BY THE AVENGERS YEARS AGO TO OVERSEE THE CRAIL TRACKING STATION. ANTHONY STARK HIMSELF SUGGESTED HIM WITH THE HIGHEST RECOMMENDATION.
NOTHING IN HIS RECORD WOULD SUGGEST THIS ABERRANT BEHAVIOR.
D...DON'T YE SEE?!
I HAD NO CHOICE... NONE!
SHE WAS WITH YE!
SHI'AR!!
DEATHCRY?
THIS IS ILLOGICAL.
ONLY A HANDFUL OF PEOPLE ON EARTH KNOW OF THE EXISTENCE OF THE SHI'AR RACE.
HOW COULD YOU HAVE LEARNED OF THEM?
ARRGHH!
O LORD-- HE KNOWS! HE KNOWS!
MR. CAMPBELL...?
LISTEN, MAN-- I DIDN'T MEAN TO HURT YE! I-- I DIDN'T!
YE'VE GOT TO HELP US! HE HAS US ALL!
"HE," MR. CAMPBELL? WHO?
HOW CAN WE HELP YOU, SIR?

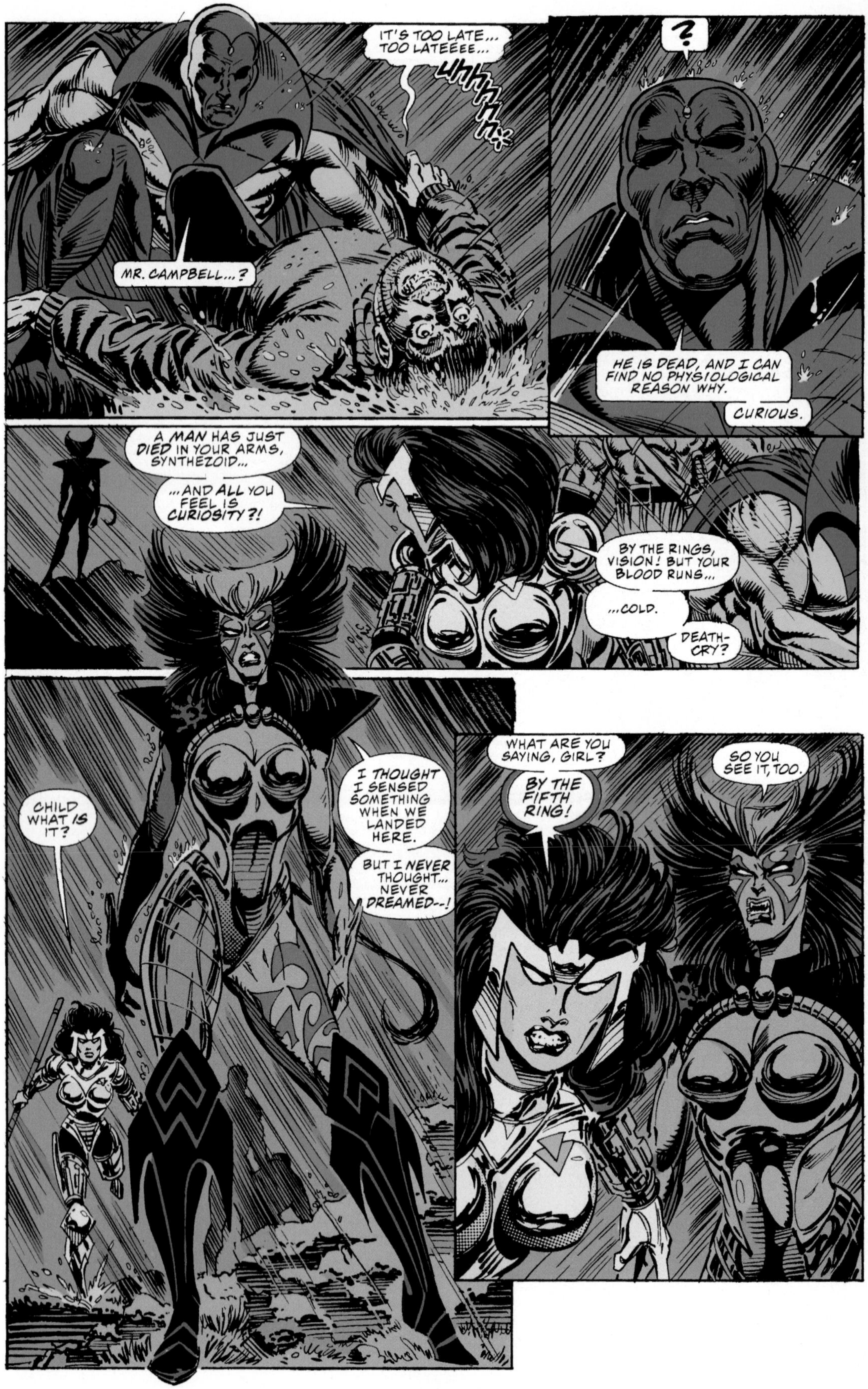
IT'S TOO LATE... TOO LATEEEE...
UHHHHH
MR. CAMPBELL...?
?
HE IS DEAD, AND I CAN FIND NO PHYSIOLOGICAL REASON WHY.
CURIOUS.
A MAN HAS JUST DIED IN YOUR ARMS, SYNTHEZOID...
...AND ALL YOU FEEL IS CURIOSITY?!
BY THE RINGS, VISION! BUT YOUR BLOOD RUNS...
...COLD.
DEATH-CRY?
CHILD WHAT IS IT?
I THOUGHT I SENSED SOMETHING WHEN WE LANDED HERE.
BUT I NEVER THOUGHT... NEVER DREAMED--!
WHAT ARE YOU SAYING, GIRL?
BY THE FIFTH RING!
SO YOU SEE IT, TOO.

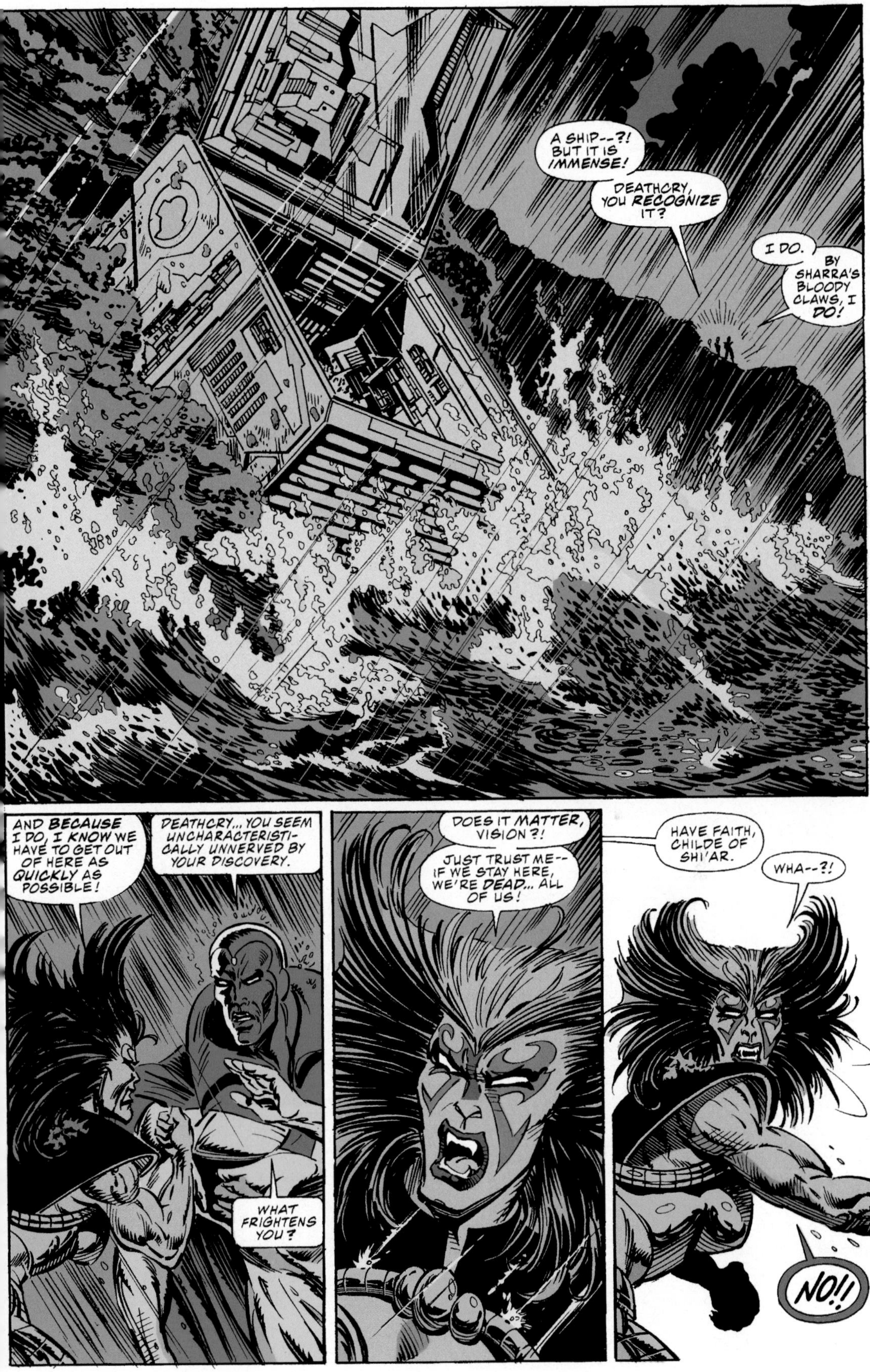
A SHIP--?! BUT IT IS IMMENSE!
DEATHCRY, YOU RECOGNIZE IT?
I DO.
BY SHARRA'S BLOODY CLAWS, I DO!
AND BECAUSE I DO, I KNOW WE HAVE TO GET OUT OF HERE AS QUICKLY AS POSSIBLE!
DEATHCRY... YOU SEEM UNCHARACTERISTI-CALLY UNNERVED BY YOUR DISCOVERY.
WHAT FRIGHTENS YOU?
DOES IT MATTER, VISION?!
JUST TRUST ME-- IF WE STAY HERE, WE'RE DEAD... ALL OF US!
HAVE FAITH, CHILDE OF SHI'AR.
WHA--?!
NO!!

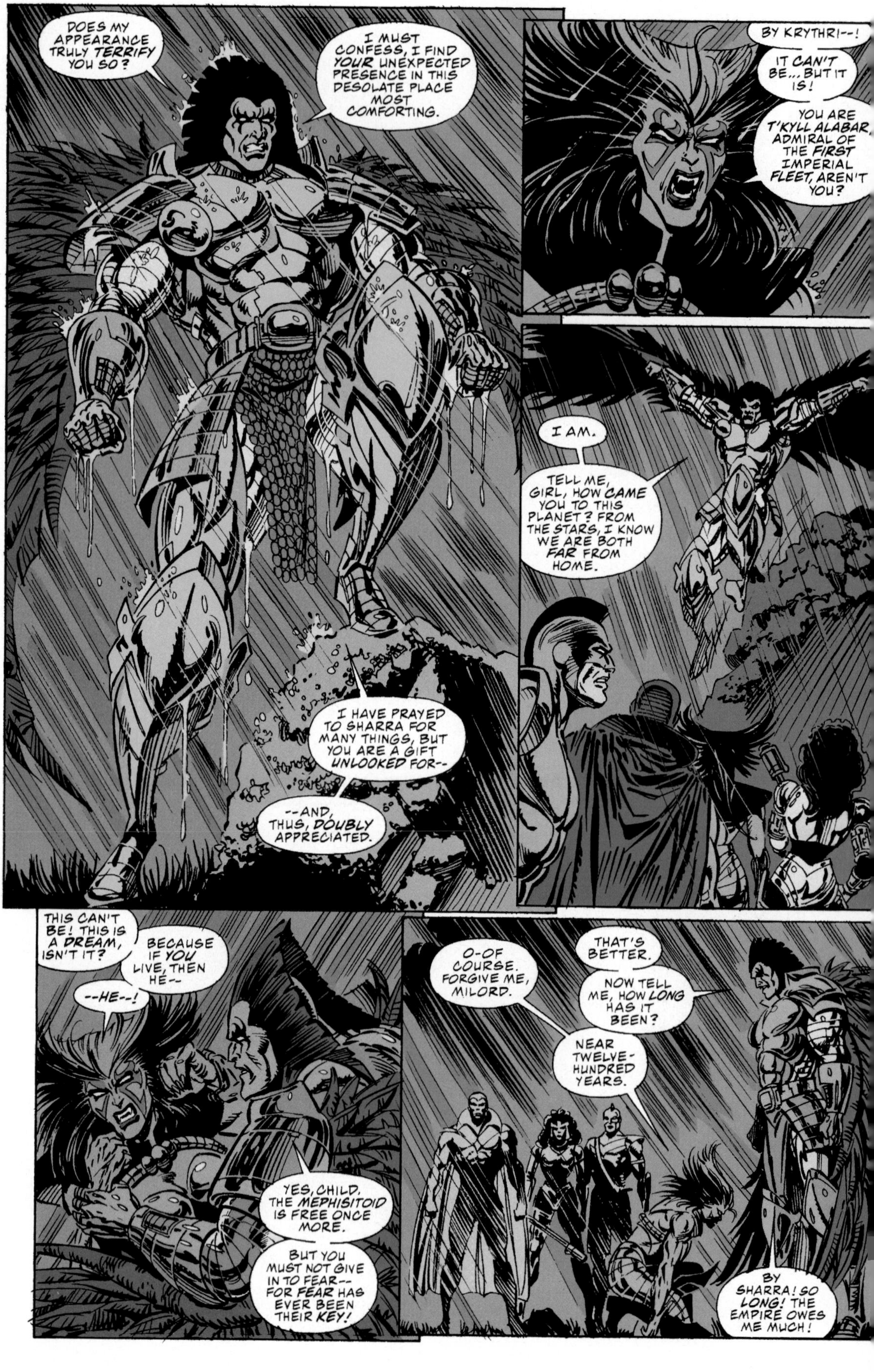
DOES MY APPEARANCE TRULY TERRIFY YOU SO?
I MUST CONFESS, I FIND YOUR UNEXPECTED PRESENCE IN THIS DESOLATE PLACE MOST COMFORTING.
I HAVE PRAYED TO SHARRA FOR MANY THINGS, BUT YOU ARE A GIFT UNLOOKED FOR--
--AND, THUS, DOUBLY APPRECIATED.
BY KRYTHRI--!
IT CAN'T BE... BUT IT IS!
YOU ARE T'KYLL ALABAR, ADMIRAL OF THE FIRST IMPERIAL FLEET, AREN'T YOU?
I AM.
TELL ME, GIRL, HOW CAME YOU TO THIS PLANET? FROM THE STARS, I KNOW WE ARE BOTH FAR FROM HOME.
THIS CAN'T BE! THIS IS A DREAM, ISN'T IT?
BECAUSE IF YOU LIVE, THEN HE--
--HE--!
YES, CHILD. THE MEPHISITOID IS FREE ONCE MORE.
BUT YOU MUST NOT GIVE IN TO FEAR-- FOR FEAR HAS EVER BEEN THEIR KEY!
O-OF COURSE. FORGIVE ME, MILORD.
THAT'S BETTER.
NOW TELL ME, HOW LONG HAS IT BEEN?
NEAR TWELVE-HUNDRED YEARS.
BY SHARRA! SO LONG! THE EMPIRE OWES ME MUCH!

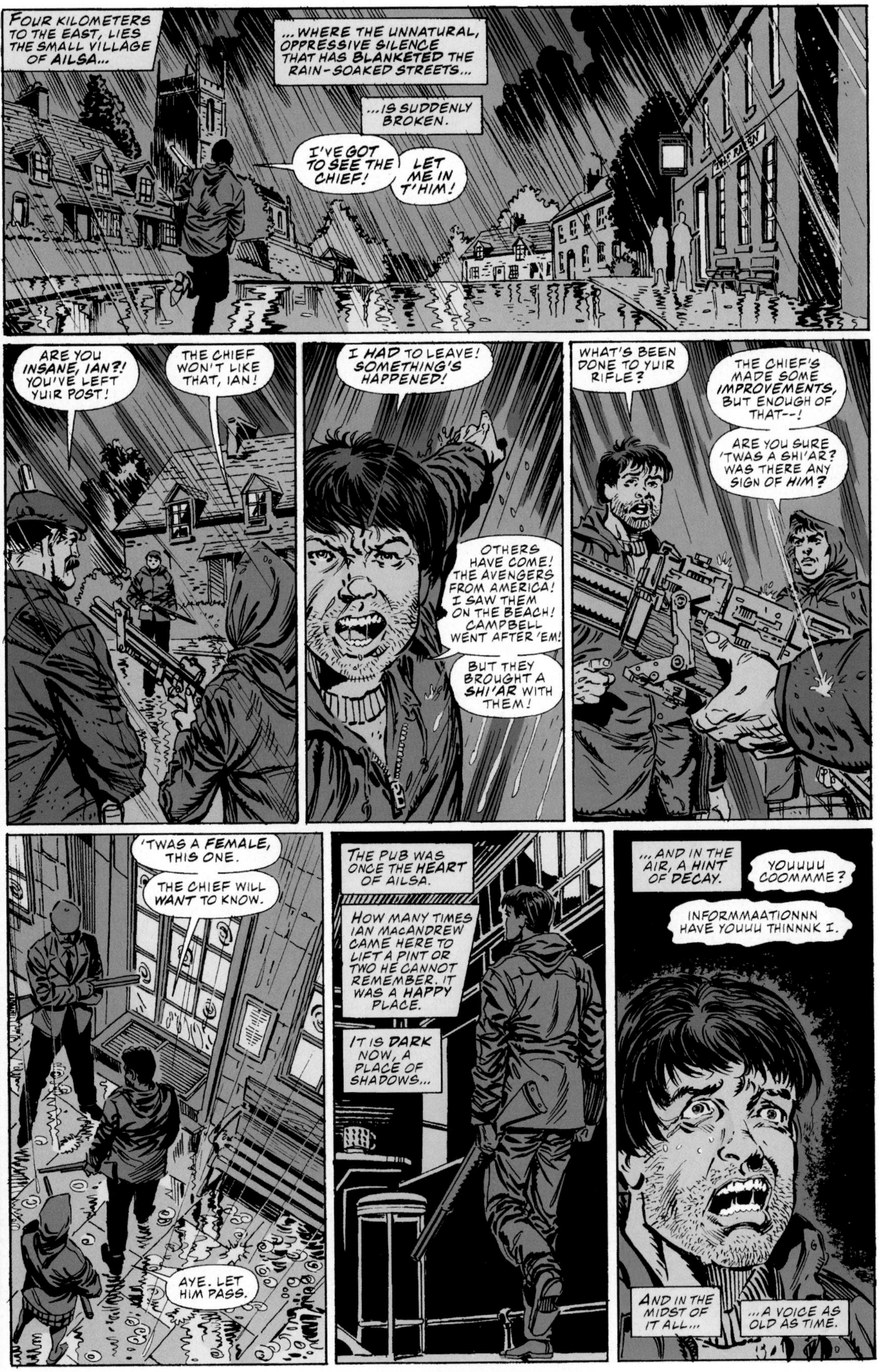
FOUR KILOMETERS TO THE EAST, LIES THE SMALL VILLAGE OF AILSA...
...WHERE THE UNNATURAL, OPPRESSIVE SILENCE THAT HAS BLANKETED THE RAIN-SOAKED STREETS...
...IS SUDDENLY BROKEN.
I'VE GOT TO SEE THE CHIEF!
LET ME IN T'HIM!
ARE YOU INSANE, IAN?! YOU'VE LEFT YUIR POST!
THE CHIEF WON'T LIKE THAT, IAN!
I HAD TO LEAVE! SOMETHING'S HAPPENED!
OTHERS HAVE COME! THE AVENGERS FROM AMERICA! I SAW THEM ON THE BEACH! CAMPBELL WENT AFTER 'EM!
BUT THEY BROUGHT A SHI'AR WITH THEM!
WHAT'S BEEN DONE TO YUIR RIFLE?
THE CHIEF'S MADE SOME IMPROVEMENTS, BUT ENOUGH OF THAT--!
ARE YOU SURE 'TWAS A SHI'AR? WAS THERE ANY SIGN OF HIM?
'TWAS A FEMALE, THIS ONE.
THE CHIEF WILL WANT TO KNOW.
AYE. LET HIM PASS.
THE PUB WAS ONCE THE HEART OF AILSA.
HOW MANY TIMES IAN MACANDREW CAME HERE TO LIFT A PINT OR TWO HE CANNOT REMEMBER. IT WAS A HAPPY PLACE.
IT IS DARK NOW, A PLACE OF SHADOWS...
...AND IN THE AIR, A HINT OF DECAY.
YOUUUU COOMMME?
INFORMMAATIONNN HAVE YOUUU THINNNK I.
AND IN THE MIDST OF IT ALL...
...A VOICE AS OLD AS TIME.

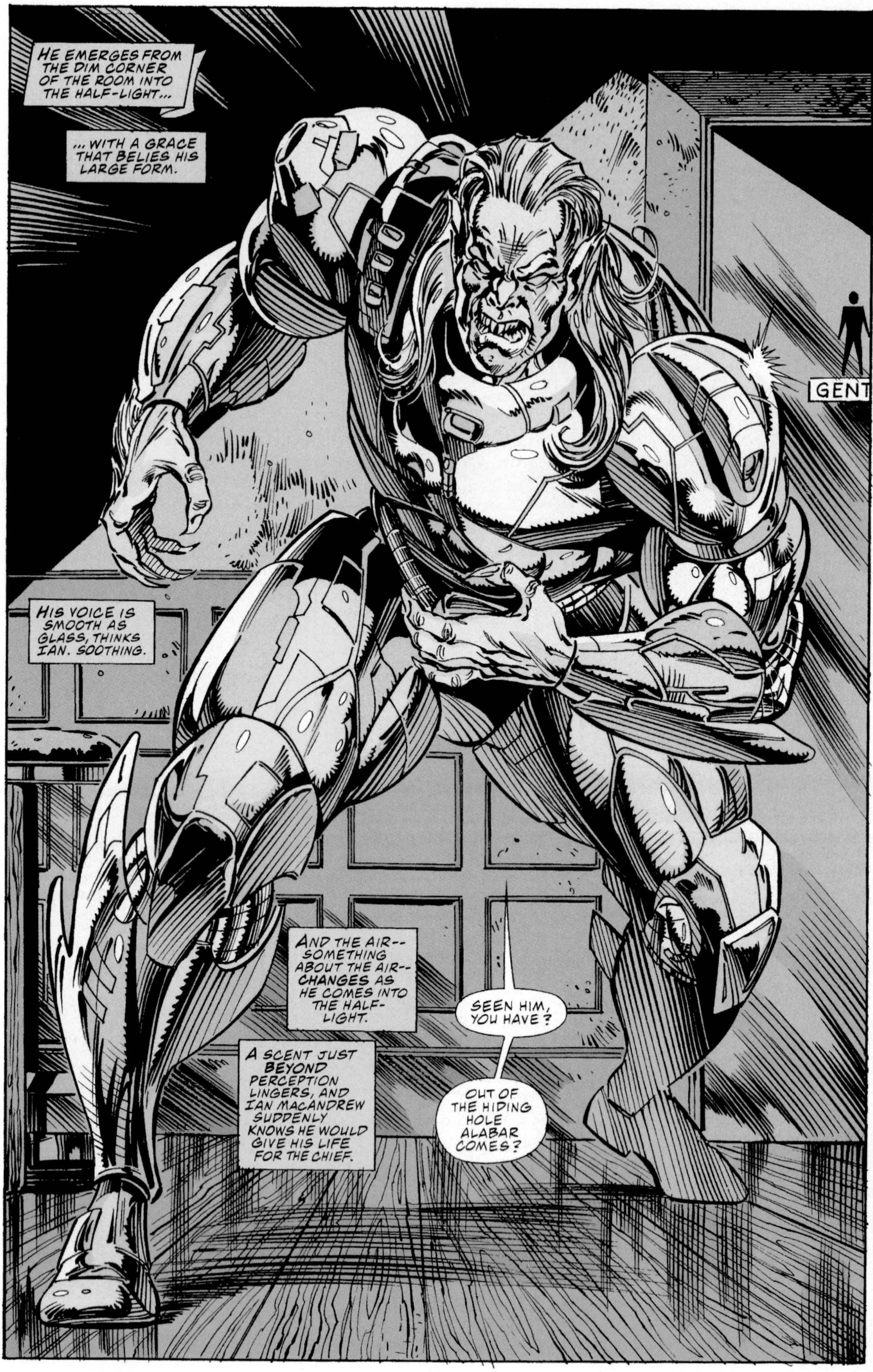
HE EMERGES FROM THE DIM CORNER OF THE ROOM INTO THE HALF-LIGHT...
...WITH A GRACE THAT BELIES HIS LARGE FORM.
GENT
HIS VOICE IS SMOOTH AS GLASS, THINKS IAN. SOOTHING.
AND THE AIR-- SOMETHING ABOUT THE AIR-- CHANGES AS HE COMES INTO THE HALF-LIGHT.
SEEN HIM, YOU HAVE?
A SCENT JUST BEYOND PERCEPTION LINGERS, AND IAN MACANDREW SUDDENLY KNOWS HE WOULD GIVE HIS LIFE FOR THE CHIEF.
OUT OF THE HIDING HOLE ALABAR COMES?

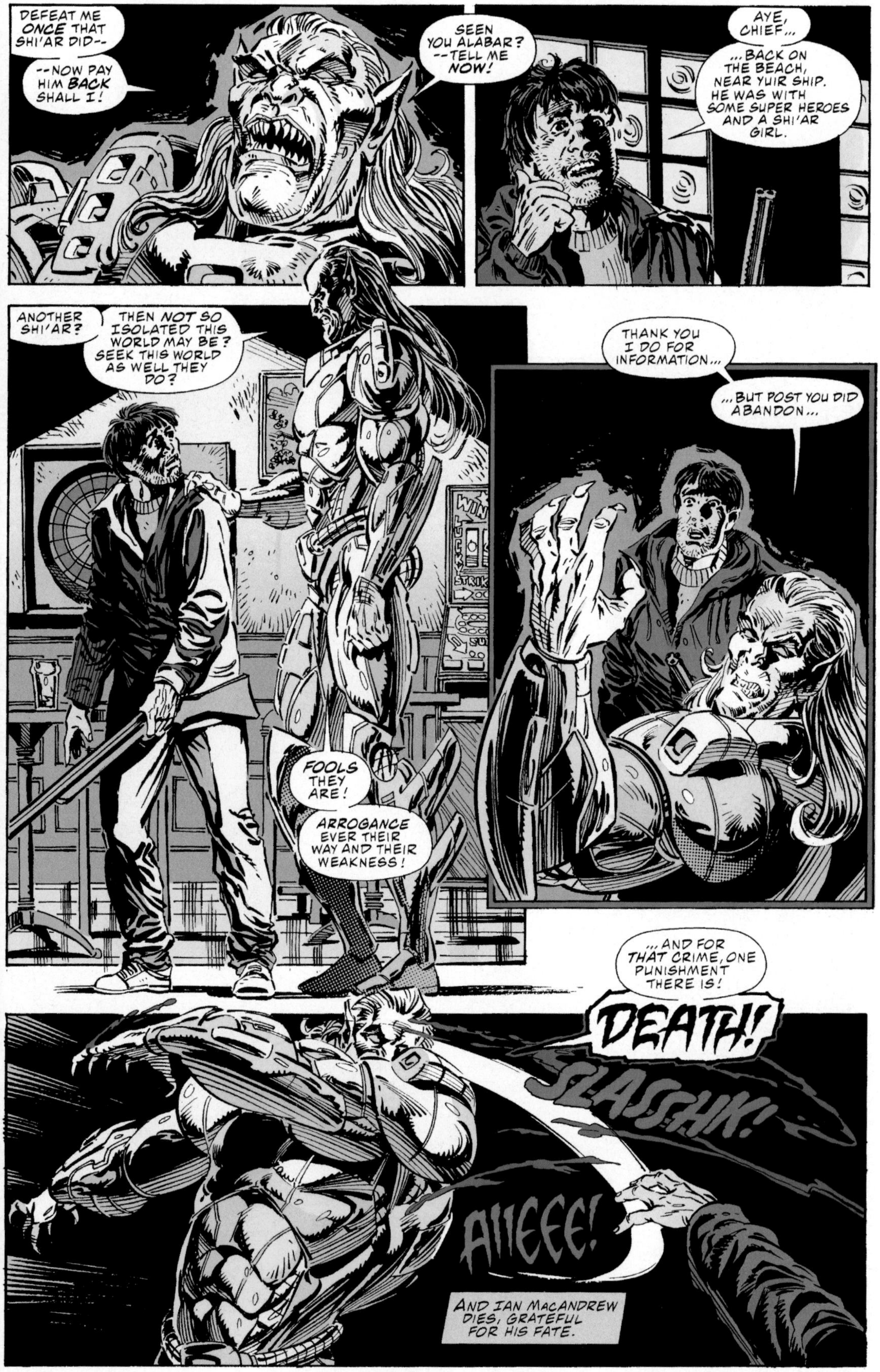
DEFEAT ME ONCE THAT SHI'AR DID--
--NOW PAY HIM BACK SHALL I!
SEEN YOU ALABAR? --TELL ME NOW!
AYE, CHIEF...
...BACK ON THE BEACH, NEAR YUIR SHIP. HE WAS WITH SOME SUPER HEROES AND A SHI'AR GIRL.
ANOTHER SHI'AR?
THEN NOT SO ISOLATED THIS WORLD MAY BE? SEEK THIS WORLD AS WELL THEY DO?
FOOLS THEY ARE!
ARROGANCE EVER THEIR WAY AND THEIR WEAKNESS!
THANK YOU I DO FOR INFORMATION...
...BUT POST YOU DID ABANDON...
...AND FOR THAT CRIME, ONE PUNISHMENT THERE IS!
DEATH!
SLASSHK!
AIIEEE!
AND IAN MACANDREW DIES, GRATEFUL FOR HIS FATE.

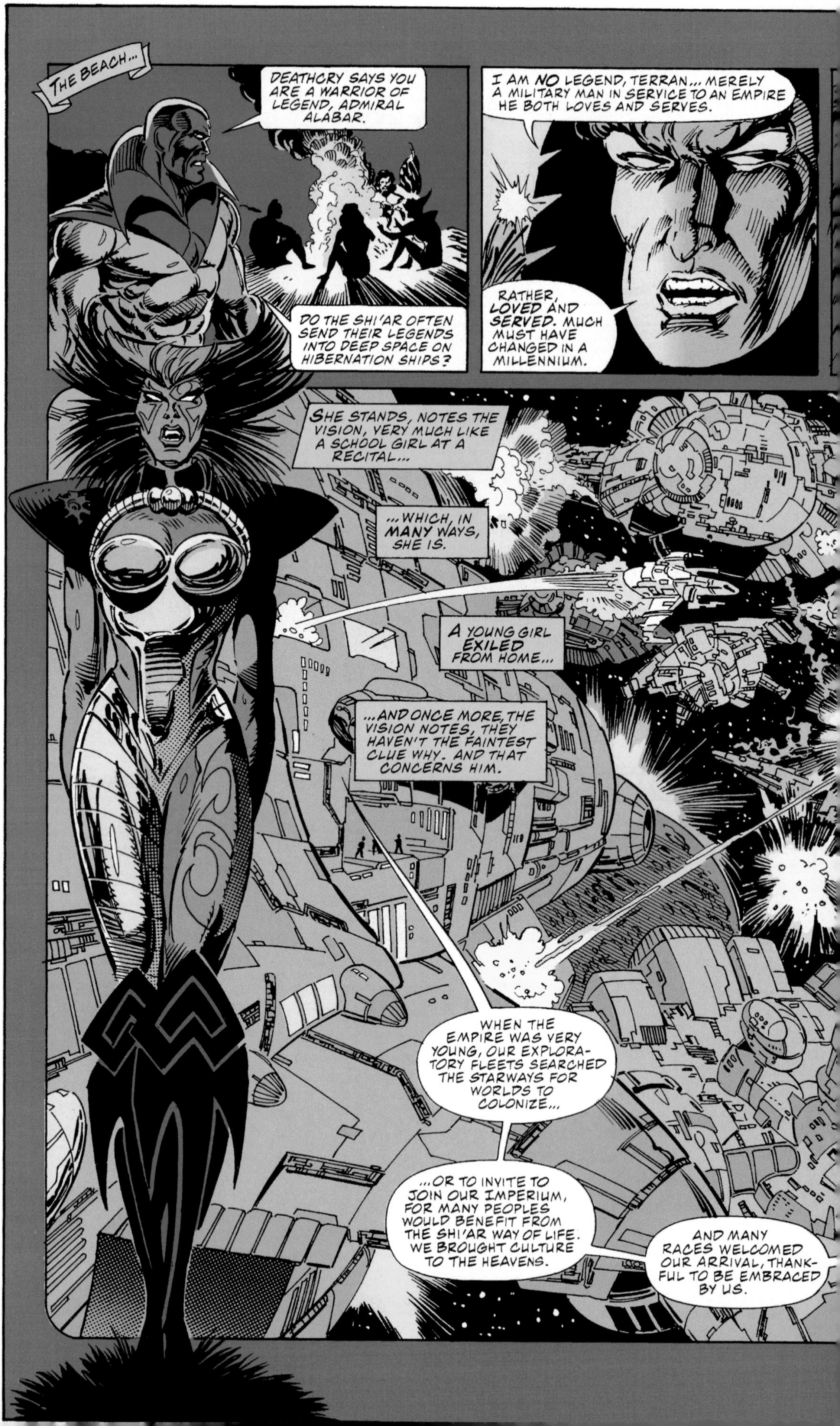
THE BEACH...
DEATHCRY SAYS YOU ARE A WARRIOR OF LEGEND, ADMIRAL ALABAR.
DO THE SHI'AR OFTEN SEND THEIR LEGENDS INTO DEEP SPACE ON HIBERNATION SHIPS?
I AM NO LEGEND, TERRAN... MERELY A MILITARY MAN IN SERVICE TO AN EMPIRE HE BOTH LOVES AND SERVES.
RATHER, LOVED AND SERVED. MUCH MUST HAVE CHANGED IN A MILLENNIUM.
SHE STANDS, NOTES THE VISION, VERY MUCH LIKE A SCHOOL GIRL AT A RECITAL...
...WHICH, IN MANY WAYS, SHE IS.
A YOUNG GIRL EXILED FROM HOME...
...AND ONCE MORE, THE VISION NOTES, THEY HAVEN'T THE FAINTEST CLUE WHY. AND THAT CONCERNS HIM.
WHEN THE EMPIRE WAS VERY YOUNG, OUR EXPLORATORY FLEETS SEARCHED THE STARWAYS FOR WORLDS TO COLONIZE...
...OR TO INVITE TO JOIN OUR IMPERIUM, FOR MANY PEOPLES WOULD BENEFIT FROM THE SHI'AR WAY OF LIFE. WE BROUGHT CULTURE TO THE HEAVENS.
AND MANY RACES WELCOMED OUR ARRIVAL, THANKFUL TO BE EMBRACED BY US.

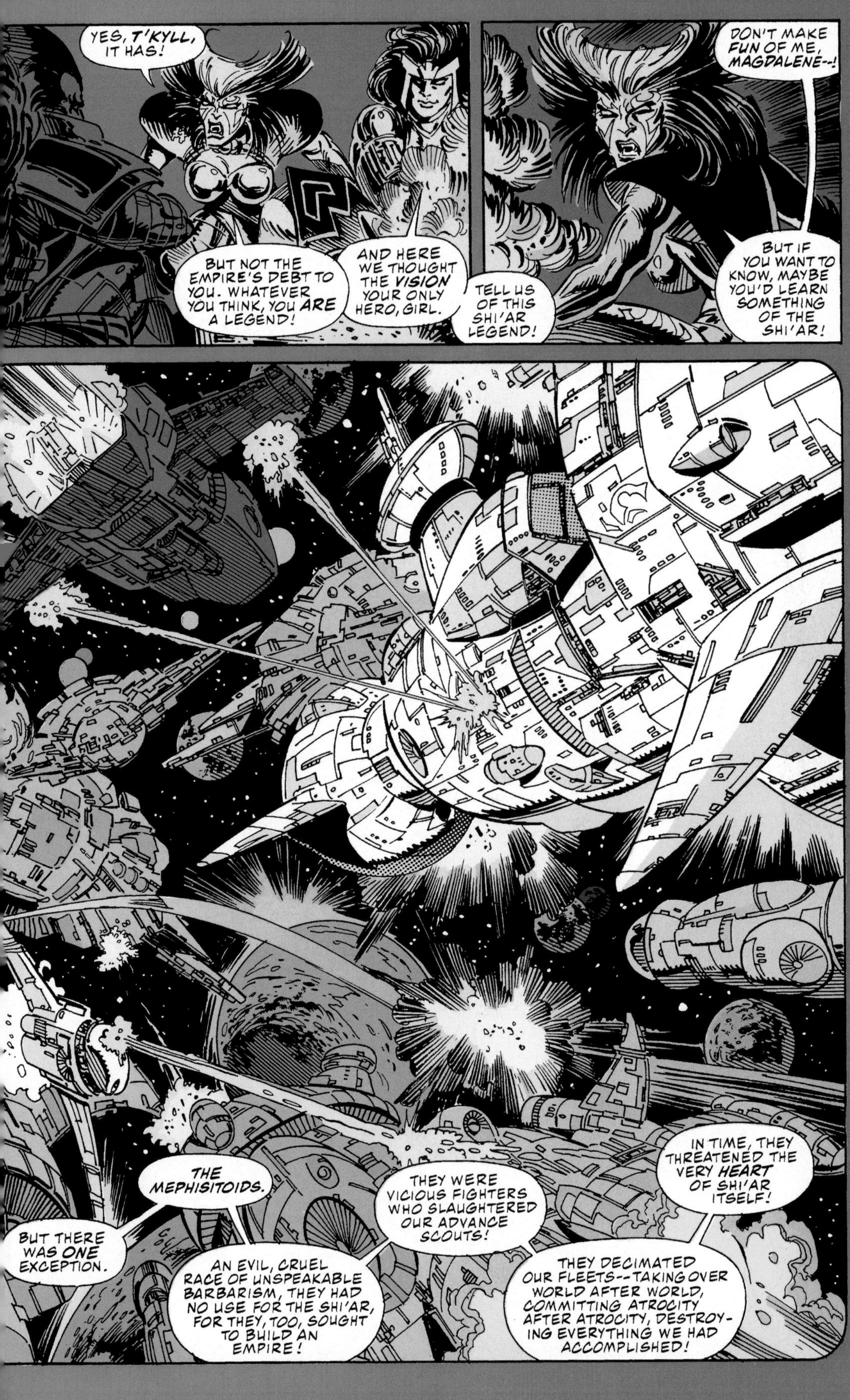
YES, T'KYLL, IT HAS!
BUT NOT THE EMPIRE'S DEBT TO YOU. WHATEVER YOU THINK, YOU ARE A LEGEND!
AND HERE WE THOUGHT THE VISION YOUR ONLY HERO, GIRL.
TELL US OF THIS SHI'AR LEGEND!
DON'T MAKE FUN OF ME, MAGDALENE--!
BUT IF YOU WANT TO KNOW, MAYBE YOU'D LEARN SOMETHING OF THE SHI'AR!
BUT THERE WAS ONE EXCEPTION.
THE MEPHISITOIDS.
AN EVIL, CRUEL RACE OF UNSPEAKABLE BARBARISM, THEY HAD NO USE FOR THE SHI'AR, FOR THEY, TOO, SOUGHT TO BUILD AN EMPIRE!
THEY WERE VICIOUS FIGHTERS WHO SLAUGHTERED OUR ADVANCE SCOUTS!
THEY DECIMATED OUR FLEETS--TAKING OVER WORLD AFTER WORLD, COMMITTING ATROCITY AFTER ATROCITY, DESTROYING EVERYTHING WE HAD ACCOMPLISHED!
IN TIME, THEY THREATENED THE VERY HEART OF SHI'AR ITSELF!

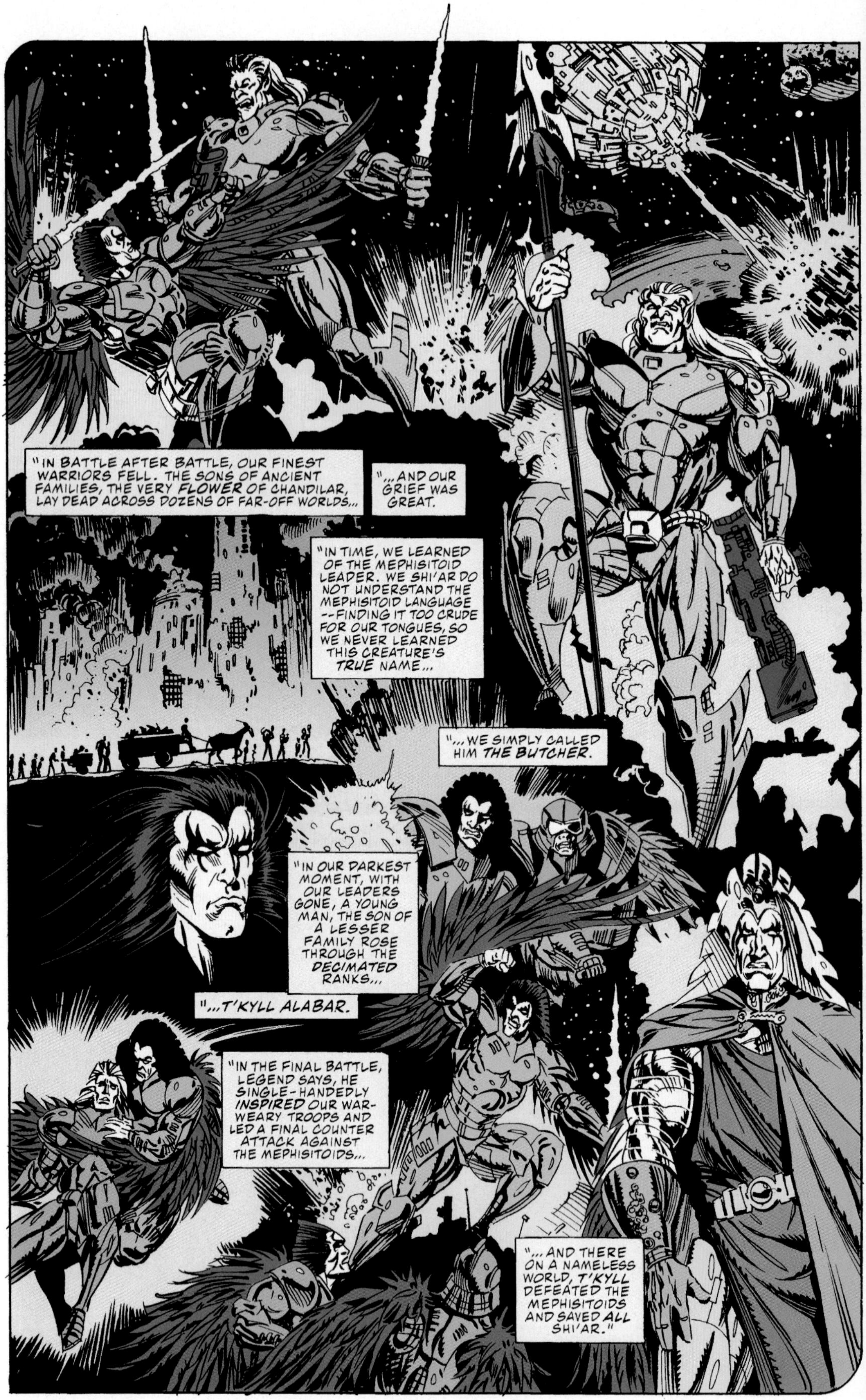
"IN BATTLE AFTER BATTLE, OUR FINEST WARRIORS FELL. THE SONS OF ANCIENT FAMILIES, THE VERY FLOWER OF CHANDILAR, LAY DEAD ACROSS DOZENS OF FAR-OFF WORLDS...
"...AND OUR GRIEF WAS GREAT.
"IN TIME, WE LEARNED OF THE MEPHISITOID LEADER. WE SHI'AR DO NOT UNDERSTAND THE MEPHISITOID LANGUAGE --FINDING IT TOO CRUDE FOR OUR TONGUES, SO WE NEVER LEARNED THIS CREATURE'S TRUE NAME...
"...WE SIMPLY CALLED HIM THE BUTCHER.
"IN OUR DARKEST MOMENT, WITH OUR LEADERS GONE, A YOUNG MAN, THE SON OF A LESSER FAMILY ROSE THROUGH THE DECIMATED RANKS...
"...T'KYLL ALABAR.
"IN THE FINAL BATTLE, LEGEND SAYS, HE SINGLE-HANDEDLY INSPIRED OUR WAR-WEARY TROOPS AND LED A FINAL COUNTER ATTACK AGAINST THE MEPHISITOIDS...
"...AND THERE ON A NAMELESS WORLD, T'KYLL DEFEATED THE MEPHISITOIDS AND SAVED ALL SHI'AR."

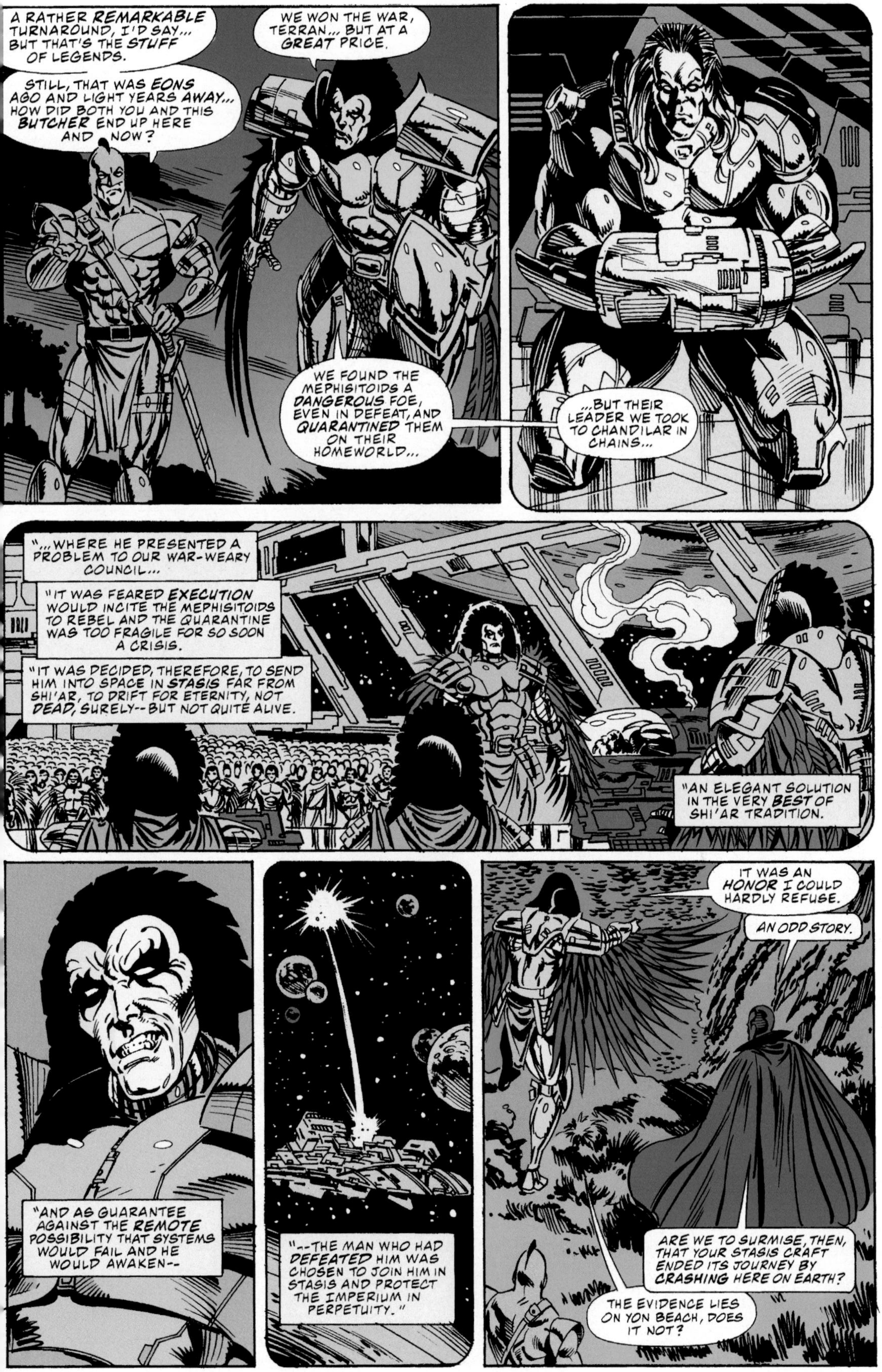
A RATHER REMARKABLE TURNAROUND, I'D SAY... BUT THAT'S THE STUFF OF LEGENDS.
STILL, THAT WAS EONS AGO AND LIGHT YEARS AWAY... HOW DID BOTH YOU AND THIS BUTCHER END UP HERE AND NOW?
WE WON THE WAR, TERRAN... BUT AT A GREAT PRICE.
WE FOUND THE MEPHISITOIDS A DANGEROUS FOE, EVEN IN DEFEAT, AND QUARANTINED THEM ON THEIR HOMEWORLD...
...BUT THEIR LEADER WE TOOK TO CHANDILAR IN CHAINS...
"...WHERE HE PRESENTED A PROBLEM TO OUR WAR-WEARY COUNCIL...
"IT WAS FEARED EXECUTION WOULD INCITE THE MEPHISITOIDS TO REBEL AND THE QUARANTINE WAS TOO FRAGILE FOR SO SOON A CRISIS.
"IT WAS DECIDED, THEREFORE, TO SEND HIM INTO SPACE IN STASIS FAR FROM SHI'AR, TO DRIFT FOR ETERNITY, NOT DEAD, SURELY--BUT NOT QUITE ALIVE.
"AN ELEGANT SOLUTION IN THE VERY BEST OF SHI'AR TRADITION.
"AND AS GUARANTEE AGAINST THE REMOTE POSSIBILITY THAT SYSTEMS WOULD FAIL AND HE WOULD AWAKEN--
"--THE MAN WHO HAD DEFEATED HIM WAS CHOSEN TO JOIN HIM IN STASIS AND PROTECT THE IMPERIUM IN PERPETUITY."
IT WAS AN HONOR I COULD HARDLY REFUSE.
AN ODD STORY.
ARE WE TO SURMISE, THEN, THAT YOUR STASIS CRAFT ENDED ITS JOURNEY BY CRASHING HERE ON EARTH?
THE EVIDENCE LIES ON YON BEACH, DOES IT NOT?

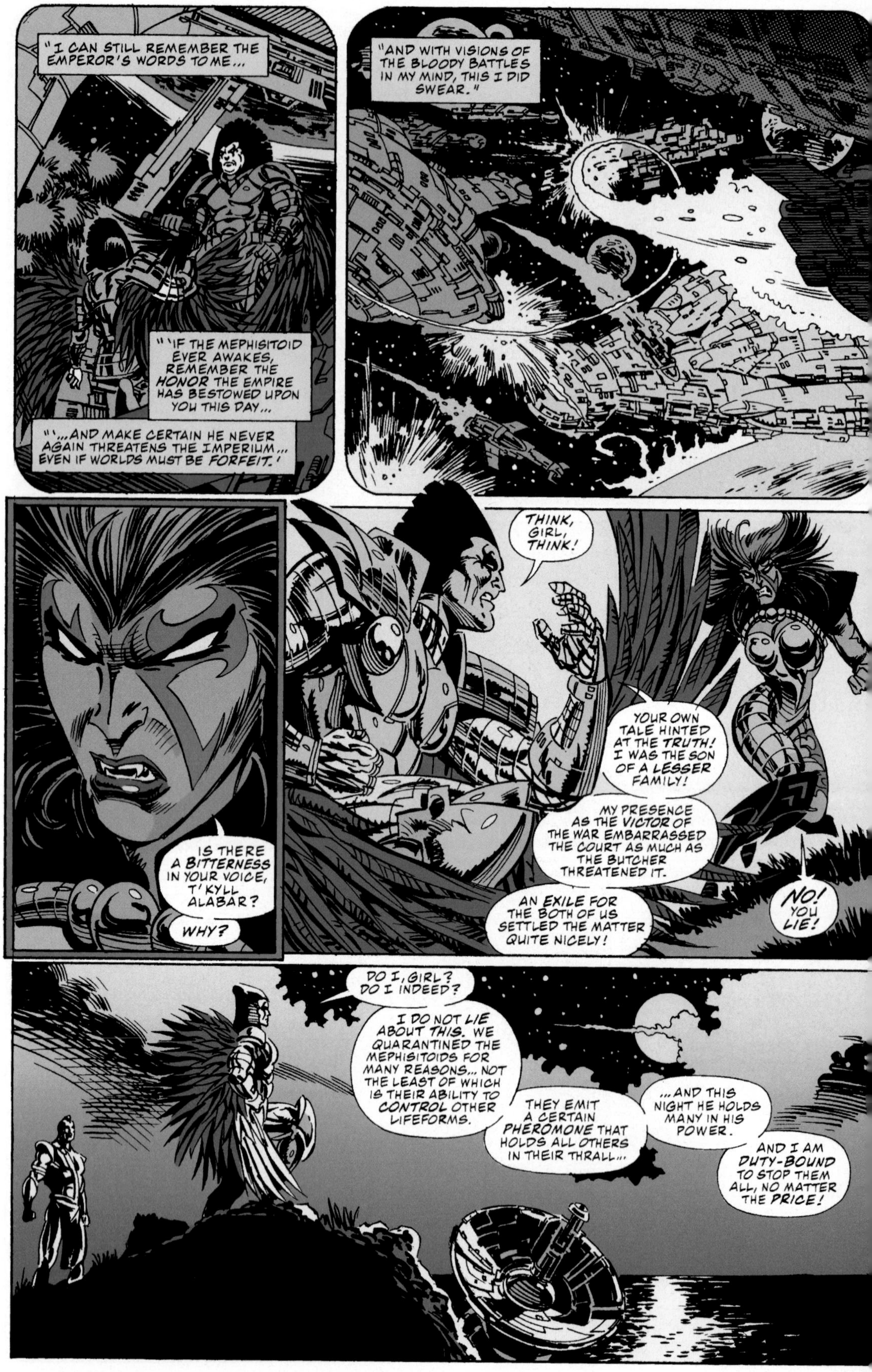
"I CAN STILL REMEMBER THE EMPEROR'S WORDS TO ME...
"'IF THE MEPHISITOID EVER AWAKES, REMEMBER THE HONOR THE EMPIRE HAS BESTOWED UPON YOU THIS DAY...
"'...AND MAKE CERTAIN HE NEVER AGAIN THREATENS THE IMPERIUM... EVEN IF WORLDS MUST BE FORFEIT.'
"AND WITH VISIONS OF THE BLOODY BATTLES IN MY MIND, THIS I DID SWEAR."
IS THERE A BITTERNESS IN YOUR VOICE, T'KYLL ALABAR?
WHY?
THINK, GIRL, THINK!
YOUR OWN TALE HINTED AT THE TRUTH! I WAS THE SON OF A LESSER FAMILY!
MY PRESENCE AS THE VICTOR OF THE WAR EMBARRASSED THE COURT AS MUCH AS THE BUTCHER THREATENED IT.
AN EXILE FOR THE BOTH OF US SETTLED THE MATTER QUITE NICELY!
NO! YOU LIE!
DO I, GIRL? DO I INDEED?
I DO NOT LIE ABOUT THIS. WE QUARANTINED THE MEPHISITOIDS FOR MANY REASONS... NOT THE LEAST OF WHICH IS THEIR ABILITY TO CONTROL OTHER LIFEFORMS.
THEY EMIT A CERTAIN PHEROMONE THAT HOLDS ALL OTHERS IN THEIR THRALL...
...AND THIS NIGHT HE HOLDS MANY IN HIS POWER.
AND I AM DUTY-BOUND TO STOP THEM ALL, NO MATTER THE PRICE!

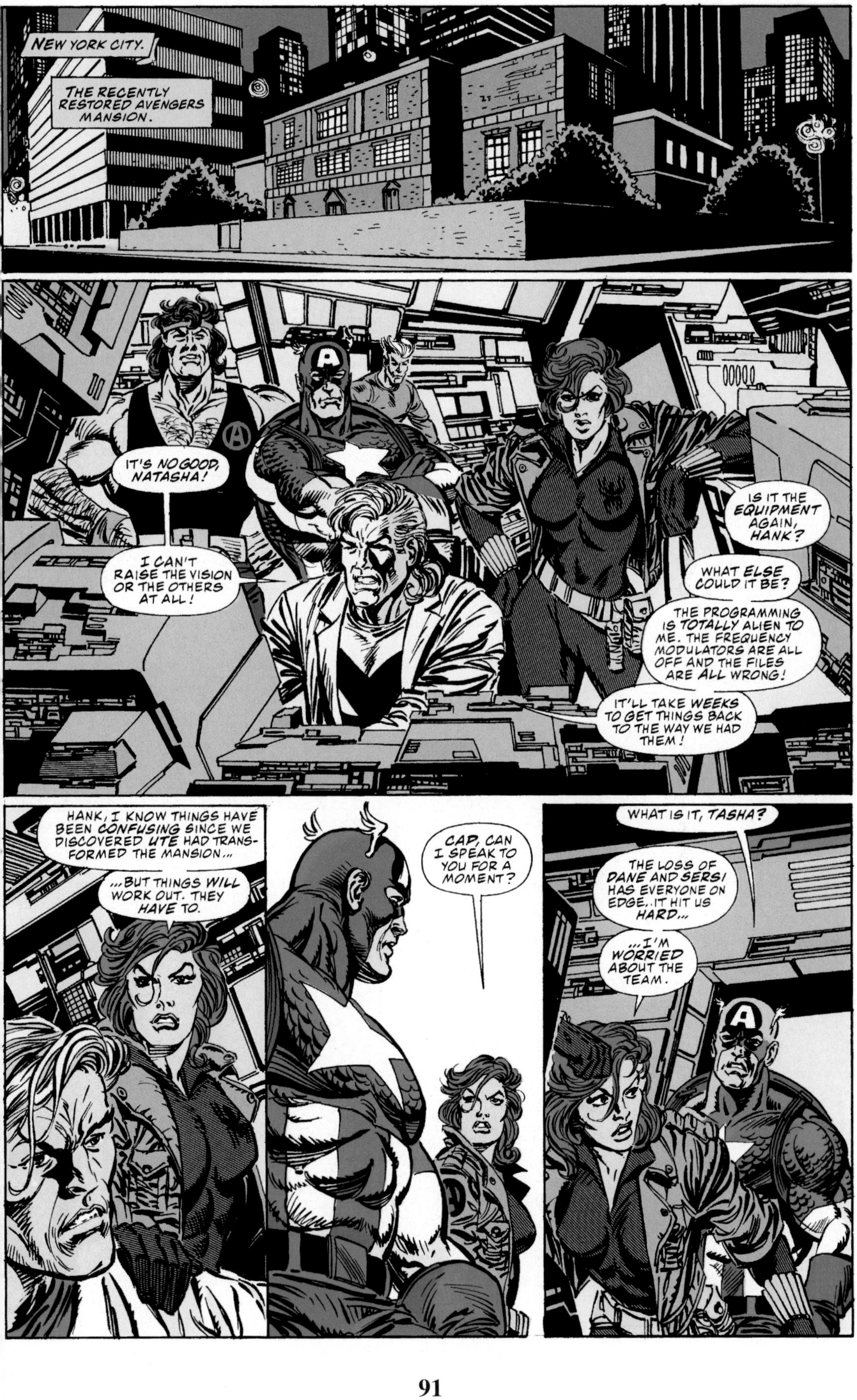
NEW YORK CITY.
THE RECENTLY RESTORED AVENGERS MANSION.
IT'S NO GOOD, NATASHA!
I CAN'T RAISE THE VISION OR THE OTHERS AT ALL!
IS IT THE EQUIPMENT AGAIN, HANK?
WHAT ELSE COULD IT BE?
THE PROGRAMMING IS TOTALLY ALIEN TO ME. THE FREQUENCY MODULATORS ARE ALL OFF AND THE FILES ARE ALL WRONG!
IT'LL TAKE WEEKS TO GET THINGS BACK TO THE WAY WE HAD THEM!
HANK, I KNOW THINGS HAVE BEEN CONFUSING SINCE WE DISCOVERED UTE HAD TRANSFORMED THE MANSION...
...BUT THINGS WILL WORK OUT. THEY HAVE TO.
CAP, CAN I SPEAK TO YOU FOR A MOMENT?
WHAT IS IT, TASHA?
THE LOSS OF DANE AND SERSI HAS EVERYONE ON EDGE.. IT HIT US HARD...
...I'M WORRIED ABOUT THE TEAM.

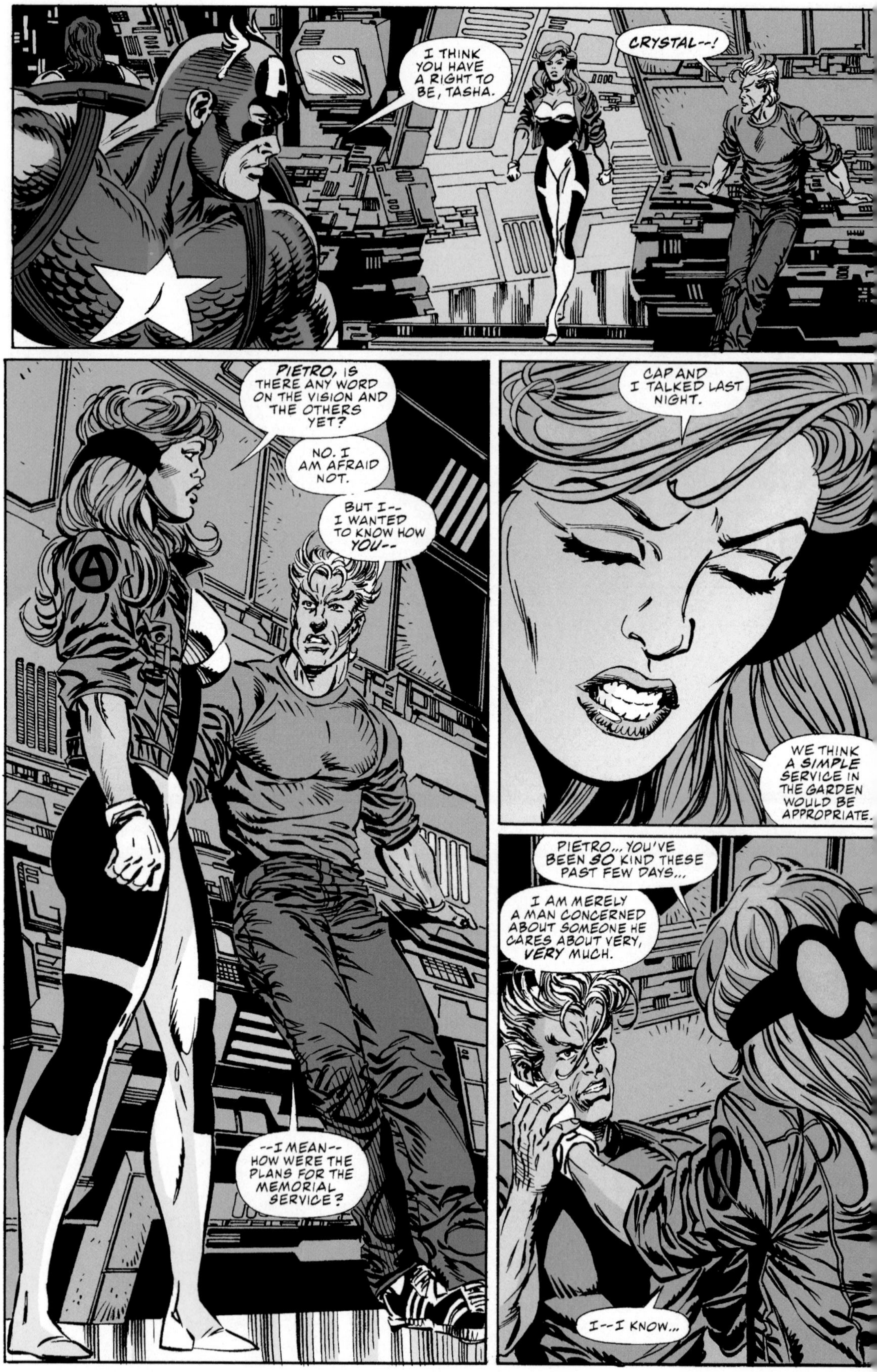
I THINK YOU HAVE A RIGHT TO BE, TASHA.
CRYSTAL--!
PIETRO, IS THERE ANY WORD ON THE VISION AND THE OTHERS YET?
NO. I AM AFRAID NOT.
BUT I-- I WANTED TO KNOW HOW YOU--
--I MEAN-- HOW WERE THE PLANS FOR THE MEMORIAL SERVICE?
CAP AND I TALKED LAST NIGHT.
WE THINK A SIMPLE SERVICE IN THE GARDEN WOULD BE APPROPRIATE.
PIETRO... YOU'VE BEEN SO KIND THESE PAST FEW DAYS...
I AM MERELY A MAN CONCERNED ABOUT SOMEONE HE CARES ABOUT VERY, VERY MUCH.
I--I KNOW...

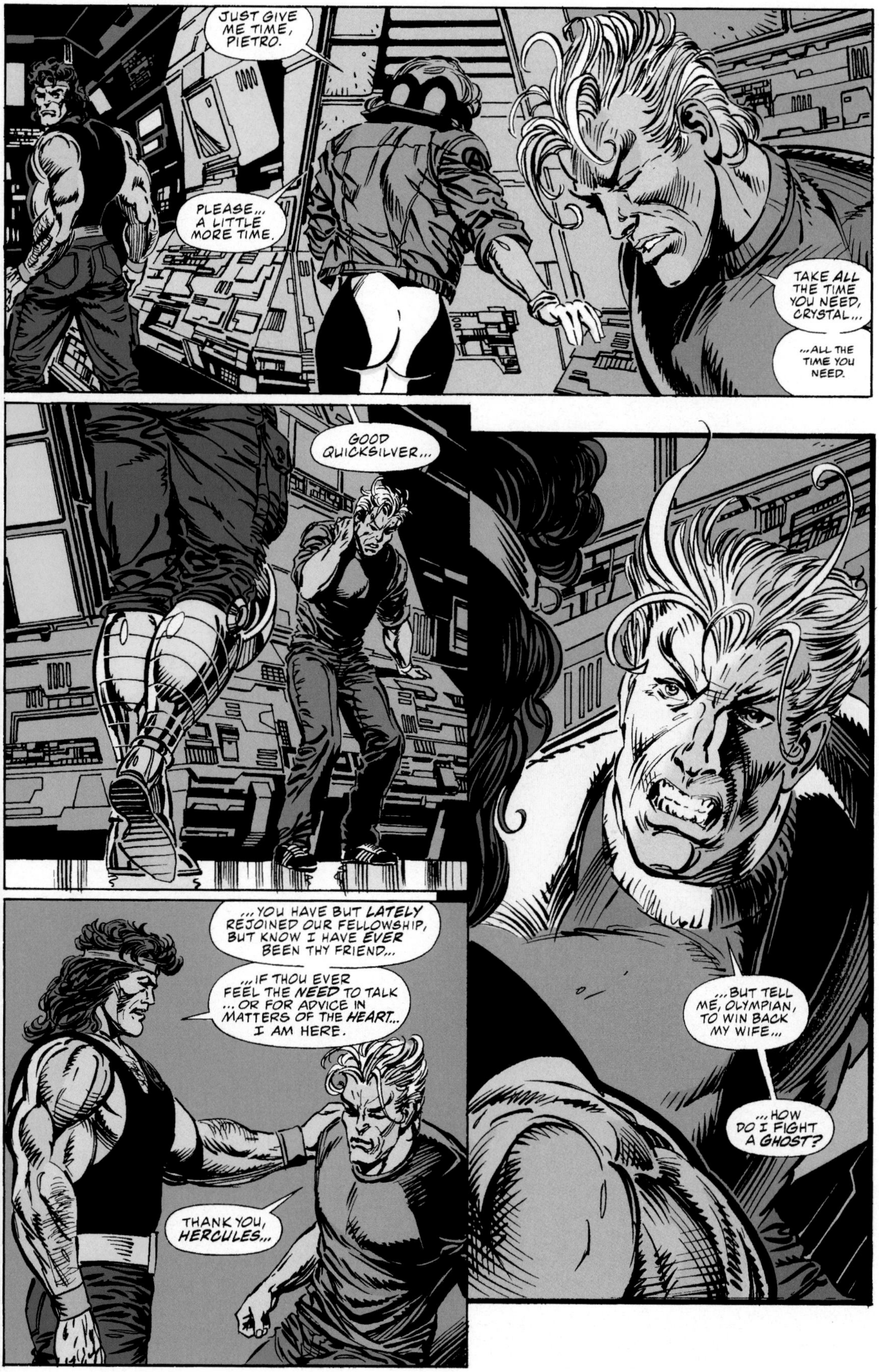
JUST GIVE ME TIME, PIETRO.
PLEASE... A LITTLE MORE TIME.
TAKE ALL THE TIME YOU NEED, CRYSTAL...
...ALL THE TIME YOU NEED.
GOOD QUICKSILVER...
...YOU HAVE BUT LATELY REJOINED OUR FELLOWSHIP, BUT KNOW I HAVE EVER BEEN THY FRIEND...
...IF THOU EVER FEEL THE NEED TO TALK ...OR FOR ADVICE IN MATTERS OF THE HEART... I AM HERE.
THANK YOU, HERCULES...
...BUT TELL ME, OLYMPIAN, TO WIN BACK MY WIFE...
...HOW DO I FIGHT A GHOST?

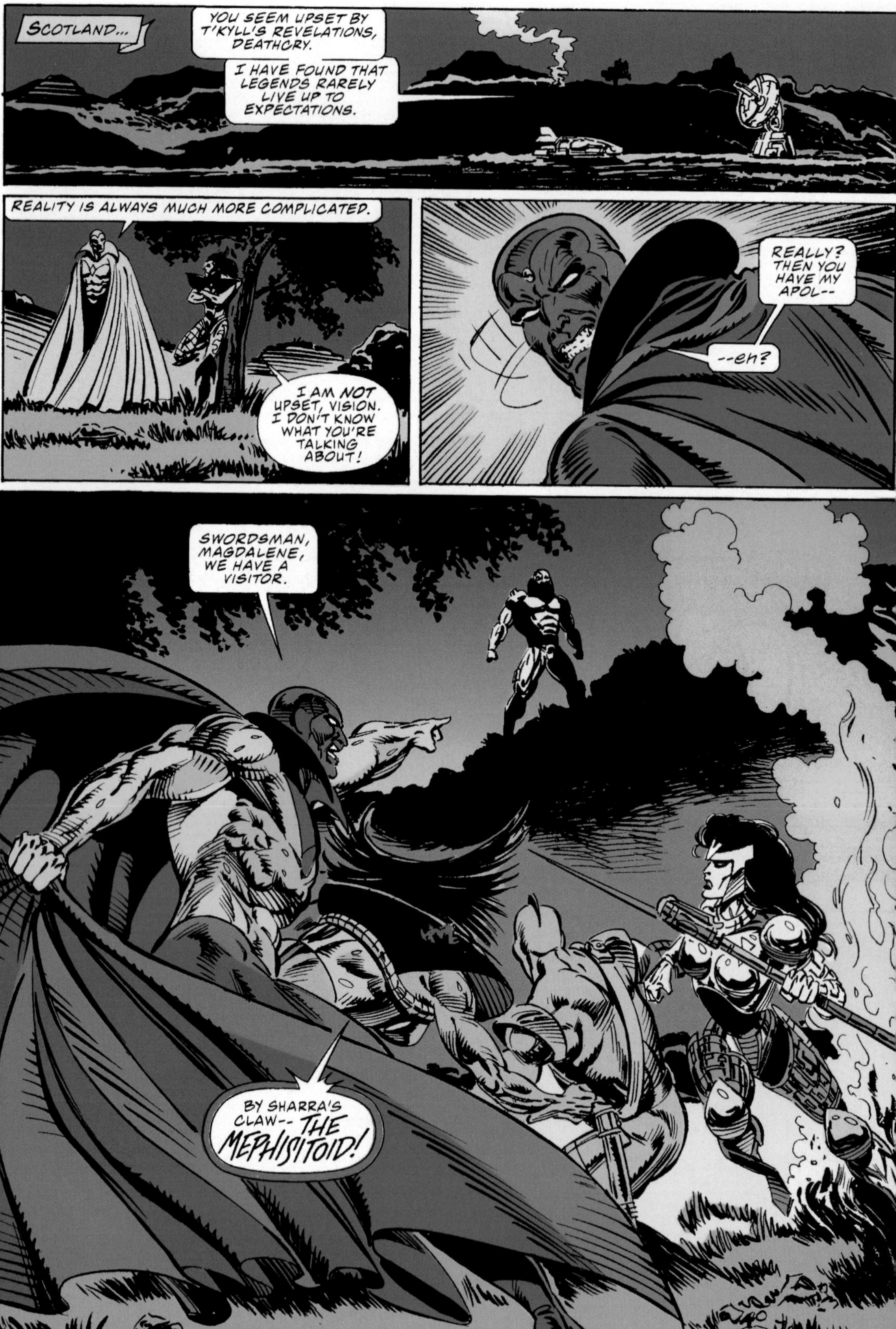

SCOTLAND...
YOU SEEM UPSET BY T'KYLL'S REVELATIONS, DEATHCRY.
I HAVE FOUND THAT LEGENDS RARELY LIVE UP TO EXPECTATIONS.
REALITY IS ALWAYS MUCH MORE COMPLICATED.
I AM NOT UPSET, VISION. I DON'T KNOW WHAT YOU'RE TALKING ABOUT!
REALLY? THEN YOU HAVE MY APOL--
--eh?
SWORDSMAN, MAGDALENE, WE HAVE A VISITOR.
BY SHARRA'S CLAW-- THE MEPHISITOID!

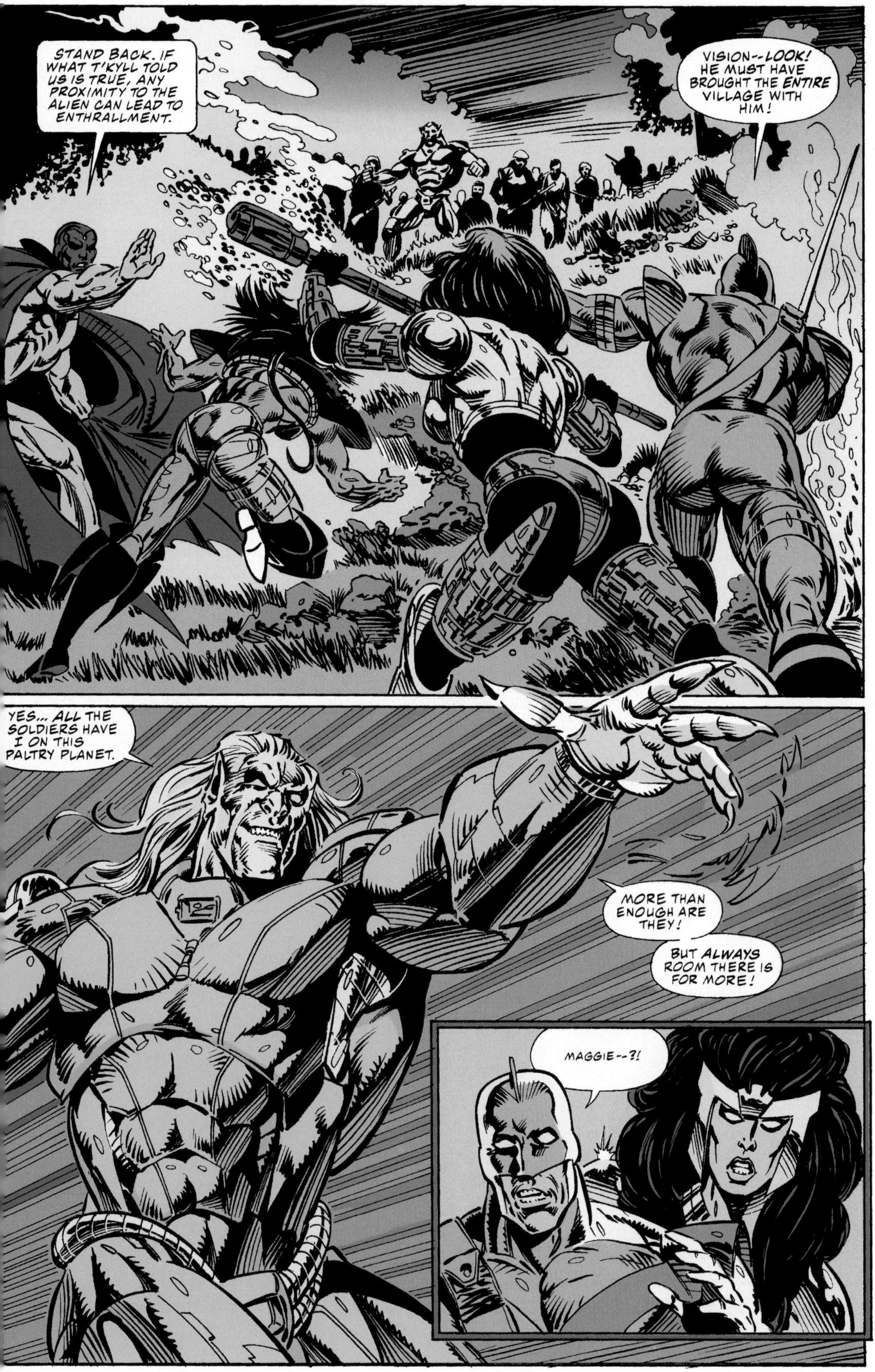
STAND BACK. IF WHAT T'KYLL TOLD US IS TRUE, ANY PROXIMITY TO THE ALIEN CAN LEAD TO ENTHRALLMENT.
VISION--LOOK! HE MUST HAVE BROUGHT THE ENTIRE VILLAGE WITH HIM!
YES... ALL THE SOLDIERS HAVE I ON THIS PALTRY PLANET.
MORE THAN ENOUGH ARE THEY!
BUT ALWAYS ROOM THERE IS FOR MORE!
MAGGIE--?!

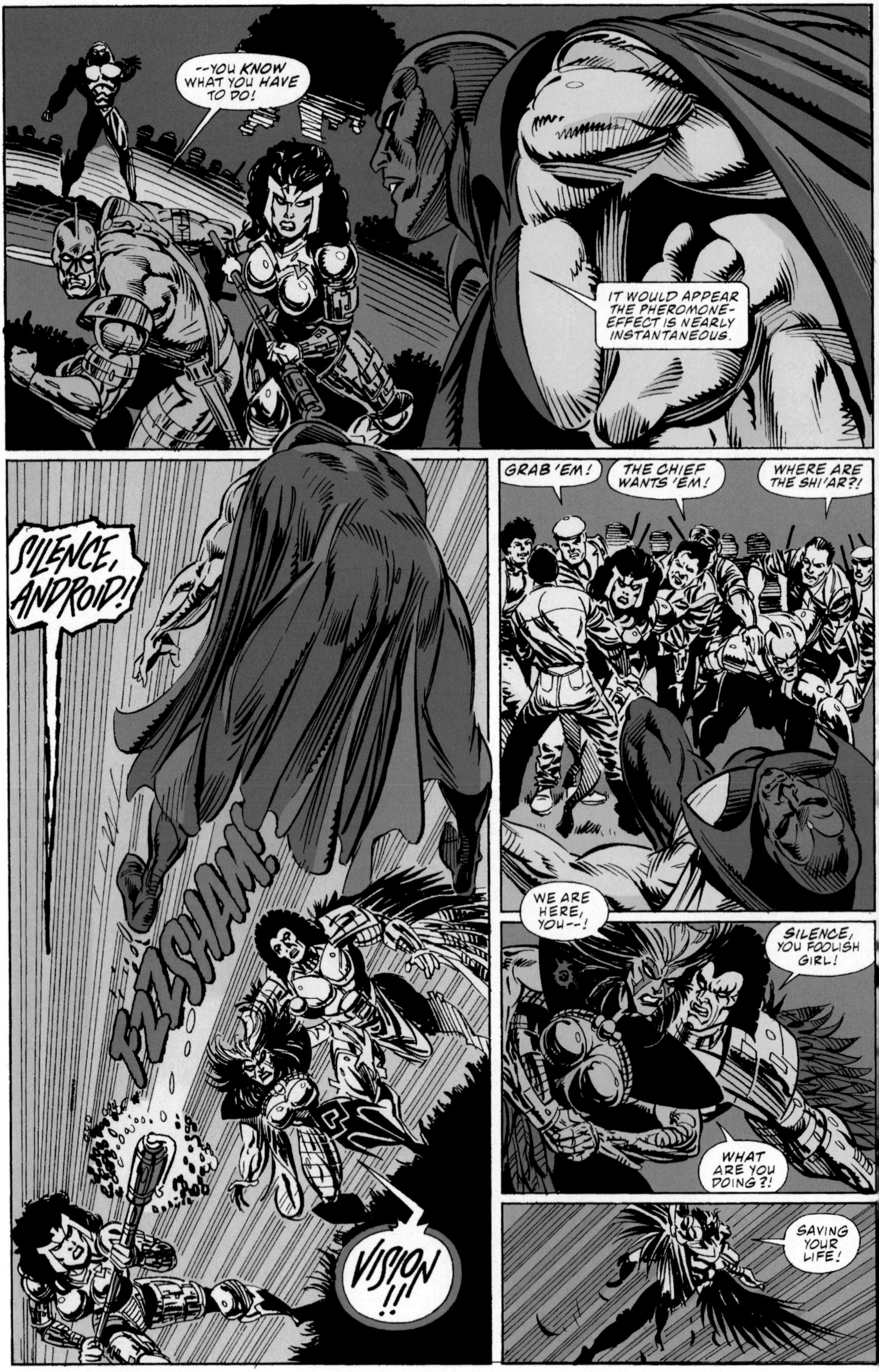
--YOU KNOW WHAT YOU HAVE TO DO!
IT WOULD APPEAR THE PHEROMONE-EFFECT IS NEARLY INSTANTANEOUS.
SILENCE, ANDROID!
FZZSHAM!
VISION!!
GRAB 'EM!
THE CHIEF WANTS 'EM!
WHERE ARE THE SHI'AR?!
WE ARE HERE, YOU--!
SILENCE, YOU FOOLISH GIRL!
WHAT ARE YOU DOING?!
SAVING YOUR LIFE!

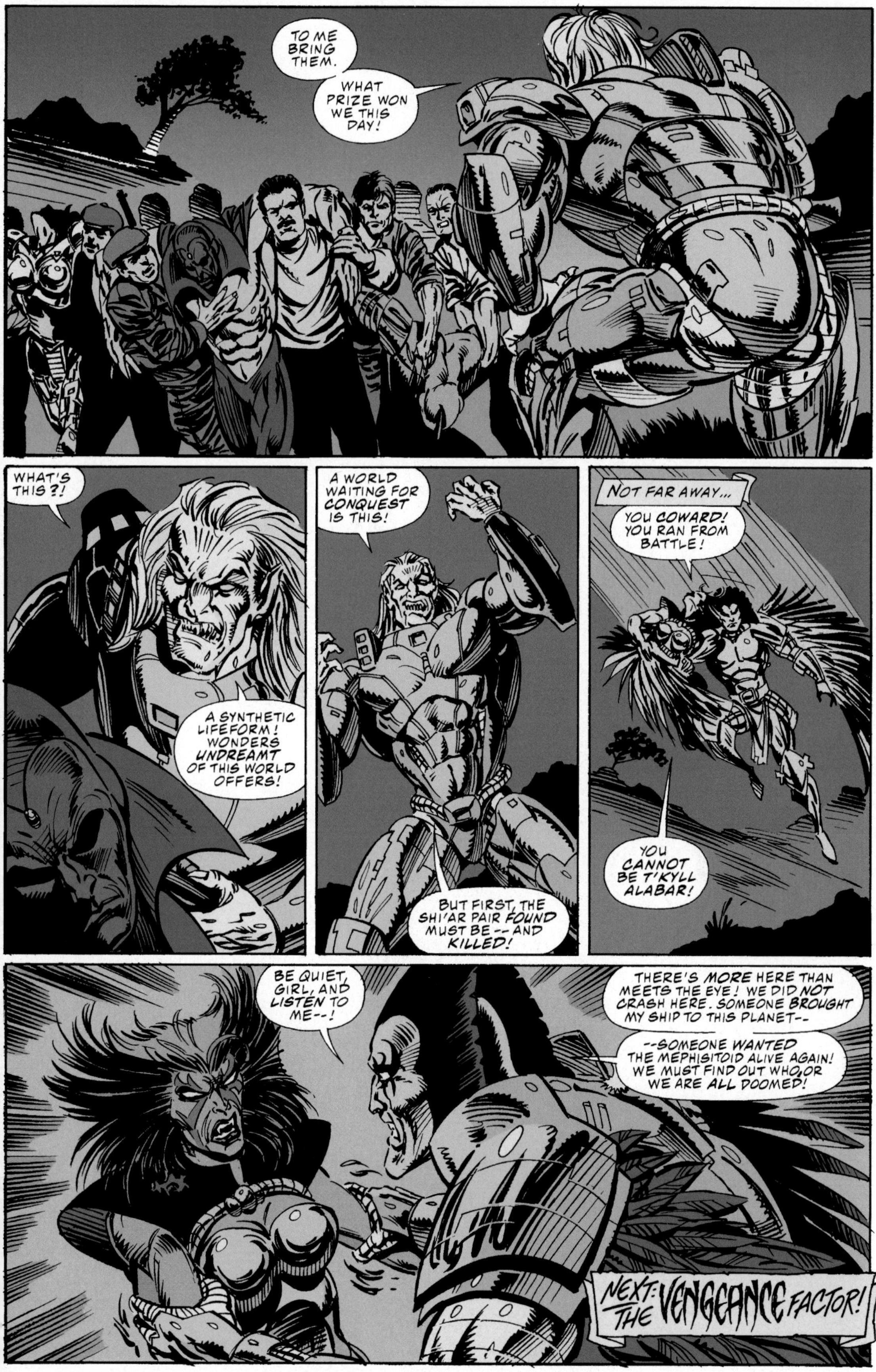

TO ME BRING THEM.
WHAT PRIZE WON WE THIS DAY!
WHAT'S THIS?!
A SYNTHETIC LIFEFORM! WONDERS UNDREAMT OF THIS WORLD OFFERS!
A WORLD WAITING FOR CONQUEST IS THIS!
BUT FIRST, THE SHI'AR PAIR FOUND MUST BE -- AND KILLED!
NOT FAR AWAY...
YOU COWARD! YOU RAN FROM BATTLE!
YOU CANNOT BE T'KYLL ALABAR!
BE QUIET, GIRL, AND LISTEN TO ME--!
THERE'S MORE HERE THAN MEETS THE EYE! WE DID NOT CRASH HERE. SOMEONE BROUGHT MY SHIP TO THIS PLANET--
--SOMEONE WANTED THE MEPHISITOID ALIVE AGAIN! WE MUST FIND OUT WHO, OR WE ARE ALL DOOMED!
NEXT: THE VENGEANCE FACTOR!

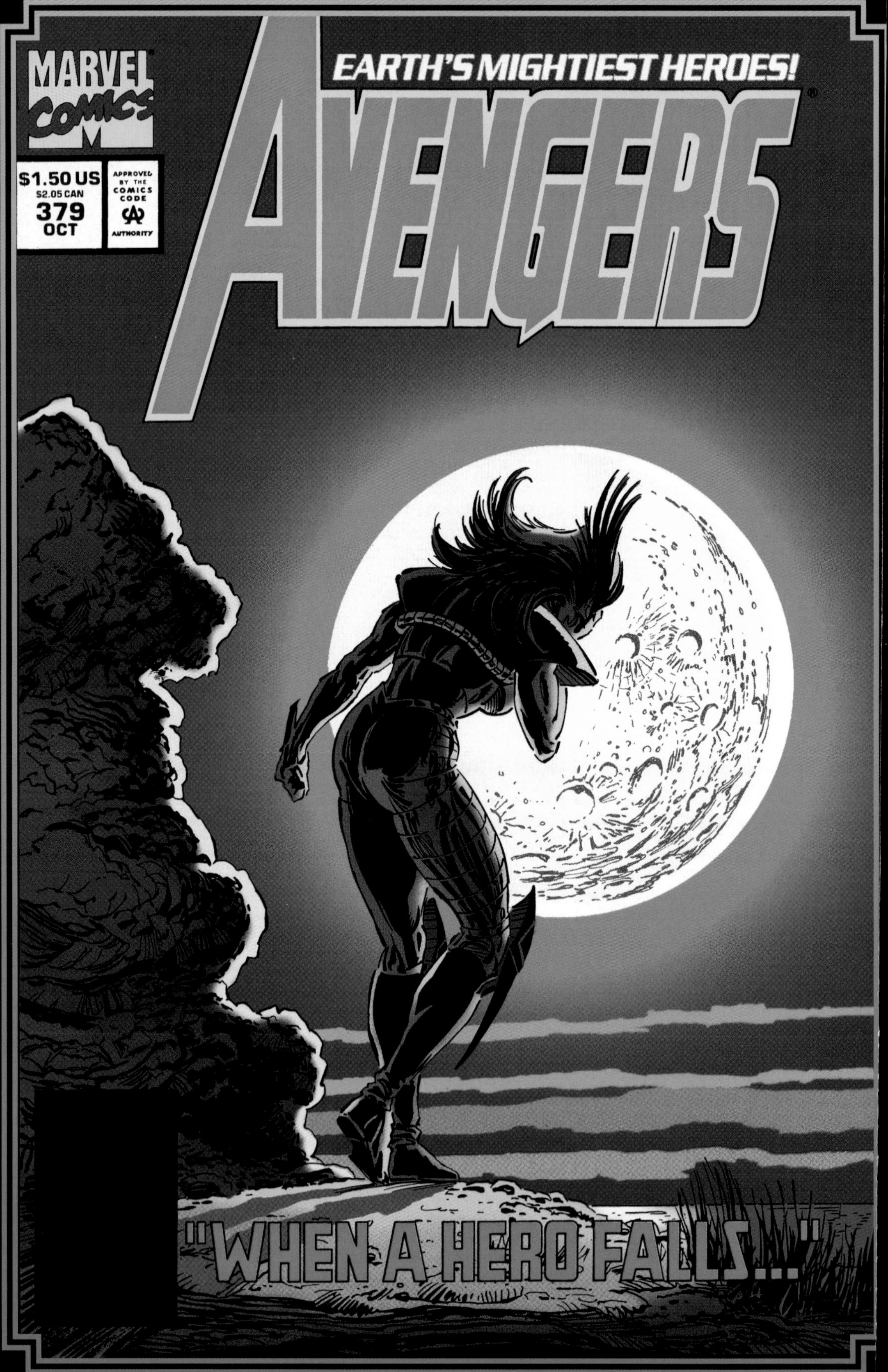
MARVEL COMICS
EARTH'S MIGHTIEST HEROES!
AVENGERS
$1.50 US
$2.05 CAN
379
OCT
APPROVED BY THE COMICS CODE AUTHORITY
"WHEN A HERO FALLS..."

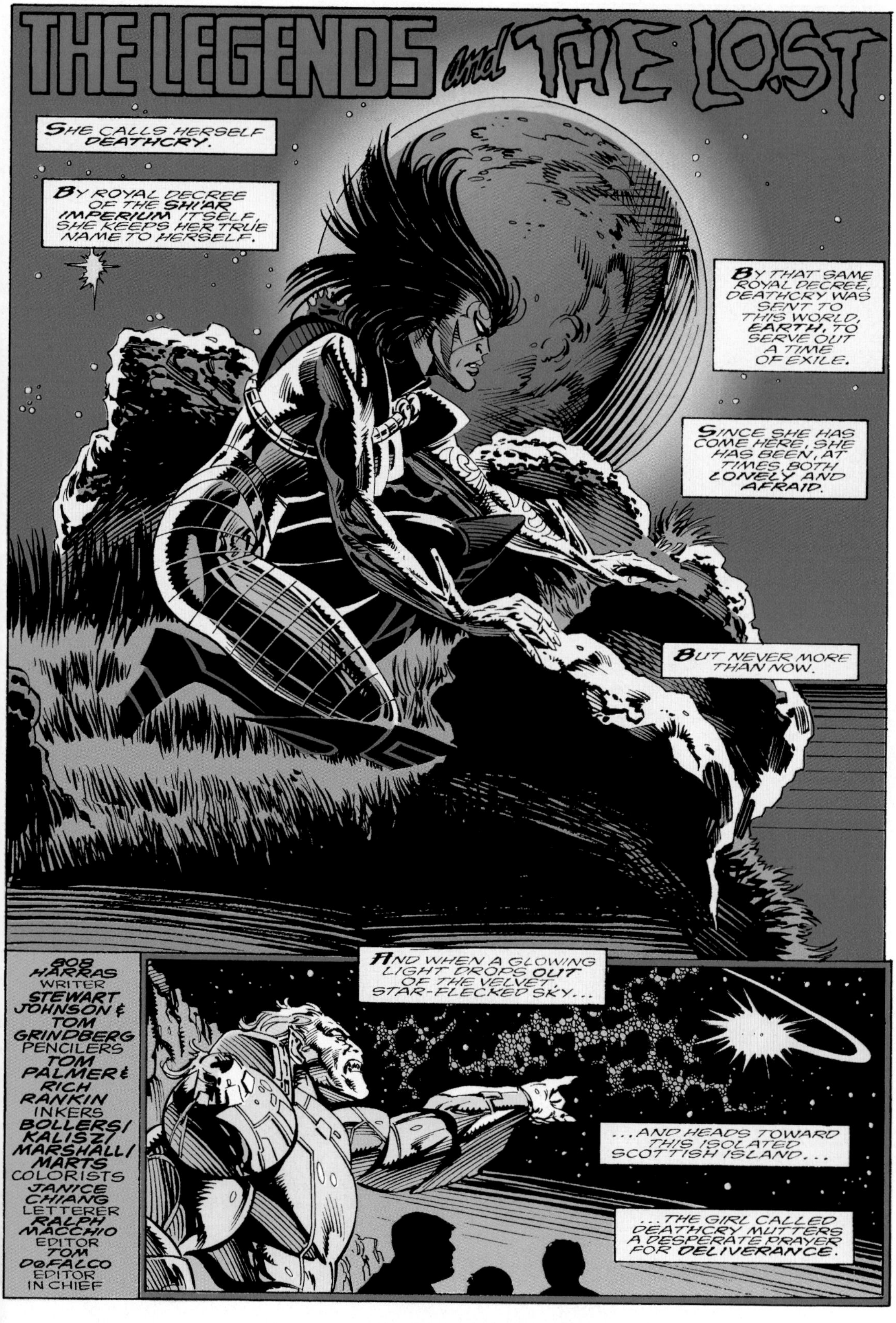

THE LEGENDS and THE LOST
SHE CALLS HERSELF DEATHCRY.
BY ROYAL DECREE OF THE SHI'AR IMPERIUM ITSELF, SHE KEEPS HER TRUE NAME TO HERSELF.
BY THAT SAME ROYAL DECREE, DEATHCRY WAS SENT TO THIS WORLD, EARTH, TO SERVE OUT A TIME OF EXILE.
SINCE SHE HAS COME HERE, SHE HAS BEEN, AT TIMES, BOTH LONELY AND AFRAID.
BUT NEVER MORE THAN NOW.
BOB HARRAS WRITER STEWART JOHNSON & TOM GRINDBERG PENCILERS TOM PALMER & RICH RANKIN INKERS BOLLERS/ KALISZ/ MARSHALL/ MARTS COLORISTS JANICE CHIANG LETTERER RALPH MACCHIO EDITOR TOM DEFALCO EDITOR IN CHIEF
AND WHEN A GLOWING LIGHT DROPS OUT OF THE VELVET, STAR-FLECKED SKY...
...AND HEADS TOWARD THIS ISOLATED SCOTTISH ISLAND...
...THE GIRL CALLED DEATHCRY MUTTERS A DESPERATE PRAYER FOR DELIVERANCE.

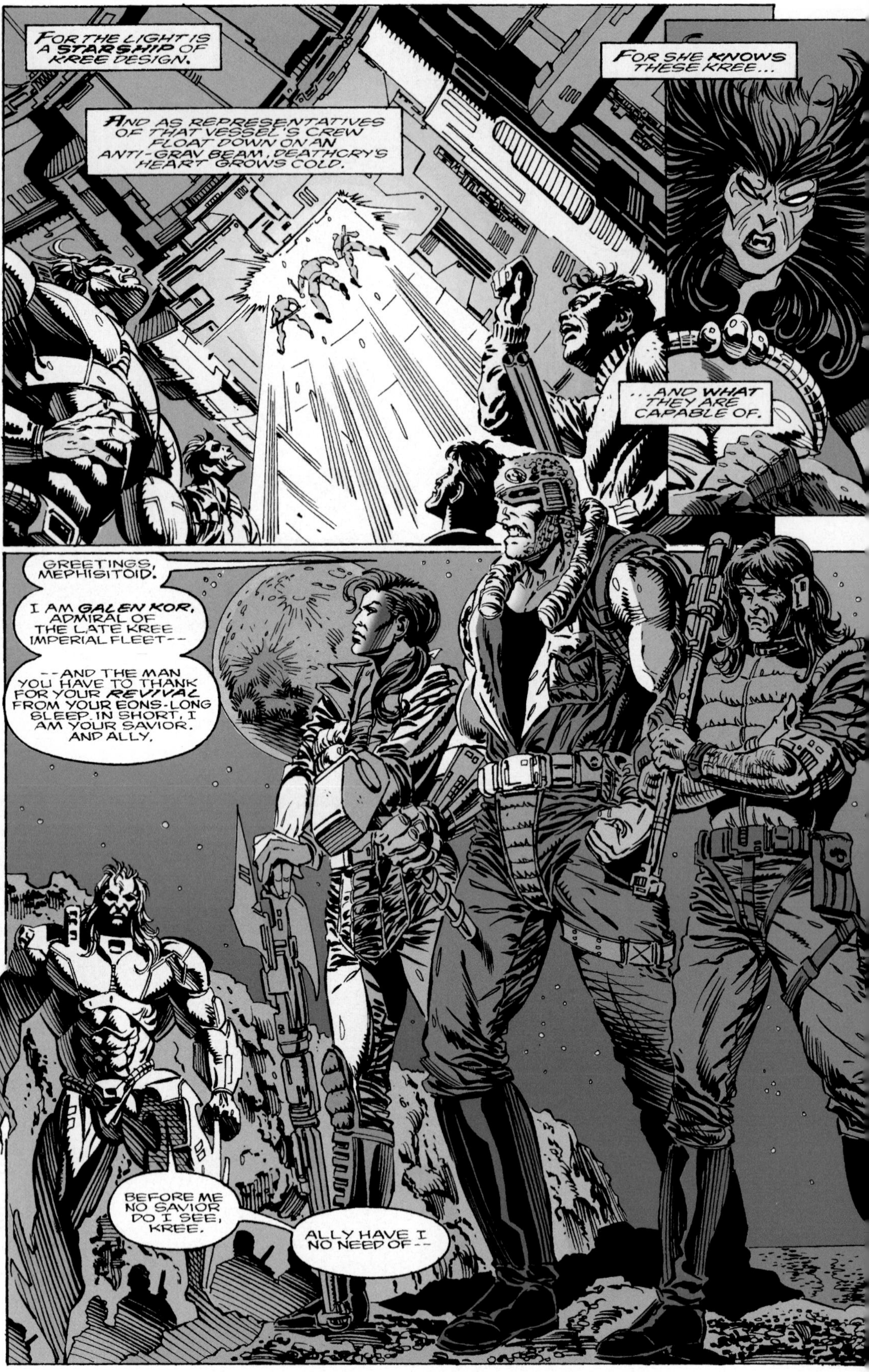
FOR THE LIGHT IS A STARSHIP OF KREE DESIGN.
AND AS REPRESENTATIVES OF THAT VESSEL'S CREW FLOAT DOWN ON AN ANTI-GRAV BEAM, DEATHCRY'S HEART GROWS COLD.
FOR SHE KNOWS THESE KREE...
...AND WHAT THEY ARE CAPABLE OF.
GREETINGS, MEPHISITOID.
I AM GALEN KOR, ADMIRAL OF THE LATE KREE IMPERIAL FLEET--
--AND THE MAN YOU HAVE TO THANK FOR YOUR REVIVAL FROM YOUR EONS-LONG SLEEP. IN SHORT, I AM YOUR SAVIOR. AND ALLY.
BEFORE ME NO SAVIOR DO I SEE, KREE.
ALLY HAVE I NO NEED OF--

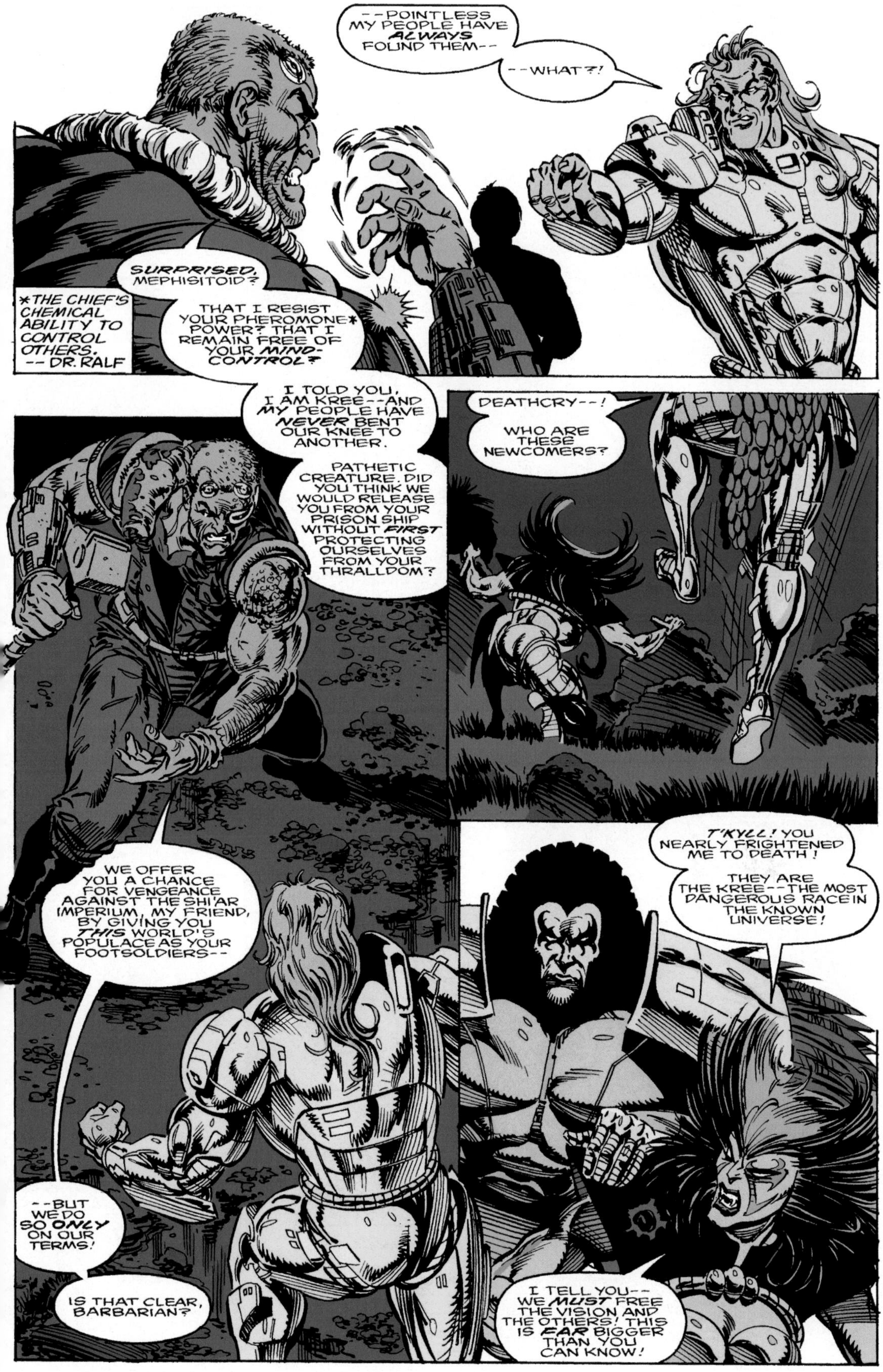
--POINTLESS MY PEOPLE HAVE ALWAYS FOUND THEM--
--WHAT?!
SURPRISED, MEPHISITOID?
*THE CHIEF'S CHEMICAL ABILITY TO CONTROL OTHERS. --DR. RALF
THAT I RESIST YOUR PHEROMONE* POWER? THAT I REMAIN FREE OF YOUR MIND-CONTROL?
I TOLD YOU, I AM KREE--AND MY PEOPLE HAVE NEVER BENT OUR KNEE TO ANOTHER.
PATHETIC CREATURE. DID YOU THINK WE WOULD RELEASE YOU FROM YOUR PRISON SHIP WITHOUT FIRST PROTECTING OURSELVES FROM YOUR THRALLDOM?
DEATHCRY--!
WHO ARE THESE NEWCOMERS?
WE OFFER YOU A CHANCE FOR VENGEANCE AGAINST THE SHI'AR IMPERIUM, MY FRIEND, BY GIVING YOU THIS WORLD'S POPULACE AS YOUR FOOTSOLDIERS--
--BUT WE DO SO ONLY ON OUR TERMS!
IS THAT CLEAR, BARBARIAN?
T'KYLL! YOU NEARLY FRIGHTENED ME TO DEATH!
THEY ARE THE KREE--THE MOST DANGEROUS RACE IN THE KNOWN UNIVERSE!
I TELL YOU--WE MUST FREE THE VISION AND THE OTHERS! THIS IS FAR BIGGER THAN YOU CAN KNOW!

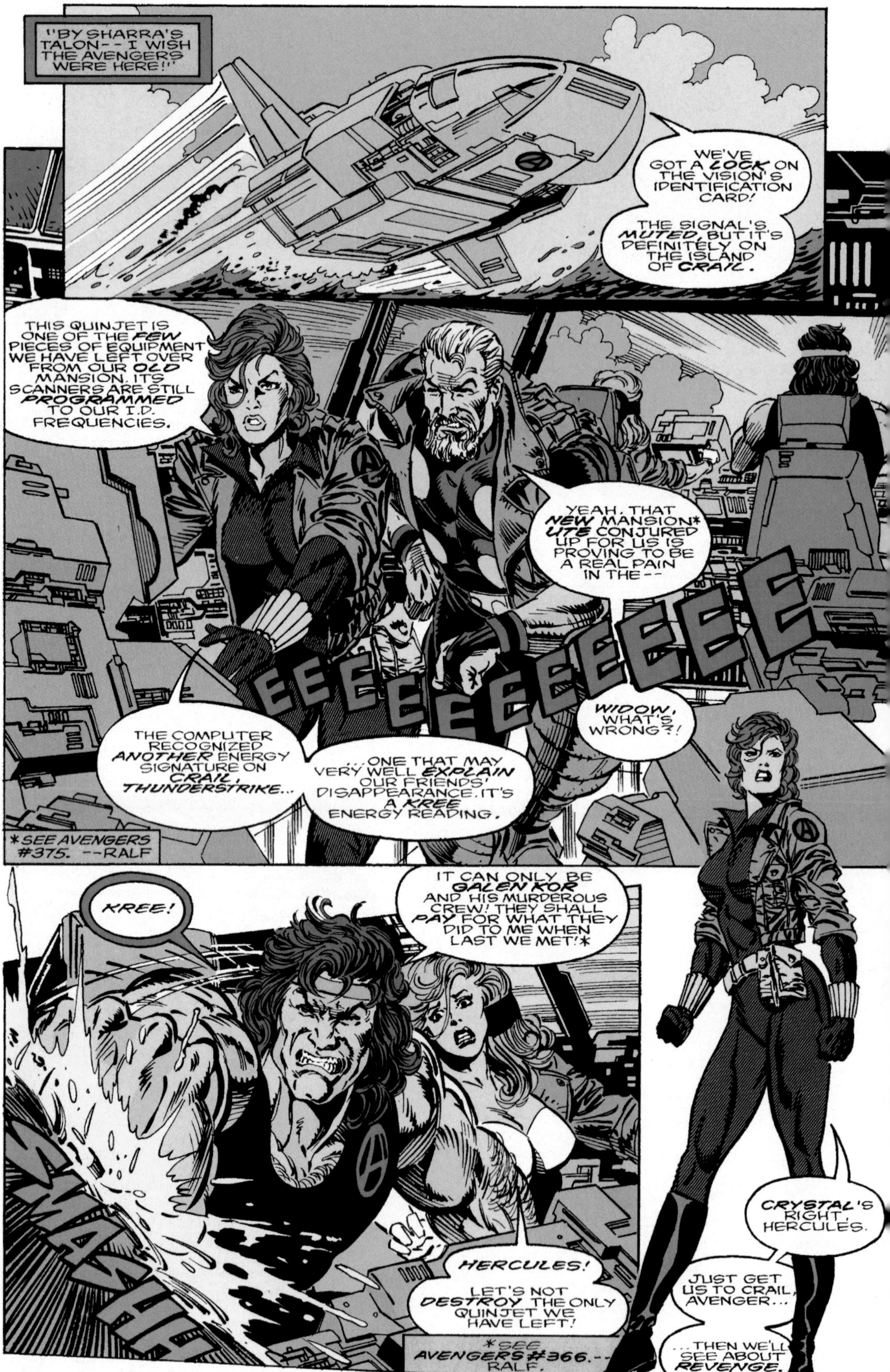

"BY SHARRA'S TALON-- I WISH THE AVENGERS WERE HERE!"
WE'VE GOT A LOCK ON THE VISION'S IDENTIFICATION CARD!
THE SIGNAL'S MUTED, BUT IT'S DEFINITELY ON THE ISLAND OF CRAIL.
THIS QUINJET IS ONE OF THE FEW PIECES OF EQUIPMENT WE HAVE LEFT OVER FROM OUR OLD MANSION. ITS SCANNERS ARE STILL PROGRAMMED TO OUR I.D. FREQUENCIES.
YEAH. THAT NEW MANSION* UTE CONJURED UP FOR US IS PROVING TO BE A REAL PAIN IN THE--
EEEEEEEEEEEEE
WIDOW, WHAT'S WRONG?!
THE COMPUTER RECOGNIZED ANOTHER ENERGY SIGNATURE ON CRAIL, THUNDERSTRIKE...
...ONE THAT MAY VERY WELL EXPLAIN OUR FRIENDS' DISAPPEARANCE. IT'S A KREE ENERGY READING.
*SEE AVENGERS #375. --RALF
KREE!
IT CAN ONLY BE GALEN KOR AND HIS MURDEROUS CREW! THEY SHALL PAY FOR WHAT THEY DID TO ME WHEN LAST WE MET!*
SMASH!
HERCULES!
LET'S NOT DESTROY THE ONLY QUINJET WE HAVE LEFT!
CRYSTAL'S RIGHT, HERCULES.
JUST GET US TO CRAIL, AVENGER...
...THEN WE'LL SEE ABOUT REVENGE.
*SEE AVENGERS #366.--RALF.

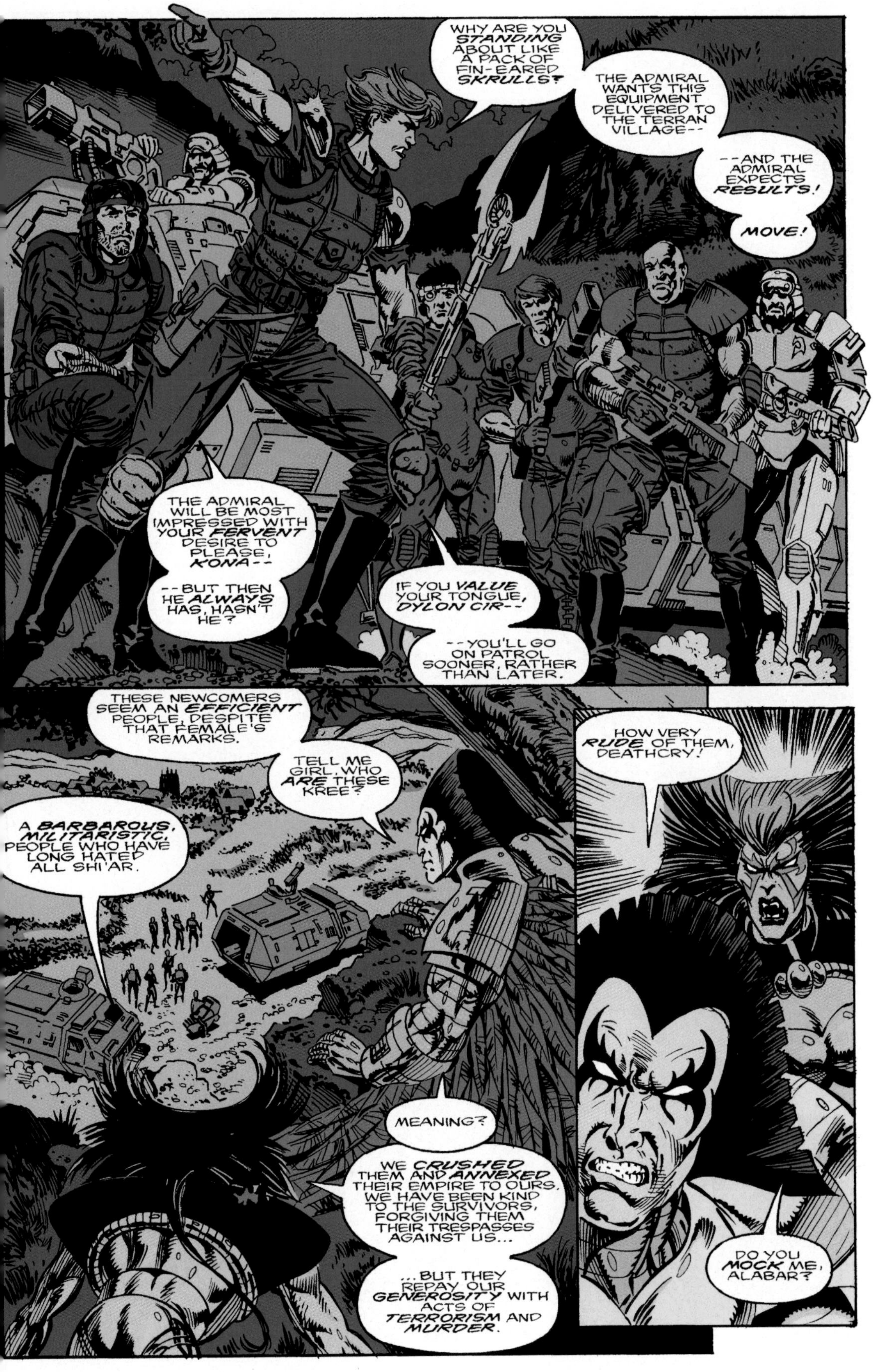
WHY ARE YOU STANDING ABOUT LIKE A PACK OF FIN-EARED SKRULLS?
THE ADMIRAL WANTS THIS EQUIPMENT DELIVERED TO THE TERRAN VILLAGE--
--AND THE ADMIRAL EXPECTS RESULTS!
MOVE!
THE ADMIRAL WILL BE MOST IMPRESSED WITH YOUR FERVENT DESIRE TO PLEASE, KONA--
--BUT THEN HE ALWAYS HAS, HASN'T HE?
IF YOU VALUE YOUR TONGUE, DYLON CIR--
--YOU'LL GO ON PATROL SOONER, RATHER THAN LATER.
THESE NEWCOMERS SEEM AN EFFICIENT PEOPLE, DESPITE THAT FEMALE'S REMARKS.
TELL ME GIRL, WHO ARE THESE KREE?
A BARBAROUS, MILITARISTIC, PEOPLE WHO HAVE LONG HATED ALL SHI'AR.
MEANING?
WE CRUSHED THEM AND ANNEXED THEIR EMPIRE TO OURS. WE HAVE BEEN KIND TO THE SURVIVORS, FORGIVING THEM THEIR TRESPASSES AGAINST US...
...BUT THEY REPAY OUR GENEROSITY WITH ACTS OF TERRORISM AND MURDER.
HOW VERY RUDE OF THEM, DEATHCRY!
DO YOU MOCK ME, ALABAR?

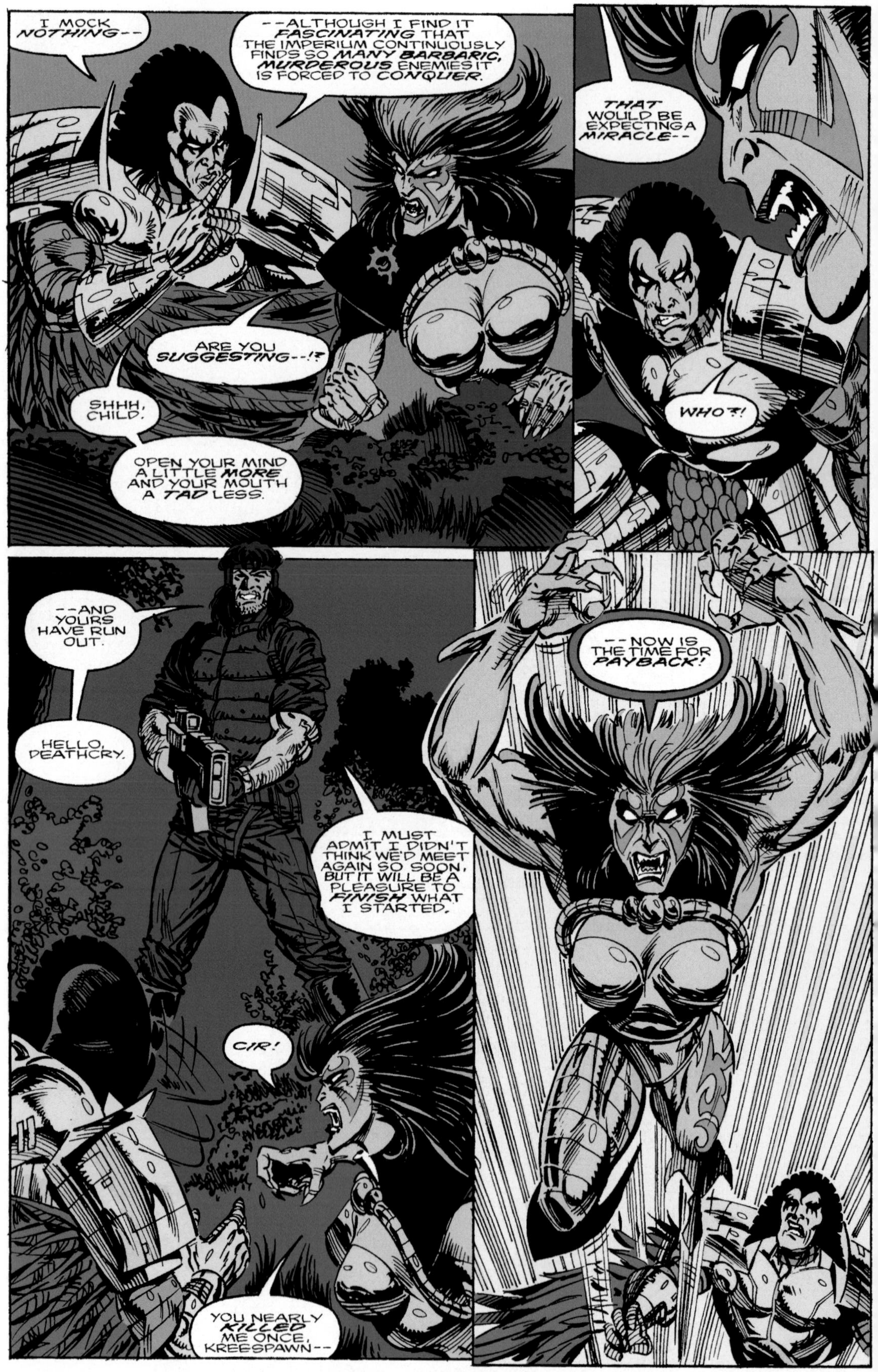
I MOCK NOTHING--
--ALTHOUGH I FIND IT FASCINATING THAT THE IMPERIUM CONTINUOUSLY FINDS SO MANY BARBARIC, MURDEROUS ENEMIES IT IS FORCED TO CONQUER.
ARE YOU SUGGESTING--!?
SHHH, CHILD.
OPEN YOUR MIND A LITTLE MORE AND YOUR MOUTH A TAD LESS.
THAT WOULD BE EXPECTING A MIRACLE--
WHO?!
--AND YOURS HAVE RUN OUT.
HELLO, DEATHCRY.
I MUST ADMIT I DIDN'T THINK WE'D MEET AGAIN SO SOON, BUT IT WILL BE A PLEASURE TO FINISH WHAT I STARTED.
CIR!
YOU NEARLY KILLED ME ONCE, KREESPAWN--
--NOW IS THE TIME FOR PAYBACK!

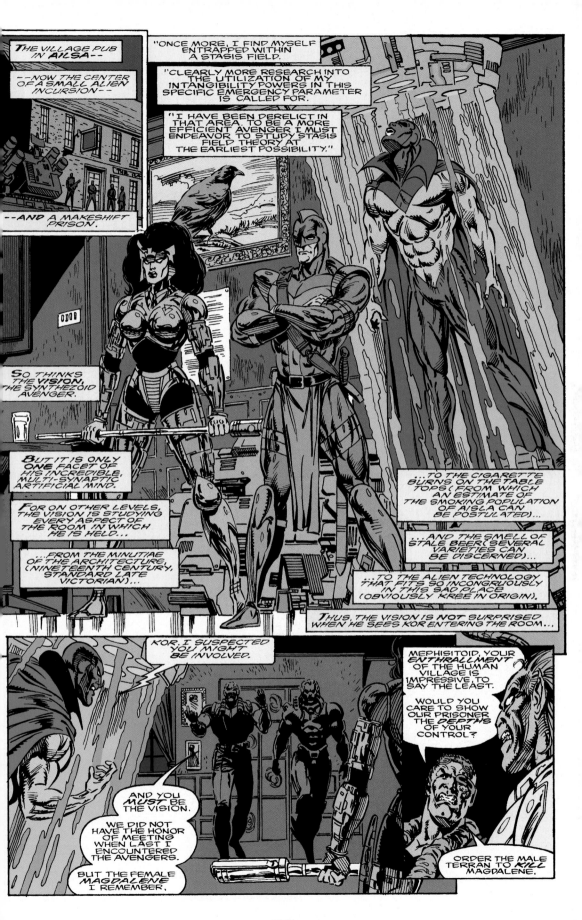

THE VILLAGE PUB IN AISLA--

--NOW THE CENTER OF A SMALL ALIEN INCURSION--

--AND A MAKESHIFT PRISON.

"ONCE MORE, I FIND MYSELF ENTRAPPED WITHIN A STASIS FIELD.

"CLEARLY MORE RESEARCH INTO THE UTILIZATION OF MY INTANGIBILITY POWERS IN THIS SPECIFIC EMERGENCY PARAMETER IS CALLED FOR.

"I HAVE BEEN DERELICT IN THAT AREA. TO BE A MORE EFFICIENT AVENGER I MUST ENDEAVOR TO STUDY STASIS FIELD THEORY AT THE EARLIEST POSSIBILITY."

SO THINKS THE VISION, THE SYNTHEZOID AVENGER.

BUT IT IS ONLY ONE FACET OF HIS INCREDIBLE, MULTI-SYNAPTIC ARTIFICIAL MIND.

FOR ON OTHER LEVELS, THE VISION IS STUDYING EVERY ASPECT OF THE ROOM IN WHICH HE IS HELD...

...FROM THE MINUTIAE OF THE ARCHITECTURE, (NINETEENTH CENTURY, STANDARD LATE VICTORIAN)...

...TO THE CIGARETTE BURNS ON THE TABLE TOPS (FROM WHICH AN ESTIMATE OF THE SMOKING POPULATION OF AISLA CAN BE POSTULATED)...

...AND THE SMELL OF STALE BEER (SEVERAL VARIETIES CAN BE DISCERNED)...

...TO THE ALIEN TECHNOLOGY THAT FITS SO INCONGRUOUSLY IN THIS SAD PLACE (OBVIOUSLY KREE IN ORIGIN).

THUS, THE VISION IS NOT SURPRISED WHEN HE SEES KOR ENTERING THE ROOM...

KOR. I SUSPECTED YOU MIGHT BE INVOLVED.

AND YOU MUST BE THE VISION. WE DID NOT HAVE THE HONOR OF MEETING WHEN LAST I ENCOUNTERED THE AVENGERS. BUT THE FEMALE MAGDALENE I REMEMBER.

MEPHISITOID, YOUR ENTHRALLMENT OF THE HUMAN VILLAGE IS IMPRESSIVE, TO SAY THE LEAST. WOULD YOU CARE TO SHOW OUR PRISONER THE DEPTHS OF YOUR CONTROL?

ORDER THE MALE TERRAN TO KILL MAGDALENE.

105

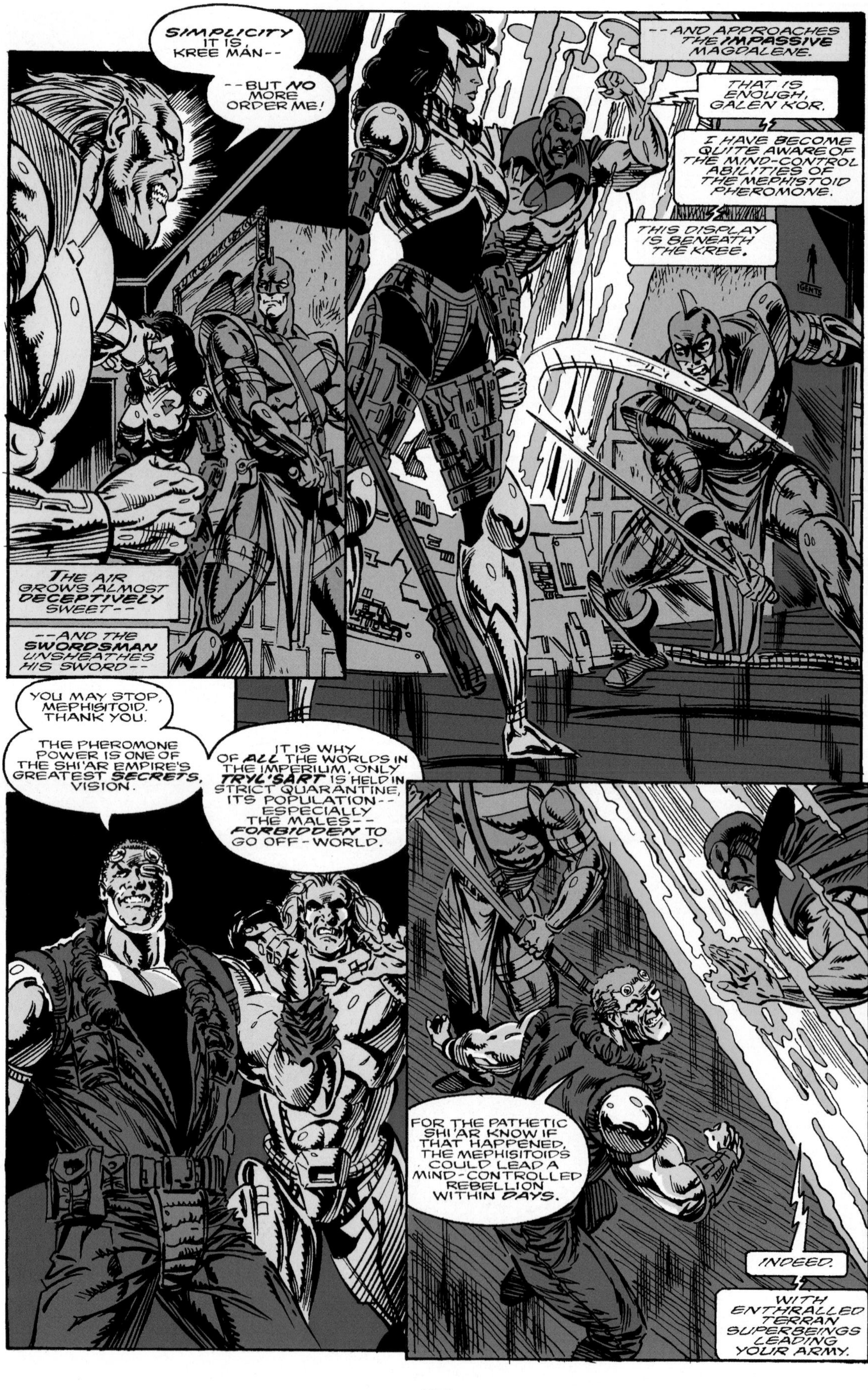
SIMPLICITY IT IS, KREE MAN--
--BUT NO MORE ORDER ME!
THE AIR GROWS ALMOST DECEPTIVELY SWEET--
--AND THE SWORDSMAN UNSHEATHES HIS SWORD--
--AND APPROACHES THE IMPASSIVE MAGDALENE.
THAT IS ENOUGH, GALEN KOR.
I HAVE BECOME QUITE AWARE OF THE MIND-CONTROL ABILITIES OF THE MEPHISTOID PHEROMONE.
THIS DISPLAY IS BENEATH THE KREE.
GENTS
YOU MAY STOP, MEPHISITOID. THANK YOU.
THE PHEROMONE POWER IS ONE OF THE SHI'AR EMPIRE'S GREATEST SECRETS, VISION.
IT IS WHY OF ALL THE WORLDS IN THE IMPERIUM, ONLY TRYL'SART IS HELD IN STRICT QUARANTINE, ITS POPULATION-- ESPECIALLY THE MALES-- FORBIDDEN TO GO OFF-WORLD.
FOR THE PATHETIC SHI'AR KNOW IF THAT HAPPENED, THE MEPHISITOIDS COULD LEAD A MIND-CONTROLLED REBELLION WITHIN DAYS.
INDEED.
WITH ENTHRALLED TERRAN SUPERBEINGS LEADING YOUR ARMY.

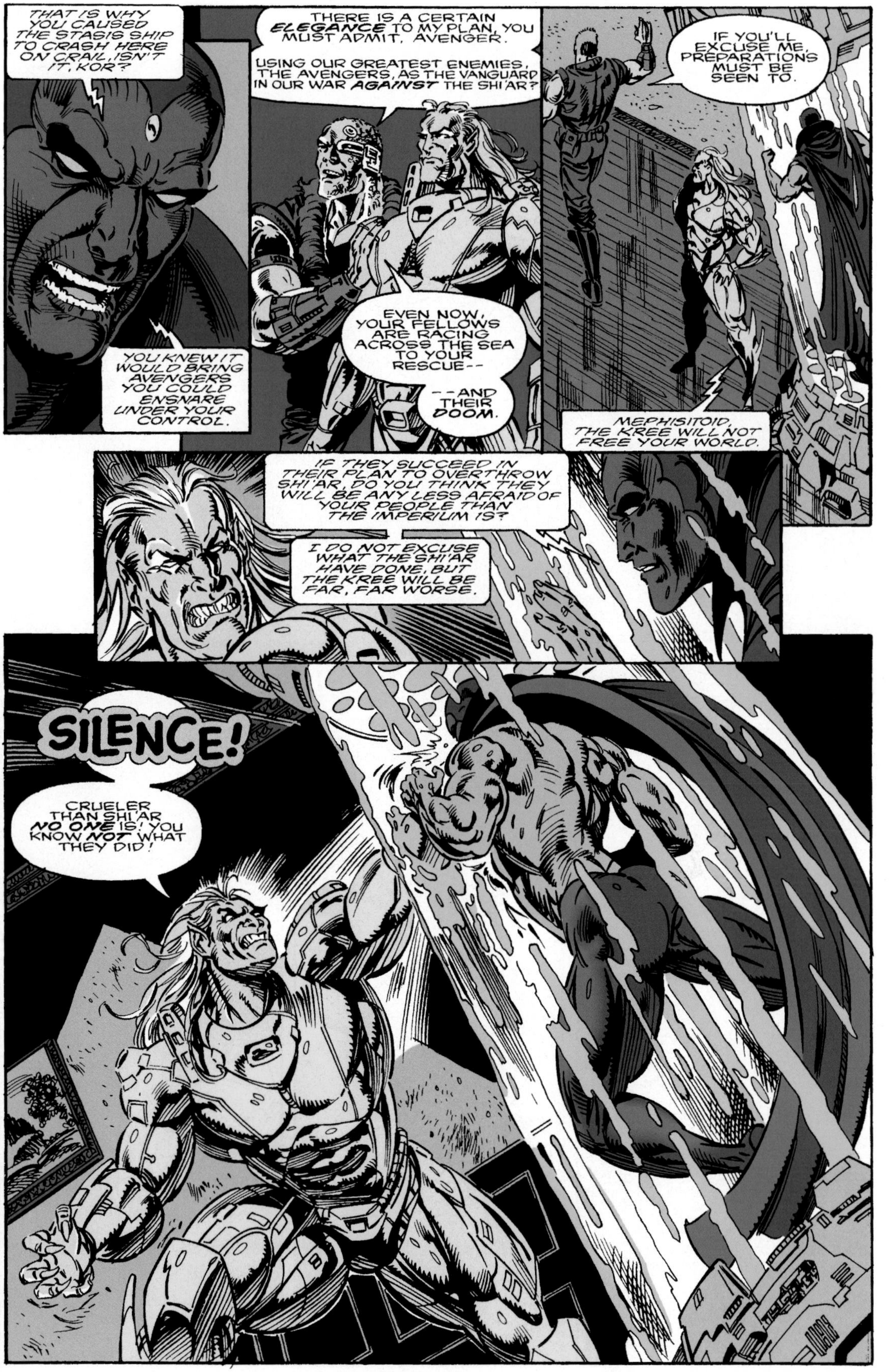

THAT IS WHY YOU CAUSED THE STASIS SHIP TO CRASH HERE ON CRAIL, ISN'T IT, KOR?
YOU KNEW IT WOULD BRING AVENGERS YOU COULD ENSNARE UNDER YOUR CONTROL.
THERE IS A CERTAIN ELEGANCE TO MY PLAN, YOU MUST ADMIT, AVENGER.
USING OUR GREATEST ENEMIES, THE AVENGERS, AS THE VANGUARD IN OUR WAR AGAINST THE SHI'AR?
EVEN NOW, YOUR FELLOWS ARE RACING ACROSS THE SEA TO YOUR RESCUE--
--AND THEIR DOOM.
IF YOU'LL EXCUSE ME, PREPARATIONS MUST BE SEEN TO.
MEPHISITOID, THE KREE WILL NOT FREE YOUR WORLD.
IF THEY SUCCEED IN THEIR PLAN TO OVERTHROW SHI'AR, DO YOU THINK THEY WILL BE ANY LESS AFRAID OF YOUR PEOPLE THAN THE IMPERIUM IS?
I DO NOT EXCUSE WHAT THE SHI'AR HAVE DONE, BUT THE KREE WILL BE FAR, FAR WORSE.
SILENCE!
CRUELER THAN SHI'AR NO ONE IS! YOU KNOW NOT WHAT THEY DID!

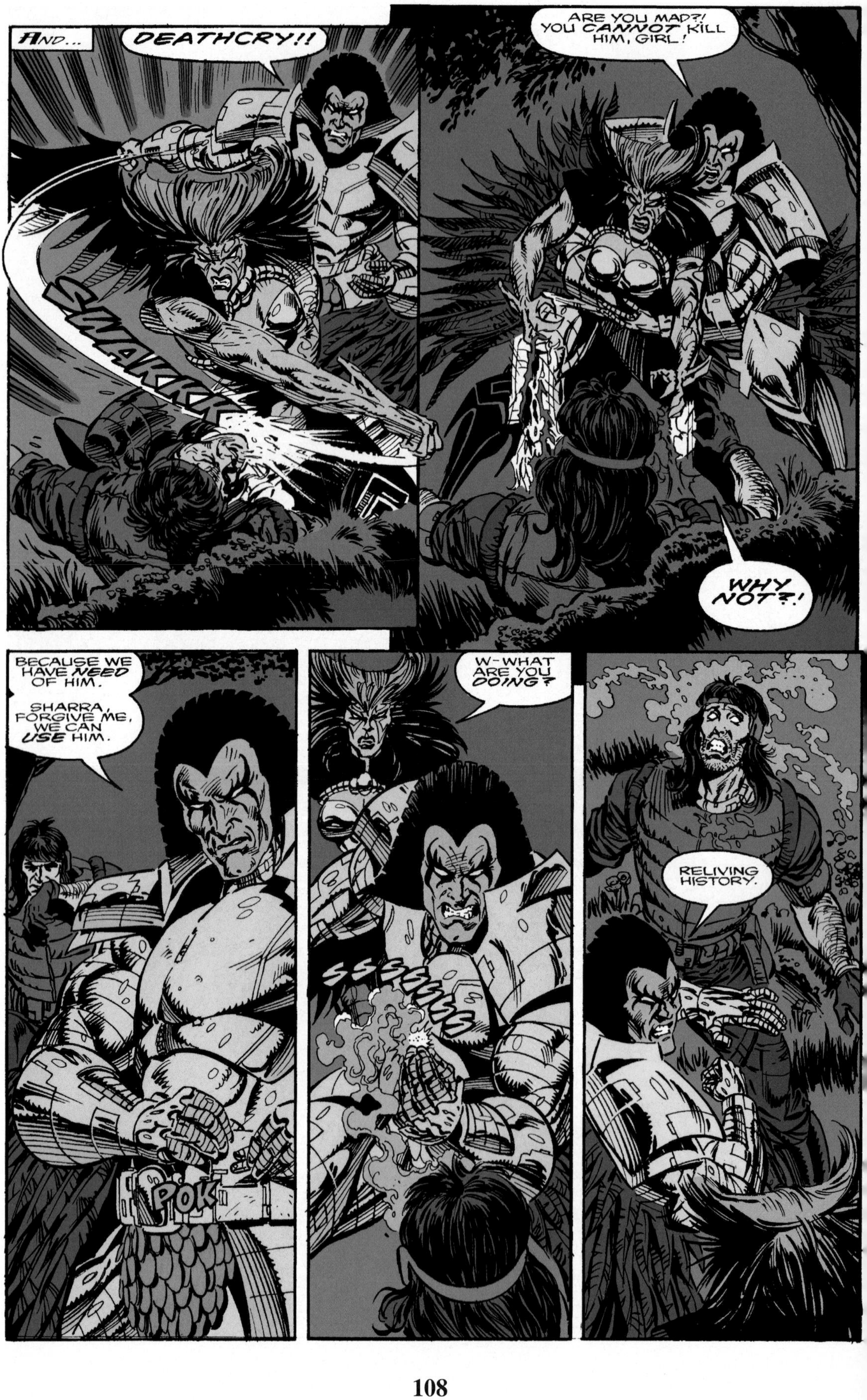
AND...
DEATHCRY!!
SHAKKK
ARE YOU MAD?! YOU CANNOT KILL HIM, GIRL!
WHY NOT?!
BECAUSE WE HAVE NEED OF HIM.
SHARRA, FORGIVE ME, WE CAN USE HIM.
POK
W-WHAT ARE YOU DOING?
SSSSSSSS
RELIVING HISTORY.

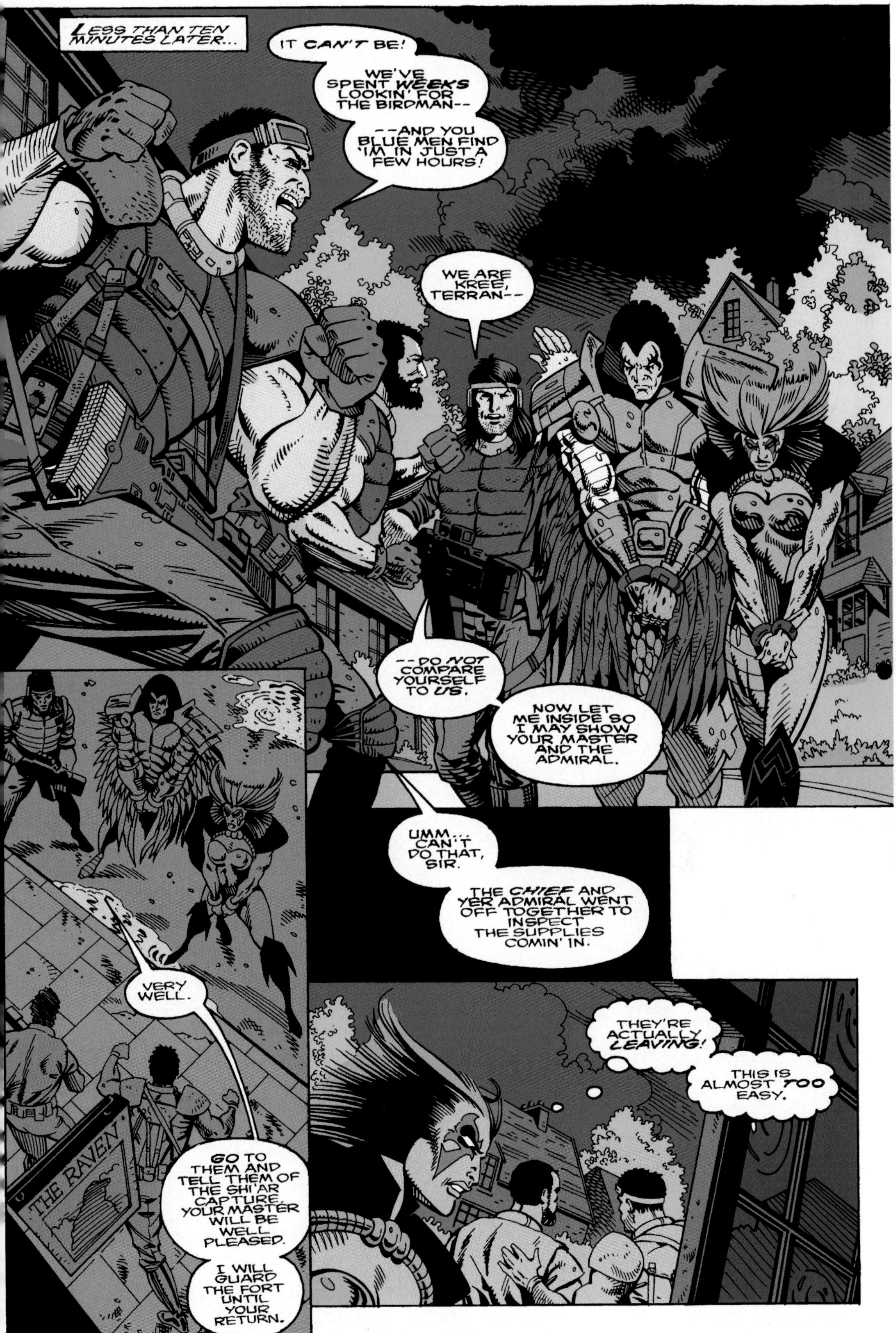
LESS THAN TEN MINUTES LATER...
IT CAN'T BE!
WE'VE SPENT WEEKS LOOKIN' FOR THE BIRDMAN--
--AND YOU BLUE MEN FIND 'IM IN JUST A FEW HOURS!
WE ARE KREE, TERRAN--
--DO NOT COMPARE YOURSELF TO US.
NOW LET ME INSIDE SO I MAY SHOW YOUR MASTER AND THE ADMIRAL.
UMM... CAN'T DO THAT, SIR.
THE CHIEF AND YER ADMIRAL WENT OFF TOGETHER TO INSPECT THE SUPPLIES COMIN' IN.
VERY WELL.
GO TO THEM AND TELL THEM OF THE SHI'AR CAPTURE. YOUR MASTER WILL BE WELL PLEASED.
I WILL GUARD THE FORT UNTIL YOUR RETURN.
THE RAVEN
THEY'RE ACTUALLY LEAVING!
THIS IS ALMOST TOO EASY.

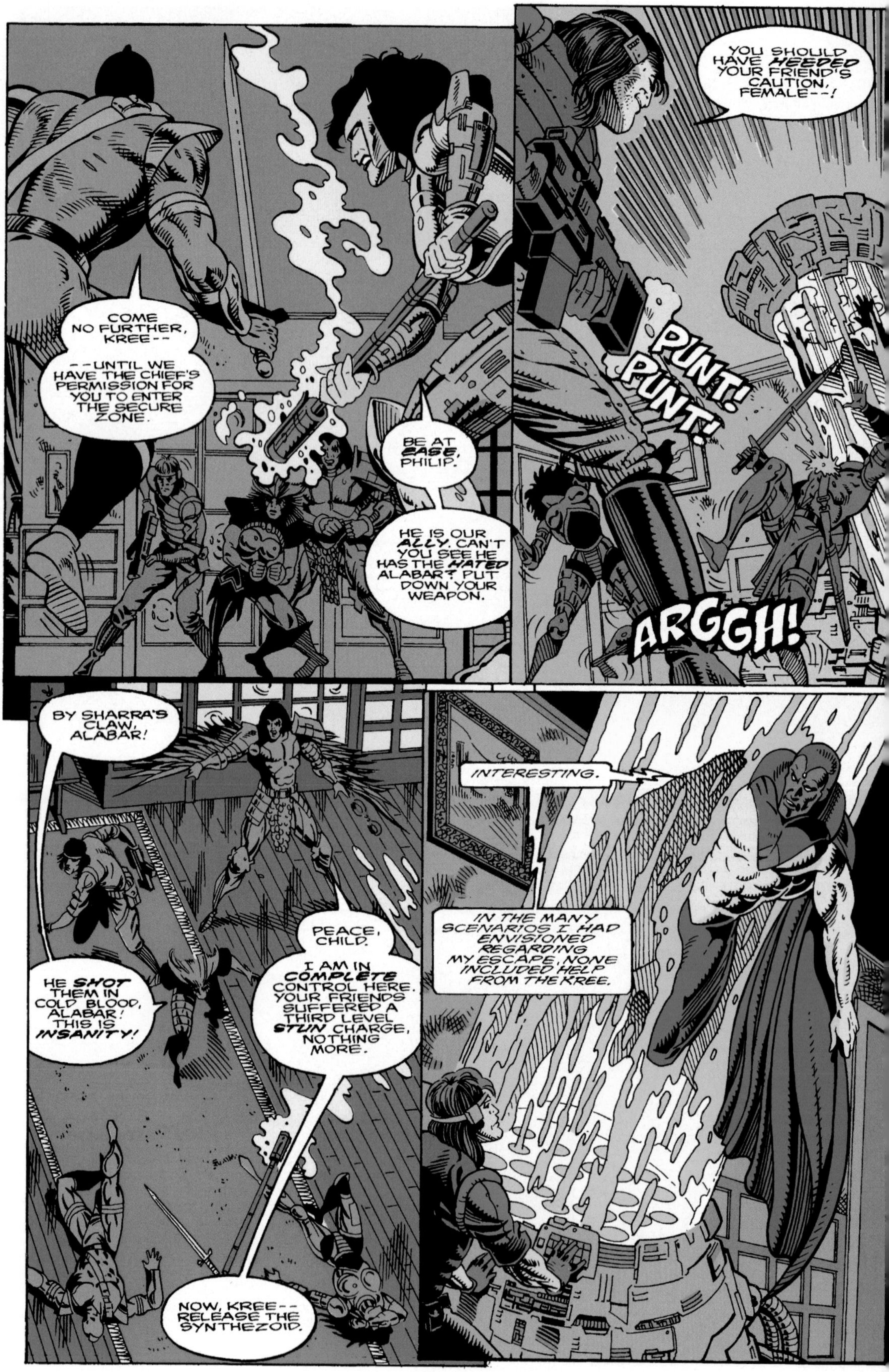
COME NO FURTHER, KREE--
--UNTIL WE HAVE THE CHIEF'S PERMISSION FOR YOU TO ENTER THE SECURE ZONE.
BE AT EASE, PHILIP.
HE IS OUR ALLY. CAN'T YOU SEE HE HAS THE HATED ALABAR? PUT DOWN YOUR WEAPON.
YOU SHOULD HAVE HEEDED YOUR FRIEND'S CAUTION, FEMALE--!
PUNT! PUNT!
ARGGH!
BY SHARRA'S CLAW, ALABAR!
HE SHOT THEM IN COLD BLOOD, ALABAR! THIS IS INSANITY!
PEACE, CHILD.
I AM IN COMPLETE CONTROL HERE. YOUR FRIENDS SUFFERED A THIRD LEVEL STUN CHARGE, NOTHING MORE.
NOW, KREE--RELEASE THE SYNTHEZOID.
INTERESTING.
IN THE MANY SCENARIOS I HAD ENVISIONED REGARDING MY ESCAPE, NONE INCLUDED HELP FROM THE KREE.

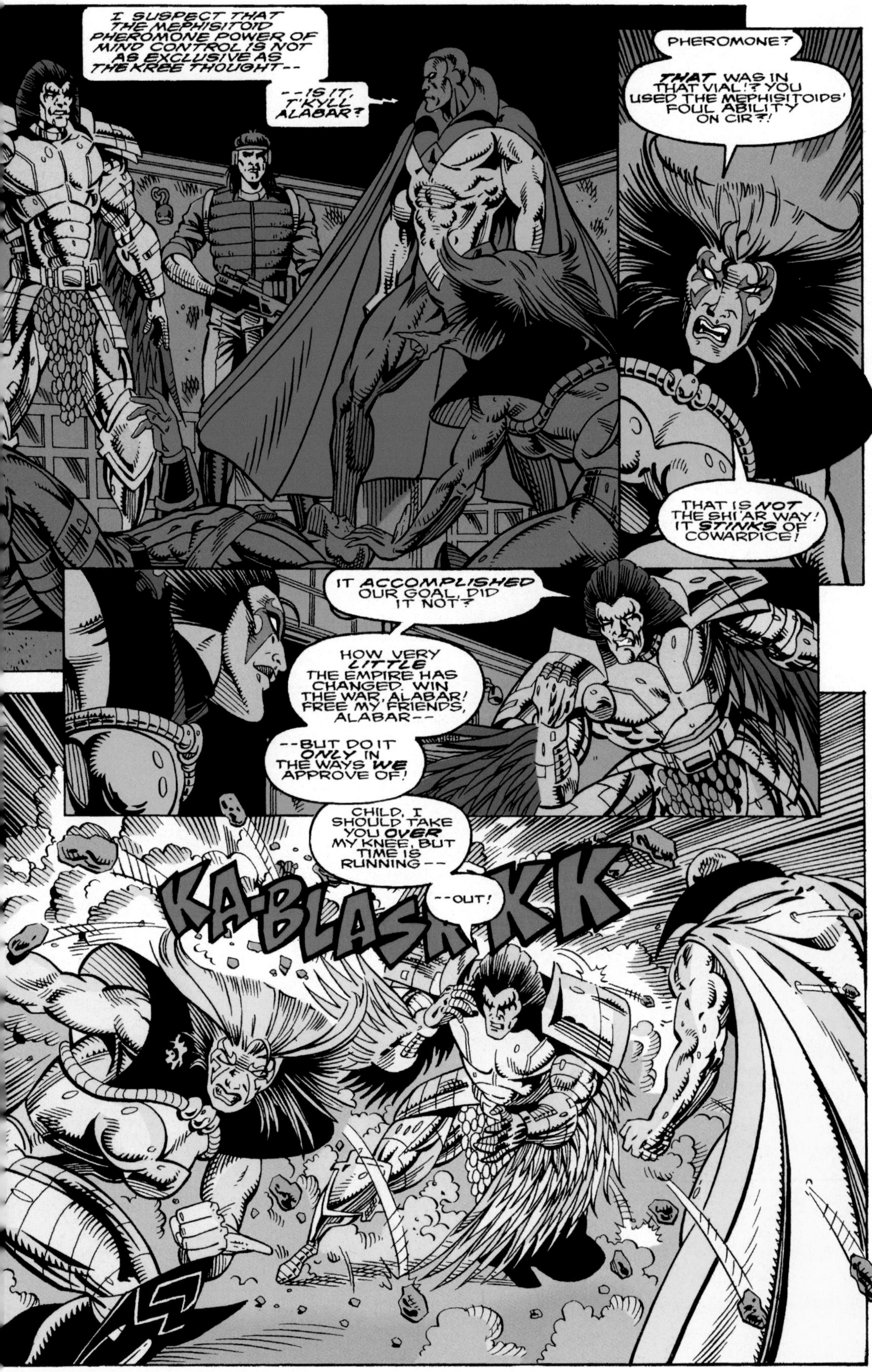
I SUSPECT THAT THE MEPHISITOID PHEROMONE POWER OF MIND CONTROL IS NOT AS EXCLUSIVE AS THE KREE THOUGHT--
--IS IT, T'KYLL ALABAR?
PHEROMONE?
THAT WAS IN THAT VIAL!? YOU USED THE MEPHISITOIDS' FOUL ABILITY ON CIR?!
THAT IS NOT THE SHI'AR WAY! IT STINKS OF COWARDICE!
IT ACCOMPLISHED OUR GOAL, DID IT NOT?
HOW VERY LITTLE THE EMPIRE HAS CHANGED. WIN THE WAR, ALABAR! FREE MY FRIENDS, ALABAR--
--BUT DO IT ONLY IN THE WAYS WE APPROVE OF!
CHILD, I SHOULD TAKE YOU OVER MY KNEE, BUT TIME IS RUNNING--
--OUT!
KA-BLASKKK

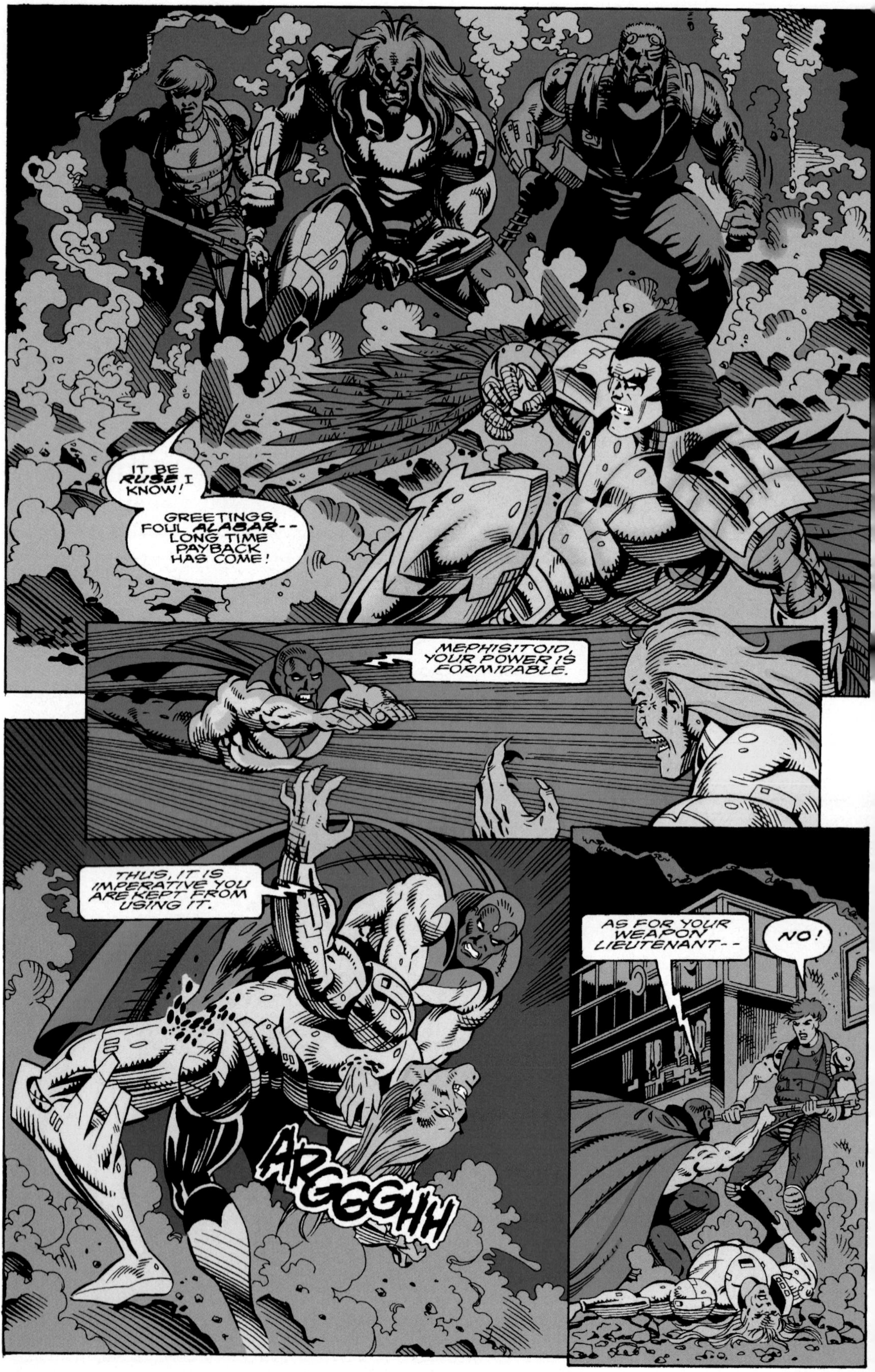
IT BE RUSE I KNOW!
GREETINGS, FOUL ALABAR-- LONG TIME PAYBACK HAS COME!
MEPHISITOID, YOUR POWER IS FORMIDABLE.
THUS, IT IS IMPERATIVE YOU ARE KEPT FROM USING IT.
ARGGGHH
AS FOR YOUR WEAPON LIEUTENANT--
NO!

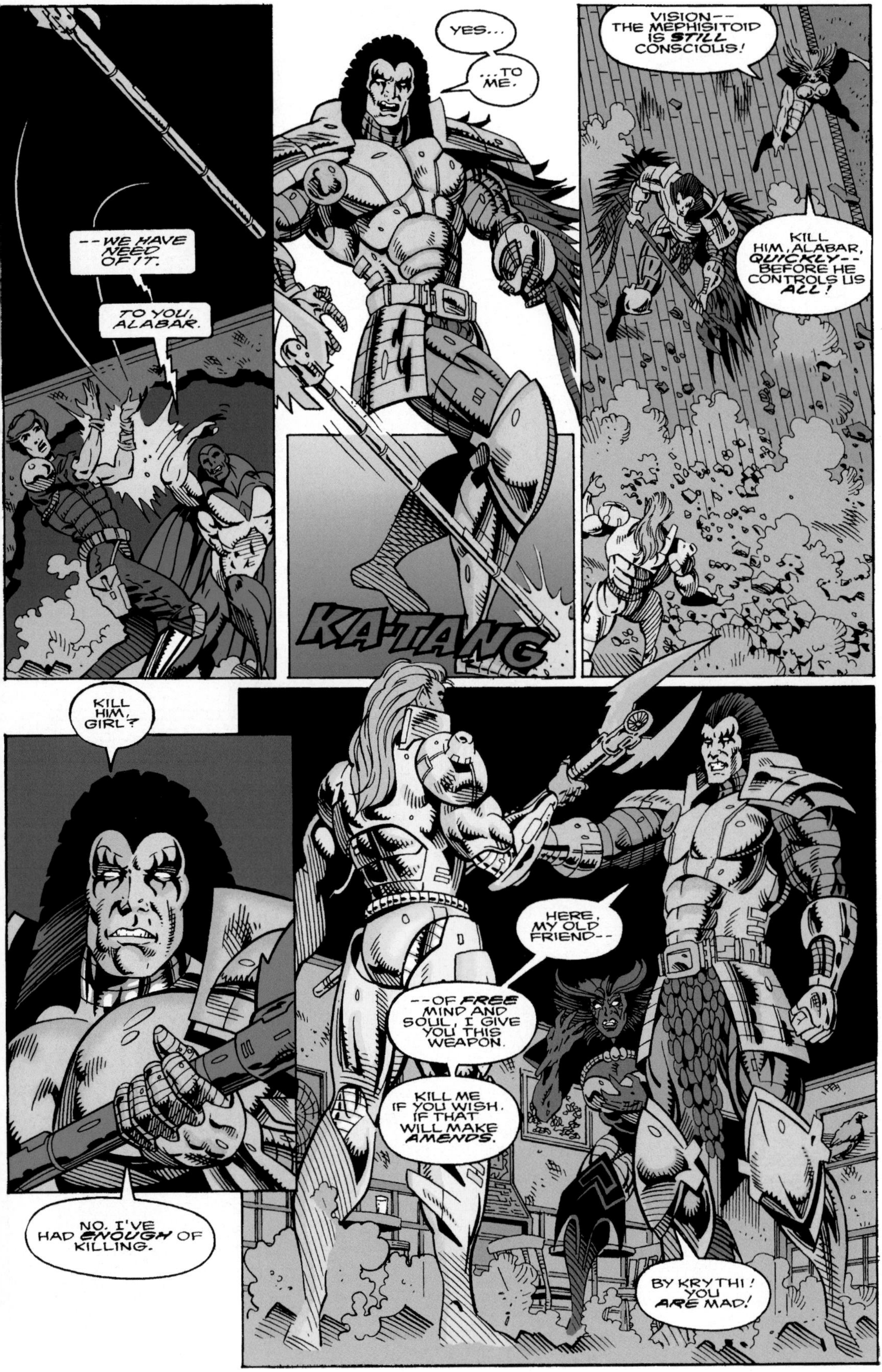
--WE HAVE NEED OF IT.
TO YOU, ALABAR.
YES...
...TO ME.
KA-TANG
VISION-- THE MEPHISITOID IS STILL CONSCIOUS!
KILL HIM, ALABAR, QUICKLY-- BEFORE HE CONTROLS US ALL!
KILL HIM, GIRL?
NO. I'VE HAD ENOUGH OF KILLING.
HERE, MY OLD FRIEND--
--OF FREE MIND AND SOUL, I GIVE YOU THIS WEAPON.
KILL ME IF YOU WISH. IF THAT WILL MAKE AMENDS.
BY KRYTHI! YOU ARE MAD!

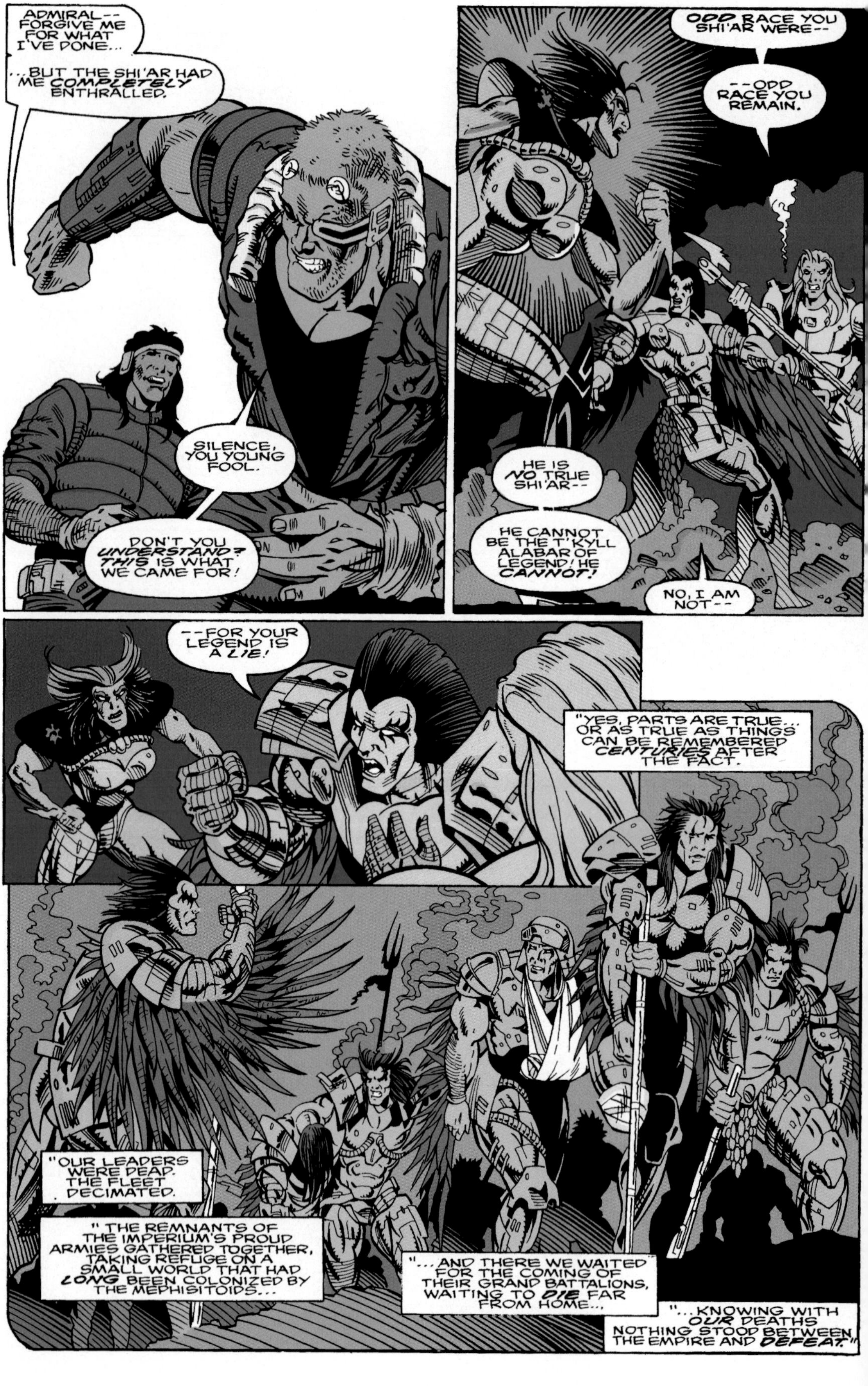
ADMIRAL-- FORGIVE ME FOR WHAT I'VE DONE...
...BUT THE SHI'AR HAD ME COMPLETELY ENTHRALLED.
SILENCE, YOU YOUNG FOOL.
DON'T YOU UNDERSTAND? THIS IS WHAT WE CAME FOR!
ODD RACE YOU SHI'AR WERE--
--ODD RACE YOU REMAIN.
HE IS NO TRUE SHI'AR--
HE CANNOT BE THE T'KYLL ALABAR OF LEGEND! HE CANNOT!
NO, I AM NOT--
--FOR YOUR LEGEND IS A LIE!
"YES, PARTS ARE TRUE... OR AS TRUE AS THINGS CAN BE REMEMBERED CENTURIES AFTER THE FACT.
"OUR LEADERS WERE DEAD. THE FLEET DECIMATED.
"THE REMNANTS OF THE IMPERIUM'S PROUD ARMIES GATHERED TOGETHER, TAKING REFUGE ON A SMALL WORLD THAT HAD LONG BEEN COLONIZED BY THE MEPHISITOIDS...
"...AND THERE WE WAITED FOR THE COMING OF THEIR GRAND BATTALIONS, WAITING TO DIE FAR FROM HOME...
"...KNOWING WITH OUR DEATHS NOTHING STOOD BETWEEN THE EMPIRE AND DEFEAT."

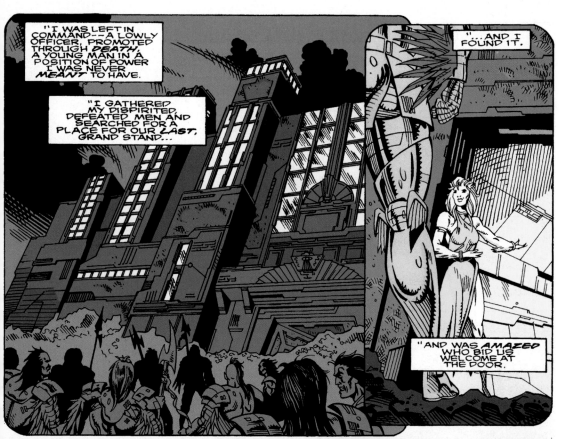

"I WAS LEFT IN COMMAND--A LOWLY OFFICER, PROMOTED THROUGH *DEATH,* A YOUNG MAN IN A POSITION OF POWER I WAS NEVER *MEANT* TO HAVE.

"I GATHERED MY DISPIRITED, DEFEATED MEN AND SEARCHED FOR A PLACE FOR OUR *LAST,* GRAND STAND...

"...AND I FOUND IT.

"AND WAS *AMAZED* WHO BID US WELCOME AT THE DOOR.

"FOR WE HAD *STUMBLED* UPON AN *ABBEY*--A PLACE OF MEPHISITOID WORSHIP HOUSED BY THE *FEMALES* OF THEIR RACE.

"WE HAD *NEVER* SEEN THEIR LIKE. FOR THE MALES HAD LONG HIDDEN THEIR MATES FROM US.

"BUT THESE WOMEN TOOK *PITY* ON US AND TOOK US IN.

"THEY CLOTHED US, FED US, *HEALED* US OUR INJURIES.

"AND SPOKE TO US OF *PEACE* BETWEEN OUR TWO PEOPLES."

THAT IS A *LIE!* A *PATHETIC* FAIRY TALE.

THE MEPHISITOIDS ARE *BARBARIANS!* THEY *KILLED* INDISCRIMINATELY.

SO *WE* THOUGHT THE SHI'AR.

115

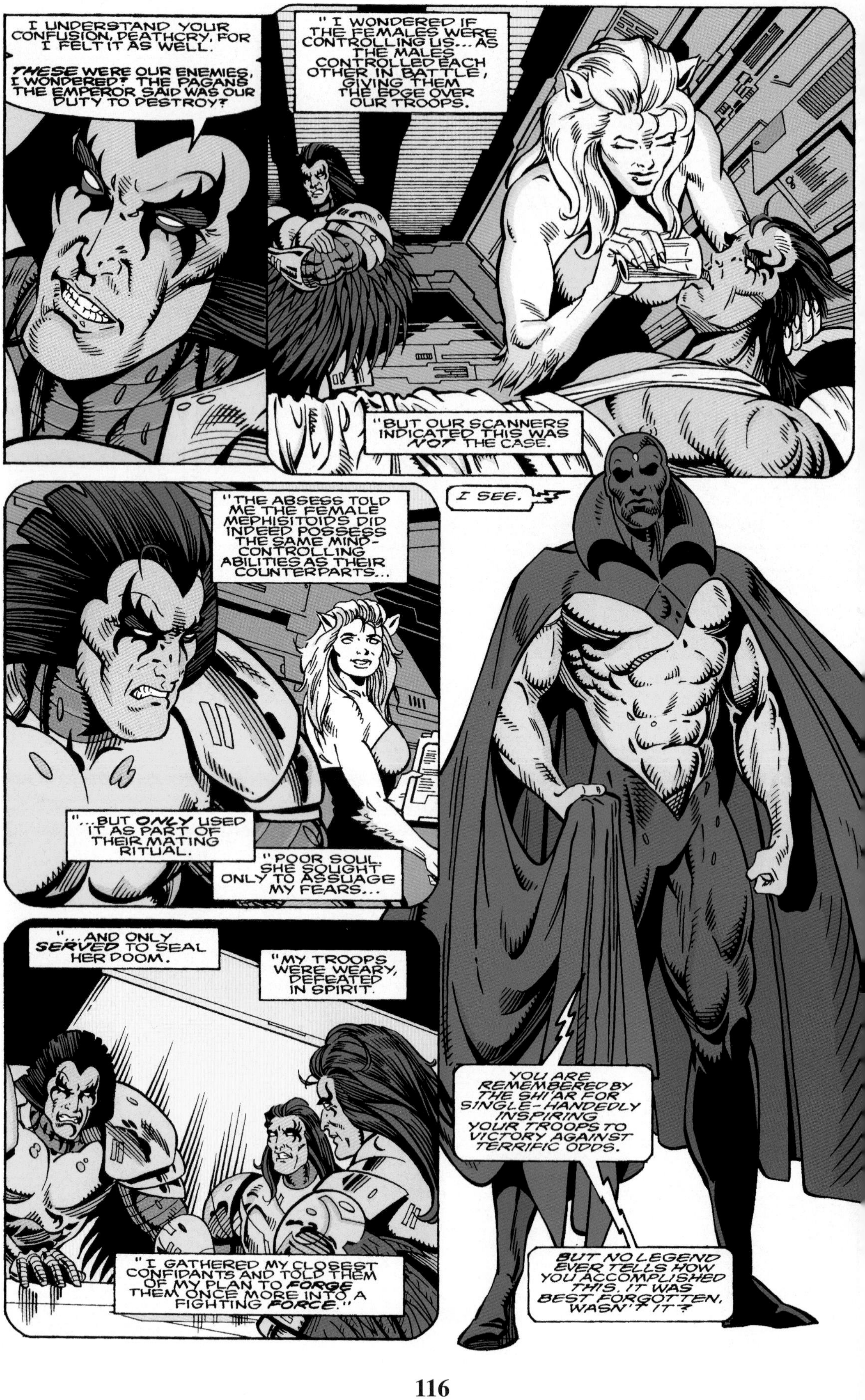
I UNDERSTAND YOUR CONFUSION, DEATHCRY, FOR I FELT IT AS WELL.
THESE WERE OUR ENEMIES, I WONDERED? THE PAGANS THE EMPEROR SAID WAS OUR DUTY TO DESTROY?
"I WONDERED IF THE FEMALES WERE CONTROLLING US... AS THE MALES CONTROLLED EACH OTHER IN BATTLE, GIVING THEM THE EDGE OVER OUR TROOPS.
"BUT OUR SCANNERS INDICATED THIS WAS NOT THE CASE.
"THE ABSESS TOLD ME THE FEMALE MEPHISITOIDS DID INDEED POSSESS THE SAME MIND-CONTROLLING ABILITIES AS THEIR COUNTERPARTS...
"...BUT ONLY USED IT AS PART OF THEIR MATING RITUAL.
"POOR SOUL. SHE SOUGHT ONLY TO ASSUAGE MY FEARS...
I SEE.
"...AND ONLY SERVED TO SEAL HER DOOM.
"MY TROOPS WERE WEARY, DEFEATED IN SPIRIT.
"I GATHERED MY CLOSEST CONFIDANTS AND TOLD THEM OF MY PLAN TO FORGE THEM ONCE MORE INTO A FIGHTING FORCE."
YOU ARE REMEMBERED BY THE SHI'AR FOR SINGLE-HANDEDLY INSPIRING YOUR TROOPS TO VICTORY AGAINST TERRIFIC ODDS.
BUT NO LEGEND EVER TELLS HOW YOU ACCOMPLISHED THIS. IT WAS BEST FORGOTTEN, WASN'T IT?

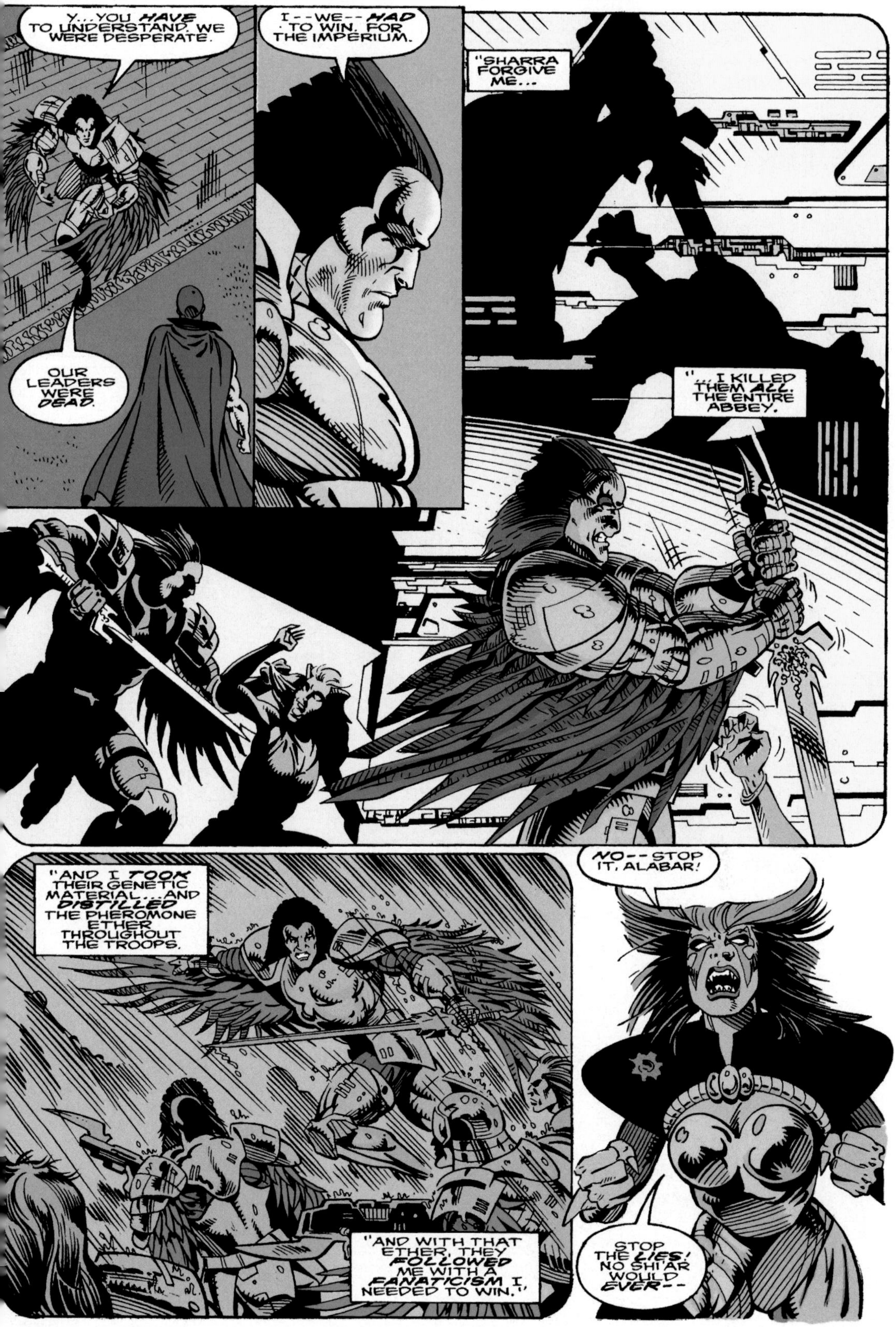

Y...YOU HAVE TO UNDERSTAND. WE WERE DESPERATE.
OUR LEADERS WERE DEAD.
I--WE--HAD TO WIN. FOR THE IMPERIUM.
"SHARRA FORGIVE ME...
"...I KILLED THEM ALL. THE ENTIRE ABBEY.
"AND I TOOK THEIR GENETIC MATERIAL...AND DISTILLED THE PHEROMONE ETHER THROUGHOUT THE TROOPS.
"AND WITH THAT ETHER, THEY FOLLOWED ME WITH A FANATICISM I NEEDED TO WIN."
NO--STOP IT, ALABAR!
STOP THE LIES! NO SHI'AR WOULD EVER--

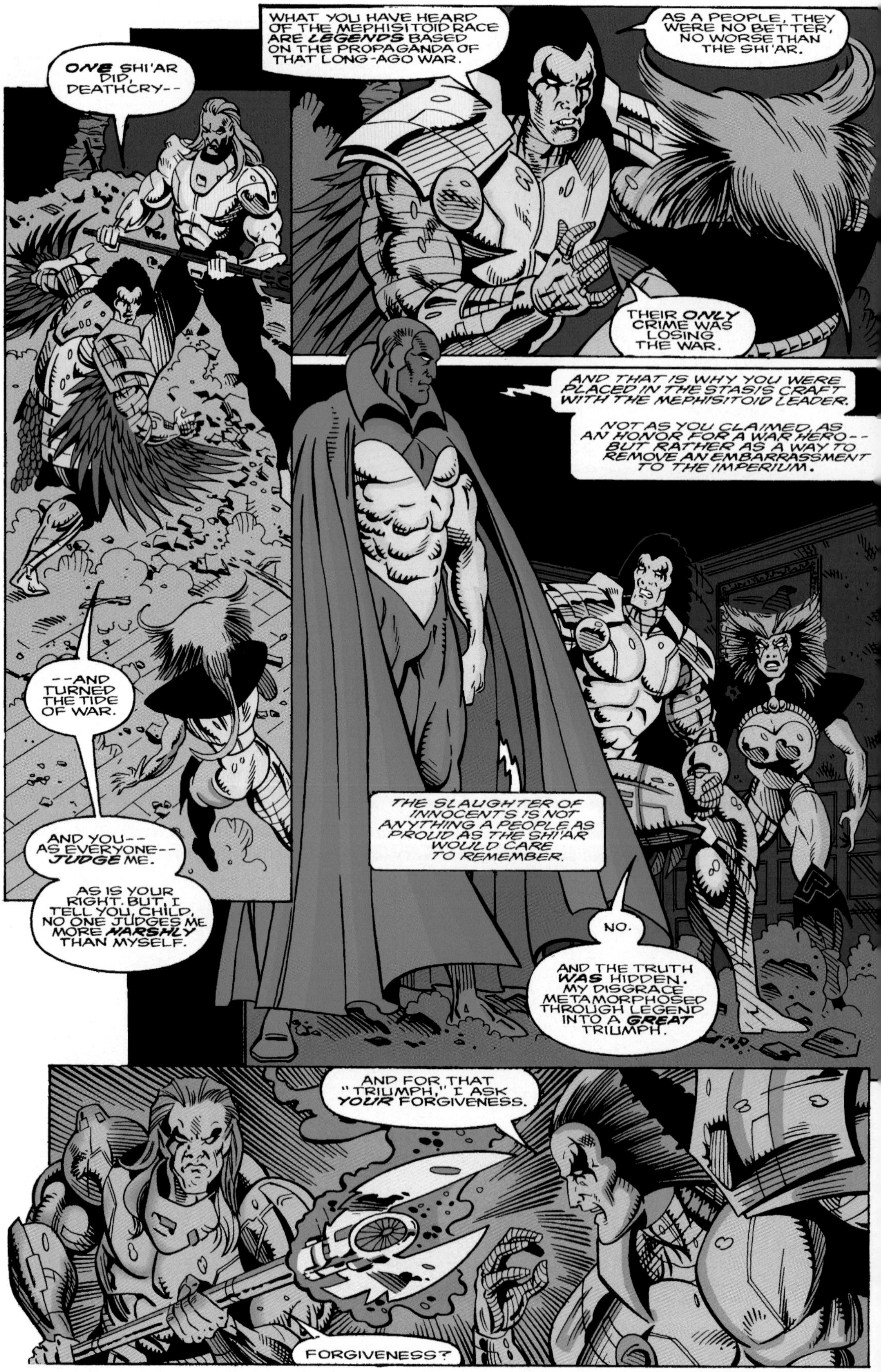
ONE SHI'AR DID, DEATHCRY--
WHAT YOU HAVE HEARD OF THE MEPHISITOID RACE ARE LEGENDS BASED ON THE PROPAGANDA OF THAT LONG-AGO WAR.
AS A PEOPLE, THEY WERE NO BETTER, NO WORSE THAN THE SHI'AR.
THEIR ONLY CRIME WAS LOSING THE WAR.
AND THAT IS WHY YOU WERE PLACED IN THE STASIS CRAFT WITH THE MEPHISITOID LEADER.
NOT AS YOU CLAIMED, AS AN HONOR FOR A WAR HERO-- BUT RATHER AS A WAY TO REMOVE AN EMBARRASSMENT TO THE IMPERIUM.
--AND TURNED THE TIDE OF WAR.
THE SLAUGHTER OF INNOCENTS IS NOT ANYTHING A PEOPLE AS PROUD AS THE SHI'AR WOULD CARE TO REMEMBER.
AND YOU-- AS EVERYONE-- JUDGE ME.
AS IS YOUR RIGHT. BUT, I TELL YOU, CHILD, NO ONE JUDGES ME MORE HARSHLY THAN MYSELF.
NO.
AND THE TRUTH WAS HIDDEN. MY DISGRACE METAMORPHOSED THROUGH LEGEND INTO A GREAT TRIUMPH.
AND FOR THAT "TRIUMPH," I ASK YOUR FORGIVENESS.
FORGIVENESS?

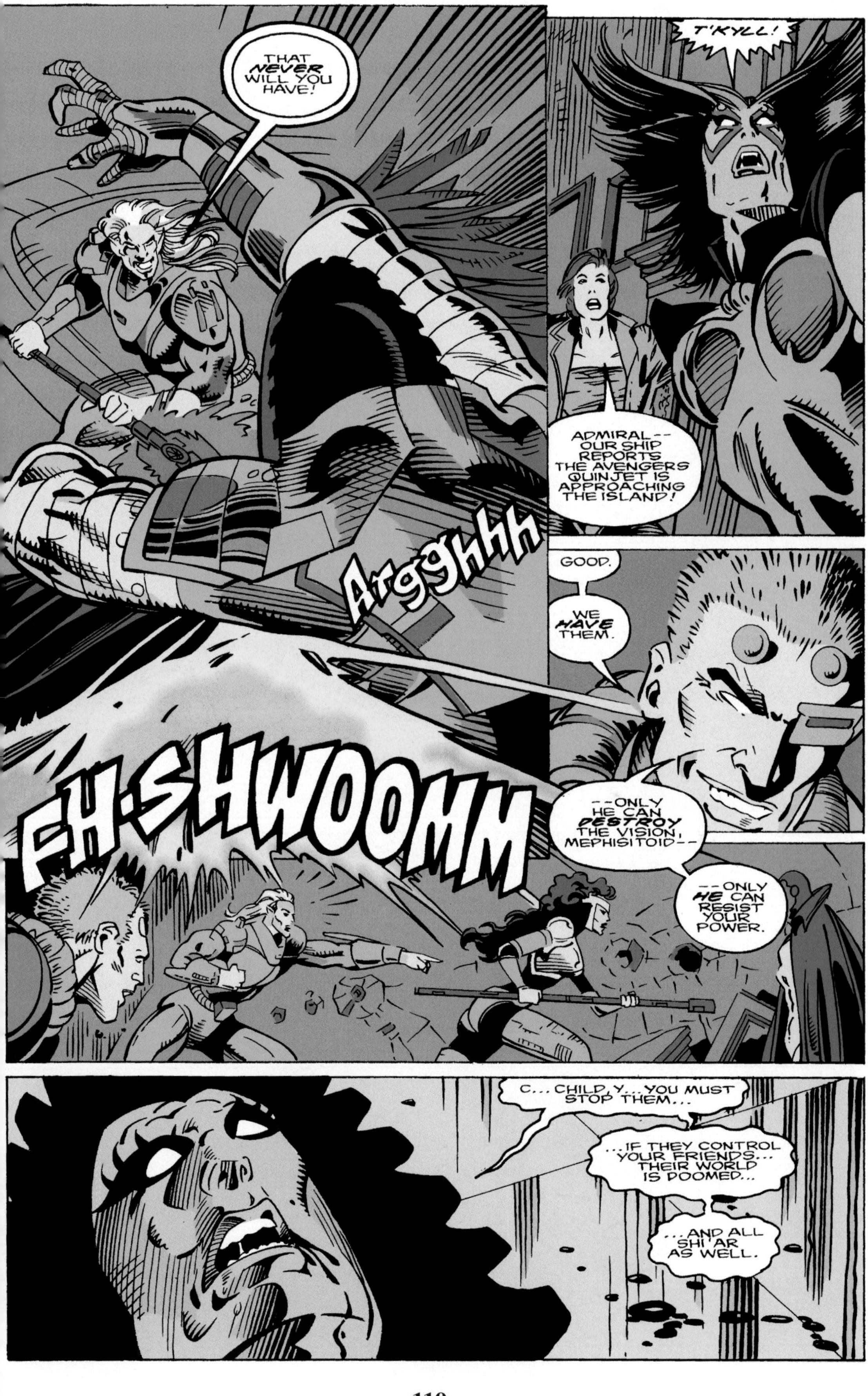
THAT NEVER WILL YOU HAVE!
Argghhh
FH-SHWOOMM
T'KYLL!
ADMIRAL-- OUR SHIP REPORTS THE AVENGERS QUINJET IS APPROACHING THE ISLAND!
GOOD.
WE HAVE THEM.
--ONLY HE CAN DESTROY THE VISION, MEPHISITOID--
--ONLY HE CAN RESIST YOUR POWER.
C... CHILD, Y... YOU MUST STOP THEM...
...IF THEY CONTROL YOUR FRIENDS... THEIR WORLD IS DOOMED...
...AND ALL SHI'AR AS WELL.

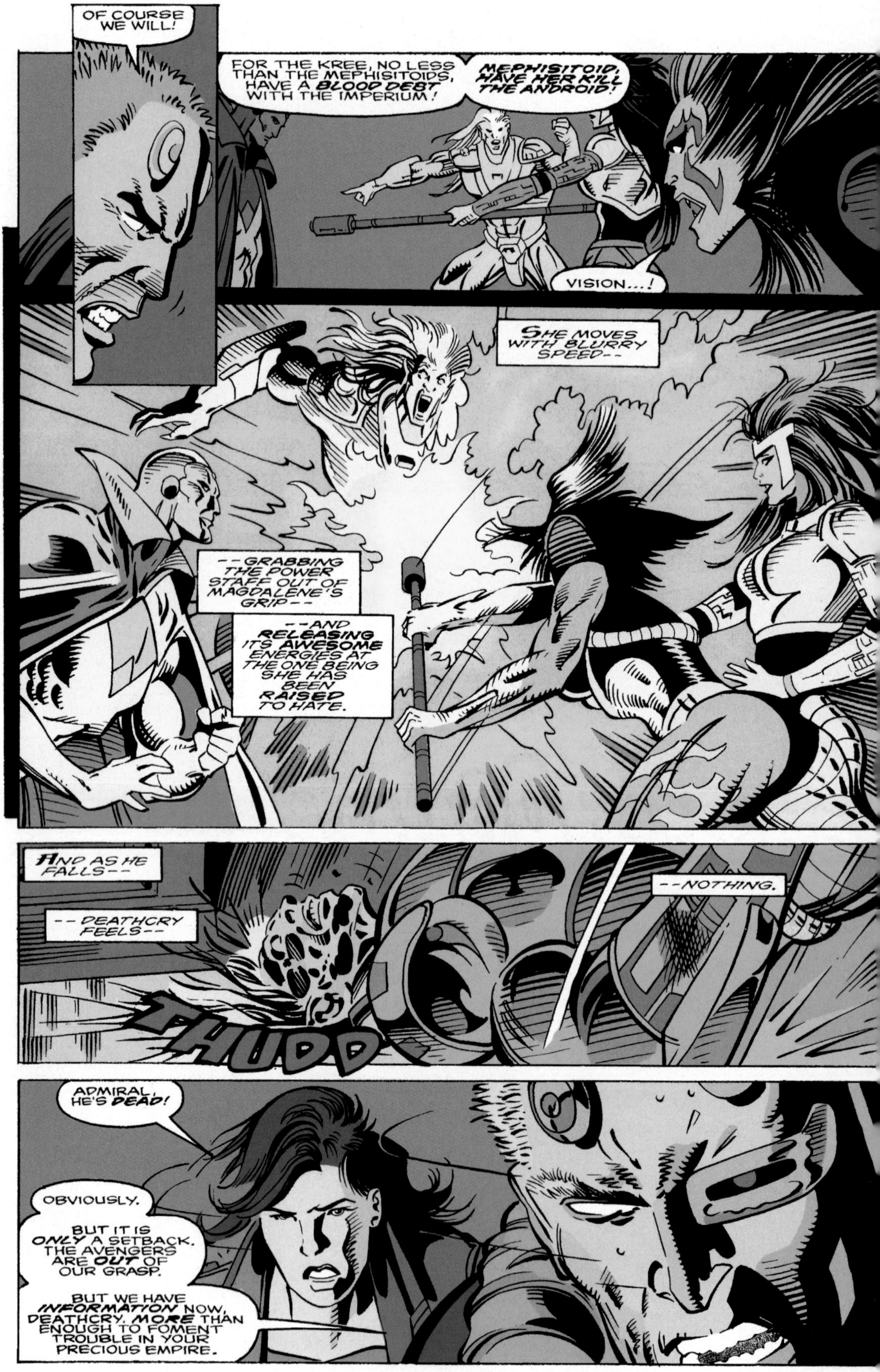

OF COURSE WE WILL!
FOR THE KREE, NO LESS THAN THE MEPHISITOIDS, HAVE A BLOOD DEST WITH THE IMPERIUM!
MEPHISITOID, HAVE HER KILL THE ANDROID!
VISION...!
SHE MOVES WITH BLURRY SPEED--
--GRABBING THE POWER STAFF OUT OF MAGDALENE'S GRIP--
--AND RELEASING IT'S AWESOME ENERGIES AT THE ONE BEING SHE HAS BEEN RAISED TO HATE.
AND AS HE FALLS--
--DEATHCRY FEELS--
--NOTHING.
THUDD
ADMIRAL, HE'S DEAD!
OBVIOUSLY.
BUT IT IS ONLY A SETBACK. THE AVENGERS ARE OUT OF OUR GRASP.
BUT WE HAVE INFORMATION NOW, DEATHCRY. MORE THAN ENOUGH TO FOMENT TROUBLE IN YOUR PRECIOUS EMPIRE.

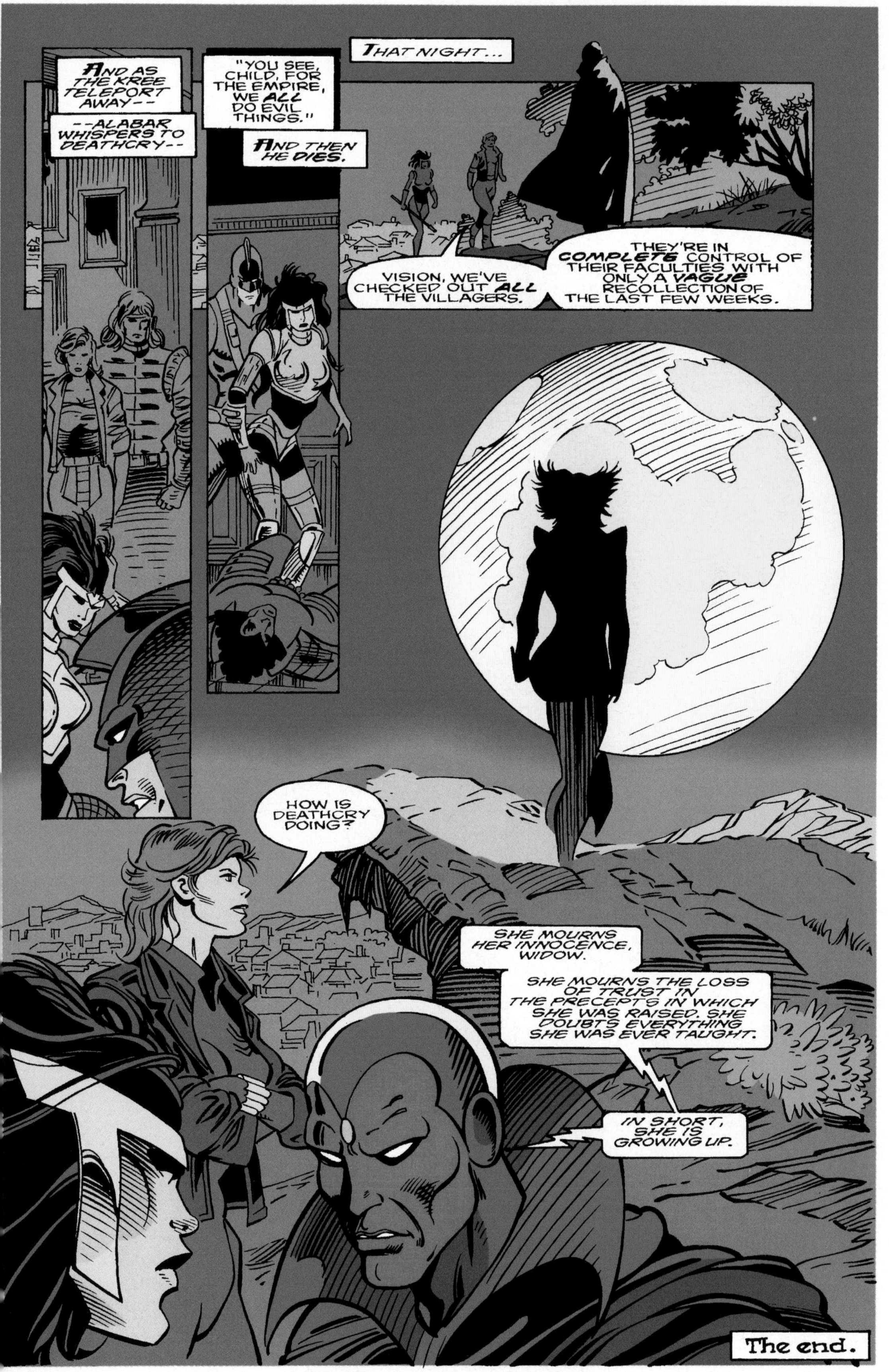
AND AS THE KREE TELEPORT AWAY--
--ALABAR WHISPERS TO DEATHCRY--
"YOU SEE, CHILD, FOR THE EMPIRE, WE ALL DO EVIL THINGS."
AND THEN HE DIES.
THAT NIGHT...
VISION, WE'VE CHECKED OUT ALL THE VILLAGERS.
THEY'RE IN COMPLETE CONTROL OF THEIR FACULTIES WITH ONLY A VAGUE RECOLLECTION OF THE LAST FEW WEEKS.
HOW IS DEATHCRY DOING?
SHE MOURNS HER INNOCENCE, WIDOW.
SHE MOURNS THE LOSS OF TRUST IN THE PRECEPTS IN WHICH SHE WAS RAISED. SHE DOUBTS EVERYTHING SHE WAS EVER TAUGHT.
IN SHORT, SHE IS GROWING UP.
The end.

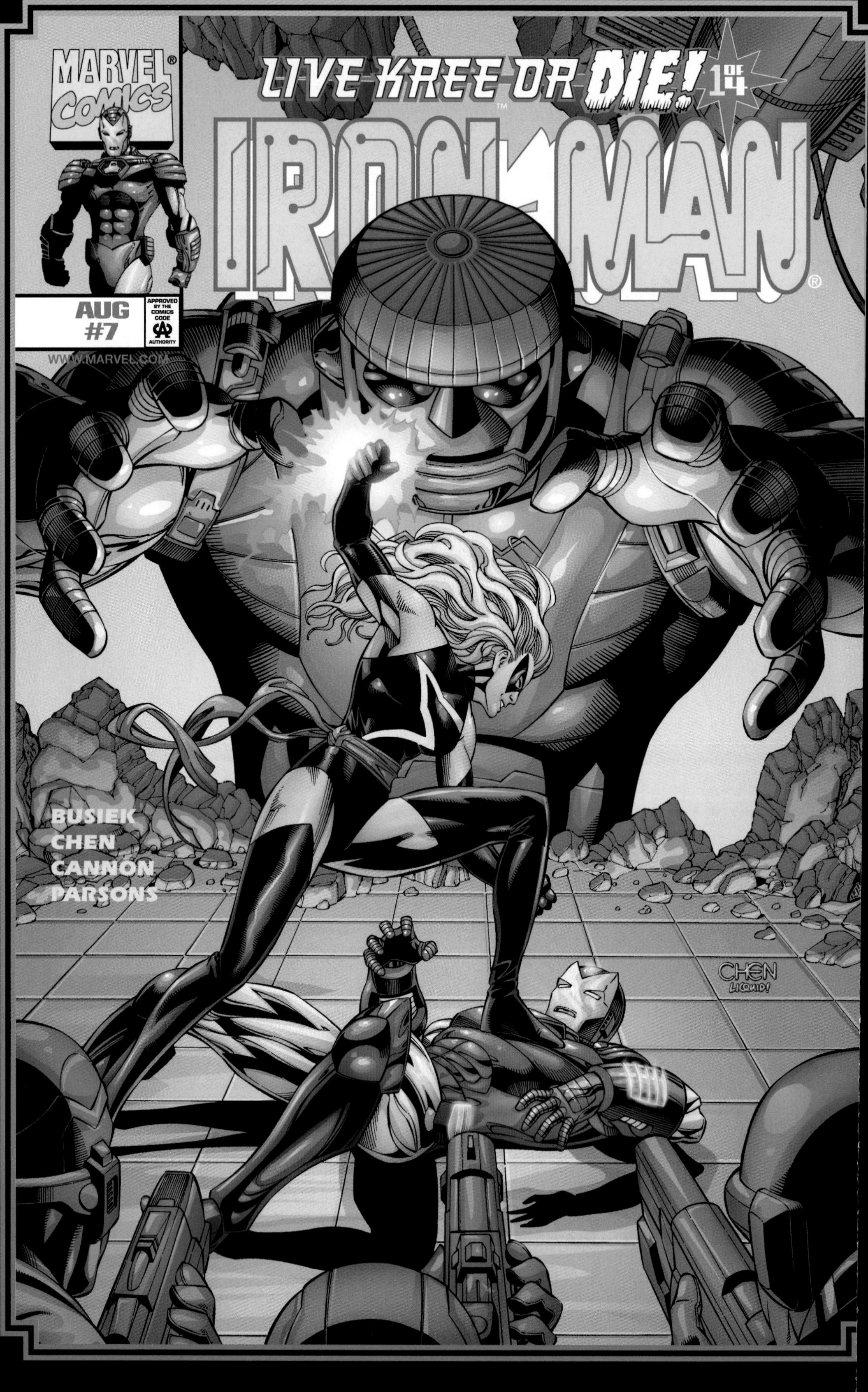
MARVEL COMICS
LIVE KREE OR DIE! 1 OF 4
IRON MAN
AUG #7
APPROVED BY THE COMICS CODE AUTHORITY
WWW.MARVEL.COM
BUSIEK
CHEN
CANNON
PARSONS
CHEN LIQUID!

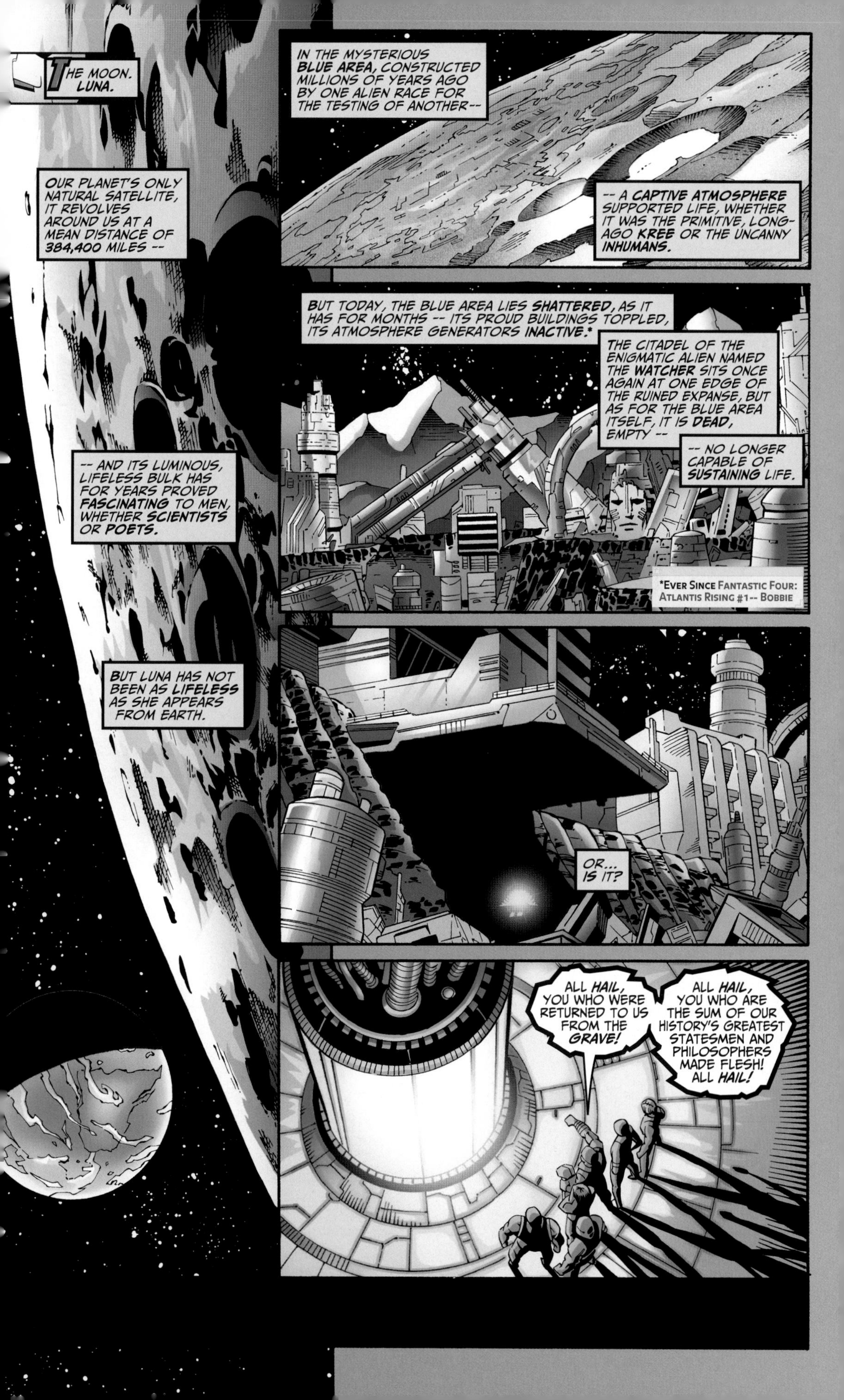
THE MOON. LUNA.
OUR PLANET'S ONLY NATURAL SATELLITE, IT REVOLVES AROUND US AT A MEAN DISTANCE OF 384,400 MILES --
-- AND ITS LUMINOUS, LIFELESS BULK HAS FOR YEARS PROVED FASCINATING TO MEN, WHETHER SCIENTISTS OR POETS.
BUT LUNA HAS NOT BEEN AS LIFELESS AS SHE APPEARS FROM EARTH.
IN THE MYSTERIOUS BLUE AREA, CONSTRUCTED MILLIONS OF YEARS AGO BY ONE ALIEN RACE FOR THE TESTING OF ANOTHER--
-- A CAPTIVE ATMOSPHERE SUPPORTED LIFE, WHETHER IT WAS THE PRIMITIVE, LONG-AGO KREE OR THE UNCANNY INHUMANS.
BUT TODAY, THE BLUE AREA LIES SHATTERED, AS IT HAS FOR MONTHS -- ITS PROUD BUILDINGS TOPPLED, ITS ATMOSPHERE GENERATORS INACTIVE.*
THE CITADEL OF THE ENIGMATIC ALIEN NAMED THE WATCHER SITS ONCE AGAIN AT ONE EDGE OF THE RUINED EXPANSE, BUT AS FOR THE BLUE AREA ITSELF, IT IS DEAD, EMPTY --
-- NO LONGER CAPABLE OF SUSTAINING LIFE.
*EVER SINCE FANTASTIC FOUR: ATLANTIS RISING #1-- BOBBIE
OR... IS IT?
ALL HAIL, YOU WHO WERE RETURNED TO US FROM THE GRAVE!
ALL HAIL, YOU WHO ARE THE SUM OF OUR HISTORY'S GREATEST STATESMEN AND PHILOSOPHERS MADE FLESH! ALL HAIL!

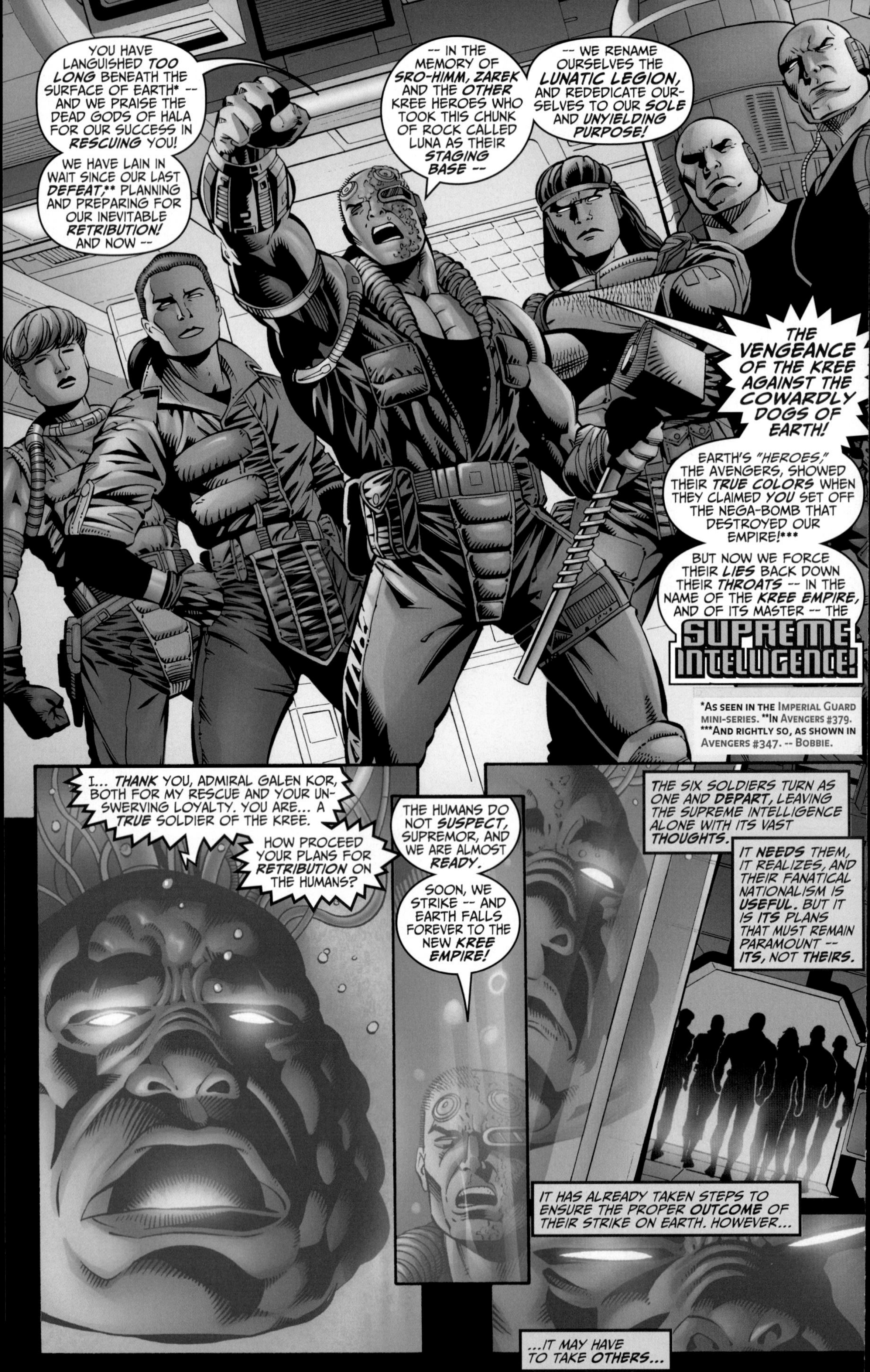

YOU HAVE LANGUISHED TOO LONG BENEATH THE SURFACE OF EARTH* -- AND WE PRAISE THE DEAD GODS OF HALA FOR OUR SUCCESS IN RESCUING YOU!
WE HAVE LAIN IN WAIT SINCE OUR LAST DEFEAT,** PLANNING AND PREPARING FOR OUR INEVITABLE RETRIBUTION! AND NOW --
-- IN THE MEMORY OF SRO-HIMM, ZAREK AND THE OTHER KREE HEROES WHO TOOK THIS CHUNK OF ROCK CALLED LUNA AS THEIR STAGING BASE --
-- WE RENAME OURSELVES THE LUNATIC LEGION, AND REDEDICATE OURSELVES TO OUR SOLE AND UNYIELDING PURPOSE!
THE VENGEANCE OF THE KREE AGAINST THE COWARDLY DOGS OF EARTH!
EARTH'S "HEROES," THE AVENGERS, SHOWED THEIR TRUE COLORS WHEN THEY CLAIMED YOU SET OFF THE NEGA-BOMB THAT DESTROYED OUR EMPIRE!***
BUT NOW WE FORCE THEIR LIES BACK DOWN THEIR THROATS -- IN THE NAME OF THE KREE EMPIRE, AND OF ITS MASTER -- THE SUPREME INTELLIGENCE!
*AS SEEN IN THE IMPERIAL GUARD MINI-SERIES. **IN AVENGERS #379. ***AND RIGHTLY SO, AS SHOWN IN AVENGERS #347. -- BOBBIE.
I... THANK YOU, ADMIRAL GALEN KOR, BOTH FOR MY RESCUE AND YOUR UNSWERVING LOYALTY. YOU ARE... A TRUE SOLDIER OF THE KREE.
HOW PROCEED YOUR PLANS FOR RETRIBUTION ON THE HUMANS?
THE HUMANS DO NOT SUSPECT, SUPREMOR, AND WE ARE ALMOST READY.
SOON, WE STRIKE -- AND EARTH FALLS FOREVER TO THE NEW KREE EMPIRE!
THE SIX SOLDIERS TURN AS ONE AND DEPART, LEAVING THE SUPREME INTELLIGENCE ALONE WITH ITS VAST THOUGHTS.
IT NEEDS THEM, IT REALIZES, AND THEIR FANATICAL NATIONALISM IS USEFUL. BUT IT IS ITS PLANS THAT MUST REMAIN PARAMOUNT -- ITS, NOT THEIRS.
IT HAS ALREADY TAKEN STEPS TO ENSURE THE PROPER OUTCOME OF THEIR STRIKE ON EARTH. HOWEVER...
...IT MAY HAVE TO TAKE OTHERS...

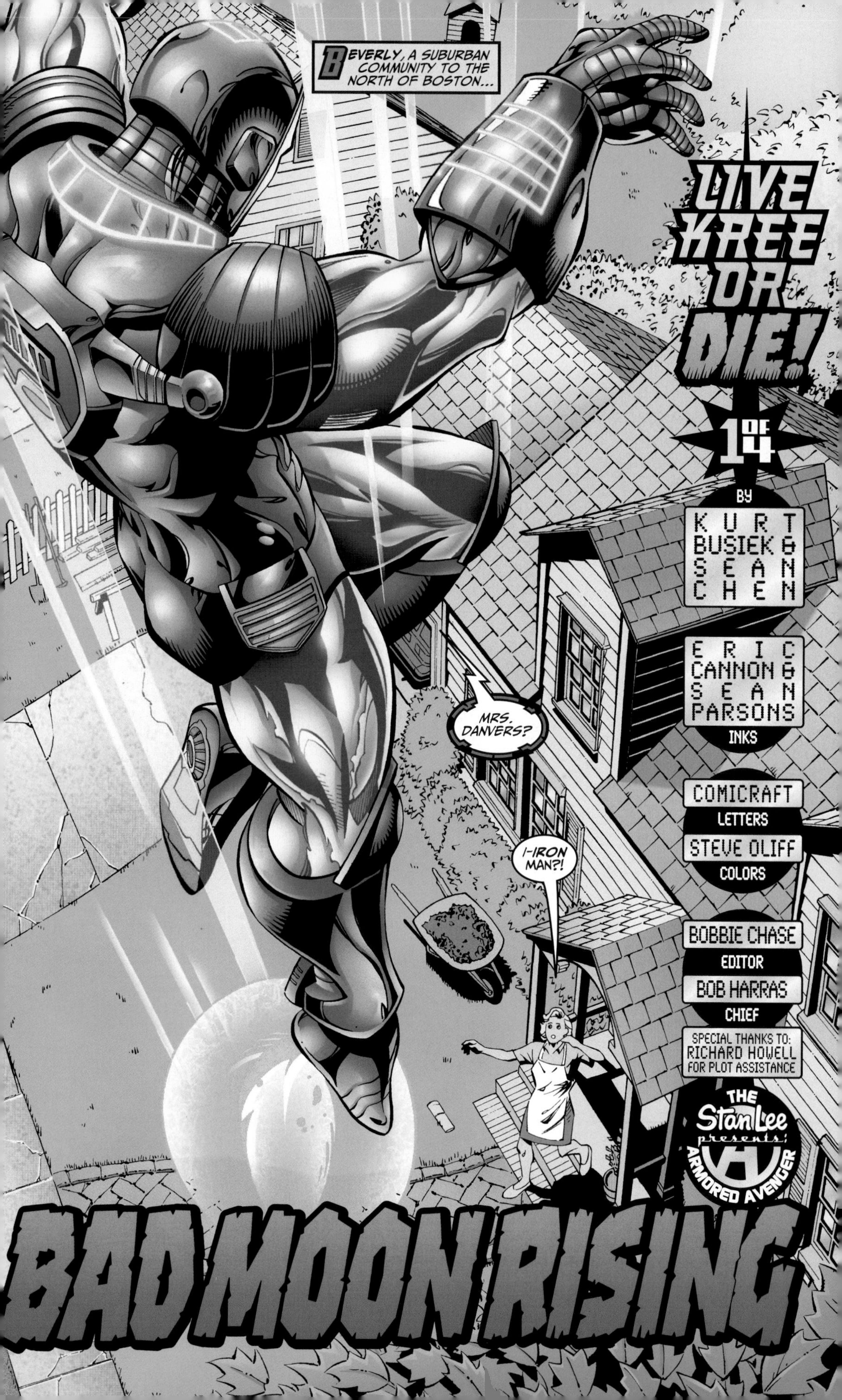
BEVERLY, A SUBURBAN COMMUNITY TO THE NORTH OF BOSTON...
LIVE KREE OR DIE!
1 OF 4
BY
KURT BUSIEK & SEAN CHEN
ERIC CANNON & SEAN PARSONS
INKS
MRS. DANVERS?
COMICRAFT
LETTERS
STEVE OLIFF
COLORS
I-IRON MAN?!
BOBBIE CHASE
EDITOR
BOB HARRAS
CHIEF
SPECIAL THANKS TO: RICHARD HOWELL FOR PLOT ASSISTANCE
THE Stan Lee presents: ARMORED AVENGER
BAD MOON RISING

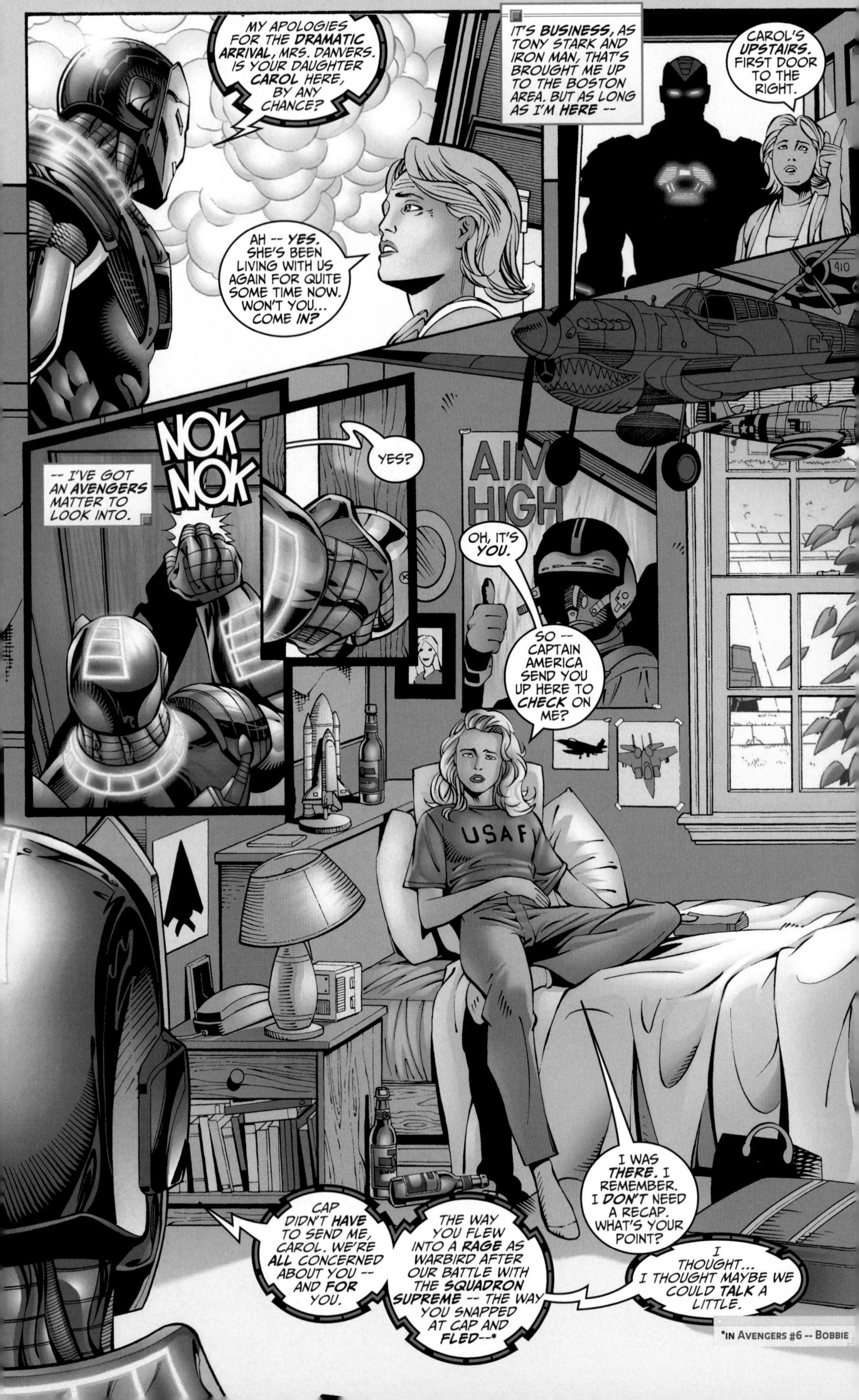

MY APOLOGIES FOR THE DRAMATIC ARRIVAL, MRS. DANVERS. IS YOUR DAUGHTER CAROL HERE, BY ANY CHANCE?
AH -- YES. SHE'S BEEN LIVING WITH US AGAIN FOR QUITE SOME TIME NOW. WON'T YOU... COME IN?
IT'S BUSINESS, AS TONY STARK AND IRON MAN, THAT'S BROUGHT ME UP TO THE BOSTON AREA. BUT AS LONG AS I'M HERE --
CAROL'S UPSTAIRS. FIRST DOOR TO THE RIGHT.
-- I'VE GOT AN AVENGERS MATTER TO LOOK INTO.
NOK NOK
YES?
AIM HIGH
OH, IT'S YOU.
SO -- CAPTAIN AMERICA SEND YOU UP HERE TO CHECK ON ME?
USAF
CAP DIDN'T HAVE TO SEND ME, CAROL. WE'RE ALL CONCERNED ABOUT YOU -- AND FOR YOU.
THE WAY YOU FLEW INTO A RAGE AS WARBIRD AFTER OUR BATTLE WITH THE SQUADRON SUPREME -- THE WAY YOU SNAPPED AT CAP AND FLED--*
I WAS THERE. I REMEMBER. I DON'T NEED A RECAP. WHAT'S YOUR POINT?
I THOUGHT... I THOUGHT MAYBE WE COULD TALK A LITTLE.
*IN AVENGERS #6 -- BOBBIE

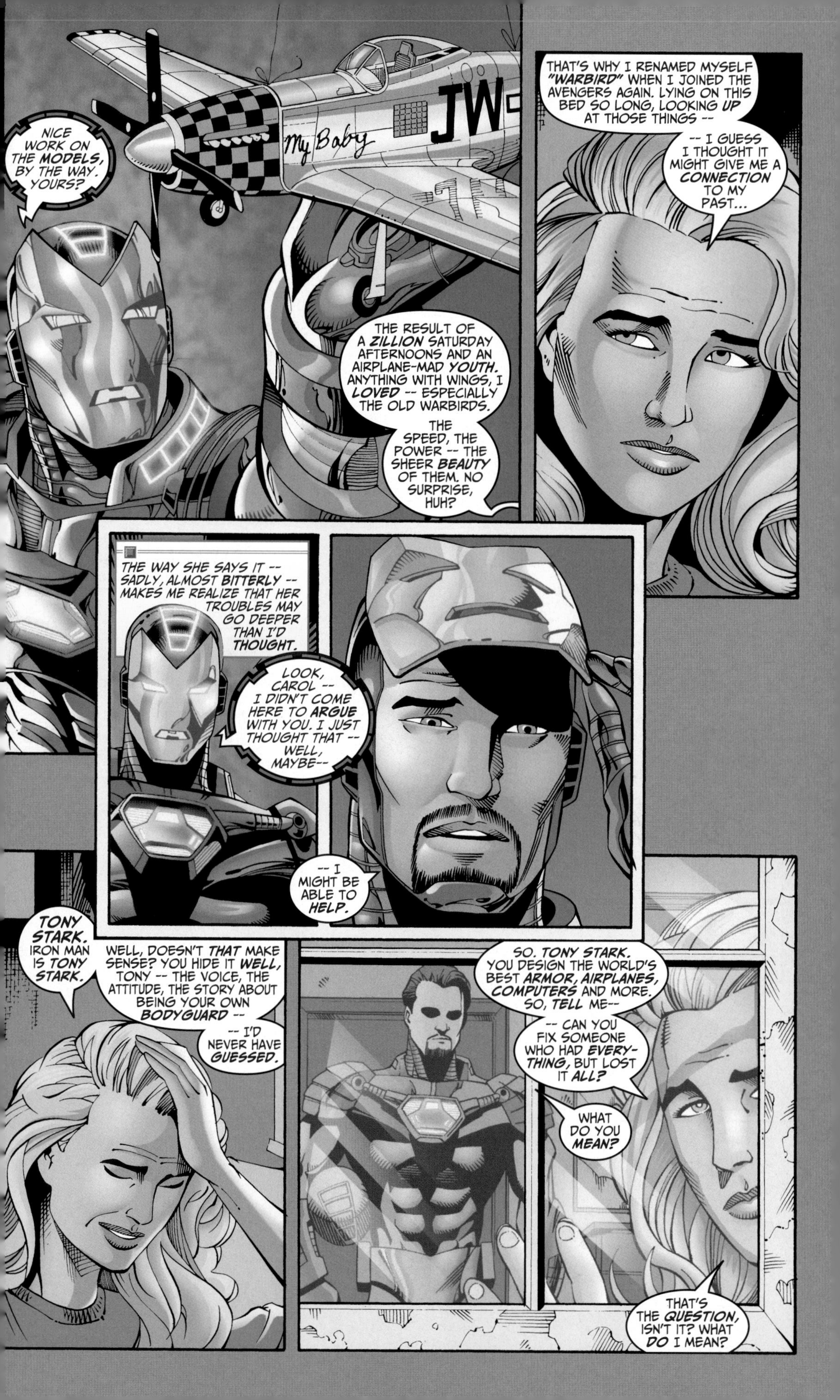

NICE WORK ON THE MODELS, BY THE WAY. YOURS?
THE RESULT OF A ZILLION SATURDAY AFTERNOONS AND AN AIRPLANE-MAD YOUTH. ANYTHING WITH WINGS, I LOVED -- ESPECIALLY THE OLD WARBIRDS.
THE SPEED, THE POWER -- THE SHEER BEAUTY OF THEM. NO SURPRISE, HUH?
THAT'S WHY I RENAMED MYSELF "WARBIRD" WHEN I JOINED THE AVENGERS AGAIN. LYING ON THIS BED SO LONG, LOOKING UP AT THOSE THINGS --
-- I GUESS I THOUGHT IT MIGHT GIVE ME A CONNECTION TO MY PAST...
THE WAY SHE SAYS IT -- SADLY, ALMOST BITTERLY -- MAKES ME REALIZE THAT HER TROUBLES MAY GO DEEPER THAN I'D THOUGHT.
LOOK, CAROL -- I DIDN'T COME HERE TO ARGUE WITH YOU. I JUST THOUGHT THAT -- WELL, MAYBE--
-- I MIGHT BE ABLE TO HELP.
TONY STARK. IRON MAN IS TONY STARK.
WELL, DOESN'T THAT MAKE SENSE? YOU HIDE IT WELL, TONY -- THE VOICE, THE ATTITUDE, THE STORY ABOUT BEING YOUR OWN BODYGUARD --
-- I'D NEVER HAVE GUESSED.
SO. TONY STARK. YOU DESIGN THE WORLD'S BEST ARMOR, AIRPLANES, COMPUTERS AND MORE. SO, TELL ME--
-- CAN YOU FIX SOMEONE WHO HAD EVERYTHING, BUT LOST IT ALL?
WHAT DO YOU MEAN?
THAT'S THE QUESTION, ISN'T IT? WHAT DO I MEAN?

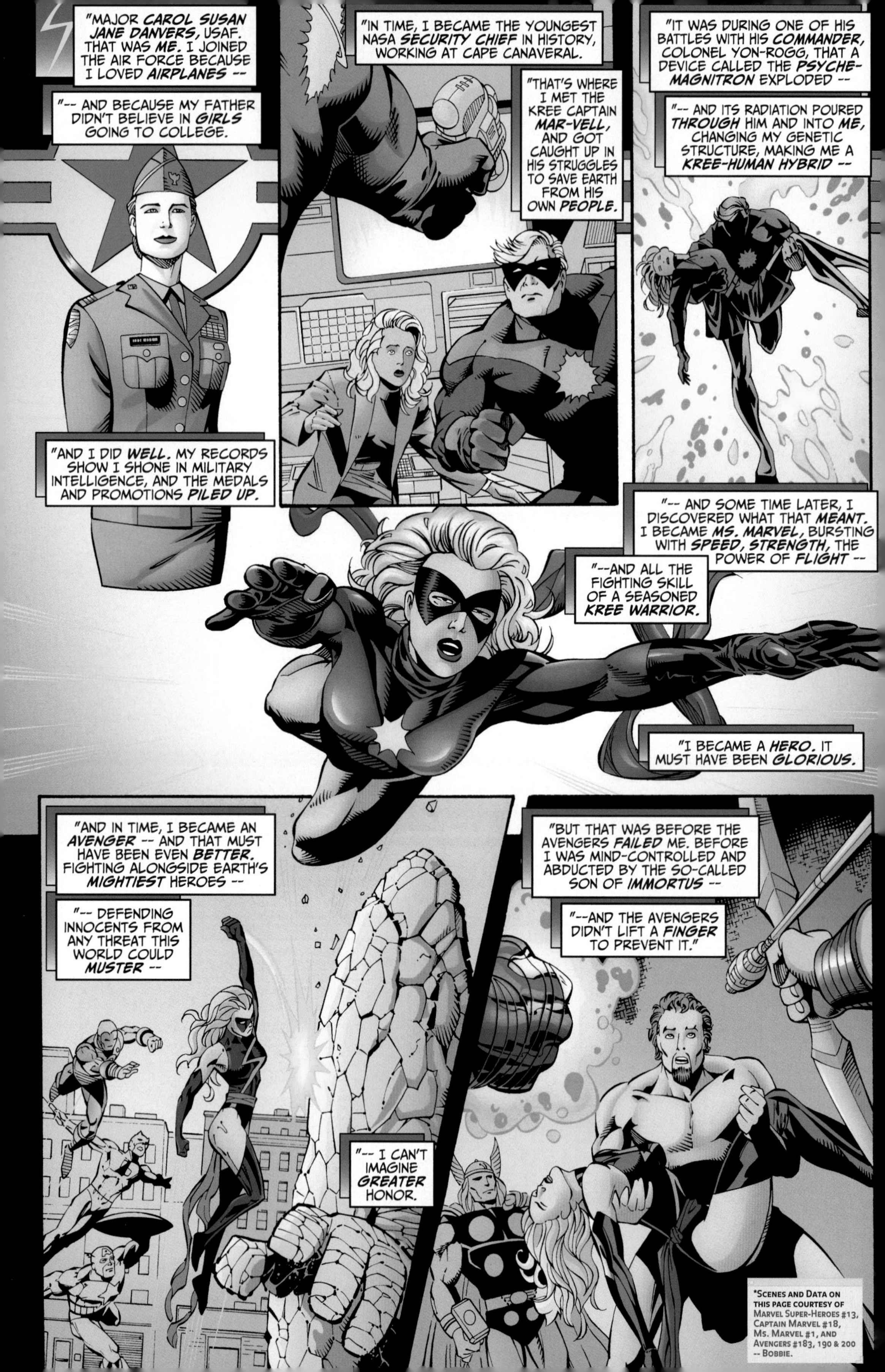
"MAJOR CAROL SUSAN JANE DANVERS, USAF. THAT WAS ME. I JOINED THE AIR FORCE BECAUSE I LOVED AIRPLANES --
"-- AND BECAUSE MY FATHER DIDN'T BELIEVE IN GIRLS GOING TO COLLEGE.
"AND I DID WELL. MY RECORDS SHOW I SHONE IN MILITARY INTELLIGENCE, AND THE MEDALS AND PROMOTIONS PILED UP.
"IN TIME, I BECAME THE YOUNGEST NASA SECURITY CHIEF IN HISTORY, WORKING AT CAPE CANAVERAL.
"THAT'S WHERE I MET THE KREE CAPTAIN MAR-VELL, AND GOT CAUGHT UP IN HIS STRUGGLES TO SAVE EARTH FROM HIS OWN PEOPLE.
"IT WAS DURING ONE OF HIS BATTLES WITH HIS COMMANDER, COLONEL YON-ROGG, THAT A DEVICE CALLED THE PSYCHE-MAGNITRON EXPLODED --
"-- AND ITS RADIATION POURED THROUGH HIM AND INTO ME, CHANGING MY GENETIC STRUCTURE, MAKING ME A KREE-HUMAN HYBRID --
"-- AND SOME TIME LATER, I DISCOVERED WHAT THAT MEANT. I BECAME MS. MARVEL, BURSTING WITH SPEED, STRENGTH, THE POWER OF FLIGHT --
"--AND ALL THE FIGHTING SKILL OF A SEASONED KREE WARRIOR.
"I BECAME A HERO. IT MUST HAVE BEEN GLORIOUS.
"AND IN TIME, I BECAME AN AVENGER -- AND THAT MUST HAVE BEEN EVEN BETTER. FIGHTING ALONGSIDE EARTH'S MIGHTIEST HEROES --
"-- DEFENDING INNOCENTS FROM ANY THREAT THIS WORLD COULD MUSTER --
"-- I CAN'T IMAGINE GREATER HONOR.
"BUT THAT WAS BEFORE THE AVENGERS FAILED ME. BEFORE I WAS MIND-CONTROLLED AND ABDUCTED BY THE SO-CALLED SON OF IMMORTUS --
"--AND THE AVENGERS DIDN'T LIFT A FINGER TO PREVENT IT."
*SCENES AND DATA ON THIS PAGE COURTESY OF MARVEL SUPER-HEROES #13, CAPTAIN MARVEL #18, MS. MARVEL #1, AND AVENGERS #183, 190 & 200 -- BOBBIE.

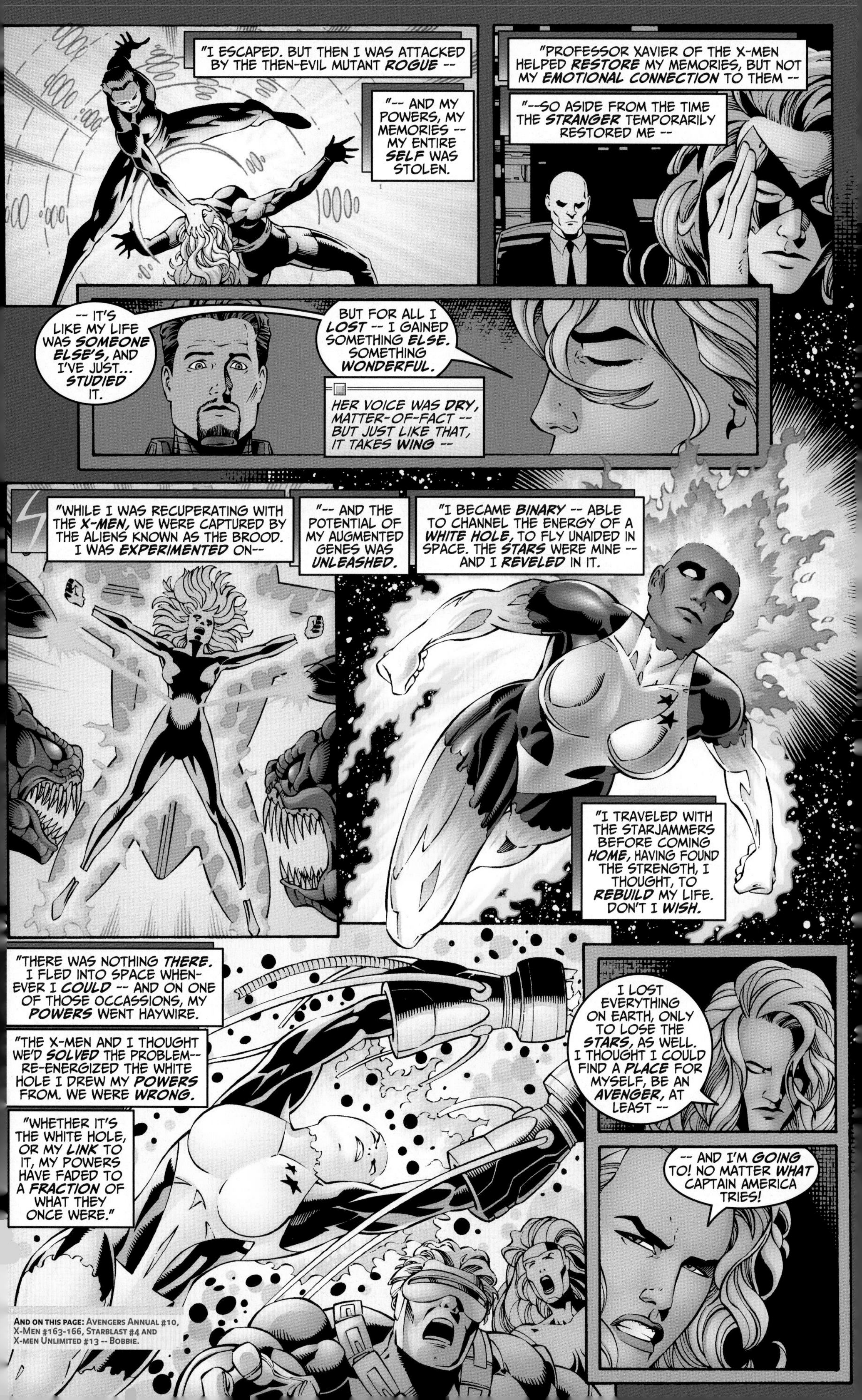
"I ESCAPED. BUT THEN I WAS ATTACKED BY THE THEN-EVIL MUTANT ROGUE --
"-- AND MY POWERS, MY MEMORIES -- MY ENTIRE SELF WAS STOLEN.
"PROFESSOR XAVIER OF THE X-MEN HELPED RESTORE MY MEMORIES, BUT NOT MY EMOTIONAL CONNECTION TO THEM --
"--SO ASIDE FROM THE TIME THE STRANGER TEMPORARILY RESTORED ME --
-- IT'S LIKE MY LIFE WAS SOMEONE ELSE'S, AND I'VE JUST... STUDIED IT.
BUT FOR ALL I LOST -- I GAINED SOMETHING ELSE. SOMETHING WONDERFUL.
HER VOICE WAS DRY, MATTER-OF-FACT -- BUT JUST LIKE THAT, IT TAKES WING --
"WHILE I WAS RECUPERATING WITH THE X-MEN, WE WERE CAPTURED BY THE ALIENS KNOWN AS THE BROOD. I WAS EXPERIMENTED ON--
"-- AND THE POTENTIAL OF MY AUGMENTED GENES WAS UNLEASHED.
"I BECAME BINARY -- ABLE TO CHANNEL THE ENERGY OF A WHITE HOLE, TO FLY UNAIDED IN SPACE. THE STARS WERE MINE -- AND I REVELED IN IT.
"I TRAVELED WITH THE STARJAMMERS BEFORE COMING HOME, HAVING FOUND THE STRENGTH, I THOUGHT, TO REBUILD MY LIFE. DON'T I WISH.
"THERE WAS NOTHING THERE. I FLED INTO SPACE WHENEVER I COULD -- AND ON ONE OF THOSE OCCASSIONS, MY POWERS WENT HAYWIRE.
"THE X-MEN AND I THOUGHT WE'D SOLVED THE PROBLEM-- RE-ENERGIZED THE WHITE HOLE I DREW MY POWERS FROM. WE WERE WRONG.
"WHETHER IT'S THE WHITE HOLE, OR MY LINK TO IT, MY POWERS HAVE FADED TO A FRACTION OF WHAT THEY ONCE WERE."
I LOST EVERYTHING ON EARTH, ONLY TO LOSE THE STARS, AS WELL. I THOUGHT I COULD FIND A PLACE FOR MYSELF, BE AN AVENGER, AT LEAST --
-- AND I'M GOING TO! NO MATTER WHAT CAPTAIN AMERICA TRIES!
AND ON THIS PAGE: AVENGERS ANNUAL #10, X-MEN #163-166, STARBLAST #4 AND X-MEN UNLIMITED #13 -- BOBBIE.

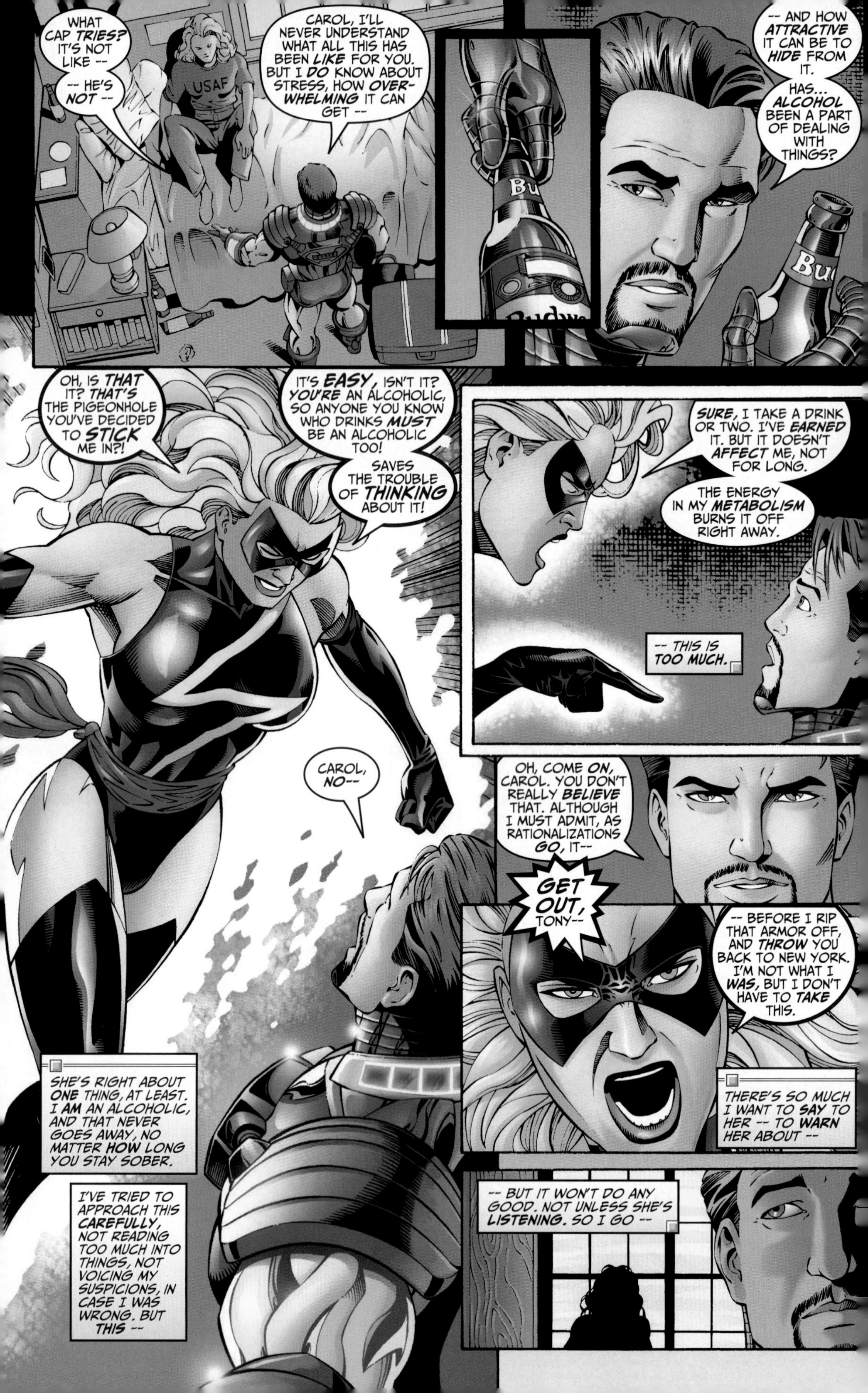

WHAT CAP TRIES? IT'S NOT LIKE --
-- HE'S NOT --
CAROL, I'LL NEVER UNDERSTAND WHAT ALL THIS HAS BEEN LIKE FOR YOU. BUT I DO KNOW ABOUT STRESS, HOW OVER-WHELMING IT CAN GET --
-- AND HOW ATTRACTIVE IT CAN BE TO HIDE FROM IT.
HAS... ALCOHOL BEEN A PART OF DEALING WITH THINGS?
OH, IS THAT IT? THAT'S THE PIGEONHOLE YOU'VE DECIDED TO STICK ME IN?!
IT'S EASY, ISN'T IT? YOU'RE AN ALCOHOLIC, SO ANYONE YOU KNOW WHO DRINKS MUST BE AN ALCOHOLIC TOO!
SAVES THE TROUBLE OF THINKING ABOUT IT!
SURE, I TAKE A DRINK OR TWO. I'VE EARNED IT. BUT IT DOESN'T AFFECT ME, NOT FOR LONG.
THE ENERGY IN MY METABOLISM BURNS IT OFF RIGHT AWAY.
-- THIS IS TOO MUCH.
CAROL, NO--
OH, COME ON, CAROL. YOU DON'T REALLY BELIEVE THAT. ALTHOUGH I MUST ADMIT, AS RATIONALIZATIONS GO, IT--
GET OUT, TONY--
-- BEFORE I RIP THAT ARMOR OFF, AND THROW YOU BACK TO NEW YORK. I'M NOT WHAT I WAS, BUT I DON'T HAVE TO TAKE THIS.
SHE'S RIGHT ABOUT ONE THING, AT LEAST. I AM AN ALCOHOLIC, AND THAT NEVER GOES AWAY, NO MATTER HOW LONG YOU STAY SOBER.
I'VE TRIED TO APPROACH THIS CAREFULLY, NOT READING TOO MUCH INTO THINGS, NOT VOICING MY SUSPICIONS, IN CASE I WAS WRONG. BUT THIS --
THERE'S SO MUCH I WANT TO SAY TO HER -- TO WARN HER ABOUT --
-- BUT IT WON'T DO ANY GOOD. NOT UNLESS SHE'S LISTENING. SO I GO --

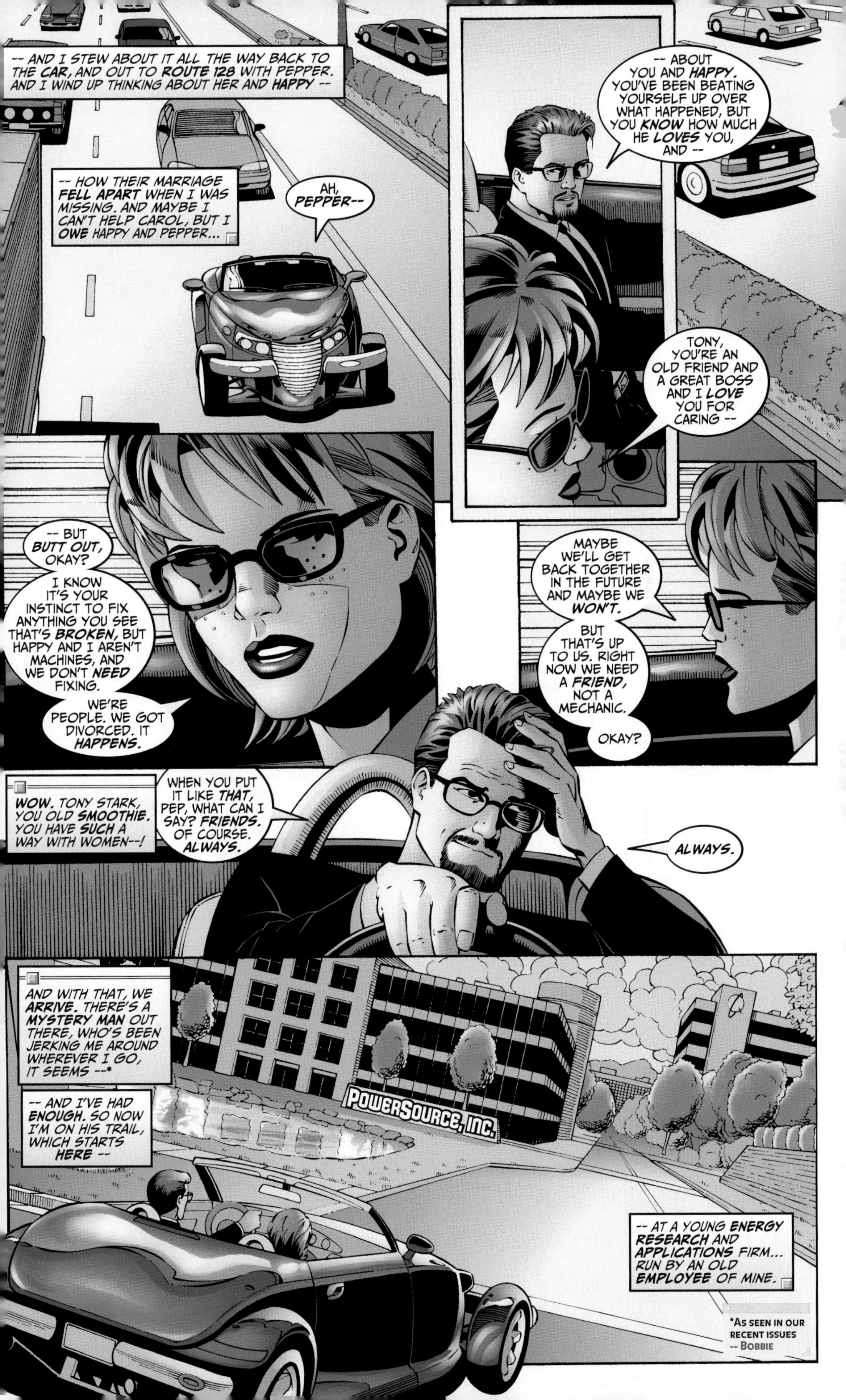
-- AND I STEW ABOUT IT ALL THE WAY BACK TO THE CAR, AND OUT TO ROUTE 128 WITH PEPPER. AND I WIND UP THINKING ABOUT HER AND HAPPY --
-- HOW THEIR MARRIAGE FELL APART WHEN I WAS MISSING. AND MAYBE I CAN'T HELP CAROL, BUT I OWE HAPPY AND PEPPER...
AH, PEPPER--
-- ABOUT YOU AND HAPPY. YOU'VE BEEN BEATING YOURSELF UP OVER WHAT HAPPENED, BUT YOU KNOW HOW MUCH HE LOVES YOU, AND --
TONY, YOU'RE AN OLD FRIEND AND A GREAT BOSS AND I LOVE YOU FOR CARING --
-- BUT BUTT OUT, OKAY?
I KNOW IT'S YOUR INSTINCT TO FIX ANYTHING YOU SEE THAT'S BROKEN, BUT HAPPY AND I AREN'T MACHINES, AND WE DON'T NEED FIXING.
WE'RE PEOPLE. WE GOT DIVORCED. IT HAPPENS.
MAYBE WE'LL GET BACK TOGETHER IN THE FUTURE AND MAYBE WE WON'T.
BUT THAT'S UP TO US. RIGHT NOW WE NEED A FRIEND, NOT A MECHANIC.
OKAY?
WOW. TONY STARK, YOU OLD SMOOTHIE. YOU HAVE SUCH A WAY WITH WOMEN--!
WHEN YOU PUT IT LIKE THAT, PEP, WHAT CAN I SAY? FRIENDS. OF COURSE. ALWAYS.
ALWAYS.
AND WITH THAT, WE ARRIVE. THERE'S A MYSTERY MAN OUT THERE, WHO'S BEEN JERKING ME AROUND WHEREVER I GO, IT SEEMS --*
-- AND I'VE HAD ENOUGH. SO NOW I'M ON HIS TRAIL, WHICH STARTS HERE --
POWERSOURCE, INC.
-- AT A YOUNG ENERGY RESEARCH AND APPLICATIONS FIRM... RUN BY AN OLD EMPLOYEE OF MINE.
*AS SEEN IN OUR RECENT ISSUES -- BOBBIE

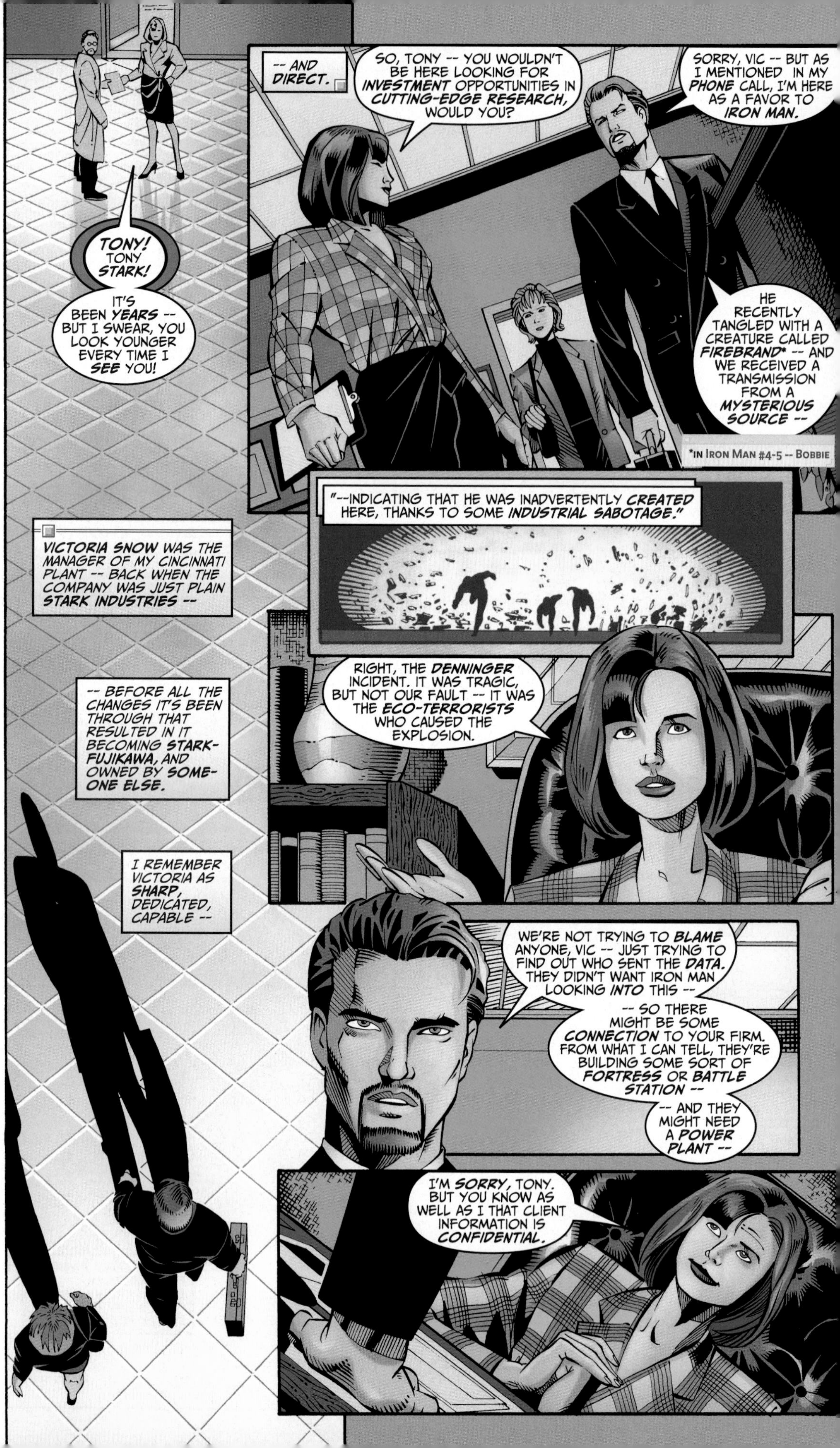
TONY! TONY STARK!
IT'S BEEN YEARS -- BUT I SWEAR, YOU LOOK YOUNGER EVERY TIME I SEE YOU!
-- AND DIRECT.
SO, TONY -- YOU WOULDN'T BE HERE LOOKING FOR INVESTMENT OPPORTUNITIES IN CUTTING-EDGE RESEARCH, WOULD YOU?
SORRY, VIC -- BUT AS I MENTIONED IN MY PHONE CALL, I'M HERE AS A FAVOR TO IRON MAN.
HE RECENTLY TANGLED WITH A CREATURE CALLED FIREBRAND* -- AND WE RECEIVED A TRANSMISSION FROM A MYSTERIOUS SOURCE --
*IN IRON MAN #4-5 -- BOBBIE
VICTORIA SNOW WAS THE MANAGER OF MY CINCINNATI PLANT -- BACK WHEN THE COMPANY WAS JUST PLAIN STARK INDUSTRIES --
-- BEFORE ALL THE CHANGES IT'S BEEN THROUGH THAT RESULTED IN IT BECOMING STARK-FUJIKAWA, AND OWNED BY SOMEONE ELSE.
I REMEMBER VICTORIA AS SHARP, DEDICATED, CAPABLE --
"--INDICATING THAT HE WAS INADVERTENTLY CREATED HERE, THANKS TO SOME INDUSTRIAL SABOTAGE."
RIGHT, THE DENNINGER INCIDENT. IT WAS TRAGIC, BUT NOT OUR FAULT -- IT WAS THE ECO-TERRORISTS WHO CAUSED THE EXPLOSION.
WE'RE NOT TRYING TO BLAME ANYONE, VIC -- JUST TRYING TO FIND OUT WHO SENT THE DATA. THEY DIDN'T WANT IRON MAN LOOKING INTO THIS --
-- SO THERE MIGHT BE SOME CONNECTION TO YOUR FIRM. FROM WHAT I CAN TELL, THEY'RE BUILDING SOME SORT OF FORTRESS OR BATTLE STATION --
-- AND THEY MIGHT NEED A POWER PLANT --
I'M SORRY, TONY. BUT YOU KNOW AS WELL AS I THAT CLIENT INFORMATION IS CONFIDENTIAL.

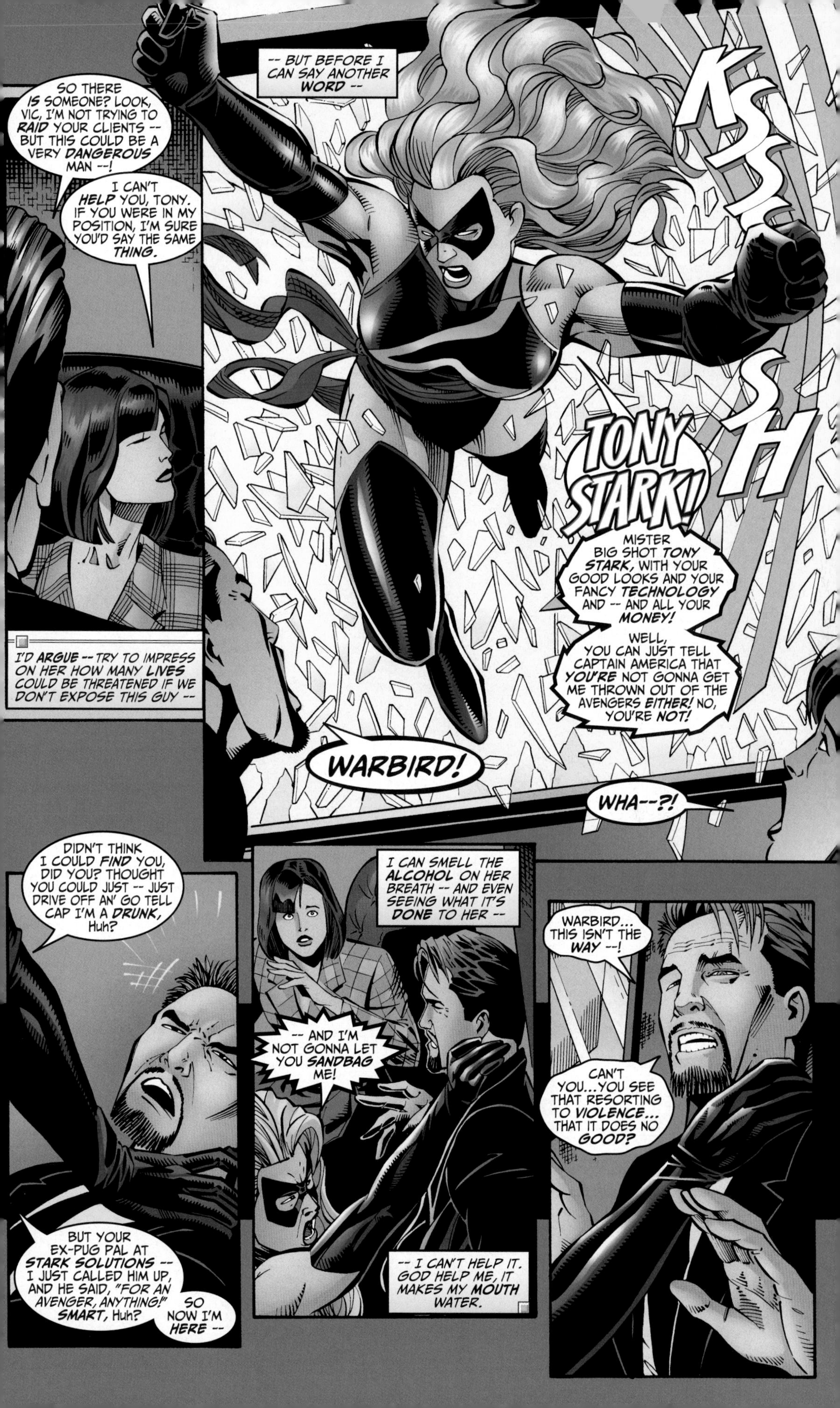
SO THERE IS SOMEONE? LOOK, VIC, I'M NOT TRYING TO RAID YOUR CLIENTS -- BUT THIS COULD BE A VERY DANGEROUS MAN --!
I CAN'T HELP YOU, TONY. IF YOU WERE IN MY POSITION, I'M SURE YOU'D SAY THE SAME THING.
I'D ARGUE -- TRY TO IMPRESS ON HER HOW MANY LIVES COULD BE THREATENED IF WE DON'T EXPOSE THIS GUY --
-- BUT BEFORE I CAN SAY ANOTHER WORD --
KSSSH
TONY STARK!
MISTER BIG SHOT TONY STARK, WITH YOUR GOOD LOOKS AND YOUR FANCY TECHNOLOGY AND -- AND ALL YOUR MONEY!
WELL, YOU CAN JUST TELL CAPTAIN AMERICA THAT YOU'RE NOT GONNA GET ME THROWN OUT OF THE AVENGERS EITHER! NO, YOU'RE NOT!
WARBIRD!
WHA--?!
DIDN'T THINK I COULD FIND YOU, DID YOU? THOUGHT YOU COULD JUST -- JUST DRIVE OFF AN' GO TELL CAP I'M A DRUNK, Huh?
BUT YOUR EX-PUG PAL AT STARK SOLUTIONS -- I JUST CALLED HIM UP, AND HE SAID, "FOR AN AVENGER, ANYTHING!" SMART, Huh?
SO NOW I'M HERE --
I CAN SMELL THE ALCOHOL ON HER BREATH -- AND EVEN SEEING WHAT IT'S DONE TO HER --
-- AND I'M NOT GONNA LET YOU SANDBAG ME!
-- I CAN'T HELP IT. GOD HELP ME, IT MAKES MY MOUTH WATER.
WARBIRD... THIS ISN'T THE WAY --!
CAN'T YOU...YOU SEE THAT RESORTING TO VIOLENCE... THAT IT DOES NO GOOD?

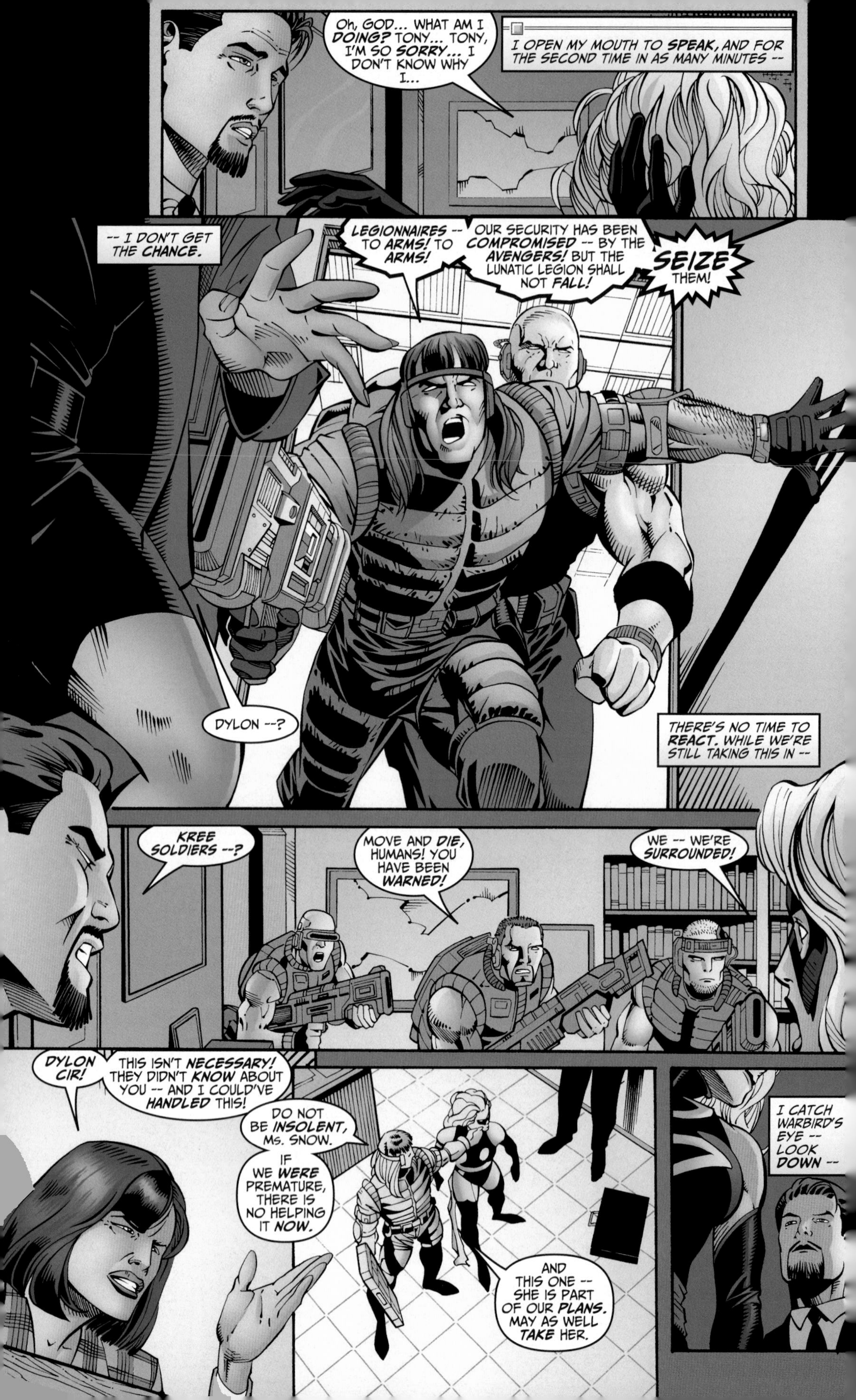

Oh, GOD... WHAT AM I DOING? TONY... TONY, I'M SO SORRY... I DON'T KNOW WHY I...
I OPEN MY MOUTH TO SPEAK, AND FOR THE SECOND TIME IN AS MANY MINUTES --
-- I DON'T GET THE CHANCE.
LEGIONNAIRES -- TO ARMS! TO ARMS!
OUR SECURITY HAS BEEN COMPROMISED -- BY THE AVENGERS! BUT THE LUNATIC LEGION SHALL NOT FALL!
SEIZE THEM!
DYLON --?
THERE'S NO TIME TO REACT. WHILE WE'RE STILL TAKING THIS IN --
KREE SOLDIERS --?
MOVE AND DIE, HUMANS! YOU HAVE BEEN WARNED!
WE -- WE'RE SURROUNDED!
DYLON CIR!
THIS ISN'T NECESSARY! THEY DIDN'T KNOW ABOUT YOU -- AND I COULD'VE HANDLED THIS!
DO NOT BE INSOLENT, Ms. SNOW.
IF WE WERE PREMATURE, THERE IS NO HELPING IT NOW.
AND THIS ONE -- SHE IS PART OF OUR PLANS. MAY AS WELL TAKE HER.
I CATCH WARBIRD'S EYE -- LOOK DOWN --

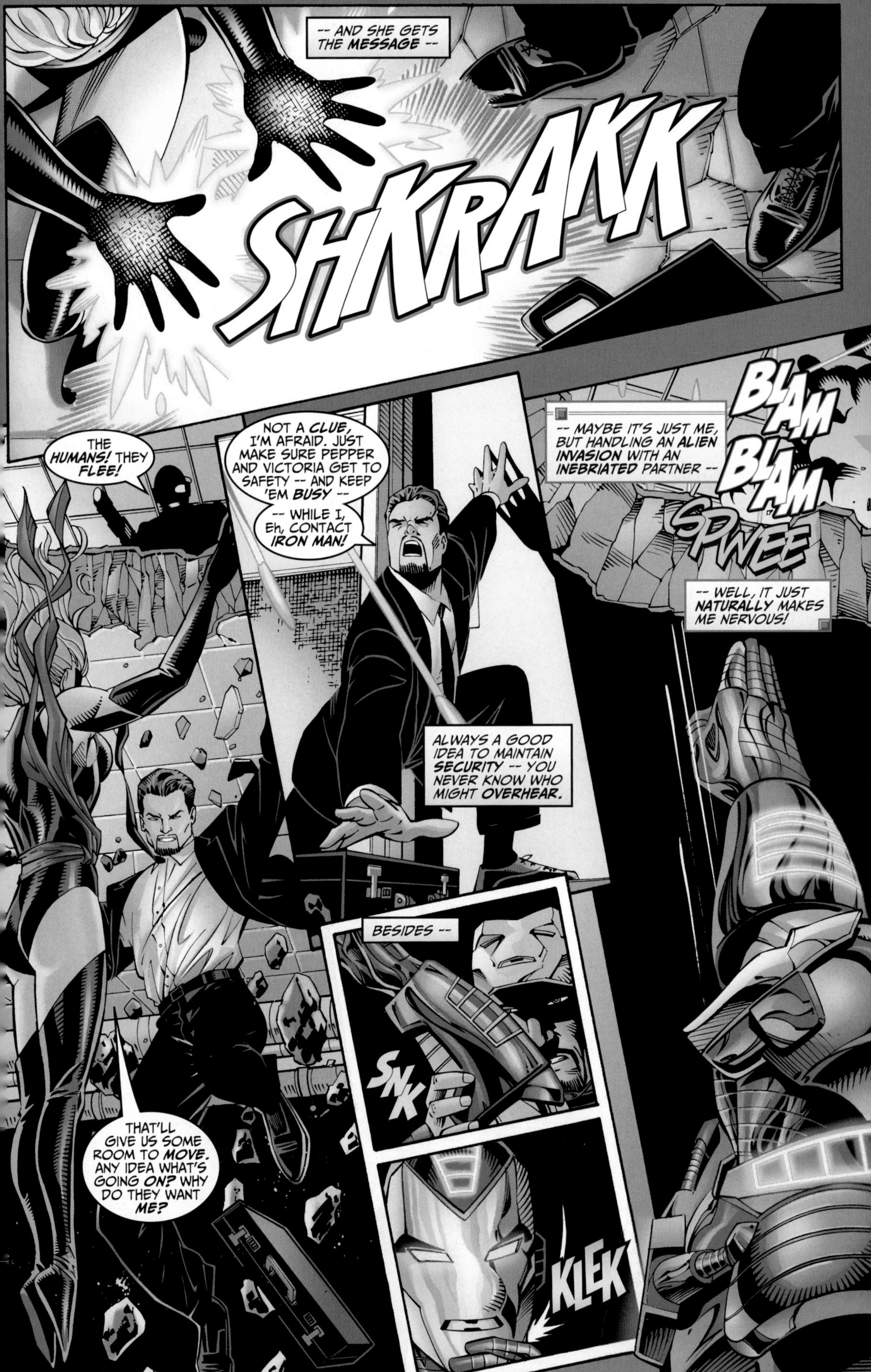
-- AND SHE GETS THE MESSAGE --
SHKRAKK
THE HUMANS! THEY FLEE!
NOT A CLUE, I'M AFRAID. JUST MAKE SURE PEPPER AND VICTORIA GET TO SAFETY -- AND KEEP 'EM BUSY --
-- WHILE I, Eh, CONTACT IRON MAN!
-- MAYBE IT'S JUST ME, BUT HANDLING AN ALIEN INVASION WITH AN INEBRIATED PARTNER --
BLAM
BLAM
SPWEE
-- WELL, IT JUST NATURALLY MAKES ME NERVOUS!
ALWAYS A GOOD IDEA TO MAINTAIN SECURITY -- YOU NEVER KNOW WHO MIGHT OVERHEAR.
THAT'LL GIVE US SOME ROOM TO MOVE. ANY IDEA WHAT'S GOING ON? WHY DO THEY WANT ME?
BESIDES --
SNK
KLEK

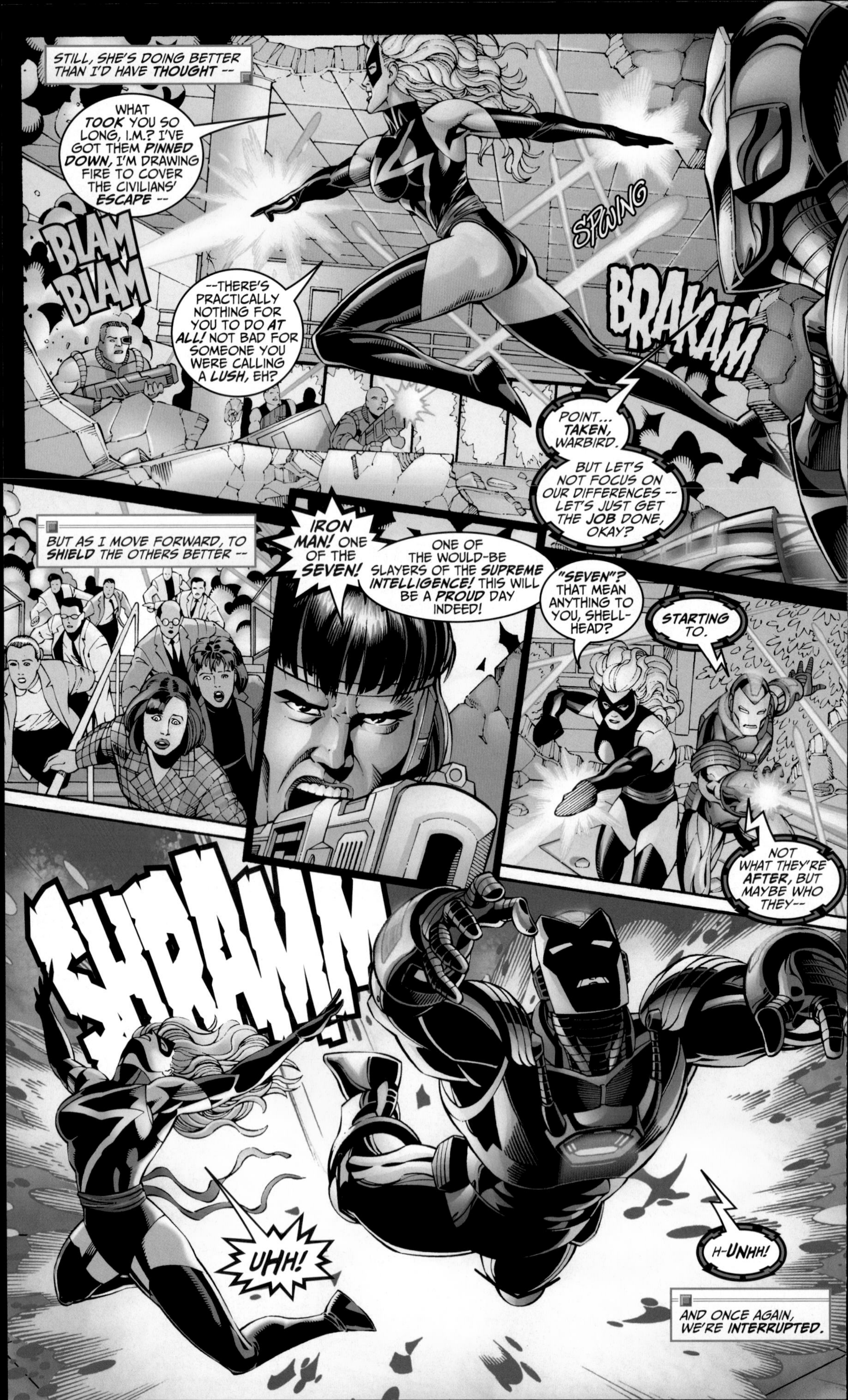

STILL, SHE'S DOING BETTER THAN I'D HAVE THOUGHT --
WHAT TOOK YOU SO LONG, I.M.? I'VE GOT THEM PINNED DOWN, I'M DRAWING FIRE TO COVER THE CIVILIANS' ESCAPE --
BLAM BLAM
--THERE'S PRACTICALLY NOTHING FOR YOU TO DO AT ALL! NOT BAD FOR SOMEONE YOU WERE CALLING A LUSH, EH?
SPWING
BRAKAM
POINT... TAKEN, WARBIRD.
BUT LET'S NOT FOCUS ON OUR DIFFERENCES -- LET'S JUST GET THE JOB DONE, OKAY?
BUT AS I MOVE FORWARD, TO SHIELD THE OTHERS BETTER --
IRON MAN! ONE OF THE SEVEN!
ONE OF THE WOULD-BE SLAYERS OF THE SUPREME INTELLIGENCE! THIS WILL BE A PROUD DAY INDEED!
"SEVEN"? THAT MEAN ANYTHING TO YOU, SHELL-HEAD?
STARTING TO.
NOT WHAT THEY'RE AFTER, BUT MAYBE WHO THEY--
SHRAMM
UHH!
H-UNHH!
AND ONCE AGAIN, WE'RE INTERRUPTED.

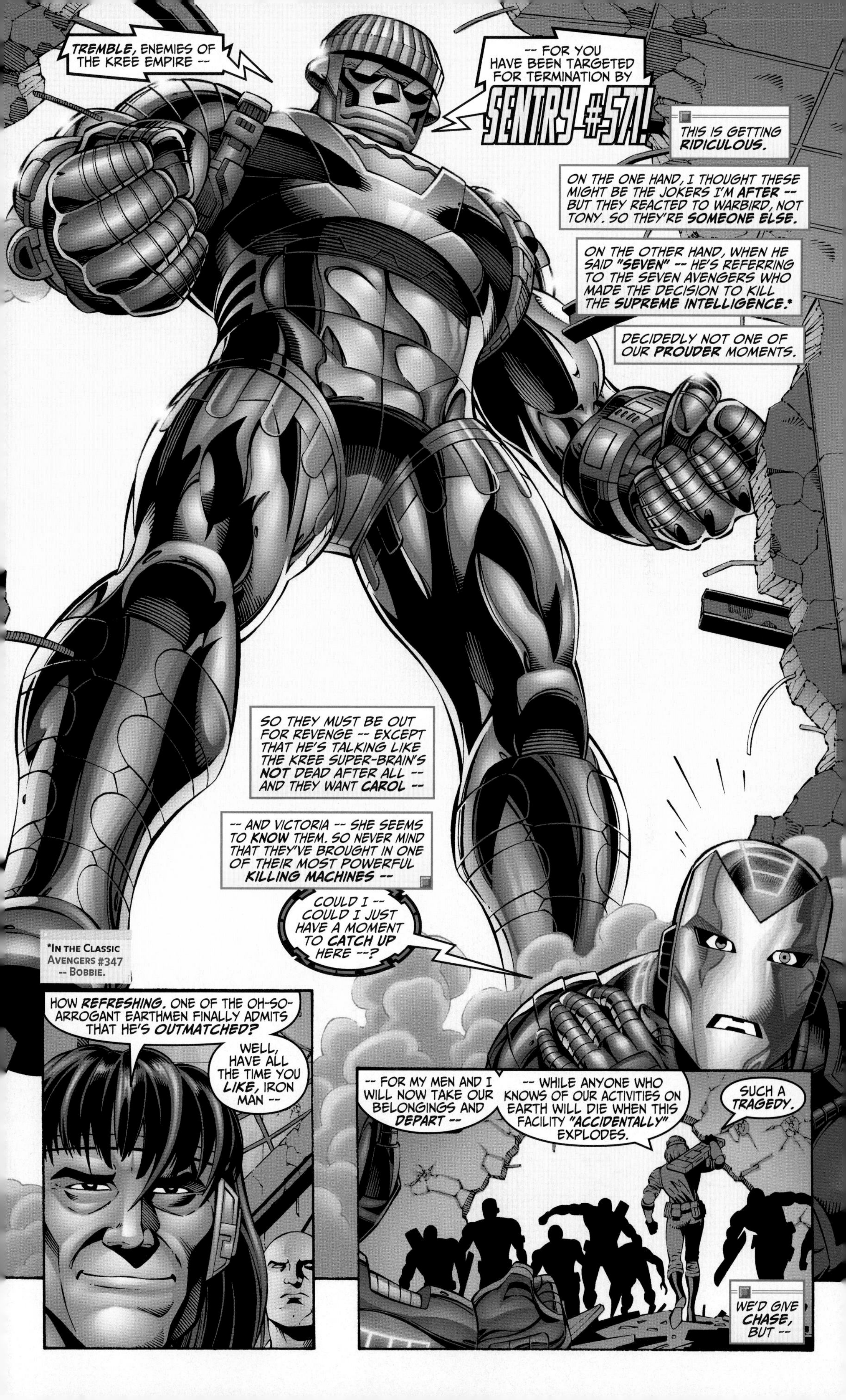
TREMBLE, ENEMIES OF THE KREE EMPIRE --
-- FOR YOU HAVE BEEN TARGETED FOR TERMINATION BY SENTRY #571!
THIS IS GETTING RIDICULOUS.
ON THE ONE HAND, I THOUGHT THESE MIGHT BE THE JOKERS I'M AFTER -- BUT THEY REACTED TO WARBIRD, NOT TONY. SO THEY'RE SOMEONE ELSE.
ON THE OTHER HAND, WHEN HE SAID "SEVEN" -- HE'S REFERRING TO THE SEVEN AVENGERS WHO MADE THE DECISION TO KILL THE SUPREME INTELLIGENCE.*
DECIDEDLY NOT ONE OF OUR PROUDER MOMENTS.
SO THEY MUST BE OUT FOR REVENGE -- EXCEPT THAT HE'S TALKING LIKE THE KREE SUPER-BRAIN'S NOT DEAD AFTER ALL -- AND THEY WANT CAROL --
-- AND VICTORIA -- SHE SEEMS TO KNOW THEM. SO NEVER MIND THAT THEY'VE BROUGHT IN ONE OF THEIR MOST POWERFUL KILLING MACHINES --
COULD I -- COULD I JUST HAVE A MOMENT TO CATCH UP HERE --?
*IN THE CLASSIC AVENGERS #347 -- BOBBIE.
HOW REFRESHING. ONE OF THE OH-SO-ARROGANT EARTHMEN FINALLY ADMITS THAT HE'S OUTMATCHED?
WELL, HAVE ALL THE TIME YOU LIKE, IRON MAN --
-- FOR MY MEN AND I WILL NOW TAKE OUR BELONGINGS AND DEPART --
-- WHILE ANYONE WHO KNOWS OF OUR ACTIVITIES ON EARTH WILL DIE WHEN THIS FACILITY "ACCIDENTALLY" EXPLODES.
SUCH A TRAGEDY.
WE'D GIVE CHASE, BUT --

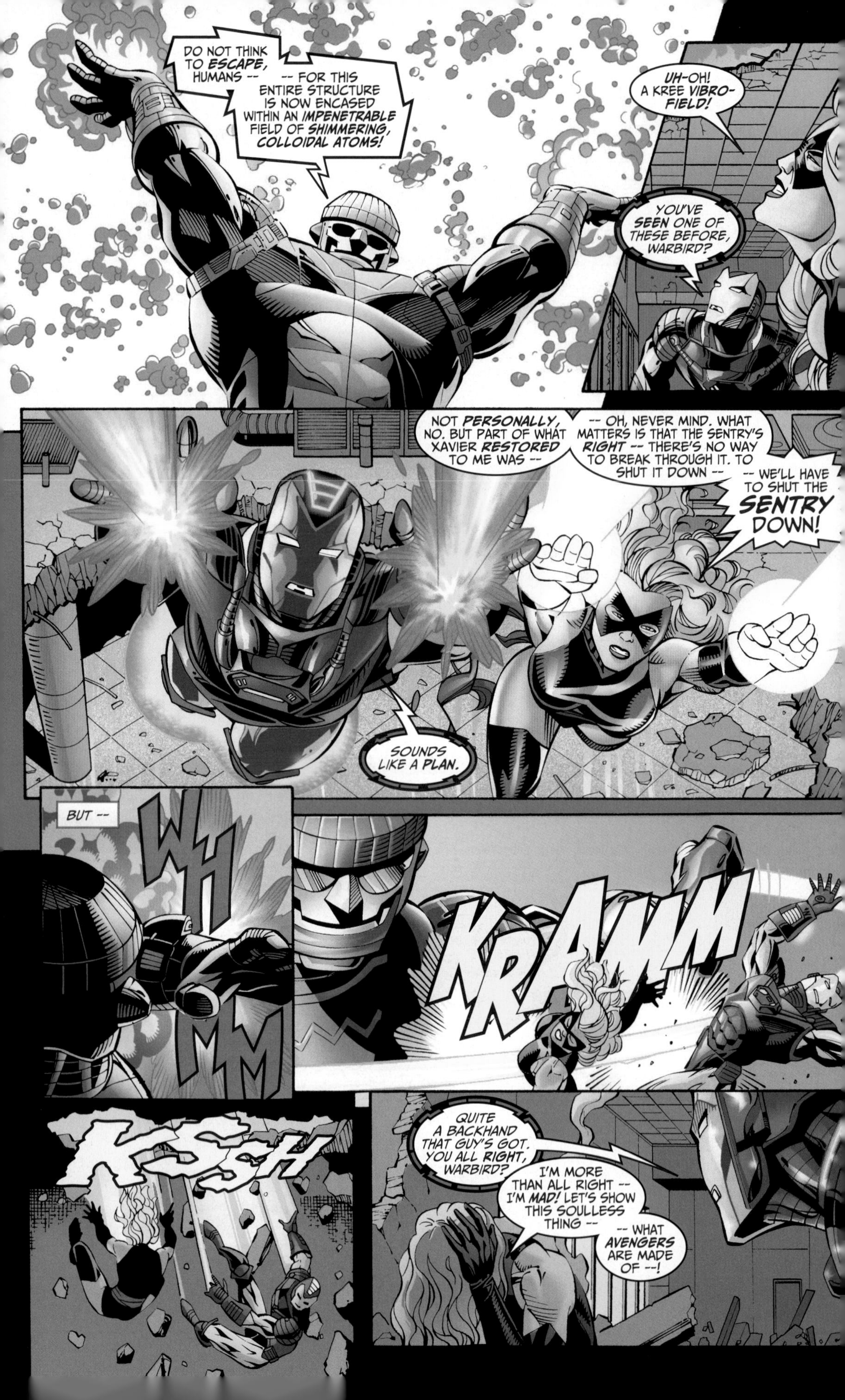
DO NOT THINK TO ESCAPE, HUMANS --
-- FOR THIS ENTIRE STRUCTURE IS NOW ENCASED WITHIN AN IMPENETRABLE FIELD OF SHIMMERING, COLLOIDAL ATOMS!
UH-OH! A KREE VIBRO-FIELD!
YOU'VE SEEN ONE OF THESE BEFORE, WARBIRD?
NOT PERSONALLY, NO. BUT PART OF WHAT XAVIER RESTORED TO ME WAS --
-- OH, NEVER MIND. WHAT MATTERS IS THAT THE SENTRY'S RIGHT -- THERE'S NO WAY TO BREAK THROUGH IT. TO SHUT IT DOWN --
-- WE'LL HAVE TO SHUT THE SENTRY DOWN!
SOUNDS LIKE A PLAN.
BUT --
WHMM
KRAMM
KSH
QUITE A BACKHAND THAT GUY'S GOT. YOU ALL RIGHT, WARBIRD?
I'M MORE THAN ALL RIGHT -- I'M MAD! LET'S SHOW THIS SOULLESS THING --
-- WHAT AVENGERS ARE MADE OF --!

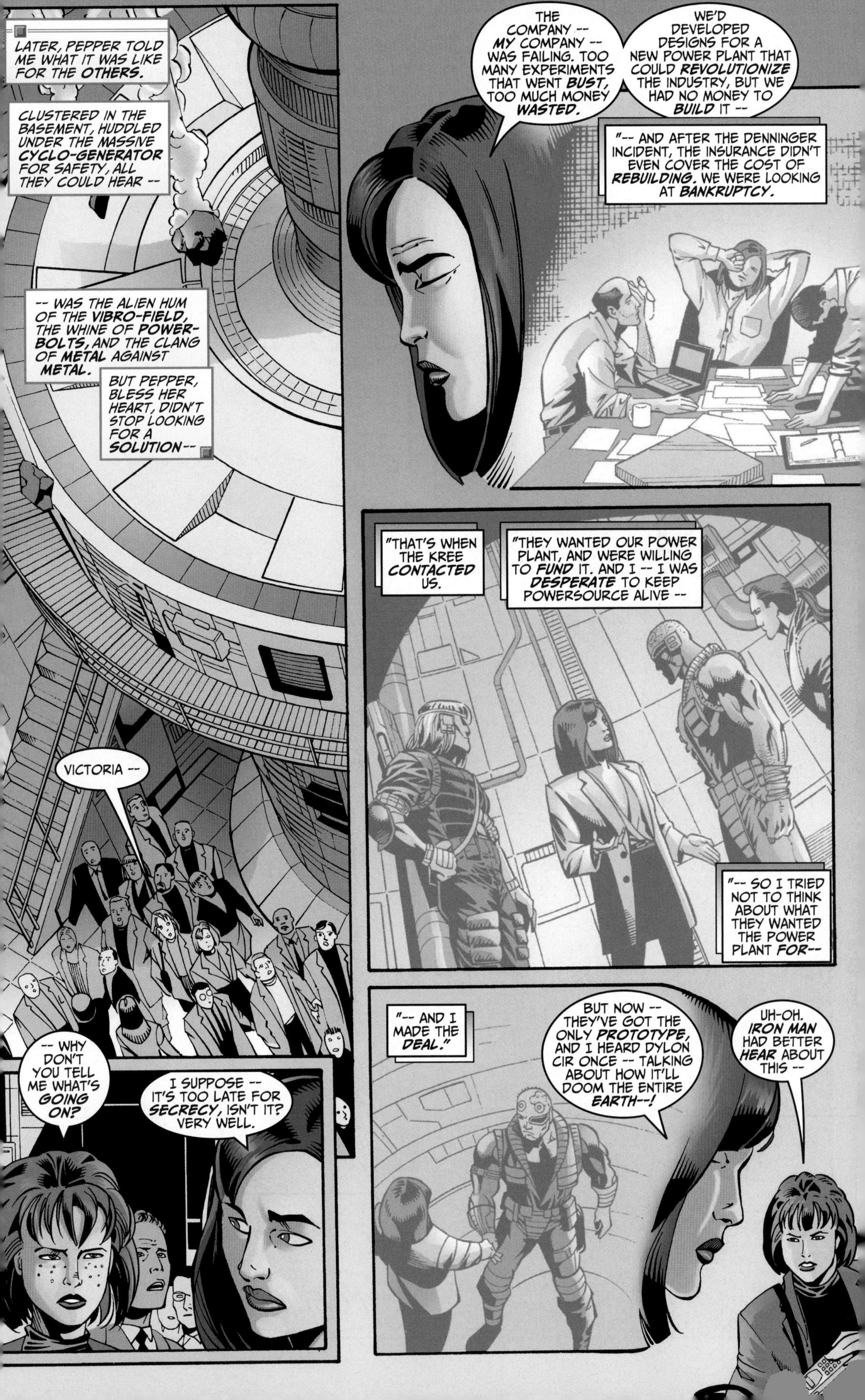

LATER, PEPPER TOLD ME WHAT IT WAS LIKE FOR THE OTHERS.
CLUSTERED IN THE BASEMENT, HUDDLED UNDER THE MASSIVE CYCLO-GENERATOR FOR SAFETY, ALL THEY COULD HEAR --
-- WAS THE ALIEN HUM OF THE VIBRO-FIELD, THE WHINE OF POWER-BOLTS, AND THE CLANG OF METAL AGAINST METAL.
BUT PEPPER, BLESS HER HEART, DIDN'T STOP LOOKING FOR A SOLUTION--
VICTORIA --
-- WHY DON'T YOU TELL ME WHAT'S GOING ON?
I SUPPOSE -- IT'S TOO LATE FOR SECRECY, ISN'T IT? VERY WELL.
THE COMPANY -- MY COMPANY -- WAS FAILING. TOO MANY EXPERIMENTS THAT WENT BUST, TOO MUCH MONEY WASTED.
WE'D DEVELOPED DESIGNS FOR A NEW POWER PLANT THAT COULD REVOLUTIONIZE THE INDUSTRY, BUT WE HAD NO MONEY TO BUILD IT --
"-- AND AFTER THE DENNINGER INCIDENT, THE INSURANCE DIDN'T EVEN COVER THE COST OF REBUILDING. WE WERE LOOKING AT BANKRUPTCY.
"THAT'S WHEN THE KREE CONTACTED US.
"THEY WANTED OUR POWER PLANT, AND WERE WILLING TO FUND IT. AND I -- I WAS DESPERATE TO KEEP POWERSOURCE ALIVE --
"-- SO I TRIED NOT TO THINK ABOUT WHAT THEY WANTED THE POWER PLANT FOR--
"-- AND I MADE THE DEAL."
BUT NOW -- THEY'VE GOT THE ONLY PROTOTYPE, AND I HEARD DYLON CIR ONCE -- TALKING ABOUT HOW IT'LL DOOM THE ENTIRE EARTH--!
UH-OH. IRON MAN HAD BETTER HEAR ABOUT THIS --

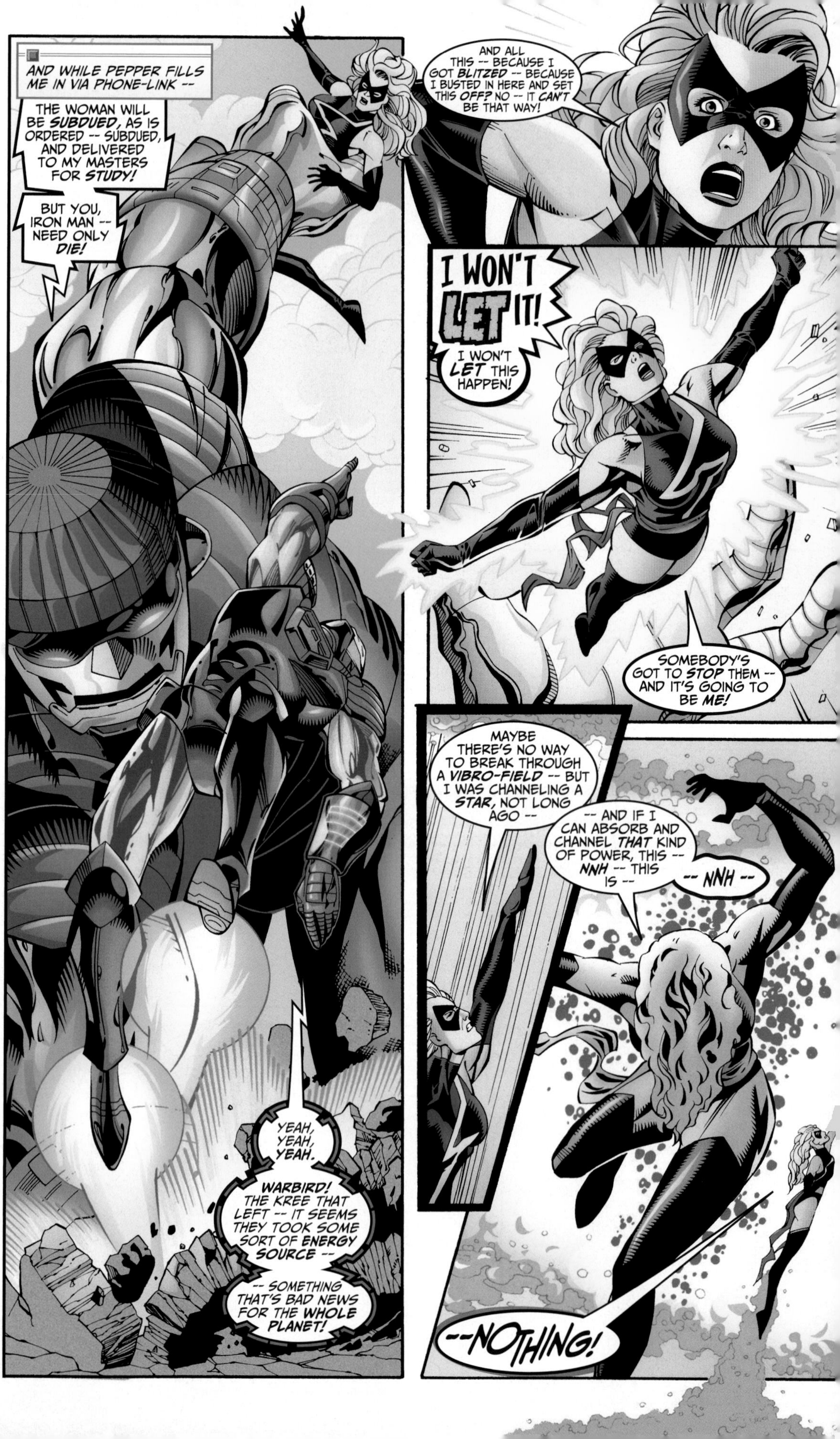

AND WHILE PEPPER FILLS ME IN VIA PHONE-LINK --
THE WOMAN WILL BE SUBDUED, AS IS ORDERED -- SUBDUED, AND DELIVERED TO MY MASTERS FOR STUDY!
BUT YOU, IRON MAN -- NEED ONLY DIE!
YEAH, YEAH, YEAH.
WARBIRD! THE KREE THAT LEFT -- IT SEEMS THEY TOOK SOME SORT OF ENERGY SOURCE --
-- SOMETHING THAT'S BAD NEWS FOR THE WHOLE PLANET!
AND ALL THIS -- BECAUSE I GOT BLITZED -- BECAUSE I BUSTED IN HERE AND SET THIS OFF? NO -- IT CAN'T BE THAT WAY!
I WON'T LET IT!
I WON'T LET THIS HAPPEN!
SOMEBODY'S GOT TO STOP THEM -- AND IT'S GOING TO BE ME!
MAYBE THERE'S NO WAY TO BREAK THROUGH A VIBRO-FIELD -- BUT I WAS CHANNELING A STAR, NOT LONG AGO --
-- AND IF I CAN ABSORB AND CHANNEL THAT KIND OF POWER, THIS -- NNH -- THIS IS --
-- NNH --
--NOTHING!

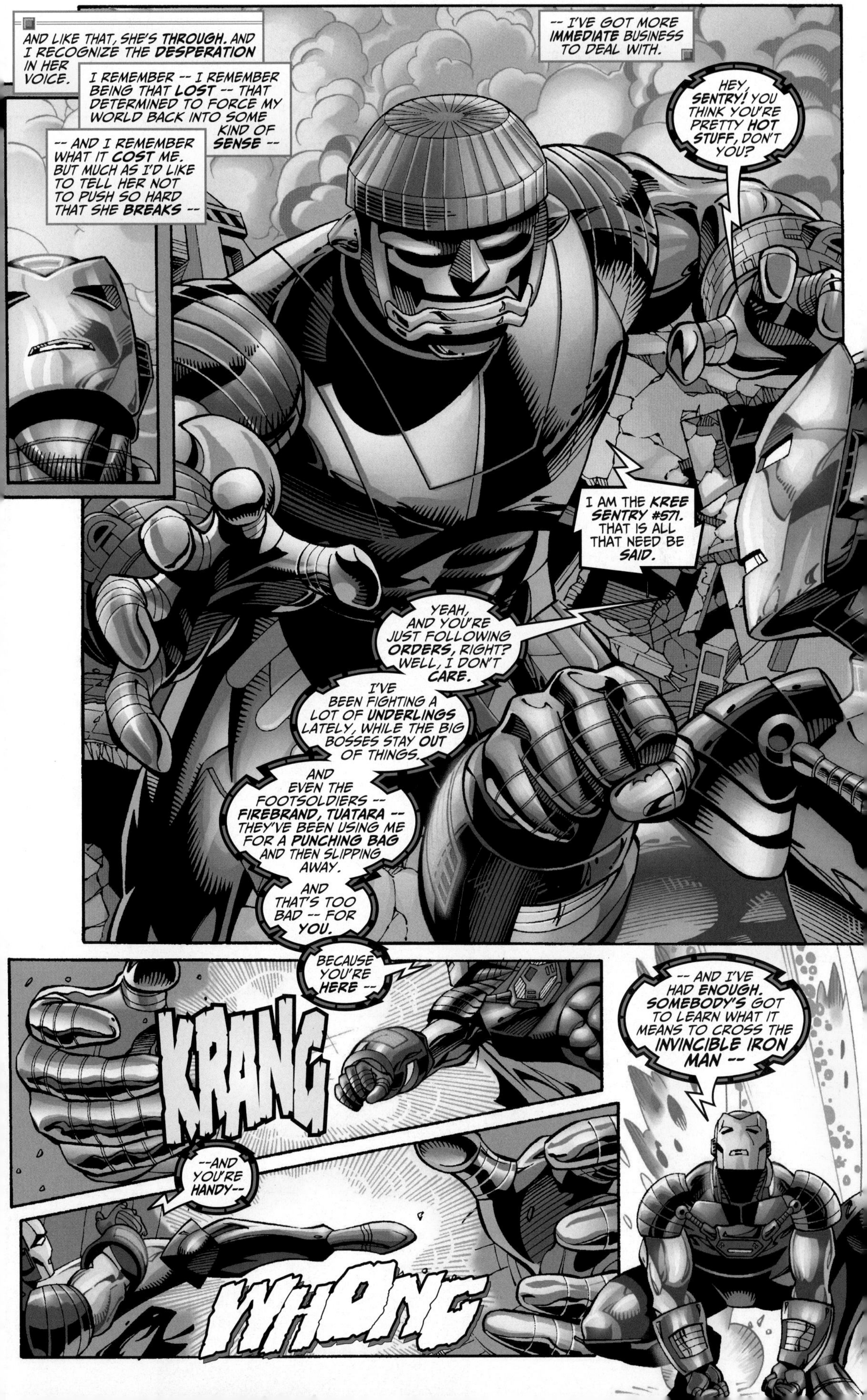

AND LIKE THAT, SHE'S THROUGH. AND I RECOGNIZE THE DESPERATION IN HER VOICE.
I REMEMBER -- I REMEMBER BEING THAT LOST -- THAT DETERMINED TO FORCE MY WORLD BACK INTO SOME KIND OF SENSE --
-- AND I REMEMBER WHAT IT COST ME. BUT MUCH AS I'D LIKE TO TELL HER NOT TO PUSH SO HARD THAT SHE BREAKS --
-- I'VE GOT MORE IMMEDIATE BUSINESS TO DEAL WITH.
HEY, SENTRY! YOU THINK YOU'RE PRETTY HOT STUFF, DON'T YOU?
I AM THE KREE SENTRY #571. THAT IS ALL THAT NEED BE SAID.
YEAH, AND YOU'RE JUST FOLLOWING ORDERS, RIGHT? WELL, I DON'T CARE.
I'VE BEEN FIGHTING A LOT OF UNDERLINGS LATELY, WHILE THE BIG BOSSES STAY OUT OF THINGS.
AND EVEN THE FOOTSOLDIERS -- FIREBRAND, TUATARA -- THEY'VE BEEN USING ME FOR A PUNCHING BAG AND THEN SLIPPING AWAY.
AND THAT'S TOO BAD -- FOR YOU.
BECAUSE YOU'RE HERE --
KRANG
--AND YOU'RE HANDY--
WHONG
-- AND I'VE HAD ENOUGH. SOMEBODY'S GOT TO LEARN WHAT IT MEANS TO CROSS THE INVINCIBLE IRON MAN --

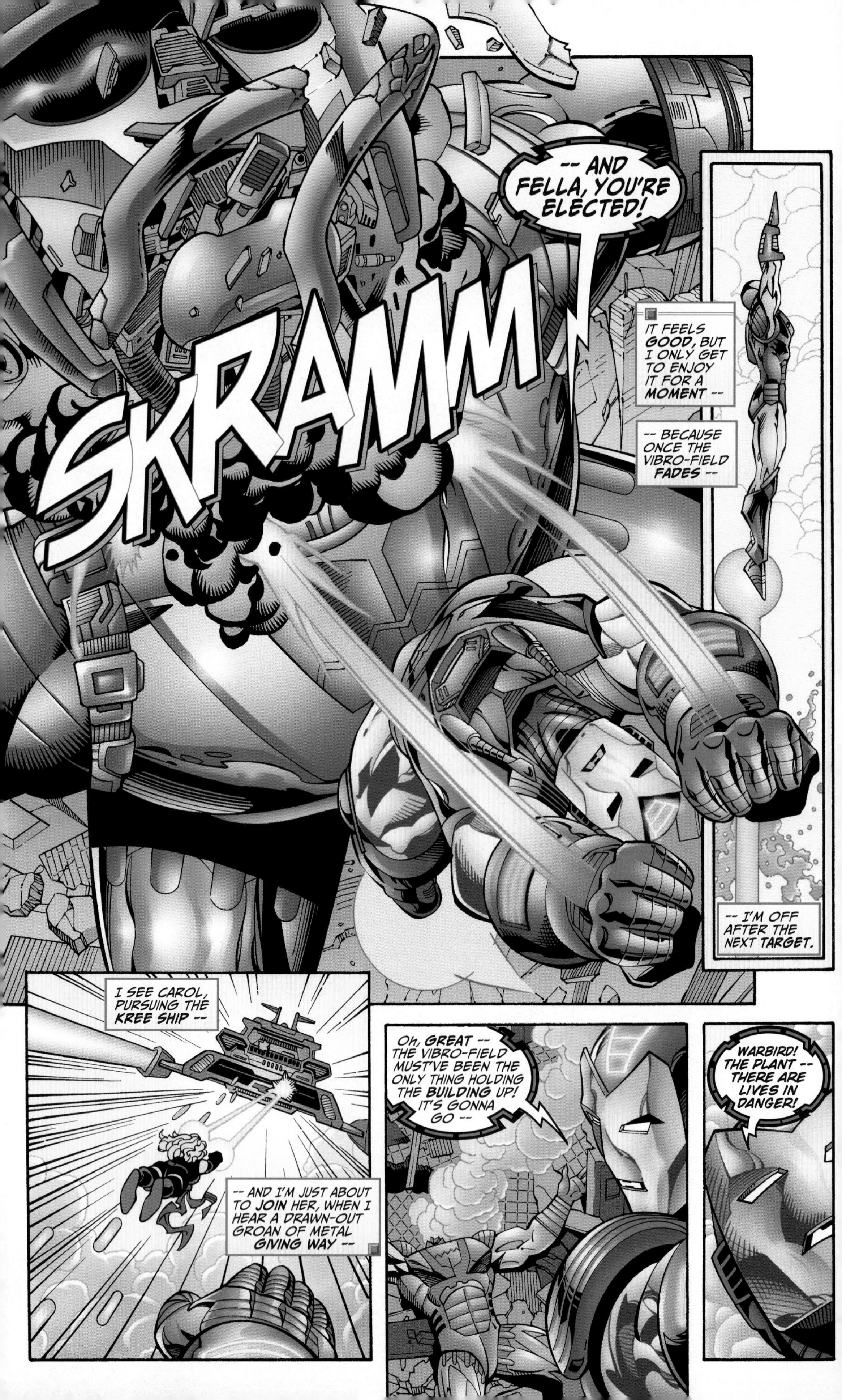
-- AND FELLA, YOU'RE ELECTED!
SKRAMM
IT FEELS GOOD, BUT I ONLY GET TO ENJOY IT FOR A MOMENT --
-- BECAUSE ONCE THE VIBRO-FIELD FADES --
-- I'M OFF AFTER THE NEXT TARGET.
I SEE CAROL, PURSUING THE KREE SHIP --
-- AND I'M JUST ABOUT TO JOIN HER, WHEN I HEAR A DRAWN-OUT GROAN OF METAL GIVING WAY --
Oh, GREAT -- THE VIBRO-FIELD MUST'VE BEEN THE ONLY THING HOLDING THE BUILDING UP! IT'S GONNA GO --
WARBIRD! THE PLANT -- THERE ARE LIVES IN DANGER!

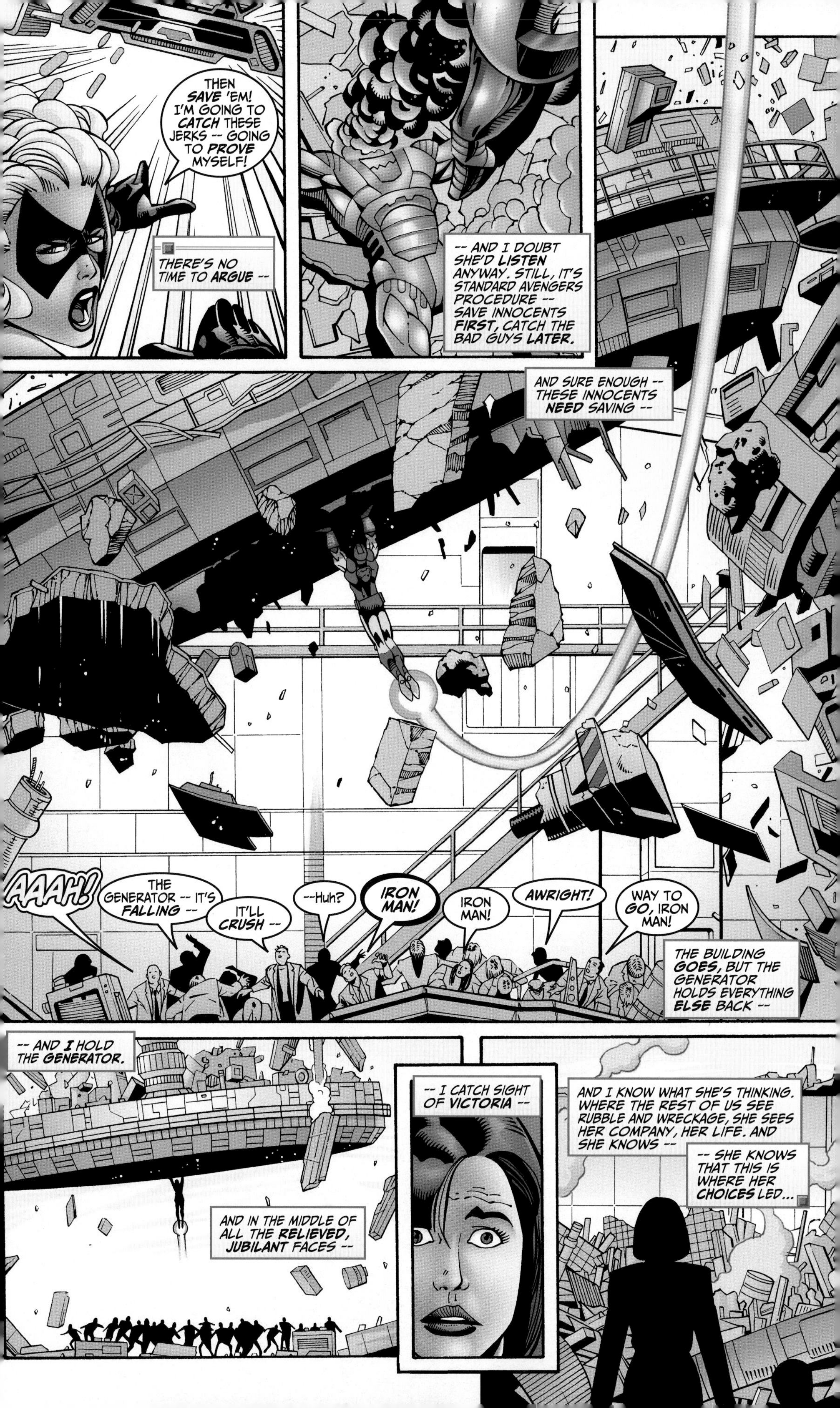
THEN SAVE 'EM! I'M GOING TO CATCH THESE JERKS -- GOING TO PROVE MYSELF!
THERE'S NO TIME TO ARGUE --
-- AND I DOUBT SHE'D LISTEN ANYWAY. STILL, IT'S STANDARD AVENGERS PROCEDURE -- SAVE INNOCENTS FIRST, CATCH THE BAD GUYS LATER.
AND SURE ENOUGH -- THESE INNOCENTS NEED SAVING --
AAAH!
THE GENERATOR -- IT'S FALLING --
IT'LL CRUSH --
--Huh?
IRON MAN!
IRON MAN!
AWRIGHT!
WAY TO GO, IRON MAN!
THE BUILDING GOES, BUT THE GENERATOR HOLDS EVERYTHING ELSE BACK --
-- AND I HOLD THE GENERATOR.
AND IN THE MIDDLE OF ALL THE RELIEVED, JUBILANT FACES --
-- I CATCH SIGHT OF VICTORIA --
AND I KNOW WHAT SHE'S THINKING. WHERE THE REST OF US SEE RUBBLE AND WRECKAGE, SHE SEES HER COMPANY, HER LIFE. AND SHE KNOWS --
-- SHE KNOWS THAT THIS IS WHERE HER CHOICES LED...

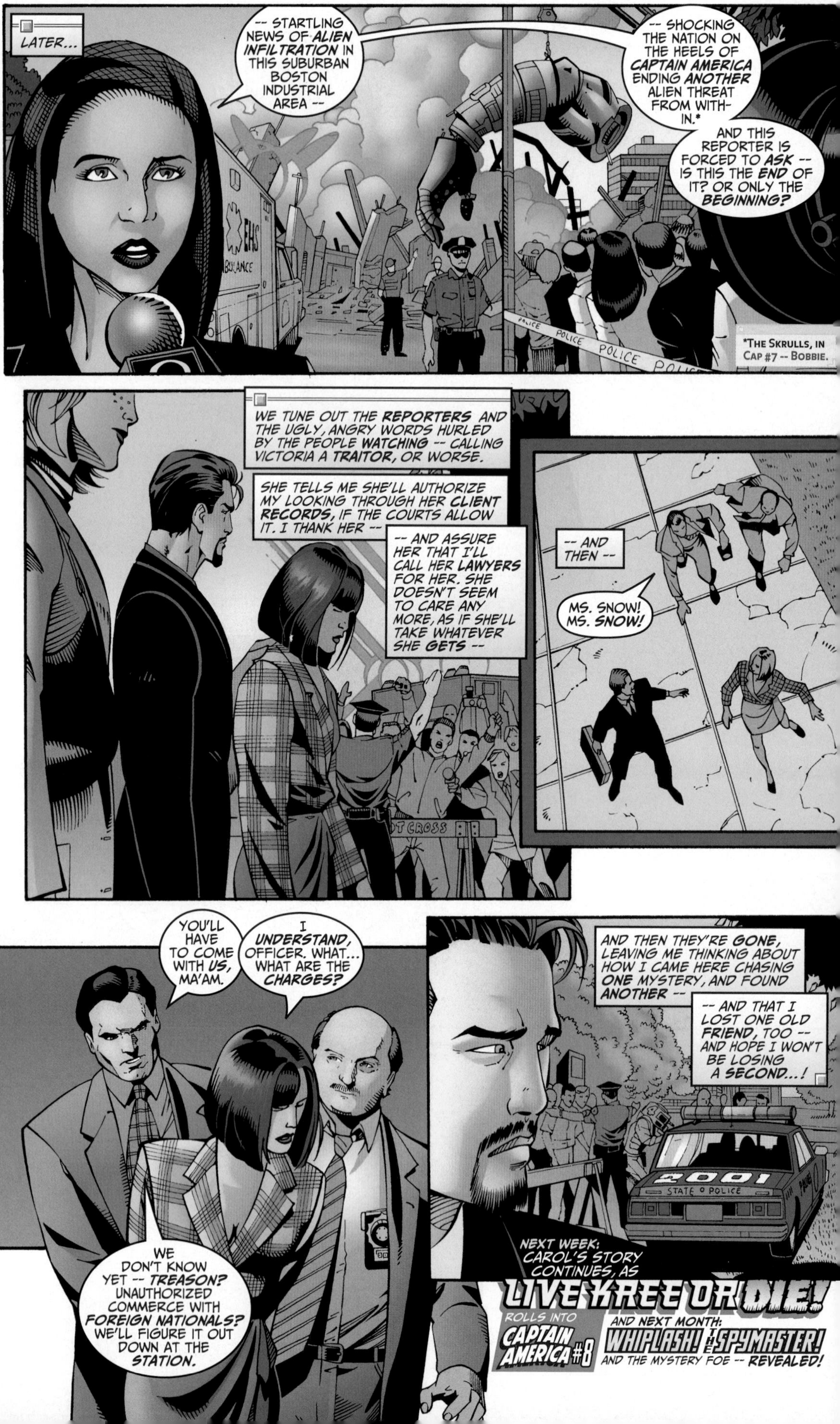
LATER...
-- STARTLING NEWS OF ALIEN INFILTRATION IN THIS SUBURBAN BOSTON INDUSTRIAL AREA --
-- SHOCKING THE NATION ON THE HEELS OF CAPTAIN AMERICA ENDING ANOTHER ALIEN THREAT FROM WITH-IN.*
AND THIS REPORTER IS FORCED TO ASK -- IS THIS THE END OF IT? OR ONLY THE BEGINNING?
*The Skrulls, in Cap #7 -- Bobbie.
POLICE POLICE POLICE
WE TUNE OUT THE REPORTERS AND THE UGLY, ANGRY WORDS HURLED BY THE PEOPLE WATCHING -- CALLING VICTORIA A TRAITOR, OR WORSE.
SHE TELLS ME SHE'LL AUTHORIZE MY LOOKING THROUGH HER CLIENT RECORDS, IF THE COURTS ALLOW IT. I THANK HER --
-- AND ASSURE HER THAT I'LL CALL HER LAWYERS FOR HER. SHE DOESN'T SEEM TO CARE ANY MORE, AS IF SHE'LL TAKE WHATEVER SHE GETS --
-- AND THEN --
MS. SNOW! MS. SNOW!
YOU'LL HAVE TO COME WITH US, MA'AM.
I UNDERSTAND, OFFICER. WHAT... WHAT ARE THE CHARGES?
WE DON'T KNOW YET -- TREASON? UNAUTHORIZED COMMERCE WITH FOREIGN NATIONALS? WE'LL FIGURE IT OUT DOWN AT THE STATION.
AND THEN THEY'RE GONE, LEAVING ME THINKING ABOUT HOW I CAME HERE CHASING ONE MYSTERY, AND FOUND ANOTHER --
-- AND THAT I LOST ONE OLD FRIEND, TOO -- AND HOPE I WON'T BE LOSING A SECOND...!
2001
STATE POLICE
NEXT WEEK: CAROL'S STORY CONTINUES, AS
LIVE KREE OR DIE!
ROLLS INTO CAPTAIN AMERICA #8
AND NEXT MONTH: WHIPLASH! THE SPYMASTER! AND THE MYSTERY FOE -- REVEALED!

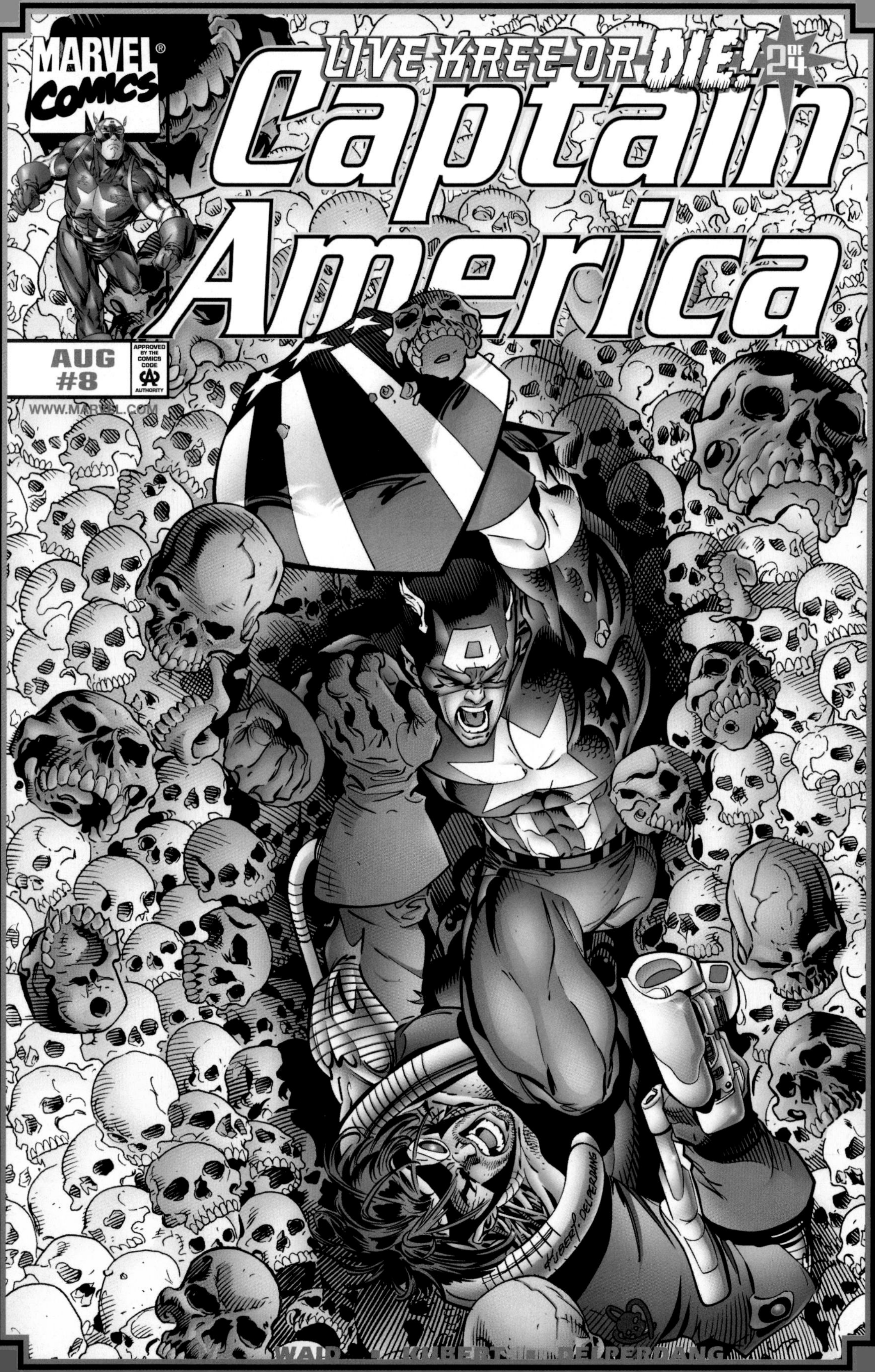
MARVEL COMICS
LIVE KREE OR DIE! 2 OF 4
Captain America
AUG #8
APPROVED BY THE COMICS CODE AUTHORITY
WWW.MARVEL.COM
WAID KUBERT DELPERDANG

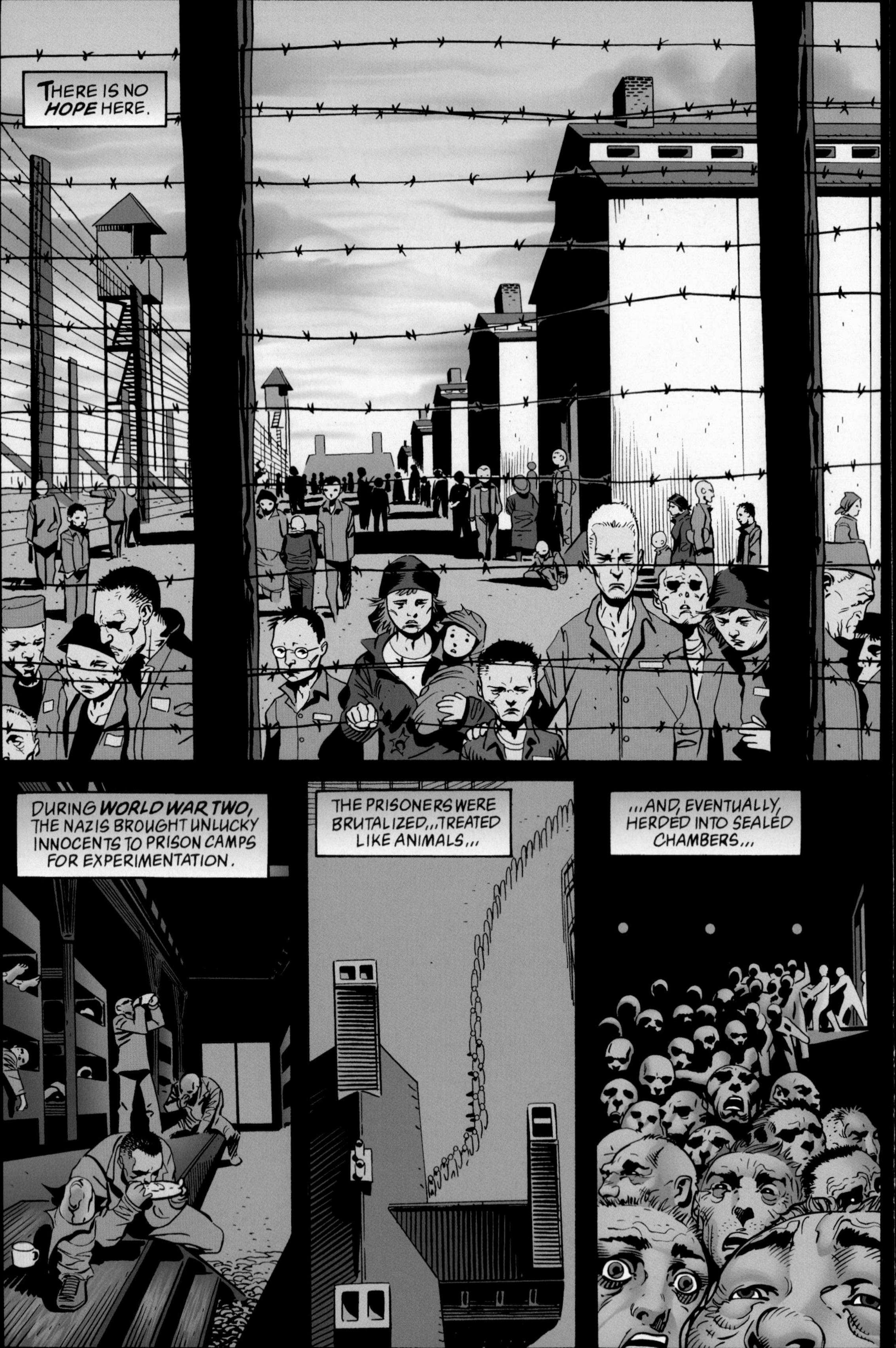
THERE IS NO HOPE HERE.
DURING WORLD WAR TWO, THE NAZIS BROUGHT UNLUCKY INNOCENTS TO PRISON CAMPS FOR EXPERIMENTATION.
THE PRISONERS WERE BRUTALIZED...TREATED LIKE ANIMALS...
...AND, EVENTUALLY, HERDED INTO SEALED CHAMBERS...

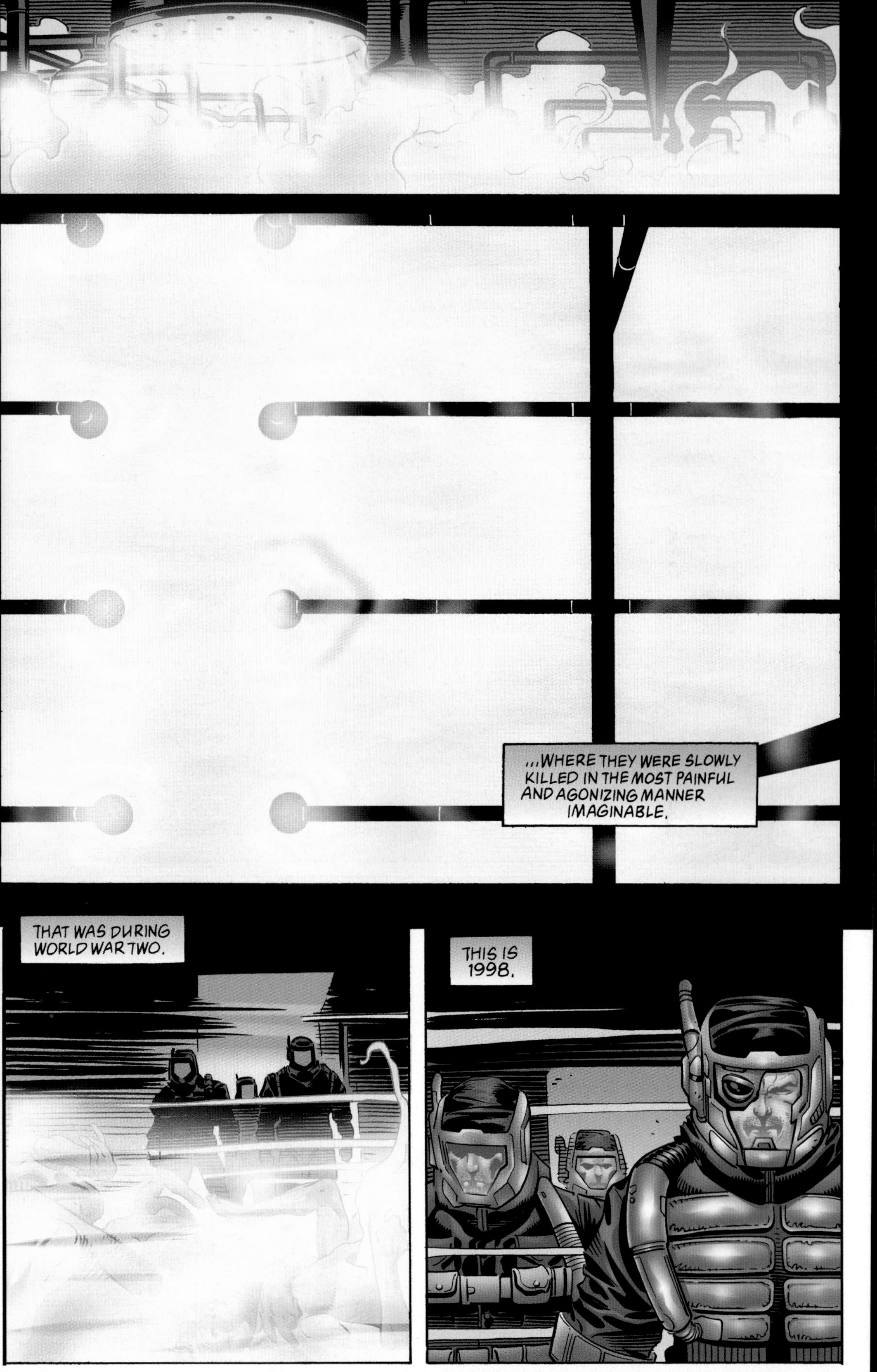
...WHERE THEY WERE SLOWLY KILLED IN THE MOST PAINFUL AND AGONIZING MANNER IMAGINABLE.
THAT WAS DURING WORLD WAR TWO.
THIS IS 1998.

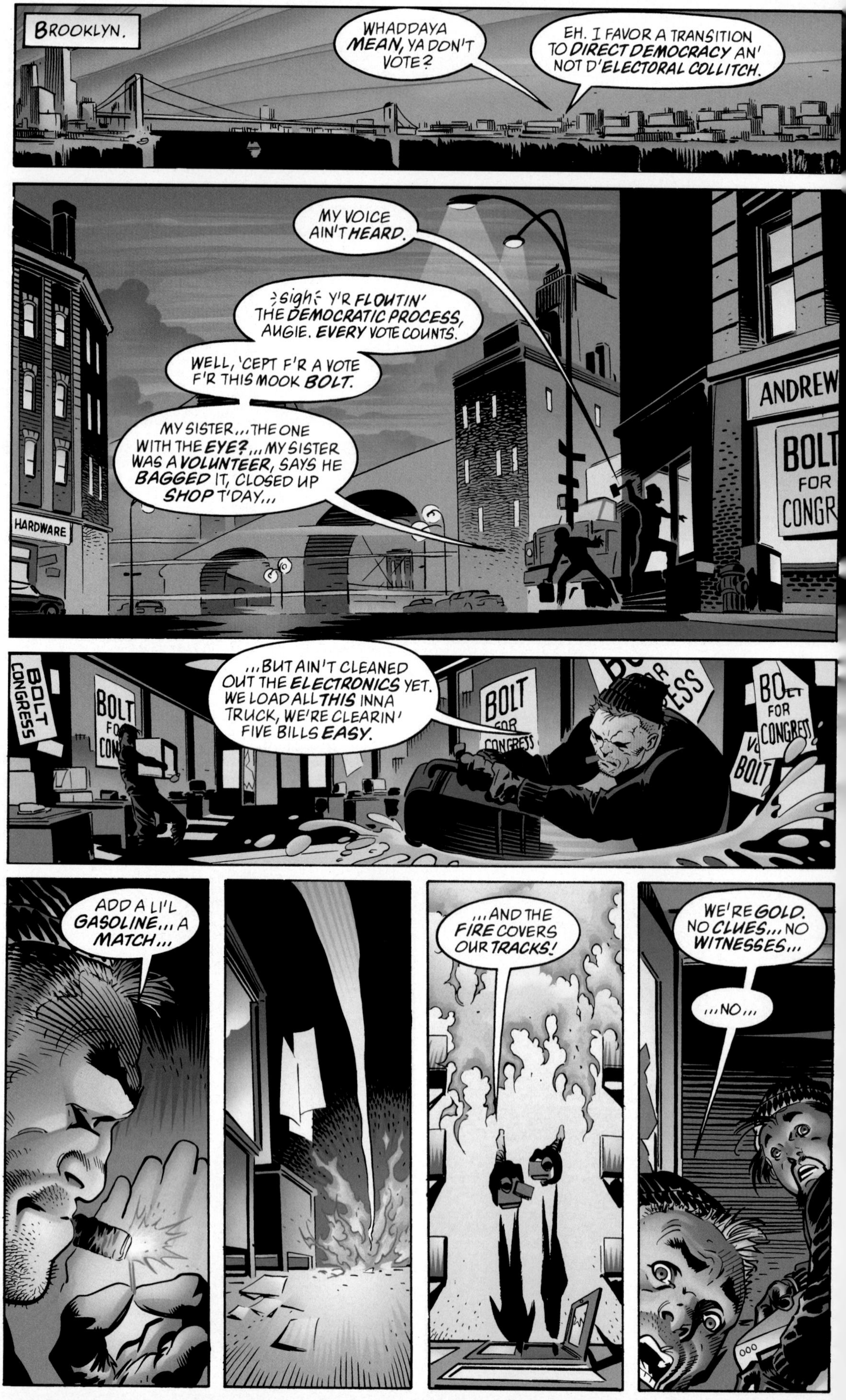
BROOKLYN.
WHADDAYA MEAN, YA DON'T VOTE?
EH. I FAVOR A TRANSITION TO DIRECT DEMOCRACY AN' NOT D'ELECTORAL COLLITCH.
MY VOICE AIN'T HEARD.
-sigh- Y'R FLOUTIN' THE DEMOCRATIC PROCESS, AUGIE. EVERY VOTE COUNTS.
WELL, 'CEPT F'R A VOTE F'R THIS MOOK BOLT.
MY SISTER... THE ONE WITH THE EYE?... MY SISTER WAS A VOLUNTEER, SAYS HE BAGGED IT, CLOSED UP SHOP T'DAY...
HARDWARE
ANDREW
BOLT FOR CONGR
...BUT AIN'T CLEANED OUT THE ELECTRONICS YET. WE LOAD ALL THIS INNA TRUCK, WE'RE CLEARIN' FIVE BILLS EASY.
BOLT CONGRESS
BOLT FOR CONGRESS
BOLT FOR CONGRESS
BOLT FOR CONGRESS
ADD A LI'L GASOLINE... A MATCH...
...AND THE FIRE COVERS OUR TRACKS!
WE'RE GOLD. NO CLUES... NO WITNESSES...
...NO...

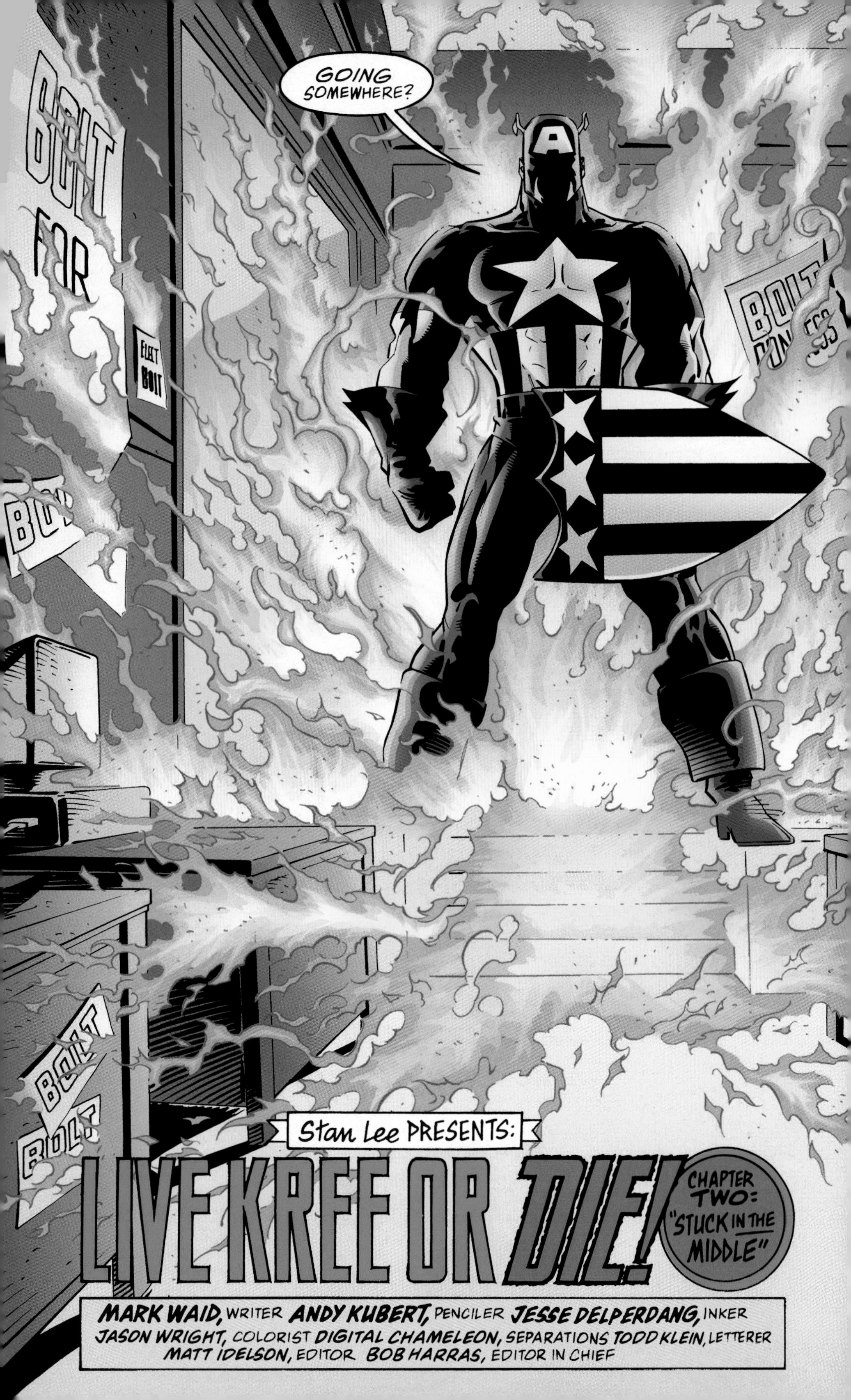
GOING SOMEWHERE?
Stan Lee PRESENTS:
LIVE KREE OR DIE!
CHAPTER TWO: "STUCK IN THE MIDDLE"
MARK WAID, WRITER ANDY KUBERT, PENCILER JESSE DELPERDANG, INKER
JASON WRIGHT, COLORIST DIGITAL CHAMELEON, SEPARATIONS TODD KLEIN, LETTERER
MATT IDELSON, EDITOR BOB HARRAS, EDITOR IN CHIEF

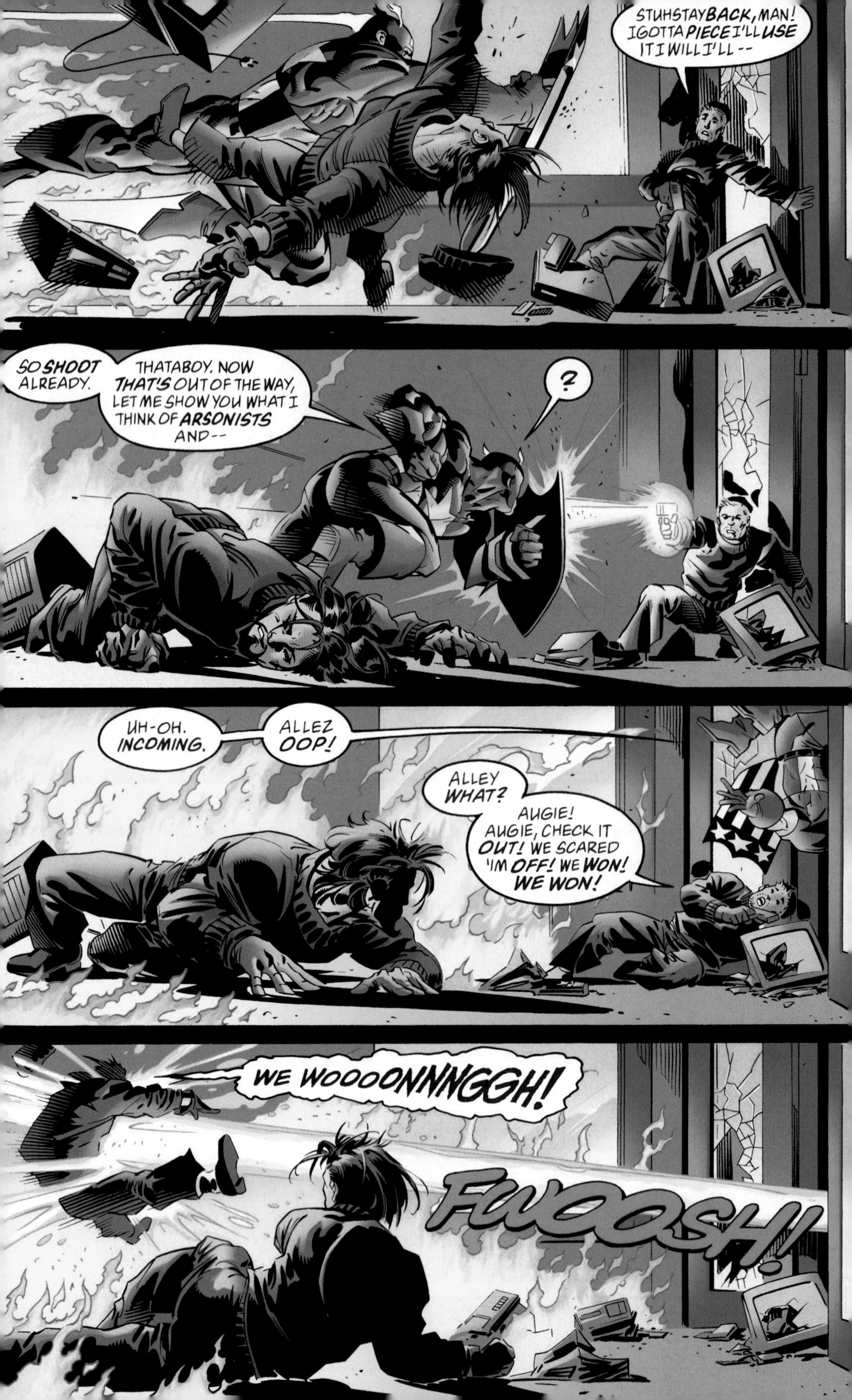
STUHSTAYBACK, MAN! IGOTTAPIECEI'LLUSE ITIWILLI'LL--
SO SHOOT ALREADY.
THATABOY. NOW THAT'S OUT OF THE WAY, LET ME SHOW YOU WHAT I THINK OF ARSONISTS AND--
?
UH-OH. INCOMING.
ALLEZ OOP!
ALLEY WHAT?
AUGIE! AUGIE, CHECK IT OUT! WE SCARED 'IM OFF! WE WON! WE WON!
WE WOOOONNNGGH!
FWOOSH!!

--AND WE'RE **DONE!** SHOW'S **OVER,** FOLKS! FIRE'S **OUT!**

AND THE CULPRITS ARE BEHIND **BARS**... THANKS TO **YOU,** CAP. WHAT BRINGS YOU HERE?

I WAS LOOKING FOR **YOU,** FRANKLY. WHY WAS YOUR OFFICE **DESERTED?**

WHY GO **ON?** CONGRESS IS OUT OF **REACH** FOR **THIS** UNLUCKY COUNCILMAN, CAP. CAMPAIGN TOOK TOO BIG A **HIT** THE OTHER DAY.

I THOUGHT I WAS GETTING YOUR **ENDORSEMENT,** RIGHT?

TURNS OUT I GOT THE NOD FROM THE SKRULL **IMPERSONATING** YOU...AND THE MEDIA'S HAVING A **FIELD DAY** WITH THAT. I'M A **LAUGHING STOCK.***

THE **DAILY NEWS** HAS ALREADY MOCKED UP MY **POLL RESULTS** ON MARS.

AILY BUGL
Wednesday, June 17, 1998
Congressional Hopeful
Endorsed by Cap Impos

*ISSUE 6.--MATT

I-- I DON'T KNOW WHAT TO **SAY.** THIS IS **EXACTLY** THE KIND OF DAMAGE I WAS **AFRAID** HE'D CAUSE.

THE SKRULL USED MY REPUTATION TO SHATTER **LIVES**...AND I **CANNOT** HAVE THAT ON MY **CONSCIENCE**...

BREE

EXCUSE ME, BOLT. AVENGERS **ALERT.**

WARBIRD? WHAT'S **WRONG?**

PRIORITY RED, CAP! I NEED **HELP--** FAST!

AUTHORIZED
FULL SECURITY CLEARANCE
AUTHORIZED
AUTHORIZED
RERS

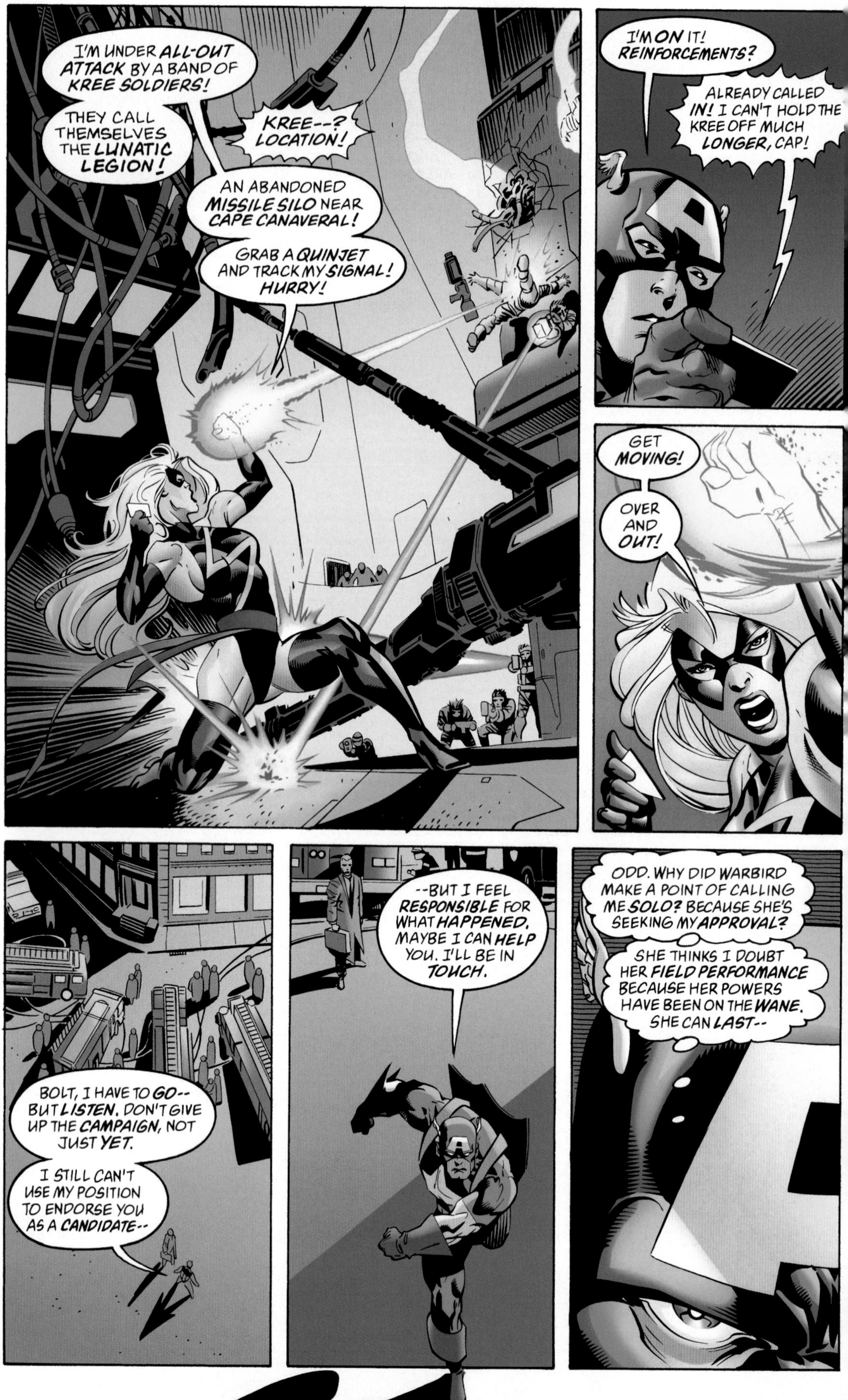

I'M UNDER ALL-OUT ATTACK BY A BAND OF KREE SOLDIERS!
THEY CALL THEMSELVES THE LUNATIC LEGION!
KREE--? LOCATION!
AN ABANDONED MISSILE SILO NEAR CAPE CANAVERAL!
GRAB A QUINJET AND TRACK MY SIGNAL! HURRY!
I'M ON IT! REINFORCEMENTS?
ALREADY CALLED IN! I CAN'T HOLD THE KREE OFF MUCH LONGER, CAP!
GET MOVING!
OVER AND OUT!
BOLT, I HAVE TO GO-- BUT LISTEN. DON'T GIVE UP THE CAMPAIGN, NOT JUST YET.
I STILL CAN'T USE MY POSITION TO ENDORSE YOU AS A CANDIDATE--
--BUT I FEEL RESPONSIBLE FOR WHAT HAPPENED. MAYBE I CAN HELP YOU. I'LL BE IN TOUCH.
ODD. WHY DID WARBIRD MAKE A POINT OF CALLING ME SOLO? BECAUSE SHE'S SEEKING MY APPROVAL?
SHE THINKS I DOUBT HER FIELD PERFORMANCE BECAUSE HER POWERS HAVE BEEN ON THE WANE. SHE CAN LAST--

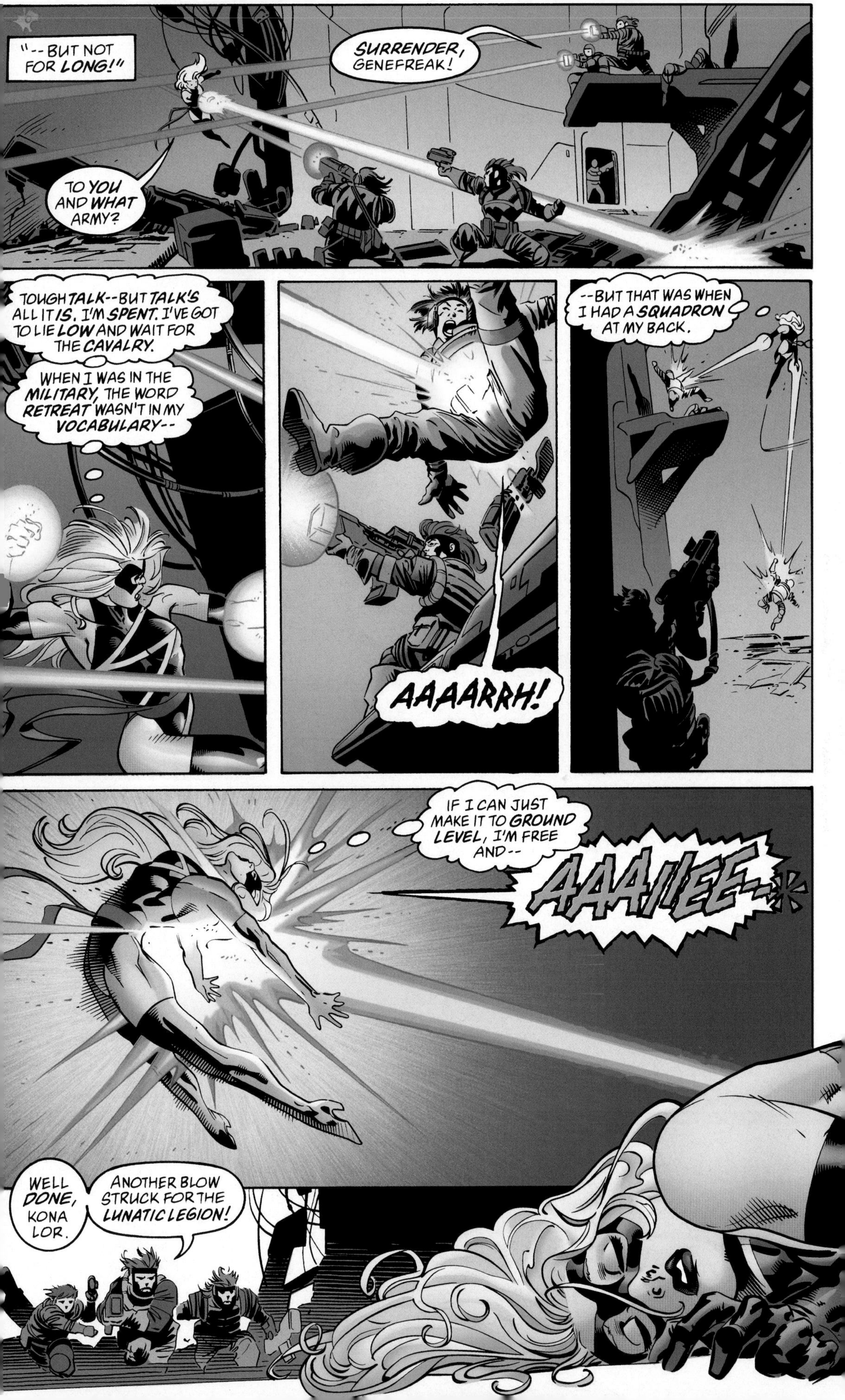
"--BUT NOT FOR LONG!"
SURRENDER, GENEFREAK!
TO YOU AND WHAT ARMY?
TOUGH TALK--BUT TALK'S ALL IT IS. I'M SPENT. I'VE GOT TO LIE LOW AND WAIT FOR THE CAVALRY.
WHEN I WAS IN THE MILITARY, THE WORD RETREAT WASN'T IN MY VOCABULARY--
AAAARRH!
--BUT THAT WAS WHEN I HAD A SQUADRON AT MY BACK.
IF I CAN JUST MAKE IT TO GROUND LEVEL, I'M FREE AND--
AAAIIEE--
WELL DONE, KONA LOR.
ANOTHER BLOW STRUCK FOR THE LUNATIC LEGION!

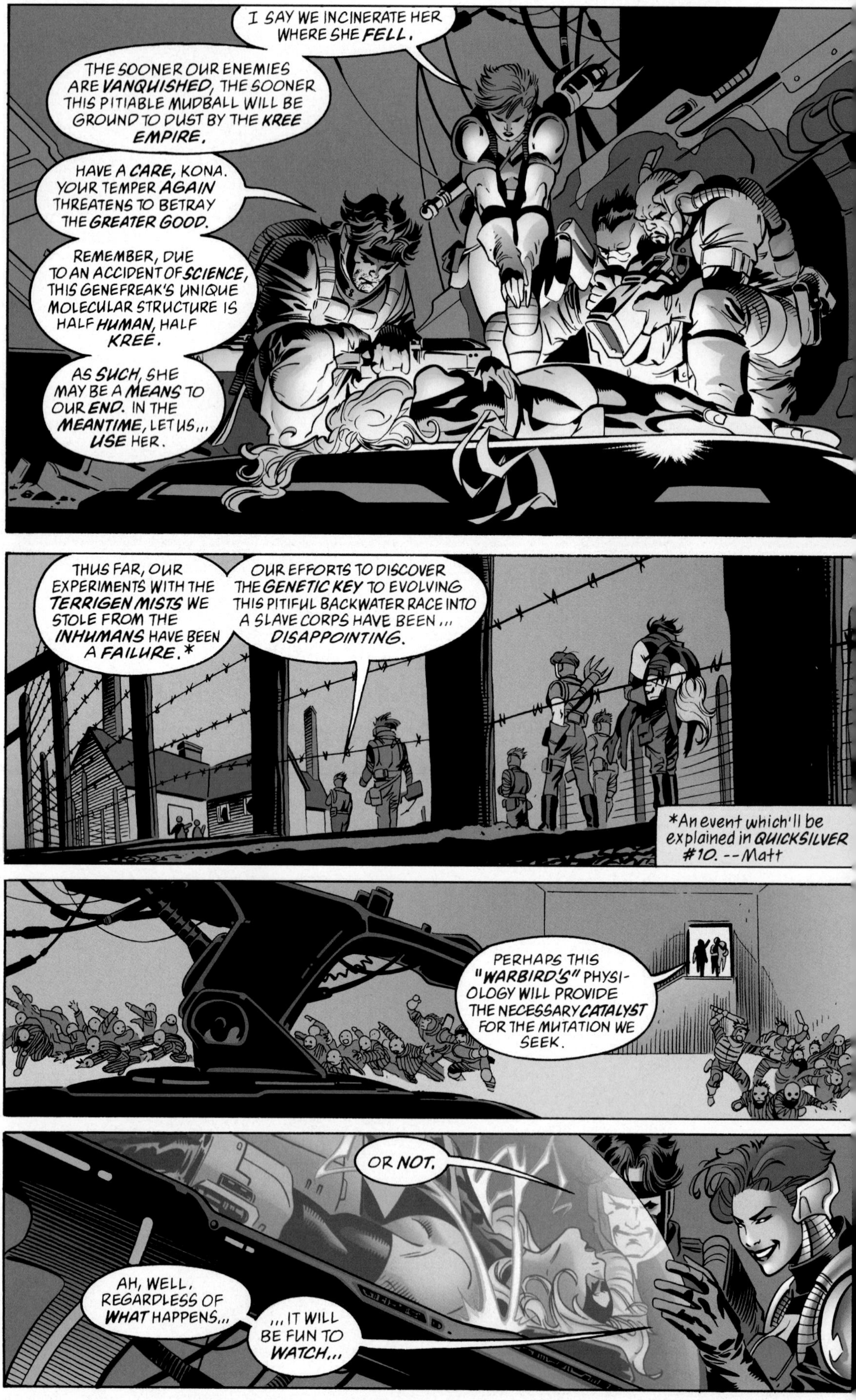
THE SOONER OUR ENEMIES ARE VANQUISHED, THE SOONER THIS PITIABLE MUDBALL WILL BE GROUND TO DUST BY THE KREE EMPIRE.
I SAY WE INCINERATE HER WHERE SHE FELL.
HAVE A CARE, KONA. YOUR TEMPER AGAIN THREATENS TO BETRAY THE GREATER GOOD.
REMEMBER, DUE TO AN ACCIDENT OF SCIENCE, THIS GENEFREAK'S UNIQUE MOLECULAR STRUCTURE IS HALF HUMAN, HALF KREE.
AS SUCH, SHE MAY BE A MEANS TO OUR END. IN THE MEANTIME, LET US... USE HER.
THUS FAR, OUR EXPERIMENTS WITH THE TERRIGEN MISTS WE STOLE FROM THE INHUMANS HAVE BEEN A FAILURE.*
OUR EFFORTS TO DISCOVER THE GENETIC KEY TO EVOLVING THIS PITIFUL BACKWATER RACE INTO A SLAVE CORPS HAVE BEEN... DISAPPOINTING.
*An event which'll be explained in QUICKSILVER #10. --Matt
PERHAPS THIS "WARBIRD'S" PHYSIOLOGY WILL PROVIDE THE NECESSARY CATALYST FOR THE MUTATION WE SEEK.
OR NOT.
AH, WELL, REGARDLESS OF WHAT HAPPENS...
...IT WILL BE FUN TO WATCH...

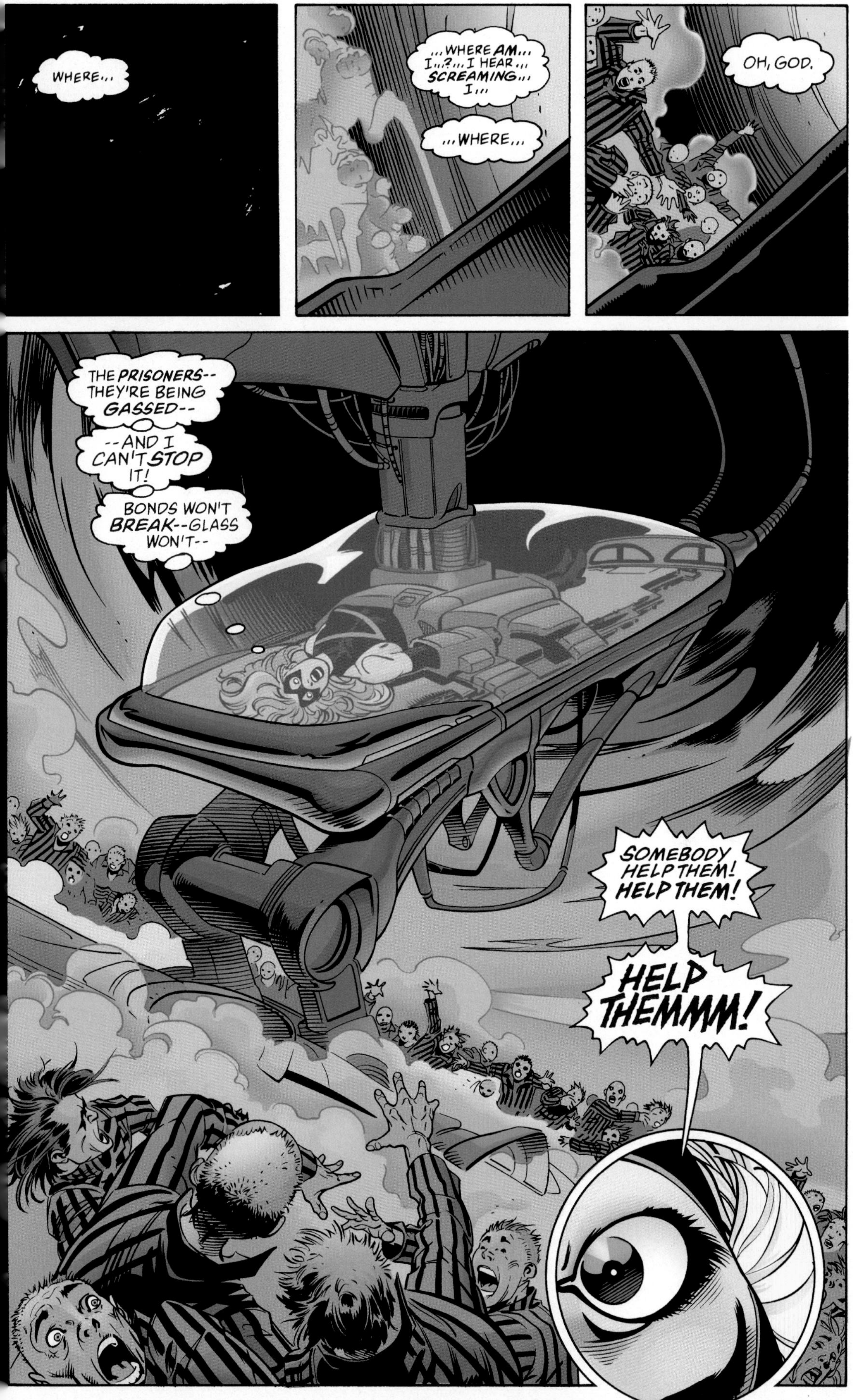
WHERE...
...WHERE AM I...?...I HEAR...SCREAMING...I...
...WHERE...
OH, GOD.
THE PRISONERS--THEY'RE BEING GASSED--
--AND I CAN'T STOP IT!
BONDS WON'T BREAK--GLASS WON'T--
SOMEBODY HELP THEM! HELP THEM!
HELP THEMMM!

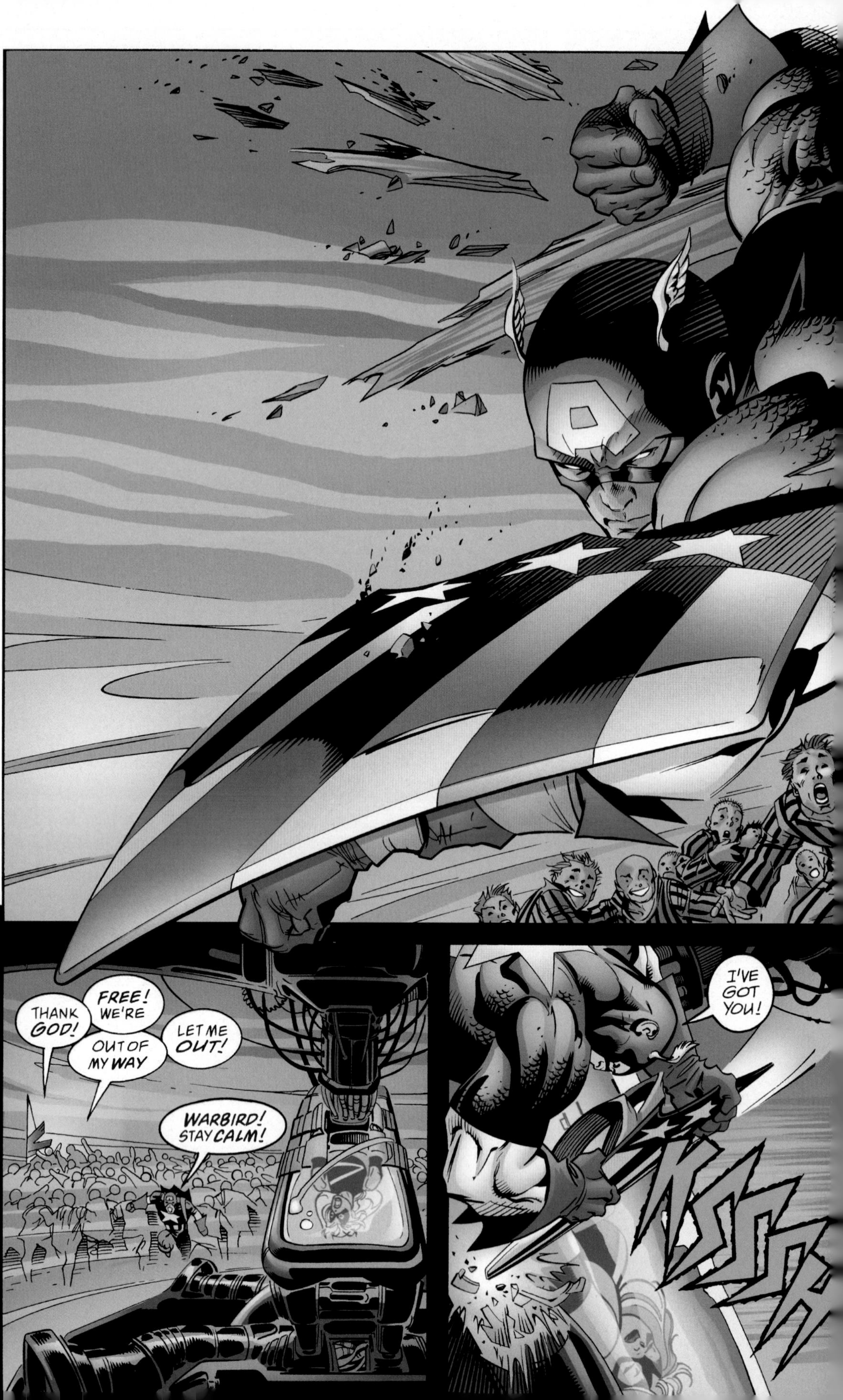
THANK GOD!
FREE! WE'RE
OUT OF MY WAY
LET ME OUT!
WARBIRD! STAY CALM!
I'VE GOT YOU!
KSSSK

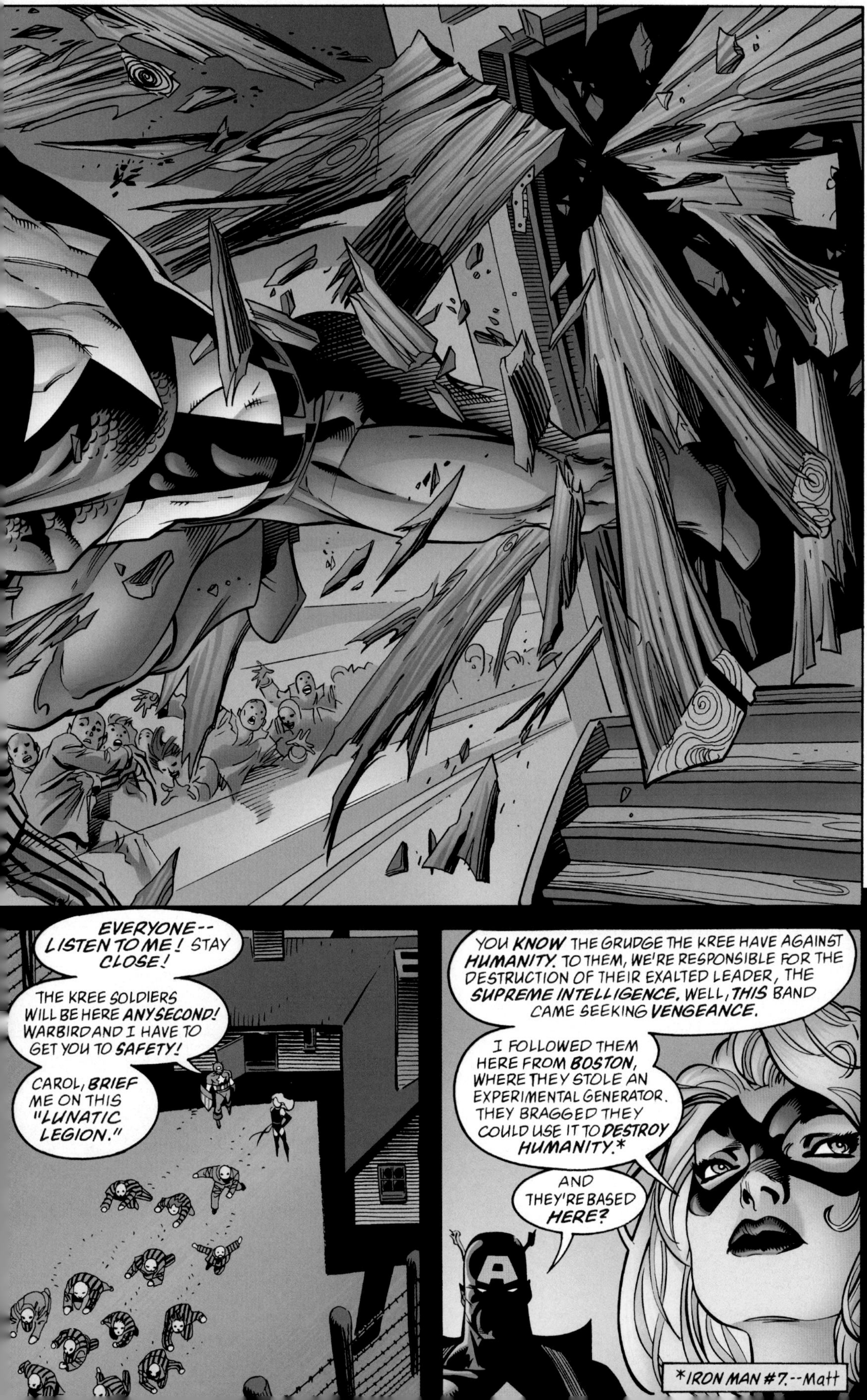
EVERYONE-- LISTEN TO ME! STAY CLOSE!
THE KREE SOLDIERS WILL BE HERE ANY SECOND! WARBIRD AND I HAVE TO GET YOU TO SAFETY!
CAROL, BRIEF ME ON THIS "LUNATIC LEGION."
YOU KNOW THE GRUDGE THE KREE HAVE AGAINST HUMANITY. TO THEM, WE'RE RESPONSIBLE FOR THE DESTRUCTION OF THEIR EXALTED LEADER, THE SUPREME INTELLIGENCE. WELL, THIS BAND CAME SEEKING VENGEANCE.
I FOLLOWED THEM HERE FROM BOSTON, WHERE THEY STOLE AN EXPERIMENTAL GENERATOR. THEY BRAGGED THEY COULD USE IT TO DESTROY HUMANITY.*
AND THEY'RE BASED HERE?
*IRON MAN #7.--Matt

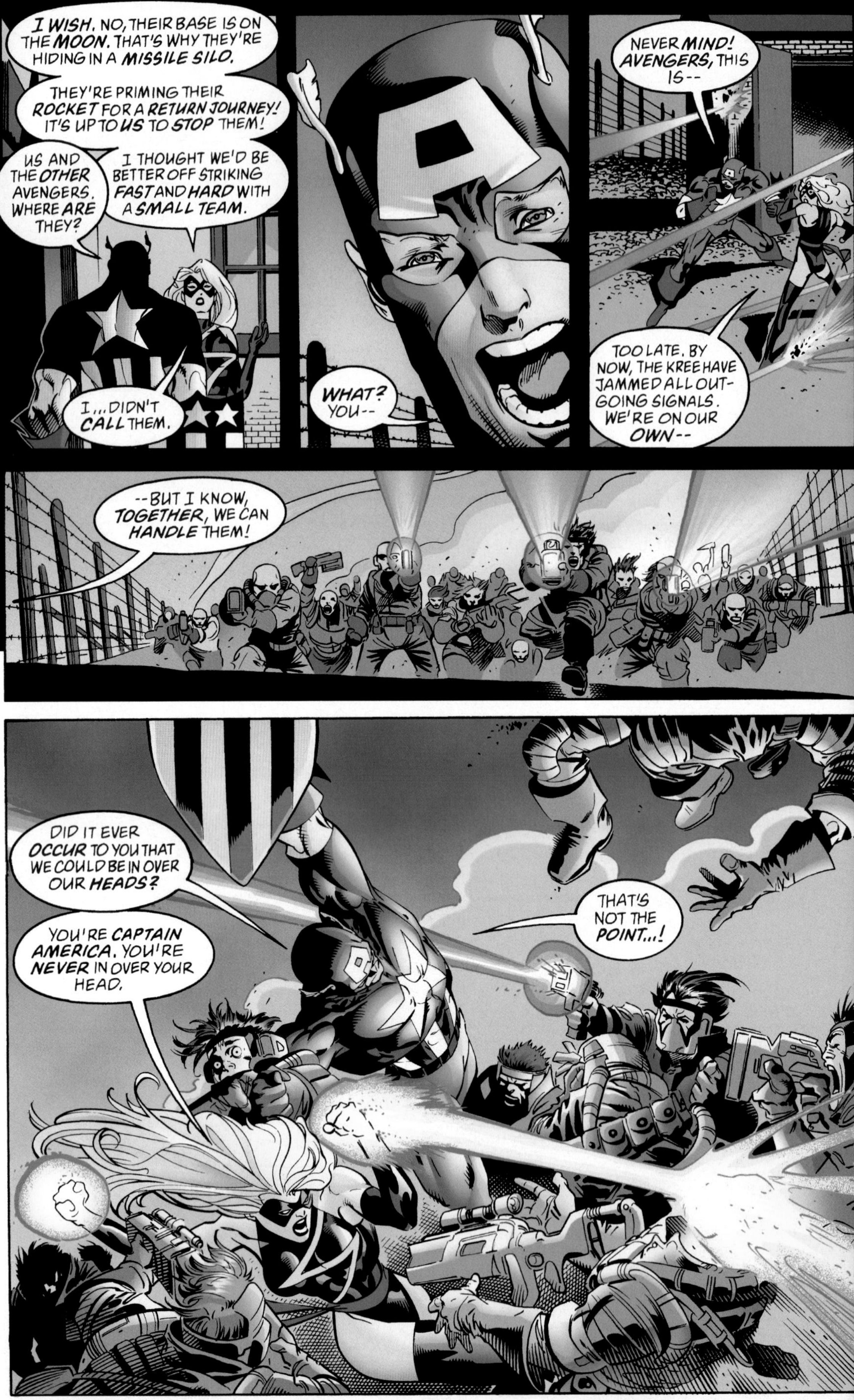
I WISH. NO, THEIR BASE IS ON THE MOON. THAT'S WHY THEY'RE HIDING IN A MISSILE SILO.
THEY'RE PRIMING THEIR ROCKET FOR A RETURN JOURNEY! IT'S UP TO US TO STOP THEM!
US AND THE OTHER AVENGERS. WHERE ARE THEY?
I THOUGHT WE'D BE BETTER OFF STRIKING FAST AND HARD WITH A SMALL TEAM.
I... DIDN'T CALL THEM.
WHAT? YOU--
NEVER MIND! AVENGERS, THIS IS--
TOO LATE. BY NOW, THE KREE HAVE JAMMED ALL OUT-GOING SIGNALS. WE'RE ON OUR OWN--
--BUT I KNOW, TOGETHER, WE CAN HANDLE THEM!
DID IT EVER OCCUR TO YOU THAT WE COULD BE IN OVER OUR HEADS?
YOU'RE CAPTAIN AMERICA. YOU'RE NEVER IN OVER YOUR HEAD.
THAT'S NOT THE POINT...!

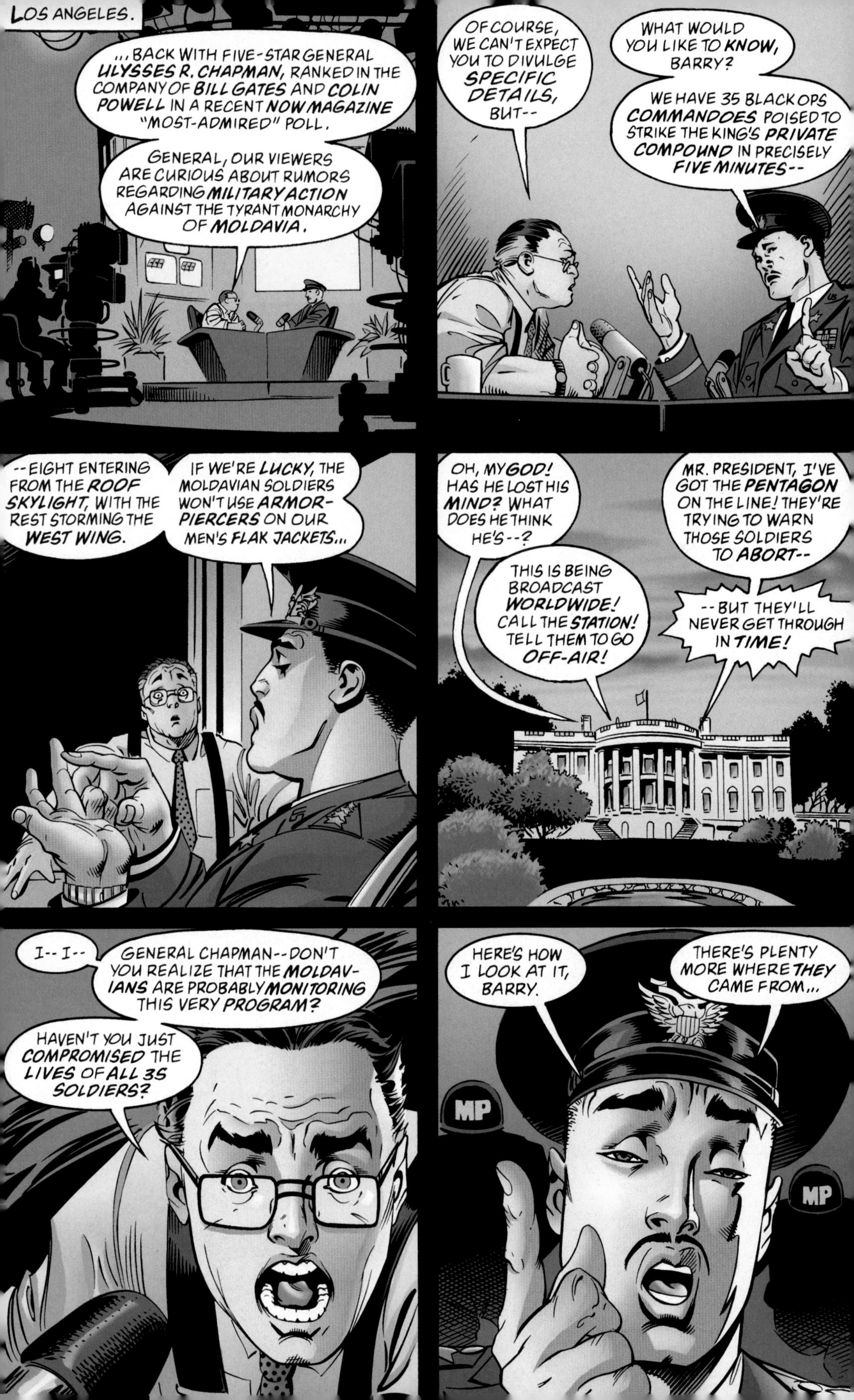
LOS ANGELES.
...BACK WITH FIVE-STAR GENERAL ULYSSES R. CHAPMAN, RANKED IN THE COMPANY OF BILL GATES AND COLIN POWELL IN A RECENT NOW MAGAZINE "MOST-ADMIRED" POLL.
GENERAL, OUR VIEWERS ARE CURIOUS ABOUT RUMORS REGARDING MILITARY ACTION AGAINST THE TYRANT MONARCHY OF MOLDAVIA.
OF COURSE, WE CAN'T EXPECT YOU TO DIVULGE SPECIFIC DETAILS, BUT--
WHAT WOULD YOU LIKE TO KNOW, BARRY?
WE HAVE 35 BLACK OPS COMMANDOES POISED TO STRIKE THE KING'S PRIVATE COMPOUND IN PRECISELY FIVE MINUTES--
--EIGHT ENTERING FROM THE ROOF SKYLIGHT, WITH THE REST STORMING THE WEST WING.
IF WE'RE LUCKY, THE MOLDAVIAN SOLDIERS WON'T USE ARMOR-PIERCERS ON OUR MEN'S FLAK JACKETS...
OH, MY GOD! HAS HE LOST HIS MIND? WHAT DOES HE THINK HE'S--?
THIS IS BEING BROADCAST WORLDWIDE! CALL THE STATION! TELL THEM TO GO OFF-AIR!
MR. PRESIDENT, I'VE GOT THE PENTAGON ON THE LINE! THEY'RE TRYING TO WARN THOSE SOLDIERS TO ABORT--
--BUT THEY'LL NEVER GET THROUGH IN TIME!
I-- I--
GENERAL CHAPMAN--DON'T YOU REALIZE THAT THE MOLDAVIANS ARE PROBABLY MONITORING THIS VERY PROGRAM?
HAVEN'T YOU JUST COMPROMISED THE LIVES OF ALL 35 SOLDIERS?
HERE'S HOW I LOOK AT IT, BARRY.
THERE'S PLENTY MORE WHERE THEY CAME FROM...
MP
MP
MP

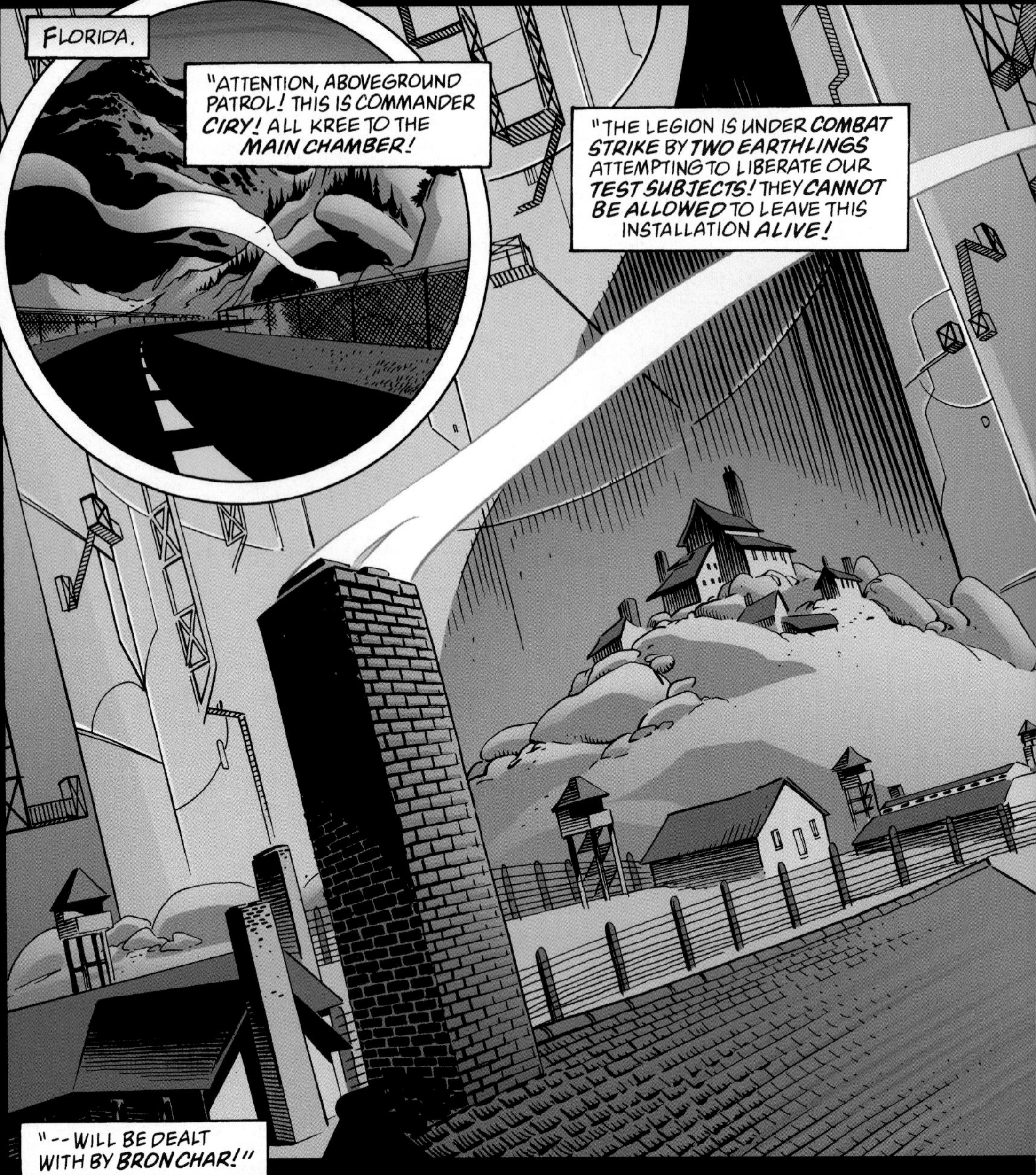
FLORIDA.
"ATTENTION, ABOVEGROUND PATROL! THIS IS COMMANDER CIRY! ALL KREE TO THE MAIN CHAMBER!
"THE LEGION IS UNDER COMBAT STRIKE BY TWO EARTHLINGS ATTEMPTING TO LIBERATE OUR TEST SUBJECTS! THEY CANNOT BE ALLOWED TO LEAVE THIS INSTALLATION ALIVE!
"--WILL BE DEALT WITH BY BRONCHAR!"

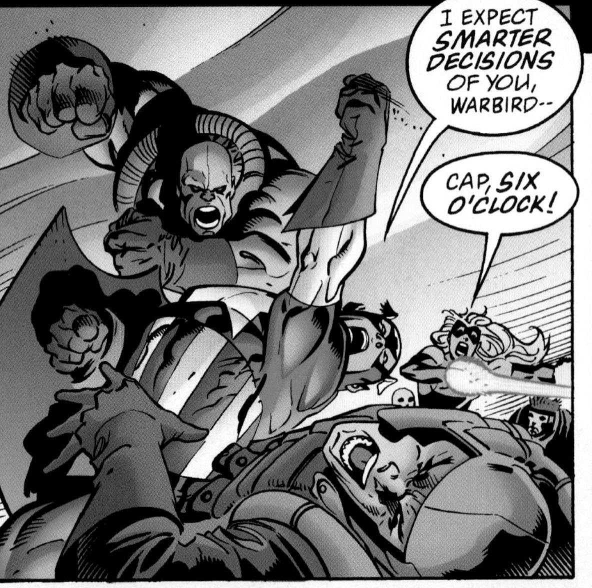
I EXPECT SMARTER DECISIONS OF YOU, WARBIRD--
CAP, SIX O'CLOCK!

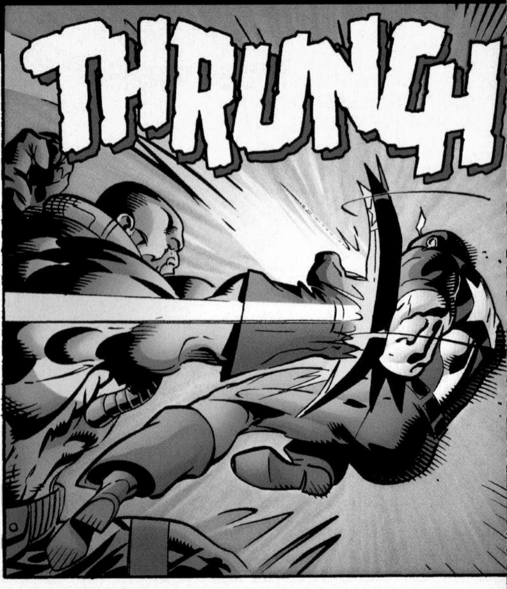
THRUNCH

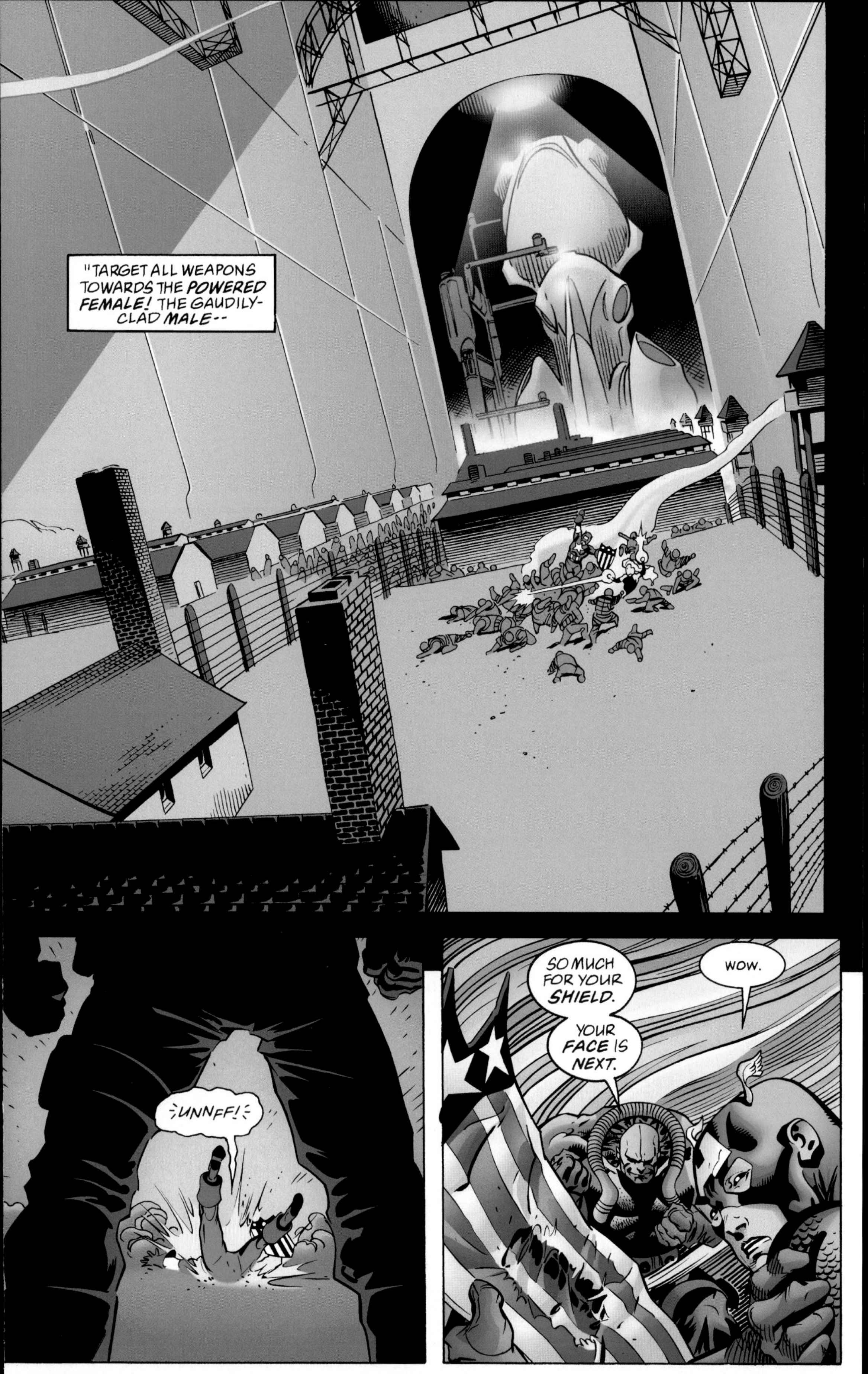
"TARGET ALL WEAPONS TOWARDS THE POWERED FEMALE! THE GAUDILY-CLAD MALE--
UNNFF!
SO MUCH FOR YOUR SHIELD.
YOUR FACE IS NEXT.
WOW.

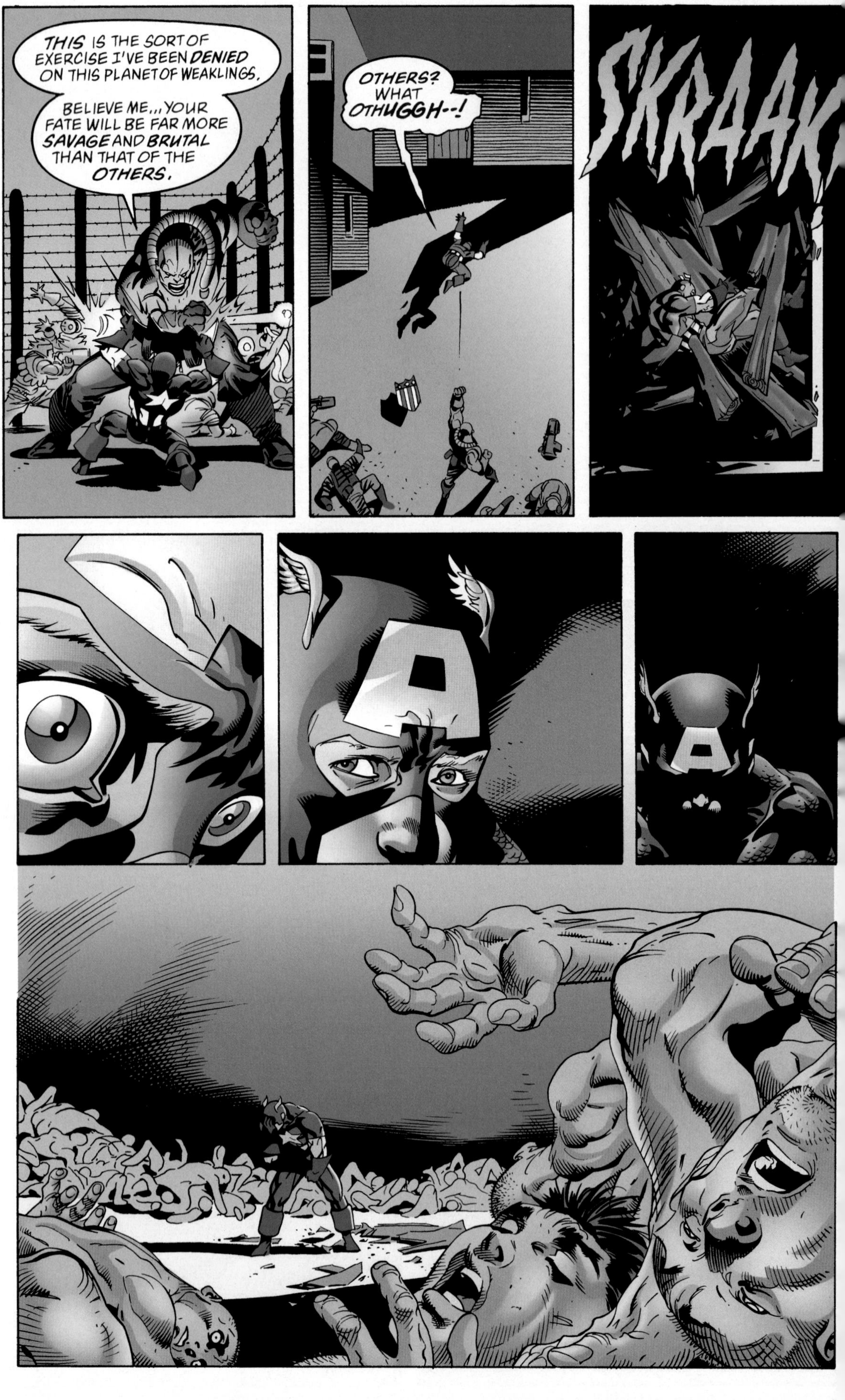
THIS IS THE SORT OF EXERCISE I'VE BEEN DENIED ON THIS PLANET OF WEAKLINGS.
BELIEVE ME... YOUR FATE WILL BE FAR MORE SAVAGE AND BRUTAL THAN THAT OF THE OTHERS.
OTHERS? WHAT OTHUGGH--!
SKRAAK

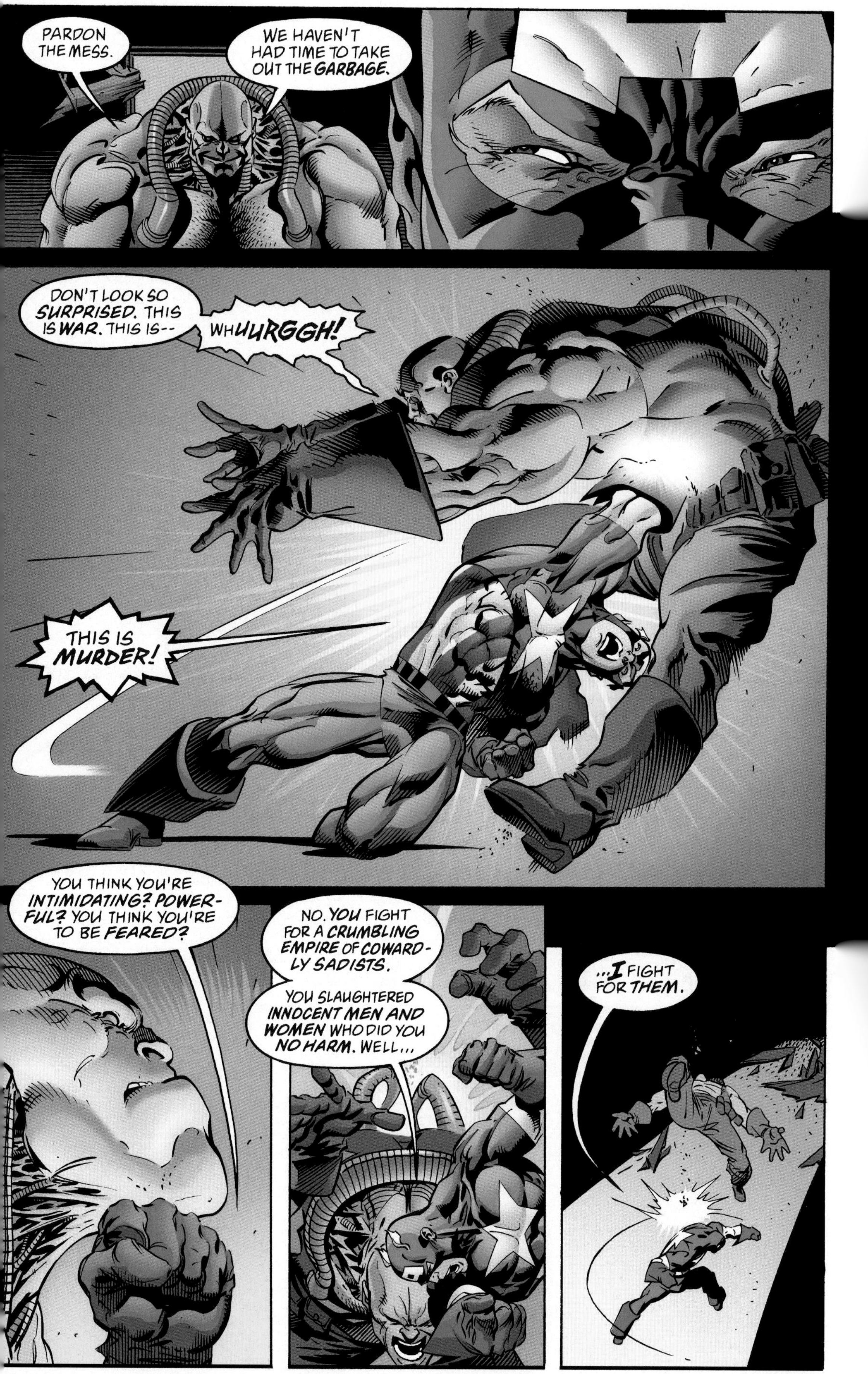
PARDON THE MESS.
WE HAVEN'T HAD TIME TO TAKE OUT THE GARBAGE.
DON'T LOOK SO SURPRISED. THIS IS WAR. THIS IS--
WHUURGGH!
THIS IS MURDER!
YOU THINK YOU'RE INTIMIDATING? POWERFUL? YOU THINK YOU'RE TO BE FEARED?
NO. YOU FIGHT FOR A CRUMBLING EMPIRE OF COWARDLY SADISTS.
YOU SLAUGHTERED INNOCENT MEN AND WOMEN WHO DID YOU NO HARM. WELL...
...I FIGHT FOR THEM.

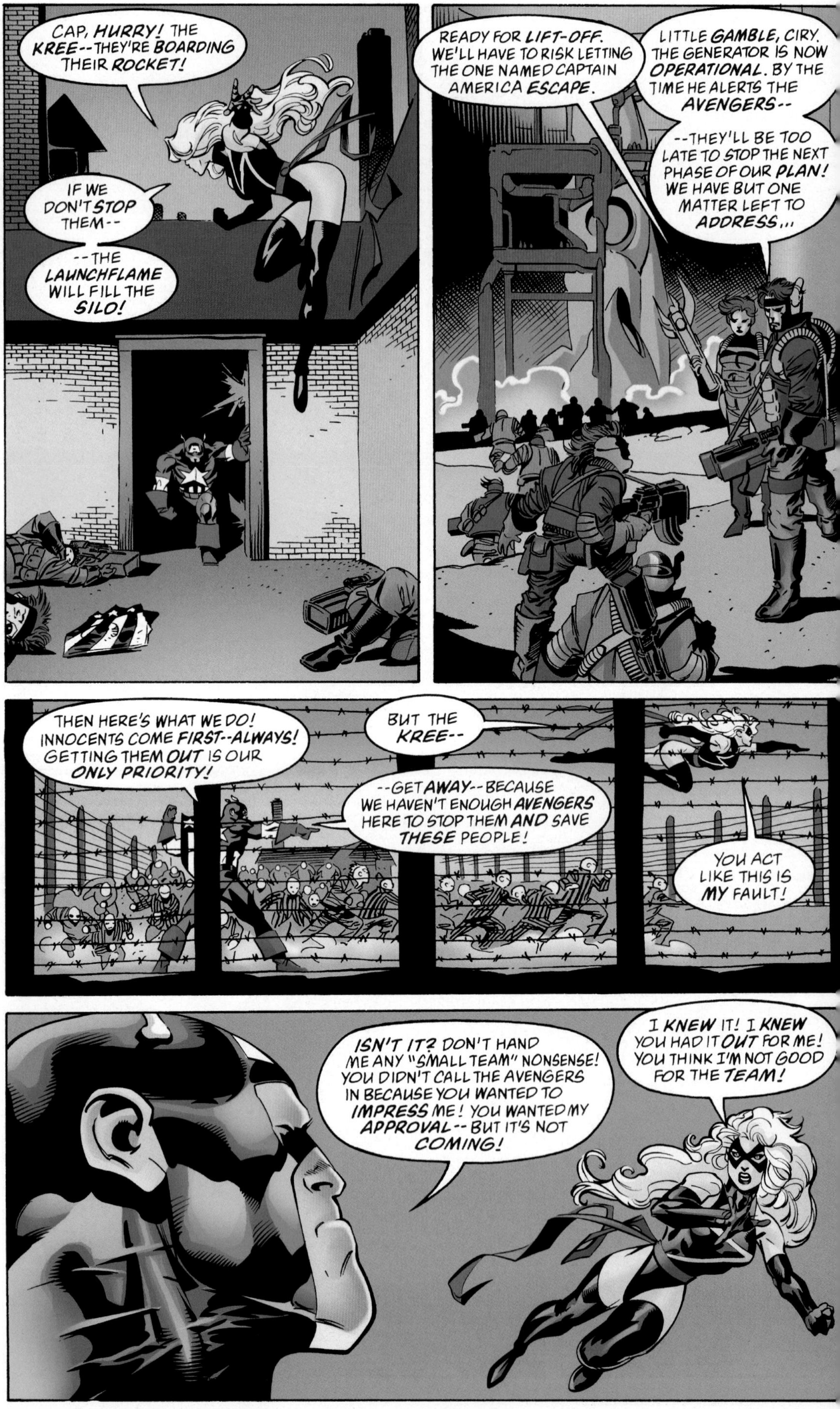

CAP, HURRY! THE KREE--THEY'RE BOARDING THEIR ROCKET!
IF WE DON'T STOP THEM--
--THE LAUNCHFLAME WILL FILL THE SILO!
READY FOR LIFT-OFF. WE'LL HAVE TO RISK LETTING THE ONE NAMED CAPTAIN AMERICA ESCAPE.
LITTLE GAMBLE, CIRY. THE GENERATOR IS NOW OPERATIONAL. BY THE TIME HE ALERTS THE AVENGERS--
--THEY'LL BE TOO LATE TO STOP THE NEXT PHASE OF OUR PLAN! WE HAVE BUT ONE MATTER LEFT TO ADDRESS...
THEN HERE'S WHAT WE DO! INNOCENTS COME FIRST--ALWAYS! GETTING THEM OUT IS OUR ONLY PRIORITY!
BUT THE KREE--
--GET AWAY--BECAUSE WE HAVEN'T ENOUGH AVENGERS HERE TO STOP THEM AND SAVE THESE PEOPLE!
YOU ACT LIKE THIS IS MY FAULT!
ISN'T IT? DON'T HAND ME ANY "SMALL TEAM" NONSENSE! YOU DIDN'T CALL THE AVENGERS IN BECAUSE YOU WANTED TO IMPRESS ME! YOU WANTED MY APPROVAL--BUT IT'S NOT COMING!
I KNEW IT! I KNEW YOU HAD IT OUT FOR ME! YOU THINK I'M NOT GOOD FOR THE TEAM!

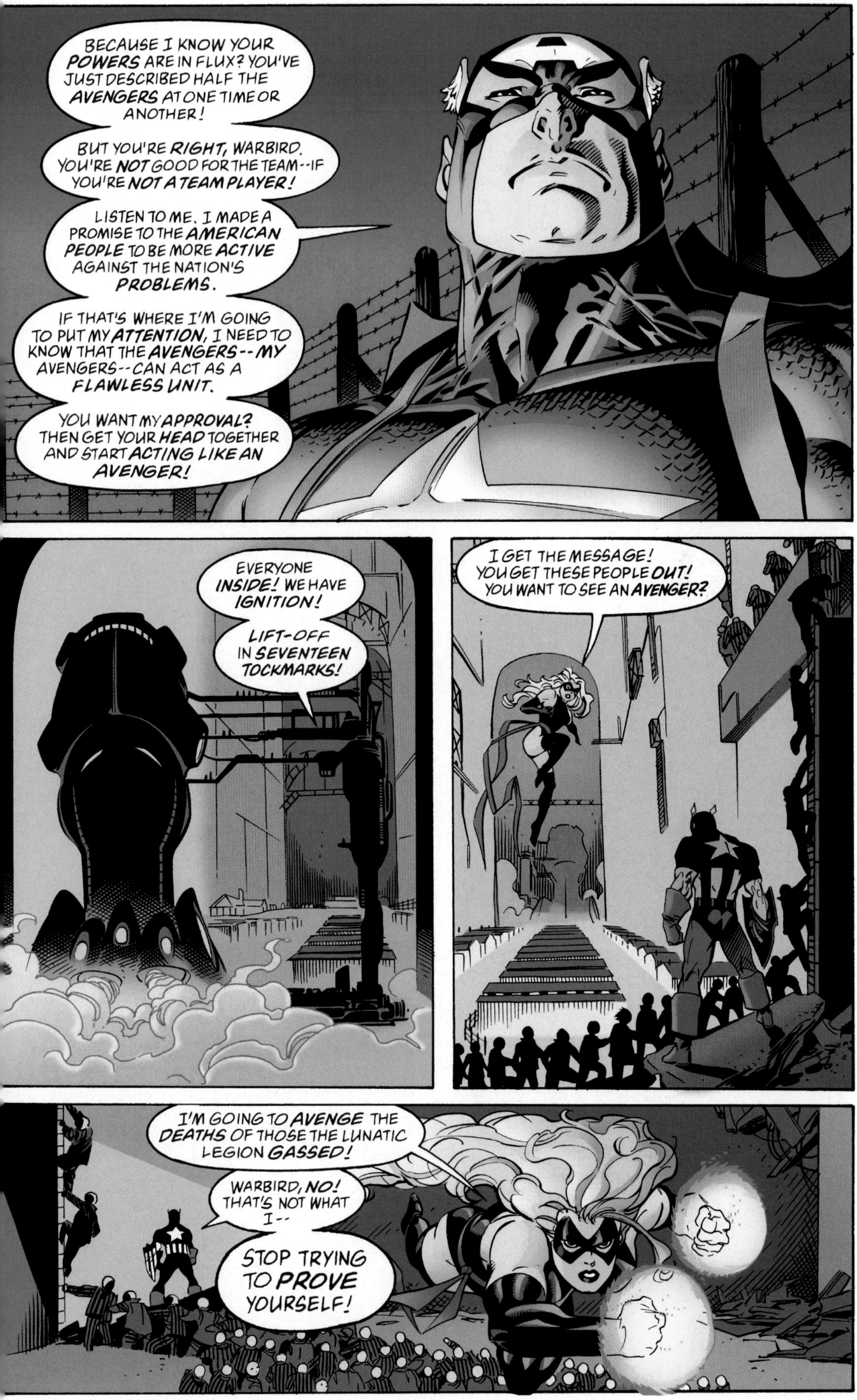
BECAUSE I KNOW YOUR POWERS ARE IN FLUX? YOU'VE JUST DESCRIBED HALF THE AVENGERS AT ONE TIME OR ANOTHER!
BUT YOU'RE RIGHT, WARBIRD. YOU'RE NOT GOOD FOR THE TEAM--IF YOU'RE NOT A TEAM PLAYER!
LISTEN TO ME. I MADE A PROMISE TO THE AMERICAN PEOPLE TO BE MORE ACTIVE AGAINST THE NATION'S PROBLEMS.
IF THAT'S WHERE I'M GOING TO PUT MY ATTENTION, I NEED TO KNOW THAT THE AVENGERS-- MY AVENGERS--CAN ACT AS A FLAWLESS UNIT.
YOU WANT MY APPROVAL? THEN GET YOUR HEAD TOGETHER AND START ACTING LIKE AN AVENGER!
EVERYONE INSIDE! WE HAVE IGNITION!
LIFT-OFF IN SEVENTEEN TOCKMARKS!
I GET THE MESSAGE! YOU GET THESE PEOPLE OUT! YOU WANT TO SEE AN AVENGER?
I'M GOING TO AVENGE THE DEATHS OF THOSE THE LUNATIC LEGION GASSED!
WARBIRD, NO! THAT'S NOT WHAT I--
STOP TRYING TO PROVE YOURSELF!

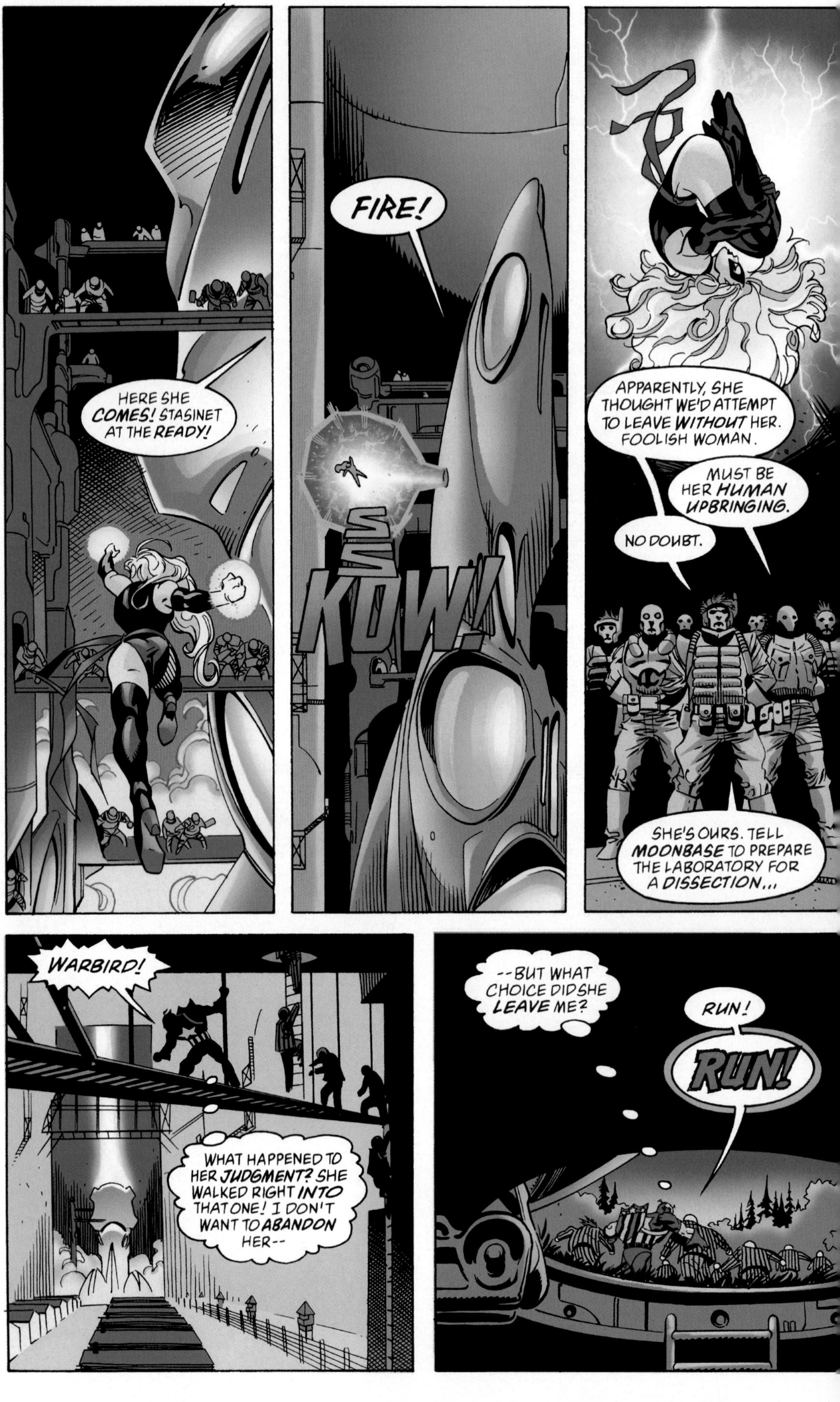
HERE SHE COMES! STASINET AT THE READY!
FIRE!
SS
KOW!
APPARENTLY, SHE THOUGHT WE'D ATTEMPT TO LEAVE WITHOUT HER. FOOLISH WOMAN.
MUST BE HER HUMAN UPBRINGING.
NO DOUBT.
SHE'S OURS. TELL MOONBASE TO PREPARE THE LABORATORY FOR A DISSECTION...
WARBIRD!
WHAT HAPPENED TO HER JUDGMENT? SHE WALKED RIGHT INTO THAT ONE! I DON'T WANT TO ABANDON HER--
--BUT WHAT CHOICE DID SHE LEAVE ME?
RUN!
RUN!

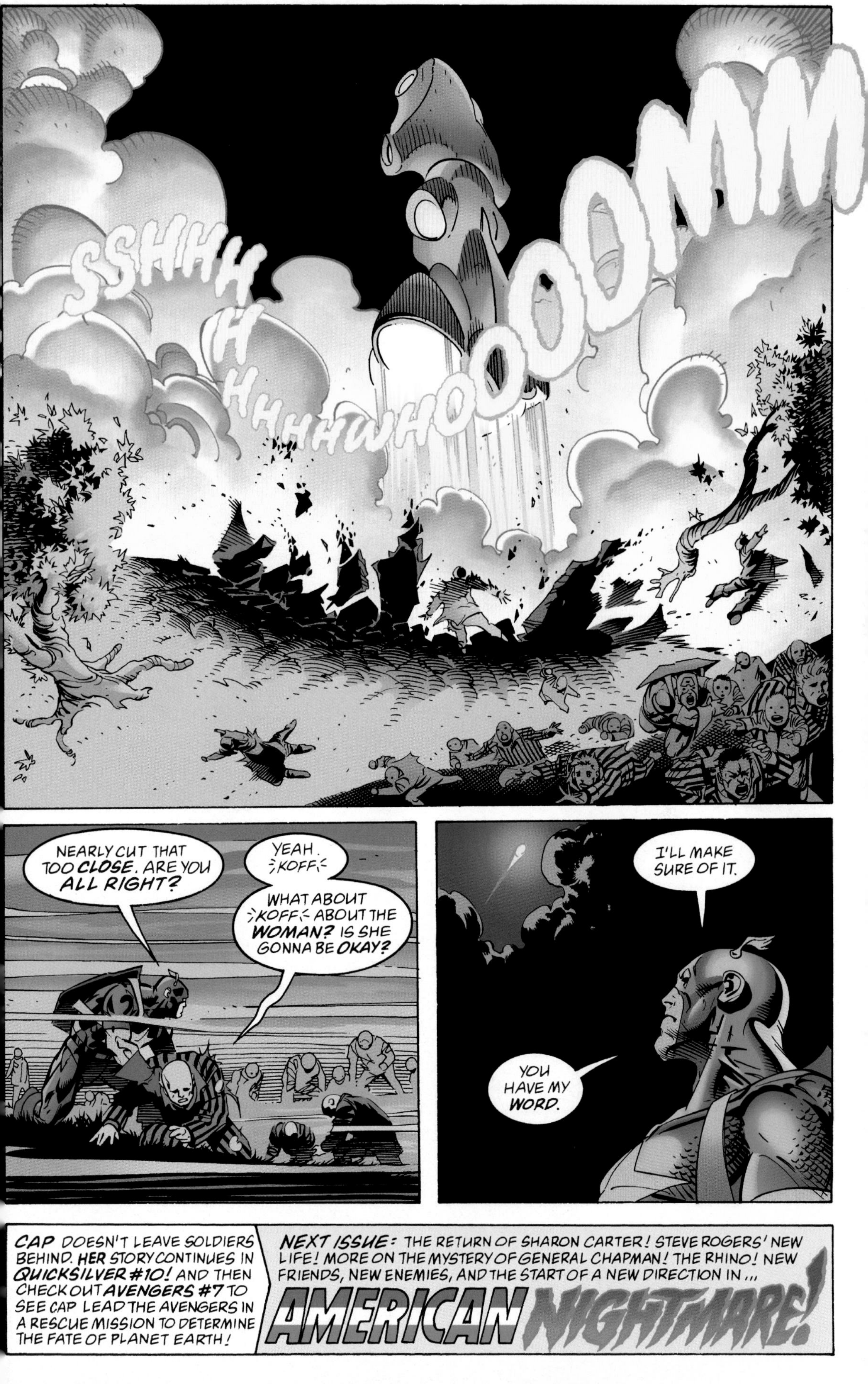
SSHHHHHHHHWHOOOOOOMMM
NEARLY CUT THAT TOO CLOSE. ARE YOU ALL RIGHT?
YEAH. KOFF
WHAT ABOUT KOFF ABOUT THE WOMAN? IS SHE GONNA BE OKAY?
I'LL MAKE SURE OF IT.
YOU HAVE MY WORD.
CAP DOESN'T LEAVE SOLDIERS BEHIND. HER STORY CONTINUES IN QUICKSILVER #10! AND THEN CHECK OUT AVENGERS #7 TO SEE CAP LEAD THE AVENGERS IN A RESCUE MISSION TO DETERMINE THE FATE OF PLANET EARTH!
NEXT ISSUE: THE RETURN OF SHARON CARTER! STEVE ROGERS' NEW LIFE! MORE ON THE MYSTERY OF GENERAL CHAPMAN! THE RHINO! NEW FRIENDS, NEW ENEMIES, AND THE START OF A NEW DIRECTION IN...
AMERICAN NIGHTMARE!

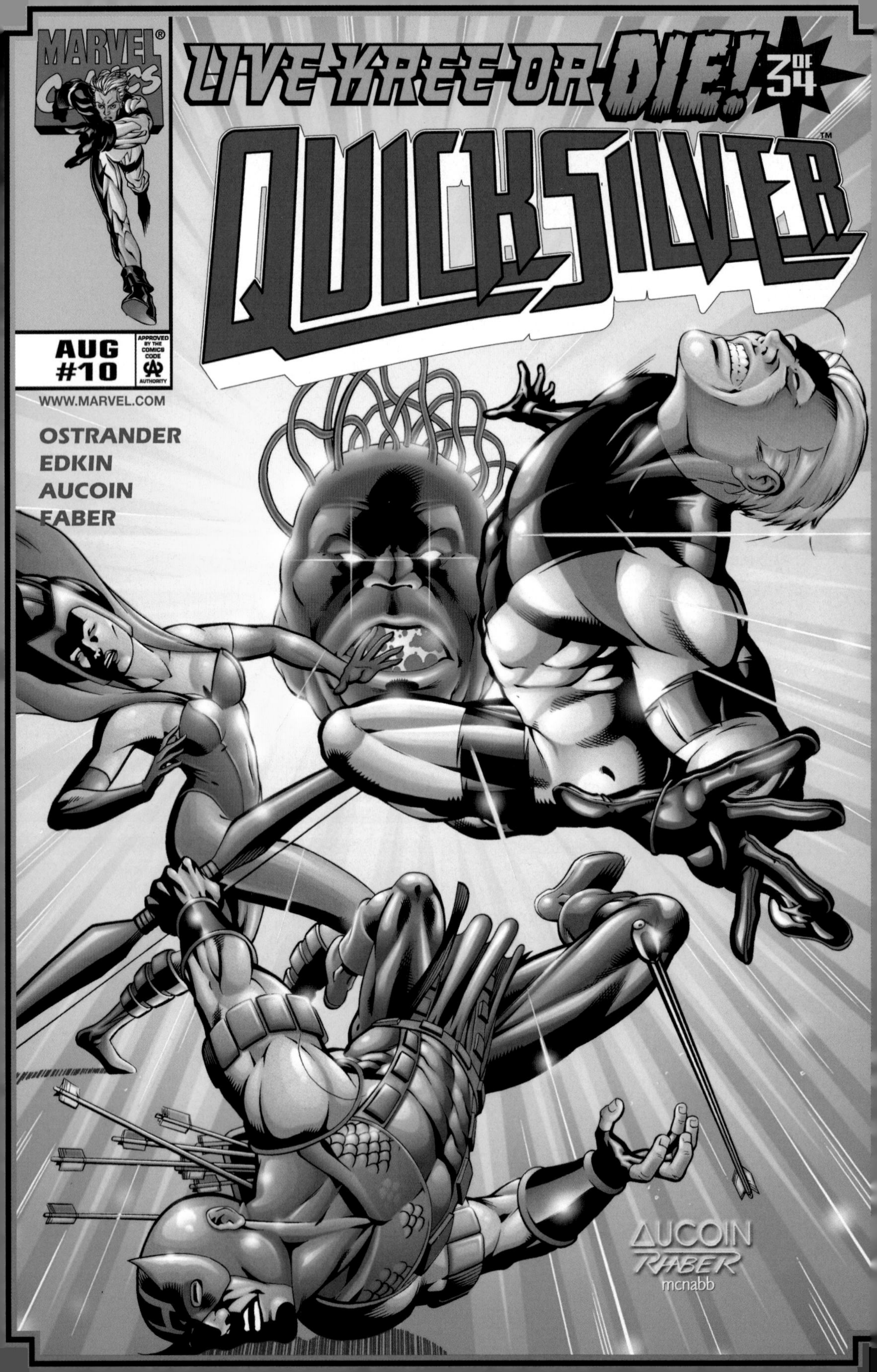
MARVEL COMICS
LIVE KREE OR DIE! 3 OF 4
QUICKSILVER™
AUG #10
APPROVED BY THE COMICS CODE AUTHORITY
WWW.MARVEL.COM
OSTRANDER
EDKIN
AUCOIN
FABER
AUCOIN
FABER
mcnabb

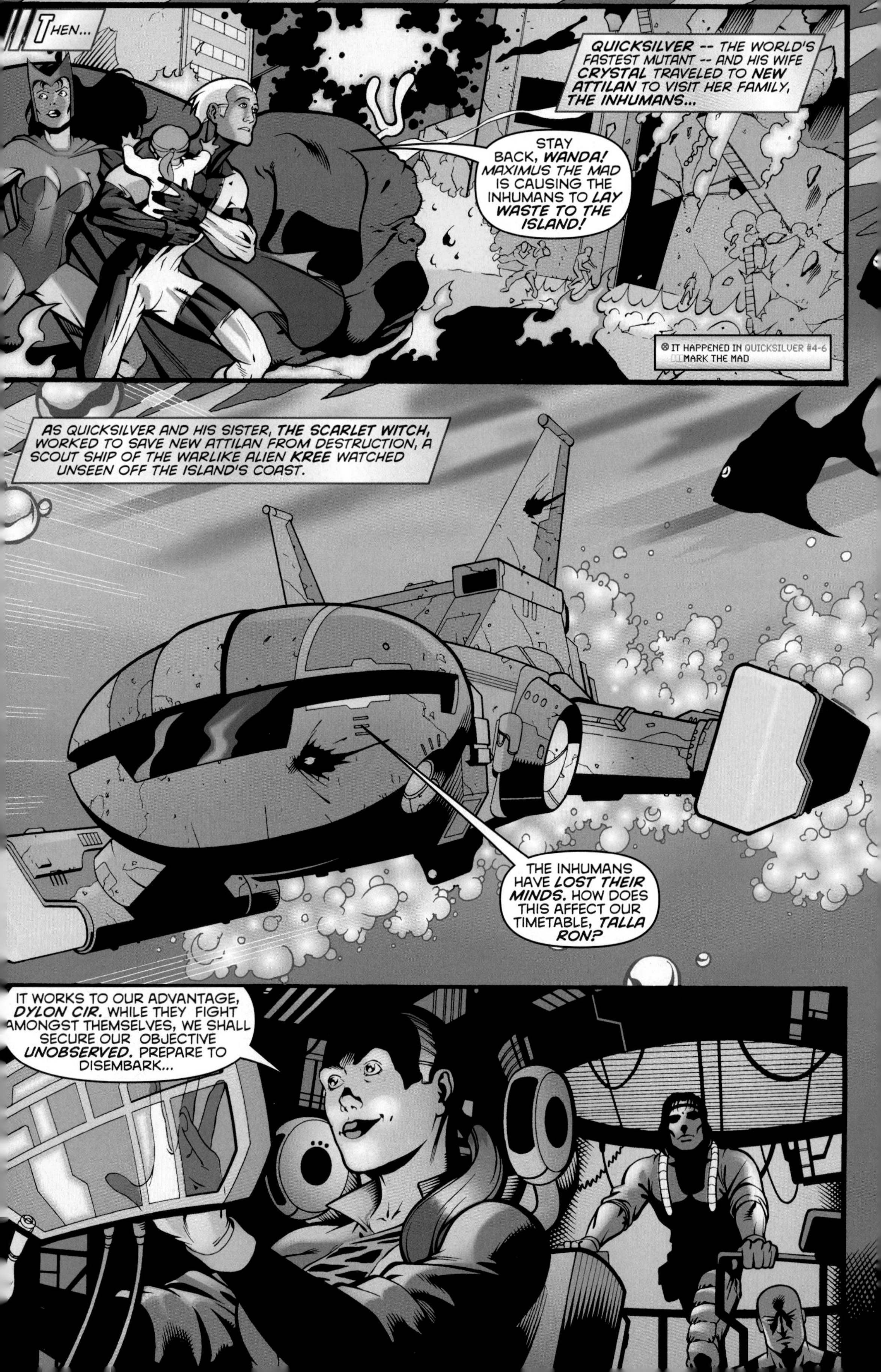
THEN...
QUICKSILVER -- THE WORLD'S FASTEST MUTANT -- AND HIS WIFE CRYSTAL TRAVELED TO NEW ATTILAN TO VISIT HER FAMILY, THE INHUMANS...
STAY BACK, WANDA! MAXIMUS THE MAD IS CAUSING THE INHUMANS TO LAY WASTE TO THE ISLAND!
IT HAPPENED IN QUICKSILVER #4-6
MARK THE MAD
AS QUICKSILVER AND HIS SISTER, THE SCARLET WITCH, WORKED TO SAVE NEW ATTILAN FROM DESTRUCTION, A SCOUT SHIP OF THE WARLIKE ALIEN KREE WATCHED UNSEEN OFF THE ISLAND'S COAST.
THE INHUMANS HAVE LOST THEIR MINDS. HOW DOES THIS AFFECT OUR TIMETABLE, TALLA RON?
IT WORKS TO OUR ADVANTAGE, DYLON CIR. WHILE THEY FIGHT AMONGST THEMSELVES, WE SHALL SECURE OUR OBJECTIVE UNOBSERVED. PREPARE TO DISEMBARK...

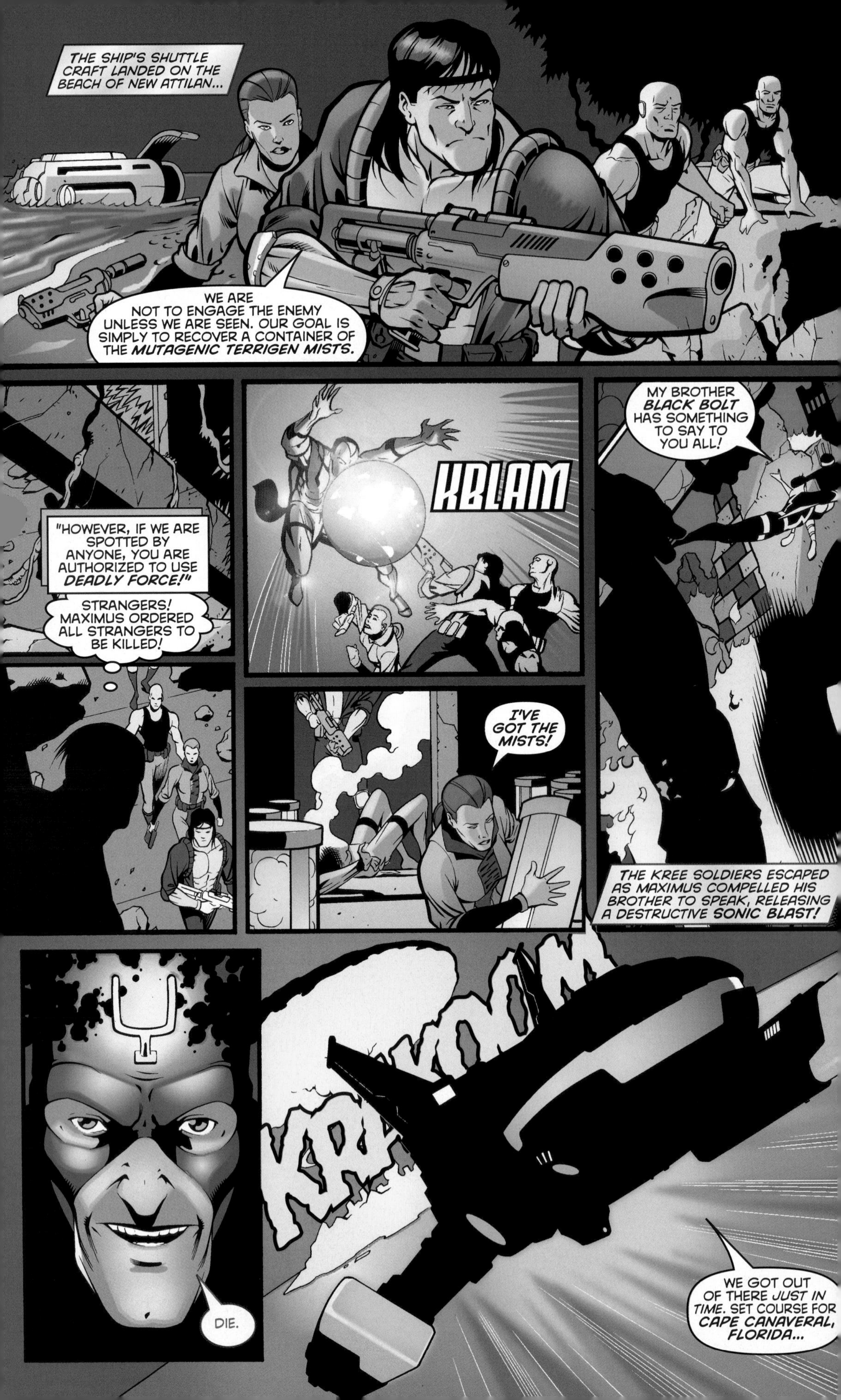
THE SHIP'S SHUTTLE CRAFT LANDED ON THE BEACH OF NEW ATTILAN...
WE ARE NOT TO ENGAGE THE ENEMY UNLESS WE ARE SEEN. OUR GOAL IS SIMPLY TO RECOVER A CONTAINER OF THE *MUTAGENIC TERRIGEN MISTS.*
"HOWEVER, IF WE ARE SPOTTED BY ANYONE, YOU ARE AUTHORIZED TO USE *DEADLY FORCE!*"
STRANGERS! MAXIMUS ORDERED ALL STRANGERS TO BE KILLED!
KBLAM
I'VE GOT THE MISTS!
MY BROTHER *BLACK BOLT* HAS SOMETHING TO SAY TO YOU ALL!
THE KREE SOLDIERS ESCAPED AS MAXIMUS COMPELLED HIS BROTHER TO SPEAK, RELEASING A DESTRUCTIVE *SONIC BLAST!*
DIE.
KRAKOOM
WE GOT OUT OF THERE *JUST IN TIME.* SET COURSE FOR *CAPE CANAVERAL, FLORIDA...*

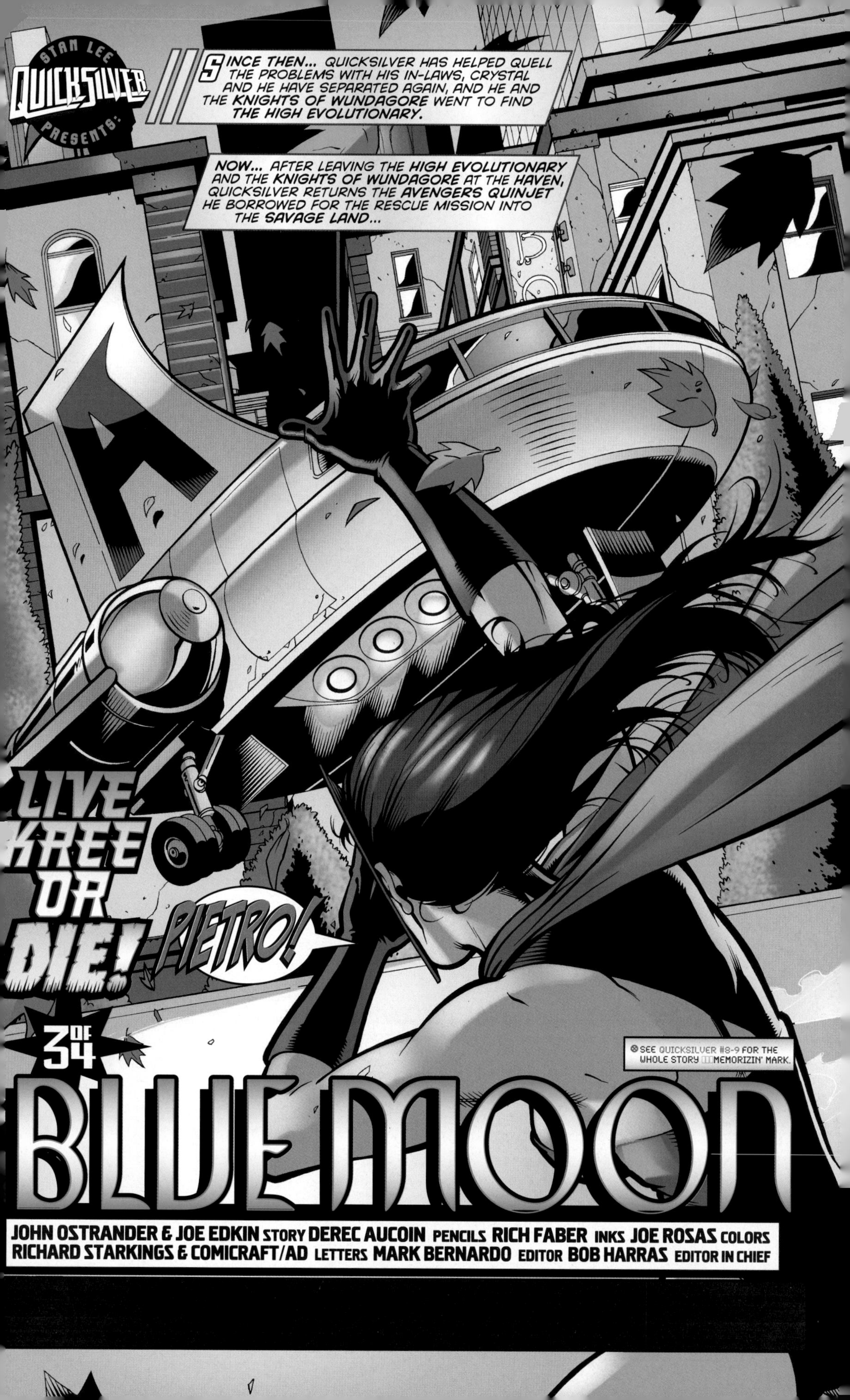
STAN LEE QUICKSILVER PRESENTS:
SINCE THEN... QUICKSILVER HAS HELPED QUELL THE PROBLEMS WITH HIS IN-LAWS, CRYSTAL AND HE HAVE SEPARATED AGAIN, AND HE AND THE KNIGHTS OF WUNDAGORE WENT TO FIND THE HIGH EVOLUTIONARY.
NOW... AFTER LEAVING THE HIGH EVOLUTIONARY AND THE KNIGHTS OF WUNDAGORE AT THE HAVEN, QUICKSILVER RETURNS THE AVENGERS QUINJET HE BORROWED FOR THE RESCUE MISSION INTO THE SAVAGE LAND...
LIVE KREE OR DIE!
PIETRO!
3 OF 4
SEE QUICKSILVER #8-9 FOR THE WHOLE STORY — MEMORIZIN' MARK.
BLUE MOON
JOHN OSTRANDER & JOE EDKIN STORY DEREC AUCOIN PENCILS RICH FABER INKS JOE ROSAS COLORS
RICHARD STARKINGS & COMICRAFT/AD LETTERS MARK BERNARDO EDITOR BOB HARRAS EDITOR IN CHIEF

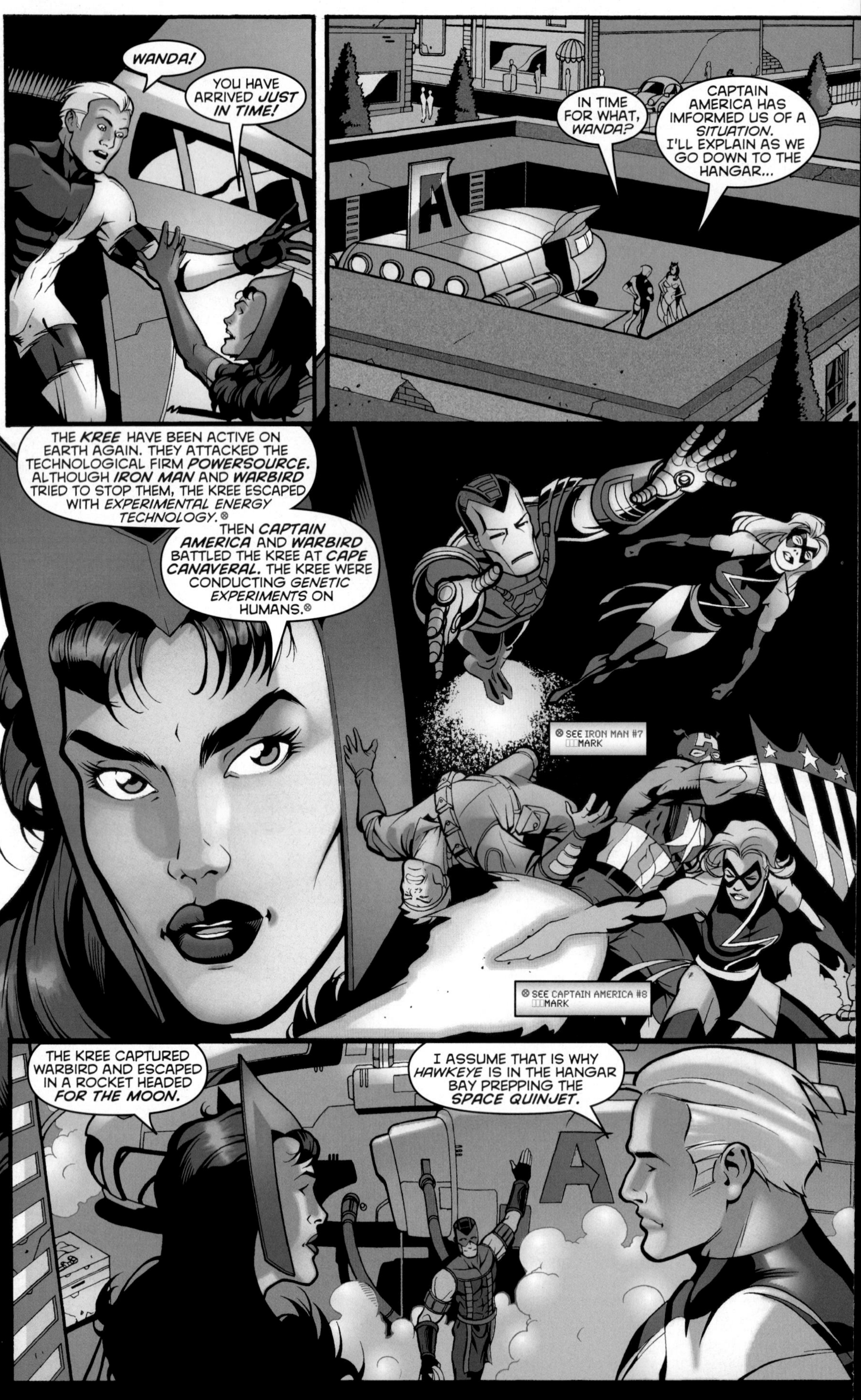
WANDA!
YOU HAVE ARRIVED JUST IN TIME!
IN TIME FOR WHAT, WANDA?
CAPTAIN AMERICA HAS INFORMED US OF A SITUATION. I'LL EXPLAIN AS WE GO DOWN TO THE HANGAR...
THE KREE HAVE BEEN ACTIVE ON EARTH AGAIN. THEY ATTACKED THE TECHNOLOGICAL FIRM POWERSOURCE. ALTHOUGH IRON MAN AND WARBIRD TRIED TO STOP THEM, THE KREE ESCAPED WITH EXPERIMENTAL ENERGY TECHNOLOGY.
THEN CAPTAIN AMERICA AND WARBIRD BATTLED THE KREE AT CAPE CANAVERAL. THE KREE WERE CONDUCTING GENETIC EXPERIMENTS ON HUMANS.
SEE IRON MAN #7 —MARK
SEE CAPTAIN AMERICA #8 —MARK
THE KREE CAPTURED WARBIRD AND ESCAPED IN A ROCKET HEADED FOR THE MOON.
I ASSUME THAT IS WHY HAWKEYE IS IN THE HANGAR BAY PREPPING THE SPACE QUINJET.

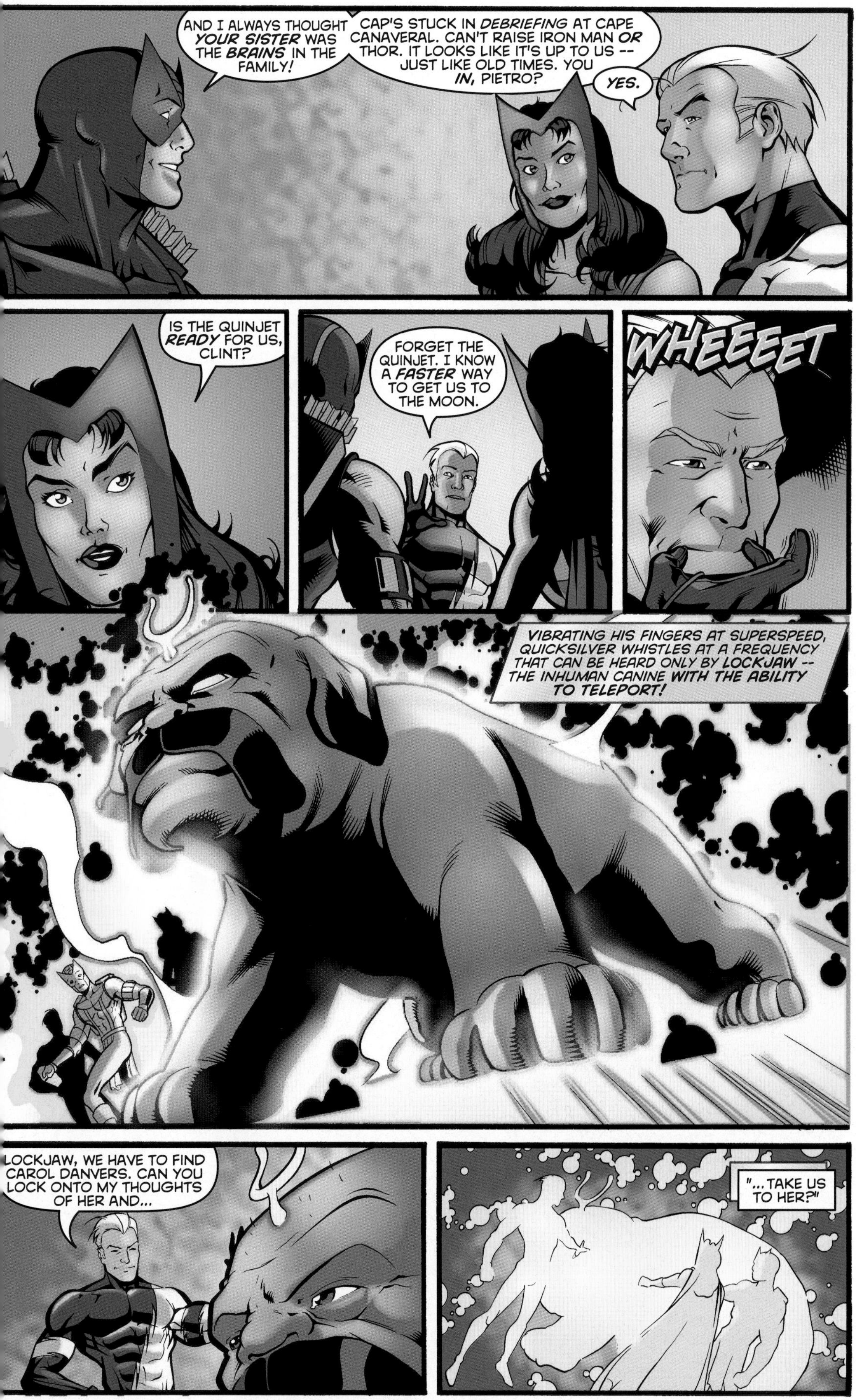

AND I ALWAYS THOUGHT YOUR SISTER WAS THE BRAINS IN THE FAMILY!
CAP'S STUCK IN DEBRIEFING AT CAPE CANAVERAL. CAN'T RAISE IRON MAN OR THOR. IT LOOKS LIKE IT'S UP TO US -- JUST LIKE OLD TIMES. YOU IN, PIETRO?
YES.
IS THE QUINJET READY FOR US, CLINT?
FORGET THE QUINJET. I KNOW A FASTER WAY TO GET US TO THE MOON.
WHEEEEET
VIBRATING HIS FINGERS AT SUPERSPEED, QUICKSILVER WHISTLES AT A FREQUENCY THAT CAN BE HEARD ONLY BY LOCKJAW -- THE INHUMAN CANINE WITH THE ABILITY TO TELEPORT!
LOCKJAW, WE HAVE TO FIND CAROL DANVERS. CAN YOU LOCK ONTO MY THOUGHTS OF HER AND...
"...TAKE US TO HER?"

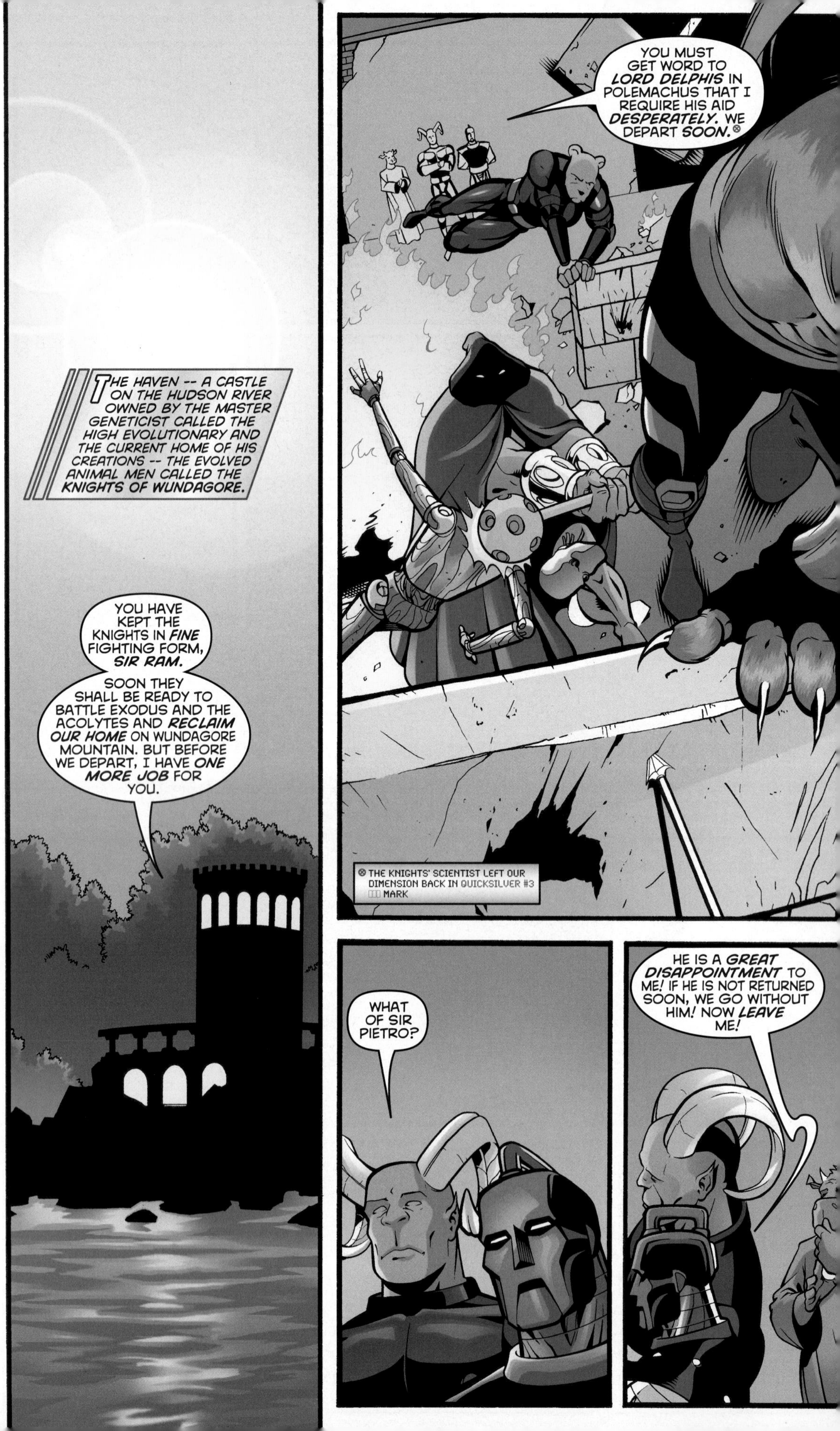
THE HAVEN -- A CASTLE ON THE HUDSON RIVER OWNED BY THE MASTER GENETICIST CALLED THE HIGH EVOLUTIONARY AND THE CURRENT HOME OF HIS CREATIONS -- THE EVOLVED ANIMAL MEN CALLED THE KNIGHTS OF WUNDAGORE.
YOU HAVE KEPT THE KNIGHTS IN FINE FIGHTING FORM, SIR RAM.
SOON THEY SHALL BE READY TO BATTLE EXODUS AND THE ACOLYTES AND RECLAIM OUR HOME ON WUNDAGORE MOUNTAIN. BUT BEFORE WE DEPART, I HAVE ONE MORE JOB FOR YOU.
YOU MUST GET WORD TO LORD DELPHIS IN POLEMACHUS THAT I REQUIRE HIS AID DESPERATELY. WE DEPART SOON.⊗
⊗ THE KNIGHTS' SCIENTIST LEFT OUR DIMENSION BACK IN QUICKSILVER #3
MARK
WHAT OF SIR PIETRO?
HE IS A GREAT DISAPPOINTMENT TO ME! IF HE IS NOT RETURNED SOON, WE GO WITHOUT HIM! NOW LEAVE ME!

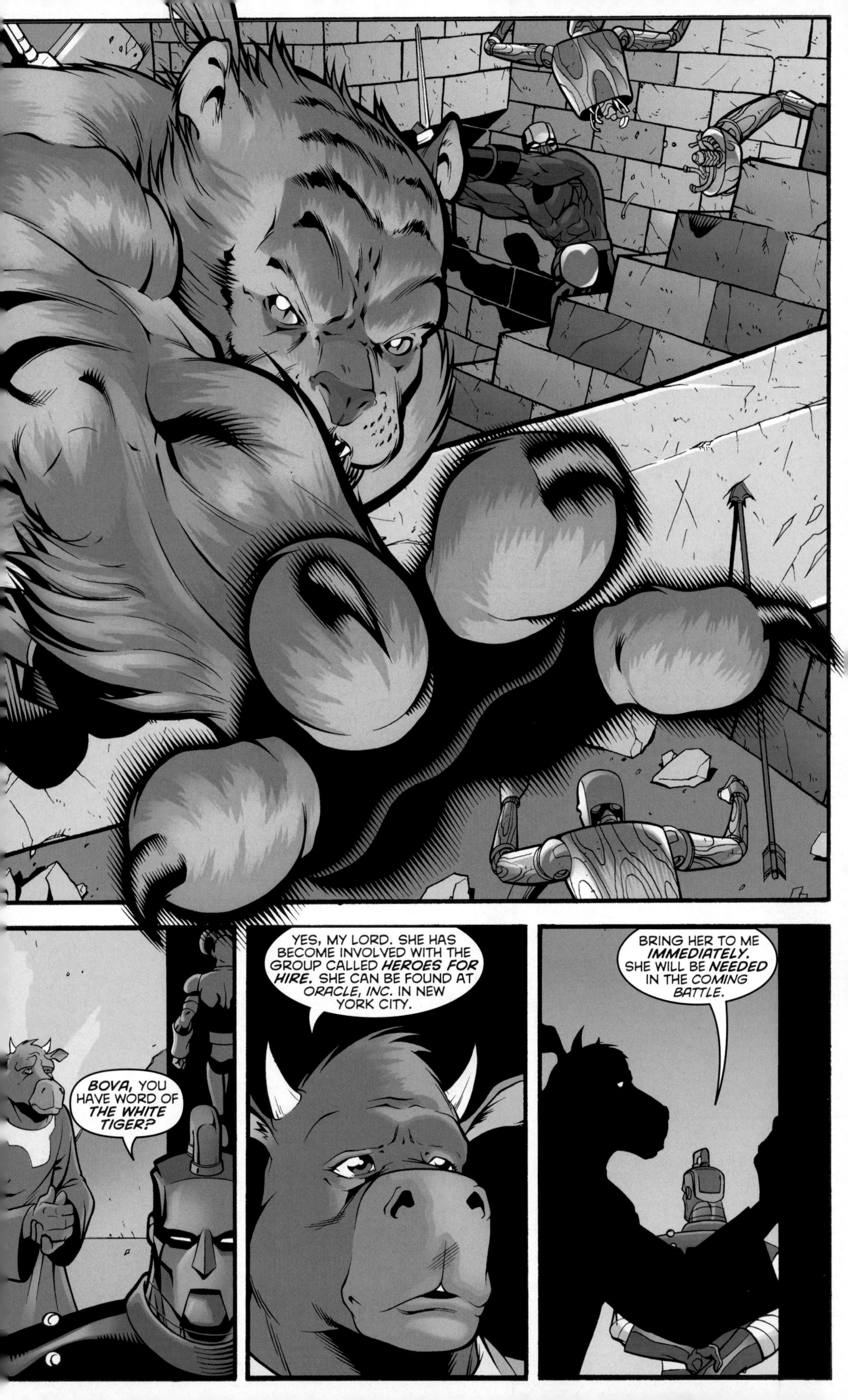
BOVA, YOU HAVE WORD OF THE WHITE TIGER?
YES, MY LORD. SHE HAS BECOME INVOLVED WITH THE GROUP CALLED HEROES FOR HIRE. SHE CAN BE FOUND AT ORACLE, INC. IN NEW YORK CITY.
BRING HER TO ME IMMEDIATELY. SHE WILL BE NEEDED IN THE COMING BATTLE.

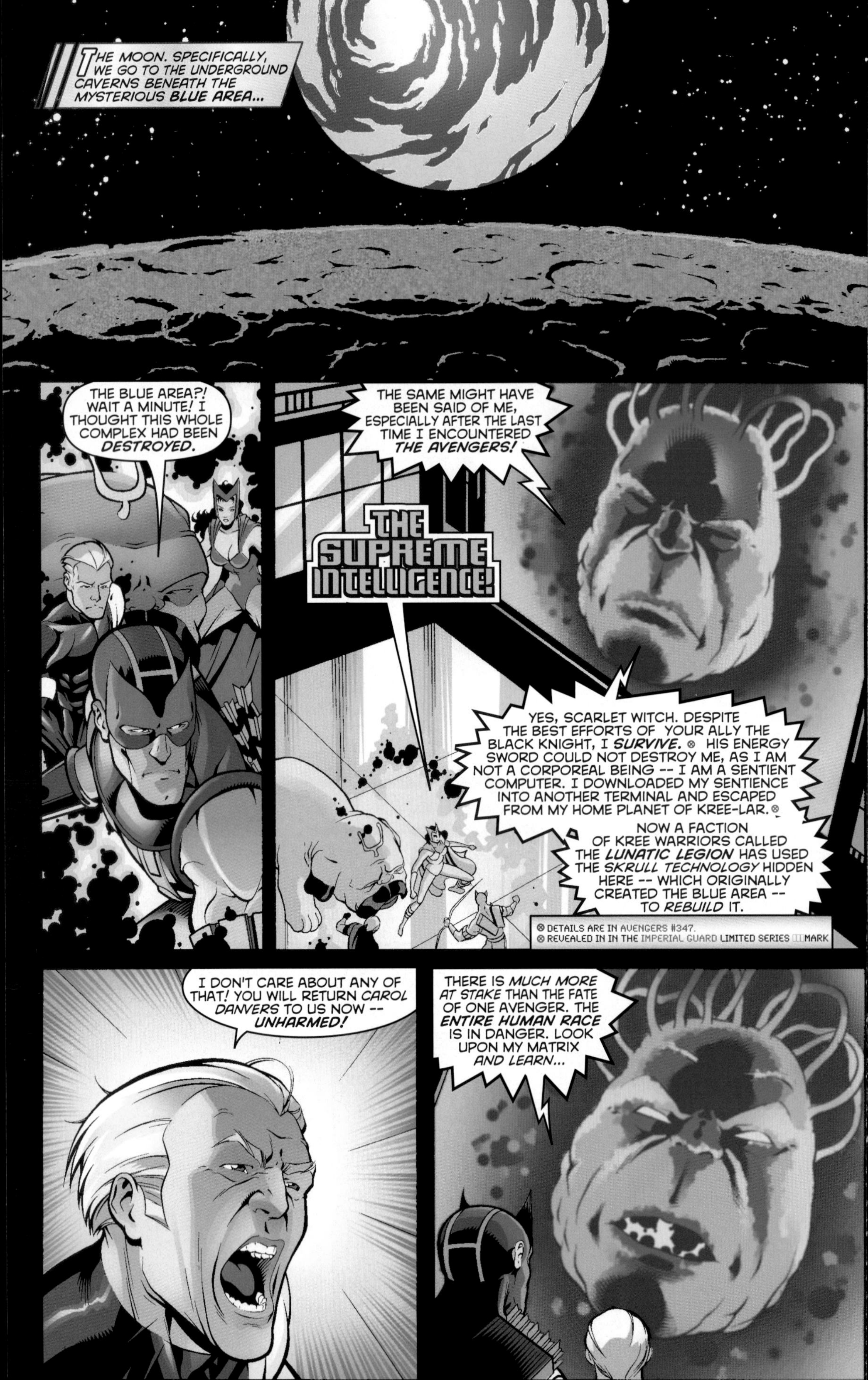

THE MOON. SPECIFICALLY, WE GO TO THE UNDERGROUND CAVERNS BENEATH THE MYSTERIOUS BLUE AREA...
THE BLUE AREA?! WAIT A MINUTE! I THOUGHT THIS WHOLE COMPLEX HAD BEEN DESTROYED.
THE SAME MIGHT HAVE BEEN SAID OF ME, ESPECIALLY AFTER THE LAST TIME I ENCOUNTERED THE AVENGERS!
THE SUPREME INTELLIGENCE!
YES, SCARLET WITCH. DESPITE THE BEST EFFORTS OF YOUR ALLY THE BLACK KNIGHT, I SURVIVE. ⊗ HIS ENERGY SWORD COULD NOT DESTROY ME, AS I AM NOT A CORPOREAL BEING -- I AM A SENTIENT COMPUTER. I DOWNLOADED MY SENTIENCE INTO ANOTHER TERMINAL AND ESCAPED FROM MY HOME PLANET OF KREE-LAR. ⊗
NOW A FACTION OF KREE WARRIORS CALLED THE LUNATIC LEGION HAS USED THE SKRULL TECHNOLOGY HIDDEN HERE -- WHICH ORIGINALLY CREATED THE BLUE AREA -- TO REBUILD IT.
⊗ DETAILS ARE IN AVENGERS #347.
⊗ REVEALED IN IN THE IMPERIAL GUARD LIMITED SERIES MARK
I DON'T CARE ABOUT ANY OF THAT! YOU WILL RETURN CAROL DANVERS TO US NOW -- UNHARMED!
THERE IS MUCH MORE AT STAKE THAN THE FATE OF ONE AVENGER. THE ENTIRE HUMAN RACE IS IN DANGER. LOOK UPON MY MATRIX AND LEARN...

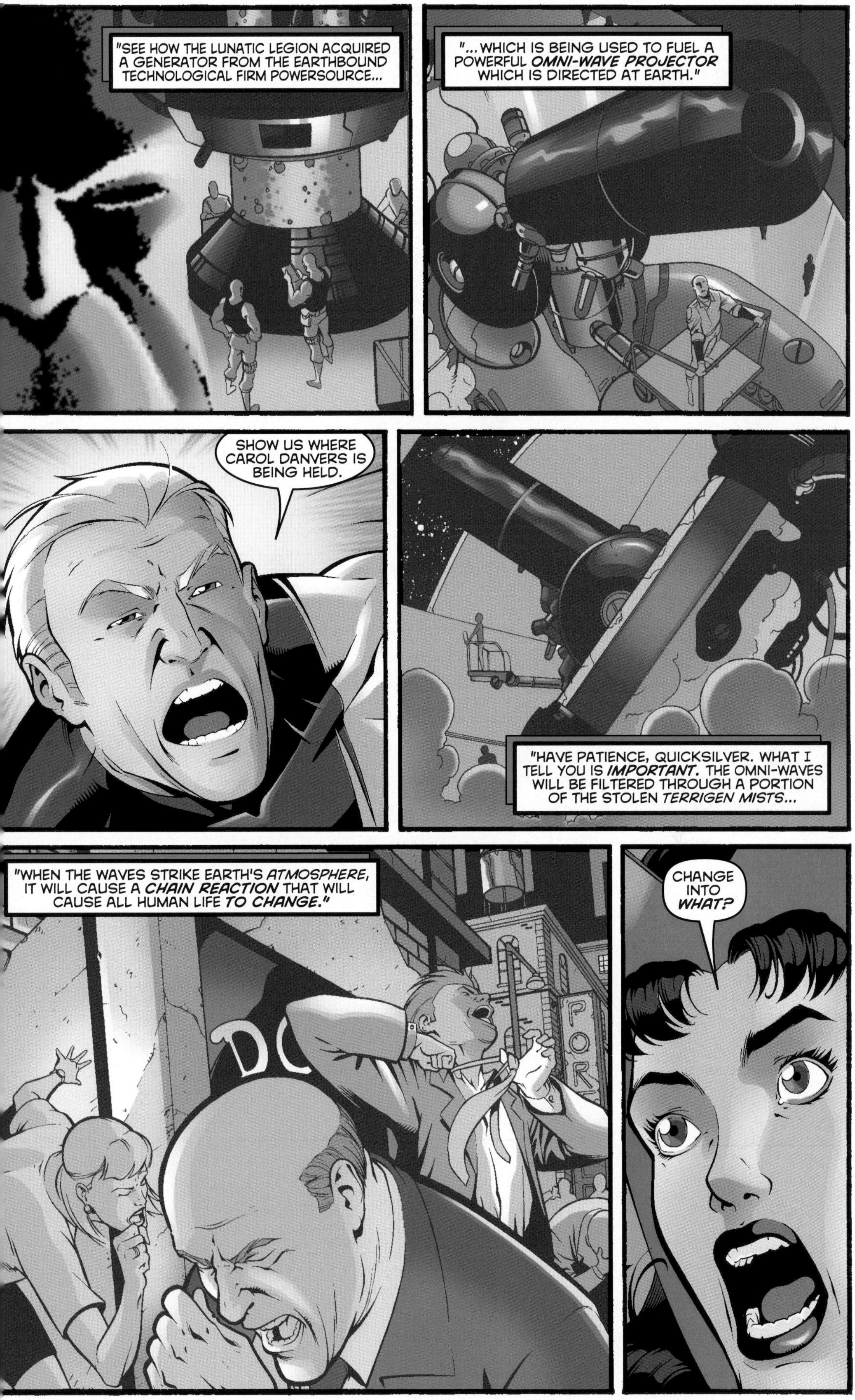
"SEE HOW THE LUNATIC LEGION ACQUIRED A GENERATOR FROM THE EARTHBOUND TECHNOLOGICAL FIRM POWERSOURCE...
"...WHICH IS BEING USED TO FUEL A POWERFUL *OMNI-WAVE PROJECTOR* WHICH IS DIRECTED AT EARTH."
SHOW US WHERE CAROL DANVERS IS BEING HELD.
"HAVE PATIENCE, QUICKSILVER. WHAT I TELL YOU IS *IMPORTANT.* THE OMNI-WAVES WILL BE FILTERED THROUGH A PORTION OF THE STOLEN *TERRIGEN MISTS*...
"WHEN THE WAVES STRIKE EARTH'S *ATMOSPHERE*, IT WILL CAUSE A *CHAIN REACTION* THAT WILL CAUSE ALL HUMAN LIFE *TO CHANGE.*"
CHANGE INTO *WHAT?*

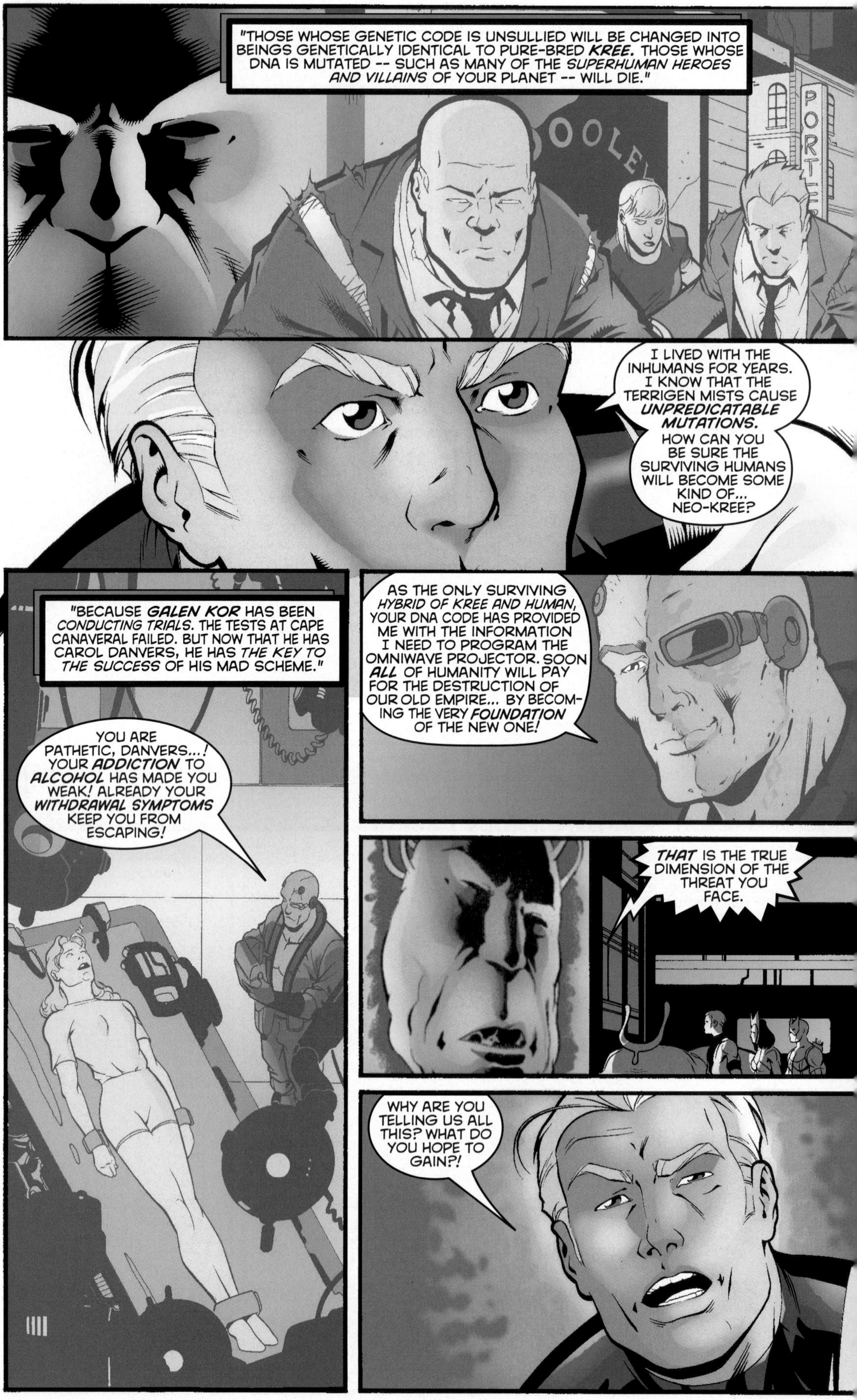
"THOSE WHOSE GENETIC CODE IS UNSULLIED WILL BE CHANGED INTO BEINGS GENETICALLY IDENTICAL TO PURE-BRED KREE. THOSE WHOSE DNA IS MUTATED -- SUCH AS MANY OF THE SUPERHUMAN HEROES AND VILLAINS OF YOUR PLANET -- WILL DIE."
PORTE
I LIVED WITH THE INHUMANS FOR YEARS. I KNOW THAT THE TERRIGEN MISTS CAUSE UNPREDICATABLE MUTATIONS. HOW CAN YOU BE SURE THE SURVIVING HUMANS WILL BECOME SOME KIND OF... NEO-KREE?
"BECAUSE GALEN KOR HAS BEEN CONDUCTING TRIALS. THE TESTS AT CAPE CANAVERAL FAILED. BUT NOW THAT HE HAS CAROL DANVERS, HE HAS THE KEY TO THE SUCCESS OF HIS MAD SCHEME."
YOU ARE PATHETIC, DANVERS...! YOUR ADDICTION TO ALCOHOL HAS MADE YOU WEAK! ALREADY YOUR WITHDRAWAL SYMPTOMS KEEP YOU FROM ESCAPING!
AS THE ONLY SURVIVING HYBRID OF KREE AND HUMAN, YOUR DNA CODE HAS PROVIDED ME WITH THE INFORMATION I NEED TO PROGRAM THE OMNIWAVE PROJECTOR. SOON ALL OF HUMANITY WILL PAY FOR THE DESTRUCTION OF OUR OLD EMPIRE... BY BECOMING THE VERY FOUNDATION OF THE NEW ONE!
THAT IS THE TRUE DIMENSION OF THE THREAT YOU FACE.
WHY ARE YOU TELLING US ALL THIS? WHAT DO YOU HOPE TO GAIN?!

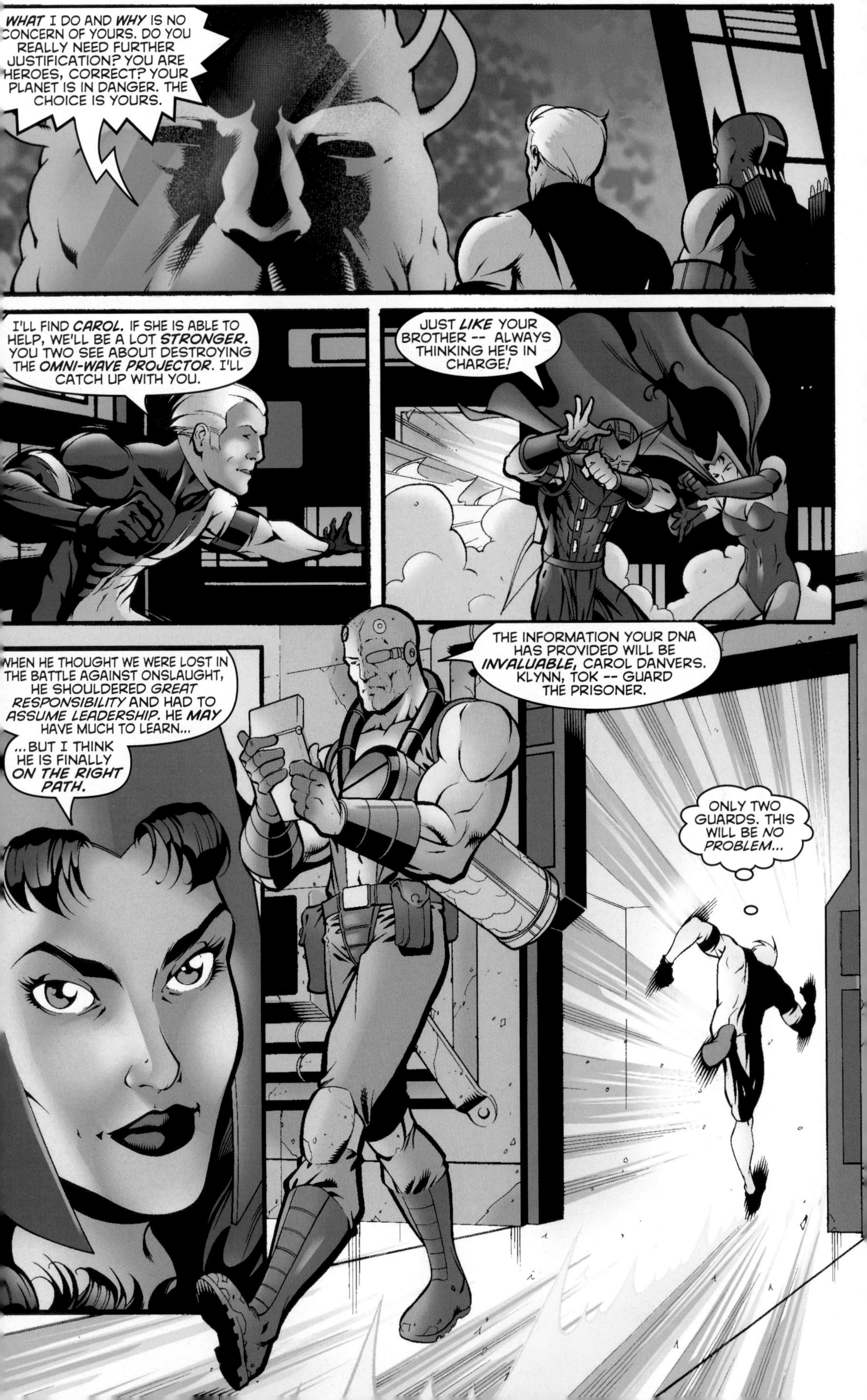
WHAT I DO AND WHY IS NO CONCERN OF YOURS. DO YOU REALLY NEED FURTHER JUSTIFICATION? YOU ARE HEROES, CORRECT? YOUR PLANET IS IN DANGER. THE CHOICE IS YOURS.
I'LL FIND CAROL. IF SHE IS ABLE TO HELP, WE'LL BE A LOT STRONGER. YOU TWO SEE ABOUT DESTROYING THE OMNI-WAVE PROJECTOR. I'LL CATCH UP WITH YOU.
JUST LIKE YOUR BROTHER -- ALWAYS THINKING HE'S IN CHARGE!
WHEN HE THOUGHT WE WERE LOST IN THE BATTLE AGAINST ONSLAUGHT, HE SHOULDERED GREAT RESPONSIBILITY AND HAD TO ASSUME LEADERSHIP. HE MAY HAVE MUCH TO LEARN...
...BUT I THINK HE IS FINALLY ON THE RIGHT PATH.
THE INFORMATION YOUR DNA HAS PROVIDED WILL BE INVALUABLE, CAROL DANVERS. KLYNN, TOK -- GUARD THE PRISONER.
ONLY TWO GUARDS. THIS WILL BE NO PROBLEM...

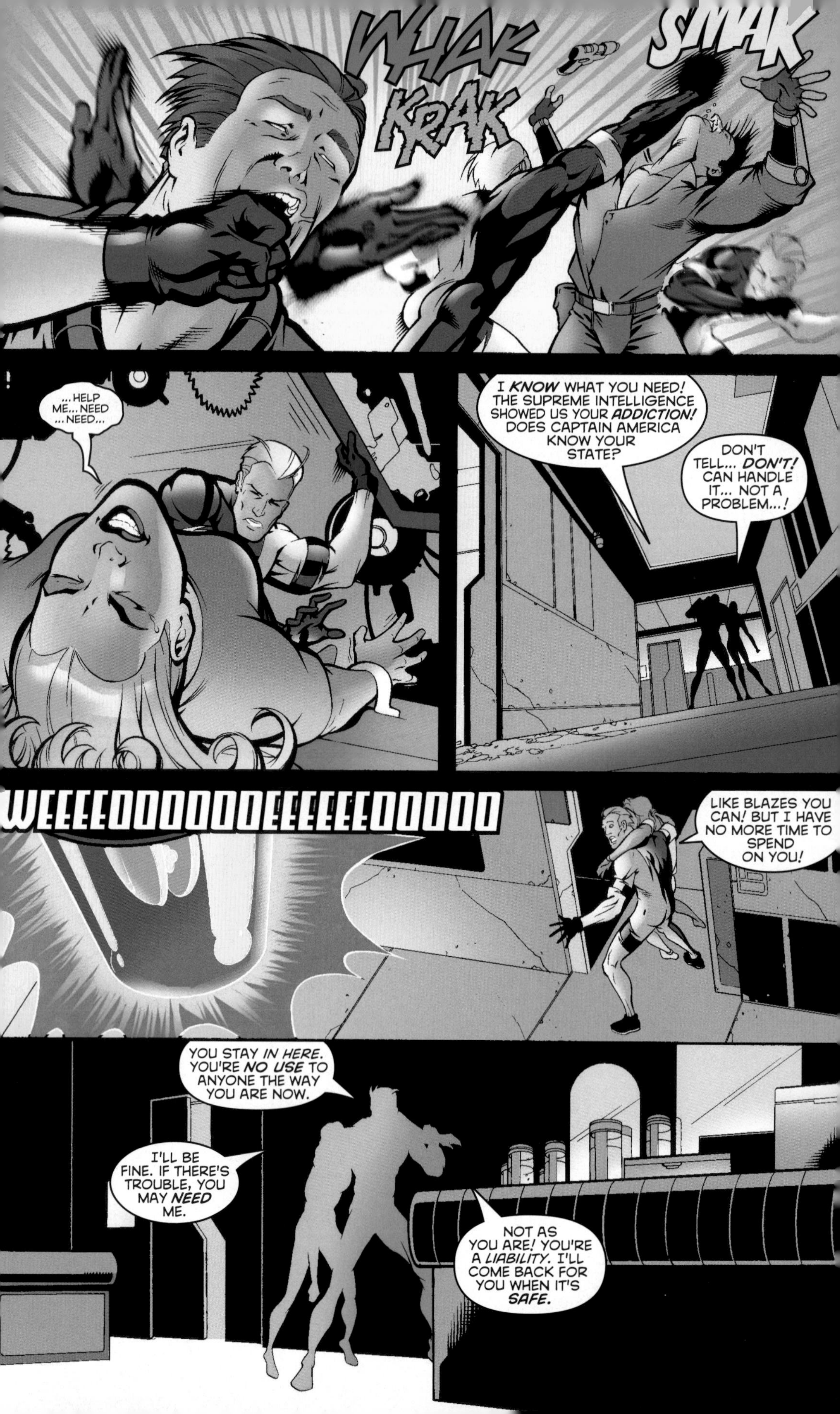
WHAK
KRAK
SMAK
...HELP ME...NEED ...NEED...
I KNOW WHAT YOU NEED! THE SUPREME INTELLIGENCE SHOWED US YOUR ADDICTION! DOES CAPTAIN AMERICA KNOW YOUR STATE?
DON'T TELL... DON'T! CAN HANDLE IT... NOT A PROBLEM...!
WEEEEOOOOOOOEEEEEEOOOOO
LIKE BLAZES YOU CAN! BUT I HAVE NO MORE TIME TO SPEND ON YOU!
YOU STAY IN HERE. YOU'RE NO USE TO ANYONE THE WAY YOU ARE NOW.
I'LL BE FINE. IF THERE'S TROUBLE, YOU MAY NEED ME.
NOT AS YOU ARE! YOU'RE A LIABILITY. I'LL COME BACK FOR YOU WHEN IT'S SAFE.

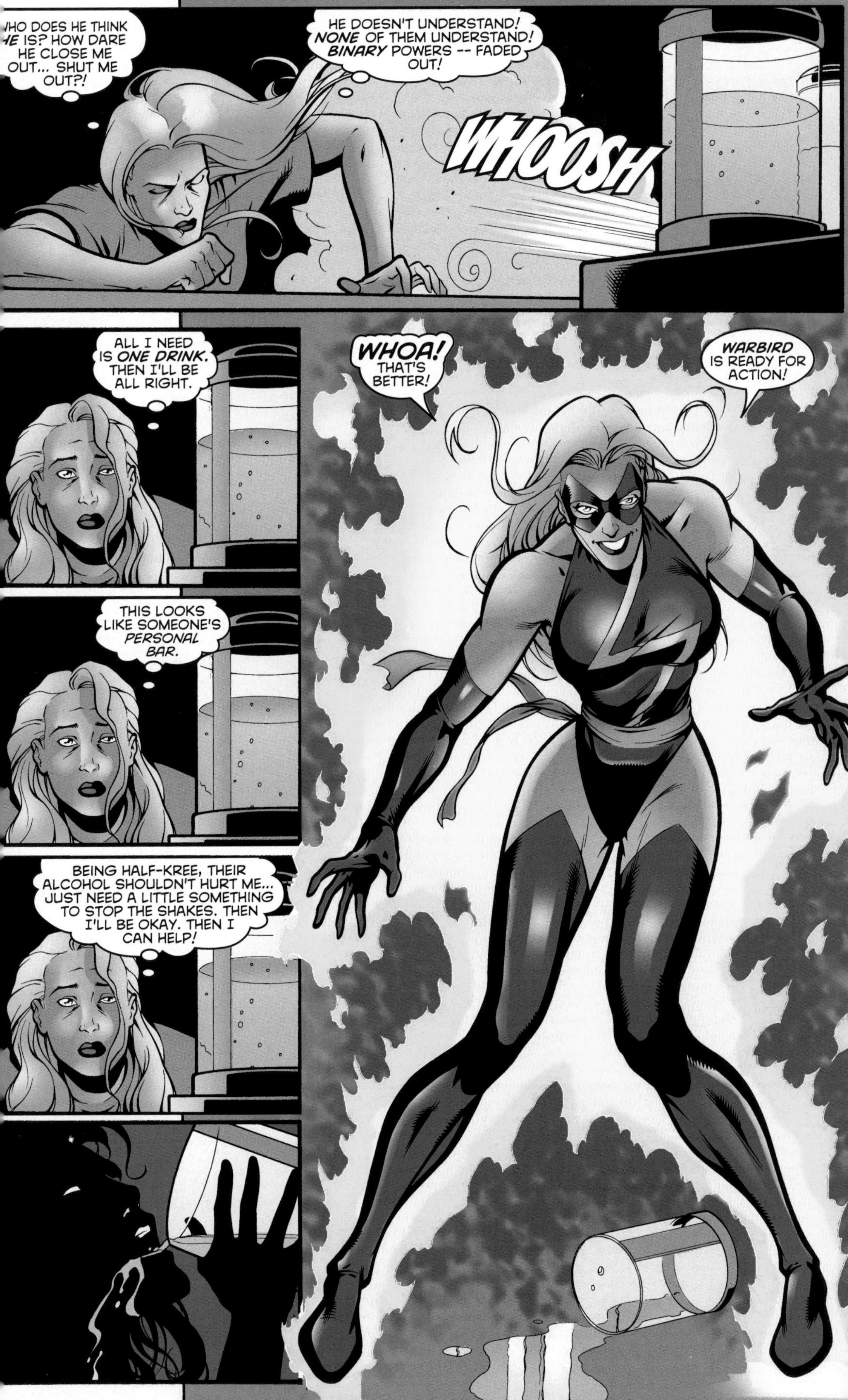

WHO DOES HE THINK HE IS? HOW DARE HE CLOSE ME OUT... SHUT ME OUT?!
HE DOESN'T UNDERSTAND! NONE OF THEM UNDERSTAND! BINARY POWERS -- FADED OUT!
WHOOSH
ALL I NEED IS ONE DRINK. THEN I'LL BE ALL RIGHT.
THIS LOOKS LIKE SOMEONE'S PERSONAL BAR.
BEING HALF-KREE, THEIR ALCOHOL SHOULDN'T HURT ME... JUST NEED A LITTLE SOMETHING TO STOP THE SHAKES. THEN I'LL BE OKAY. THEN I CAN HELP!
WHOA! THAT'S BETTER!
WARBIRD IS READY FOR ACTION!

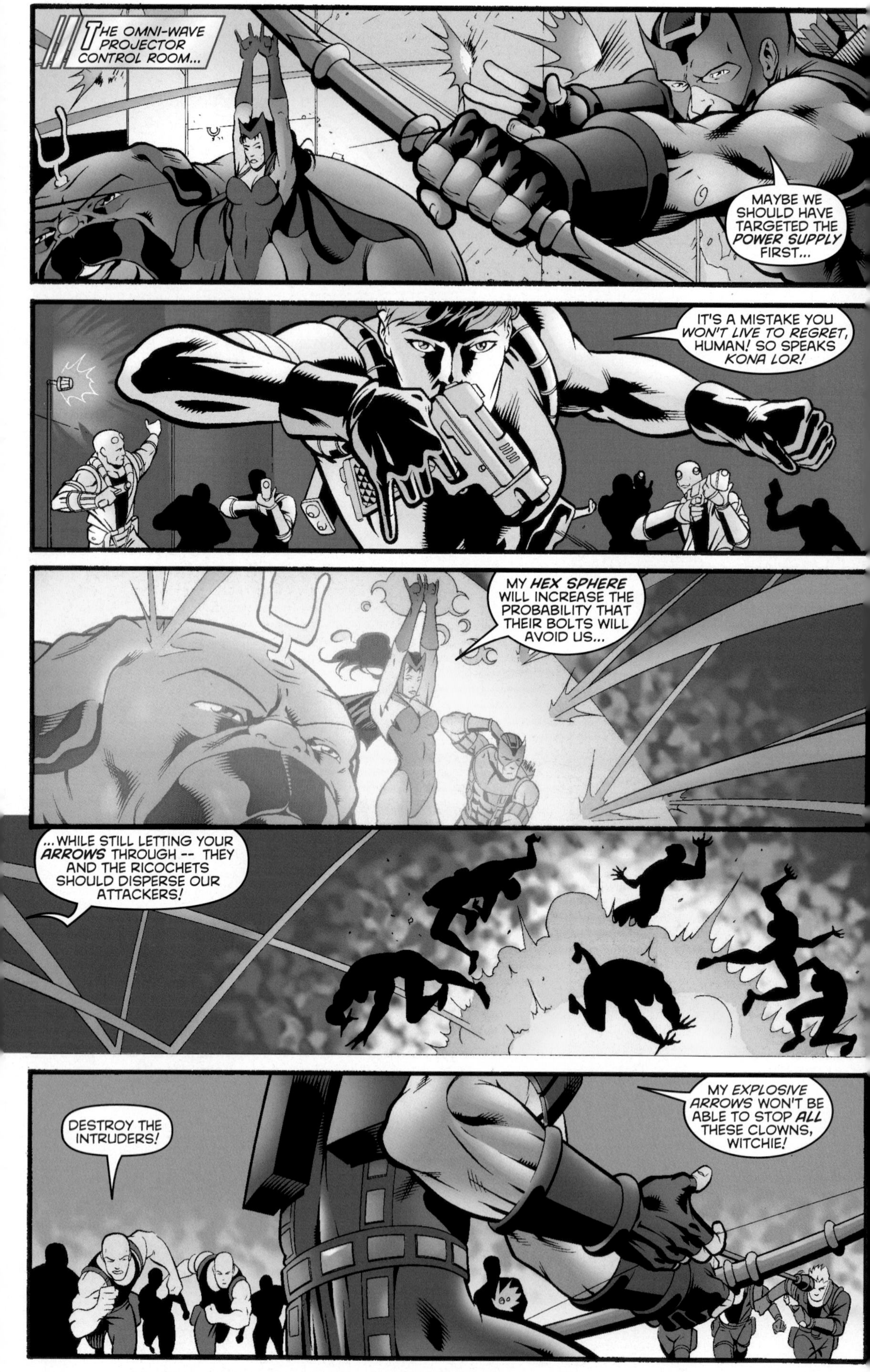
THE OMNI-WAVE PROJECTOR CONTROL ROOM...
MAYBE WE SHOULD HAVE TARGETED THE POWER SUPPLY FIRST...
IT'S A MISTAKE YOU WON'T LIVE TO REGRET, HUMAN! SO SPEAKS KONA LOR!
MY HEX SPHERE WILL INCREASE THE PROBABILITY THAT THEIR BOLTS WILL AVOID US...
...WHILE STILL LETTING YOUR ARROWS THROUGH -- THEY AND THE RICOCHETS SHOULD DISPERSE OUR ATTACKERS!
MY EXPLOSIVE ARROWS WON'T BE ABLE TO STOP ALL THESE CLOWNS, WITCHIE!
DESTROY THE INTRUDERS!

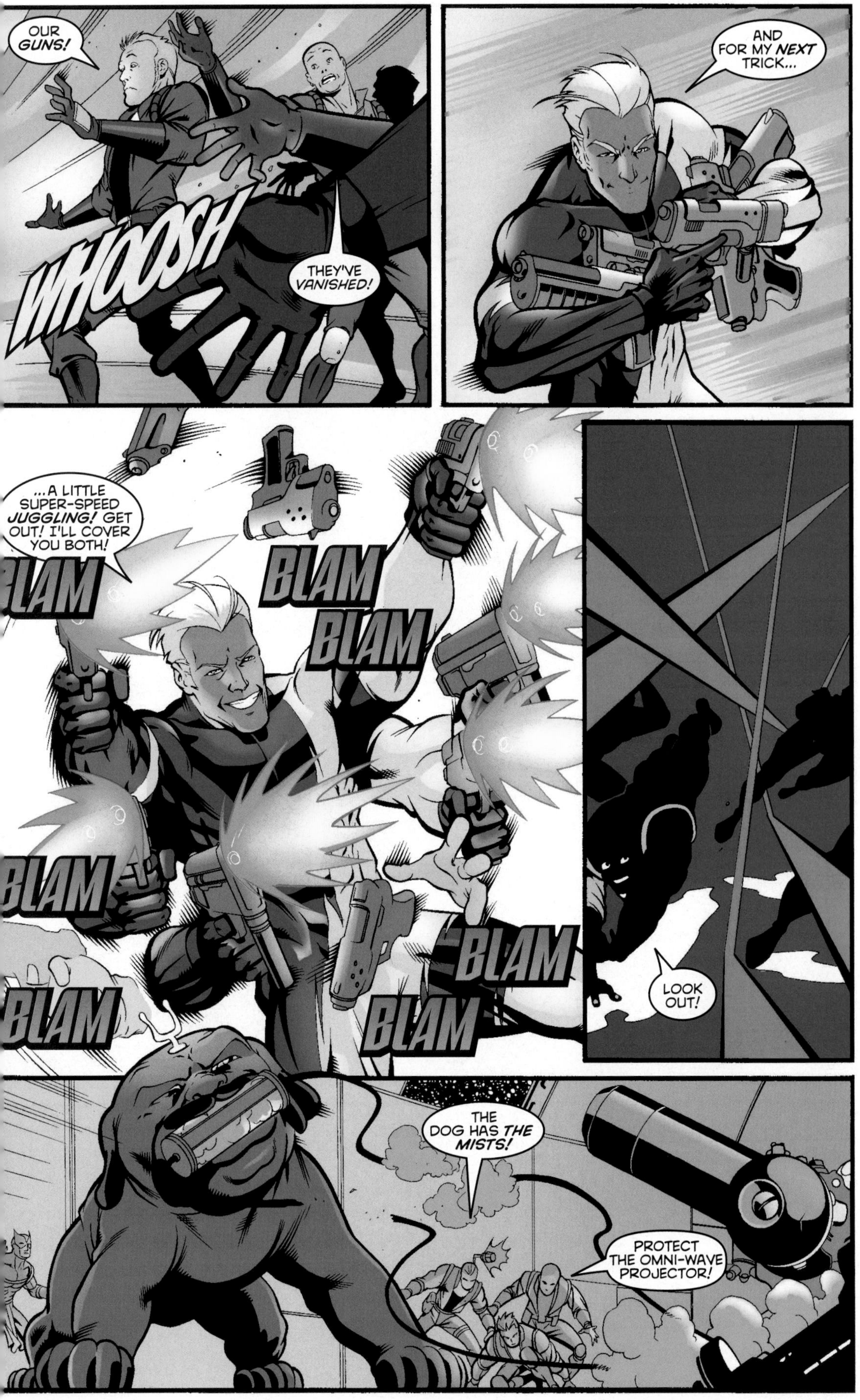
OUR GUNS!
WHOOSH
THEY'VE VANISHED!
AND FOR MY NEXT TRICK...
...A LITTLE SUPER-SPEED JUGGLING! GET OUT! I'LL COVER YOU BOTH!
BLAM
BLAM
BLAM
BLAM
BLAM
BLAM
BLAM
LOOK OUT!
THE DOG HAS THE MISTS!
PROTECT THE OMNI-WAVE PROJECTOR!

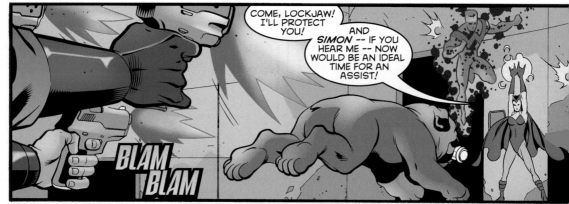

COME, LOCKJAW! I'LL PROTECT YOU!

AND *SIMON* -- IF YOU HEAR ME -- NOW WOULD BE AN IDEAL TIME FOR AN ASSIST!

BLAM BLAM

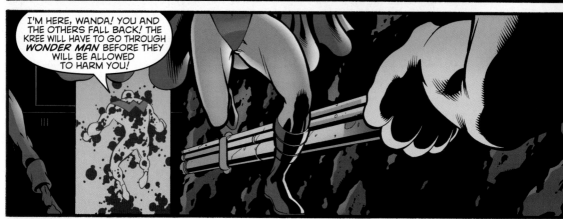

I'M HERE, WANDA! YOU AND THE OTHERS FALL BACK! THE KREE WILL HAVE TO GO THROUGH *WONDER MAN* BEFORE THEY WILL BE ALLOWED TO HARM YOU!

IT STILL CREEPS ME OUT WHEN YOUR SISTER CAUSES *WONDER MAN* TO *MANIFEST* FROM OUT OF THIN AIR!® HE'S *SUPPOSED* TO BE *DEAD!*

WE HAVE *MORE PRESSING THINGS* TO WORRY ABOUT. THE GUNS I CONFISCATED ARE OUT OF CHARGES, AND CAROL DANVERS IS ... INCAPACITATED.

® SEE AVENGERS #3
▢▢ MARK

WE MUST *IMMOBILIZE* THE OMNI-WAVE PROJECTOR! JUST BECAUSE LOCKJAW HAS TAKEN THE MISTS DOESN'T MEAN THE PROJECTOR *CAN'T* DO EARTH HARM!

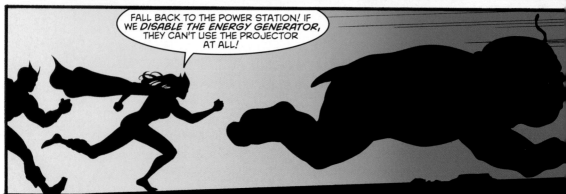

FALL BACK TO THE POWER STATION! IF WE *DISABLE THE ENERGY GENERATOR,* THEY CAN'T USE THE PROJECTOR AT ALL!

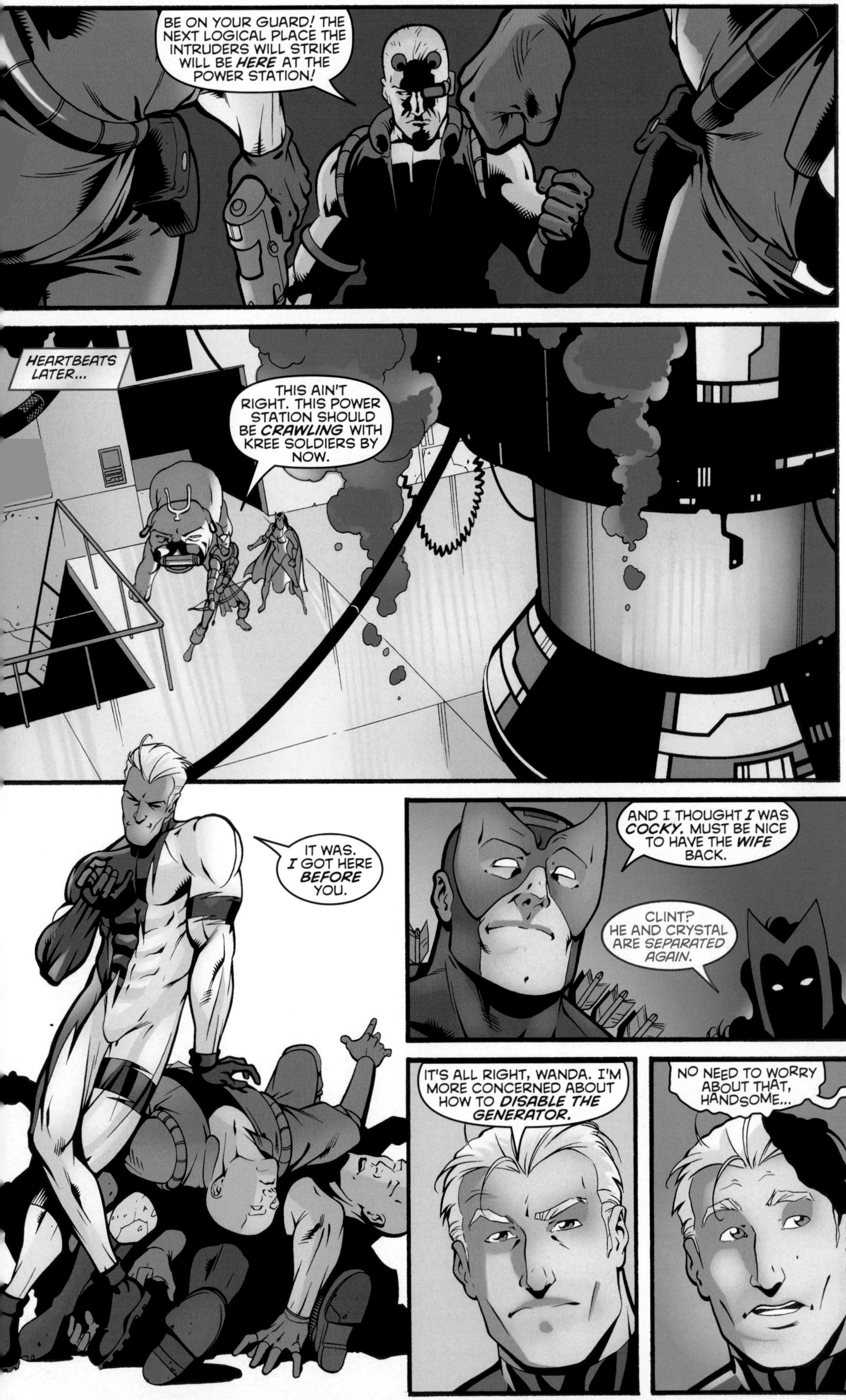
BE ON YOUR GUARD! THE NEXT LOGICAL PLACE THE INTRUDERS WILL STRIKE WILL BE *HERE* AT THE POWER STATION!
HEARTBEATS LATER...
THIS AIN'T RIGHT. THIS POWER STATION SHOULD BE *CRAWLING* WITH KREE SOLDIERS BY NOW.
IT WAS. *I* GOT HERE *BEFORE* YOU.
AND I THOUGHT *I* WAS *COCKY*. MUST BE NICE TO HAVE THE *WIFE* BACK.
CLINT? HE AND CRYSTAL ARE *SEPARATED AGAIN.*
IT'S ALL RIGHT, WANDA. I'M MORE CONCERNED ABOUT HOW TO *DISABLE THE GENERATOR.*
NO NEED TO WORRY ABOUT THAT, HANDSOME...

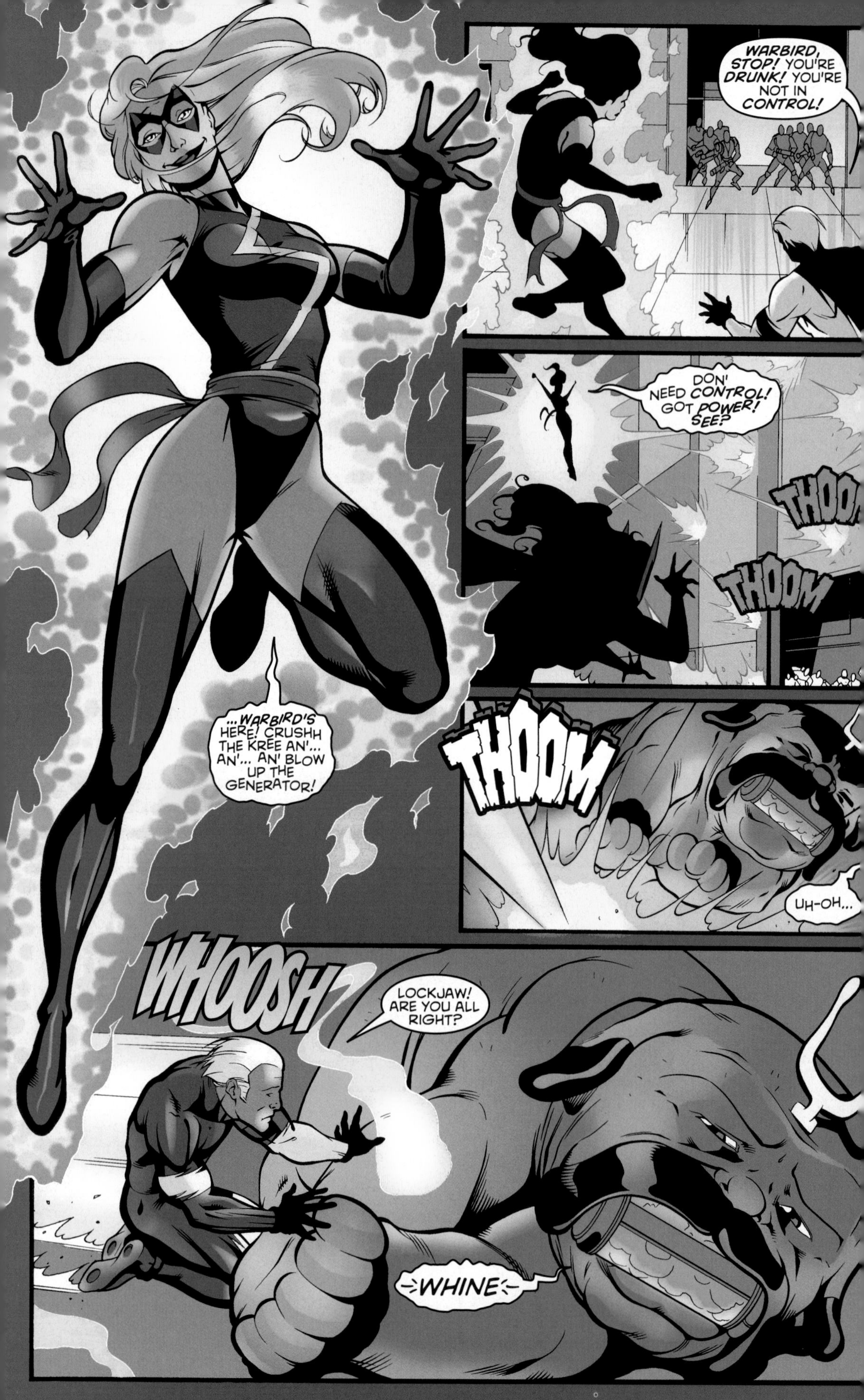
WARBIRD, STOP! YOU'RE DRUNK! YOU'RE NOT IN CONTROL!
...WARBIRD'S HERE! CRUSHH THE KREE AN'... AN'... AN' BLOW UP THE GENERATOR!
DON' NEED CONTROL! GOT POWER! SEE?
THOOM
THOOM
THOOM
UH-OH...
WHOOSH
LOCKJAW! ARE YOU ALL RIGHT?
-WHINE-

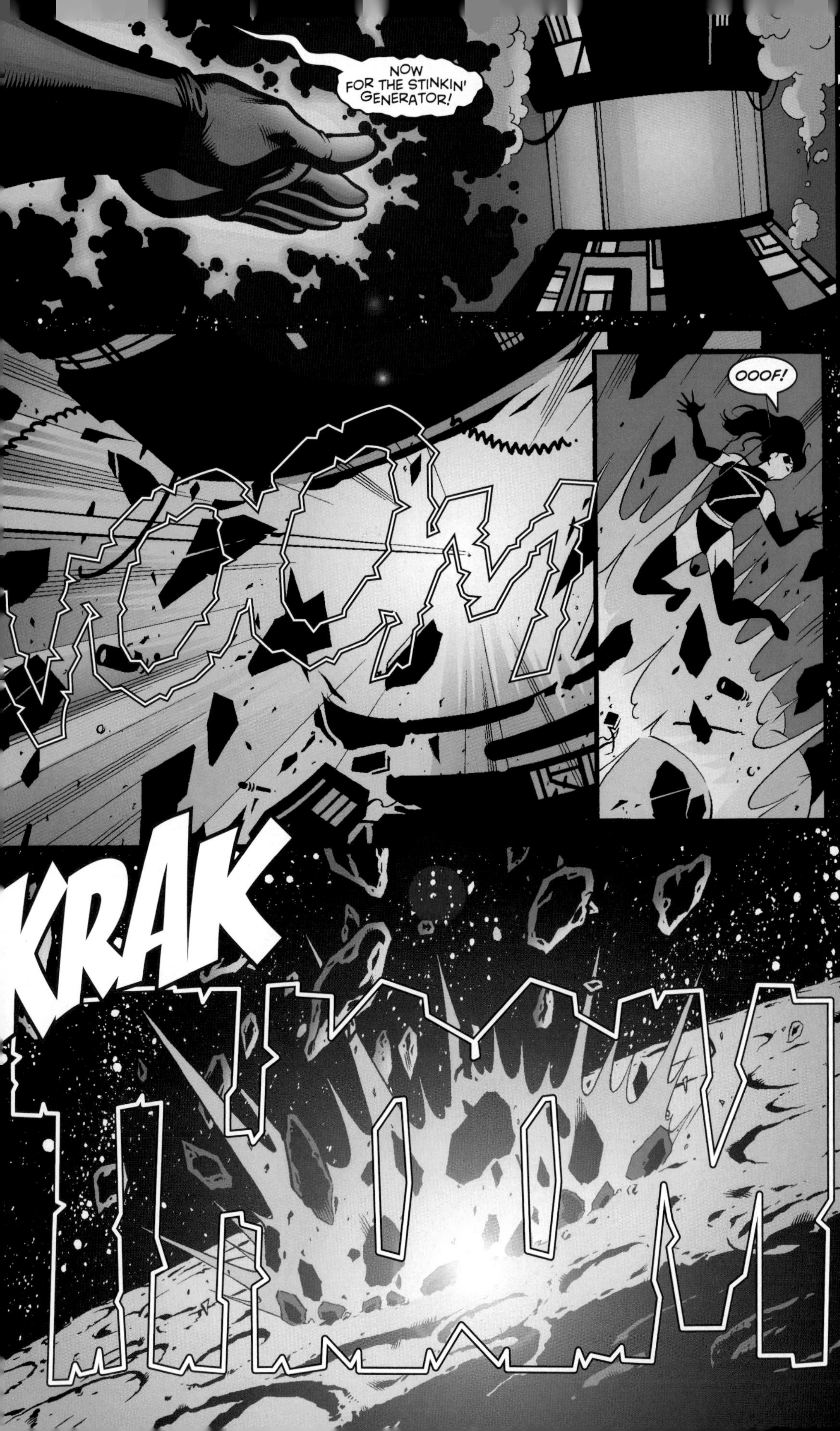
NOW FOR THE STINKIN' GENERATOR!
VOOM
OOOF!
KRAK
THOOM

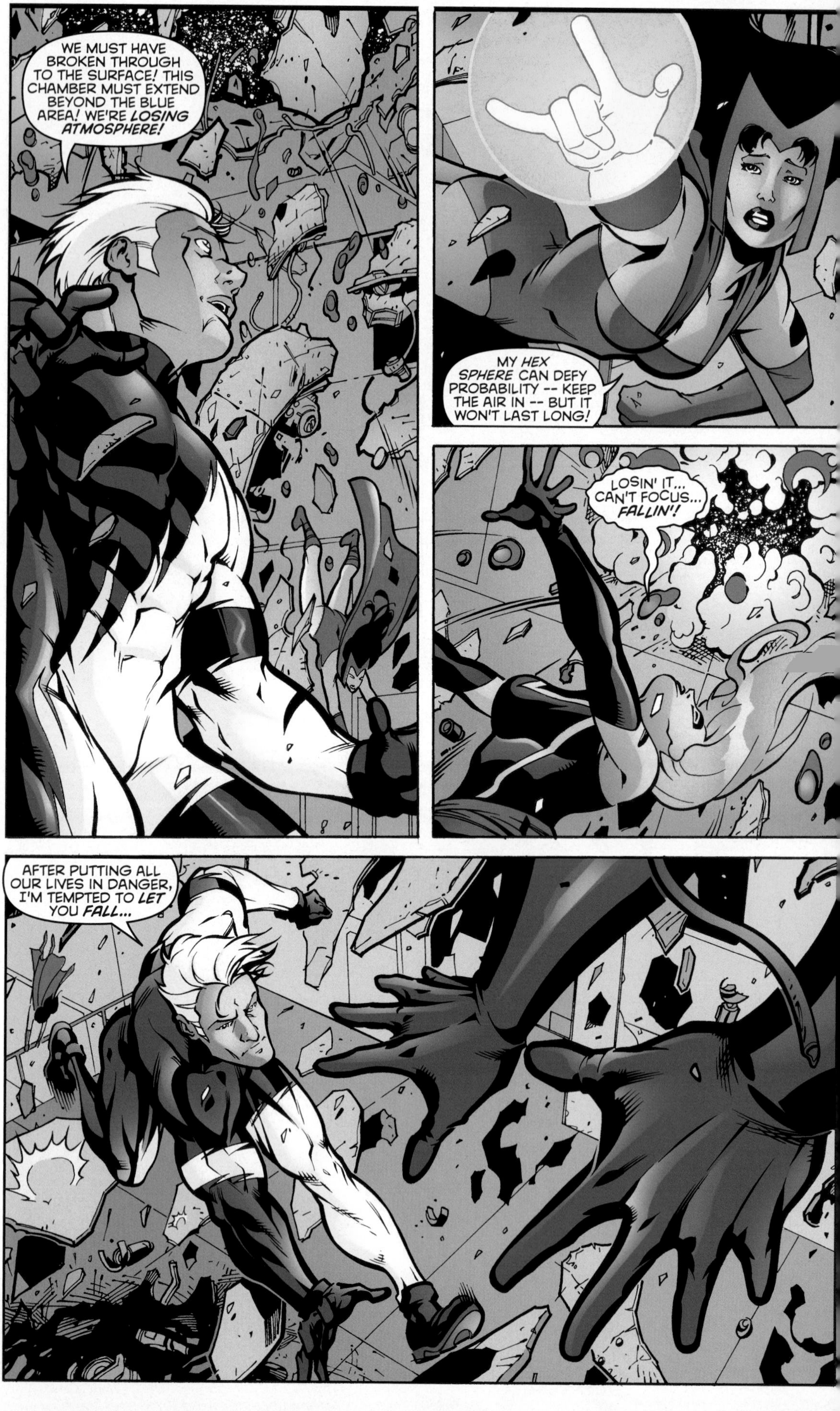
WE MUST HAVE BROKEN THROUGH TO THE SURFACE! THIS CHAMBER MUST EXTEND BEYOND THE BLUE AREA! WE'RE *LOSING ATMOSPHERE!*
MY *HEX SPHERE* CAN DEFY PROBABILITY -- KEEP THE AIR IN -- BUT IT WON'T LAST LONG!
LOSIN' IT... CAN'T FOCUS... *FALLIN'!*
AFTER PUTTING ALL OUR LIVES IN DANGER, I'M TEMPTED TO *LET* YOU *FALL*...

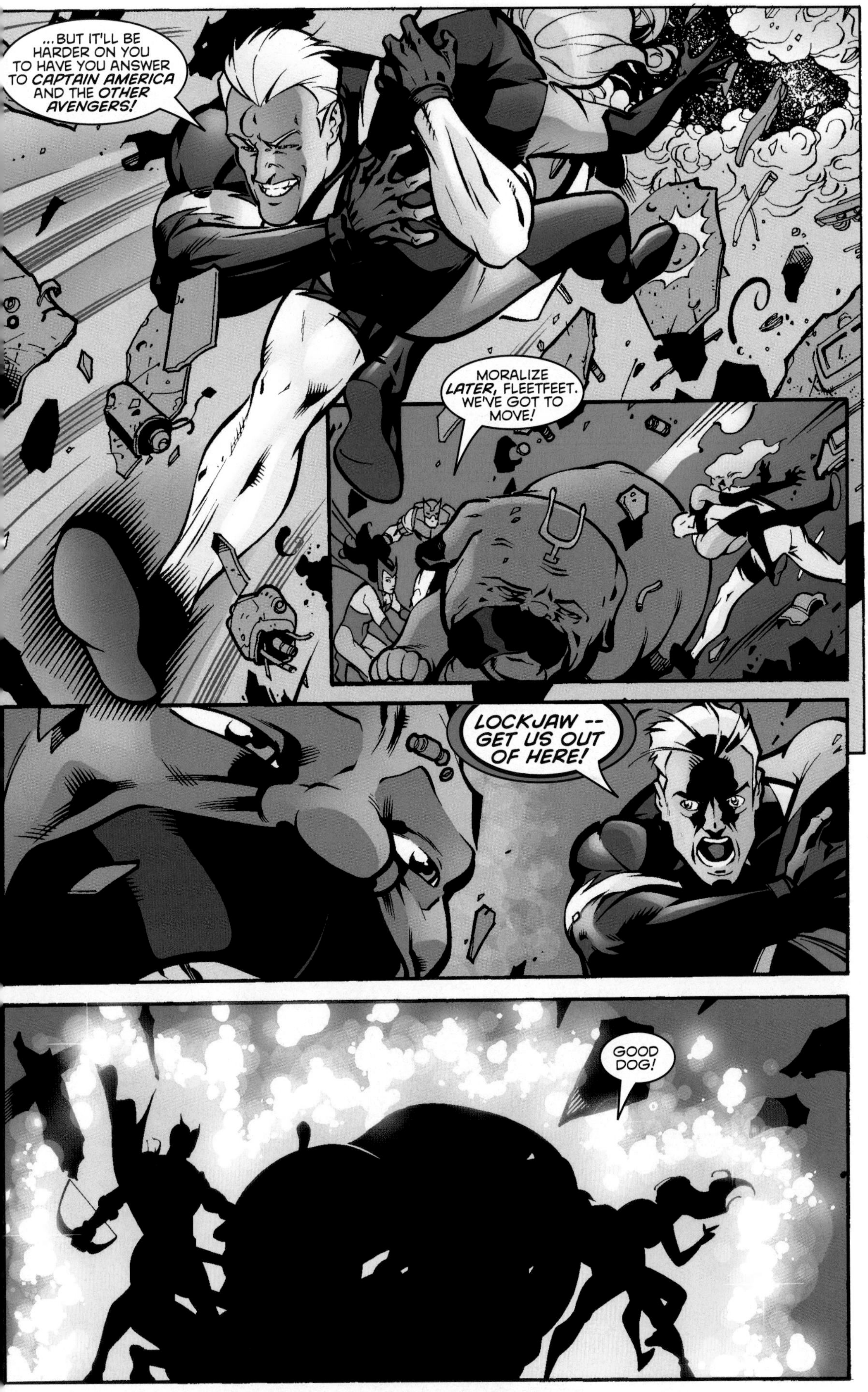
...BUT IT'LL BE HARDER ON YOU TO HAVE YOU ANSWER TO CAPTAIN AMERICA AND THE OTHER AVENGERS!
MORALIZE LATER, FLEETFEET. WE'VE GOT TO MOVE!
LOCKJAW -- GET US OUT OF HERE!
GOOD DOG!

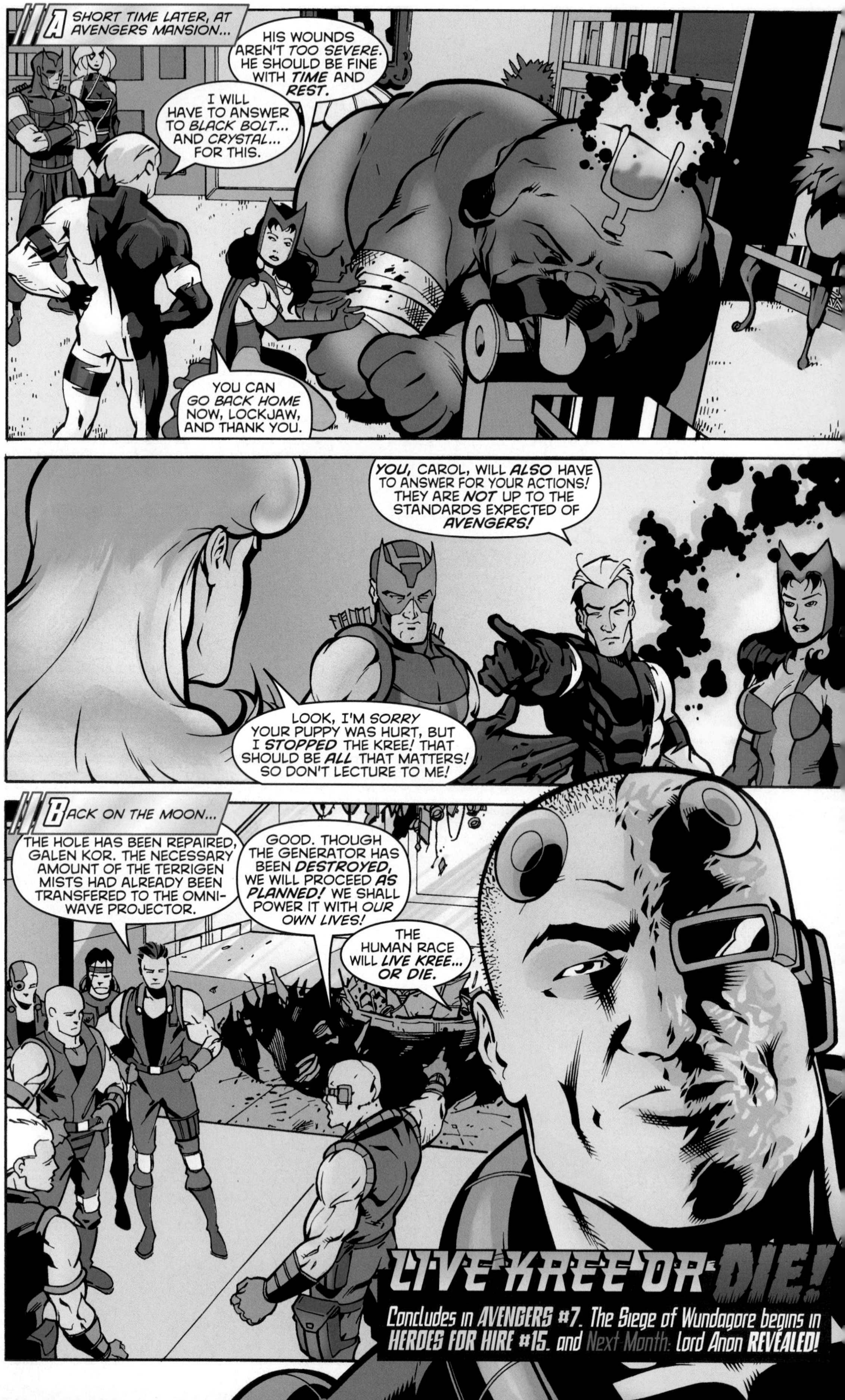
A SHORT TIME LATER, AT AVENGERS MANSION...
HIS WOUNDS AREN'T TOO SEVERE. HE SHOULD BE FINE WITH TIME AND REST.
I WILL HAVE TO ANSWER TO BLACK BOLT... AND CRYSTAL... FOR THIS.
YOU CAN GO BACK HOME NOW, LOCKJAW, AND THANK YOU.
YOU, CAROL, WILL ALSO HAVE TO ANSWER FOR YOUR ACTIONS! THEY ARE NOT UP TO THE STANDARDS EXPECTED OF AVENGERS!
LOOK, I'M SORRY YOUR PUPPY WAS HURT, BUT I STOPPED THE KREE! THAT SHOULD BE ALL THAT MATTERS! SO DON'T LECTURE TO ME!
BACK ON THE MOON...
THE HOLE HAS BEEN REPAIRED, GALEN KOR. THE NECESSARY AMOUNT OF THE TERRIGEN MISTS HAD ALREADY BEEN TRANSFERED TO THE OMNI-WAVE PROJECTOR.
GOOD. THOUGH THE GENERATOR HAS BEEN DESTROYED, WE WILL PROCEED AS PLANNED! WE SHALL POWER IT WITH OUR OWN LIVES!
THE HUMAN RACE WILL LIVE KREE... OR DIE.
LIVE KREE OR DIE!
Concludes in AVENGERS #7. The Siege of Wundagore begins in HEROES FOR HIRE #15. and Next Month: Lord Anon REVEALED!

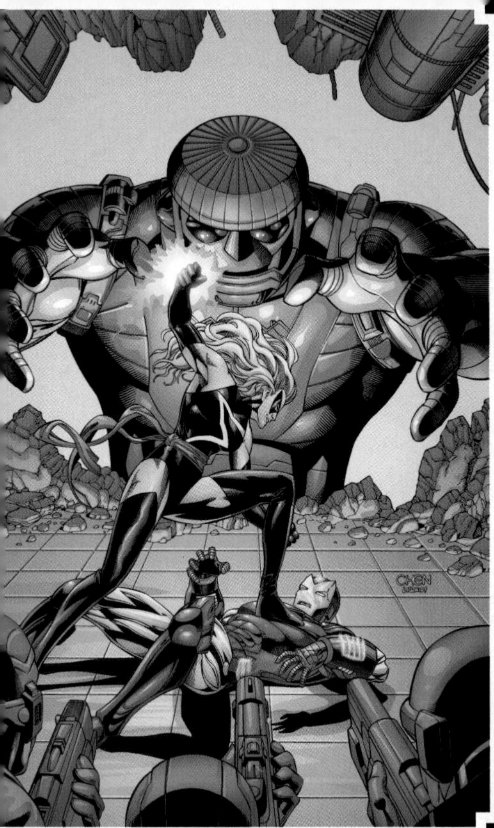
CHEN
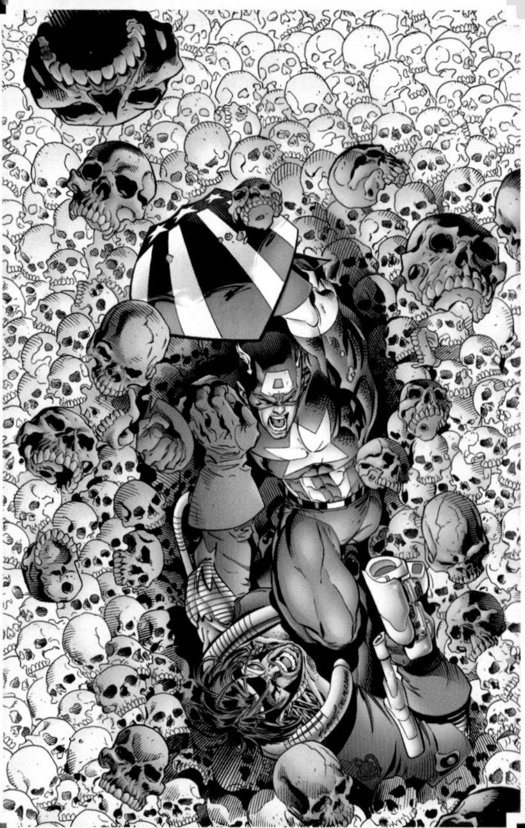
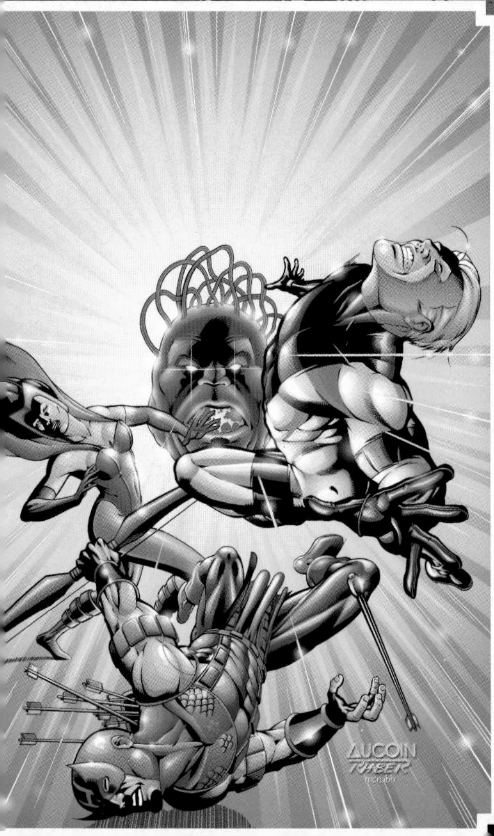
AUCOIN
RABER
mcnabb
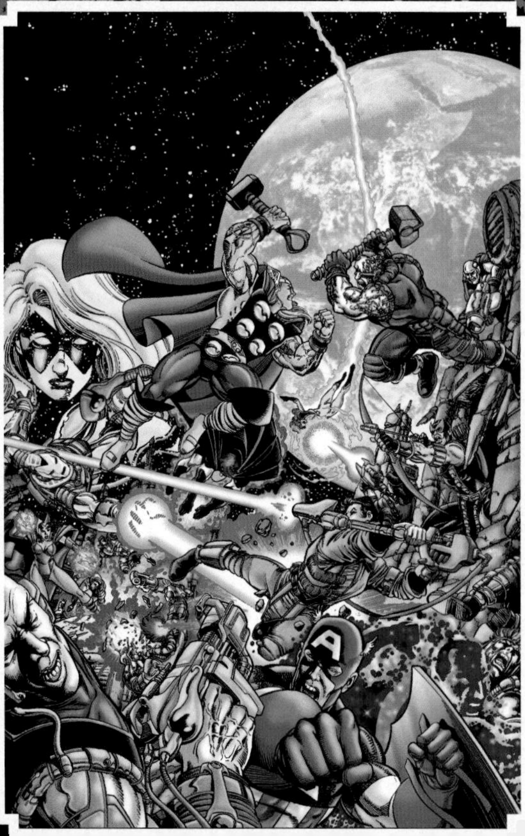

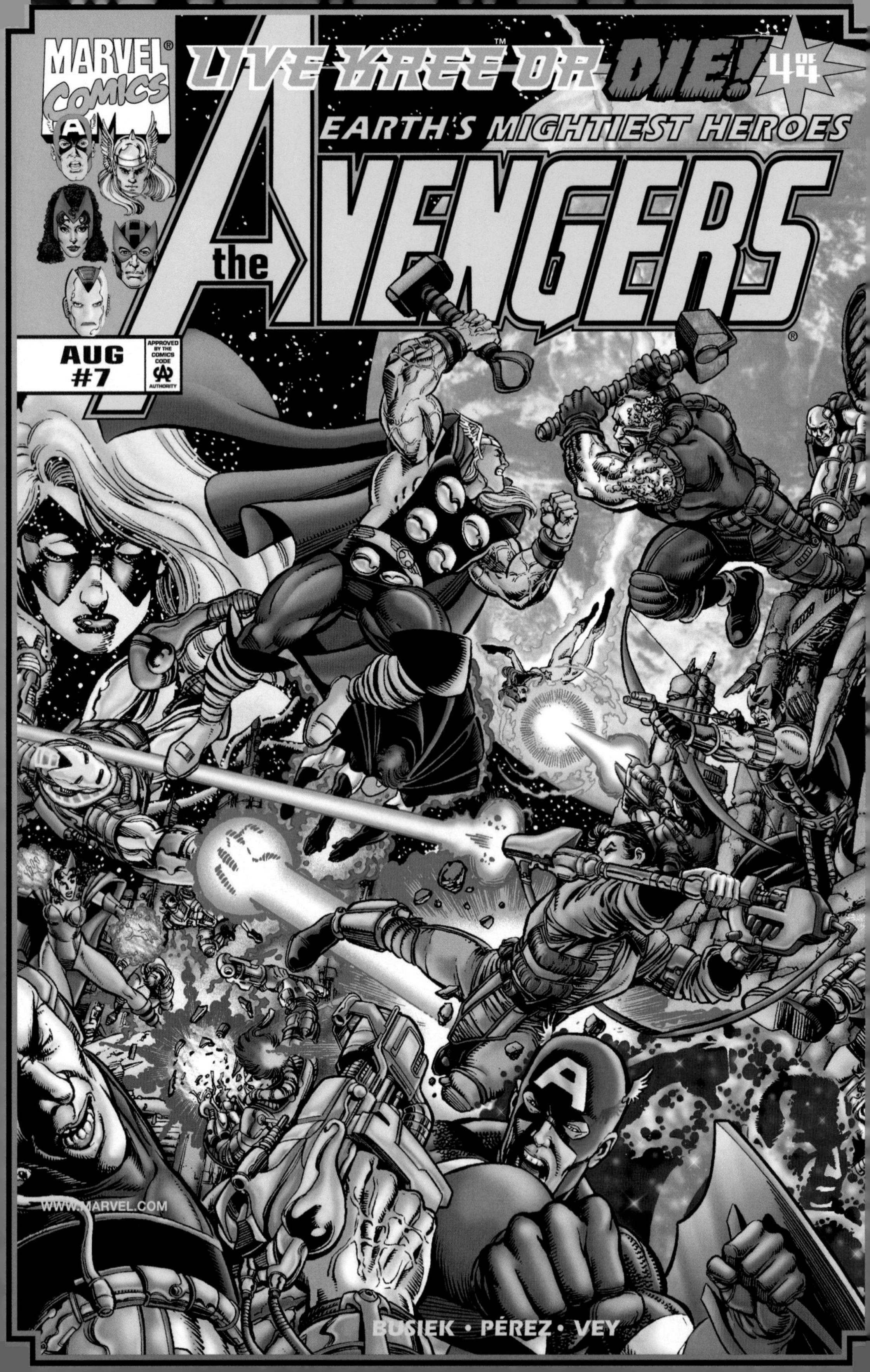

MARVEL COMICS
LIVE KREE OR DIE!
4 OF 4
EARTH'S MIGHTIEST HEROES
the AVENGERS
AUG #7
APPROVED BY THE COMICS CODE AUTHORITY
WWW.MARVEL.COM
BUSIEK • PÉREZ • VEY

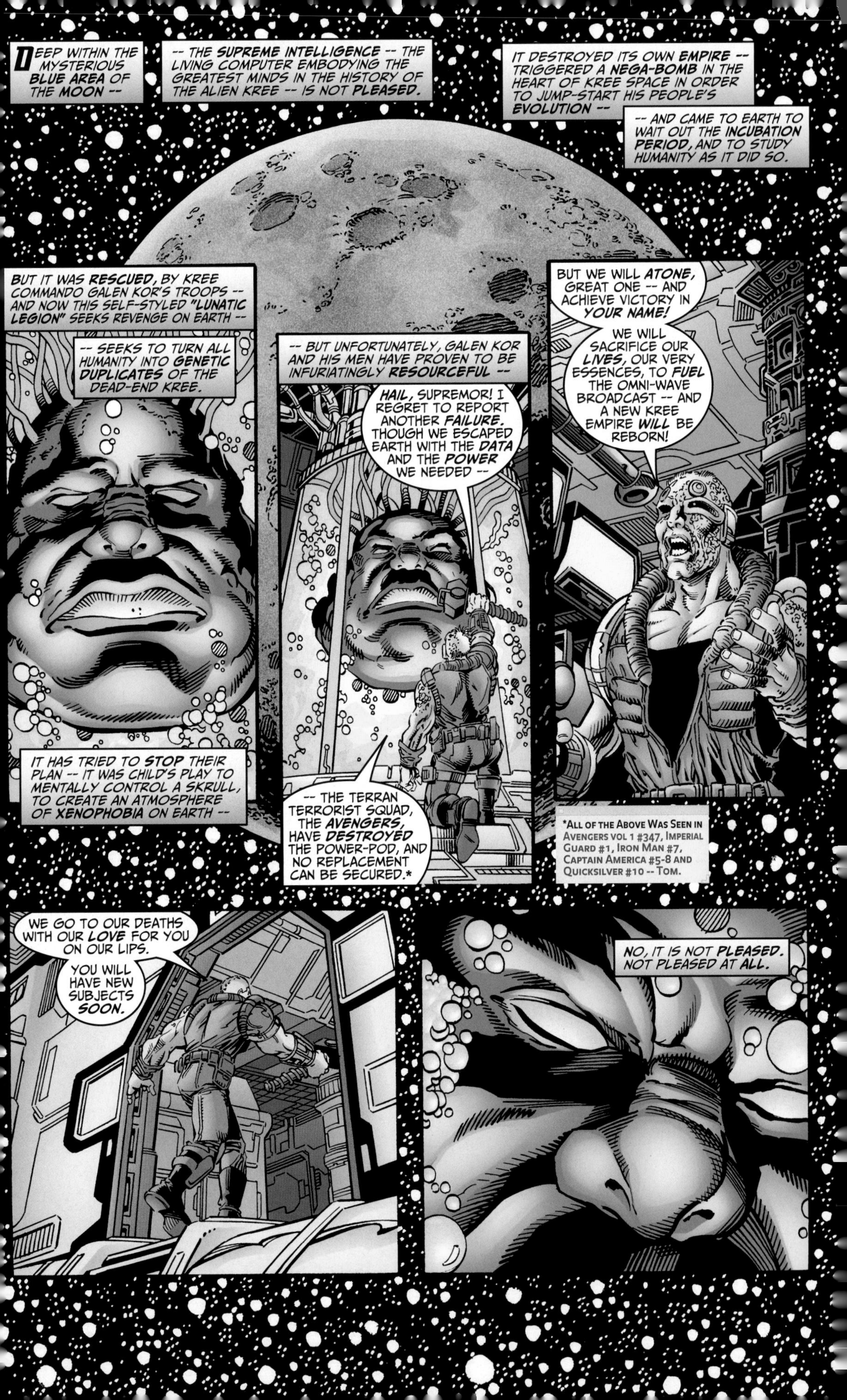
DEEP WITHIN THE MYSTERIOUS BLUE AREA OF THE MOON --
-- THE SUPREME INTELLIGENCE -- THE LIVING COMPUTER EMBODYING THE GREATEST MINDS IN THE HISTORY OF THE ALIEN KREE -- IS NOT PLEASED.
IT DESTROYED ITS OWN EMPIRE -- TRIGGERED A NEGA-BOMB IN THE HEART OF KREE SPACE IN ORDER TO JUMP-START HIS PEOPLE'S EVOLUTION --
-- AND CAME TO EARTH TO WAIT OUT THE INCUBATION PERIOD, AND TO STUDY HUMANITY AS IT DID SO.
BUT IT WAS RESCUED, BY KREE COMMANDO GALEN KOR'S TROOPS -- AND NOW THIS SELF-STYLED "LUNATIC LEGION" SEEKS REVENGE ON EARTH --
-- SEEKS TO TURN ALL HUMANITY INTO GENETIC DUPLICATES OF THE DEAD-END KREE.
IT HAS TRIED TO STOP THEIR PLAN -- IT WAS CHILD'S PLAY TO MENTALLY CONTROL A SKRULL, TO CREATE AN ATMOSPHERE OF XENOPHOBIA ON EARTH --
-- BUT UNFORTUNATELY, GALEN KOR AND HIS MEN HAVE PROVEN TO BE INFURIATINGLY RESOURCEFUL --
HAIL, SUPREMOR! I REGRET TO REPORT ANOTHER FAILURE. THOUGH WE ESCAPED EARTH WITH THE DATA AND THE POWER WE NEEDED --
-- THE TERRAN TERRORIST SQUAD, THE AVENGERS, HAVE DESTROYED THE POWER-POD, AND NO REPLACEMENT CAN BE SECURED.*
BUT WE WILL ATONE, GREAT ONE -- AND ACHIEVE VICTORY IN YOUR NAME!
WE WILL SACRIFICE OUR LIVES, OUR VERY ESSENCES, TO FUEL THE OMNI-WAVE BROADCAST -- AND A NEW KREE EMPIRE WILL BE REBORN!
*ALL OF THE ABOVE WAS SEEN IN AVENGERS VOL 1 #347, IMPERIAL GUARD #1, IRON MAN #7, CAPTAIN AMERICA #5-8 AND QUICKSILVER #10 -- TOM.
WE GO TO OUR DEATHS WITH OUR LOVE FOR YOU ON OUR LIPS.
YOU WILL HAVE NEW SUBJECTS SOON.
NO, IT IS NOT PLEASED. NOT PLEASED AT ALL.

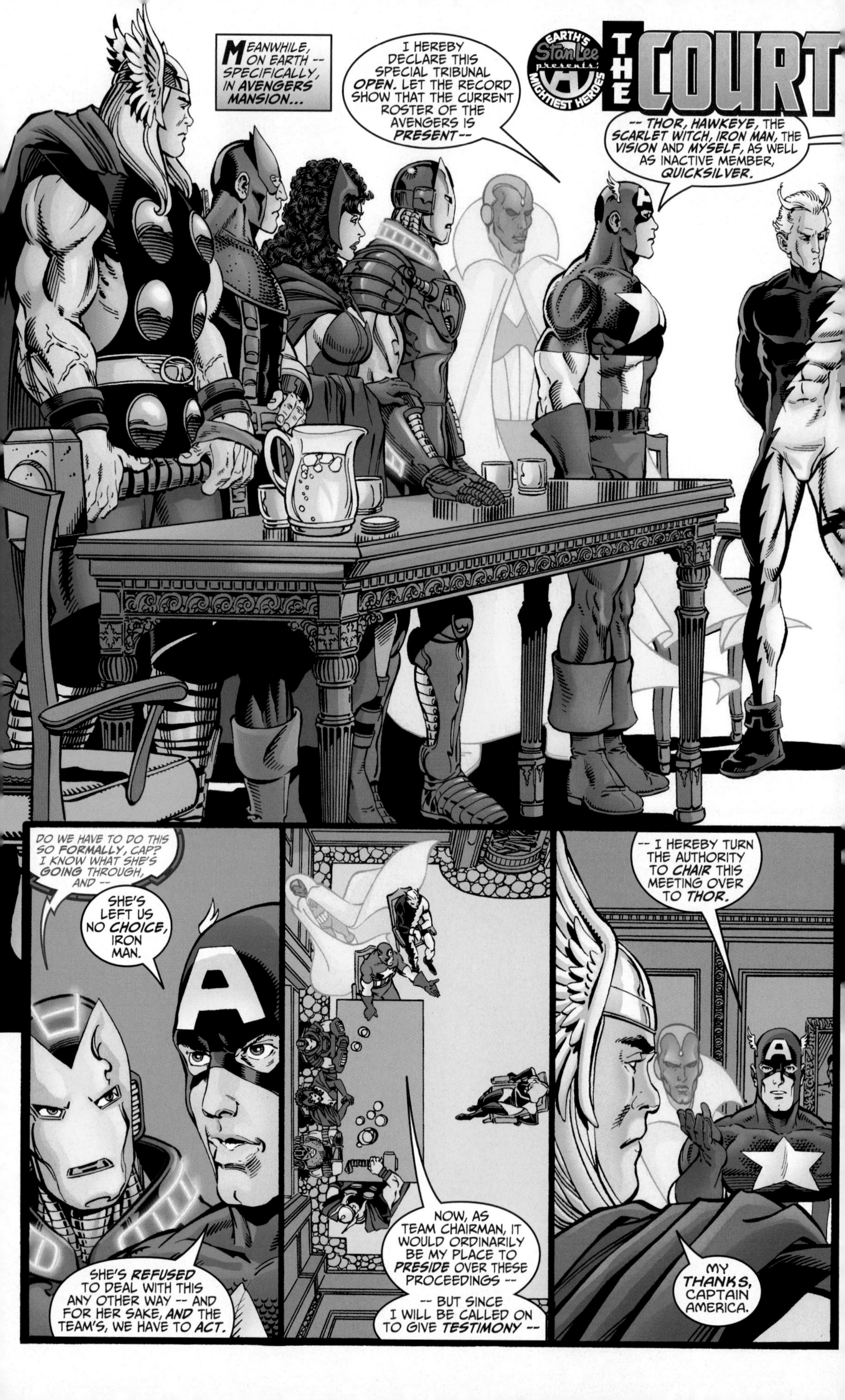
MEANWHILE, ON EARTH -- SPECIFICALLY, IN AVENGERS MANSION...
I HEREBY DECLARE THIS SPECIAL TRIBUNAL OPEN. LET THE RECORD SHOW THAT THE CURRENT ROSTER OF THE AVENGERS IS PRESENT--
EARTH'S MIGHTIEST HEROES
Stan Lee presents:
THE COURT
-- THOR, HAWKEYE, THE SCARLET WITCH, IRON MAN, THE VISION AND MYSELF, AS WELL AS INACTIVE MEMBER, QUICKSILVER.
DO WE HAVE TO DO THIS SO FORMALLY, CAP? I KNOW WHAT SHE'S GOING THROUGH, AND --
SHE'S LEFT US NO CHOICE, IRON MAN.
SHE'S REFUSED TO DEAL WITH THIS ANY OTHER WAY -- AND FOR HER SAKE, AND THE TEAM'S, WE HAVE TO ACT.
NOW, AS TEAM CHAIRMAN, IT WOULD ORDINARILY BE MY PLACE TO PRESIDE OVER THESE PROCEEDINGS --
-- BUT SINCE I WILL BE CALLED ON TO GIVE TESTIMONY --
-- I HEREBY TURN THE AUTHORITY TO CHAIR THIS MEETING OVER TO THOR.
MY THANKS, CAPTAIN AMERICA.

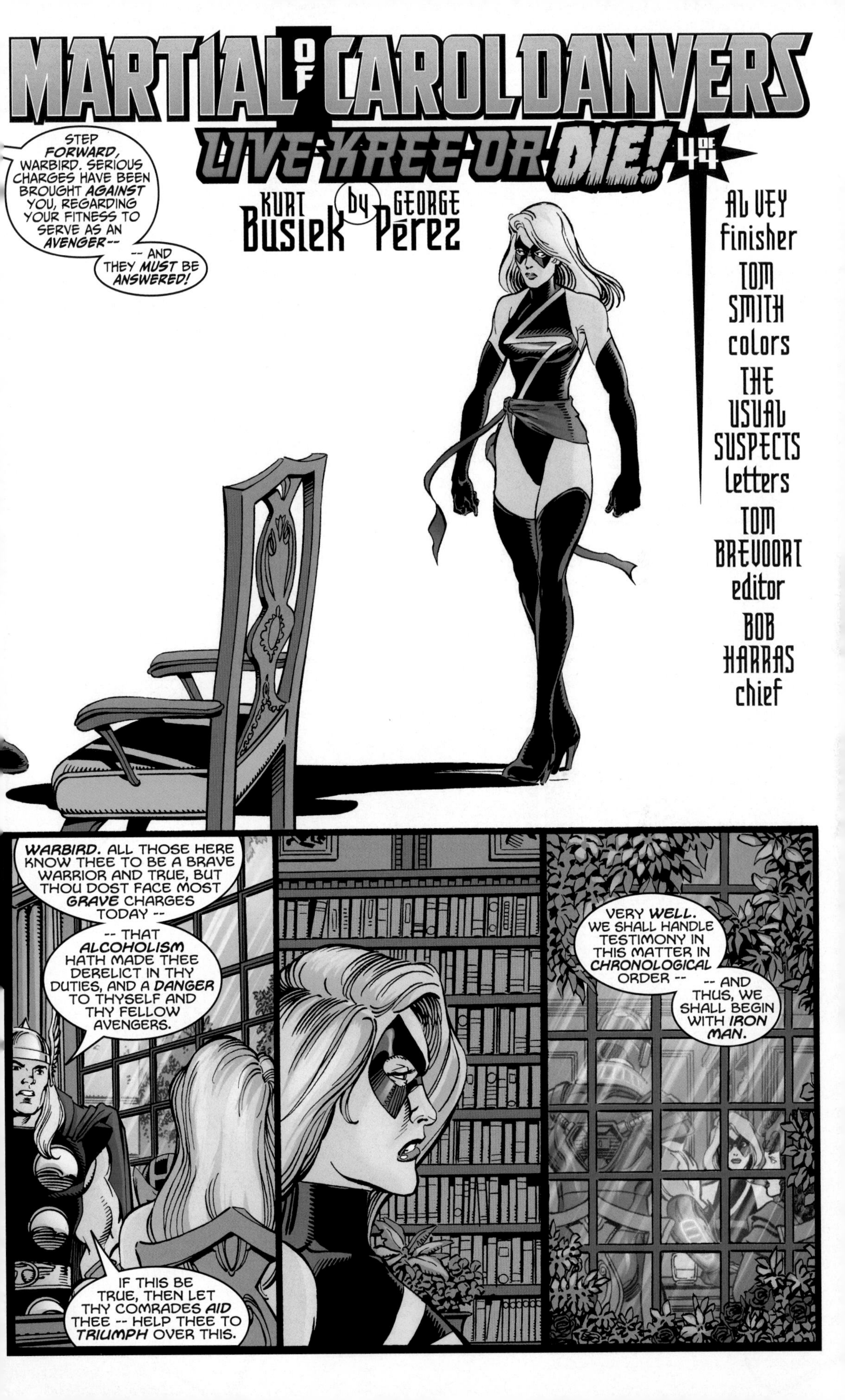

MARTIAL OF CAROL DANVERS
LIVE KREE OR DIE! 4 OF 4
KURT BUSIEK by GEORGE PÉREZ
STEP FORWARD, WARBIRD. SERIOUS CHARGES HAVE BEEN BROUGHT AGAINST YOU, REGARDING YOUR FITNESS TO SERVE AS AN AVENGER--
-- AND THEY MUST BE ANSWERED!
AL VEY finisher
TOM SMITH colors
THE USUAL SUSPECTS letters
TOM BREVOORT editor
BOB HARRAS chief
WARBIRD. ALL THOSE HERE KNOW THEE TO BE A BRAVE WARRIOR AND TRUE, BUT THOU DOST FACE MOST GRAVE CHARGES TODAY --
-- THAT ALCOHOLISM HATH MADE THEE DERELICT IN THY DUTIES, AND A DANGER TO THYSELF AND THY FELLOW AVENGERS.
IF THIS BE TRUE, THEN LET THY COMRADES AID THEE -- HELP THEE TO TRIUMPH OVER THIS.
VERY WELL. WE SHALL HANDLE TESTIMONY IN THIS MATTER IN CHRONOLOGICAL ORDER --
-- AND THUS, WE SHALL BEGIN WITH IRON MAN.

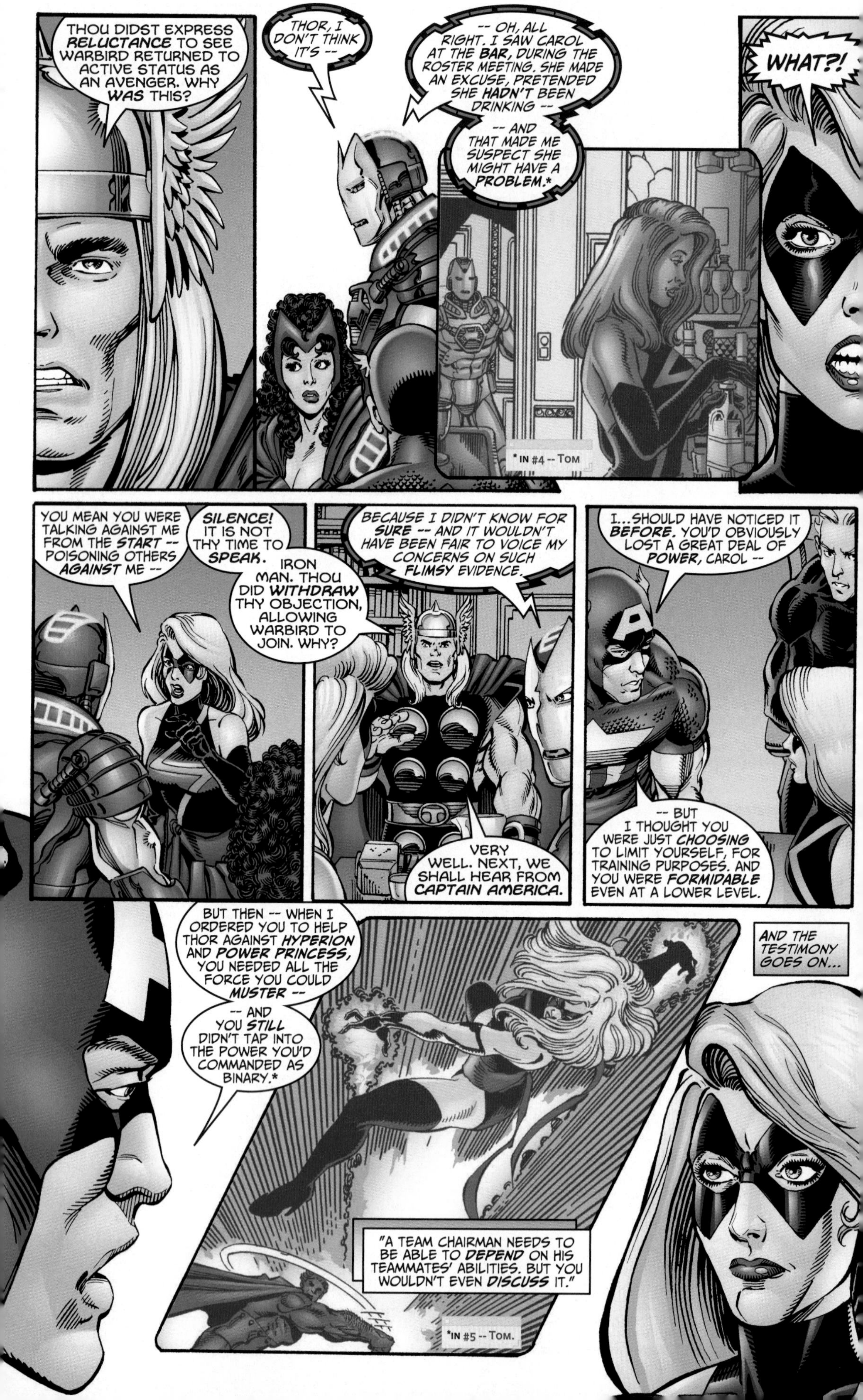
THOU DIDST EXPRESS RELUCTANCE TO SEE WARBIRD RETURNED TO ACTIVE STATUS AS AN AVENGER. WHY WAS THIS?
THOR, I DON'T THINK IT'S --
-- OH, ALL RIGHT. I SAW CAROL AT THE BAR, DURING THE ROSTER MEETING. SHE MADE AN EXCUSE, PRETENDED SHE HADN'T BEEN DRINKING --
-- AND THAT MADE ME SUSPECT SHE MIGHT HAVE A PROBLEM.*
*IN #4 -- TOM
WHAT?!
YOU MEAN YOU WERE TALKING AGAINST ME FROM THE START -- POISONING OTHERS AGAINST ME --
SILENCE! IT IS NOT THY TIME TO SPEAK.
IRON MAN. THOU DID WITHDRAW THY OBJECTION, ALLOWING WARBIRD TO JOIN. WHY?
BECAUSE I DIDN'T KNOW FOR SURE -- AND IT WOULDN'T HAVE BEEN FAIR TO VOICE MY CONCERNS ON SUCH FLIMSY EVIDENCE.
VERY WELL. NEXT, WE SHALL HEAR FROM CAPTAIN AMERICA.
I...SHOULD HAVE NOTICED IT BEFORE. YOU'D OBVIOUSLY LOST A GREAT DEAL OF POWER, CAROL --
-- BUT I THOUGHT YOU WERE JUST CHOOSING TO LIMIT YOURSELF, FOR TRAINING PURPOSES. AND YOU WERE FORMIDABLE EVEN AT A LOWER LEVEL.
BUT THEN -- WHEN I ORDERED YOU TO HELP THOR AGAINST HYPERION AND POWER PRINCESS, YOU NEEDED ALL THE FORCE YOU COULD MUSTER --
-- AND YOU STILL DIDN'T TAP INTO THE POWER YOU'D COMMANDED AS BINARY.*
"A TEAM CHAIRMAN NEEDS TO BE ABLE TO DEPEND ON HIS TEAMMATES' ABILITIES. BUT YOU WOULDN'T EVEN DISCUSS IT."
*IN #5 -- TOM.
AND THE TESTIMONY GOES ON...

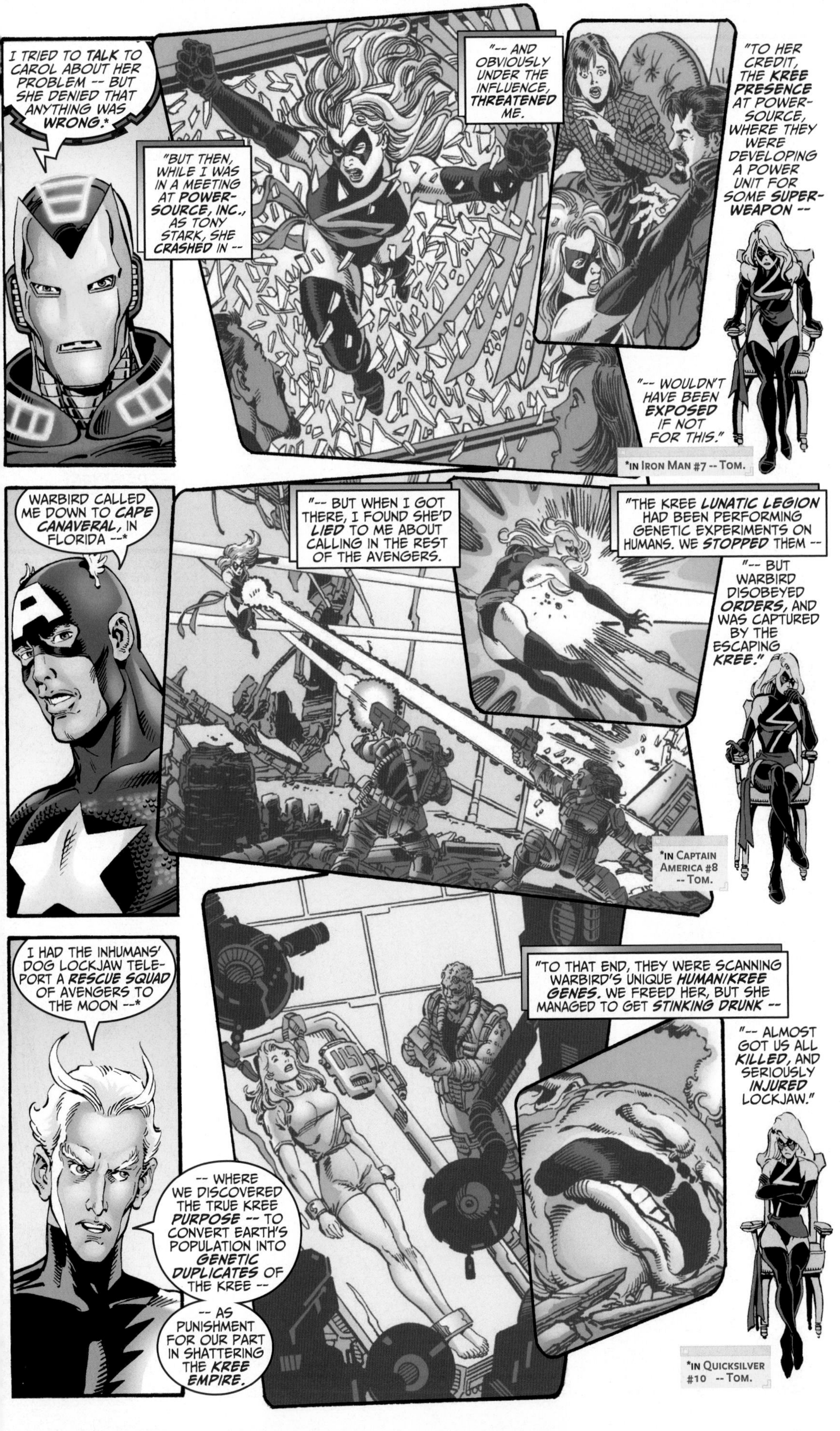

I TRIED TO TALK TO CAROL ABOUT HER PROBLEM -- BUT SHE DENIED THAT ANYTHING WAS WRONG.*
"BUT THEN, WHILE I WAS IN A MEETING AT POWER-SOURCE, INC., AS TONY STARK, SHE CRASHED IN --
"-- AND OBVIOUSLY UNDER THE INFLUENCE, THREATENED ME.
"TO HER CREDIT, THE KREE PRESENCE AT POWER-SOURCE, WHERE THEY WERE DEVELOPING A POWER UNIT FOR SOME SUPER-WEAPON --
"-- WOULDN'T HAVE BEEN EXPOSED IF NOT FOR THIS."
*IN IRON MAN #7 -- TOM.
WARBIRD CALLED ME DOWN TO CAPE CANAVERAL, IN FLORIDA --*
"-- BUT WHEN I GOT THERE, I FOUND SHE'D LIED TO ME ABOUT CALLING IN THE REST OF THE AVENGERS.
"THE KREE LUNATIC LEGION HAD BEEN PERFORMING GENETIC EXPERIMENTS ON HUMANS. WE STOPPED THEM --
"-- BUT WARBIRD DISOBEYED ORDERS, AND WAS CAPTURED BY THE ESCAPING KREE."
*IN CAPTAIN AMERICA #8 -- TOM.
I HAD THE INHUMANS' DOG LOCKJAW TELE-PORT A RESCUE SQUAD OF AVENGERS TO THE MOON --*
-- WHERE WE DISCOVERED THE TRUE KREE PURPOSE -- TO CONVERT EARTH'S POPULATION INTO GENETIC DUPLICATES OF THE KREE --
-- AS PUNISHMENT FOR OUR PART IN SHATTERING THE KREE EMPIRE.
"TO THAT END, THEY WERE SCANNING WARBIRD'S UNIQUE HUMAN/KREE GENES. WE FREED HER, BUT SHE MANAGED TO GET STINKING DRUNK --
"-- ALMOST GOT US ALL KILLED, AND SERIOUSLY INJURED LOCKJAW."
*IN QUICKSILVER #10 -- TOM.

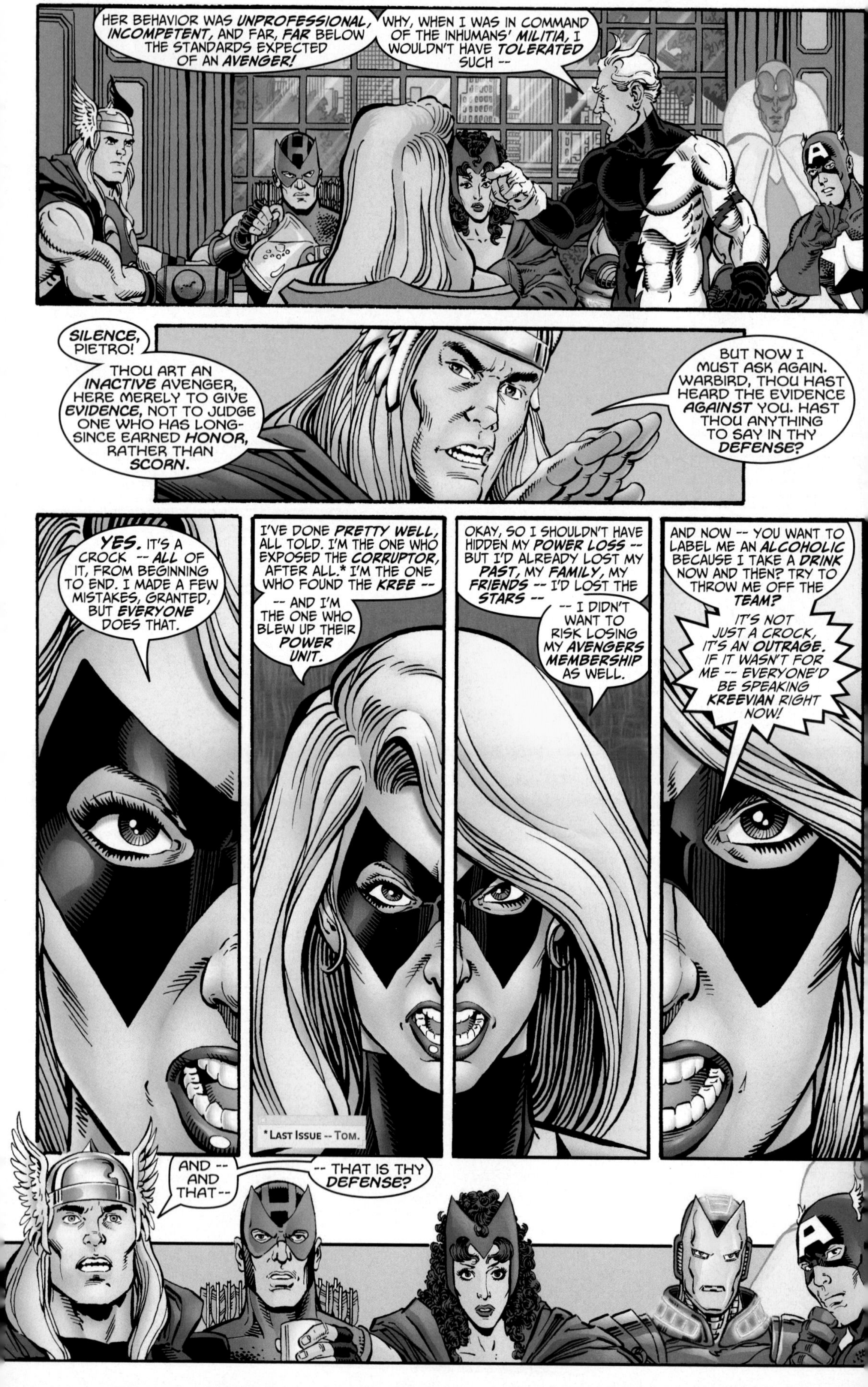
HER BEHAVIOR WAS UNPROFESSIONAL, INCOMPETENT, AND FAR, FAR BELOW THE STANDARDS EXPECTED OF AN AVENGER!
WHY, WHEN I WAS IN COMMAND OF THE INHUMANS' MILITIA, I WOULDN'T HAVE TOLERATED SUCH --
SILENCE, PIETRO!
THOU ART AN INACTIVE AVENGER, HERE MERELY TO GIVE EVIDENCE, NOT TO JUDGE ONE WHO HAS LONG-SINCE EARNED HONOR, RATHER THAN SCORN.
BUT NOW I MUST ASK AGAIN. WARBIRD, THOU HAST HEARD THE EVIDENCE AGAINST YOU. HAST THOU ANYTHING TO SAY IN THY DEFENSE?
YES. IT'S A CROCK -- ALL OF IT, FROM BEGINNING TO END. I MADE A FEW MISTAKES, GRANTED, BUT EVERYONE DOES THAT.
I'VE DONE PRETTY WELL, ALL TOLD. I'M THE ONE WHO EXPOSED THE CORRUPTOR, AFTER ALL.* I'M THE ONE WHO FOUND THE KREE --
-- AND I'M THE ONE WHO BLEW UP THEIR POWER UNIT.
*LAST ISSUE -- TOM.
OKAY, SO I SHOULDN'T HAVE HIDDEN MY POWER LOSS -- BUT I'D ALREADY LOST MY PAST, MY FAMILY, MY FRIENDS -- I'D LOST THE STARS --
-- I DIDN'T WANT TO RISK LOSING MY AVENGERS MEMBERSHIP AS WELL.
AND NOW -- YOU WANT TO LABEL ME AN ALCOHOLIC BECAUSE I TAKE A DRINK NOW AND THEN? TRY TO THROW ME OFF THE TEAM?
IT'S NOT JUST A CROCK, IT'S AN OUTRAGE. IF IT WASN'T FOR ME -- EVERYONE'D BE SPEAKING KREEVIAN RIGHT NOW!
AND -- AND THAT--
-- THAT IS THY DEFENSE?

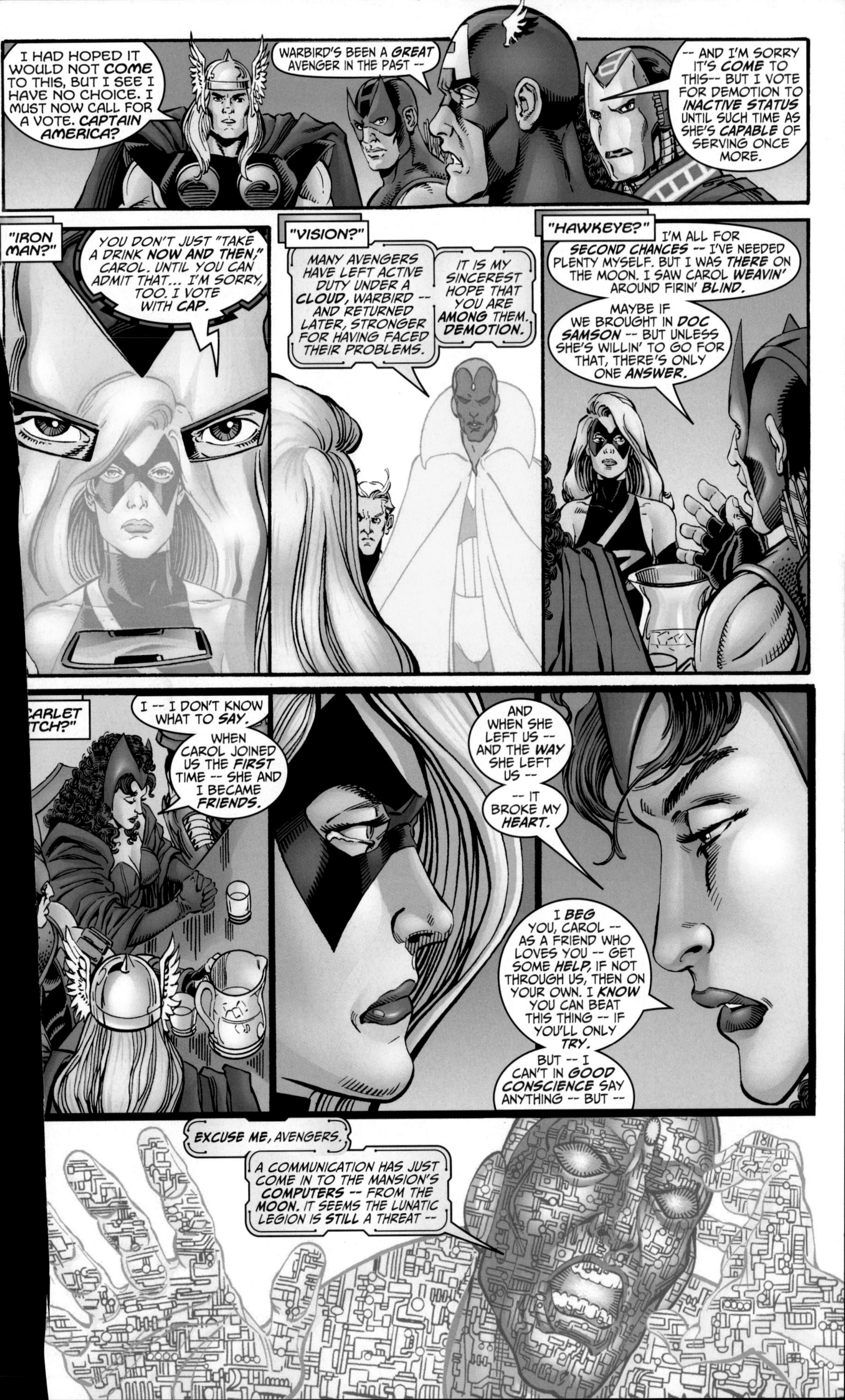
I HAD HOPED IT WOULD NOT COME TO THIS, BUT I SEE I HAVE NO CHOICE. I MUST NOW CALL FOR A VOTE. CAPTAIN AMERICA?
WARBIRD'S BEEN A GREAT AVENGER IN THE PAST --
-- AND I'M SORRY IT'S COME TO THIS-- BUT I VOTE FOR DEMOTION TO INACTIVE STATUS UNTIL SUCH TIME AS SHE'S CAPABLE OF SERVING ONCE MORE.
"IRON MAN?"
YOU DON'T JUST "TAKE A DRINK NOW AND THEN," CAROL. UNTIL YOU CAN ADMIT THAT... I'M SORRY, TOO. I VOTE WITH CAP.
"VISION?"
MANY AVENGERS HAVE LEFT ACTIVE DUTY UNDER A CLOUD, WARBIRD -- AND RETURNED LATER, STRONGER FOR HAVING FACED THEIR PROBLEMS.
IT IS MY SINCEREST HOPE THAT YOU ARE AMONG THEM. DEMOTION.
"HAWKEYE?"
I'M ALL FOR SECOND CHANCES -- I'VE NEEDED PLENTY MYSELF. BUT I WAS THERE ON THE MOON. I SAW CAROL WEAVIN' AROUND FIRIN' BLIND.
MAYBE IF WE BROUGHT IN DOC SAMSON -- BUT UNLESS SHE'S WILLIN' TO GO FOR THAT, THERE'S ONLY ONE ANSWER.
CARLET TCH?"
I -- I DON'T KNOW WHAT TO SAY.
WHEN CAROL JOINED US THE FIRST TIME -- SHE AND I BECAME FRIENDS.
AND WHEN SHE LEFT US -- AND THE WAY SHE LEFT US --
-- IT BROKE MY HEART.
I BEG YOU, CAROL -- AS A FRIEND WHO LOVES YOU -- GET SOME HELP, IF NOT THROUGH US, THEN ON YOUR OWN. I KNOW YOU CAN BEAT THIS THING -- IF YOU'LL ONLY TRY.
BUT -- I CAN'T IN GOOD CONSCIENCE SAY ANYTHING -- BUT --
EXCUSE ME, AVENGERS.
A COMMUNICATION HAS JUST COME IN TO THE MANSION'S COMPUTERS -- FROM THE MOON. IT SEEMS THE LUNATIC LEGION IS STILL A THREAT --

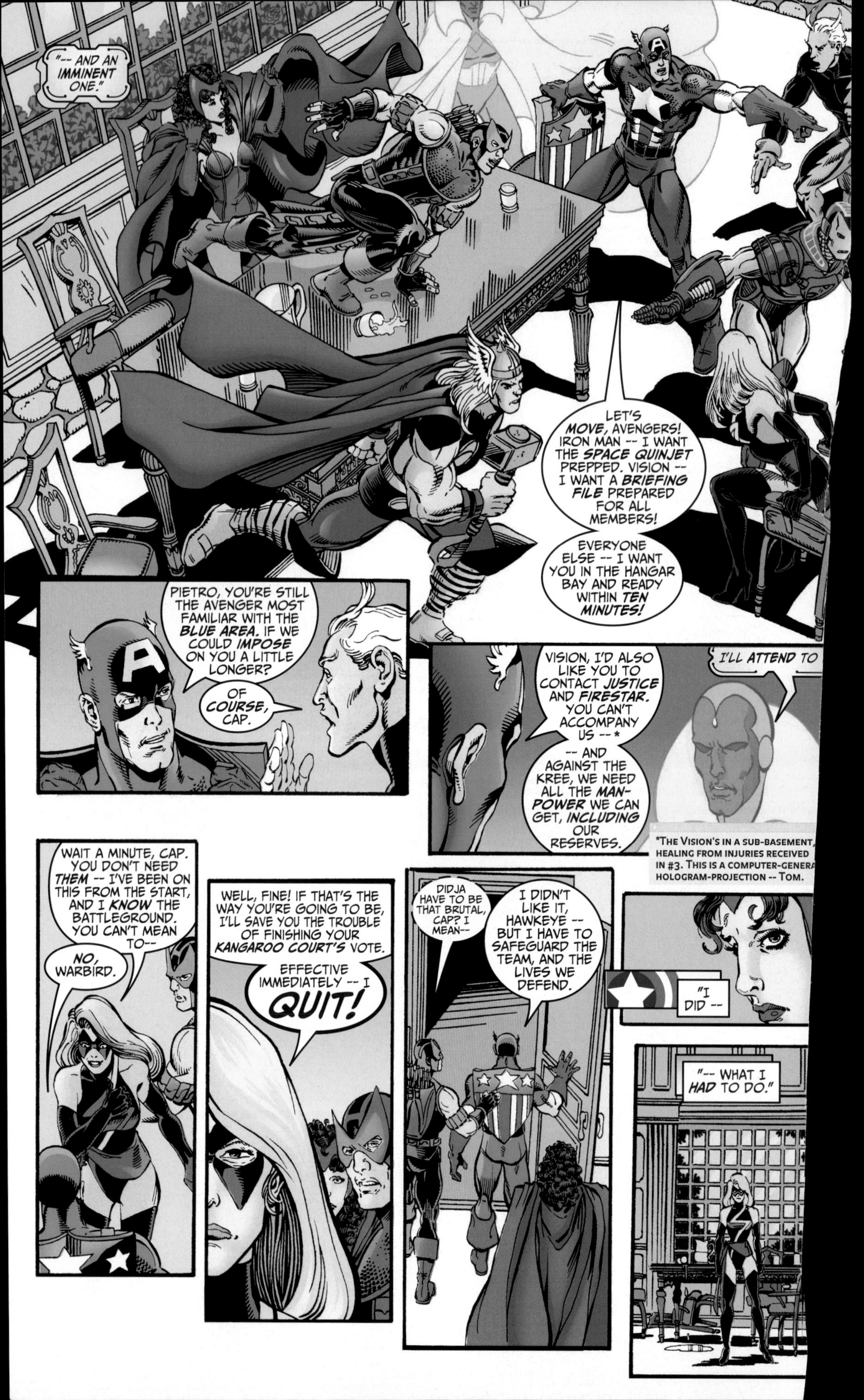
"-- AND AN IMMINENT ONE."
LET'S MOVE, AVENGERS! IRON MAN -- I WANT THE SPACE QUINJET PREPPED. VISION -- I WANT A BRIEFING FILE PREPARED FOR ALL MEMBERS!
EVERYONE ELSE -- I WANT YOU IN THE HANGAR BAY AND READY WITHIN TEN MINUTES!
PIETRO, YOU'RE STILL THE AVENGER MOST FAMILIAR WITH THE BLUE AREA. IF WE COULD IMPOSE ON YOU A LITTLE LONGER?
OF COURSE, CAP.
VISION, I'D ALSO LIKE YOU TO CONTACT JUSTICE AND FIRESTAR. YOU CAN'T ACCOMPANY US -- *
-- AND AGAINST THE KREE, WE NEED ALL THE MAN-POWER WE CAN GET, INCLUDING OUR RESERVES.
I'LL ATTEND TO
*THE VISION'S IN A SUB-BASEMENT, HEALING FROM INJURIES RECEIVED IN #3. THIS IS A COMPUTER-GENERA HOLOGRAM-PROJECTION -- TOM.
WAIT A MINUTE, CAP. YOU DON'T NEED THEM -- I'VE BEEN ON THIS FROM THE START, AND I KNOW THE BATTLEGROUND. YOU CAN'T MEAN TO--
NO, WARBIRD.
WELL, FINE! IF THAT'S THE WAY YOU'RE GOING TO BE, I'LL SAVE YOU THE TROUBLE OF FINISHING YOUR KANGAROO COURT'S VOTE.
EFFECTIVE IMMEDIATELY -- I QUIT!
DIDJA HAVE TO BE THAT BRUTAL, CAP? I MEAN--
I DIDN'T LIKE IT, HAWKEYE -- BUT I HAVE TO SAFEGUARD THE TEAM, AND THE LIVES WE DEFEND.
"I DID --
"-- WHAT I HAD TO DO."

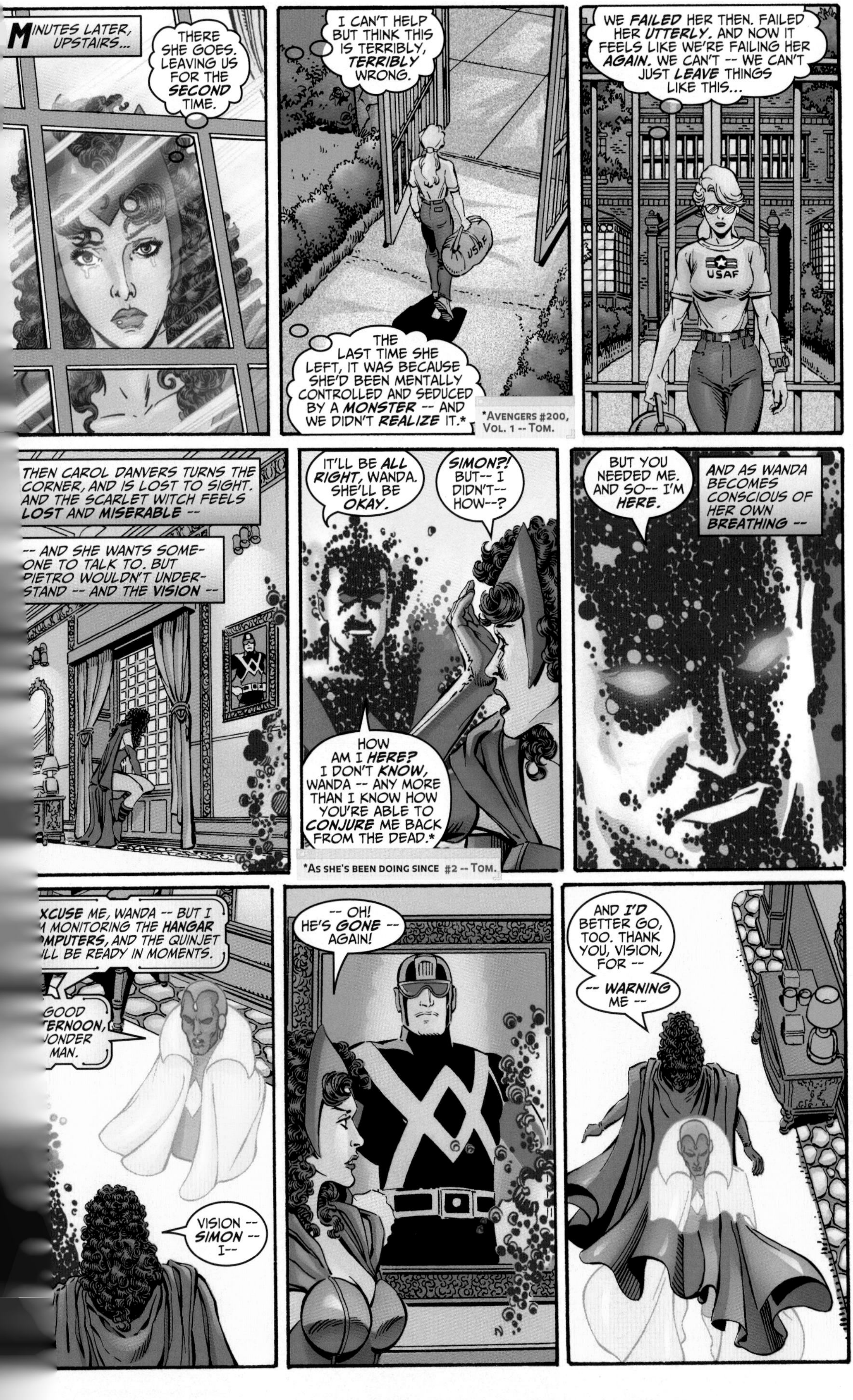
MINUTES LATER, UPSTAIRS...
THERE SHE GOES. LEAVING US FOR THE SECOND TIME.
I CAN'T HELP BUT THINK THIS IS TERRIBLY, TERRIBLY WRONG.
THE LAST TIME SHE LEFT, IT WAS BECAUSE SHE'D BEEN MENTALLY CONTROLLED AND SEDUCED BY A MONSTER -- AND WE DIDN'T REALIZE IT.*
*AVENGERS #200, VOL. 1 -- TOM.
WE FAILED HER THEN. FAILED HER UTTERLY. AND NOW IT FEELS LIKE WE'RE FAILING HER AGAIN. WE CAN'T -- WE CAN'T JUST LEAVE THINGS LIKE THIS...
USAF
USAF
THEN CAROL DANVERS TURNS THE CORNER, AND IS LOST TO SIGHT. AND THE SCARLET WITCH FEELS LOST AND MISERABLE --
-- AND SHE WANTS SOMEONE TO TALK TO. BUT PIETRO WOULDN'T UNDERSTAND -- AND THE VISION --
IT'LL BE ALL RIGHT, WANDA. SHE'LL BE OKAY.
SIMON?! BUT-- I DIDN'T-- HOW--?
HOW AM I HERE? I DON'T KNOW, WANDA -- ANY MORE THAN I KNOW HOW YOU'RE ABLE TO CONJURE ME BACK FROM THE DEAD.*
*AS SHE'S BEEN DOING SINCE #2 -- TOM.
BUT YOU NEEDED ME. AND SO-- I'M HERE.
AND AS WANDA BECOMES CONSCIOUS OF HER OWN BREATHING --
XCUSE ME, WANDA -- BUT I M MONITORING THE HANGAR OMPUTERS, AND THE QUINJET ILL BE READY IN MOMENTS.
GOOD TERNOON, ONDER MAN.
VISION -- SIMON -- I--
-- OH! HE'S GONE -- AGAIN!
AND I'D BETTER GO, TOO. THANK YOU, VISION, FOR --
-- WARNING ME --

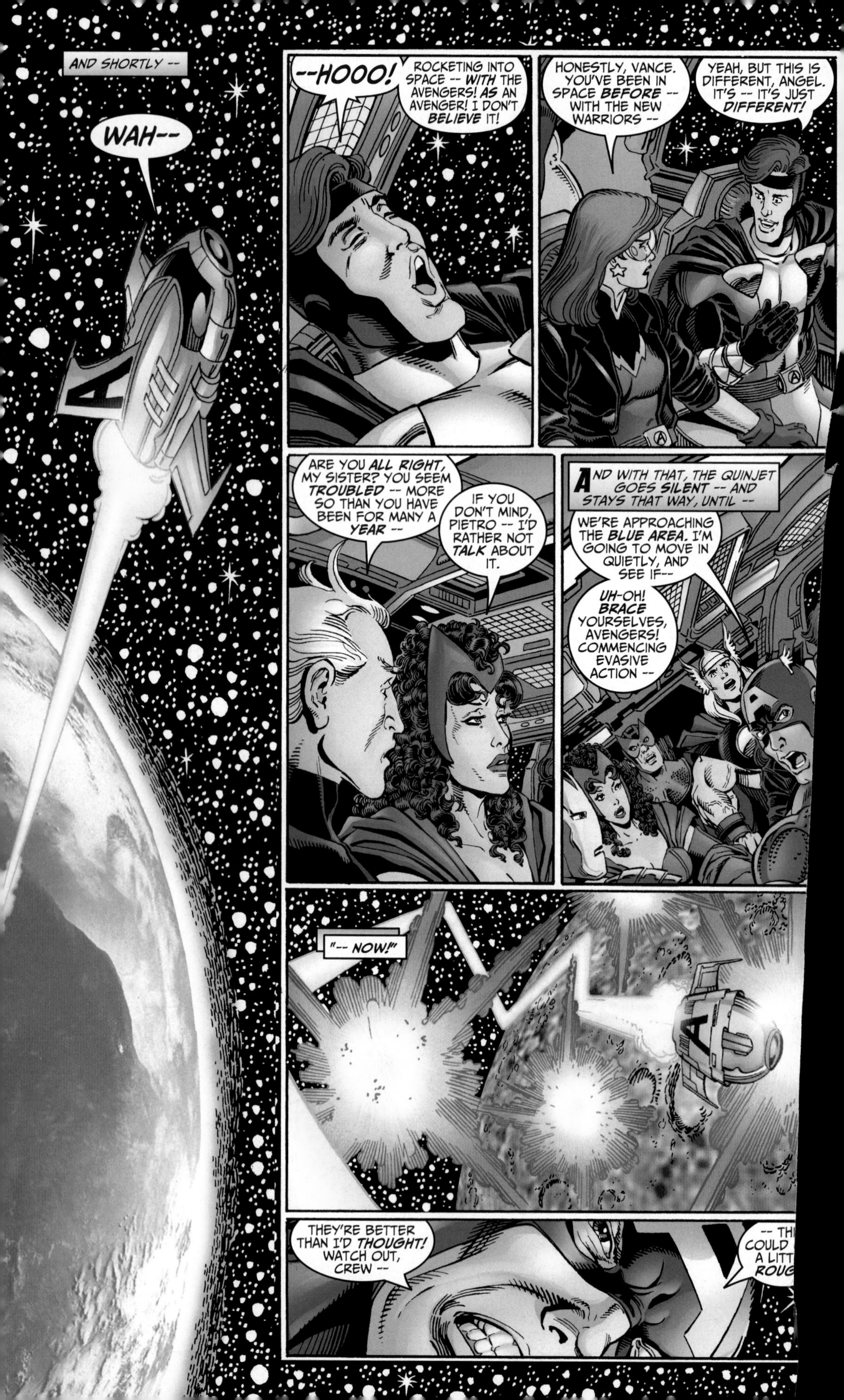
AND SHORTLY --
WAH--
--HOOO!
ROCKETING INTO SPACE -- WITH THE AVENGERS! AS AN AVENGER! I DON'T BELIEVE IT!
HONESTLY, VANCE. YOU'VE BEEN IN SPACE BEFORE -- WITH THE NEW WARRIORS --
YEAH, BUT THIS IS DIFFERENT, ANGEL. IT'S -- IT'S JUST DIFFERENT!
ARE YOU ALL RIGHT, MY SISTER? YOU SEEM TROUBLED -- MORE SO THAN YOU HAVE BEEN FOR MANY A YEAR --
IF YOU DON'T MIND, PIETRO -- I'D RATHER NOT TALK ABOUT IT.
AND WITH THAT, THE QUINJET GOES SILENT -- AND STAYS THAT WAY, UNTIL --
WE'RE APPROACHING THE BLUE AREA. I'M GOING TO MOVE IN QUIETLY, AND SEE IF--
UH-OH! BRACE YOURSELVES, AVENGERS! COMMENCING EVASIVE ACTION --
"-- NOW!"
THEY'RE BETTER THAN I'D THOUGHT! WATCH OUT, CREW --
COULD

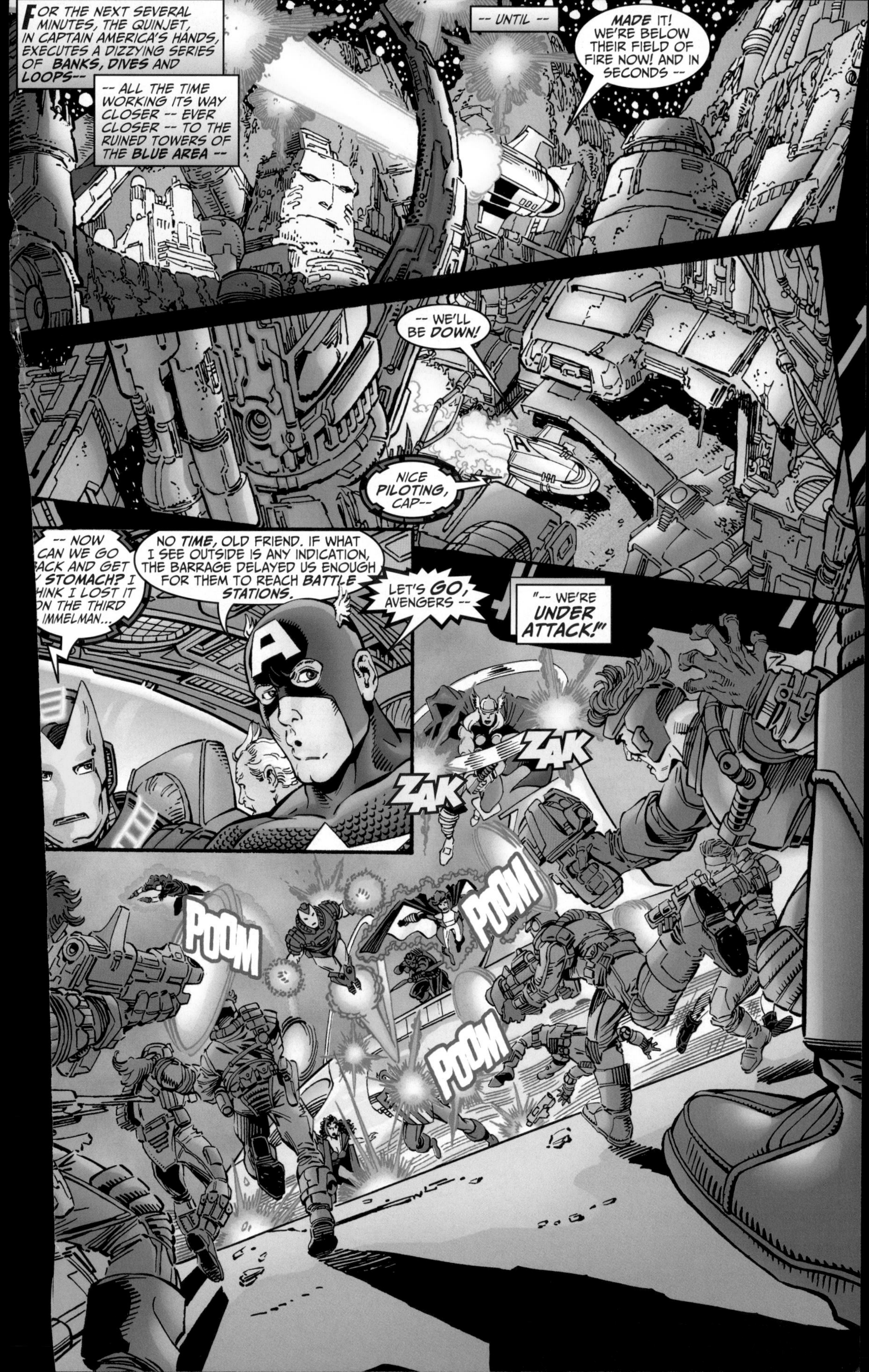

FOR THE NEXT SEVERAL MINUTES, THE QUINJET, IN CAPTAIN AMERICA'S HANDS, EXECUTES A DIZZYING SERIES OF BANKS, DIVES AND LOOPS--
-- ALL THE TIME WORKING ITS WAY CLOSER -- EVER CLOSER -- TO THE RUINED TOWERS OF THE BLUE AREA --
-- UNTIL --
MADE IT! WE'RE BELOW THEIR FIELD OF FIRE NOW! AND IN SECONDS --
-- WE'LL BE DOWN!
NICE PILOTING, CAP--
-- NOW CAN WE GO ACK AND GET Y STOMACH? I HINK I LOST IT ON THE THIRD IMMELMAN...
NO TIME, OLD FRIEND. IF WHAT I SEE OUTSIDE IS ANY INDICATION, THE BARRAGE DELAYED US ENOUGH FOR THEM TO REACH BATTLE STATIONS.
LET'S GO, AVENGERS --
"-- WE'RE UNDER ATTACK!"
ZAK
ZAK
POOM
POOM
POOM

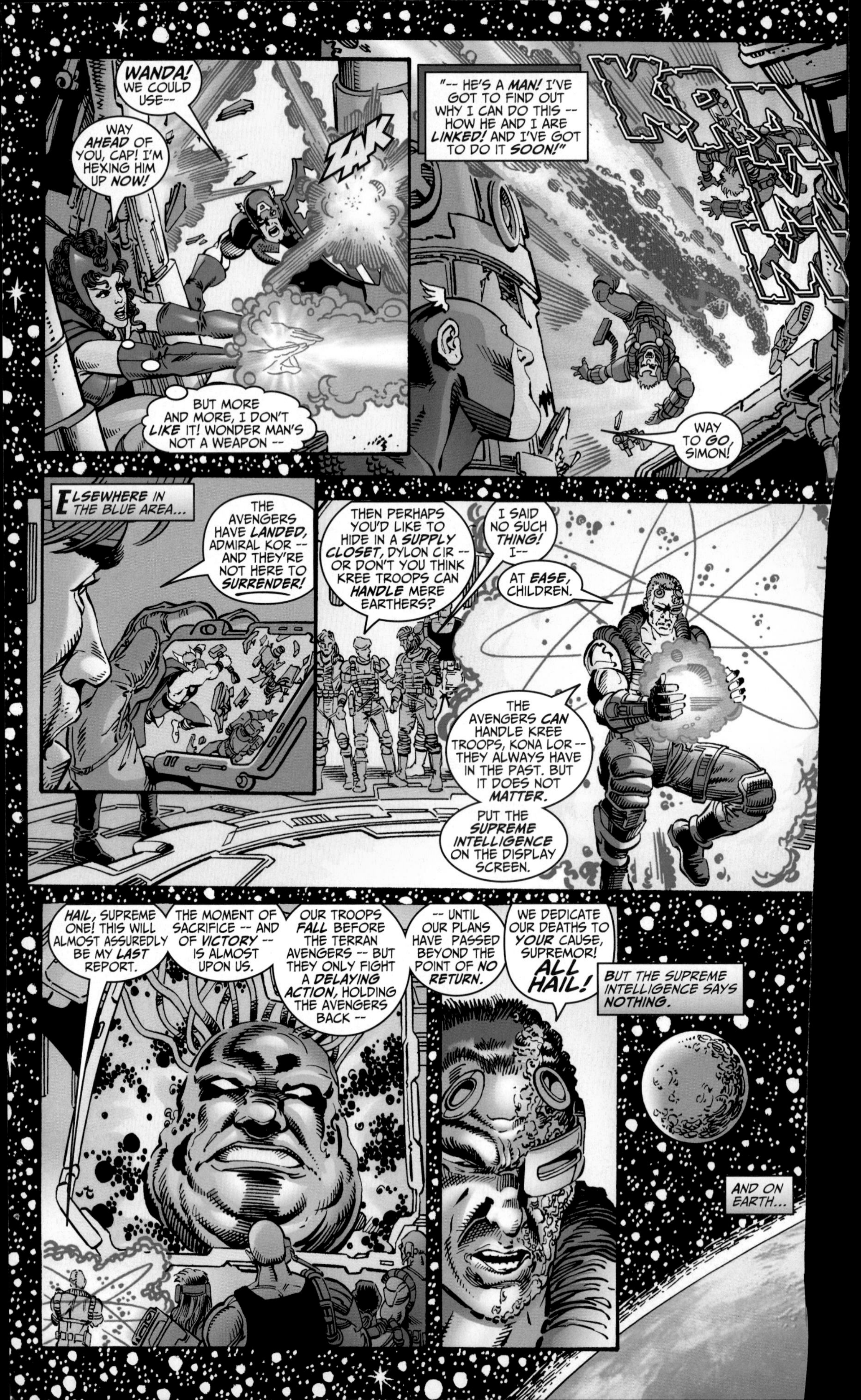

WANDA! WE COULD USE--
WAY AHEAD OF YOU, CAP! I'M HEXING HIM UP NOW!
ZAK
BUT MORE AND MORE, I DON'T LIKE IT! WONDER MAN'S NOT A WEAPON --
"-- HE'S A MAN! I'VE GOT TO FIND OUT WHY I CAN DO THIS -- HOW HE AND I ARE LINKED! AND I'VE GOT TO DO IT SOON!"
WAY TO GO, SIMON!
ELSEWHERE IN THE BLUE AREA...
THE AVENGERS HAVE LANDED, ADMIRAL KOR -- AND THEY'RE NOT HERE TO SURRENDER!
THEN PERHAPS YOU'D LIKE TO HIDE IN A SUPPLY CLOSET, DYLON CIR -- OR DON'T YOU THINK KREE TROOPS CAN HANDLE MERE EARTHERS?
I SAID NO SUCH THING! I--
AT EASE, CHILDREN.
THE AVENGERS CAN HANDLE KREE TROOPS, KONA LOR -- THEY ALWAYS HAVE IN THE PAST. BUT IT DOES NOT MATTER.
PUT THE SUPREME INTELLIGENCE ON THE DISPLAY SCREEN.
HAIL, SUPREME ONE! THIS WILL ALMOST ASSUREDLY BE MY LAST REPORT.
THE MOMENT OF SACRIFICE -- AND OF VICTORY -- IS ALMOST UPON US.
OUR TROOPS FALL BEFORE THE TERRAN AVENGERS -- BUT THEY ONLY FIGHT A DELAYING ACTION, HOLDING THE AVENGERS BACK --
-- UNTIL OUR PLANS HAVE PASSED BEYOND THE POINT OF NO RETURN.
WE DEDICATE OUR DEATHS TO YOUR CAUSE, SUPREMOR! ALL HAIL!
BUT THE SUPREME INTELLIGENCE SAYS NOTHING.
AND ON EARTH...

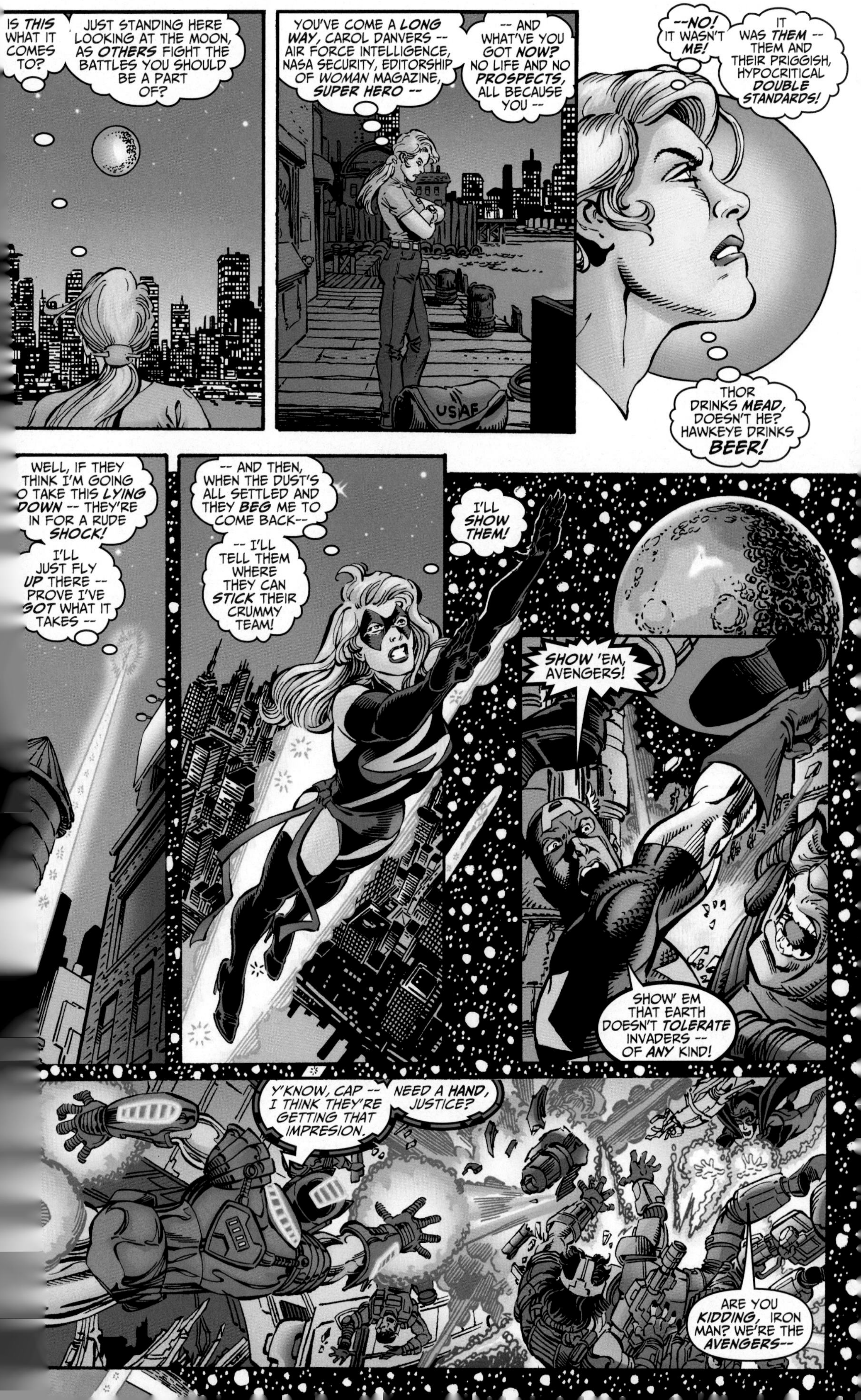

IS THIS WHAT IT COMES TO?
JUST STANDING HERE LOOKING AT THE MOON, AS OTHERS FIGHT THE BATTLES YOU SHOULD BE A PART OF?
YOU'VE COME A LONG WAY, CAROL DANVERS -- AIR FORCE INTELLIGENCE, NASA SECURITY, EDITORSHIP OF WOMAN MAGAZINE, SUPER HERO --
-- AND WHAT'VE YOU GOT NOW? NO LIFE AND NO PROSPECTS, ALL BECAUSE YOU --
USAF
--NO! IT WASN'T ME!
IT WAS THEM -- THEM AND THEIR PRIGGISH, HYPOCRITICAL DOUBLE STANDARDS!
THOR DRINKS MEAD, DOESN'T HE? HAWKEYE DRINKS BEER!
WELL, IF THEY THINK I'M GOING O TAKE THIS LYING DOWN -- THEY'RE IN FOR A RUDE SHOCK!
I'LL JUST FLY UP THERE -- PROVE I'VE GOT WHAT IT TAKES --
-- AND THEN, WHEN THE DUST'S ALL SETTLED AND THEY BEG ME TO COME BACK--
-- I'LL TELL THEM WHERE THEY CAN STICK THEIR CRUMMY TEAM!
I'LL SHOW THEM!
SHOW 'EM, AVENGERS!
SHOW' EM THAT EARTH DOESN'T TOLERATE INVADERS -- OF ANY KIND!
Y'KNOW, CAP -- I THINK THEY'RE GETTING THAT IMPRESION.
NEED A HAND, JUSTICE?
ARE YOU KIDDING, IRON MAN? WE'RE THE AVENGERS--

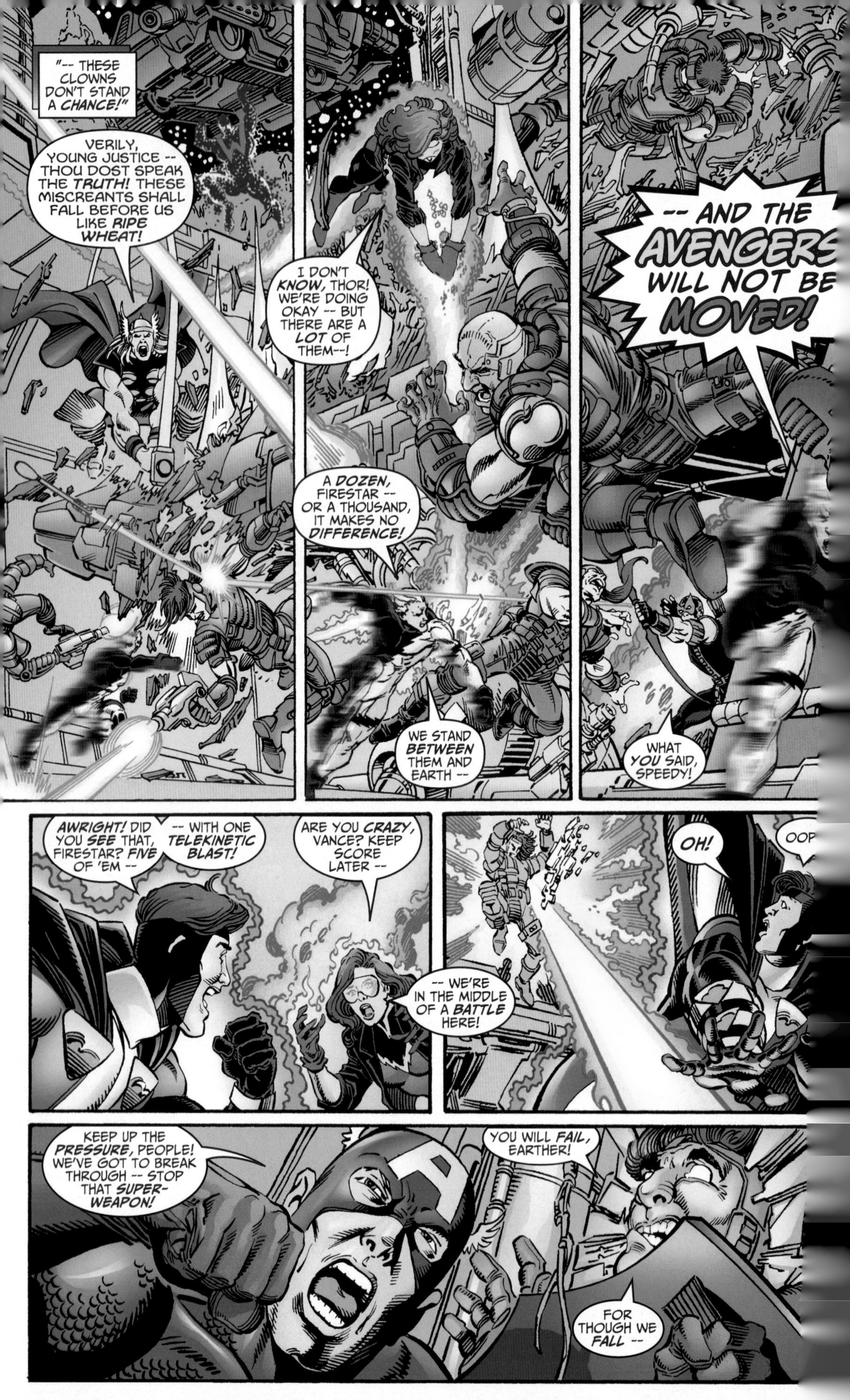
"-- THESE CLOWNS DON'T STAND A CHANCE!"
VERILY, YOUNG JUSTICE -- THOU DOST SPEAK THE TRUTH! THESE MISCREANTS SHALL FALL BEFORE US LIKE RIPE WHEAT!
I DON'T KNOW, THOR! WE'RE DOING OKAY -- BUT THERE ARE A LOT OF THEM--!
A DOZEN, FIRESTAR -- OR A THOUSAND, IT MAKES NO DIFFERENCE!
WE STAND BETWEEN THEM AND EARTH --
-- AND THE AVENGERS WILL NOT BE MOVED!
WHAT YOU SAID, SPEEDY!
AWRIGHT! DID YOU SEE THAT, FIRESTAR? FIVE OF 'EM --
-- WITH ONE TELEKINETIC BLAST!
ARE YOU CRAZY, VANCE? KEEP SCORE LATER --
-- WE'RE IN THE MIDDLE OF A BATTLE HERE!
OH!
OOP
KEEP UP THE PRESSURE, PEOPLE! WE'VE GOT TO BREAK THROUGH -- STOP THAT SUPER-WEAPON!
YOU WILL FAIL, EARTHER!
FOR THOUGH WE FALL --

-- OUR SACRIFICE -- BRINGS ABOUT VICTORY--!

HUH?

THAT *EFFECT*, CAP! I'VE SEEN IT BEFORE -- OR SOMETHING LIKE IT!

IT WAS AROUND CAPTAIN MARVEL -- WHEN HE CREATED AN *OMNI-WAVE PROJECTOR*!

*SHE GLIMPSED IT IN *AVENGERS* VOL. 1 #96 -- TOM.

OD'S BLOOD! AND 'TIS NOT MERELY *ONE* OF THEM WHO DOTH VANISH -- -- BUT *ALL* OF THE *FALLEN*!

THEY'RE NOT JUST *VANISHING*, THOR! UNLESS I MISS MY GUESS -- THEY'RE *CONVERTING* THEM-SELVES TO *ENERGY*!

BUT -- *WHY*?

YOU WEREN'T HERE WHEN WE RESCUED *WARBIRD*, IRON MAN!

"THIS MUST BE CONNECTED TO *THEIR* OMNI-WAVE PROJECTOR -- AND I KNOW WHERE IT IS! *QUICKLY*, AVENGERS --

"-- *FOLLOW ME*!"

THE AVENGERS CHARGE FORWARD AS ONE --

AND, FAR ELOW --

THE AIR IS GETTING *THIN*. BUT STILL, THE WOMAN CALLED WARBIRD *FORGES* AHEAD --

-- DRAWING ON HER INTERNAL POWER RESERVES, CLOSING OFF HER NEED TO *BREATHE* --

-- FORCING *HERSELF* FORWARD --

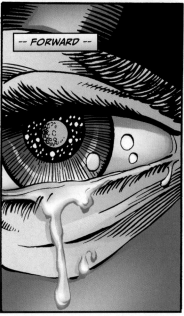

-- FORWARD --

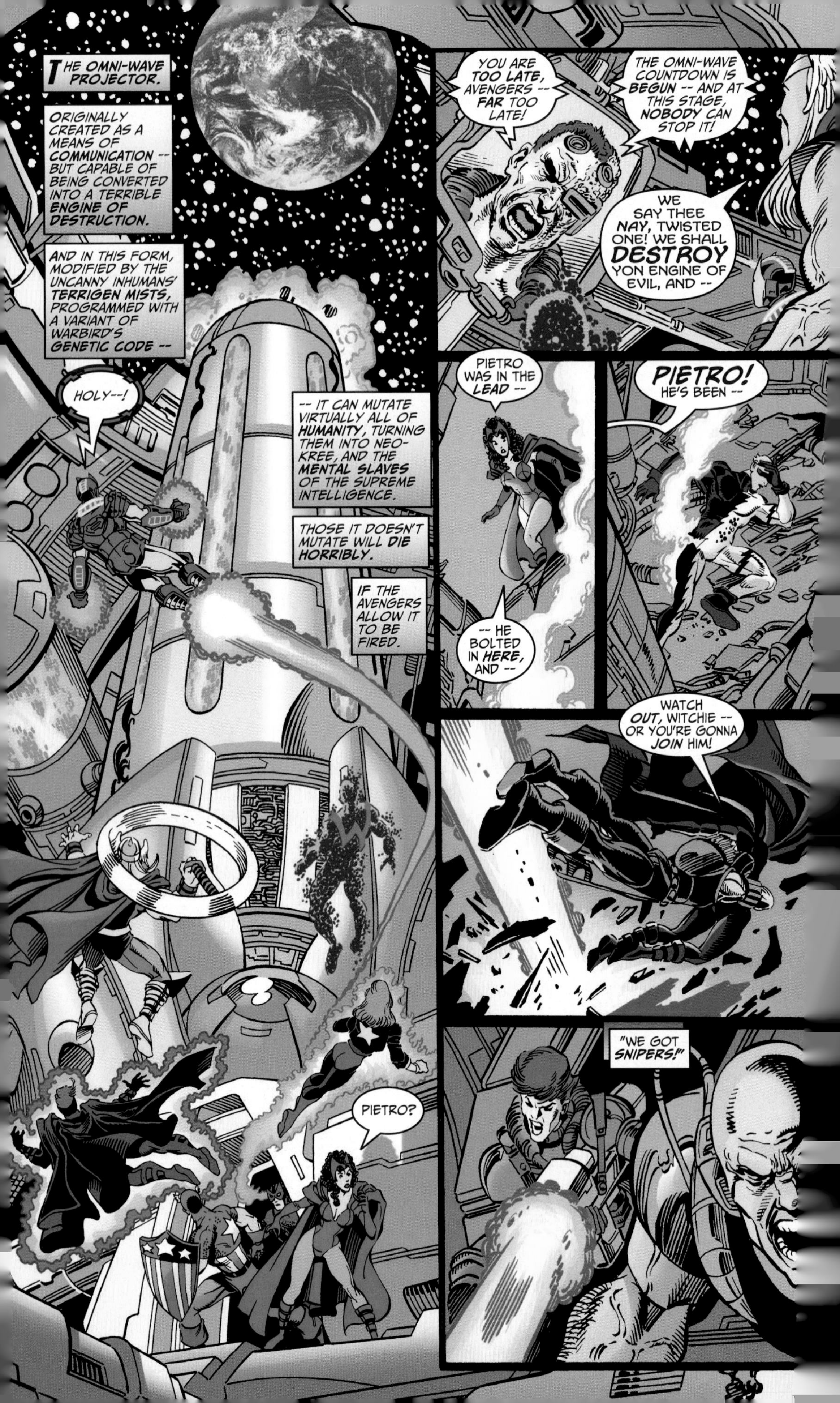

THE OMNI-WAVE PROJECTOR.
ORIGINALLY CREATED AS A MEANS OF COMMUNICATION -- BUT CAPABLE OF BEING CONVERTED INTO A TERRIBLE ENGINE OF DESTRUCTION.
AND IN THIS FORM, MODIFIED BY THE UNCANNY INHUMANS' TERRIGEN MISTS, PROGRAMMED WITH A VARIANT OF WARBIRD'S GENETIC CODE --
HOLY--!
-- IT CAN MUTATE VIRTUALLY ALL OF HUMANITY, TURNING THEM INTO NEO-KREE, AND THE MENTAL SLAVES OF THE SUPREME INTELLIGENCE.
THOSE IT DOESN'T MUTATE WILL DIE HORRIBLY.
IF THE AVENGERS ALLOW IT TO BE FIRED.
PIETRO?
YOU ARE TOO LATE, AVENGERS -- FAR TOO LATE!
THE OMNI-WAVE COUNTDOWN IS BEGUN -- AND AT THIS STAGE, NOBODY CAN STOP IT!
WE SAY THEE NAY, TWISTED ONE! WE SHALL DESTROY YON ENGINE OF EVIL, AND --
PIETRO WAS IN THE LEAD --
-- HE BOLTED IN HERE, AND --
PIETRO! HE'S BEEN --
WATCH OUT, WITCHIE -- OR YOU'RE GONNA JOIN HIM!
"WE GOT SNIPERS!"

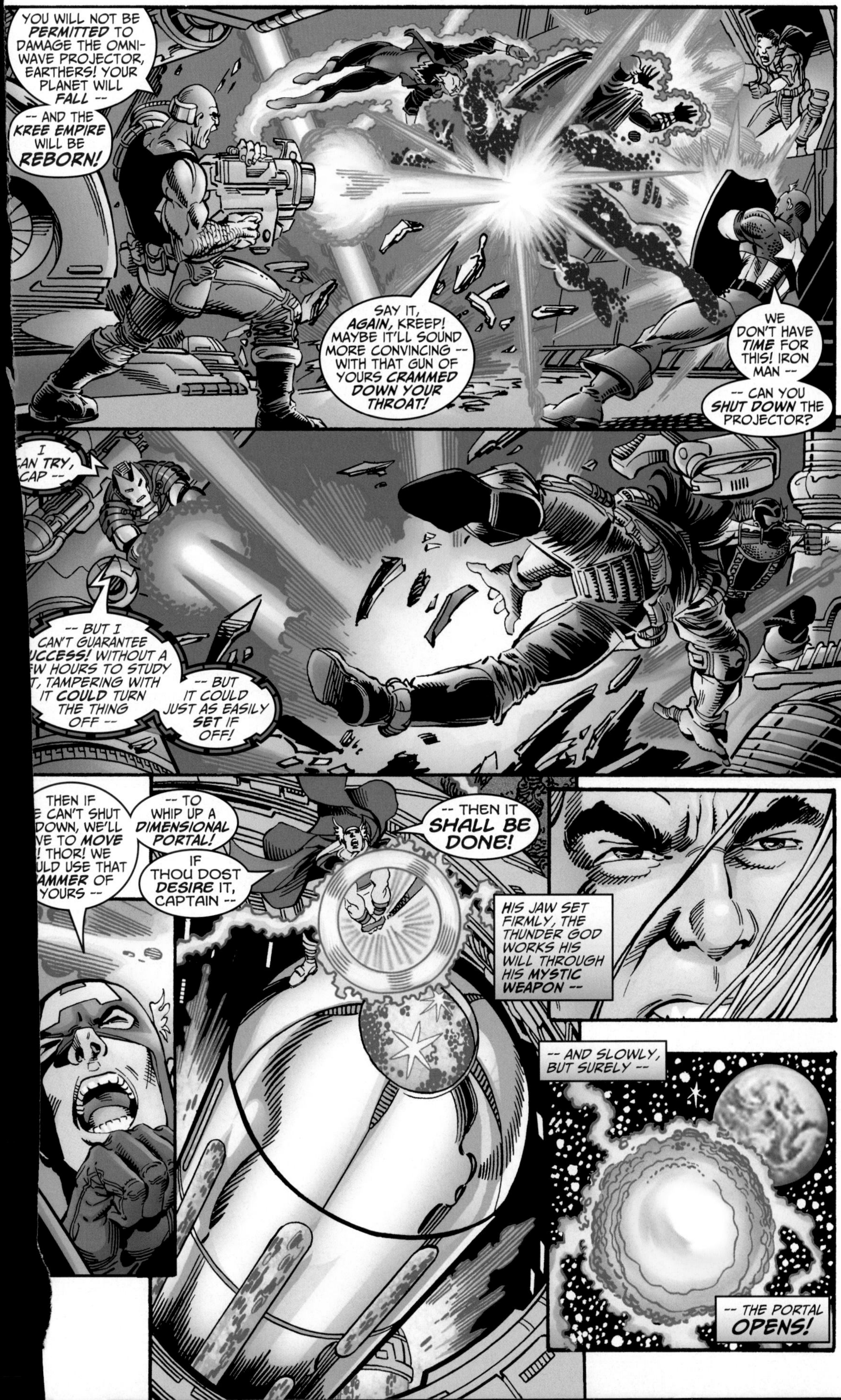

YOU WILL NOT BE PERMITTED TO DAMAGE THE OMNI-WAVE PROJECTOR, EARTHERS! YOUR PLANET WILL FALL --
-- AND THE KREE EMPIRE WILL BE REBORN!
SAY IT, AGAIN, KREEP! MAYBE IT'LL SOUND MORE CONVINCING -- WITH THAT GUN OF YOURS CRAMMED DOWN YOUR THROAT!
WE DON'T HAVE TIME FOR THIS! IRON MAN --
-- CAN YOU SHUT DOWN THE PROJECTOR?
I CAN TRY, CAP --
-- BUT I CAN'T GUARANTEE UCCESS! WITHOUT A EW HOURS TO STUDY T, TAMPERING WITH IT COULD TURN THE THING OFF --
-- BUT IT COULD JUST AS EASILY SET IF OFF!
THEN IF E CAN'T SHUT DOWN, WE'LL VE TO MOVE ! THOR! WE ULD USE THAT AMMER OF YOURS --
-- TO WHIP UP A DIMENSIONAL PORTAL!
IF THOU DOST DESIRE IT, CAPTAIN --
-- THEN IT SHALL BE DONE!
HIS JAW SET FIRMLY, THE THUNDER GOD WORKS HIS WILL THROUGH HIS MYSTIC WEAPON --
-- AND SLOWLY, BUT SURELY --
-- THE PORTAL OPENS!

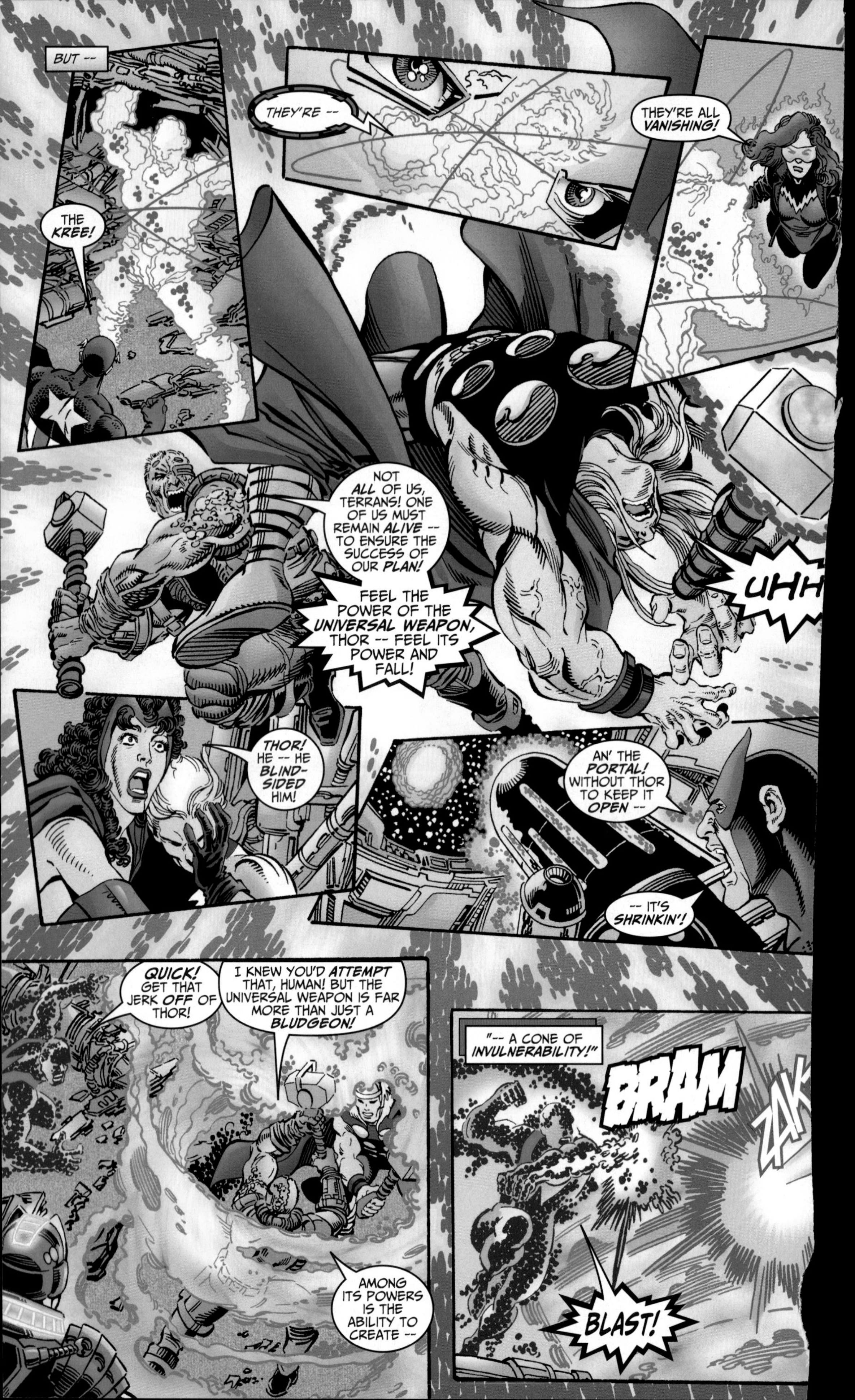
BUT --
THE KREE!
THEY'RE --
THEY'RE ALL VANISHING!
NOT ALL OF US, TERRANS! ONE OF US MUST REMAIN ALIVE -- TO ENSURE THE SUCCESS OF OUR PLAN!
FEEL THE POWER OF THE UNIVERSAL WEAPON, THOR -- FEEL ITS POWER AND FALL!
UHH
THOR! HE -- HE BLIND-SIDED HIM!
AN' THE PORTAL! WITHOUT THOR TO KEEP IT OPEN --
-- IT'S SHRINKIN'!
QUICK! GET THAT JERK OFF OF THOR!
I KNEW YOU'D ATTEMPT THAT, HUMAN! BUT THE UNIVERSAL WEAPON IS FAR MORE THAN JUST A BLUDGEON!
AMONG ITS POWERS IS THE ABILITY TO CREATE --
"-- A CONE OF INVULNERABILITY!"
BRAM
ZAK
BLAST!

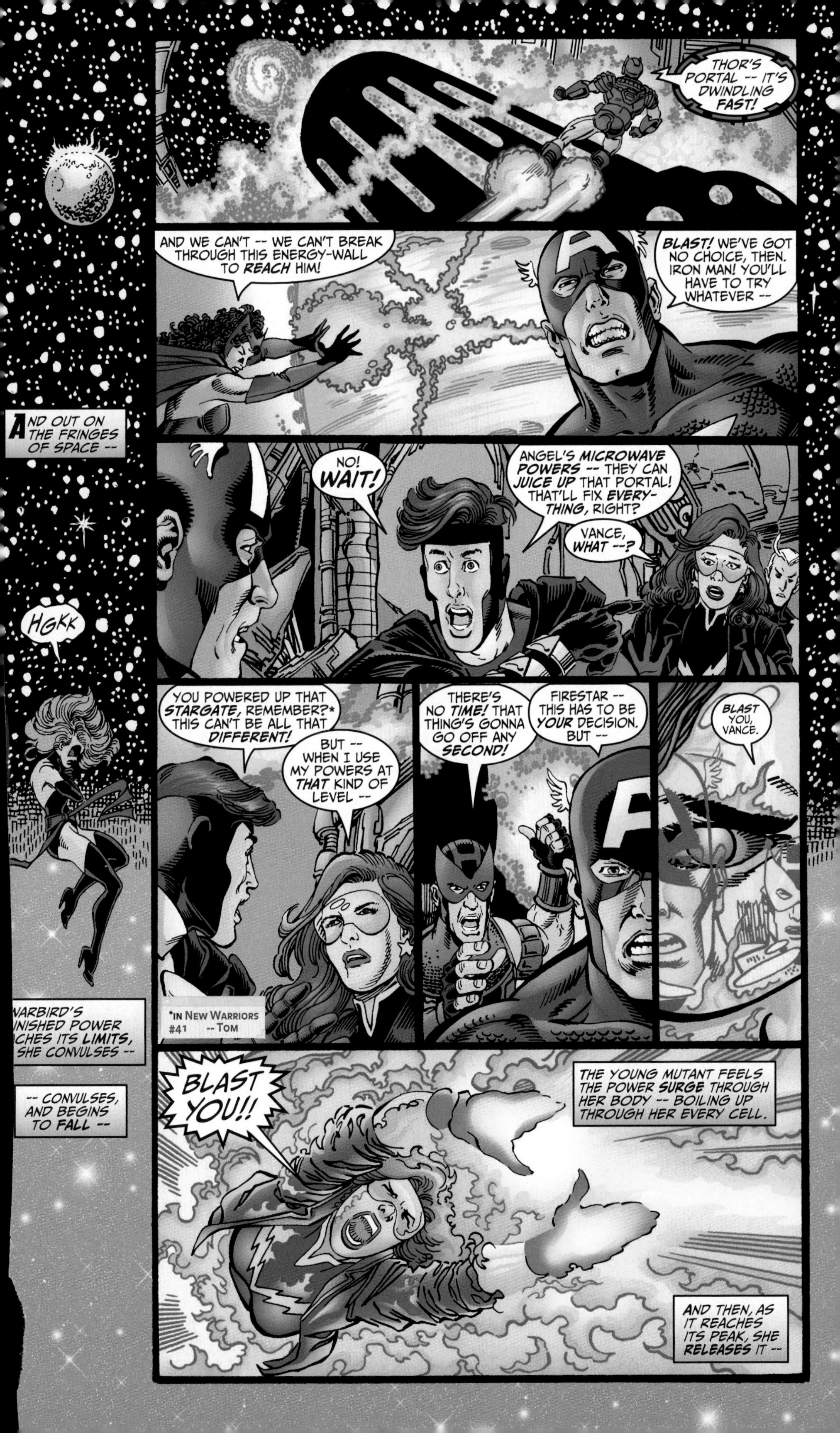
THOR'S PORTAL -- IT'S DWINDLING FAST!
AND WE CAN'T -- WE CAN'T BREAK THROUGH THIS ENERGY-WALL TO REACH HIM!
BLAST! WE'VE GOT NO CHOICE, THEN. IRON MAN! YOU'LL HAVE TO TRY WHATEVER --
AND OUT ON THE FRINGES OF SPACE --
NO! WAIT!
ANGEL'S MICROWAVE POWERS -- THEY CAN JUICE UP THAT PORTAL! THAT'LL FIX EVERYTHING, RIGHT?
VANCE, WHAT --?
HGKK
YOU POWERED UP THAT STARGATE, REMEMBER?* THIS CAN'T BE ALL THAT DIFFERENT!
BUT -- WHEN I USE MY POWERS AT THAT KIND OF LEVEL --
*IN NEW WARRIORS #41 --TOM
THERE'S NO TIME! THAT THING'S GONNA GO OFF ANY SECOND!
FIRESTAR -- THIS HAS TO BE YOUR DECISION. BUT --
BLAST YOU, VANCE.
WARBIRD'S INISHED POWER ICHES ITS LIMITS, SHE CONVULSES --
-- CONVULSES, AND BEGINS TO FALL --
BLAST YOU!!
THE YOUNG MUTANT FEELS THE POWER SURGE THROUGH HER BODY -- BOILING UP THROUGH HER EVERY CELL.
AND THEN, AS IT REACHES ITS PEAK, SHE RELEASES IT --

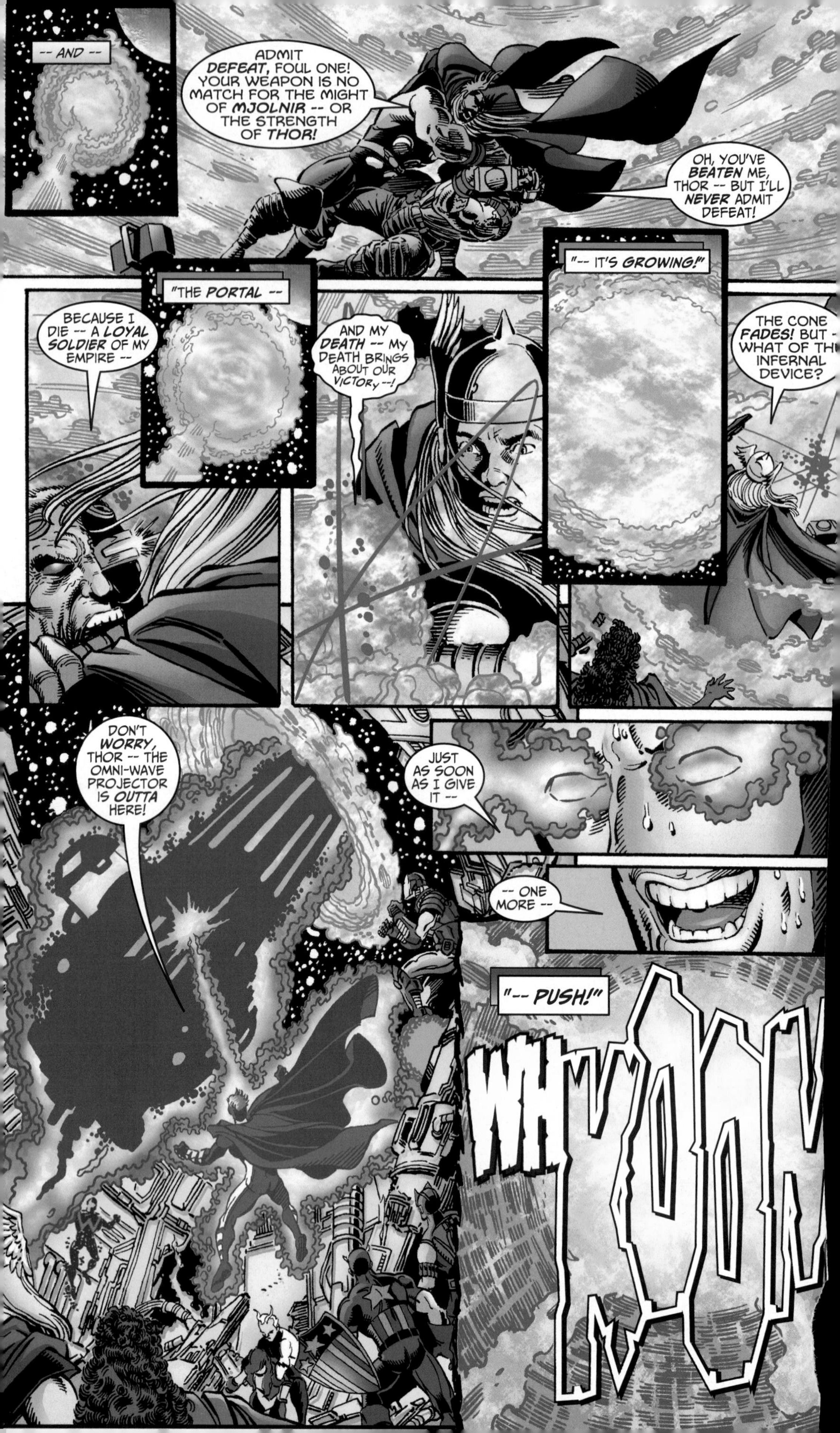
-- AND --
ADMIT DEFEAT, FOUL ONE! YOUR WEAPON IS NO MATCH FOR THE MIGHT OF MJOLNIR -- OR THE STRENGTH OF THOR!
OH, YOU'VE BEATEN ME, THOR -- BUT I'LL NEVER ADMIT DEFEAT!
BECAUSE I DIE -- A LOYAL SOLDIER OF MY EMPIRE --
"THE PORTAL --
AND MY DEATH -- MY DEATH BRINGS ABOUT OUR VICTORY--!
"-- IT'S GROWING!"
THE CONE FADES! BUT -- WHAT OF THE INFERNAL DEVICE?
DON'T WORRY, THOR -- THE OMNI-WAVE PROJECTOR IS OUTTA HERE!
JUST AS SOON AS I GIVE IT --
-- ONE MORE --
"-- PUSH!"
WHOOM

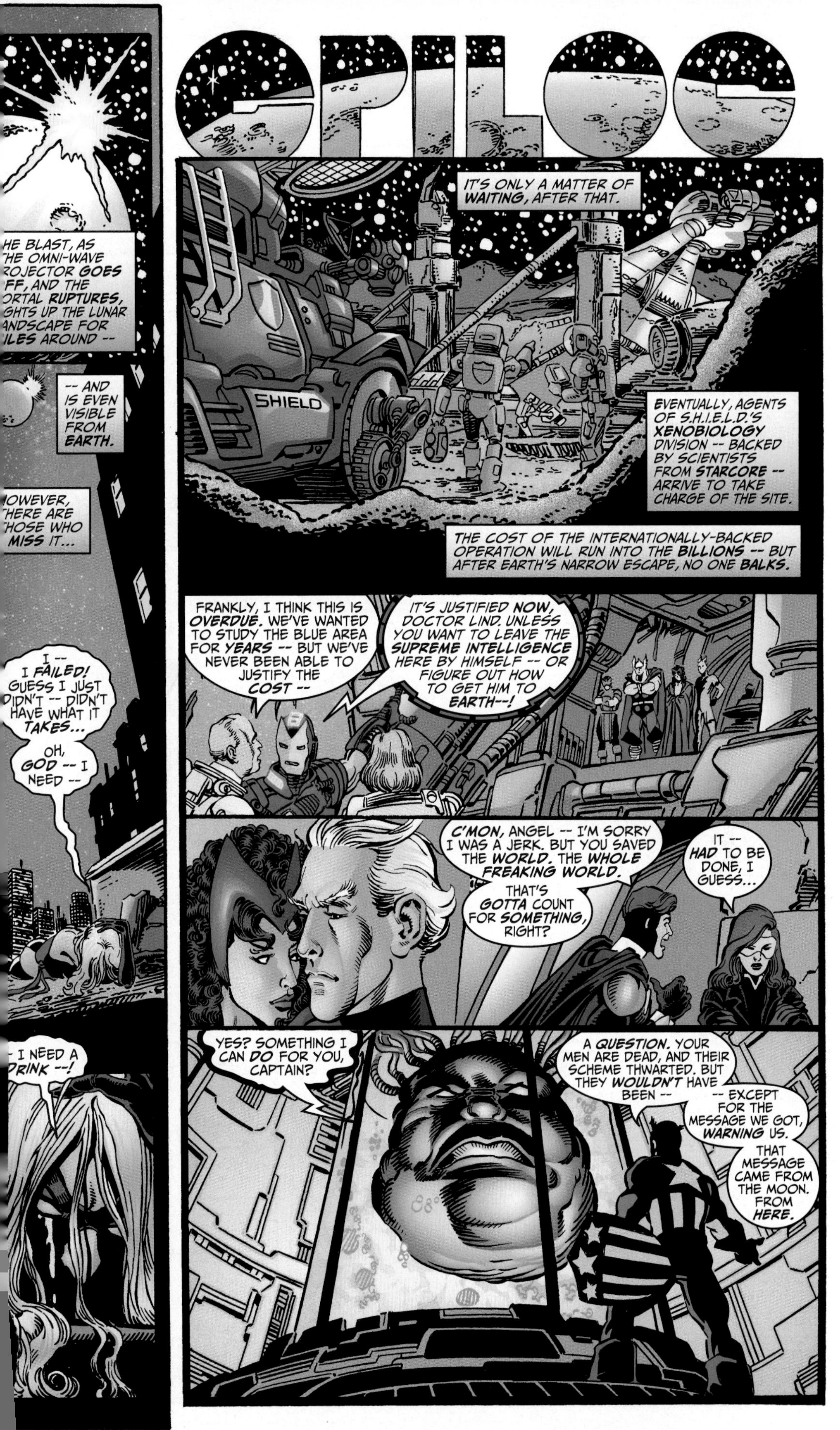
EPILOG
HE BLAST, AS THE OMNI-WAVE ROJECTOR GOES FF, AND THE ORTAL RUPTURES, GHTS UP THE LUNAR ANDSCAPE FOR ILES AROUND --
-- AND IS EVEN VISIBLE FROM EARTH.
OWEVER, THERE ARE THOSE WHO MISS IT...
I -- I FAILED! GUESS I JUST DIDN'T -- DIDN'T HAVE WHAT IT TAKES...
OH, GOD -- I NEED --
- I NEED A DRINK --!
IT'S ONLY A MATTER OF WAITING, AFTER THAT.
SHIELD
EVENTUALLY, AGENTS OF S.H.I.E.L.D.'S XENOBIOLOGY DIVISION -- BACKED BY SCIENTISTS FROM STARCORE -- ARRIVE TO TAKE CHARGE OF THE SITE.
THE COST OF THE INTERNATIONALLY-BACKED OPERATION WILL RUN INTO THE BILLIONS -- BUT AFTER EARTH'S NARROW ESCAPE, NO ONE BALKS.
FRANKLY, I THINK THIS IS OVERDUE. WE'VE WANTED TO STUDY THE BLUE AREA FOR YEARS -- BUT WE'VE NEVER BEEN ABLE TO JUSTIFY THE COST --
IT'S JUSTIFIED NOW, DOCTOR LIND. UNLESS YOU WANT TO LEAVE THE SUPREME INTELLIGENCE HERE BY HIMSELF -- OR FIGURE OUT HOW TO GET HIM TO EARTH--!
C'MON, ANGEL -- I'M SORRY I WAS A JERK. BUT YOU SAVED THE WORLD. THE WHOLE FREAKING WORLD.
THAT'S GOTTA COUNT FOR SOMETHING, RIGHT?
IT -- HAD TO BE DONE, I GUESS...
YES? SOMETHING I CAN DO FOR YOU, CAPTAIN?
A QUESTION. YOUR MEN ARE DEAD, AND THEIR SCHEME THWARTED. BUT THEY WOULDN'T HAVE BEEN --
-- EXCEPT FOR THE MESSAGE WE GOT, WARNING US.
THAT MESSAGE CAME FROM THE MOON. FROM HERE.

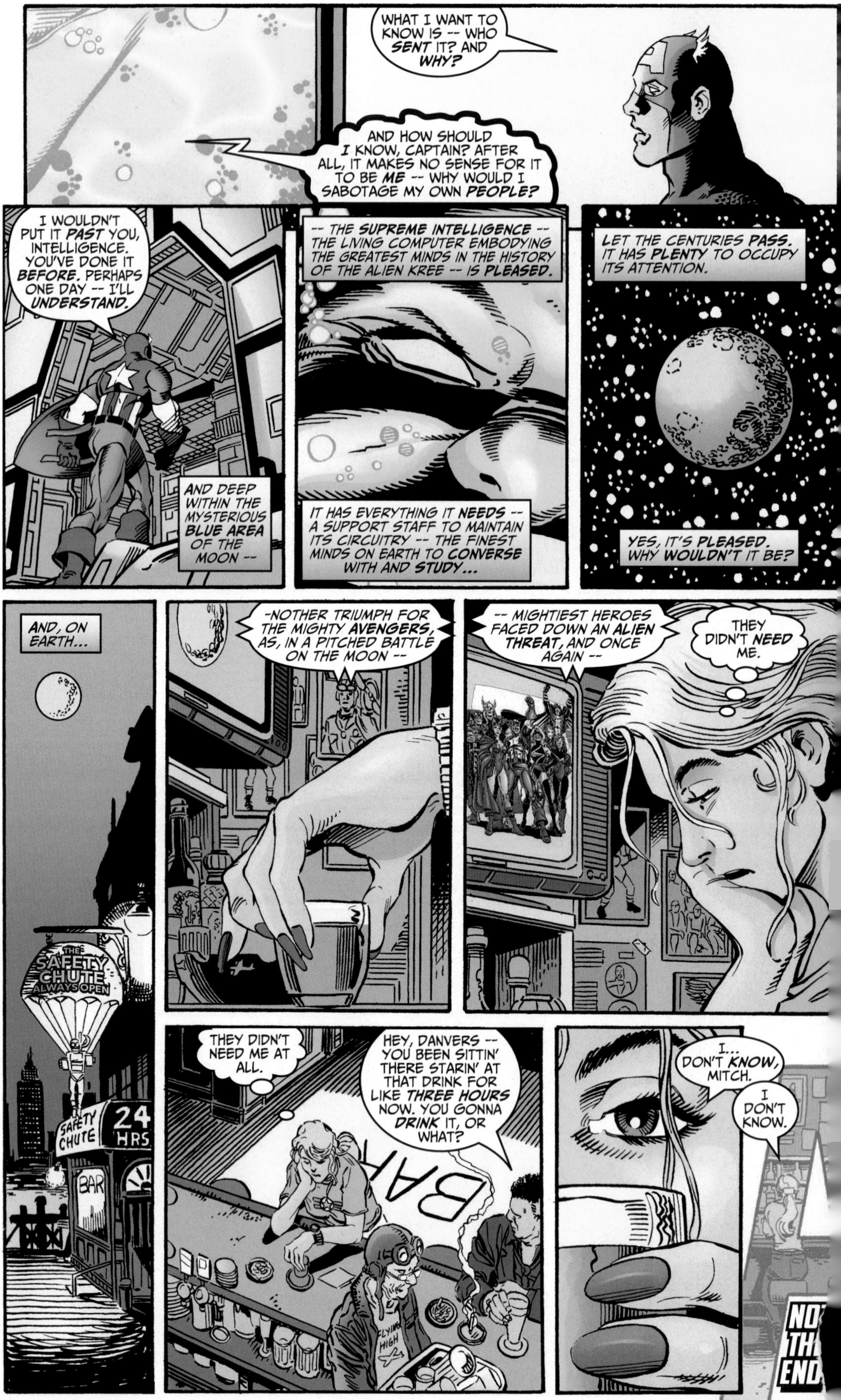

WHAT I WANT TO KNOW IS -- WHO SENT IT? AND WHY?
AND HOW SHOULD I KNOW, CAPTAIN? AFTER ALL, IT MAKES NO SENSE FOR IT TO BE ME -- WHY WOULD I SABOTAGE MY OWN PEOPLE?
I WOULDN'T PUT IT PAST YOU, INTELLIGENCE. YOU'VE DONE IT BEFORE. PERHAPS ONE DAY -- I'LL UNDERSTAND.
AND DEEP WITHIN THE MYSTERIOUS BLUE AREA OF THE MOON --
-- THE SUPREME INTELLIGENCE -- THE LIVING COMPUTER EMBODYING THE GREATEST MINDS IN THE HISTORY OF THE ALIEN KREE -- IS PLEASED.
IT HAS EVERYTHING IT NEEDS -- A SUPPORT STAFF TO MAINTAIN ITS CIRCUITRY -- THE FINEST MINDS ON EARTH TO CONVERSE WITH AND STUDY...
LET THE CENTURIES PASS. IT HAS PLENTY TO OCCUPY ITS ATTENTION.
YES, IT'S PLEASED. WHY WOULDN'T IT BE?
AND, ON EARTH...
THE SAFETY CHUTE ALWAYS OPEN
SAFETY CHUTE
24 HRS
BAR
-NOTHER TRIUMPH FOR THE MIGHTY AVENGERS, AS, IN A PITCHED BATTLE ON THE MOON --
-- MIGHTIEST HEROES FACED DOWN AN ALIEN THREAT, AND ONCE AGAIN --
THEY DIDN'T NEED ME.
THEY DIDN'T NEED ME AT ALL.
HEY, DANVERS -- YOU BEEN SITTIN' THERE STARIN' AT THAT DRINK FOR LIKE THREE HOURS NOW. YOU GONNA DRINK IT, OR WHAT?
FLYING HIGH
I... DON'T KNOW, MITCH.
I DON'T KNOW.

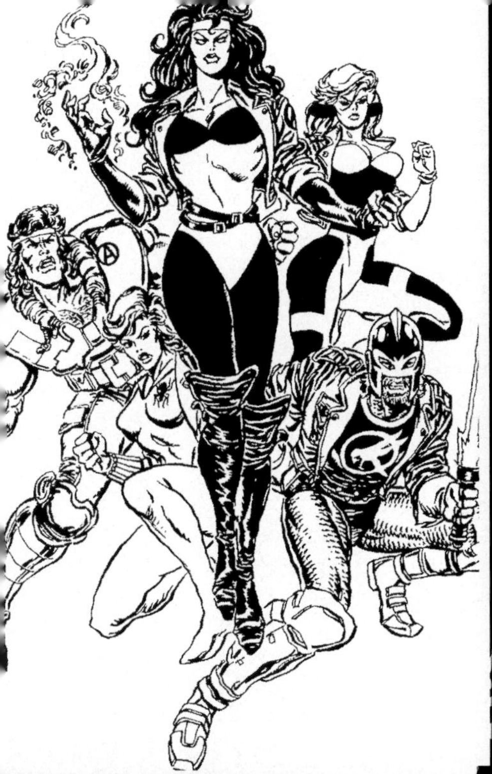

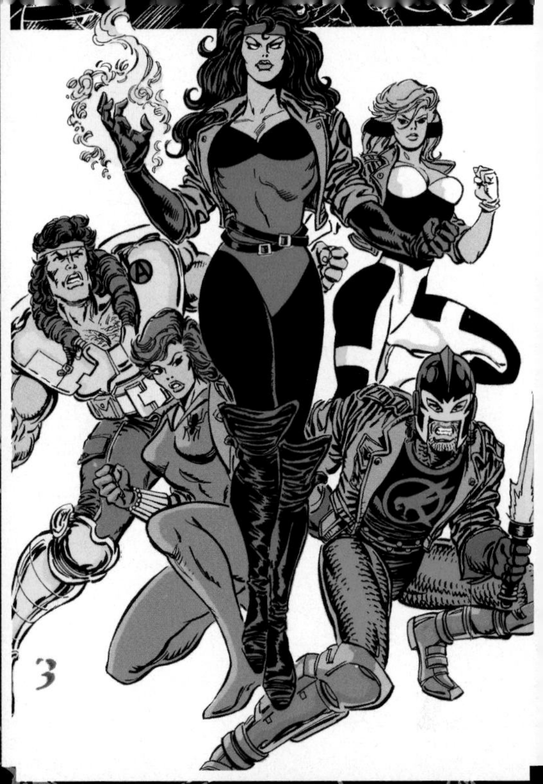

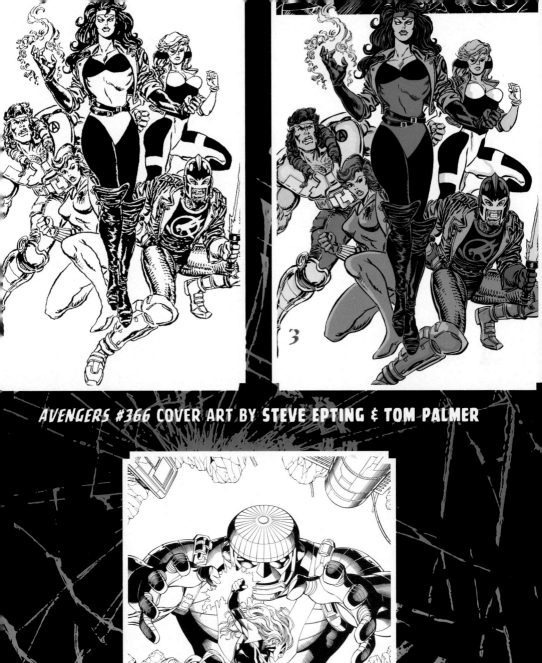

AVENGERS #366 COVER ART BY STEVE EPTING & TOM PALMER

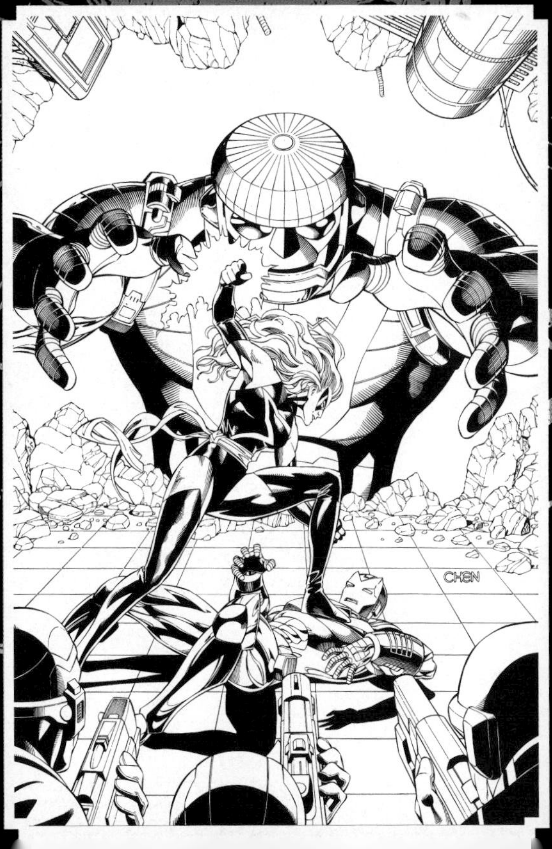
CHEN

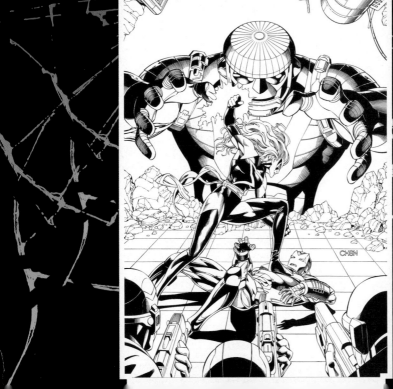

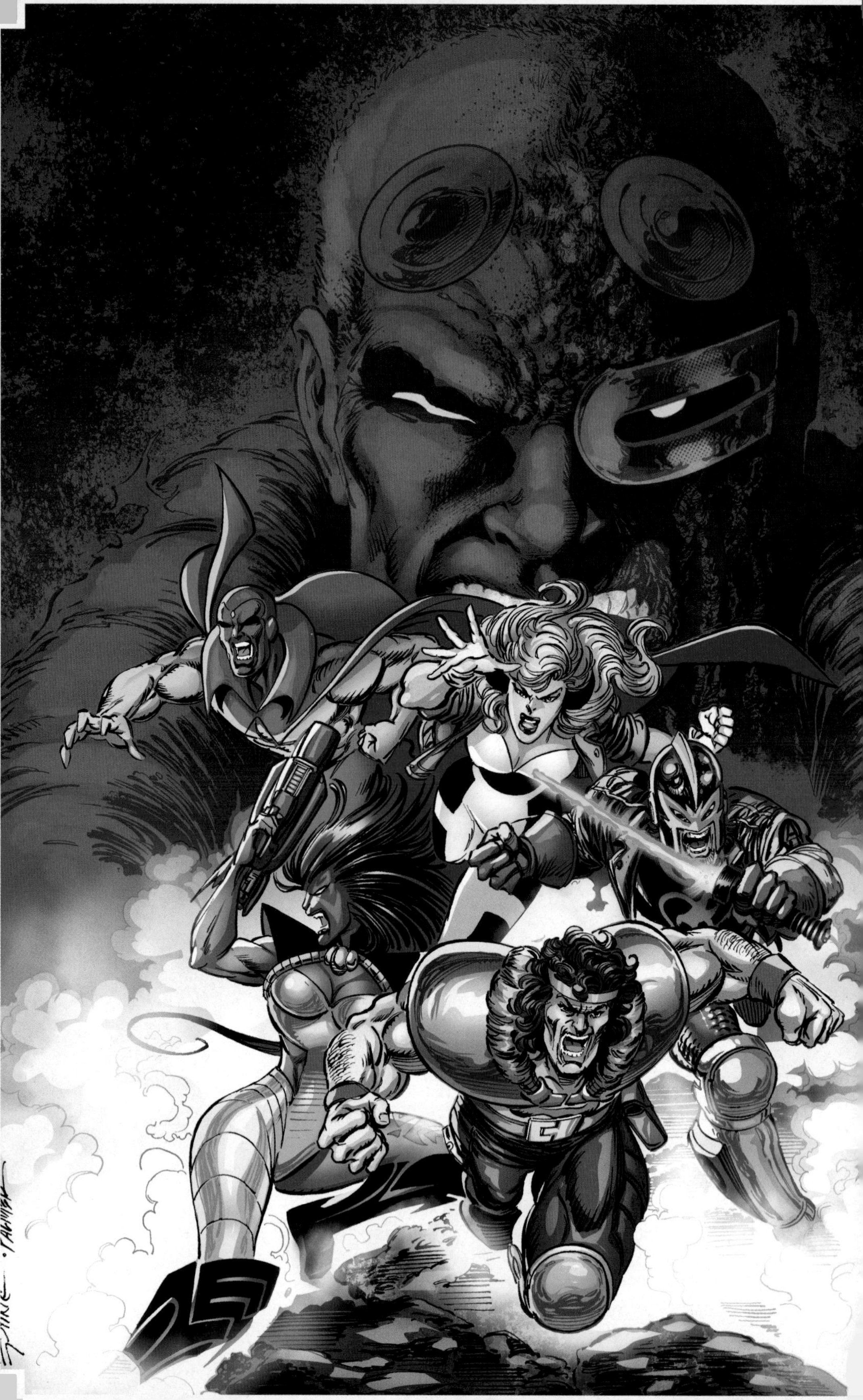